Quick Access Menu

Using *A Speaker's Guidebook*

The menu to the left briefly displays the book's content. Each menu box corresponds to a tabbed divider in the text. The dividers contain more detailed lists of contents in each section and are followed by "Speaker's Preview" pages that offer executive-like summaries of the subsequent chapters. At the back of the book, you will find:

- The index
- A list of feature boxes and checklists
- A list of sample speeches
- A list of visual guides

Where Students Learn

Go to the interior back cover to learn how you can get access to LaunchPad and look for these icons throughout the book.

LearningCurve, an adaptive quizzing program.

Video—a curated collection of video clips and full-length speech videos, including "needs improvement" clips.

Readings in LaunchPad—additional resources and reference materials, such as visual guides and documentation help.

To Find Out More

For more on using the book's reference aids and digital tools, turn to "How to Use This Book" (p. v).

A SPEAKER'S GUIDEBOOK

Text and Reference

SEVENTH EDITION

A SPEAKER'S GUIDEBOOK

Text and Reference

Dan O'Hair
University of Kentucky

Rob Stewart
Texas Tech University

Hannah Rubenstein

bedford/st.martin's
Macmillan Learning
Boston | New York

For Bedford/St. Martin's

Vice President, Editorial, Macmillan Learning Humanities: Edwin Hill
Senior Program Director for Communication: Erika Gutierrez
Director of Content Development: Jane Knetzger
Senior Development Manager: Susan McLaughlin
Senior Developmental Editor: Lorraina Morrison
Editorial Assistant: Kimberly Roberts
Marketing Manager: Kayti Corfield
Senior Content Project Manager: Harold Chester
Workflow Manager: Lisa McDowell
Production Supervisor: Bob Cherry
Media Project Manager: Sarah O'Connor
Editorial Services: Lumina Datamatics Inc.
Composition: Lumina Datamatics Inc.
Photo Researcher: Terri Wright, Lumina Datamatics Inc.
Permissions Editor: Angela Boehler
Permissions Assistant: Allison Ziebka
Senior Art Director: Anna Palchik
Text Design: Alisha Webber
Cover Design: John Callahan
Printing and Binding: RR Donnelley and Sons

Printed in China.

2 1 0 9 8 7
f e d c b a

For information, write: Bedford/St. Martin's, 75 Arlington Street, Boston, MA 02116

ISBN: 978-1-319-05941-5

Acknowledgments

Text acknowledgments and copyrights appear at the back of the book on page 503, which constitutes an extension of the copyright page. Art acknowledgments and copyrights appear on the same page as the art selections they cover.

At the time of publication all Internet URLs published in this text were found to accurately link to their intended Web site. If you do find a broken link, please forward the information to kimberly.roberts@macmillan.com so that it can be corrected for the next printing.

How to Use This Book and Digital Resources

A Speaker's Guidebook: Text and Reference has been carefully designed to help you easily and quickly access the information you need to prepare speeches and presentations. The text may be used in a public speaking course, in other college courses, in your working life after college, and in your civic activities in your community. Digital tools such as adaptive quizzing and sample speech videos are integrated throughout the book and through the LaunchPad platform. See the inside back cover to learn more about access.

The Main Menu and Table of Contents

The twelve tab dividers (discussed in more detail on the next page) allow the book to flip open easily, and the book's binding lets it lie flat. On the inside front cover you will find the **Main Menu** that offers a listing of the thirty-one chapters in the text, color-coded to the corresponding tab, and a visual link to help you find each one. For even more information or to find a specific topic, simply turn to the full **table of contents** on p. xxv.

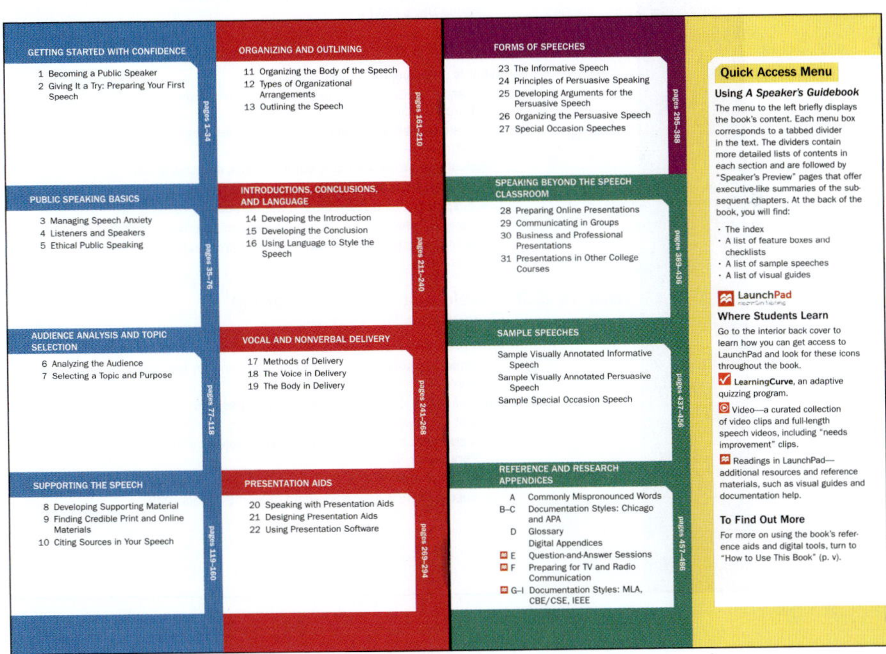

Quick Access Menu

Using *A Speaker's Guidebook*

The menu to the left briefly displays the book's content. Each menu box corresponds to a tabbed divider in the text. The dividers contain more detailed lists of contents in each section and are followed by "Speaker's Preview" pages that offer executive-like summaries of the subsequent chapters. At the back of the book, you will find:

- The index
- A list of feature boxes and checklists
- A list of sample speeches
- A list of visual guides

LaunchPad

Where Students Learn

Go to the interior back cover to learn how you can get access to LaunchPad and look for these icons throughout the book.

LearningCurve, an adaptive quizzing program.

Video—a curated collection of video clips and full-length speech videos, including "needs improvement" clips.

Readings in LaunchPad—additional resources and reference materials, such as visual guides and documentation help.

To Find Out More

For more on using the book's reference aids and digital tools, turn to "How to Use This Book" (p. v).

The Tabs

A Speaker's Guidebook is divided into twelve tabbed sections that are arranged into four color banks—blue, orange, purple, and green. Each section opens with a tab divider; the front of the tab divider identifies the tab name and the chapters contained in that section. The back indicates chapter titles and detailed information about major topics covered. To find the specific information you want, look for the appropriate tab and open the book to it.

The back of each tab divider offers a table of contents for the chapters within that tabbed section. The Speaker's Preview pages for the chapters within the section follow each tab divider.

FORMS OF SPEECHES (295–388)

FORMS OF SPEECHES

SPEAKER'S PREVIEW

Speaker's Preview Sections

You may well find one of the most useful features of *A Speaker's Guidebook* to be its Speaker's Preview pages that immediately follow each tab divider. **Speaker's Preview** pages offer a quick review of the most important information in subsequent chapters through summaries and key terms. A list of **key terms** in the chapters appears at the end of the Speaker's Preview pages, just before the opening of the first chapter within that tabbed section.

To refer to the full in-text coverage of a topic, simply flip to the page indicated in parentheses.

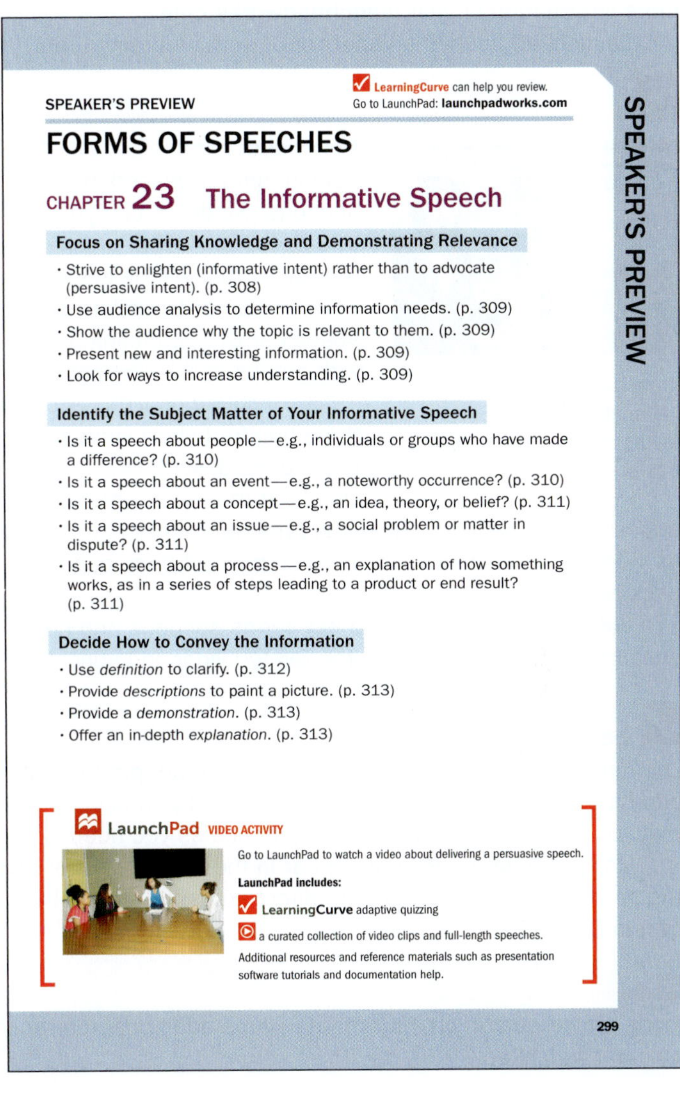

LearningCurve can help you review.
Go to LaunchPad: **launchpadworks.com**

SPEAKER'S PREVIEW

SPEAKER'S PREVIEW

FORMS OF SPEECHES

CHAPTER 23 The Informative Speech

Focus on Sharing Knowledge and Demonstrating Relevance

- Strive to enlighten (informative intent) rather than to advocate (persuasive intent). (p. 308)
- Use audience analysis to determine information needs. (p. 309)
- Show the audience why the topic is relevant to them. (p. 309)
- Present new and interesting information. (p. 309)
- Look for ways to increase understanding. (p. 309)

Identify the Subject Matter of Your Informative Speech

- Is it a speech about people—e.g., individuals or groups who have made a difference? (p. 310)
- Is it a speech about an event—e.g., a noteworthy occurrence? (p. 310)
- Is it a speech about a concept—e.g., an idea, theory, or belief? (p. 311)
- Is it a speech about an issue—e.g., a social problem or matter in dispute? (p. 311)
- Is it a speech about a process—e.g., an explanation of how something works, as in a series of steps leading to a product or end result? (p. 311)

Decide How to Convey the Information

- Use *definition* to clarify. (p. 312)
- Provide *descriptions* to paint a picture. (p. 313)
- Provide a *demonstration*. (p. 313)
- Offer an in-depth *explanation*. (p. 313)

LaunchPad VIDEO ACTIVITY

Go to LaunchPad to watch a video about delivering a persuasive speech.

LaunchPad includes:

LearningCurve adaptive quizzing

a curated collection of video clips and full-length speeches.

Additional resources and reference materials such as presentation software tutorials and documentation help.

299

LaunchPad for *A Speaker's Guidebook:* launchpadworks.com

LaunchPad is an easy-to-use platform that offers digital tools to support the speechmaking process, including adaptive quizzes, model full-length speech videos, student video clips, and video quizzes. LaunchPad can be packaged with *A Speaker's Guidebook*, or purchased separately—see the inside back cover for more information or visit **launchpadworks.com.**

LaunchPad houses a variety of powerful learning tools, including:

Video

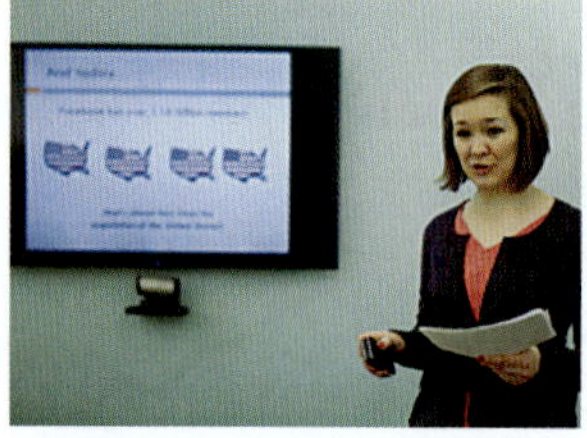

Anna Davis delivers the informative speech "Social Media, Social Identity, and Social Causes."

New videos, professionally shot for the seventh edition, are introduced in the Speaker's Preview sections. Students can go to LaunchPad to view this series of videos, which give students a taste of the topics that will be covered in the part. The videos use humor to explore such topics as managing speech anxiety, outlining a speech, and interacting with groups in the workplace.

LaunchPad provides access to more than three hundred short video clips illustrating speech techniques described in the book. A list of video clips that map to important speechmaking topics appears after the index. Speeches that are printed in the book and available as videos in LaunchPad are listed on the last book page across from the inside back cover.

Video icons appear in the Key Terms sections and near sample speeches to encourage students to watch the related video in LaunchPad.

LearningCurve

LearningCurve is an online learning tool that adapts to what you already know and helps you learn the topics that you need to practice. LearningCurve ensures that you receive as much targeted practice as you need.

Icons for **LearningCurve** appear in the Speaker's Preview sections and at the beginning of each chapter to direct students to adaptive quizzes for each part in LaunchPad.

Readings in LaunchPad

Icons are present in chapters that include additional reference materials, available in LaunchPad.

Visual Guides

Visual Guides walk you through the most challenging aspects of the speech-making process—from research and organization through creating presentation aids. A complete list of visual guides is available at the end of this book.

FROM IDEA TO SPEECH

How to Transform an Idea into a Polished Speech

The authors of *A Speaker's Guidebook* worked on this speech project with Professor Gary Russell of Quincy University, a liberal arts university in Illinois. Professor Russell asked student Teresa Gorrell to work with us on her speech of introduction. Our goal was to show how a student can take a first draft of a speech and improve it. We wanted to see how Teresa could improve the language of her speech, as well as the delivery.

Teresa Chooses Her Topic

First, Teresa did some brainstorming, to decide what part of her life she'd like to speak about in her speech of introduction.

Teresa commented, "Based on the sample speeches of introduction that I was sent by my professor, I have gathered that my speech purpose should be to introduce myself by sharing a personal story concerning some life-shaping, character-forming aspect."

With this understanding, Teresa did some thinking and narrowed her options to two ideas for a direction to take.

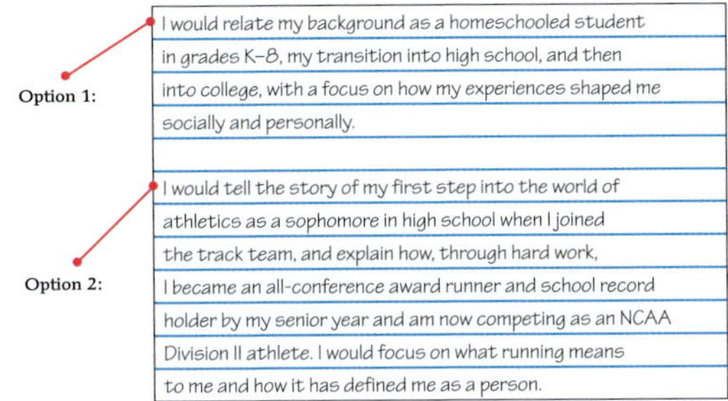

Option 1:
I would relate my background as a homeschooled student in grades K–8, my transition into high school, and then into college, with a focus on how my experiences shaped me socially and personally.
Option 2:
I would tell the story of my first step into the world of athletics as a sophomore in high school when I joined the track team, and explain how, through hard work, I became an all-conference award runner and school record holder by my senior year and am now competing as an NCAA Division II athlete. I would focus on what running means to me and how it has defined me as a person.

Teresa Drafts Her Speech

Teresa's first draft speech was compelling, but the authors thought that she could add more colorful language and details to the introduction. The authors advised Teresa to "set the scene," so that the audience could imagine her daily routine.

26

Checklists, Boxed Features, and Full-Text Speeches

Valuable checklists, appearing in each chapter and providing students with easy-to-reference tips and advice on speech techniques and related content, are a pedagogical hallmark of *A Speaker's Guidebook*. Throughout *A Speaker's Guidebook* you will also find three types of special boxed features. *A Cultural Perspective* explores the many ways that culture informs public speaking; *ESL Speaker's Notes* offer detailed guidance for non-native speakers; and *Ethically Speaking* boxes offer students ways to ensure an ethical stance when speaking. Throughout, you also will find ten full-text sample speeches, seven of them by fellow student speakers, which can serve as models to help you learn the art and craft of creating your own speeches. **For a full list of the checklists, boxes, and sample speeches, refer to the end of the book.**

A Cultural Perspective

ESL Speaker's Notes

Ethically Speaking

Photos: (passport) Charles Taylor/Shutterstock; (globe) NASA Goddard Space Flight Center; (column) Radu Bercan/Shutterstock

Preface

A Speaker's Guidebook: Text and Reference is a groundbreaking public speaking text that offers better solutions to the wide range of challenges that students face. Adopted at more than 850 schools since the first edition was published in 2001, the book grew out of the realization that public speaking courses are not ends in themselves. The authors strive to help students go beyond merely meeting the requirements of the course—with guidance for delivering presentations in their other college courses, in their working lives after college, and in the vital roles they may play in their communities. The book functions not only as a brief yet comprehensive classroom text but also as a unique and useful post-classroom reference, one that will prove an invaluable resource in any public speaking situation graduates may face.

The key goal of *A Speaker's Guidebook* has always been to effectively address the fundamental challenges of public speaking, both inside and outside the speech classroom. And we recognize that as times have changed—especially due to advances in technology—the challenges of both formal public speaking and presentational speaking in the classroom and workplace have evolved as well. Thus, with the support of hundreds of instructors nationwide, we have developed a book that students use and keep, that reinforces basic skills while providing cutting-edge coverage, and that helps students apply what they've learned to their own speeches.

Enduring Features

The following features have made *A Speaker's Guidebook: Text and Reference* extremely successful in its first six editions.

An Invaluable Reference beyond the Speech Classroom

A Speaker's Guidebook features a unique, user-friendly design, convenient and accessible reference features throughout, and extensive reference and research appendices. The information in *A Speaker's Guidebook* is designed for quick and easy retrieval. Twelve tabbed dividers allow the book to flip open easily, and a comb binding lets it lie flat. A **Main Menu** on the inside front cover listing all tabs and chapters, paired with a full **table of contents** beginning on p. xxv, quickly directs students to the sections they need.

Speaker's Preview pages at the beginning of each tabbed section allow students to quickly access and preview the most important information they will learn in each chapter; convenient cross-references to chapter content enable readers to flip quickly to a full discussion of the material. In the new edition, we revised these sections to better mirror the needs of students.

Every chapter in *A Speaker's Guidebook* contains helpful **Checklists** that offer step-by-step directions, Self-Assessments, and content review checks. Widely praised by reviewers for their precision and conciseness, these checklists help students and professionals both plan their speeches and assess their efforts.

The **Sample Speeches** appendix and a wealth of **Reference** appendices allow students to easily access practical information.

A Comprehensive Classroom Text

A Speaker's Guidebook addresses every topic included in the standard public speaking texts—and truly much more. Although we designed the coverage to be accessible, we didn't lose sight of the need for comprehensiveness. *A Speaker's Guidebook* covers all the traditional topics, including listening; speaking ethically; managing speech anxiety; analyzing the audience; selecting a topic and purpose; locating and using supporting materials; organizing and outlining ideas; using language; constructing informative, persuasive, or ceremonial speech types; creating presentation aids; and delivering the speech. The textbook also includes the most current coverage of public speaking topics that will help students in their future careers and work in other courses, including using presentation software, delivering online presentations, preparing business and professional presentations, and speaking in other courses.

To give students advice that is grounded in the theory of speech communication throughout the text, we have included references to both current communication research and classical rhetorical theory, using this research as the basis for concrete suggestions in real-world speaking situations. Examples range from coverage of individual contemporary theorists and their work to down-to-earth discussions of classical theory.

Because persuasive speaking is a major aspect of most speech courses, *A Speaker's Guidebook* offers three full chapters on persuasion, more than any other text. Chapter 24 introduces the student to contemporary and classical approaches to persuasion, Chapter 25 to forming arguments, and Chapter 26 to organizing the persuasion speech.

Finally, *A Speaker's Guidebook* recognizes the importance of solid sample speeches, and it provides ten in total. Speeches include two speeches of introduction, three informative speeches, four persuasive speeches, and two special occasion speeches. Each of the full-text model speeches offers textual annotations that help students understand the language, organization, and arguments used in the speech. The seven visually annotated speeches also include photographs of speakers delivering their presentations and connect to the videos available in LaunchPad. These visual annotations go beyond the traditional printed page by bringing the elements and analysis of speech delivery into clear focus.

Public Speaking and Diverse Voices

A Speaker's Guidebook also offers students a wealth of resources to help them adapt their speeches to the cultural requirements of the speech situation. Along with a text-wide emphasis on cultural values and diverse voices, **A Cultural**

Perspective boxes feature such topics as addressing cultural orientation in the persuasive speech, delivery and culture, differing perspectives on plagiarism, and cultural variations in nonverbal communication.

Special consideration has also been given to the non-native speaker. **ESL Speaker's Notes** boxes focus on critical areas of concern to speakers whose first language is not English and offer practical ways to address those concerns. Sample features include "Avoiding the Pitfalls of Manuscript Delivery" and "Vocal Variety and the Non-Native Speaker." Another characteristic that defines *A Speaker's Guidebook* is its strong focus on ethics. Chapter 5, "Ethical Public Speaking," includes an in-depth consideration of the role that values play in the ethical quality of speeches. **Ethically Speaking** boxes also appear throughout the text, continually reminding students that ethical conduct must apply to all aspects of the speechmaking process.

A Superior Resource for a Lifetime of Public Speaking

Along with providing students with an accessible, up-to-date classroom guide, *A Speaker's Guidebook* contains many features that will make it an invaluable resource in other college courses and *after* the public speaking course.

More about public speaking on the job. *A Speaker's Guidebook* gives students more in-depth preparation than any other text for the kinds of speaking situations they are likely to encounter on the job. Chapter 28 offers detailed guidance on preparing online presentations; Chapter 30 is devoted to business and professional reports and proposals, and Chapter 31 familiarizes students with the different types of on-the-job audiences.

"Presentations in Other College Courses." Chapter 31 provides guidance for creating the kinds of oral presentations students are likely to deliver in other college courses, from the social sciences and humanities to science and engineering. Separate sections describe typical presentation assignments in scientific and mathematical, technical, social science, arts and humanities, education, and nursing and allied health courses.

Extensive help with the research process. Useful for any college course, print and online appendices provide advice on how to cite sources in a variety of reference styles, from APA to MLA to Chicago and more. Appendices E and F offer guidance on handling question-and-answer sessions and in preparing students for speaking in mediated communication situations such as television and radio. Appendices E–I are available within LaunchPad.

The Story of the New Edition

In the seventh edition of *A Speaker's Guidebook,* print and digital tools converge to help students with every aspect of the speechmaking process, including an enhanced online learning platform that seamlessly integrates e-Book content,

Francis Miller/The LIFE Picture Collection/Getty Images

In the photo shown here, civil rights leader Martin Luther King Jr. delivers his "I Have a Dream" speech on August 28, 1963, at the Lincoln Memorial in Washington, D.C. Awarded the Nobel Peace Prize in 1964, King is one of the most admired and respected American public speakers. King's words have influenced social movements throughout the world.

adaptive quizzes, and video. With students' needs foremost in mind, revised chapters on persuasion, as well as on fundamentals such as listening, ethical speechmaking, audience analysis, topic selection and development, and outlining contain newly relevant examples and even more accessible guidance. Once again, the authors have streamlined the text to make chapters more engaging for students to read and understand. The seventh edition continues the authors' collective efforts to review the literature and incorporate the most reliable and up-to-date research studies and scholarship.

Revised as well is a visually appealing and highly relevant collection of speech videos on topics ranging from how emigrants use cell phones to survive their perilous search for refuge, to being a socially conscious consumer. Included once again is a "before" and "after" student speech—an early "needs improvement" version and a second more-polished version. The sample student speech videos are accompanied by quiz questions that test understanding of concepts. These speech video resources help students focus on how to strengthen their own speeches by analyzing model speech techniques and "needs improvement" speeches.

Roy Rochlin/Getty Images

Bassem Youssef is an Egyptian comedian and satirist who now lives in the United States and speaks about politics and equality. In this photo, he was discussing his show "The Democracy Handbook" at the AOL Speaker Series.

LaunchPad features a collection of new brief videos designed to pique students' interest and involvement in core topics in the speechmaking process. These relatable and humorous vignettes, professionally shot for the new edition, provide students with a down-to-earth preview of topics covered in the parts. Included in LaunchPad are critical thinking questions for students to answer.

The seventh edition of *A Speaker's Guidebook* is available in a variety of digital formats, including LaunchPad. LaunchPad combines an interactive e-Book, full-length speech videos and video clips, reference tools, LearningCurve adaptive quizzes, and online readings such as reference and research appendices that help support research in one convenient learning program.

Even Stronger Coverage of Public Speaking Fundamentals

- **Sample speech outlines in all formats.** The seventh edition of *A Speaker's Guidebook* now contains speeches outlined in each of the three outline formats: full sentence and key word outlines appear in Chapter 13, and a new phrase outline of a student speech organized in Monroe's Motivational Sequence design appears in Chapter 26.

- **The latest scholarship on listening.** Fully revised in the last edition and made even more accessible in this one, Chapter 4, "Listeners and Speakers," stresses the centrality of listening in the communication act, the crucial role of selective perception and steps students can take to counter it, and reflects an effort to represent current scholarship on listening-processing strategies and approaches to the listening event published in the literature.

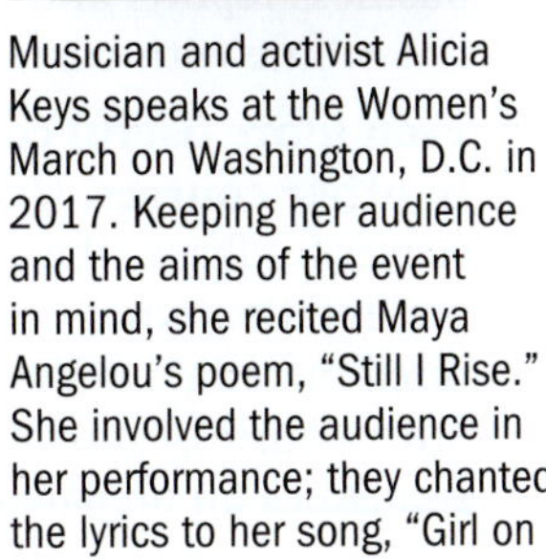
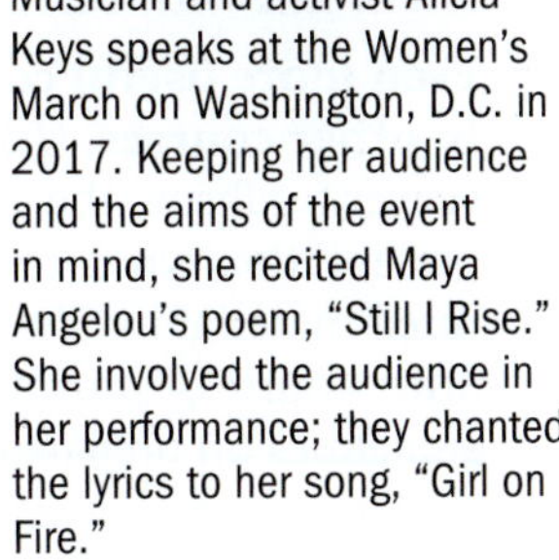

Theo Wargo/Getty Images

Musician and activist Alicia Keys speaks at the Women's March on Washington, D.C. in 2017. Keeping her audience and the aims of the event in mind, she recited Maya Angelou's poem, "Still I Rise." She involved the audience in her performance; they chanted the lyrics to her song, "Girl on Fire."

- **Additional emphasis on organizational arrangements.** *A Speaker's Guidebook* contains two full chapters (12 and 26) on organizational arrangements, revised in this edition for increased clarity. Two comprehensive new tables further enhance student learning. In Chapter 12, "One Topic (A Speech About Immigration) Organized Six Ways" provides students with a concrete demonstration of how one topic can be organized using six different patterns, thus easing students' entry into this sometimes daunting aspect of speechmaking.
- **Interactive communication ethics, updated with the foundations.** The revised Chapter 5 retains its popular basic structure while offering student speakers tangible new tools with which to engage in ethical decision making. A newly revised overview of major ethical theories, each reflecting differing standards by which to distinguish ethical from nonethical behavior in communication, enables students not just to read about what they "should" or "should not" do, but to reflect on and actively engage their own values when considering the role of ethics in the speechmaking process.
- **New coverage on building speaker credibility.** The seventh edition adds to existing coverage of classical theories of ethos and contemporary theories of speaker credibility with a new section in Chapter 24 on building credibility during a speech, from initial to derived to terminal credibility.
- **Theory and practice of persuasion carefully streamlined to drive home core principles and demonstrate their application to building a persuasive speech.** Persuasion lies at the heart of public speaking, but learning about it can be daunting for the first-time student. In three successive chapters, each carefully revised in this edition for increased accessibility and ever-more relevant examples, students learn about the following: classical and contemporary persuasive appeals, from ethos, pathos, and logos to needs, motives, and routes of mental engagement (Chapter 24); constructing arguments using effective claims, evidence, and warrants that incorporate these appeals (Chapter 25); and choosing organizational patterns to maximize appeals for specific audiences (Chapter 26). New

tables and dynamic figures provide students with the criteria they need to make effective choices.

- **Focus on business and professional presentations**. The authors completely re-envisioned Chapter 30 with new coverage of business reports and proposals, bringing material in line with current practice.
- **Even more useful coverage of presentations in other courses.** Using multidisciplinary reviewer feedback, the authors have added new presentation types, omitted others, and reorganized material in Chapter 31, "Presentations in other courses," providing students with precise guidelines on preparing specialized oral presentations assigned in science, mathematics, and technical courses, as well as courses on the social sciences, arts and humanities, education, and nursing and allied health.

Jacob Hahn gives his persuasive speech "Becoming a Socially Conscious Consumer." The full text and a new outline of the speech are included in Chapter 26, and the full-length speech video and relevant video clips are available in LaunchPad.

Cutting-Edge Coverage of the New Public Speaking Realities

Students live in a digital age in which the realities of preparing and delivering presentations continue to evolve. A growing number of instructors are teaching an online public speaking course for the first time, and more and more students (and professionals) are expected to prepare and deliver mediated presentations, creating new challenges across the board. In this edition, we have further updated our groundbreaking coverage of online presentations and using presentation aids.

- **Chapter 9, "Finding Credible Print and Online Materials," reflects how students search for sources, and stresses doing it credibly.** Offering an approach to searching for supporting materials aligned with the way that students do their research today—online—a newly revised Chapter 9 demonstrates where, how, and most importantly, *why* students should seek reliable and credible resources, both print and digital.
- **Revised chapters show students how to create presentations in up-to-date versions of Prezi, Apple Keynote, and Microsoft PowerPoint.** Chapters 20–22 focus on presentation aids and software and show students how to create and deliver effective presentations while avoiding technical glitches.
- **An updated chapter on online presentations.** Chapter 28 provides students with the most helpful tips and guidance on how to prepare online speeches—whether for use in an online class, for a recorded presentation, or for a virtual meeting. Introduced in the fifth edition, this Chapter 28 has been fully revised in the seventh edition of *A Speaker's Guidebook* to reflect current practices.

A Multifaceted Digital Experience Brings It All Together

Digital resources for *A Speaker's Guidebook* are available in LaunchPad, a dynamic platform that combines a curated collection of video, homework assignments, e-Book content, and the LearningCurve adaptive quizzing program in a simple design. LaunchPad can be packaged with *A Speaker's Guidebook*, or it can be purchased separately.

- **Relevant videos are available by e-Book chapter.** After students read about speech techniques, they can view videos that model these concepts.
- **LearningCurve's adaptive quizzing provides a personalized learning experience.** In every chapter, call-outs prompt students to tackle the LearningCurve quizzes to test their knowledge and reinforce learning of the material. Based on research on how students learn, LearningCurve motivates students to engage with course materials and learn important concepts. LearningCurve for *A Speaker's Guidebook* is organized by part, so students can review a range of topics.
- **Instructors can create reading, video, or quiz assignments easily.** LaunchPad provides premade assignment that instructors can use as-is or as a starting point for their own assignments.
- **With LaunchPad, instructors can upload and embed their own content.** Instructors can add their own readings, videos, and custom content to the ready-made content that exists in LaunchPad.
- **The Gradebook in LaunchPad enables instructors to track and analyze student progress.** Instructors can also keep an eye on their class's progress throughout the semester—reviewing progress for the whole class, individual students, or individual assignments.

Video Collection in LaunchPad Helps Students Apply What They Learn to Their Own Speeches

- **Informative and persuasive speech videos** accompanied by questions show how speakers can polish every aspect of their speeches—by demonstrating effective introductions, conclusions, transitions, supporting material, patterns of organization, citation of sources, use of presentation aids, and techniques of delivery. These polished and professionally shot speech videos offer topics of real interest to students, such as social media, freeganism, and ethical manufacturing. Full-text versions of the speeches are printed in the book, with electronic transcripts and closed captioning in LaunchPad. Mirroring new realities, the speech on preventing cyberbullying is given as an online presentation, showing the process of setting up the presentation and techniques for keeping a remote audience engaged.

- **A comprehensive video collection containing a variety of clips and full-length student speeches** highlights typical issues—in model speeches that show expert speech techniques and "needs improvement clips"—in order for students to develop their own skills.

Digital and Print Formats

For more information on these formats and packaging information, please visit the online catalog at **macmillanlearning.com/communication**.

LaunchPad for *A Speaker's Guidebook* is a dynamic new platform that dramatically enhances teaching and learning. LaunchPad combines the full e-Book, which includes *The Essential Guide to Rhetoric*, with carefully chosen videos, quizzes, activities, instructor's resources, and LearningCurves. To get access to the videos, quizzes, and multimedia resources, package LaunchPad with the print version of *A Speaker's Guidebook* or order LaunchPad on its own. Learn more at **launchpadworks.com**.

***A Speaker's Guidebook* is available as a print text.** To get the most out of the book, package LaunchPad with the text.

***A Speaker's Guidebook* e-Book option.** *A Speaker's Guidebook* is available in a range of new e-Book formats for computers, tablets, and e-readers. For more information, see **macmillanlearning.com**.

Resources for Students and Instructors

Online Resources for Students

For more information on Student Resources or to learn about package options, please visit the online catalog at **macmillanlearning.com/communication**.

LaunchPad for *A Speaker's Guidebook*. This easy-to-use learning platform includes an interactive e-Book, adaptive quizzing, a comprehensive collection of speech videos, and more. Visit **launchpadworks.com** for more information.

Print Resources for Students

***The Essential Guide to Rhetoric*, Second Edition** by Christian O. Lundberg, University of North Carolina, Chapel Hill and William M. Keith, University of Wisconsin, Milwaukee. This highly regarded guide is a powerful addition to the public speaking class, providing an accessible and balanced overview of key historical and contemporary rhetorical theories. Written by two leaders in the field, the guide uses concrete, relevant examples and jargon-free language to bring these concepts to life.

***The Essential Guide to Presentation Software,* Second Edition,** by Allison Bailey, University of North Georgia, and Rob Patterson, University of Virginia. This completely revised guide shows students how presentation software can be used to support, not overtake, their speeches. Sample screens and practical advice on using PowerPoint, Prezi, and other presentation tools make this an indispensable resource for students preparing electronic visual aids.

***The Essential Guide to Interpersonal Communication,* Second Edition,** by Steven McCornack and Kelly Morrison, ***The Essential Guide to Group Communication,* Third Edition,** by Andrea Davis, Dan O'Hair, and Mary Wiemann. These brief and readable guides offer succinct yet comprehensive coverage of key aspects of interpersonal, group, and intercultural communication, covering basic concepts and theories backed by current scholarship.

The Essential Guide to Intercultural Communication, by Jennifer Willis-Rivera (University of Wisconsin, River Falls). This useful guide offers an overview of key communication areas, including perception, verbal and nonverbal communication, interpersonal relationships, and organizations, from a uniquely intercultural perspective. Enhancing the discussion are contemporary and fun examples drawn from real life, as well as an entire chapter devoted to intercultural communication in popular culture.

***Media Career Guide: Preparing for Jobs in the 21st Century,* Eleventh Edition,** by Sherri Hope Culver, Temple University. Practical, student-friendly, and revised for recent trends in the job market—like the role of social media in a job search—this guide includes a comprehensive directory of media jobs, practical tips, and career guidance for students considering a major in communication studies and mass media.

***Research and Documentation in the Digital Age with 2016 MLA Update,* Sixth Edition,** by Diana Hacker, late of Prince George's Community College, and Barbara Fister, Gustavus Adolphus College. This handy booklet covers everything students need for college research assignments at the library and on the Internet, including advice for finding and evaluating Internet sources.

Resources for Instructors

For more information or to order or download the Instructor Resources, please visit the online catalog at **macmillanlearning.com/communication**.

Online Instructor's Resource Manual by LeAnne Lagasse, Texas Tech University; Jennifer Emerling Bone, State University of New York, Oneonta; Elaine Wittenberg-Lyles, University of Texas, San Antonio; and Melinda Villagran, George Mason University. Available in LaunchPad or downloadable online, this revised comprehensive manual is a valuable resource for new and experienced instructors alike. It offers extensive advice on topics such as helping students use their public speaking skills to become more engaged citizens, ideas for preparation and practice to reduce speech anxiety, setting and achieving student learning goals, managing the classroom, facilitating group discussion, understanding culture and gender considerations, dealing with ESL students, evaluating speeches (for both instructors and students), and evaluating Internet resources. In addition, each chapter of the main text is broken down into chapter challenges, detailed outlines, suggestions for facilitating class discussion from topics covered in feature boxes, additional activities and exercises, and recommended supplementary resources. The new edition includes more guidelines for first-time instructors, advice for integrating technology into the speech class, and expanded suggestions for videos and other classroom resources.

Computerized Test Bank by LeAnne Lagasse, Texas Tech University; Jennifer Emerling Bone, State University of New York, Oneonta; and Merry Buchanan, University of Central Oklahoma. *A Speaker's Guidebook* offers a complete testing program, available in LaunchPad or downloadable online, for Windows and Macintosh environments. Each chapter includes multiple-choice, true-false, and fill-in-the-blank exercises, as well as essay questions. Sample final examinations are also included in the testing program.

Lecture Slides for A Speaker's Guidebook. Available in LaunchPad or as a download, each chapter's slides include the most important points from the text, as well as key figures.

Custom solutions. Qualified adopters can customize *A Speaker's Guidebook* and make it their own by adding their own content or mixing it with ours. To learn more, visit **macmillanlearning.com/catalog/preview/curriculumsolutions**.

Professional Development Series

***ESL Students in the Public Speaking Classroom: A Guide for Instructors,* Second Edition,** by Robbin Crabtree, Fairfield University, and David Allen Sapp, Fairfield University, with Robert Weissberg, New Mexico State University. This guidebook provides support for new and experienced instructors of public speaking courses whose classrooms include ESL and other linguistically diverse students. Based on landmark research and years of their own teaching experience, the authors provide insights about the variety of non-native English-speaking students (including speakers of global English varieties), practical techniques that can be used to help these students succeed in their assignments, and ideas for leveraging this cultural asset for the education of *all* students in the public speaking classroom.

Coordinating the Communication Course: A Guidebook by Deanna L. Fassett, San José State University, and John T. Warren, Southern Illinois University, Carbondale. This resource offers practical advice on every topic central to the coordinator/director role.

Acknowledgments

We are especially thankful for the contributions of several individuals who helped us develop this edition of *A Speaker's Guidebook*. Thanks to Kevin Ayotte of California State University, Fresno, and Brian Kanouse of Keene State College for their contributions to the sample speeches. Thanks to Gary Russell, Quincy University, for his help with the sample speech of introduction. We would like to thank Teri Varner of St. Edward's University and her students for their contributions to the sample speeches. We are also grateful to Kelley Cowden from the University of Kentucky for her helpful suggestions. Thank you to LeAnne Lagasse of Texas Tech University for her excellent work on the *Instructor's Resource Manual* (originally created by Elaine Wittenberg-Lyles of the University of Texas at San Antonio and Melinda Villagran of George Mason University, and revised for the third edition by Jennifer Emerling Bone of the State University of New York, Oneonta) and Test Bank (originally created by Tom Howard of the University of Oklahoma and Merry Buchanan of the University of Central Oklahoma, and updated by Jennifer Emerling Bone). Thanks to Annette Joseph of Pace University for writing the new video activities for this edition.

We very much appreciate the assistance of the hundreds of reviewers whose feedback and advice allowed us to make *A Speaker's Guidebook: Text and Reference*, Seventh Edition, better. Please see the following pages for a list of these reviewers.

The seventh edition of *A Speaker's Guidebook* demanded constant attention and labor from the dedicated team at Bedford/St. Martin's. Thanks to Vice President, Editorial, Edwin Hill. Senior Program Director Erika Guiterrez has now been the guiding spirit for the book for nearly fifteen years, and we are ever grateful for her countless editorial, marketing, and sales contributions to its success. Thanks to Senior Development Manager Susan McLaughlin for her insights and guidance during this revision. Once again, Senior Development Editor Lorraina Morrison led the development process, orchestrating direction, spearheading another superb series of speech videos, and laboring over countless key details, and we feel fortunate and grateful for her efforts. Thanks to freelance editor Brian Baker for his creative input and for Deborah Heimann for copyediting the text. We also thank Editorial Assistant Kimberly Roberts for her help and dedication. We feel very fortunate that Harold Chester, Senior Content Project Manager, once again expertly guided the text through a complicated production process under the direction of Lisa Kinne and Elise S. Kaiser. Thanks to Thomas Kane, Senior New Media Editor for helping us to develop LaunchPad. We are very grateful to Kayti Corfield, Marketing Manager, for her sales and marketing efforts.

Reviewers and Survey Respondents, Seventh Edition

Jen Anderson, Bellevue College
Sarah Cole, Framingham State University
Susan Emel, Baker University
Neva Gronert, Arapahoe Community College
Jennifer Hallett, Young Harris College
Carla Harrell, Old Dominion University
Mariko Izumi, Columbus State University
Annette Joseph, Pace University
Nancy Legge, Idaho State University
Peg McCree, Middle Tennessee State University
Kimberly McInerney, Indiana University South Bend
Kevin Mitchell, College of Southern Nevada
Emanuel Pantelidis, Pace University
Keith Poole, Isothermal Community College
Terri Scrima, Arapahoe Community College
Mary-Beth Taylor, Central Maine Community College
Alan Teitleman, South Piedmont Community College

Reviewers and Survey Respondents, Sixth Edition

Rebecca Aarestad, *Waubun High School;* Karen Alman, *Wenatchee Valley College;* Oluwunmi Ariyo, *Vance Granville Community College;* Marlene Atkins, *The Illinois Institute of Art, Schaumburg;* Kathy Berggren, *Cornell University,* Aria Bernstein, *Georgia Perimeter College;* Steven Bisch, *Washington State University Tri Cities;* Becky Behm, *Alexandria Technical and Community College;* Esther Boucher, *Worchester Polytechnic Institute;* Greg Brecht, *University of South Florida St. Petersburg;* Carol Brown, *Centralia College;* Carolyn Calhoon Dillahunt, *Yakima Valley Community College;* Marybeth Callison, *University of Georgia;* Diane Carter, *University of Idaho;* Linda Carvalho Cooley, *Reedley College;* Anthony Cavaluzzi, *SUNY Adirondack;* Melinda Christianson, *Underwood School;* Jeanne Christie, *Western Connecticut State University;* John Castagna, *Penn State Abington;* Steven Cohen, *University of Maryland;* Diana Cooley, *Lone Star College, North Harris;* Dustin Crosby, *Southern Oregon University;* Anna Cross, *Portsmouth Public Schools;* Mittie Jane Crouch, *Tidewater Community College;* Paul Crowley, *Spartanburg Community College;* Rose Crnkovich, *Trinity High School;* Kevin Cummings, *Mercer University;* Staci Dinerstein, *William Patterson University;* Donna Elkins, *Jefferson Community and Technical College;* Sarah Engle, *Liverpool High School;* Emilie Falc, *Winona State University;* Julie Floyd, *Central Georgia Technical College;* Amy Gall, *St. Louis Christian College;* Ellen Gabrielleschi, *Clarke University;* Jerry Gibbens, *Williams Baptist College;* Beate Gilliar, *Manchester University;* Cheryl Golemo, *Harper College;* Alan Gousie, *Community College of Rhode Island;* Orsini Gonzalez, *City College;* Robin Grantham, *Georgia Military College;* Jennifer Hallett, *Young Harris College;* Debra Harper-LeBlanc, *Lone Star College, Greenspoint Center;* Carla Harrell, *Old Dominion University;* Richard Harris, *Southeastern University;* Richard Harrison, *Kilgore College;* Marcia Hines-Colvin, *Saint Mary's University of Minnesota;* Gregory Hudson, *Cincinnati State;* Jessica Hurless, *Casper College;* Susan Isaacs, *Union College;* Kathleen Jacquette, *Farmingdale State College;* Marlena Karami, *Roxbury Community College;* Veronica Koehn, *Oregon Institute of Technology;*

Beth Konrad, *Loyola University Chicago;* Kelly Lancaster, *School of Art and Design;* Ross Larson, *Carthage College;* Darren Linvill, *Clemson University;* Shane Martin, *Fitchburg State University*; Amanda Martinez, *Davidson College;* Chandra Massner, *University of Pikeville;* Monica Maxwell, *Georgetown University;* Julia McDermott-Swanson, *Santa Rosa Junior College;* Jamie McKown, *College of the Atlantic;* Ellen Mroz, *Community College of Rhode Island;* Diorah Nelson, *Hillsborough Community College;* Charles Parker, *Friends University;* Elaine Pascale, *Suffolk University;* Shelli Pentimall Bookler, *Bucks County Community College;* Brandi Quesenberry, *Virginia Tech;* Gail G. Reid, *University of West Georgia;* Donald Rhoads, *Thaddeus Stevens College of Technology*; R. Joseph Rodriguez, *University of Texas at Austin;* Sue Roeglin, *Georgetown University;* Gary Russell, *Quincy University;* Gerald Savage, *Illinois State University;* Lynn Scramuzza, *University of Scranton;* Gretchen Skivington, *Great Basin College;* Julie Suek, *Lower Columbia College;* Gregory Thomas, *Morgan Community College;* Shauna Vey, *New York City College of Technology CUNY;* Fred Whiting, *Art Institute of Washington, DC;* Jon A. Williams, *Niagara County Community College;* Kathleen Williams, *Bergen Community College;* Ty Williams, *St. Philip's College.*

Reviewers and Survey Respondents, Fifth Edition

Diane Auten, Allan Hancock College; Diane M. Badzinski, Colorado Christian University; Raymond Bell, Calhoun Community College; Jeffrey D. Brand, Millikin University; Lacinda Brese, Southeastern Oklahoma State University; Jennifer L. Chakroff, Lasell College; Jeannette Duarte, Rio Hondo College; Richard E. Edwards, Baylor University; Donna Elkins, Jefferson Community and Technical College; Nancy M. Fisher, Ohio State University; David S. Fusani, Erie Community College; Jeffery Gentry, Rogers State University; Kim Gerhardt, San Diego Mesa College; Steven Grant, Florida State College at Jacksonville; Carla Harrell, Old Dominion University; Constance G. Hudspeth, Rollins College and Valencia Community College; Carie Kapellusch, Texas Christian University; Carol Koris, Johnson & Wales University; Steve Madden, Coastal Carolina University; Brian R. McGee, College of Charleston; Teresa Metzger, California State University San Marcos; Alexa G. Naramore, University of Cincinnati; Clayton Coke Newell, University of Saint Francis; Nikki Poppen-Eagan, Pierce College; Mark Ristroph, Augusta Technical College; Gary E. Russell, Quincy University; Jeffrey VanCleave, University of Kentucky; Teri Lynn Varner, St. Edward's University; John T. Warren, Southern Illinois University, Carbondale; and Allyson Zadeh, Front Range Community College.

Contents

Video LearningCurve adaptive quizzing LaunchPad readings

PUBLIC SPEAKING BASICS

LearningCurve

SUPPORTING THE SPEECH

ORGANIZING AND OUTLINING

LearningCurve

INTRODUCTIONS, CONCLUSIONS, AND LANGUAGE LearningCurve

PRESENTATION AIDS

FORMS OF SPEECHES

SAMPLE SPEECHES

REFERENCE AND RESEARCH APPENDICES

GETTING STARTED WITH CONFIDENCE

In the photo shown here, civil rights leader Martin Luther King Jr. delivers his "I Have a Dream" speech on August 28, 1963, at the Lincoln Memorial in Washington, D.C. Awarded the Nobel Peace Prize in 1964, King is one of the most admired and respected American public speakers. King's words have influenced social movements throughout the world. **Francis Miller/The LIFE Picture Collection/Getty Images**

GETTING STARTED WITH CONFIDENCE

SPEAKER'S PREVIEW

LearningCurve can help you review!
Go to LaunchPad: **launchpadworks.com**

GETTING STARTED WITH CONFIDENCE

CHAPTER 1 Becoming a Public Speaker

Recognize the Many Benefits of Public Speaking

- Gain real-life skills that lead to greater confidence and satisfaction. (p. 8)
- Advance your professional goals. (p. 8)
- Gain the oral communication skills employers so highly value in a college graduate. (p. 8)

Enhance Your Career as a Student

- Hone your researching, writing and outlining, reasoning, critical thinking, and listening skills. (p. 8)
- Deliver better oral presentations in other courses, including speaking in science and mathematics, technical, social science, arts and humanities, education, nursing and allied health, and business courses. (p. 8)

Find New Opportunities for Civic Engagement

- Use public speaking to become more involved in addressing issues you care about. (p. 9)
- Become a more active participant in our democracy. (p. 9)
- Learn the rules of engagement for effective and ethical public discourse. (p. 9)

Recognize the Classical Roots of Public Speaking

- Rhetoric first flourished in the Greek city-state of Athens in the fifth century B.C.E. and referred to making effective speeches, particularly those of a persuasive nature. (p. 10)

LaunchPad VIDEO ACTIVITY

Go to LaunchPad to watch a video about the importance of the public speaking course.

LaunchPad includes:

LearningCurve adaptive quizzing

a curated collection of video clips and full-length speeches.

Additional resources and reference materials such as presentation software tutorials and documentation help.

- Public speaking played a central role in the development of democracy in ancient Greece and Rome and remains an essential tool in safeguarding democracy today. (p. 10)
- The ancient Greek agora and the Roman forum exist today as physical spaces, such as town halls, as well as virtual forums streamed to listeners online. (p. 10)
- The *canons of rhetoric*, a five-part speechmaking process developed in ancient Greece, remain relevant for today's public speaker. (p. 11)

Draw on the Familiar Skills of Conversation and Composition

- Consider that in both conversation and writing, you try to uncover the audience's interests and needs before speaking. (p. 12)
- Consider that in both conversation and writing, you check to make certain that you are understood, and adjust your speech to the listeners and to the occasion. (p. 12)
- Much of what you've learned about organizing written papers can be applied to organizing your speeches. (p. 13)

Recognize Unique Aspects of Public Speaking

- More so than writers, successful speakers generally use familiar words, easy-to-follow sentences, and transitional words and phrases. (p. 13)
- Spoken language is often more interactive and inclusive of the audience than written language. (p. 13)

Become an Inclusive Speaker

- Try to identify and respectfully address the diversity of values and viewpoints held by audience members. (p. 13)
- Work toward making every member of the audience feel recognized and included in your message. (p. 13)

Recognize Public Speaking as a Category of Communication

- As in *conversation* (*dyadic communication*), you attempt to make yourself understood, involve and respond to your conversational partner, and take responsibility for what you say. (p. 14)
- As in *small group communication*, you address a group of people who are focused on you and expect you to clearly discuss issues that are relevant to the topic and to the occasion. (p. 14)
- As in *mass communication*, you address a group with whom you have little or no interaction, as on television and radio. (p. 14)
- In *public speaking*, a speaker delivers a message with a specific purpose to an audience of people who are present during the delivery of the speech. (p. 14)

Recognize That Public Speaking Is an Interactive Communication Process

- Understand elements of *source*, *receiver*, *message*, and *channel* and how they interact in public speaking. (p. 14)
- Understand and plan for the *rhetorical situation* — the circumstance that calls for a public response (the speech). (p. 16)

Recognize the Similarities and Differences between Public Speaking and the Other Forms of Communication

- Opportunities for feedback are fewer than in conversation or in small group communication, and greater than in mass communication. (p. 16)
- Preparation required is greater than in other forms of communication. (p. 16)
- The degree of formality tends to be greater than in other forms of communication. (p. 16)

CHAPTER 2 Giving It a Try: Preparing Your First Speech

Use This Overview to Construct and Deliver Your First Speech

- Analyze the audience. (p. 18)
- Select a topic. (p. 18)
- Determine the speech purpose. (p. 19)
- Compose a thesis statement. (p. 19)
- Develop the main points. (p. 20)
- Gather supporting material. (p. 20)
- Separate the speech into its major parts: introduction, body, and conclusion. (p. 20)
- Outline the speech using coordinate and subordinate points. (p. 21)
- Consider presentation aids. (p. 23)
- Practice delivering the speech. (p. 23)

KEY TERMS

Chapter 1

rhetoric
oratory
agora
forum
public forum
forensic oratory
deliberative oratory
epideictic oratory
canons of rhetoric
invention
arrangement
style
memory
delivery
culture
cultural intelligence
dyadic communication
small group communication
mass communication
public speaking
source
encoding
receiver
decoding
feedback
message
channel
noise
shared meaning
context
rhetorical situation
audience-centered perspective

Chapter 2

audience analysis
general speech purpose
specific speech purpose
thesis statement
main points
supporting material
introduction
body (of speech)
conclusion
coordination
subordination
coordinate points
subordinate points
organizational pattern
working outline
speaking outline
presentation aids

Go to LaunchPad: **launchpadworks.com** to watch the video clips for this chapter.

1 Becoming a Public Speaker

LearningCurve can help you review!
Go to LaunchPad: **launchpadworks.com**

As a student of public speaking, you are joining a very large and venerable club. People have studied public speaking in one form or another for well over two thousand years. Indeed, public speaking may be the single most studied skill in history! Since before the time of Aristotle, the brilliant Greek thinker who laid the groundwork for modern public communication (384–322 B.C.E.), and Roman statesmen and orators such as Cicero (106–43 B.C.E.), people have used public speaking to enlighten, persuade, entertain, and move others to act.

Martin Luther King Jr. was certainly a member of this ancient club. He was not only one of America's greatest civil rights leaders but one of its most gifted public speakers. His "I Have A Dream" speech, delivered during the March on Washington in the waning days of August 1963, awed the huge (250,000-person) crowd rallying for racial equality and economic opportunity, as well as the millions more who watched it on the wavy lines of their black-and-white television sets. Of every color and creed and from all walks of life, the audience listened raptly as Reverend King, speaking in the cadenced rhythm of the Bible, shared the phrase "I have a dream" in eight successive sentences.

Time has done nothing to diminish the power of King's speech, which took just seventeen minutes to deliver. The words stir us still, symbolizing not only the struggle for racial justice but the power of speech to move people and change the course of history.

Our own frenzied era of electronic communication and social-media saturation has not in any way diminished the need for this singularly effective form of communication, and public speaking remains an indispensable vehicle for the expression of ideas. Whatever people care deeply about, it offers a way to communicate their concerns to others. Indeed, few other activities offer quite the same opportunity to make one's voice heard.

This guidebook offers the tools you need to create and deliver effective speeches, from presentations made to fellow students, co-workers, or fellow citizens to major addresses. Here you will discover the basic building blocks of any good speech and acquire the skills to deliver presentations in a variety of specialized contexts—from the college classroom to the civic, business and professional, and personal arenas. You'll also find proven techniques to build your confidence by overcoming the anxiety associated with public speaking.

Why Study Public Speaking?

The ability to speak confidently and convincingly in public is a crucial skill for anyone who wants to take an active role in the classroom, workplace, and community. As you master the techniques of speaking in front of audiences, you'll find that it is a powerful vehicle for personal and professional growth.

Gain a Vital Life Skill

Skill in public speaking will give you an unmistakable edge in life, leading to greater confidence and satisfaction. Whether you want to do well in an interview, stand up with poise in front of classmates or in other group situations, assume a leadership role in your work or civic life, or parlay your skills in your community or other personal venues, public speaking offers you a way to fulfill your goals. Business magnate Warren Buffett passionately extols the role that public speaking has played in his success:

> Be sure to do it, whether you like it or not . . . do it until you get comfortable with it. . . . Public speaking is an asset that will last you 50 or 60 years, and it's a necessary skill; and if you don't like doing it, that will also last you 50 or 60 years. . . . Once you tackle the fear and master the skill, you can run the world. You can walk into rooms, command people, and get them to listen to you and your great ideas.[1]

Advance Your Professional Goals

Today public speaking is both a vital life skill and a potent weapon in career development. Dozens of surveys of managers and executives reveal that ability in oral and written communication is the most important skill they look for in a new employee. In a recent survey of 318 mid- to large-scale employers, conducted on behalf of the Association of American Colleges and Universities (AAC&U), 93 percent ranked the ability to communicate clearly, think critically, and solve complex problems as more important than an undergraduate's major.[2] Likewise, employer surveys across many occupations confirm the value of well-developed skill in oral communication, making the public speaking course potentially the most valuable one you can take during your undergraduate career. See Table 1.1.

Enhance Your Career as a Student

Preparing speeches develops numerous skills that you can (and will) apply in other courses. As in the speech class, other courses, some in your major, also require that you research and write about topics, analyze audiences, outline and organize ideas, and support claims. These and other skill sets covered in this guidebook, such as working with presentation media and controlling voice and body during delivery, are valuable in any course that includes an oral-presentation component, from English composition to nursing or engineering. Guidelines for speaking across the curriculum, including speaking in science

TABLE 1.1

Skills Employers Rate as Most Important	%
Effective verbal communication	85
Working well in teams	83
Effective written communication	82
Ethics in thoughts and actions	81
Skills in reasoning and critical thinking	81
Application of concepts learned to real-world situations	80

Data from: Hart Research Associates, "Falling Short? College Learning and Career Success: Selected Findings from Online Surveys of Employers and College Students Conducted on Behalf of the Association of American Colleges & Universities," January 20, 2015, www.aacu.org/sites/default/files/files/LEAP/2015employer studentsurvey.pdf.

and mathematics, technical, social science, arts and humanities, education, nursing and allied health, and business courses, are the focus of Chapter 31, "Speaking in Your Other Courses."

Find New Opportunities for Civic Engagement

Perhaps unique among the body of knowledge you will acquire as a student, public speaking offers you ways to enter the public conversation about social concerns and become a more engaged citizen. Public speaking gives you a voice that can be heard and counted. Climate change, energy, government debt, immigration reform—such large civic issues require our considered judgment and action. Yet too many of us leave it up to politicians, journalists, and other "experts" to make decisions about critical issues such as these. Overall, voting patterns in the United States are substantially lower than in most other established democracies around the world, with only between 50 and 60 percent of the population voting in presidential elections over the past 50 years.[3] This even held true in the last highly contentious presidential election between Hilary Clinton and Donald Trump. Voting rates in congressional, state, and local elections can be as low as 5 percent.[4] Those ages 18 to 29 years old are least likely to vote in nonpresidential elections. When we as citizens speak up in sufficient numbers, including making our voices heard through our votes, democracy functions better and change that truly reflects the will of the people occurs. Leaving pressing social issues to others, on the other hand, is an invitation to special interest groups who may or may not act with our best interests in mind.

As you study public speaking, you will have the opportunity to research topics that are meaningful to you, consider alternate viewpoints, and decide where you stand and how you want to act on important issues. You will learn to distinguish between argument that advances constructive goals and uncivil speech that serves merely to inflame and demean others. You will practice, in short, the "rules of engagement" for effective public discourse.[5] As you do, you

TABLE 1.2 Civic Engagement on the Web

Change.org	Change.org bills itself as the world's largest petition platform, "empowering people everywhere to create the change they want to see."
DoSomething.org	DoSomething.org, a youth organization with over five million members in 130 countries, spearheads voluntary social change campaigns. Its motto is "Any cause, anytime, anywhere."
Goodnet.org	Goodnet, Gateway to Doing Good, is an online hub that aims to help you "activate your goodness." The Goodnet Directory offers a listing of services for volunteering, charity, causes, and social action.

will gain confidence in your ability to join your voice with others in pursuit of issues you care about.

Table 1.2, "Civic Engagement on the Web," lists websites devoted to education about key policy issues and candidates and to engagement in social causes.

The Classical Roots of Public Speaking

Originally, the practice of giving speeches was known as **rhetoric** or **oratory**. Rhetoric first flourished in the Greek city-state of Athens in the fifth century B.C.E. and referred to making effective speeches, particularly those of a persuasive nature. It would later assume an equally dominant role in Roman society, where patrician families educated their sons in the necessary art of oratory.

Athens was the site of the Western world's first democracy, and it was through public speaking that its free, land-owning males made it a reality. Meeting in a public square called the **agora**, the Athenians spoke with great skill on issues of public policy, and their belief that citizenship demands active participation in public affairs endures in modern democracies to this day. Following the eventual conquest of Greece (ca. 146 B.C.E.), citizens in the Roman republic used oratory to create the world's first known representative democracy. Assembling in a public space called a **forum**, the Romans used public speaking to lobby for civic issues and debate political perspectives. These days, the term **public forum** denotes a variety of venues for the discussion of issues of public interest, including traditional physical spaces such as town halls as well as virtual forums online. Today we use the Internet as a global public forum or agora.[6]

The Canons of Rhetoric

For the Greeks, oratory was the means by which they settled civil disputes, determined public policy, and established laws. In cases involving major crimes, for example, juries usually included five hundred members.[7] People served as their own advocates, so their chances of persuading jurors to vote in their favor depended on the quality of their speaking skills. The Greeks called this kind of advocating or legal speech **forensic oratory**; speech given in legislative or political contexts, **deliberative oratory**; and speech delivered in special ceremonies, such as celebrations and funerals, **epideictic oratory**. The great Athenian leader-general Pericles, for example, used his considerable powers of political persuasion, or *deliberative oratory*, to convince Athenians to rebuild the Acropolis and erect other great temples, such as the Parthenon, that would endure and amaze the world for centuries to come. These aren't just ancient practices; in much the same way today, we use different types of persuasive speeches to, among other things, appeal to juries, create legislation, and mark special occasions.

Greek and Roman teachers divided the process of preparing a speech into five parts—*invention*, *arrangement*, *style*, *memory*, and *delivery*—called the **canons of rhetoric**. These parts correspond to the order in which they believed a speech should be put together. **Invention** refers to discovering the types of evidence and arguments you will use to make your case to an audience. **Arrangement** is organizing the evidence and arguments in ways that are best suited to the topic and the audience. **Style** is the way the speaker uses language to express the speech ideas. **Memory** is the practice of the speech until it can be artfully delivered. Finally, **delivery** is the vocal and nonverbal behavior you use when speaking. The Romans later renamed these canons *inventio* (discovering the speech material), *dispositio* (arranging the material), *elocutio* (styling the speech), *memoria* (remembering all the various lines of argument to prove a case), and *pronuntiatio* (vocal and nonverbal delivery). To read more on the classical canons, see Table 1.3, "Classical Rhetoric on the Web," which lists several sites on the Web devoted to classical rhetoric.

A Rich and Relevant Heritage

Although founding scholars such as Aristotle and Cicero surely didn't anticipate the ever-present PowerPoint or Prezi slideshow that accompanies so many contemporary speeches, the speechmaking structure they bequeathed to us as the canons of rhetoric remain remarkably intact. Often identified by terms other than the original, these canons nonetheless continue to be taught in current books on public speaking, including this guidebook. To read more on

TABLE 1.3 Classical Rhetoric on the Web

Silva Rhetoricae rhetoric.byu.edu	Sponsored by Brigham Young University, this site offers detailed descriptions of the canons of rhetoric, along with entries of thousands of rhetorical terms.
Virtual Salt: A Handbook of Rhetorical Devices www.virtualsalt.com/rhetoric.htm	Virtual Salt contains definitions and examples of more than sixty traditional rhetorical devices useful for improving your speeches.
A Glossary of Rhetorical Terms with Examples (University of Kentucky, Division of Classics) www.uky.edu/AS/Classics/rhetoric.html	From the University of Kentucky Classics Department, this site offers brief definitions of rhetorical strategies and a number of examples to illustrate each concept.

TABLE 1.4 The Classic Canons of Rhetoric and Speechmaking Today

The Canons of Rhetoric	Addressed in *A Speaker's Guidebook*
1. *Invention* (Selecting and adapting speech material to the audience; constructing arguments)	Chapter 6: Analyzing the Audience Chapter 7: Selecting a Topic and Purpose Chapter 8: Developing Supporting Materials Chapter 9: Finding Credible Print and Online Materials Chapter 10: Citing Sources in Your Speech Chapter 24: The Persuasive Speech Chapter 25: Developing Arguments for the Persuasive Speech
2. *Arrangement* (Ordering the speech)	Chapter 11: Organizing the Body of the Speech Chapter 12: Types of Organizational Arrangements Chapter 13: Outlining the Speech Chapter 26: Organizing the Persuasive Speech
3. *Style* (Use of language, including figures of speech)	Chapter 16: Using Language to Style the Speech
4. *Memory* (Practice of the speech)	Chapter 17: Methods of Delivery Chapter 18: The Voice in Delivery
5. *Delivery* (Vocal and nonverbal delivery)	Chapter 19: The Body in Delivery

where the canons are addressed in this text, see Table 1.4, "The Classic Canons of Rhetoric and Speechmaking Today."

Learning to Speak in Public

None of us is born knowing how to deliver a successful speech. Rather, public speaking is an acquired skill that improves with practice. It is also a skill that shares much in common with other familiar activities, such as conversing and writing, and it can be much less daunting when you realize that you can draw on expertise you already have.

Draw on Conversational Skills

In several respects, planning and delivering a speech resembles engaging in a particularly important conversation. When speaking to a friend, you automatically check to make certain you are understood and adjust your meaning accordingly. You also tend to discuss issues that are appropriate to the circumstances. When a relative stranger is involved, however, you try to get to know his or her interests and attitudes before revealing any strong opinions. These instinctive adjustments to your *audience*, *topic*, and *occasion* represent critical steps in creating a speech. Although public speaking requires more planning, both the conversationalist and the public speaker try to uncover the audience's interests and needs before speaking.

Draw on Skills in Composition

Preparing a speech also has much in common with writing. Both depend on having a focused sense of who the audience is.[8] Both speaking and writing often require that you research a topic, offer credible evidence, employ effective transitions, and devise persuasive appeals. The principles of organizing a speech parallel those of organizing an essay, including offering a compelling introduction, a clear thesis statement, supporting ideas, and a thoughtful conclusion.

Develop an Effective Oral Style

Although public speaking has much in common with everyday conversation and with writing, a speech is a unique form of communication characterized by an oral style of language. Spoken language is simpler, more rhythmic, more repetitious, and more interactive than either conversation or writing.[9] More so than writers, effective speakers use familiar words and easy-to-follow sentences. Repetition in even the briefest speeches is key, and speakers routinely repeat key words and phrases to emphasize ideas and help listeners follow along.

Spoken language also is often more *interactive* and inclusive of the audience than written language. Audience members want to know what the speaker thinks and feels and that he or she recognizes them and, importantly, relates the message to them. Speakers accomplish this by making specific references to themselves and to the audience. Yet because public speaking usually occurs in more formal settings than does everyday conversation, listeners expect a somewhat more formal style of communication from the speaker. When you give a speech, listeners expect you to speak in a clear, recognizable, and organized fashion. Thus, in contrast to conversation, in order to develop an effective oral style you must practice the words you will say and the way you will say them.

Effective public speakers, engaging conversationalists, and compelling writers share an important quality: They keep their focus on offering something of value for the audience!

Demonstrate Respect for Difference

Every audience member wants to feel that the speaker has his or her particular needs and interests at heart, and to feel recognized and included in the speaker's message. To create this sense of inclusion, a public speaker must be able to address diverse audiences with sensitivity, demonstrating respect for differences in identity and **culture**—the language, beliefs, values, norms, behaviors, and even material objects that are passed from one generation to the next. As David C. Thomas and Kerr Inkson explain, more than ever, public speakers must cultivate their **cultural intelligence**, which they define as

> being skilled and flexible about understanding a culture, learning more about it from your ongoing interactions with it, and gradually reshaping your thinking to be more sympathetic to the culture and to be more skilled and appropriate when interacting with others from the culture.[10]

Striving for inclusion and adopting an audience-centered perspective will bring you closer to the goal of every public speaker—establishing a genuine connection with the audience.

Public Speaking as a Form of Communication

Public speaking is one of four categories of human communication; the other categories include dyadic, small group, and mass communication.

- **Dyadic communication** happens between two people, as in a conversation.
- **Small group communication** involves a small number of people who can see and speak directly with one another.
- **Mass communication** occurs between a speaker and a large audience of unknown people who are usually not present with the speaker, or who are part of such an immense crowd that there can be little or no interaction between speaker and listener. Mass public rallies and television and radio news broadcasts are examples of mass communication.
- In **public speaking**, a speaker delivers a message with a specific purpose to an audience of people who are present during the delivery of the speech. Public speaking always includes a speaker who has a reason for speaking, an audience that gives the speaker its attention, and a message that is meant to accomplish a specific purpose. Public speakers address audiences largely without interruption and take responsibility for the words and ideas being expressed.

Public Speaking as an Interactive Communication Process

In any communication event, including public speaking, several elements are present and interact with one another. These include the source, the receiver, the message, the channel, and shared meaning (see Figure 1.1).

The **source**, or sender, is the person who creates a message. Creating, organizing, and producing the message is called **encoding**—the process of converting thoughts into words.

The recipient of the source's message is the **receiver**, or audience. The process of interpreting the message is called **decoding**. Audience members decode the meaning of the message selectively, based on their own experiences and attitudes. **Feedback**, the audience's response to a message, can be conveyed both verbally and nonverbally.

The **message** is the content of the communication process: thoughts and ideas put into meaningful expressions, expressed verbally and nonverbally.

The medium through which the speaker sends a message is the **channel**. If a speaker delivers a message in front of a live audience, the channel is the air through which sound waves travel. Other channels include phones, televisions, computers, written communication including text messages, and the Internet.

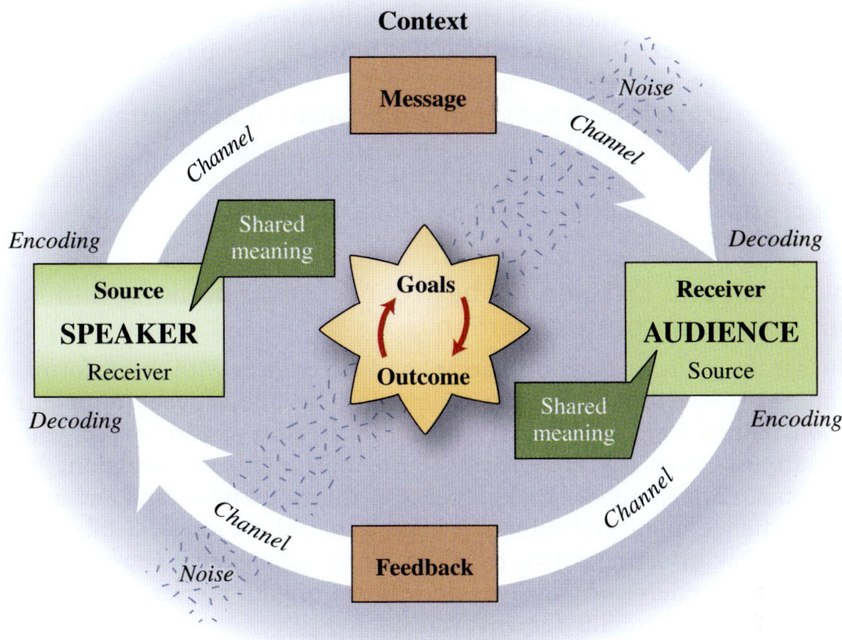

FIGURE 1.1 The Communication Process

Noise is any interference with the message. Noise can disrupt the communication process through physical sounds such as cell phones ringing and people talking, through psychological distractions such as heated emotions, or through environmental interference such as a frigid room or the presence of unexpected people.

Shared meaning is the mutual understanding of a message between speaker and audience. The lowest level of shared meaning exists when the speaker has merely caught the audience's attention. As the message develops, a higher degree of shared meaning is possible. Thus listener and speaker together truly make a speech a speech—they "co-create" its meaning.

Two other factors are critical to consider when preparing and delivering a speech—context and goals. **Context** includes anything that influences the speaker, the audience, the occasion—and thus, ultimately, the speech. In classroom speeches, context would include (among other things) recent events on campus or in the outside world, the physical setting, the order and timing of speeches, and the cultural orientations of audience members. Successful communication can never be divorced from the concerns and expectations of others.

Part of the context of any speech is the situation that created the need for it in the first place. All speeches are delivered in response to a specific

rhetorical situation, or a circumstance calling for a spoken, often public response.[11] Bearing the rhetorical situation in mind ensures that you maintain an **audience-centered perspective**—that is, that you keep the needs, values, and attitudes of your listeners firmly in focus.

A clearly defined *speech purpose* or goal—what you want the audience to learn or do as a result of the speech—is a final prerequisite for an effective speech. Establishing a speech purpose early on will help you proceed through speech preparation and delivery with a clear focus in mind.

Similarities and Differences between Public Speaking and Other Forms of Communication

Public speaking shares both similarities and differences with other forms of communication. Like *small group communication*, public speaking requires that you address a group of people who are focused on you and expect you to clearly discuss issues that are relevant to the topic and to the occasion. As in *mass communication*, public speaking requires that you understand and appeal to the audience members' interests, attitudes, and values. And like *dyadic communication*, or conversation, public speaking requires that you attempt to make yourself understood, involve and respond to your conversational partners, and take responsibility for what you say.

A key feature of any type of communication is sensitivity to the listeners. Whether you are talking to one person in a coffee shop or giving a speech to a hundred people, your listeners want to feel that you care about their interests, desires, and goals. Skilled conversationalists do this, and so do successful public speakers. Similarly, skilled conversationalists are in command of their information and present it in a way that is organized and easy to follow, believable, relevant, and interesting. Public speaking is no different. Moreover, the audience will expect you to be knowledgeable and unbiased about your topic and to express your ideas clearly.

Although public speaking shares many characteristics of other types of communication, several factors distinguish public speaking from other forms of communication. These include (1) opportunities for feedback, (2) level of preparation, and (3) degree of formality.

Public speaking presents different opportunities for *feedback*, or listener response to a message, than do dyadic, small group, or mass communication. Opportunities for feedback are abundant both in conversation and in small group interactions. Partners in conversation continually respond to one another in back-and-forth fashion; in small groups, participants expect interruptions for purposes of clarification or redirection. However, because the receiver of the message in mass communication is physically removed from the messenger, feedback is delayed until after the event, as in TV ratings.

Public speaking offers a middle ground between low and high levels of feedback. Public speaking does not permit the constant exchange of information between listener and speaker that happens in conversation, but audiences can and do provide ample verbal and nonverbal cues to what they are thinking and feeling. Facial expressions, vocalizations (including laughter or disapproving noises), gestures, applause, and a range of body movements all signal the audience's response to the speaker. The perceptive speaker reads these cues and tries to adjust his or her remarks accordingly. Feedback is more restricted in public speaking situations than in dyadic and small group communication, and *preparation* must be more careful and extensive. In dyadic and small group communication, you can always shift the burden to your conversational partner or to other group members. Public speaking offers no such shelter, and lack of preparation stands out starkly.

Public speaking also differs from other forms of communication in terms of its *degree of formality*. In general, speeches tend to occur in more formal settings than do other forms of communication. Formal gatherings such as graduations lend themselves to speeches; they provide a focus and give form—a "voice"—to the event. In contrast, with the exception of formal interviews, dyadic communication (or conversation) is largely informal. Small group communication also tends to be less formal than public speaking, even in business meetings.

Thus public speaking shares many features of everyday conversation, but because the speaker is the focal point of attention in what is usually a formal setting, listeners expect a more systematic presentation than they do in conversation or small group communication. As such, public speaking requires more preparation and practice than the other forms of communication.

2 Giving It a Try: Preparing Your First Speech

LearningCurve can help you review!
Go to LaunchPad: **launchpadworks.com**

Public speaking is an applied art, and every speaking opportunity, including that provided by the classroom, offers you valuable hands-on experience. To help you get started as quickly as possible, this chapter previews the steps involved in putting together any speech or presentation, whether it be a brief first speaking assignment in the classroom or a longer address in a public setting. Subsequent chapters expand on these steps.

A Brief Overview of the Speechmaking Process

Whatever type of speech you are asked to prepare, in school and out, the basic building blocks remain the same, as seen in Figure 2.1. Everything begins with analyzing the audience.

Analyze the Audience

We give speeches in order to communicate with groups of people—our audiences. And because audiences are composed of people with personalities, interests, and opinions all their own, every audience is unique. The first task in preparing any speech, then, is to do **audience analysis**, a process of learning about your listeners relative to the speech topic and occasion. The formal process involves strategies such as interviewing or surveying audience members (see Chapter 6, "Analyzing the Audience"). For a brief first speech, however, your own powers of observation may be your best tool. If possible, ask someone familiar with the audience about their current interests and concerns. Consider some simple *demographic characteristics*, such as the ratio of males to females, age ranges, and apparent cultural and/or socioeconomic differences among audience members. Use what you learn about these characteristics as you select your topic and draft the speech, focusing on ways you can relate it meaningfully to your audience.

Select a Topic

Unless the topic has been assigned, the next step is to decide what you want to speak about. Selecting a topic can be overwhelming, but there are ways to make it easier. First, consider the speech purpose and occasion. What topics will be suitable to your audience's needs and wants in these circumstances?

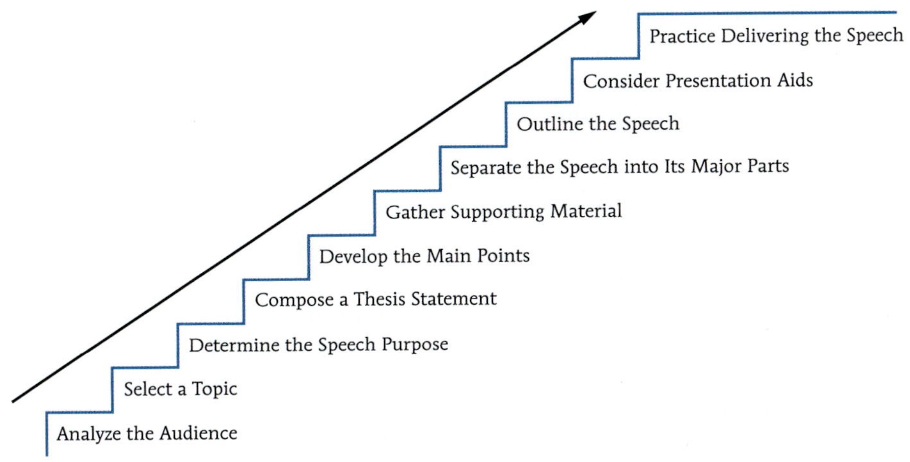

FIGURE 2.1 Steps in the Speechmaking Process

Using these parameters, use your interests and expertise to guide you in selecting something to speak about (see Chapter 7 for a discussion on finding topics).

Determine the Speech Purpose

With topic in hand, you will need to decide what you want to accomplish with your speech. For any given topic, you should direct your speech toward one of three **general speech purposes**: *to inform*, *to persuade*, or *to mark a special occasion*. Thus, consider whether your general purpose is to simply give your audience information about the topic; to convince them to accept one position to the exclusion of other positions; or to commemorate an occasion such as a wedding, a funeral, or an awards event.

You should also have a **specific speech purpose**—what you want the audience to learn or do as a result of your speech. For example, if your general purpose is to inform, your specific purpose might be "to inform my audience about how self-driving cars will likely impact auto insurance policies." If your general purpose is to persuade, the specific purpose could be "to convince my audience why they should support tighter regulation on insuring self-driving vehicles."

Compose a Thesis Statement

Next, compose a **thesis statement** that clearly expresses the central idea of your speech. While the specific purpose focuses your attention on the *outcome* you want to achieve with the speech, the thesis statement directly expresses, in a single sentence, what the speech is *about*.

GENERAL PURPOSE: To inform

SPECIFIC PURPOSE: To inform my audience about three critical steps we can take to combat identity theft.

THESIS STATEMENT: The best way to combat identity theft is to review your monthly financial statements, periodically check your credit report, and secure your personal information in both digital and print form.

As you develop your speech, use both your thesis statement and specific speech purpose as guides to ensure that you are on track with what you've set out to do.

Develop the Main Points

Organize your speech around two or three **main points**. These are the primary pieces of knowledge (in an informative speech) or the key claims (in a persuasive speech). If you prepare a clear thesis for your speech, the main points will be easily identifiable.

THESIS STATEMENT: The best way to combat identity theft is to review your monthly financial statements, periodically check your credit report, and secure your personal information in both digital and print form.

I. Review your monthly bank statements, credit card bills, and similar financial records to be aware of all transactions.

II. Check your consumer credit report at least twice a year.

III. Keep your personally identifying digital and print information highly secure.

Gather Supporting Material

Illustrate the main points with **supporting material** that clarifies, elaborates, and verifies your ideas. Supporting material potentially includes the entire world of information available to you. Unless your speech is autobiographical, research your topic to provide evidence for your assertions and lend credibility to your message (see Chapter 9, "Finding Credible Print and Online Materials").

Arrange the Speech into Its Major Parts

Every speech will have an *introduction*, a *body*, and a *conclusion* (see Table 2.1). Develop each part separately, then bring them together using transition statements (see Chapters 14 and 15 on developing the introduction and conclusion).

The **introduction** serves to draw the audience's interest to the topic, the speaker, and your thesis (see Chapter 14). The speech **body** contains the main points and supporting points, arranged to reflect the speech's thesis. Use the supporting material you have gathered to clarify, elaborate, or substantiate your points. The **conclusion** restates the thesis and reiterates how the main points confirm it. Because the conclusion represents your last opportunity to affect your listeners about your topic in a memorable way, end on a strong note (see Chapter 15).

TABLE 2.1 Developing Speech Parts

Introduction	Body	Conclusion
• Pique the audience's attention and interest with a quotation, short story, an example, or other means of gaining their attention described in Chapter 14. • Introduce yourself and your topic. • Preview the thesis and main points. (Use a transition statement to signal the start of the speech body.)	• Develop the main points and illustrate each one with relevant supporting material. • Organize your ideas and evidence in a structure that suits your topic, audience, and occasion. • (Use transitions to move between main points and to the conclusion.)	• Review the thesis and reiterate how the main points confirm it. • Leave your audience with something to think about.

Outline the Speech

An outline is a plan for arranging the elements of your speech in support of your thesis. Outlines are based on the principle of **coordination** and **subordination**—the logical placement of ideas relative to their importance to one another. **Coordinate points** are of equal importance and are indicated by their parallel alignment. Any main point or subpoint should have at least one other point coordinate to it—that is, your speech should have two or more main points, and for each main point there should be two or more subpoints. **Subordinate points**, or subpoints, offer evidence ("support") for the main points and are identified in outlines by their placement below and to the right of the points they support. (For a full discussion of outlining, see Chapter 13.) In an outline, they appear as follows.

COORDINATE POINTS

I. Main Point 1
II. Main Point 2
    A. Subpoint 1
    B. Subpoint 2

SUBORDINATE POINTS

I. Main Point 1
    A. First level of subordination
        1. Second level of subordination
        2. Second level of subordination
            a. Third level of subordination
            b. Third level of subordination

As your speeches become more detailed, you will need to select an appropriate **organizational pattern** (see Chapters 13 and 26 on outlining and organizing speeches). You will also need to consider developing both *working* and *speaking* outlines (see Chapter 13 on outlining a speech). **Working outlines** generally contain points stated in complete or close-to-complete sentences. **Speaking outlines** are far briefer and are usually prepared using either short phrases or key words.

Following is a working full-sentence outline of the body of a speech created by a beginning public speaking student for a speech of introduction (see speech below).

TOPIC: Speech of Introduction for Ashley White

SPEECH PURPOSE: To inform

SPECIFIC SPEECH PURPOSE: To inform my audience about overcoming obstacles posed by physical limitations to find another path to personal and professional fulfillment.

Introduction

We are on a lifelong journey to find our identity. On this journey, we look for those things that make us unique, that bring us success, and that hold us back, and we discover how they define our personality. We set standards for ourselves and observe our boundaries. *(Captures audience attention—in this case, by presenting her story as a universal quest for identity and fulfillment. This creates a common bond with the audience and encourages listeners to identify with what's to come.)*

We take so many extraordinary measures, but when exactly are we supposed to discover who we are? Is there a specific moment? Is there an initiation age? Is it ever certain? What happens if what defines us must suddenly be let go? How do we find new purpose with what is left? *(States thesis statement and previews main points. In a brief speech, the preview may not systematically preview each main point but instead serve as a transition to them, as occurs in Ashley's speech.)*

Body

I. I have always identified myself as a dancer.
   - A. Since age three I have been in dance classes, but since birth I have danced.
   - B. Few people outside of the discipline understand the commitment that dance affords its chosen ones.
   - C. Dance becomes more than a hobby; it is self-defining.

II. My dance teacher was the first to notice the curve, and I was formally diagnosed with scoliosis at the age of ten . . .
   - A. Scoliosis is a lateral curvature of the spine . . .
     - 1. Scoliosis often gets worse during adolescent growth . . .
     - 2. The condition affects girls and boys . . .
   - B. At eleven, I was wearing a back brace . . .

C. Adolescence is a difficult time to deal with any anomaly . . .
  1. The brace made me feel different . . .
  2. Dance class was my only time of liberation . . .

D. In college I received troubling news . . .
  1. My curve had worsened and it was time for surgery . . .
  2. The doctor informed me that dancing professionally would not be likely . . .

III. . . . Amongst all this emotional turmoil, I have found a new passion. . . .
  A. This art is expressed in the kitchen, not in the dance studio . . .
  B. Cooking and dancing require many of the same skills . . .

Conclusion

(*Restates the thesis in a memorable way.*) This transition of redefining myself has been a difficult one, and I have learned that it is actually an ongoing one. Being in touch with oneself requires constant learning, redefining, and reapplying, and not just being dedicated to a single interest.

(*Leaves the audience with a motivating message.*) This lifelong journey I am on? I know now that this is just the beginning of finding my own identity.

Consider Presentation Aids

As you prepare your speech, consider whether using visual, audio, or a combination of different **presentation aids** will help the audience understand your points (see Chapter 20 on using presentation aids).

Practice Delivering the Speech

Preparation and practice are necessary for the success of every speech. You will want to feel and appear "natural" to your listeners, an effect best achieved by rehearsing both the verbal and nonverbal delivery of your speech at least six times (see Chapters 18 and 19 on use of the voice and body in speech delivery). For a four- to six-minute speech, that's only twenty to thirty minutes of actual practice time, figuring in re-starts and pauses.

CHECKLIST

RECORD THE SPEECH TO BOLSTER CONFIDENCE

Many experts agree that watching and listening to recordings of your own speeches can assist in pinpointing your strengths and weaknesses and building confidence in public speaking. Observing your speech helps make it real and, therefore, less scary.

If you own a smart phone, it probably includes an audio and/or video recorder; otherwise, libraries loan computers with recording capabilities. Use it as you practice so you can assess your verbal delivery (see Chapter 18 for detailed guidelines on recording your speech).

ESL SPEAKER'S NOTES

Identifying Linguistic Issues as You Practice Your Speech

NASA Goddard Space Flight Center

When practicing a speech with an audio or video recorder, second-language speakers of English may wish to pay added attention to pronunciation and articulation as they listen. *Pronunciation* is the correct formation of word sounds. *Articulation* is the clarity or forcefulness with which the sounds are made, regardless of whether they are pronounced correctly. If possible, try to arrange an appointment with an instructor or another student to help you identify key linguistic issues in your speech practice tape or video.

Each of us will speak a second language a bit differently from native speakers. That is, we will have some sort of accent. This should not concern you in and of itself. What is important is identifying which specific features of your pronunciation, if any, interfere with your ability to make yourself understandable. Once you have listened to your speech tape and identified which words you tend to mispronounce, you can work to correct the problem.

As you listen to your recording, watch as well for your articulation of words. ESL students whose first languages don't differentiate between the /sh/ sound and its close cousin /ch/, for example, may say "share" when they mean "chair" or "shoes" when they mean "choose."[1] It is therefore important that you also check to make sure that you are using the correct meaning of the words you have selected for your speech.

1. Based on Robbin Crabtree and Robert Weissberg, *ESL Students in the Public Speaking Classroom* (Boston: Bedford/St. Martin's, 2000), 23.

Take the Plunge

As you prepare for your first speech, it is important to follow each step in the speechmaking process described in the previous section. Take note of your progress and be aware of your feelings about the whole process—from the time the assignment is given to the few minutes immediately following the speech.

SELF-ASSESSMENT CHECKLIST

MY FIRST SPEECH

Consider each item in the following checklist in two ways—as something to accomplish during preparation, and as something to consider after you have presented your speech. Use this self-assessment tool to improve future speeches by isolating areas where you need improvement.

Introduction

_____ 1. How will/did I capture attention?

_____ 2. What is/was my thesis statement?

_____ 3. What will/did I say to relate the topic to the audience?

_____ 4. What will/did I say to preview the main points of the speech?

_____ 5. What will/did I say to make the transition from my introduction to my first main point?

Body

_____ 1. Is/was the arrangement of my main points clear and logical?

_____ 2. Do I have/Did I use appropriate support material for each point?

_____ 3. What transition statements will/did I use between main points?

Conclusion

_____ 1. How will/did I restate the thesis/purpose of my speech?

_____ 2. What will/did I say to summarize the main points?

_____ 3. What memorable thought will/did I end the speech with?

Delivery

_____ 1. What will/did I do to assure consistent eye contact?

_____ 2. What will/did I do to project appropriate vocal qualities (rate and volume, clear articulation)?

_____ 3. What will/did I do to ensure proper posture, gestures, and general movement?

My overall assessment of this speech is: _____

What I consider strengths in this speech: _____

Elements I need to improve on: _____

Goals for my next speech: _____

How to Transform an Idea into a Polished Speech

The authors of *A Speaker's Guidebook* worked on this speech project with Professor Gary Russell of Quincy University, a liberal arts university in Illinois. Professor Russell asked student Teresa Gorrell to work with us on her speech of introduction. Our goal was to show how a student can take a first draft of a speech and improve it. We wanted to see how Teresa could improve the language of her speech, as well as the delivery.

Teresa Chooses Her Topic

First, Teresa did some brainstorming, to decide what part of her life she'd like to speak about in her speech of introduction.

Teresa commented, "Based on the sample speeches of introduction that I was sent by my professor, I have gathered that my speech purpose should be to introduce myself by sharing a personal story concerning some life-shaping, character-forming aspect."

With this understanding, Teresa did some thinking and narrowed her options to two ideas for a direction to take.

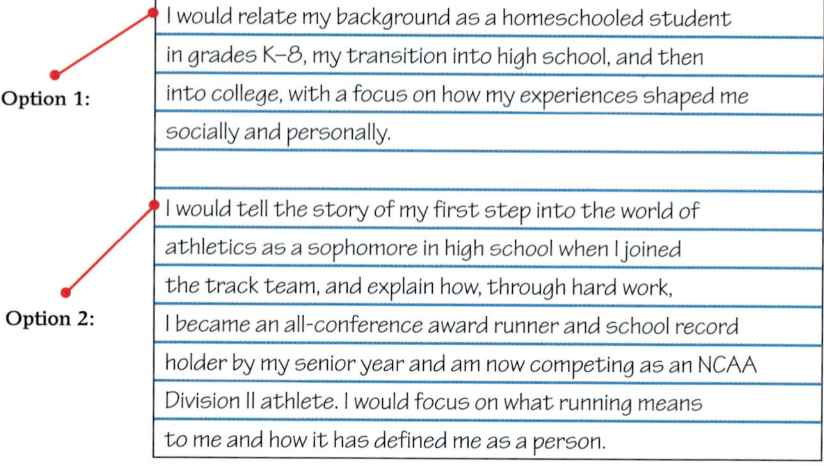
Option 1:
I would relate my background as a homeschooled student in grades K–8, my transition into high school, and then into college, with a focus on how my experiences shaped me socially and personally.
Option 2:
I would tell the story of my first step into the world of athletics as a sophomore in high school when I joined the track team, and explain how, through hard work, I became an all-conference award runner and school record holder by my senior year and am now competing as an NCAA Division II athlete. I would focus on what running means to me and how it has defined me as a person.

Teresa Drafts Her Speech

Teresa's first draft speech was compelling, but the authors thought that she could add more colorful language and details to the introduction. The authors advised Teresa to "set the scene," so that the audience could imagine her daily routine.

Original Introduction

I used to go to school every day wearing slippers. My bedroom doubled as my classroom. My mother was my teacher and my father was my principal. The reason for this is because I was homeschooled.

Revised Introduction

resa ds ore tails.

esa ds orful scrip- ns.

Growing up, my typical school day was very different, compared to what most kids experienced. I'd roll out of bed, slide my feet into some slippers, and run downstairs. I ate breakfast in my pajamas, and then watched TV with my sisters until my mom said that we needed "to hurry up and get ready for school!" At the sound of the school bus wheezing to a stop at the street corner, I'd press my nose against the window pane and watch the neighborhood kids board, one by one, weighed down by overstuffed backpacks and colorful lunchboxes. I lingered at the window until I could no longer see anything but a blur of yellow trailing off in the distance.

Teresa revised her introduction by

- Introducing the idea that a day of learning at home was different than what most kids experienced.
- Adding more details about her daily routine, such as getting up in the morning, playing with her siblings, and then watching the bus from her window.
- Emphasizing the image of her watching the bus take the other neighborhood children to school.

Edited Conclusion

The authors liked the conclusion but thought that the image of a building might be out of place. Since Teresa didn't mention that symbol earlier in her speech, the authors advised her to close with an image already discussed in the speech. Teresa decided to connect back to the opening of the speech and the image of the neighborhood children riding the bus to school.

Original Conclusion

While no experience can fully prepare a person for change, I believe that my formative time in high school prepared me well for college. In high school, I built upon the foundation laid by my homeschool education. By becoming involved in groups, taking on leadership roles, and deliberately developing my character, I fashioned myself into a better version of me. Now, in college, I am continuing to build up that structure. I am erecting an edifice tall and proud, a symbol of my struggles, my lessons, and my triumphs.

Revised Conclusion

Now that I'm in college, my morning routine has reverted back to my homeschool days. Every morning I roll out of bed, push my feet into some slippers, and eat breakfast in my pajamas. Then I rush to dress and get ready for the day. Walking at the edge of campus on my way to class, I watch children across the street trudging up the giant steps to a big yellow bus. My eyes stay fixed on the school bus as it shuts its doors and rolls away. The sight always brings me back to those memories of having my nose pressed against a glass pane, peering out into the "real world" and wondering what it was like. Through my struggles and lessons in high school, it's as though the glass has been broken. I've entered the real world, and I'm still in the process of defining who I am and where I fit in it. My past experiences will continue to guide me as I become the person I dream to be.

Teresa connects images back to the beginning of speech.

While revising the conclusion, Teresa worked on:

- Connecting the images back to the beginning of the speech.
- Reiterating what she's learned from the transition from being homeschooled to attending public high school.
- Using concrete language like "big yellow bus" and "nose pressed against the glass pane" that allows listeners to imagine her surroundings.

The first time Teresa gave her speech, she stood behind a podium, so it was difficult for the audience to see her gestures.

After a lot of practice, Teresa gave her speech again. She improved her delivery by walking around the classroom and using open gestures.

To see Teresa deliver her first draft speech and compare it with her final speech, go to **launchpadworks.com**

SPEECH OF INTRODUCTION

To see Teresa Gorrell deliver her speech, go to **launchpadworks.com**

Homeschooled to High School: My Journey of Growth and Change

TERESA GORRELL
Quincy University

Growing up, my typical school day was very different, compared to what most kids experienced. I'd roll out of bed, slide my feet into some slippers, and run downstairs. I ate breakfast in my pajamas, and then watched television with my sisters until my mom said that we needed "to hurry up and get ready for school!" At the sound of the school bus wheezing to a stop at the street corner, I'd press my nose against the window pane and watch the neighborhood kids board, one by one, weighed down by overstuffed backpacks and cartoon-themed lunchboxes. I lingered at the window until I could no longer see anything but a blur of yellow trailing off in the distance. •

• Teresa uses a personal story to gain her audience's attention and draw them into her speech. This introductory anecdote sets the tone for the entire speech.

Teresa uses animated gestures to emphasize her story.

Finally, it was time to start my own school day. I grabbed my notebook and gathered around the dining room table with my siblings. My mother brought out our textbooks and whatever else was needed for that day's assignments.

Our homeschooling day had begun. •

• Here Teresa introduces her topic and transitions into the body of her speech.

For me, being homeschooled was truly a joy. My family used a rigorous curriculum, but I truly relished the challenge. I worked at my own pace, progressing more quickly in the subjects that were easier for me and spending more time on the tougher ones. It was also fun to be able to spend so much time with my sisters.

This routine lasted from my preschool years until seventh grade. But then, things started to get tough. The coursework became increasingly difficult and the workload sometimes seemed crushing. By the end of my eighth-grade school year, I fell behind and had to work through the summer months to catch up. •

• Teresa speaks of both the joys and the challenges she experienced as a homeschooler, evoking the tension she felt in response to a major change in her life.

As a result of these events, at the start of my ninth-grade year, my parents decided to enroll me in the local public high school. This decision was quite upsetting: I'd enjoyed being homeschooled, despite the demanding work. The idea of change intimidated

Her smile and friendly demeanor connect with the audience.

me, and I was anxious about leaving the comfortable familiarity of my home. I fought my parents' decision fiercely, but their minds were made up. •

• Teresa gets to the crux of her speech – her transition from homeschooling to public school.

One of my major fears as I walked through the doors on my first day of public school was entering the social scene. It's not as if I had been completely isolated from the world the first fourteen years of my life. I belonged to a 4-H club, went to Sunday school, and played community softball. However, these activities didn't adequately prepare me for the culture shock I experienced upon starting public school. I'd rarely been exposed to the kind of language that I began hearing in everyday conversation among my peers and sometimes even from my teachers.

For the most part, I had to make friends from scratch. I was self-conscious; and I felt like I was always being inspected like a specimen under a microscope. •

• By stating some specific feelings that she experienced, Teresa gives authenticity to her story, promoting her credibility with the audience.

As time went on, I slowly acclimated to my new environment. I joined school-sponsored clubs, which gave me the opportunity to bond with my peers. • I learned to appreciate the differences of those around me and I became more comfortable around my classmates and teachers.

• Teresa uses the phrase "As time went on," to give a sense of movement and continuity to her story while also providing a transition to new main point.

Teresa makes eye contact with audience members in all parts of the room.

As I continued to participate in school clubs and activities, I wanted to become more deeply involved. I began to take on leadership roles within these groups. I worked extensively with group members in planning and organizing, which forced me to polish my communication and cooperation skills. I proved to others and to myself that I was a capable leader.

Confidence was certainly not a trait I held prior to my freshman year of high school. However, in the process of branching out and exercising leadership, I began to trust my capabilities. •

• In two brief sentences, Teresa sums up her earlier challenges and how she overcame them and previews her next point – her growing confidence as a person and a leader.

Today, that feeling of self-assurance infuses all aspects of my life. I can now face unfamiliar situations with composure. I can deliver an impromptu speech, perform on stage, or introduce myself to someone new without a qualm. Becoming self-confident has strengthened me as a communicator, as a leader, and as an individual. • Looking back, I'm certain that the transition from a lifetime of homeschooling to the public school system was the most difficult challenge I've ever faced. Yet I don't regret assuming the challenge. My high school experiences formed me, helping me to grow as a communicator, as a leader, and as an individual.

• Here Teresa offers concrete examples of how she has overcome the challenges and uncertainties she faced earlier, reinforcing her central idea of growth and change.

This past fall, I ventured out on another new expedition into another unknown realm — that of college. There's so much to adapt to in the college setting. Dorm life certainly holds its fair share of potential for culture shock and personality conflicts. A first-year freshman college student must learn to balance extracurricular activities with studies and other responsibilities. The college years are an era of independence, a time of new freedoms and choices.

Taking her speech seriously, Teresa dresses in a polished and pulled together way.

While no experience can fully prepare a person for change, I believe that my formative time in high school prepared me well for college. In high school, I built upon the foundation laid by my homeschool education. By becoming involved in groups, taking on leadership roles, and deliberately developing my character, I fashioned myself into a better version of me.

Now that I'm in college, my morning routine has reverted back to my homeschool days. Every morning I roll out of bed, push my feet into some slippers, and eat breakfast in my pajamas. Then I rush to dress and get ready for the day.

Walking at the edge of campus on my way to class, I watch children across the street trudging up the giant steps to a big yellow bus. My eyes stay fixed on the school bus as it shuts its doors and rolls away. The sight always brings me back to those memories of having my nose pressed against a glass pane, peering out into the "real world" and wondering what it was like. Through my struggles and lessons in high school, it's as though the glass has been broken. I've entered the real world, and I'm still in the process of defining who I am and where I fit in it. My past experiences will continue to guide me as I become the person I dream to be. •

• Teresa returns to the same imagery, first offered in the introduction, of her morning routine as a homeschooled child. But Teresa adds a dramatic twist: She's no longer a child on the outside but a confident college student who's "broken through glass." Concluding a speech by using elements of the introduction brings the speech full circle, while offering a strong final image that leaves a lasting impression on the audience.

SAMPLE VISUALLY ANNOTATED INTRODUCTORY SPEECH

To see Ashley White deliver her speech, go to Launchpad: **launchpadworks.com**

The Dance of Life

ASHLEY WHITE

Warm smile connects with audience

We are on a lifelong journey to find our identity. On this journey, we look for those things that make us unique, that bring us success, and that hold us back, and we discover how they define our personality. We set standards for ourselves and observe our boundaries. We take so many extraordinary measures, but when exactly are we supposed to discover who we are? Is there a specific moment? Is there an initiation age? Is it ever certain? What happens if what defines us must suddenly be let go? How do we find new purpose with what is left? •

• Even though the speaker's topic is herself, she draws the audience in with the personal pronoun "We." This captures the audience's attention and makes listeners feel included. The speaker's use of a series of rhetorical questions is a dramatic way to introduce her thesis—the search for identity and purpose in life—and to preview the main points.

Quick pause to glance at notecard

I have always identified myself as a dancer. Since age three I have been in dance classes, but since birth I have danced. It is not a path for the faint of heart, and yet seldom are dancers taken very seriously. Few people outside of the discipline understand the commitment, the scrutiny, the self-sacrifice, the physical and emotional pain—and the unspeakable joy—that dance affords its chosen ones. Dance truly does offer an inexpressible enjoyment, whether performed in the classroom, in rehearsal, or on stage. It becomes more than a hobby. It is self-defining. •

• The speaker's first main point introduces dance as her passion.

My dance teacher was the first to notice the curve, and then I was formally diagnosed with scoliosis at the age of ten. Scoliosis is a lateral curvature of the spine ranging from slight to severe. It often gets worse during adolescent growth and stops worsening when growth stops. It affects girls and boys, but it is not life threatening. •

• The speaker introduces her second main point, that she developed scoliosis. She adds drama by signaling, in story form, that something has gone wrong with her chosen path.

Effective gestures underscore emotion

At eleven, I was wearing a back brace at night, and at twelve, both day and night. Adolescence is a difficult time to deal with any anomaly. During a time when everyone was trying to fit the norm, the brace made me feel different. This caused me much anxiety and depression. Dance class was my only time of liberation, which made my desire to dance even stronger. •

I stopped wearing the brace once I got to high school because I had stopped growing; but during my second semester of college I received troubling news. My curve had worsened by fifteen degrees in four years, and it was time to consider surgery. The doctor informed me from the start that, with the surgery, dancing professionally would not be likely, although I would be able to dance recreationally. He also advised that without the surgery, my spine would continue to curve, leaving me with lifelong discomfort and misshapenness. I went through with the surgery in July 2007. The doctors placed two titanium rods on either side of my spine, held in place by hooks. Two months later, I am still recovering and have little pain. •

• In a surprise twist, the speaker tells us that she has found a new passion. This is her third main point.

Ashley turns to address audience members in all corners of the room

I am thankful for my overall health, for the success of the surgery, that one day soon I will dance again, and that amongst all this emotional turmoil, I have found a new passion. This art is expressed in the kitchen, not in the dance studio, and my training begins here at Johnson and Wales University. Cooking and dancing require many of the same skills: discipline, artistry, technique. •

However, knowledge of food can also provide me with endless career opportunities, where as a dancer I might never have worked steadily. This transition of redefining myself has been a difficult one, and I have learned that it is actually an ongoing one. Being in touch with oneself requires constant learning, redefining, and reapplying, and not just being dedicated to a single interest. This lifelong journey I am on? I know now that this is just the beginning of finding my own identity. •

• The speaker concludes by returning to the theme she introduced in her introduction: the quest for identity.

PUBLIC SPEAKING BASICS

Bassem Youssef is an Egyptian comedian and satirist who now lives in the United States and speaks about politics and equality. In this photo, he was discussing his show "The Democracy Handbook" at the AOL Speaker Series. Roy Rochlin/Getty Images

PUBLIC SPEAKING BASICS

SPEAKER'S PREVIEW

LearningCurve can help you review.
Go to LaunchPad: **launchpadworks.com**

PUBLIC SPEAKING BASICS

CHAPTER 3 Managing Speech Anxiety

Understand What Makes Us Anxious about Public Speaking

- A lack of public speaking experience: It can be difficult to put into perspective the anxiety that often precedes new experiences. (p. 43)
- Feeling different: Remember, even seasoned speakers feel anxiety. (p. 44)
- Being the center of attention: The audience won't notice things about you that you don't want to reveal. (p. 44)

Pinpoint the Onset of Your Anxiety and Plan to Overcome It

- Some people become anxious upon hearing that they must give a speech (pre-preparation anxiety). (p. 45)

  Don't allow your anxiety to deter you from planning your speech.
- For some, anxiety occurs as they begin to prepare the speech (preparation anxiety). (p. 46)

  Beware of avoidance and procrastination.
- Some people begin to feel anxious when it is time to rehearse the speech (pre-performance anxiety). (p. 46)

  Practice your speech to build confidence.
- Many people experience public speaking anxiety only when they begin to deliver the speech (performance anxiety). (p. 46)

  Practice stress-control breathing and other relaxation techniques.

Use Proven Strategies to Build Your Confidence

- Plan your presentation thoroughly. (p. 47)
- Rehearse often until you know how you want to express yourself. (p. 47)
- Lessen anxiety by using positive thoughts prior to delivery. (p. 47)

Go to LaunchPad to watch a video about managing speech anxiety.

LaunchPad includes:

LearningCurve adaptive quizzing

a curated collection of video clips and full-length speeches.

Additional resources and reference materials such as presentation software tutorials and documentation help.

Use Visualization and Relaxation Techniques to Control Anxiety

- Visualize a positive outcome. (p. 48)
- Consider meditation, stress-control breathing, and natural gestures. (p. 50)

Enjoy the Occasion

- You have the chance to influence others. (p. 51)
- Use feedback from others constructively to note your strengths and discover where your speechmaking can be improved. (p. 51)

CHAPTER 4 Listeners and Speakers

Recognize the Importance of Listening

- Skill in listening is linked to leadership potential. (p. 52)
- Listening to speeches takes focus and skill. (p. 53)
- Listening scholars note different types of listening linked to different purposes: understanding, evaluation and action, support, pleasure. (p. 53)
- *Active listening* is focused and purposeful. (p. 53)

Understand the Difference between Hearing and Listening

- *Hearing* is the physiological process of perceiving sound; *listening* is a conscious act of receiving, constructing meaning from, and responding to spoken and nonverbal messages. (p. 53)

Recognize That We Listen Selectively

- People pay attention to what they hold to be important. (p. 54)
- People pay attention to information that touches their beliefs and experiences. (p. 54)
- People ignore or downplay information that contradicts their beliefs. (p. 54)

Anticipate Common Obstacles to Listening

- Plan ahead in order to minimize the impact of external distractions such as noise, movement, light, darkness, heat or cold, and so forth. (p. 54)
- Try not to let internal distractions, such as daydreaming, time pressures, emotional turmoil, or fatigue, disrupt your concentration. (p. 54)
- Beware of listening defensively: Wait for the speaker to finish before devising your own mental arguments. (p. 54)

- Refrain from multitasking, such as checking your cell phone. (p. 56)
- Guard against scriptwriting and defensive listening. (p. 56)
- Beware of laziness and overconfidence. (p. 56)

Practice Active Listening Strategies

- Set listening goals that encourage action. (p. 58)
- Listen for main ideas and take notes. (p. 59)

Evaluate Evidence and Reasoning

- Evaluate the speaker's evidence for accuracy and credibility. (p. 59)
- Analyze the speaker's assumptions and biases. (p. 59)
- Assess the speaker's reasoning: Look for weak arguments. (p. 59)
- Consider alternate perspectives. (p. 59)
- Summarize and assess the relevant facts and evidence before deciding how you will act on the speaker's information or argument. (p. 59)

Strive for the Open Exchange of Ideas

- Think about sharing ideas with the audience rather than delivering a monologue. (p. 59)

Offer Constructive and Compassionate Feedback

- Be honest and fair in your evaluation. (p. 60)
- Do not judge the message's content on the basis of the speaker's communication style. (p. 60)
- Be compassionate in your criticism: Start with something positive; be selective in your criticism; and focus on the speech, not on the speaker. (p. 60)

CHAPTER 5 Ethical Public Speaking

Take Responsibility for Your Words

- Be morally accountable to yourself and your audience for your message. (p. 62)
- Accept responsibility for the stands you take. (p. 62)

Demonstrate Competence and Character

- Display good character (ethos). (p. 63)
- Develop a solid grasp of your subject (competence). (p. 63)

- Display sound reasoning skills. (p. 63)
- Present information honestly and without manipulation. (p. 63)
- Be genuinely interested in the welfare of your listeners. (p. 63)

Respect Your Listeners' Values

- Consider the audience's values as you plan your speech. (p. 63)
- Be aware that conflicting values lie at the heart of many controversial issues. (p. 63)
- When your topic is controversial, consider both sides of an issue. (p. 64)

Be Aware of Different Ethical Perspectives

- Three prominent ethical theories—consequentialist ethics, rules-based ethics, and virtue ethics—propose different standards and rationales for making ethical choices. (p. 64)
- Discover your own values using the instruments in the text. (p. 65)

Contribute to Positive Public Discourse

- Advance constructive goals. (p. 66)
- Avoid introducing invective and other conversation stoppers into public discourse. (p. 67)
- Follow the rules of engagement for civil public discourse. (p. 67)

Use Your Rights of Free Speech Responsibly

- As a public speaker, you face balancing your rights of free speech with the responsibilities that accompany these rights. (p. 67)
- The First Amendment provides protection both to truthful speakers and to speakers whose words are inflammatory and offensive. (p. 67)
- Be aware that certain types of speech are illegal:

  Speech that provokes people to violence ("fighting words")

  Speech that can be proved to harm an individual's reputation (slander or defamatory statements)

  Words spoken with a reckless disregard for the truth (p. 67)

Avoid Hate Speech in Any Form

- *Hate speech* is any offensive communication directed against people's racial, ethnic, religious, gender, or other characteristics. (p. 67)
- Avoid ethnocentrism and any hint of stereotyping. (p. 67)

Observe the Ground Rules for Ethical Speaking

- Demonstrate dignity and integrity in your own character and accord it to each audience member. (p. 69)

- Tell the truth, don't distort information, and acknowledge sources. (p. 70)
- Show respect for audience members. (p. 70)
- Be accountable for what you say. (p. 70)
- Acknowledge alternative and opposing views. (p. 70)
- Be civic-minded. (p. 71)

Avoid Plagiarism

- Orally acknowledge any source that requires credit in written form: other people's ideas, opinions, theories, evidence, and research; direct quotations; paraphrased information; facts and statistics. (p. 72)
- Know how to directly quote, paraphrase, or summarize a source. (p. 72)

Understand the Rules of Fair Use and Copyright

- Copyright law protects *intellectual property* (original authorship). (p. 74)
- The *fair use* doctrine permits limited use of copyrighted materials without permission; such material must be orally credited in your speech. (p. 74)

KEY TERMS

Chapter 3

public speaking anxiety (PSA)
illusion of transparency
pre-preparation anxiety
preparation anxiety
pre-performance anxiety
anxiety stop-time technique
performance anxiety
trait anxiety
visualization
"fight or flight response"

Chapter 4

active listening
hearing/listening
selective perception
listening distraction
defensive listening
critical thinking
dialogic communication

Chapter 5

responsibility
ethics
communication ethics
ethos
source credibility
values
ethical theory
consequentialist ethics
rules-based ethics
virtue ethics
public discourse
invective
conversation stopper
"rules of engagement"
free speech
First Amendment
hate speech
"fighting words"
slander
reckless disregard for the truth

SPEAKER'S PREVIEW

ethnocentrism
stereotypes
speech codes
dignity
integrity
civic virtues
trustworthiness
respect
responsibility
fairness
civic-minded
plagiarism
intellectual property
direct quotation
paraphrase
summary
copyright
public domain
fair use

Go to LaunchPad: **launchpadworks.com** to watch the video clips for this chapter.

3 Managing Speech Anxiety

LearningCurve can help you review!
Go to LaunchPad: **launchpadworks.com**

> *When you face your fear, most of the time you will discover that it was not really such a big threat after all.* —Les Brown, speaker, author, DJ, politician

Contrary to what most of us think, feeling nervous about giving a speech is considered one of the less severe social anxieties.[1] Nervous energy can boost performance, as it does for the singer Adele, who has fought stage fright since age sixteen. She channels her nervous energy into powerful performances by breathing with her diaphragm instead of her chest,[2] a technique many people delivering a speech find enormously helpful. This chapter introduces specific techniques that speakers use to minimize their tension.

> I imagine my audience taking in the information I'm presenting like a toddler tasting a new food for the first time. When I focus on their interest and wonderment, I am engaged in their experience and don't notice my fear or anxiety. —*Sam Torrez, student*

Identify What Makes You Anxious

Anxiety about giving a speech is one of the less severe types of *social anxiety*—a state of uneasiness brought on by fear. Some of us tend to be more anxious than others about public speaking because of our particular psychological traits, life experiences, or even genetic factors. Researchers have identified several factors that underlie a fear of public speaking: a lack of public speaking experience, or having had a negative experience; feeling different from members of the audience; and uneasiness about being the center of attention.[3] Each factor can precipitate **public speaking anxiety (PSA)**—"a situation-specific social anxiety that arises from the real or anticipated enactment of an oral presentation."[4] Fortunately, we can learn techniques to tame this anxiety and make it work for us. The first step is to identify what makes us anxious.

Lack of Positive Experience

If you are new to public speaking or have had unpleasant experiences, anxiety about what to expect is only natural. And without positive experiences to draw on, it's hard to put this anxiety into perspective. It's a bit of a vicious circle. Some people react by deciding to avoid making speeches altogether, yet gaining more experience is key to overcoming speech anxiety.

Feeling Different

The prospect of getting up in front of an audience makes many of us extra-sensitive to our personal idiosyncrasies, such as a less-than-perfect haircut, a slight lisp, or an accent. We may even believe that no one could possibly be interested in anything we have to say.

As inexperienced speakers, we become anxious because we assume that being different somehow means being inferior. Actually, everyone is different from everyone else in many ways, and nearly everyone experiences some nervousness about giving a speech.

> I control my anxiety by mentally viewing myself as being 100 percent equal to my classmates. —*Lee Morris, student*

Being the Center of Attention

Certain audience behaviors—such as chatting with a neighbor or checking text messages during a presentation—can cause us as speakers to think that we lost the audience's attention by doing something wrong; we wonder about our mistakes and whether others noticed these supposed flaws. Researchers have termed this tendency the **illusion of transparency**—when a speaker thinks his or her anxiety is more noticeable than it is.[5] Left unchecked, this kind of self-consciousness can distract us from the speech itself, with all our attention now focused on "me." We then become more sensitive to things that might be wrong—and that makes us feel even more conspicuous, which in turn increases our anxiety! Actually, an audience rarely notices anything about us that we don't want to reveal.

> It's always scary to speak in front of others, but you just have to remember that everyone is human. . . . Nobody wants you to fail; they're not waiting on you to mess up. —*Mary Parrish, student*

Pinpoint the Onset of Public Speaking Anxiety

Different people become anxious at different times during the speechmaking process. Some people start to feel anxious as soon as they learn that they will have to give a speech. Others don't really get nervous until they approach the podium. Even the kind of speech assigned (e.g., being called on to deliver off-the-cuff remarks versus reading from prepared remarks) may be a factor in when and how much a speaker feels anxious.[6] By pinpointing the onset of speech anxiety, you can manage it promptly with specific anxiety-reducing techniques (see Figure 3.1).

CHECKLIST

RECOGNIZING AND OVERCOMING YOUR UNDERLYING FEARS ABOUT PUBLIC SPEAKING

Problem	Solution
Are you intimidated by a lack of experience?	✓ Prepare well and practice your speech several times in front of at least one other person. This actual experience delivering your speech will help build your confidence.
Are you worried about appearing different from others?	✓ Remember that everyone is different from everyone else. Dress appropriately for the occasion and be well groomed to make a good impression.
Are you uncomfortable about being the center of attention?	✓ Focus on the speech and not on yourself, and remember that the audience won't notice anything about you that you don't want to reveal.

Pre-Preparation Anxiety

Some people feel anxious the minute they know they will be giving a speech. **Pre-preparation anxiety** can be a problem when we delay planning for the speech, or when it so preoccupies us that we miss vital information needed to fulfill the speech assignment. If this form of anxiety affects you, start very early using the stress-reducing techniques described later in this chapter.

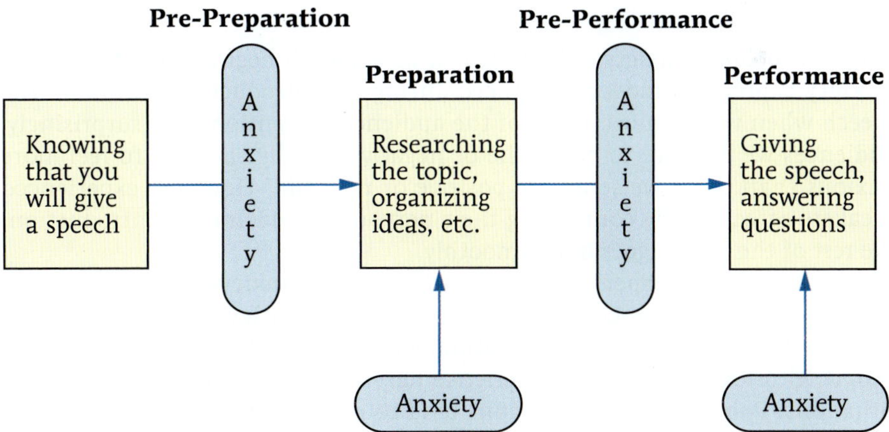

FIGURE 3.1 Where Anxiety Can Occur in the Speechmaking Process

Preparation Anxiety

For a few people, anxiety arises only when they actually begin to prepare for the speech. These individuals might feel overwhelmed by the amount of time and planning required or hit a roadblock that puts them behind schedule. Preparation pressures produce a cycle of stress, procrastination, and outright avoidance, all of which contribute to **preparation anxiety**. Research has shown, however, that for most speakers, anxiety is lowest during the preparation phase,[7] suggesting that the best way to gain a sense of control and confidence is to immerse yourself in the speech's preparation. But over-preparation can also be an indicator of poorly managed anxiety.[8] If you find yourself practicing endlessly, shift your focus to the anxiety-reducing techniques described below.

Pre-Performance Anxiety

Some people experience anxiety as they rehearse their speech. This is when the reality of the situation sets in: They worry that the audience will be watching and listening only to them; or they feel that their ideas aren't as focused or as interesting as they should be, and they sense that time is short. If this **pre-performance anxiety** is strong enough, some may even decide to stop rehearsing too soon. If you experience heightened anxiety at this point, consider using **anxiety stop-time technique**: Allow your anxiety to present itself for up to a few minutes until you declare time for confidence to step in so you can proceed to complete your practice.[9]

> I experience anxiety before, during, and after the speech. My "before speech" anxiety begins the night before my speech, but then I begin to look over my notecards, and I start to realize that I am ready for this speech. I practice one more time and I tell myself I am going to be fine. —*Paige Mease, student*

Performance Anxiety

For most people, anxiety is highest just as a speech begins.[10] **Performance anxiety** is probably most pronounced during the introduction portion of the speech when we are most aware of the audience's attention. Not surprisingly, audiences we perceive to be hostile or negative usually cause us to feel more anxious than those we sense are positive or neutral.[11] However, experienced speakers agree that by controlling their nervousness during the introduction, the rest of the speech goes quite smoothly.

Each of us will experience more or less speech anxiety at these four different points in the process depending mainly on our level of **trait anxiety**. People with high trait anxiety are naturally anxious much of the time, whereas people with low trait anxiety experience nervousness usually only in unusual situations. Public speaking situations tend to make people nervous regardless of their level of trait anxiety. But they can be more challenging for high trait-anxious individuals than for low trait-anxious persons. For instance, researchers have shown that low trait-anxious people get nervous when starting a speech but gain confidence throughout the speech. Regardless of your level of trait anxiety, when anxiety about a speech strikes, the important thing to remember is that you can manage the anxiety and control the time and effort you put into planning, rehearsing, and delivering a successful speech.

Use Proven Strategies to Build Your Confidence

A number of proven strategies exist to help you rein in your fears about public speaking, from *meditation* and *visualization* to other forms of relaxation techniques. The first step in taming speech anxiety is to have a thorough plan for each presentation. As professional speaker Lenny Laskowski sums it up in the 9 Ps, "Prior Proper Preparation Prevents Poor Performance of the Person Putting on the Presentation."[12]

Prepare and Practice

Preparation should begin as soon as possible after a speech is assigned. If you are confident that you know your material and have adequately rehearsed your delivery, you're far more likely to feel confident at the podium. Once you have prepared the speech, you should rehearse it several times. Recent research shows that students who practiced their speeches in front of small audiences of three to eight people received significantly higher evaluations of their classroom speeches than students who didn't practice or practiced in different ways.[13] And although practicing didn't directly produce lower speech anxiety, the overall better performance outcomes for those who did practice suggest that even the more anxious students were better able to control their anxiety. Speech coach John Robert Colombo emphasizes that the best way to work out your fear of speaking is to *overwork* it[14]—practice as often as you can, and, in the future, accept as many speaking engagements as appropriate.

> Knowing your material is crucial! The worst anxiety comes when you feel unprepared. You just can't help but be nervous, at least a little. If you are confident about what you're speaking, the anxiety fades and you'll feel more comfortable.
>
> —*Shea Michelle Allen, student*

Modify Thoughts and Attitudes

Negative thoughts about speechmaking increase speech anxiety, but positive thoughts reduce it. As you prepare for and deliver your speech, envision it as a valuable, worthwhile, and challenging activity. Encourage yourself with positive self-talk.[15] That is, remind yourself of all the reasons that public speaking is helpful personally, socially, and professionally. Think of speechmaking as a kind of ordinary conversation instead of a formal performance. In this way, you will feel less threatened and more relaxed about the process.[16] And with each successive speech experience, your thoughts and attitudes about public speaking will be increasingly favorable.

ESL SPEAKER'S NOTES

Confidence and Culture: When English Isn't Your First Language

NASA Goddard Space Flight Center

For native English speakers, the fear of being at center stage is normal. If you are a non-native speaker, public speaking anxiety can create an added challenge, but also an opportunity.[1] It is important to know that you are not alone.

Try to think about public speaking as an opportunity to learn more about the English language and how to use it. Following are some tips that all novice speakers, regardless of whether English is their first language, will find helpful.

1. Take your time and speak slowly as you introduce the purpose and the main points of your speech. This will give your listeners time to get used to your voice and to focus on your message.
2. Practice saying any English words that may be troublesome for you five times. Then say the words again, five times. Progress slowly until each word becomes clearer and easier to pronounce. This type of practice will give you time to work on any accent features you might want to improve.[2]
3. Avoid using jargon (see Chapter 16, "Using Language to Style Speech"). Learn to use a thesaurus to find *synonyms*, or words that mean the same thing, that are simpler and easier to pronounce.
4. Offer words from your native language as a way of drawing attention to a point you're making. This helps the audience appreciate your native language and your accent. For example, the Spanish word *corazón* has a more lyrical quality than its English counterpart, *heart*. Capitalize on the beauty of your native tongue.

1. T. Docan-Morgan and T. Schmidt, "Reducing Public Speaking Anxiety for Native and Non-Native English Speakers: The Value of Systematic Desensitization, Cognitive Restructuring, and Skills Training," *Cross-Cultural Communication* 8 (2012): 16–19.
2. J. E. Flege, J. M. Munro, and I. R. A. MacKay, "Factors Affecting Strength of Perceived Foreign Accent in a Second Language," *Journal of the Acoustical Society of America* 97 (1995): 3125ff.

> Just before a speech those feelings of anxiety undoubtedly try to sneak in. The way I keep them from taking over is to not let my mind become negative! As long as I keep positive thoughts of confidence in my head, anxiety doesn't stand a chance!
> —*Morgan Verdery, student*

Visualize Success

Visualization—the practice of summoning feelings and actions consistent with successful performance—is a highly effective method of reducing speech anxiety.[17, 18] Speech communication researchers have developed scripts for visualizing success and increasing positive expectations associated with a public speaking occasion; one such script is below. It requires you, the speaker, to close your eyes and visualize a series of positive feelings and actions that will occur on the day of your speech. Practicing the mental exercise of seeing yourself give a successful speech will help you prepare with confidence and strengthen your positive attitudes and expectations for speechmaking.

> Close your eyes and allow your body to get comfortable in the chair in which you are sitting. Take a deep, comfortable breath and hold it . . . now slowly release it through your nose. Now take another deep breath and make certain that you are breathing from the diaphragm . . . hold it . . . now slowly release it and note how you feel while doing this. Now one more deep breath . . . hold it . . . and release it slowly . . . and begin your normal breathing pattern. Shift around if you need to get comfortable again.
>
> Now begin to visualize the beginning of a day in which you are going to give an informative speech. See yourself getting up in the morning, full of energy, full of confidence, looking forward to the day's challenges. As you dress, you think about how dressing well makes you look and feel good about yourself. As you are driving, riding, or walking to the speech setting, note how clear and confident you feel. You feel thoroughly prepared to discuss the topic that you will be presenting today.
>
> Now you see yourself standing or sitting in the room where you will present your speech, talking very comfortably and confidently with others in the room. The people to whom you will be presenting your speech appear to be quite friendly and are very cordial in their greetings and conversations prior to the presentation. You feel absolutely sure of your material and of your ability to present the information in a forceful, convincing, positive manner.
>
> Now you see yourself approaching the area from which you will present. You are feeling very good about this presentation and see yourself move eagerly forward. All of your audiovisual materials are well organized, well planned, and clearly aid your presentation.[19]

Activate the Relaxation Response

Before, during, and sometimes after a speech you may experience rapid heart rate and breathing, dry mouth, faintness, freezing-up, or other uncomfortable sensations. These physiological reactions result from the "**fight or flight response**"—the body's automatic response to threatening or fear-inducing events. These sensations indicate the body is preparing to confront a threat head-on ("fight") or to make a hasty escape from the threat ("flight").[20] Research shows that you can counteract these sensations by activating a relaxation response using techniques such as meditation and controlled breathing.[21] The opposite of fight or flight, the relaxation response is a state of deep physical rest that decreases stress. Just as you would warm up before taking a lengthy jog, use the following relaxation techniques before, and even during, your speech to help slow your heart rate and breathing rate, lower your blood pressure, increase blood flow to major muscles, and reduce muscle tension. These more relaxed physiological sensations help you feel better[22] and result in better concentration and sharper performance.

LaunchPad
Go to LaunchPad to listen to the Relaxation Audio Download: **launchpadworks.com**

Briefly Meditate

You can calm yourself considerably before delivering a presentation with this brief meditation exercise:

1. Sit comfortably in a quiet place.
2. Relax your muscles, moving from neck to shoulders to arms to back to legs.
3. Choose a word, phrase, or prayer associated with your belief system (e.g., "Namaste," "Om," "Hail Mary, full of grace"). Breathe slowly and say it until you become calm (about ten to twenty minutes).

Use Stress-Control Breathing

When you feel stressed, the center of your breathing tends to move from the abdomen to the upper chest, and the chest and shoulders rise—leaving you with a reduced supply of air and feeling out of breath. *Stress-control breathing* gives you more movement in the stomach than in the chest. Try it in two stages.

Stage One Inhale air and let your abdomen go out. Exhale air and let your abdomen go in. Do this for a while until you get into the rhythm of it.

Stage Two As you inhale, use a soothing word such as *calm* or *relax*, or a personal mantra, like this: "Inhale *calm*, abdomen out, exhale *calm*, abdomen in." Go slowly, taking about three to five seconds with each inhalation and exhalation.

Begin practicing stress-control breathing several days before a speech event. Then, once the occasion arrives, begin stress-control breathing while awaiting your turn at the podium. And you can continue the breathing pattern as you approach the podium, and once more while you're arranging your notes and getting ready to begin.

> I have two ways to cope with my nervousness before I'm about to speak. I take a couple deep breaths through my stomach; I breathe in through my nose and out of my mouth. This allows more oxygen to the brain so you can think clearly. I also calm myself down by saying, "Everything will be okay, and the world is not going to crumble before me if I mess up." —*Jenna Sanford, student*

Use Movement to Minimize Anxiety

During delivery, you can use controlled movements with your hands and body to release nervousness (see Chapter 19, "The Body in Delivery").

Practice Natural Gestures

Practice natural gestures such as holding up your index finger when stating your first main point. Think about what you want to say as you do this, instead of thinking about how you look or feel.

Move as You Speak

You don't have to stand perfectly still behind the podium when you deliver a speech. Walk around as you make some of your points. Movement relieves tension and helps hold the audience's attention. Some actual exercise a few hours prior to your speech can sharpen your mental focus, leaving you more limber and better able to move naturally.[23]

Enjoy the Occasion

Most people ultimately find that giving speeches can indeed be fun. It's satisfying and empowering to influence people, and a good speech is a sure way to do this. All of the time and effort that go into preparing and delivering a speech, from the moment the assignment is made to the moment you step away from the podium, make public speaking both challenging and exciting. Think of it in this way, and chances are you will find much pleasure in it.

Learn from Feedback

Speech evaluations help to identify ways to improve what you do. You can learn a lot through self-evaluation, but self-perceptions can be distorted,[24] so objective evaluations by others often are more helpful. In your speech class, your speech assignments will be evaluated by your instructor, of course, and probably by your classmates as well. Both sources will provide practical feedback to help you improve your next speeches. Ultimately, all speakers rely on audience feedback to evaluate the effectiveness of their speeches.

CHECKLIST

PREPARING TO SPEAK WITH CONFIDENCE

Your confidence will grow with each successful completion of a speech assignment, but both confidence and success result mainly from diligent preparation. Follow these general steps as part of your plan for each speech.

- ✓ *Prepare and practice.* Start early, even when selecting your topic, to decide when and where you will practice your speech.
- ✓ *Modify thoughts and attitudes.* Keep positive thoughts, concentrating on what makes sense as you develop your topic, and on the positive outcomes expected from your speech.
- ✓ *Visualize success.* Practice an optimistic frame of mind, seeing yourself with well-developed speech points that you deliver enthusiastically and effectively.
- ✓ *Utilize relaxation techniques.* Use stress-control breathing and natural hand and body movement while speaking.
- ✓ *Learn from the task and enjoy it.* Consider each speech assignment a learning opportunity to enrich future academic and career objectives.

4 Listeners and Speakers

LearningCurve can help you review!
Go to LaunchPad: **launchpadworks.com**

What would it be like to give a speech that no one heard? Merely posing this question points to the central role of listeners in a speech. In fact, all successful communication is two-way, including that of public speaking. Listeners and speakers are interdependent: As speakers, we need an audience, and as listeners, we need someone to whom we can listen. But the relationship between speaking and listening goes deeper than this. Connecting with audience members requires that we know what they care about, which in turn necessitates our taking the time to learn about, or listen to, them. We do this by analyzing the audience before preparing the speech (see Chapter 6 on analyzing the audience) and by being responsive to listeners during it.

As a listener, connecting with a speaker also takes focus. We can decide to tune out the speaker and ignore the message, uncritically accept or hypercritically reject whatever is said, or bring our full attention and critical faculties to bear. Thus it is listener and speaker together who truly make a speech possible.

Recognize the Centrality of Listening

More than any other single communication act, we listen. We listen to *gain understanding*, to *evaluate and act on information*, to *provide support*, and to *experience the sheer pleasure of receiving sound*, as in listening to music[1] (see Table 4.1). College students in the United States spend more time listening (about 24 percent) than they do on any other communication activity, such as speaking (20 percent), using the Internet (13 percent), writing (9 percent), or reading (8 percent).[2] Listening is also the number one activity employees do during the workday, taking precedence over twenty other frequently observed workplace behaviors.[3] Managers overwhelmingly associate listening skills with leadership potential, promoting employees who display them and hiring new entrants who appear to possess them.[4] Competent listeners tend to be efficient and successful in both their personal and professional lives and tend to be better problem solvers and more engaged citizens.[5]

As you can see, focusing on the art of listening will serve you well in many arenas other than public speaking. The public speaking classroom itself is the perfect place to hone your listening skills. Here you can practice **active listening**—listening that is focused and purposeful—as you attend to your classmates' speeches. You will be able to observe what will and won't work for your speech, and offer constructive criticism. You can watch for "listenable language"[6] in others' speeches and experiment with it in your own, preparing speeches for the ear rather than the eye—the listener rather than the reader (see Chapter 16, "Using Language to Style the Speech").

TABLE 4.1 Types of Listening

Type of Listening	Function	Example
Comprehensive listening	To gain understanding	Listening to a lecture; asking for instructions or directions
Critical listening	To critically evaluate or make judgments about and act on information; to be a responsible receiver of information	Listening critically to explanations in an informative speech or arguments in a persuasive speech; identifying bias and logical fallacies, and making decisions about your own point of view
Empathic listening	To provide support	Listening compassionately to a friend express grief over loss; sharing feelings with friends and family
Appreciative listening	To experience pleasure and enjoyment	Listening to music or another art form

Understand the Difference between Hearing and Listening

Many of us assume that listening comes naturally. But *hearing* and *listening* are two distinct processes. **Hearing** is the physiological, largely involuntary process of perceiving sound. Hearing loss is a major condition for young and old alike, affecting over 5 million children and adolescents ages 6–19 and 26 million adults ages 20–69.[7] Being sensitive to audience members' ability to hear you, by speaking at a rate and volume sufficient for your audience, is an important aspect of "listening" to audience members. So too is being sensitive to nonnative speakers of English, who may have difficulty understanding your words because of your speech rate, articulation, and/or pronunciation patterns (see Chapter 18, "The Voice in Delivery"). But while hearing has to do with the intelligibility of sounds, **listening** is the conscious act of receiving, constructing meaning from, and responding to spoken and nonverbal messages.[8] Listening involves consciously *selecting* what you will listen to, *giving it your attention*, *processing* and *understanding* it, *remembering* the information, and *responding* to it—either verbally, nonverbally, or through both channels.[9] During a speech, for example, speakers are highly attuned to the body language of audience members and can read a great deal from it (see Chapter 6 Checklist, "Respond to the Audience as You Speak," p. 91).

Recognize That We Listen Selectively

Can you recall sharing reactions with a friend about a guest speaker at your college or a televised speech by a politician and noticing that even though you both heard the same speaker, you formed quite different impressions? In any given situation, no two listeners will process information in exactly the same way. The reason lies in **selective perception**—people pay attention selectively to certain messages while ignoring others.[10] Several factors influence what we listen to and what we ignore.

1. *We pay attention to what we hold to be important.* We are most motivated to listen to others if we think that what is being said affects us or reflects our interests, needs, values, attitudes, and beliefs.
2. *We pay attention to information that touches our beliefs and expectations* and ignore, downplay, or even belittle messages that contradict them.

The idea that perceptions are, by their very nature, subject to our biases and expectations does not mean we must be blinded by them. To a certain extent, selective perception is simply human nature, but in your dual roles as listener and speaker there are constructive steps you can take to counter it: For example, as a *listener*, examine your expectations and motivations to hear things a certain way, and ask yourself whether you are really hearing what the speaker is saying. Focus on evaluating the message without prejudgment, and be alert to screening out parts of the speaker's messages that don't immediately align with your views. As a *speaker*, give the audience good reasons to care about your message. Focus on demonstrating the topic's relevance to the audience. In so far as possible, use audience analysis to anticipate and address audience attitudes and beliefs.

Anticipate Obstacles to Listening

Selective perception is hardly our only obstacle to listening, whether to a speech or to something else. Active listening isn't possible under conditions that distract us. In any listening situation, try to identify and overcome some common obstacles, whether they be from competing noise in the environment, attempts to multitask, or a defensive attitude.

Minimize External and Internal Distractions

A **listening distraction** is anything that competes for attention we are trying to give to something else. External distractions originate outside of us, in the

ESL SPEAKER'S NOTES

Learning by Listening and Feedback

NASA Goddard Space Flight Center

As any language student knows, listening and feedback are the keys to learning. Using textbooks to study usage and grammar is important, but it is through the *spoken language*—hearing it and speaking it—that we gain fluency; and it is through *feedback* from others that we discover whether or not we have been understood.

Listening to the speeches of colleagues or classmates, as well as those broadcast on YouTube, TV, radio, TED talks, or podcasts, can help hone the skills needed to become a better speaker. Nearly all college libraries own many recorded and online materials made specifically for ESL speakers. Among the many helpful sites you will find on the Internet is the *Merriam-Webster Online Dictionary* (www.merriam-webster.com), which includes an audio feature that allows you to hear the correct pronunciation of words.

As you listen to these resources, you can

- Build your vocabulary
- Improve pronunciation through guided repetition
- Learn new *idioms*, or informal expressions, used by native speakers of English
- Observe body posture, gestures, intonation, and other nonverbal aspects of delivery[1]

When preparing for classroom speeches, recording your speech can be especially helpful. Begin by reviewing it alone, then with the instructor and/or another native speaker. Listen for the following.

- *Pronunciation*: Are your words intelligible?
- *Rate of speaking*: Are you speaking too fast or too slow for others to understand you?
- *Grammar*: Are there mistakes that will distort your meaning? Use feedback to discover this.[2]

1. See also Melissa Beall, "Perspectives on Intercultural Listening," in *Listening and Human Communication in the Twenty-First Century*, ed. Andrew. D. Wolvin (Boston: Wiley-Blackwell, 2010), 225–38.
2. Robbin D. Crabtree and David Alan Sapp, *ESL Students in the Public Speaking Classroom*, 2nd ed. (Bedford/St. Martin's, 2000).

environment, while internal distractions occur within our own thoughts and feelings.

External listening distractions, such as the din of jackhammers or competing conversations, can significantly interfere with our ability to listen, so try to anticipate and plan for them. For example, if you struggle to see or hear over noise or at a distance, arrive early and sit in the front. As for *internal*

CHECKLIST

DEALING WITH DISTRACTIONS DURING DELIVERY OF A SPEECH

Problem: **Passing distractions** (chatting, entry of latecomers)

✓ *Solution:* Pause until distraction recedes

Problem: **Ongoing noise** (construction)

✓ *Solution:* Raise speaking volume

Problem: **Sudden distraction** (collapsing chair, falling object)

✓ *Solution:* Minimize response and proceed

Problem: **Audience interruption** (raised hand, prolonged comment)

✓ *Solution:* Acknowledge audience reaction and either follow up or defer response to conclusion of speech

listening distractions, so often we attend an event, whether it be a class lecture or a major speech, and fail to follow the speaker's words. We might be tired or upset about something that occurred prior to the event. To reduce these kinds of impediments to listening, make some intentions for yourself. Remind yourself to avoid daydreaming and monitor yourself for lapses in attention. Ideally, plan on being well rested for any important speaking event you attend.

Refrain from Multitasking

Whether attending a speech or engaging in conversation, you cannot listen well while multitasking. Activities such as checking a cell phone or calendar, finishing an assignment, or responding to a text divert our attention from the message and reduce our ability to interpret it accurately. Just as you can't focus on driving while texting, you cannot focus on listening while focusing on other tasks.

Guard against Scriptwriting and Defensive Listening

When we, as listeners, engage in *scriptwriting*, we focus on what we, rather than the speaker, will say next.[11] Similarly, people who engage in **defensive listening** decide either that they won't like what the speaker is going to say or that they know better. When you find yourself scriptwriting or listening to a speech with a defensive posture, remind yourself that effective listening precedes effective rebuttal. Try waiting for the speaker to finish before devising your own arguments.

Beware of Laziness and Overconfidence

Laziness and overconfidence can manifest themselves in several ways: We may expect too little from speakers, ignore important information, or display an arrogant attitude. Later, we discover that we missed important information.

ETHICALLY SPEAKING

The Responsibilities of Listening in the Public Arena

Radu Bercan/Shutterstock

As a speaker you have the power of the podium, but as a listener you also have considerable power that you can wield constructively or destructively. An example of the latter includes rude listening behaviors such as heckling, name-calling, interrupting out of turn, and other breaches in civility. Beyond short-circuiting communication, these acts can easily lead to explosive results—from menacing clashes among activists on opposite sides of a cause to eruptions at town hall meetings and other civic venues.

The ability to dissent from prevailing opinion is one of the hallmarks of a free society. As listeners, we are ethically bound to refrain from disruptive and intimidating tactics that are meant to silence those with whom we disagree. If we find the arguments of others morally offensive, we are equally bound to speak up in refutation. Only in this manner can we preserve the freedom to express our ideas. Clearly, the power to listen can translate into being socially responsible or socially destructive.

Work to Overcome Cultural Barriers

Differences in dialects or accents, nonverbal cues, word choices, and even physical appearance can serve as barriers to listening to a speaker, but they need not do so if you keep your focus on the message rather than the messenger: Refrain from judging a speaker on the basis of his or her accent, appearance, or demeanor; focus instead on what is actually being said. When possible, reveal your needs to the speaker by asking questions.

A CULTURAL PERSPECTIVE

Listening Styles and Cultural Differences

charles taylor/Shutterstock

Research suggests that both innate behavioral traits and culture influence how we listen to one another. For example, most people listen in a habitual style, which tends to mirror aspects of their innate temperaments:[1]

- *People-oriented listeners* tend to listen supportively and with sensitivity to feelings and emotions.
- *Action-oriented listeners* are task oriented—they are alert to errors and focus, sometimes impatiently, on what needs to be done.
- *Content-oriented listeners* enjoy evaluating information and making reasoned judgments on it.
- *Time-oriented listeners* want brevity—their goal is getting the message in the least amount of time.

(continued on next page)

At the same time, research suggests a link between our listening styles and a culture's predominant communication style.[2] A study of young adults in the United States, Germany, and Israel[3] found distinct listening style preferences that mirrored key value preferences, or preferred states of being, of each culture (see Chapter 6 on cultural values and national differences, p. 94). For example, Germans tended toward action-oriented listening, Israelis displayed a content-oriented style, and Americans exhibited both people- and time-oriented styles. While preliminary in nature, and not valid as a means of stereotyping or essentializing (e.g., to reduce to essentials) a given culture's group behavior, these findings confirm the cultural component of all forms of communication, including listening. They also point to the need to focus on intercultural understanding as you learn about your audience.

1. Kittie Watson, Larry Barker, and James Weaver, "The Listening Styles Profile (LPP16): Development and Validation of an Instrument to Assess Four Listening Styles," *International Journal of Listening* 9 (1995): 1–13.
2. Christian Kiewitz, James B. Weaver III, Hans-Bernd Brosius, and Gabriel Weimann, "Cultural Differences in Listening Style Preferences: A Comparison of Young Adults in Germany, Israel, and the United States," *International Journal of Public Opinion Research* 9, no. 3 (1997): 233–47, search.proquest.com/docview/60068159?accountid=10965; and Margarete Imhof and Laura Ann Janusik, "Development and Validation of the Imhof-Janusik Listening Concepts Inventory to Measure Listening Conceptualization Differences between Cultures," *Journal of Intercultural Communication Research* 35, no. 2 (2006): 79–98.
3. Kiewitz et al., "Listening Style Preferences."

Practice Active Listening

Active listening is a skill you can cultivate, a habit of mind of consciously receiving, constructing meaning from, and responding to messages. Setting listening goals, listening for main ideas, and watching for nonverbal cues are practical steps you can take to become more adept at listening actively.

Set Listening Goals

Setting listening goals helps you prepare to get the most from a listening situation. What do you need and expect from the listening situation? Keep these goals in mind as you listen. Try to state your listening goals in a way that encourages action. Table 4.2 illustrates the steps in setting listening goals.

TABLE 4.2 Steps in Setting Listening Goals
Identify your listening needs: "I must know my classmate's speech central idea, purpose in speaking, main points, and organizational pattern of main points in order to complete and hand in a written evaluation."
Identify why listening will help you: "I will get a better grade on the evaluation and do better on my own speech assignment if I am able to identify and evaluate the thesis, main points, purpose, and organizational pattern of Suzanne's speech."
Make an action statement (goal): "I will minimize distractions and practice the active listening steps during Suzanne's speech. I will take careful notes during her speech and ask questions about anything I do not understand."
Assess goal achievement: "I did identify the components of the speech I decided to focus upon and wrote about them in class."

Listen for Main Ideas

To ensure that you hear and retain the speaker's most important points, try these strategies:

- *Listen for introductions, transitions, and conclusions to alert you to the main points.* Most speakers will preview their main points in the *introduction*, giving the listener a chance to recognize them: "I have three points I want to make tonight. First, . . ." *Transitions* can also alert the listener to the fact that a main point is about to be discussed: "Now let's consider interest rates. . . ." *Conclusions* are a valuable place to recheck your memory of the main points: "Let me recap those three rules for living overseas. . . ."
- *Take notes on the speaker's main points.* Several different methods of note taking—bullet, column, and outline—can be helpful.

Evaluate Evidence and Reasoning

Purposeful, focused listening and critical thinking go hand in hand. **Critical thinking** is the ability to evaluate claims on the basis of well-supported reasons, to look for flaws in arguments, and to resist claims that have no supporting evidence.

As you listen to speeches, use your critical faculties to

- *Evaluate the speaker's evidence.* Is it accurate? Are the sources credible? Can the evidence be tracked?
- *Analyze the speaker's assumptions and biases.* What lies behind the speaker's assertions? Does the evidence support these assertions?
- *Assess the speaker's reasoning.* Does it make sense? Does it betray faulty logic? Does it rely on fallacies in reasoning? (See Chapter 25 to review logical fallacies.)
- *Consider multiple perspectives.* Is there another way to view the argument? How do other viewpoints compare with the speaker's?
- *Summarize and assess the relevant facts and evidence.* If the speaker asks for an action on the part of listeners (as is often the case in persuasive speeches; see Chapter 24), decide how you will act on the basis of the evidence. Will you be more apt to act on the evidence itself, or in line with what you think most people will do?

Strive for the Open Exchange of Ideas

In contrast to *monologue*, in which we try to impose what we think on another person or group of people, **dialogic communication** is the open sharing of ideas in an atmosphere of respect.[12] True dialogue encourages both speaker and listener to reach conclusions together. For the speaker, this means approaching a speech not as an argument that must be "won," but as an opportunity to achieve understanding with audience members. For listeners, it means maintaining an open mind and listening with empathy.[13] This will enable the speaker to deliver the message without impediment.

Offer Constructive and Compassionate Feedback

By critically evaluating the speeches of others, you'll not only help them, but you will be better able to assess your own strengths and weaknesses as a speaker.

Be Honest and Fair in Your Evaluation

Keep in mind the need to be honest and fair in your evaluation. Sometimes we have a tendency to focus on certain aspects of a speech and, as a result, minimize some of the most important elements. Focusing on a topic that you really like or dislike, for example, may cause you to place undue importance on that speech element. It is also important to remain open to ideas and beliefs that differ from your own. This openness will help your ideas prosper and improve your role as a citizen engaged with public issues. You can always learn something from differing viewpoints, and, likewise, honest and fair listeners will learn from your viewpoints.

Adjust to the Speaker's Style

Each of us has a unique communication style, a way of presenting ourselves through a mix of verbal and nonverbal signals. As listeners, we form impressions of speakers based on this communication style. Depending on our own preferences, we may find some speakers dull, others dynamic, still others off-putting, and so on. Adjusting to a speaker means not judging the content of that speaker's message based on his or her communication style. As listeners, it's up to us to identify which impressions create the most difficulty and then develop techniques for overcoming any listening problems. Accents, awkward grammatical phrases, and word choice are not good reasons to "tune out" a speaker. Maintaining respect for all types of speakers is a sign of good listening.

Be Compassionate in Your Criticism

How can you critically evaluate a presentation in a way that's constructive rather than cruel? Consider the following approach.

- *Start by saying something positive.* The benefits of this are twofold: You'll boost the speaker's self-confidence, and he or she will probably be more receptive to the criticism you do offer.
- *Be selective in your criticism.* Make specific rather than global statements. Rather than statements such as, "I just couldn't get into your topic," give the speaker something he or she can learn from: "I wanted more on why the housing market is falling. . . ."
- *Focus on the speech, not the speaker.* When you offer criticism, be sure to focus your remarks on the content of the speech rather than on characteristics of the speaker. It is fair to suggest improvements in delivery, but be certain that your remarks are constructive and not personal.

CHECKLIST

PEER EVALUATION FORM

In the space below, offer your evaluation of the speaker. Make your evaluation honest but constructive, providing the sort of feedback that you would find helpful if you were the speaker.

Did the speaker seem confident? Yes Somewhat No
Suggestions: ______________________________

____

Did the speaker use appropriate volume? Yes Somewhat No
Suggestions: ______________________________

____

Did the speaker use good eye contact? Yes Somewhat No
Suggestions: ______________________________

____

Did the speaker use effective vocal expression? Yes Somewhat No
Suggestions: ______________________________

____

Did the speaker use appropriate gestures and facial expressions? Yes Somewhat No
Suggestions: ______________________________

____

Was the speaker's introduction effective? Yes Somewhat No
Suggestions: ______________________________

____

Was the speaker's conclusion effective? Yes Somewhat No
Suggestions: ______________________________

____

Could you easily identify and remember the speaker's main points? Yes Somewhat No
Suggestions: ______________________________

____

Did the speaker's organizational patterns make sense to you? Yes Somewhat No
Suggestions: ______________________________

____

Did the speaker use effective supporting evidence? Yes Somewhat No
Suggestions: ______________________________

____

The best thing about the speaker was: ______________________________

____

The best thing about the speech was: ______________________________

____

Recommendations for improvement: ______________________________

____

5 Ethical Public Speaking

LearningCurve can help you review!
Go to LaunchPad: **launchpadworks.com**

One of the most consistent expectations that we as listeners bring to any speech situation is that the speaker will be honest and straightforward with us. Why else give our attention to someone unless we believe that he or she is sincere? Yet, while we assume an attitude of trust, we instinctively remain alert to hints that might signal dishonesty. As we listen to the actual words the speaker utters, for example, we are simultaneously evaluating his or her posture, tone of voice, gaze, and other potential markers signs of sincerity (or lack thereof). If we are honest with ourselves, we are also examining our own potential biases or preconceptions toward the speaker and message.

Why should you be concerned about demonstrating to listeners that you are worthy of their trust? As ethicist Michael Josephson has noted, there are both practical and moral reasons for maintaining an ethical stance in public speaking.[1] At the practical level, you must establish credibility with listeners before they will accept, or even listen to, your message. Credibility is based on trust, honesty, and believability. You also have a moral obligation to treat your listeners as deserving of your respect and goodwill.

Take Responsibility for Your Words

When we have an audience's attention, we are in the unusual position of being able to influence or persuade people and, at times, move them to act—for better or for worse. With this power to affect the minds and hearts of others comes **responsibility**—"a moral obligation to behave correctly towards or in respect of a person or thing."[2] Taking responsibility for your words lies at the heart of **ethics**—the study of moral conduct, and how a given culture or group within it believes people should act toward one another. Narrowing this large field of study to public speaking, **communication ethics** addresses our ethical responsibilities when seeking influence over other people and for which there are positive and negative, or "right" or "wrong," choices of action.[3] It refers to the duties and obligations we have toward our audience and ourselves as well as the responsibilities we have as listeners.

Demonstrate Competence and Character

Ethics is derived from the Greek word **ethos**, meaning "character." Writing in the fourth century B.C.E., Aristotle said the foremost duty speakers have toward their audience is to demonstrate *positive ethos*, or good character. In fact, if audience members were to listen to and trust them at all, the speaker needed to establish his or her ethos immediately, at the beginning of the speech. Speakers were said to possess positive ethos when they displayed the "virtues" of *competence* (as demonstrated by their firm grasp of the subject matter), *good moral character* (as reflected in their trustworthiness, honest presentation of the message, and lack of ulterior motives), and *goodwill* (as demonstrated by their attitude of respect toward the audience and concern for their common good).

Thus, for the ancient Greeks, speakers were regarded positively only when they were well prepared, honest, and respectful toward their audience. Some 2,400 years later, surprisingly little has changed. Current research on **source credibility**, a contemporary term for ethos, reveals that people place their greatest trust in speakers who

- have a solid grasp of the subject,
- display sound reasoning skills,
- are honest and straightforward, and
- are genuinely interested in the welfare of their listeners.[4]

Listeners tend to distrust speakers who deviate even slightly from these qualities. Notice that merely being an expert or even honest is not enough to inspire listeners' trust. We trust only those speakers who we believe have our best interests in mind.

Respect Your Listeners' Values

Our sense of ethics, of right and wrong actions, is a reflection of our **values**—our most enduring judgments or standards of what's good and bad in life and of what's important to us. Values shape how we see the world, drive much of our behavior,[5] and form the basis on which we judge the actions of others. For example, if we highly value equality among people, we will strive to treat others as equal and will judge those who do not share this value as to some degree wanting.

Because our values are so closely linked to our sense of self, consideration of the audience's values is an important aspect of preparing an ethical speech. No member of an audience wants his or her values attacked, treated without respect, or even merely unacknowledged. Yet conflicting values lie at the heart of many controversies that today's public speakers might address, making it difficult to speak about certain topics without challenging cherished beliefs. The more diverse the society, the greater these clashes will tend to be. One only has to think of the so-called *values divide* in the United States between "red states" (representing conservative values) and "blue states" (representing liberal values). In fact, according to a Pew Research Center Values Survey, Americans' values and basic beliefs "are more polarized along partisan lines than at any point in the past 25 years."[6] The United States is a country of immigrants, for example, but nearly half of the population believes that "too many" immigrants threaten traditional U.S. values and customs, while only a quarter of college-educated Americans agree.[7] Some of us are pleased that same-sex marriage is legal in the United States, while others strive to overturn the 2015 Supreme Court ruling permitting it.

As you plan speeches on controversial topics, anticipate that audience members will hold a range of values that will differ not only from your own but from each other's, and proceed with sensitivity. Audience analysis is key to discovering and planning for these differences. Only by anticipating audience members' attitudes toward a controversial issue can you form a strategy for avoiding offense (see Chapter 6 on how to identify and appeal to audience members' values).

Evaluate Frameworks for Ethical Decision Making

Ethics addresses questions of what we "should" or "ought" to do, including as public speakers. It attempts the difficult task of applying standards of correct conduct to new and confusing circumstances.[8] As a novice speaker, you might wonder, "Should I flash a gory photograph on a screen without warning to convince audience members not to text and drive? Should I bother to check the credibility of a source before offering it to the audience? Is it ethical to present only one side of an argument?"

Ethical theories attempt to answer questions such as these, proposing criteria or standards with which to distinguish ethical from nonethical behavior. Three major theoritical approaches are *consequentialist*, *rules-based*, and *virtue ethics*. Mirroring the diverse perspectives people bring to ethical quandaries, the approaches differ in the ethical standards they offer and values they prioritize. However, each offers something constructive to think about when forming decisions about ethical issues.

- **Consequentialist ethics** suggests that it is primarily the *outcome* or *consequence* of our conduct that ultimately determines its rightness. From this perspective, ethical acts are those that maximize a good outcome. A hallmark of consequentialist ethics is "the greatest good for the greatest number of people." Applied to public speaking, providing the most useful or relevant information you can discover about a topic, for as many in the audience as possible, is one way of ensuring an ethical speech from a consequentialist perspective.
- **Rules-based ethics** focuses on our duty to do what is *inherently right*, as established in widely accepted moral rules or norms, such as those in the Ten Commandments, the Eightfold Path of Buddhism, or even a university honor code. From a rules-based perspective, a good outcome is not as important as "doing what is right." One way to apply a rules-based standard of ethics in your speech is to check it against the standards specified by the course instructor or university handbook, or by the National Communication Association's credo for ethical communication. To find the NCA's credo for ethical communication, go to **launchpadworks.com**.

- **Virtue ethics** emphasizes the role of individual moral character in guiding ethical decisions. Introduced by Aristotle as democracy emerged in Greece, virtue ethics grew out of the need to cultivate civic-minded persons who could "rule and be ruled" in an ethical manner.[9] Then, as today, virtue ethics suggests that when we strive to develop positive character traits ("virtues") such as truthfulness, civility, modesty, courage, and intellectual integrity, we can rely on our own good character and practical wisdom to do the right thing. Using virtue ethics as a measure of a speech, you might check for lapses in judgment. Do you act with honesty and integrity toward the audience? Do you stay true to yourself? Are your speech aims positive, and does your message contribute to the common good?

Note that by themselves, the frameworks are limited and cannot address all of your concerns. As you consider ethical issues related to a speech you are preparing, it can be more useful to frame your choice using multiple approaches until you reach a solution with which you are comfortable.

Bring Your Own Values into Focus

Analyzing the underlying values that lead you to a position on an issue can help you gain a deeper understanding of why you feel as you do. It can also help to clarify the values of your audience members.

Through extensive research, psychologist Milton Rokeach identified thirty-six values important to a large cross section of people, distinguishing between two kinds of values: instrumental and terminal. *Instrumental values* are socially desirable behavioral characteristics, such as being courageous. *Terminal values* are desirable states of being, such as living a comfortable life.

To bring some of your personal values into focus, complete the self-assessment exercise in the accompanying checklist. To identify which values mean the most to you, rank both terminal and instrumental values from least to most important. Then compare what you care about with what your audience analysis indicates that your listeners might value (see Figure 5.1). Where your values overlap those of your audience, you may be able to identify some common ground from which to present your topic.

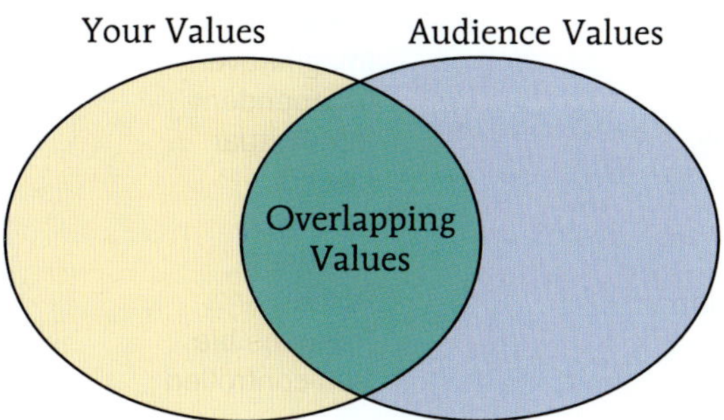

FIGURE 5.1 Comparing Values

Contribute to Positive Public Discourse

An important measure of ethical speaking is whether it contributes something positive to **public discourse** – speech involving issues of importance to the larger community, such as debates on campus about race relations or immigration reform.

What might constitute a positive contribution to public debates of this nature? Perhaps most important is the *advancement of constructive goals*. An ethical speech appeals to the greater good rather than to narrow self-interest. Speaking merely to inflame and demean others, on the other hand, as so often occurred in the most recent presidential campaign of 2016, degrades the quality of public discourse. During the campagn, candidates resorted to

SELF-ASSESSMENT CHECKLIST

IDENTIFYING VALUES

As a way of uncovering where your values lie, rank each item from *1* to *10* (from least to most important). From these, select your top five values and write them down in the circle labeled "Your Values" in Figure 5.1. Repeat the exercise, but this time rank each value in terms of how important you think it is to your audience. Select the top five of these values and place them in the circle labeled "Audience Values." Finally, draw arrows to the overlapping area to indicate where your highest values (of those listed) coincide with those you think are most important to your listeners.

Terminal Values: (States of being you consider important)	**Instrumental Values: (Characteristics you value in yourself and others)**
A comfortable life	Ambitious
An exciting life	Broad-minded
A sense of accomplishment	Capable
A world at peace	Cheerful
A world of beauty	Clean
Equality	Courageous
Family security	Forgiving
Freedom	Helpful
Happiness	Honest
Inner harmony	Imaginative
Mature love	Independent
National security	Intellectual
Pleasure	Logical
Salvation	Loving
Self-respect	Obedient
Social recognition	Polite
True friendship	Responsible
Wisdom	Self-controlled

Information from: Milton Rokeach, *Value Survey* (Sunnydale, CA: Halgren Tests, 1967).

personal or *ad hominen* attacks rather than sticking with the issues at hand. Stooping to **invective**, or verbal attacks, and relying on such fallacies of reasoning as ad hominen attacks (see Chapter 25, "Developing Arguments for the Persuasive Speech") serve as **conversation stoppers**—speeches designed to discredit, demean, and belittle those with whom one disagrees. Such speeches breach the acceptable "**rules of engagement**" for public conversations. Originally used as a military term, the rules of engagement can be applied to the ways we relate to one another in the public arena: "Comparable to the orders about the circumstances in which soldiers may use their weapons are the rights and responsibilities to speak, to speak the truth, to disclose one's purposes, to respond to others, to respond coherently, to listen, and to understand."[10]

Use Your Rights of Free Speech Responsibly

The United States vigorously protects **free speech**—defined as the right to be free from unreasonable constraints on expression[11]—thereby assuring protection both to speakers who treat the truth with respect and to those whose words are inflammatory and offensive.

Though often legally protected under the **First Amendment** (which guarantees freedoms concerning religion, expression of ideas, and rights of assembly and petition), racist, sexist, or ageist slurs, gay-bashing, and other forms of negative or hate speech are clearly unethical. **Hate speech** is any offensive communication—verbal or nonverbal—that is directed against people's racial, ethnic, religious, gender, or other characteristics.

While the First Amendment offers protection to many forms of offensive speech, certain types of speech are not only unethical but actually illegal, including the following:

- Speech that incites people to imminent violence, or so-called "**fighting words**"[12]
- Speech that expresses blackmail, perjury, child pornography, or obscenity[13]
- Speech that can be proved to be defamatory or potentially harmful to an individual's reputation at work or in the community, called **slander**

How can you tell if your speech contains defamatory language? If you are talking about public figures or a matter of public concern, you will not be legally liable unless it can be shown that you spoke with a **reckless disregard for the truth**—that is, if you knew that what you were saying was false but said it anyway. If your comments refer to private persons, it will be easier for them to assert a claim for defamation. You will then have the burden of proving that what you said was true.

Avoid Ethnocentrism and Stereotyping

Speakers who exhibit **ethnocentrism** act as though everyone shares their point of view and points of reference. They may tell jokes that require a certain context or refer only to their own customs. Ethical speakers, by contrast, assume differences and address them respectfully.

Generalizing about an apparent characteristic of a group and applying that generalization to all of its members is another serious affront to people's dignity. When such racial, ethnic, gender, or other **stereotypes** roll off the speaker's tongue, they pack a wallop of indignation and pain for the people to whom they refer. In addition, making *in-group* and *out-group* distinctions, with respect shown only to those in the in-group, can make listeners feel excluded or, worse, victimized. Speaking as though all audience members share the same religious and political beliefs, for instance, and treating those beliefs as superior to those held by others, is but one example of making in-group and out-group distinctions. Hate speech is the ultimate vehicle for promoting in-group and out-group distinctions.

While there are various approaches to evaluating ethical behavior, common to all of them are the fundamental moral precepts of not harming others and telling the truth.

ETHICALLY SPEAKING

Speech Codes on Campus: Protection or Censorship?

Radu Bercan/Shutterstock

The existence of speech codes at U.S. colleges and universities has long been at the center of the debate over free speech versus censorship. On the one side are those who resist restrictions of any kind, often in support of the constitutional rights of the First Amendment. On the other side are advocates of speech codes and other policies that limit what students and faculty can and cannot say and do. These advocates argue that **speech codes**—university regulations prohibiting expressions that would be constitutionally protected in society at large—are necessary to ensure a tolerant and safe environment.

Since the 1980s, thousands of schools, both public and private, have instituted speech codes prohibiting certain forms of offensive speech and acts deemed intimidating or hostile to individuals or groups. Many of these early codes were found to be unconstitutional, but constitutionally questionable new codes continue to crop up. In 2016, for example, the Foundation for Individual Rights in Education (FIRE) found that 49 percent of the nation's four hundred largest and most prestigious colleges and universities maintain policies that "seriously infringe on the free speech rights of students."[1] This figure has actually gone down fairly dramatically; in 2010 FIRE found that 70 percent of the schools surveyed infringed on constitutionally protected speech. While speech codes on campuses have declined overall, FIRE claims that too many universities continue to punish students and faculty for constitutionally protected speech and expression.[2]

Many colleges and universities—even those that are public, and thus legally bound to protect students' First Amendment rights—limit student protests and demonstrations to designated areas on campus called "free speech zones"; these, too, are subject to ongoing legal challenges. In 2015, for example, Missouri enacted the Campus Free Expression Act (CAFÉ Act), which prohibits that state's public institutions of higher learning from restricting students' speech activities to free speech zones. One of only a few states to do so thus far, the act deems the outdoor areas of campuses as traditional public forums, in which "any person who wishes to engage in noncommercial expressive activity on campus shall be permitted to do so freely, as long as . . . conduct is not unlawful and does not . . . disrupt the functioning of the institution."[3] Given the First Amendment, should free speech be limited to such zones? Why or why not? And what types of speech should be limited outside of such zones?

And what about that speech topic you might have in mind? At Central Connecticut State University, student John Wahlberg was asked to prepare a speech on a topic covered by the mainstream media. Wahlberg chose to argue that had students at Virginia Tech been allowed to carry concealed weapons on campus during the 2007 shootings at that campus, the shooter might have been killed before killing as many students as he did. Believing that Wahlberg's opinions made the class "uncomfortable," his professor reported him to campus police, who ordered him to explain his beliefs.[4]

Restrictions on speech on campus raise important ethical questions. University administrators who support speech codes claim that they are necessary to protect students from intimidation, to ensure equal opportunity, and to enforce the norms of a civil society. Detractors argue that limits on free speech prevent students with unpopular or politically incorrect views from freely expressing themselves. What do you think?

1. "Spotlight on Speech Codes, 2016: The State of Free Speech on Our Nation's Campuses," Foundation for Individual Rights in Education (FIRE), accessed May 10, 2016, www.thefire.org/spotlight-on-speech-codes-2016/.
2. Ibid.
3. Missouri Senate Bill No. 93, 98th General Assembly, "Campus Free Expression Act," March 31, 2015, www.senate.mo.gov/15info/pdf-bill/perf/SB93.pdf.4.
4. Jay Bergman, "Free Speech under Fire at Universities," *Hartford Courant*, March 17, 2009 Jon B. Gould, "Returning Fire," *Chronicle of Higher Education*, April 20, 2007, www.chronicle.com/weekly/v53/i33/33b01301.htm.

Observe the Ground Rules for Ethical Speaking

Ethical speech rests on a foundation of dignity and integrity. **Dignity** refers to bearing and conduct that are respectful to self and others. Audience members instinctively distrust speakers who act without dignity and who fail to make them feel worthy and respected as individuals. **Integrity** signals the speaker's incorruptibility—that he or she will avoid compromising the truth for the sake of personal expediency.[14] Speaking ethically also requires that we adhere to certain moral ground rules, or "pillars of character," including being *trustworthy, respectful, responsible, fair,* and *civic-minded.*[15] These bear close resemblance to the **civic virtues**, or characteristics thought to exemplify excellence of character so important in the early democracy of Greece, and they remain equally critical to upholding our own democracy today (the word *virtue* derives from the Greek word *arete*, or excellence).

Be Trustworthy

Trustworthiness is a combination of honesty and dependability. We find speakers trustworthy when we sense that they are honest about their intentions and don't sacrifice the truth to achieve their aims. They support their points truthfully and don't present misleading or false information. Manipulating data to achieve a particular purpose is untrustworthy, as are any attempts to deceive an audience by misrepresentation, omission, or making up of information (see Chapter 8 on the ethical use of statistics).

Truth telling can be an especially difficult issue in persuasive speeches (see Chapters 24–26). When the goal is to try to persuade others, the temptation is to fashion the information in a way that fits the goal, even if it means omitting a fact here or there that would convince the audience otherwise. But all kinds of speeches, not just persuasive ones, should be built on the truth. Acknowledging sources is also an essential aspect of being a trustworthy speaker (see rules for avoiding plagiarism later in this chapter).

Demonstrate Respect

Speakers demonstrate **respect** by treating audience members with civility and courtesy.[16] Respectful speakers address listeners as unique human beings, refrain from any form of personal attack, and focus on issues rather than personalities. They also allow the audience autonomy, or the power of rational choice. Sensationalist or lurid appeals rob audience members of this power. In most cases, it's not necessary to use graphic pictures or upsetting verbal descriptions just to make a point.

Make Responsible Speech Choices

Responsibility means being accountable for what you say. For example, will learning about your topic in some way benefit listeners? Do you use sound evidence and reasoning? (See Chapter 25 on developing arguments.) Do you offer emotional appeals because they are appropriate rather than to shore up otherwise weak arguments? (See Chapter 24 on persuasive speaking.)

Demonstrate Fairness

Fairness refers to making a genuine effort to see all sides of an issue and acknowledging the information listeners need in order to make informed decisions. Most subjects are complicated and multifaceted; rarely is there only one right or wrong way to view a topic.

Be Civic-Minded

Being **civic-minded** means caring about your community, as expressed in your speeches and in your deeds. It means recognizing that things don't get better unless people volunteer their efforts to improve things. At the broadest level, being civic-minded is essential to the democratic process because democracy depends on our participation in it.

Avoid Plagiarism

Crediting sources is a crucial aspect of any speech. **Plagiarism** — the use of other people's ideas or words without acknowledging the sources — is unethical.

A CULTURAL PERSPECTIVE

Comparing Cultural Values

charles taylor/Shutterstock

Do the criteria for an ethical speaker outlined in this chapter — that is, displaying the qualities of trustworthiness, respect, responsibility, and fairness — apply equally in every culture? For example, does telling the truth always take precedence over other qualities, such as protecting the interests of your clan or group, or simply being eloquent? Are ethical standards for speeches merely a product of a particular culture? What about the concept of plagiarism? In the United States, speakers who fail to acknowledge their sources meet with harsh criticism and often suffer severe consequences, even if, as in the case of several recent college presidents and professors, the speakers are otherwise highly respected.[1] But conceptions of plagiarism differ by culture. In Asian societies such as China, for example, ideas are not always seen as the sole property of someone but are sometimes seen as belonging to the collective. Students in Chinese culture, for example, learn to memorize what famous philosophers or scholars have said and cite them directly, without attribution, in their written and spoken work. Doing this signals that the student understands the source. In some instances citing the source could be considered an insult to the intelligence of the audience.[2]

Can you think of other examples in which ideas of ethical speech expressed in this chapter are not necessarily shared by other cultures? Do you personally hold values for ethical speech that are different from those cited here?

1. See, for example, "Board Reprimands College President for Plagiarism," *Diverse Issues in Higher Education*, February 15, 2016, www.diverseeducation.com/article/81263/.
2. Noelle, Vance, "Cross-Cultural Perspectives on Source Referencing and Plagiarism," Research Starters Education: Academic Topic Overviews, accessed October 19, 2016, http://subjectguides.wcupa.edu/ld.php?content_id=2185825. For an instructive article about plagiarism in China, in which the author disputes the notion of cultural relativity regarding plagiarism in that country, see Dilin Liu, "Plagiarism in ESOL Students: Is Cultural Conditioning Truly the Major Culprit?" *ELT* 59 (2005): 234–41.

You are obviously plagiarizing when you simply cut and paste material from sources into your speech and represent it as your own. But it is also plagiarism to copy material into your speech draft from a source (such as a magazine article or website) and then change and rearrange words and sentence structures here and there to make it appear as if it were your own.[17]

As we've noted, however, conceptions of what constitute plagiarism do differ by culture. In schools and universities in the United States, strict policies require students to acknowledge the source of other people's ideas or words. Chinese students who study in the United States, whose cultural conception of quoting famous philosophers and scholars without attribution is different from ours,[18] sometimes struggle with learning the Western conventions regarding **intellectual property** (original authorship). When you present plagiarized material as your own speech material, you abuse the trust that an audience places in you. More than any other single action, acknowledging sources lets listeners know that you are trustworthy and will represent both fact and opinion fairly and responsibly.

Rules for Avoiding Plagiarism

The rule for avoiding plagiarism as a public speaker is straightforward: *Any sources that require credit in written form should be acknowledged in oral form.* These sources include direct quotations, as well as paraphrased and summarized information—any facts and statistics, ideas, opinions, or theories gathered and reported by others. For each source that requires citation, you need to include the *author or origin of the source*, the *title or a description of the source*, the *type of source* (magazine, book, personal interview, website, etc.), and the *date of the source.*

Oral presentations need not include full bibliographic references (i.e., full names, dates, titles, volume, and page numbers). However, you should include complete references in a bibliography or at the end of the speech outline. (For more on creating a written bibliography for your speeches, see Chapter 13, on outlining a speech, and Appendices B–C and H–I, on documentation styles.) Rules for avoiding plagiarism apply equally to print and online sources.

Citing Quotations, Paraphrases, and Summaries

When citing other people's ideas, you can present them in one of three ways.

- **Direct quotations** are verbatim—or word for word—presentations of statements made by someone else. Direct quotes should always be acknowledged in a speech.
- A **paraphrase** is a restatement of someone else's ideas, opinions, or theories in the speaker's own words. Because paraphrases alter the *form* but not the *substance* of another person's ideas, you must acknowledge the original source.
- A **summary** is a brief overview of someone else's ideas, opinions, or theories. While a paraphrase contains approximately the same number

of words as the original source material stated in the speaker's own words, a summary condenses the same material, distilling only its essence.

Note how a speaker could paraphrase and summarize, *with credit*, the following excerpt from an article published in the *New Yorker* titled "Strange Fruit: The Rise and Fall of Açai," by John Calapinto.

Original Version:

> Açai was virtually unknown outside Brazil until 10 years ago, when Ryan and Jeremy Black, two brothers from Southern California, and their friend Edmund Nichols began exporting it to the United States. Since then, the fruit has followed a cycle of popularity befitting a teenage pop singer: a Miley Cyrus–like trajectory from obscurity to hype, critical backlash, and eventual ubiquity. Embraced as a "superfruit"—a potent combination of cholesterol-reducing fats and anti-aging antioxidants—açai became one of the fastest-growing foods in history. . . .

Compare the original version of the excerpt to how it could be properly quoted, paraphrased, or summarized in a speech. Oral citation language is bolded for easy identification.

Direct Quotation:

> **As John Calapinto states in an article titled "Strange Fruit: The Rise and Fall of Açai," published in the May 30, 2011, issue of the *New Yorker*,** "The fruit has followed a cycle of popularity befitting a teenage pop singer: a Miley Cyrus–like trajectory from obscurity to hype, critical backlash, and eventual ubiquity."

Oral Paraphrase:

> **In an article titled "Strange Fruit: The Rise and Fall of Açai," published in the May 30, 2011, issue of the *New Yorker*, John Calapinto explains that** until two brothers from Southern California named Ryan and Jeremy Black, along with their friend Edmund Nichols, began exporting açai to the

CHECKLIST

CORRECTLY QUOTE, PARAPHRASE, AND SUMMARIZE INFORMATION

- ✔ If *directly* quoting a source, repeat the source word for word and acknowledge whose words you are using.
- ✔ If *paraphrasing* someone else's ideas, restate the ideas in your own words and acknowledge the source.
- ✔ If *summarizing* someone else's ideas, briefly describe their essence and acknowledge the source.

United States ten years ago, it was unknown here. Now, says Calapinto, açai is seen as a "superfruit" that can help with everything from lowering cholesterol to fighting aging through its antioxidant properties.

Oral Summary:

In an article titled "Strange Fruit: The Rise and Fall of Açai," published in the May 30, 2011, issue of the *New Yorker*, John Calapinto says that açai, a fruit grown in Brazil that was unknown in this country until ten years ago, is now marketed as a "superfruit" that has powerful health benefits.

Fair Use, Copyright, and Ethical Speaking

Copyright is a legal protection afforded original creators of literary and artistic works fixed in a tangible medium of expression.[19] When including copyrighted materials in your speeches—such as reproductions of graphs or photographs, a video or sound clip, and so forth—you must determine when and if you need permission to use such works.

When a work is copyrighted, you may not reproduce, distribute, or display it without permission from the copyright holder or you will be liable for copyright infringement. For any work created from 1978 to the present, the copyright is good for the author's lifetime plus fifty years. After that time, unless extended, the work falls into the **public domain**, which means that anyone may reproduce it. Not subject to copyright are federal (but *not* state or local) government publications, common knowledge, and select other categories.

An exception to the prohibitions of copyright restrictions is the doctrine of **fair use**, which permits the limited use of copyrighted works without permission for the purposes of scholarship, criticism, comment, news reporting, teaching, and research. This means that when preparing speeches for the classroom, you have much more latitude to use other people's creative work without seeking their permission, but you must include credit in all cases, including display of the copyright symbol (©) on any copyrighted handouts or visual aids you include in your speech. Different rules apply to the professional speaker, whose use of copyrighted materials is considered part of a for-profit "performance."

In terms of crediting any visual aids you might display during your speech, bear in mind that you must accurately credit both the *source of the data* as well as the *creator of its graphic display*. If you generate your own tables and charts, using data from another source, then you are the creator of the display and need only credit the source of the data. However, suppose that for a speech on women in the sciences you locate a graph in *Time* magazine that visually illustrates the percentage of men versus women who receive PhDs in the sciences and engineering. The source of the data is a federal government agency, which falls within the public domain. As the creator of the graph, *Time* magazine owns the copyright for this particular display of the data and as such must be credited.

The long and short of it? If you are a professional public speaker who makes use of copyrighted materials in your speeches, you must obtain copyright clearance. For speeches created for one-time use in the classroom or for other nonprofit, educational purposes, accurately crediting your sources will often suffice. (For more on copyright, visit the U.S. Copyright Office online at www.copyright.gov.)

SELF-ASSESSMENT CHECKLIST

AN ETHICAL INVENTORY

- ✓ Have you distorted any information to make your point?
- ✓ Have you acknowledged each of your sources?
- ✓ Does your speech focus on issues rather than on personalities?
- ✓ Have you tried to foster a sense of inclusion?
- ✓ Is your topic socially constructive? Civic-minded?
- ✓ Do any of your arguments contain fallacies of reasoning? (see pp. 353–54)
- ✓ Is the content of your message as accurate as you can make it?
- ✓ Do you avoid speech that demeans those with whom you disagree?

AUDIENCE ANALYSIS AND TOPIC SELECTION

Musician and activist Alicia Keys speaks at the Women's March on Washington, D.C. in 2017. Keeping her audience and the aims of the event in mind, she recited Maya Angelou's poem, "Still I Rise." She involved the audience in her performance; they chanted the lyrics to her song, "Girl on Fire." **Theo Wargo/Getty Images**

AUDIENCE ANALYSIS AND TOPIC SELECTION

SPEAKER'S PREVIEW

LearningCurve can help you review.
Go to LaunchPad: **launchpadworks.com**

AUDIENCE ANALYSIS AND TOPIC SELECTION

CHAPTER 6 Analyzing the Audience

Learn about Your Audience and Adapt Your Message Accordingly

- Seek out information about your audience in order to give a speech that will be meaningful to them. (p. 83)
- Maintain an audience-centered perspective as you prepare all aspects of a speech. (p. 83)

Investigate Audience Psychology

- Understand the nature of attitudes, beliefs, and values, and the central role they play in audience receptivity to a message. (p. 84)
- Seek information on audience members' relevant attitudes, beliefs, and values about the topic and related issues. (p. 84)
- Appeal directly to important audience values related to your topic. (p. 84)

Gauge Listeners' Feelings toward the Topic

- Assess listeners' attitudes toward the topic (p. 85)
- Assess listeners' knowledge of the topic and adapt accordingly (p. 86)

Gauge Listeners' Feelings toward You as the Speaker

- Anticipate how audience members will perceive you and strive to establish credibility, or ethos. (p. 86)
- Look for ways to create identification. (p. 87)
- Stress mutual bonds (p. 87)
- Use personal pronouns to forge a sense of inclusion. (p. 87)

LaunchPad VIDEO ACTIVITY

Go to LaunchPad to watch a video about analyzing your audience.

LaunchPad includes:

LearningCurve adaptive quizzing

a curated collection of video clips and full-length speeches.

Additional resources and reference materials such as presentation software tutorials and documentation help.

SPEAKER'S PREVIEW

Gauge Listeners' Feelings toward the Occasion

- Consider the audience's expectations of the speech. (p. 87)
- Consider whether the audience is captive or voluntary; adjust accordingly. (p. 88)

Adapt the Message to Audience Demographics

- Consider audience members' *age*, *ethnic and cultural background*, *socioeconomic status*, *religious and political affiliations*, *gender*, *group affiliations*, and *disability*. (p. 88)

Appeal to Your Target Audience

- Identify whom in the audience you are most likely to influence. (p. 88)
- Focus on target audience but aim to make topic relevant to all listeners. (p. 88)

Address the Age Range of Your Audience

- Appeal to concerns and motivations of audience age range. (p. 88)

Consider Cultural Background

- Appeal to the relevant ethnic and cultural composition of your audience. (p. 89)

Consider the Socioeconomic Status of Your Audience

- Consider that listeners' attitudes may be closely tied to occupational status and income level. (p. 90)
- Use examples that are appropriate to the audience's level of education. (p. 90)

Consider Religious and Political Affiliations

- Identify potential religious and political sensitivities; tread carefully. (p. 90)

Avoid Judgments Based on Gender Stereotypes and Avoid Sexist Language

- Treat gender-related issues evenly. (p. 92)
- Consider the audience's group affiliations and appeal to the interests and values they reflect. (p. 92)

Consider How Disability May Affect Audience Members

- Use language and examples that are respectful of persons with disabilities. (p. 92)

Adapt to Cultural Values

- Identify listeners' cultural values and orientation and adapt your speech accordingly. (p. 94)
- Consult cross-cultural polls to further identify audience attitudes. (p. 95)

Gather Information about Your Audience from a Variety of Sources

- Conduct interviews. (p. 98)
- Survey the audience using questionnaires. (p. 98)
- Look for information about the audience in published sources. (p. 100)

Investigate the Logistics of the Speech Setting

- Find out in advance what the physical setting will be like. (p. 101)
- Plan appropriately for the length and timing of your speech. (p. 101)
- Consider the rhetorical situation of the speech. (p. 101)

CHAPTER 7 Selecting a Topic and Purpose

Select a Topic and Purpose Appropriate to the Audience, Occasion, and Rhetorical Situation

- Know precisely what you will cover. (p. 103)
- Be clear about the purpose and goals of the speech. (p. 103)

Consider Various Approaches to Discovering Topics

- Consider your personal interests, but ensure the topic will interest the audience. (p. 104)
- Consider current events and controversial issues. (p. 104)
- Investigate grassroots issues in the community. (p. 104)
- Avoid overused and trivial topics. (p. 106)
- Brainstorm with word association, topic mapping, and Internet tools to generate ideas. (p. 106)

Select from the Three General Speech Purposes

- Use an informative speech to increase audience understanding and awareness. (p. 110)
- Use a persuasive speech to effect change in audience attitudes, beliefs, values, or behavior. (p. 110)
- Use a special occasion speech when the specific event calls for entertainment, celebration, commemoration, inspiration, or setting a social agenda. (p. 111)

Narrow the Topic

- Narrow your topic to align with audience expectations and interests, occasion, and time constraints. (p. 112)
- Consider using topic mapping and search engines to research and narrow topics. (p. 114)
- Form a *specific speech purpose*—a statement of what you want the audience to gain from the speech. (p. 117)

Formulate the Thesis Statement

- State the thesis as a single, declarative sentence that poses the central idea of your speech. (p. 118)
- Use the thesis to help you develop main points. (p. 118)
- Make the thesis statement relevant and motivating by adding key words or phrases and considering audience interests. (p. 118)

KEY TERMS

Chapter 6

audience analysis
audience-centered perspective
psychographics
demographics
attitudes
beliefs
values
identification
captive audience
voluntary audience
target audience
audience segmentation
generational identity
co-culture
socioeconomic status (SES)
gender
sexist language
gender stereotypes
persons with disabilities (PWD)
cultural values
individualistic culture
collectivist culture
uncertainty avoidance
high-uncertainty avoidance culture
low-uncertainty avoidance culture
power distance
interview
questionnaire
closed-ended question
fixed-alternative question
scale question
open-ended question

Chapter 7

brainstorming
word association
topic mapping
general speech purpose
informative speech
persuasive speech
special occasion speech
specific speech purpose
thesis statement

Go to LaunchPad: **launchpadworks.com** to watch the video clips for this chapter.

6 Analyzing the Audience

LearningCurve can help you review!
Go to LaunchPad: **launchpadworks.com**

Advertisers are shrewd analysts of people's needs and wants. They extensively research our buying habits, opinions, and aspirations to identify what motivates us; only then, when their investigation is complete, do they craft the actual advertisement. In at least one sense, to make a successful speech or presentation, you too must function like an advertiser. To spark interest and sustain the audience's involvement in your message, you also must investigate and appeal to your audience.

Audience analysis is the process of gathering and analyzing information about audience members' attributes and motivations *with the explicit aim of preparing your speech in ways that will be meaningful to them*. This is the single most critical aspect of preparing for any speech. What are your listeners' attitudes with respect to your topic? What might they need or want to know? How will their values influence their response to your presentation? How much do audience members have in common with one another?

Assume an Audience-Centered Perspective

One of the most important psychological principles you can learn as a speaker is that audience members, and people in general, tend to evaluate information in terms of their own—rather than the speaker's—point of view, at least until they are convinced to take a second look[1] (see discussion of selective perception on p. 54. Establishing a connection with your listeners thus starts with seeking to understand their outlook and motivations and letting this information guide you in constructing your speech. You may want to convince your classmates to support a cause, but unless you know something about their perspectives on the topic, you won't be able to appeal to them effectively.

Assuming an **audience-centered perspective** does not mean, however, that you must abandon your own convictions or cater to the audience's whims. Pandering to your audience will only undermine your credibility in the eyes of the audience. Think of audience analysis as an opportunity to get to know and establish common ground with audience members, just as you might do with a new acquaintance. The more you find out about someone, the more you can discover what you share in common and how you differ.

Being audience-centered and using audience analysis throughout the entire speech preparation process — from selection and treatment of the speech topic to making decisions about how you will organize, word, and deliver it — will help you prepare a presentation that your audience will want to hear.

Adapt Your Message to Audience Psychographics

To analyze an audience, speakers investigate both psychological and demographic factors. **Psychographics** include the opinions and aspirations we hold that so intererest advertisers, as well as audience members' *attitudes, beliefs*, and *values* (including as they relate to the topic, speaker, and occasion). **Demographics** are the statistical characteristics of a given population, such as age, ethnic or cultural background, and socioeconomic status (see pp. 88–90).

Appeal to Audience Members' Attitudes, Beliefs, and Values

The audience members' attitudes, beliefs, and values provide crucial clues to how receptive they will be toward your topic and your position on it. While intertwined, attitudes, beliefs, and values reflect distinct mental states that reveal a great deal about us. **Attitudes** are our general evaluations of people, ideas, objects, or events.[2] To evaluate something is to judge it as relatively good or bad, useful or useless, or desirable or undesirable. People generally act in accordance with their attitudes (although the degree to which they do so depends on many factors).[3] If your listeners have a positive attitude toward gun ownership, for example, they're likely to own a gun and want to listen to your speech opposing stricter gun laws.

Attitudes are based on **beliefs** — the ways in which people perceive reality.[4] They are our feelings about what is true or real. Whereas attitudes deal with how we feel about some activity or entity ("Yoga is good" or "Regular church/mosque/synagogue attendance is good"), beliefs refer to our level of confidence about the very existence or validity of something ("I believe God exists" or "I'm not so sure that God exists"). The less faith listeners have that something exists — a UFO, for instance — the less open they are to hearing about it.

Both attitudes and beliefs are shaped by **values** — our most enduring judgments about what's good in life, as shaped by our culture and our unique experiences within it. We have fewer values than either attitudes or beliefs, but they are more deeply felt and resistant to change. We feel our values strongly and use them as a compass to direct our behavior. In addition, we have positive attitudes toward our values and strive to realize them. *Personal values* mirror our feelings about religious, political, social, and civic matters. *Cultural values* (also called "core values") reflect values deemed important by many members of a culture, imbuing them with distinct identities. In the United States, for example, researchers have identified a set of cultural values prevalent in the dominant culture, including *achievement and success, equal opportunity, material* *comfort, hard work, practicality and efficiency, change and progress, science, democracy,* and *freedom*[5] (see p. 94 for more on cultural values). For some of us—a minority of 37 percent in the United States[6]—the sanctity of marriage between a man and a woman is a cultural value. For others, the value of social justice supersedes that of material comfort. Whatever the nature of our values, they are central to our sense of who we are.

"If the Value Fits, Use It"

Evoking some combination of the audience's values, attitudes, and beliefs in the speeches you deliver will make them more personally relevant and motivating. For example, a recent large-scale survey of values related to the environment reveals that Americans overwhelmingly feel responsible to preserve the environment for future generations, to protect nature as God's creation, and to ensure that their families enjoy a healthy environment. Using this information, the Biodiversity Project, an organization that helps environmental groups raise public awareness, counsels speakers to appeal directly to these values in their presentations, offering the following as an example.

> You care about your family's health (value #1 as identified in survey), and you feel a responsibility to protect your loved ones' quality of life (value #2). The local wetland provides a sanctuary to many plants and animals. It helps to clean our air and water and provides a space of beauty and serenity (value #3). All of this is about to be destroyed by irresponsible development.[7]

Gauge Listeners' Feelings toward the Topic, Speaker, and Occasion

With any speech, it's important to assess the audience's feelings and expectations toward (1) the topic of your speech, (2) you as the speaker, and (3) the speech occasion. Doing this will help you anticipate listeners' reactions and develop the speech accordingly.

Gauge Listeners' Feelings toward the Topic

Consideration of the audience's attitudes (and beliefs and values) about a topic is key to offering a speech that will resonate with them (see Chapter 7, "Selecting a Topic and Purpose"). Is your topic one with which the audience is familiar, or is it new to them? Do your listeners hold positive, negative, or neutral attitudes toward the topic? That is, do they care a lot, a little, or not at all about your topic? As a rule, audience members are more interested in and pay greater attention to topics toward which they have positive attitudes and that are in keeping with their values and beliefs. The less we know about something, the more indifferent we tend to be. It is easier (though not simple) to spark interest in an indifferent audience than it is to turn negative attitudes around.

Once you assess the audience's knowledge level and attitudes toward the topic (using tools such as interviews and questionnaires; see p. 98), adjust the speech accordingly (see also the table in Chapter 24 for persuasive strategies for appealing to different audiences).

If the Topic Is *New* to Listeners,

- Start by showing why the topic is relevant to them.
- Relate the topic to familiar issues and ideas about which they already hold positive attitudes.

If Listeners Know *Relatively Little* about the Topic,

- Stick to the basics and include background information.
- Steer clear of jargon and define unclear terms.
- Repeat important points, summarizing information often.

If Listeners Are *Negatively Disposed* toward the Topic,

- Focus on establishing rapport and credibility.
- Don't directly challenge listeners' attitudes; instead begin with areas of agreement.
- Discover why they have a negative bias in order to tactfully introduce the other side of the argument.
- Offer solid evidence from sources they are likely to accept.
- Give good reasons for developing a positive attitude toward the topic.[8]

If Listeners Hold *Positive Attitudes* toward the Topic,

- Stimulate the audience to feel even more strongly by emphasizing the side of the argument with which they already agree.
- Tell stories with vivid language that reinforces listeners' attitudes.[9]

If Listeners Are a *Captive Audience*,

- Motivate listeners to pay attention by stressing what is most relevant to them.
- Pay close attention to the length of your speech.

Gauge Listeners' Feelings toward You as the Speaker

How audience members feel about you will also have significant bearing on their responsiveness to your message. A speaker who is well liked can gain at least an initial hearing even if listeners are unsure of what to expect from the message itself. Conversely, an audience that feels negatively toward the speaker will disregard even the most important or interesting message. We tend to put up barriers against people whom we hold in low regard.

To create positive audience attitudes toward you, first display the characteristics of speaker credibility (ethos) described in Chapter 4. Listeners have a natural desire to identify with the speaker and to feel that he or she shares their perceptions,[10] so look for ways to establish a common bond, or feeling of **identification**, between you and the audience. Use eye contact and body movements to include the audience in your message. Share a personal story, emphasize a shared role, and otherwise stress mutual bonds. Use personal pronouns such as *we, you, I,* and *me* to forge a connection and feeling of inclusion (see "Use Personal Pronouns" on p. 231).

Many times, especially when the topic is controversial, a speaker will create identification by emphasizing those aspects of the topic about which the audience members are likely to agree. When speaking to an audience of abortion rights activists, for example, then-Senator Hillary Clinton called on opposing sides in the debate to find "common ground" by focusing on education and abstinence.

> We should all be able to agree that we want every child born in this country and around the world to be wanted, cherished, and loved. The best way to get there is to do more to educate the public about reproductive health, about how to prevent unsafe and unwanted pregnancies.[11]

Clinton clearly was attempting to reach out beyond her core constituency and achieve some measure of identification with those who oppose abortion. Notice, too, how Clinton uses the personal pronoun *we* to encourage identification with the speech goal (see Chapter 16 for more on the power of inclusive language) and to build a sense of community within the audience. Even your physical presentation can foster identification. We're more apt to identify with the speaker who dresses like us (or in a manner we aspire to) than with someone whose style and grooming seem strange or displeasing.

Gauge Listeners' Feelings toward the Occasion

Depending on the circumstances calling for the speech, people will bring different sets of expectations and emotions to it. For example, imagine being a businessperson attending a conference—it's your third night away from home, you're tired from daylong meetings, and now you're expected to listen to company executives explain routine production charges for the coming fiscal year.

CHECKLIST

APPEAL TO AUDIENCE ATTITUDES, BELIEFS, AND VALUES

Have you . . .

✔ Investigated audience members' attitudes, beliefs, and values toward your topic?

✔ Assessed the audience's level of knowledge about the topic?

✔ Considered strategies to address positive, negative, and neutral responses to your speech topic?

✔ Considered appealing directly to audience members' values in your speech?

In contrast, picture attending a speech of your own free will to listen to a speaker you've long admired. Members of a **captive audience**, who are required to hear the speaker, may be less positively disposed to the occasion than members of a **voluntary audience**, who are present by choice. Whether planning a business presentation or classroom speech, failure to anticipate and adjust for the audience's expectations risks alienating them.

Adapt Your Message to Audience Demographics

Collecting psychological data about audience members takes you partway through an audience analysis. Equally important is to learn demographic (e.g., statistical or quantifiable) information about them. Recall that *demographics* are the statistical characteristics of a given population. At least eight demographic characteristics are typically considered when analyzing speech audiences: *age, ethnic and cultural background, socioeconomic status* (including *income, occupation*, and *education*), *religious and political affiliations, gender, group affiliations*, and *disability. Depending on the topic and speech goal*, other traits—for example, sexual orientation and place of residence—may be important to investigate as well.

Appeal to Your Target Audience

Knowing where audience members fall in relation to audience demographics will help you identify your **target audience**—those individuals within the broader audience whom you are most likely to influence in the direction you seek. Mass communicators rely upon **audience segmentation**—dividing a general audience into smaller groups to identify target audiences with similar characteristics, wants, and needs. But whether used by advertisers selling iPads, advocacy groups selling cleaner air, or you as a public speaker, segmentation is a crucial tool for those attempting to reach an audience.

Consider a speech delivered to your classmates about lowering fees for campus parking violations. Your target audience will be those persons in the class who drive, rather than bicycle or walk, to campus. Whenever you appeal to a target audience, however, aim to make the topic relevant to other audience members. For example, you might mention that lower fees will benefit non-drivers in the future, should they bring cars to campus. You may not be able to please everyone, but you should be able to establish a connection with your target audience.

Age

Age can be a very important factor in determining how listeners will react to a topic. Each age group brings with it its own concerns, psychological drives, and motivations. The quest for identity in adolescence (around the ages of 12–20), for example, differs markedly from the need to establish stable careers and relationships in early adulthood (ages 20–40). Similarly, adults in their middle years (40–65), sometimes called the "sandwich generation," tend to grapple with a full plate of issues related to career, children, aging parents, and an increased awareness of mortality. And as we age (65 and older), physical changes and changes in lifestyle (from work to retirement) assume greater prominence.

Age-specific concerns affect attitudes toward many social issues, from the role that government should play (more younger than older voters want a bigger government) to Social Security and Medicare benefits (more older than younger voters want to preserve existing arrangements).[12]

People of the same generation often share a familiarity with significant individuals, local and world events, noteworthy popular culture, and so forth. Thus, being aware of the **generational identity** of your audience, such as the Baby Boomers (those born between 1946 and 1964), millennials (those born between 1980 and 1999), or Generation Z (those born since 2000), allows you to develop points that are relevant to the experiences and interests of the widest possible cross section of your listeners. Table 6.1 lists some of the prominent characteristics and values of today's generations.

Ethnic or Cultural Background

An understanding of and sensitivity to the ethnic and cultural composition of your audience are key factors in delivering a successful (and ethical) speech. As a speaker in a multicultural and multiethnic society, expect that your audience

TABLE 6.1 Generational Identity and Today's Generations

Generation	Born	Characteristics
Traditional	1925–1945	Respect for authority and duty, disciplined, strong sense of right and wrong
Baby Boomer	1946–1964	Idealistic, devoted to career, self-actualizing, values health and wellness
Generation X	1965–1979	Seeks work-life balance, entrepreneurial, technically savvy, flexible, questions authority figures, skeptical
Generation Y/Millennials	1980–1999	Technically savvy, optimistic, self-confident, educated, appreciative of diversity, entrepreneurial, respectful of elders, short attention spans
Generation Z	2000–	Comfortable with the highest level of technical connectivity, naturally inclined to collaborate online, boundless faith in power of technology to make things possible

See, for example, "Millennials, Gen X and Baby Boomers: Who's Working at Your Company and What Do They Think About Ethics?" Ethics Resource Center, 2009 National Business Ethics Survey Supplemental Research Brief, http://ethics.org/files/u5/Gen-Diff.pdf; Dennis McCafferty, "Workforce Preview: What to Expect from Gen Z," *Baseline Magazine*, April 4, 2013, www.baselinemag.com/it-management/slideshows/workforce-preview-what-to-expect-from-gen-z; and "Generations in the Workplace in the United States and Canada," *Catalyst*, May 1, 2012, www.catalyst.org/knowledge/generations-workplace-united-states-canada.

will include members of different national origins. Some audience members may have a great deal in common with you. Others may be fluent in a language other than yours and may struggle to understand you. Some members of the audience may belong to a distinct **co-culture**, a social community whose values and style of communicating may or may not mesh with your own. All will want to feel recognized by you, the speaker. (For guidelines on adapting to diverse audiences, see p. 93, "Adapt to Diverse Audiences.")

Socioeconomic Status

Socioeconomic status (SES) includes income, occupation, and education. Knowing roughly where an audience falls in terms of these key variables can be critical in effectively targeting your message.

Income

Income determines people's experiences on many levels. It directly affects how they are housed, clothed, and fed and determines what they can afford. Beyond this, income has a ripple effect, influencing many other aspects of life. For example, depending on income, home ownership is either a taken-for-granted budget item or an out-of-reach dream. The same is true for any activity dependent on income. Given how pervasively income affects people's life experiences, insight into this aspect of an audience's makeup can be quite important.

Occupation

In most speech situations, the *occupation* of audience members is an important and easily identifiable demographic characteristic that you as a speaker should try to determine in advance. The nature of people's work has a lot to do with what interests them. Occupational interests are tied to several other areas of social concern, such as politics, the economy, education, and social reform. Personal attitudes, beliefs, and goals are also closely tied to occupational standing.

Education

Level of *education* strongly influences people's ideas, perspectives, and range of abilities. Higher levels of education appears to be associated with greater fluctuation in personal values, beliefs, and goals. Higher levels of education leads to increased lifetime earnings, decreased levels of crime, better health outcomes, and greater civic engagement;[13] such factors may be important to consider when preparing a speech. Depending upon audience members' level of education, your speech may treat topics at a higher or lower level of sophistication, with fewer or more clarifying examples and illustrations.

Religion

Beliefs and practices, and sometimes social and political views, vary by religious traditions, making *religion* another key demographic variable. At least a dozen major religious traditions coexist in the United States.[14] A major change in the United States over the past several decades is the decline in religious observance among adults under age thirty, with fully a third of persons in this group identifying as unaffiliated, or "religious nones," in 2015, along with 23 percent of all U.S. adults.[15] While members of the same spiritual tradition will most likely agree on the major spiritual tenets of their faith, they will not agree on all religiously based issues. People who identify themselves as Catholic disagree on birth control and divorce, Jews disagree on whether to recognize same-sex unions, and so forth. Awareness of an audience's general religious orientation can be especially helpful when your speech touches on a topic as potentially controversial as religion itself. Capital punishment, same-sex marriage, and teaching about the origins of humankind—all are rife with religious overtones and implications.

Political Affiliation

As with religion, beware of making unwarranted assumptions about an audience's *political values and beliefs*. Some people like nothing better than a lively debate about public-policy issues. Others avoid anything that smacks of politics. And many people are very touchy about their views on political issues. Conservative individuals hold certain views that liberals dispute, and the chasm between far right and far left is great indeed. Thus, if your topic involves politics, you'll need to obtain background on your audience's political views.

CHECKLIST

RESPOND TO THE AUDIENCE AS YOU SPEAK

Audience analysis continues as you deliver your speech. During your speech, monitor the audience for signs of how they are receiving your message. Look for bodily clues as signs of interest or disengagement.

- ✔ Large smiles and eye contact suggest a liking for and agreement with the speaker.
- ✔ Arms closed across the chest may signal disagreement.
- ✔ Averted glances, slumped posture, looking at a cell phone or other mobile device, and squirming usually indicate disengagement.
- ✔ Engage with the audience when it appears they aren't with you.
- ✔ Invite one or two listeners to briefly relate their own experiences on the topic.[1]
- ✔ Share a story linked to the topic to increase identification.

1. Nick Morgan, *Working the Room: How to Move People to Action through Audience-Centered Speaking* (Cambridge, MA: Harvard Business School Press, 2003), 181–97.

Gender

Gender is another important factor in audience analysis, if only as a reminder to avoid the minefield of *gender stereotyping*. Distinct from the fixed physical characteristics of biological sex, **gender** is our social and psychological sense of ourselves as males or females.[16] Making assumptions about the preferences, abilities, and behaviors of your audience members based on their presumed gender can seriously undermine their receptivity to your message. Using **sexist language**, language that casts males or females into roles on the basis of sex alone, will also swiftly alienate many listeners. Equally damaging to credibility is the inclusion of overt **gender stereotypes**—oversimplified and often severely distorted ideas about the innate nature of what it means to be male or female. Beyond ensuring that you treat issues of gender evenly, try to anticipate the audience members' attitudes with respect to gender and plan accordingly.

Group Affiliations

The various groups to which audience members belong—whether social, civic, work-related, or religiously or politically affiliated—reflect their interests and values and so provide insight into what they care about.

- *Social clubs* include any grouping of people who gather to share a common interest and activities, from book clubs to college fraternities and sororities.
- *Civic organizations* promote some aspect of social welfare. Examples include Lions' and Rotary Clubs, Habitat for Humanity, League of United Latin American Citizens (LULAC), and the National Association for the Advancement of Colored People (NAACP).
- *Professional associations* seek to further the interests of a particular profession, from firefighters and police to lawyers and clergy.
- *Social networking groups* maintain preestablished interpersonal relationships and build new ones online through social networking sites such as Facebook, LinkedIn, and Twitter.
- *Online communities* enable people in different geographic locations around the world without preestablished relationships to "congregate" in virtual space to share interests, work toward goals, and provide fellowship.

Disability

According to the U.S. Census Bureau, more than 19 percent of the population, or about fifty-seven million people (excluding persons who are institutionalized), have some sort of physical, mental, or employment disability; more than half of these have a severe disability.[17] About 9 percent of undergraduates (not including veterans) are counted as disabled.[18] Problems

CHECKLIST

REVIEWING YOUR SPEECH IN LIGHT OF AUDIENCE DEMOGRAPHICS

- ✔ Have you reviewed your topic in light of the age range and generational identity of your listeners? Do you use examples they will recognize and find relevant?
- ✔ Have you considered the ethnic and cultural composition of your audience and reviewed your use of language and examples in light of it?
- ✔ Are your explanations and examples at a level appropriate to the audience's sophistication and education?
- ✔ Do you make any unwarranted assumptions about the audience's political or religious values and beliefs?
- ✔ Does your topic carry religious or political overtones that are likely to stir your listeners' emotions in a negative way?
- ✔ Is your speech free of generalizations based on gender?
- ✔ Does your language reflect sensitivity toward people with disabilities?

range from sight and hearing impairments to constraints on physical mobility and employment. Thus disability is another demographic variable to consider when analyzing an audience. Keep **persons with disabilities (PWD)** in mind when you speak, and use language and examples that afford them respect and dignity.

Adapt to Diverse Audiences

In the United States, over one-third of the population, or 116 million persons, belong to a racial or ethnic minority group, or one designated by the U.S. Census Bureau as other than "non-Hispanic White."[19] Additionally, 42.2 million people, or 13.9 percent of the U.S. population, are foreign-born (see Figure 6.1). California leads the nation, with 27 percent of its residents foreign-born; New York, Texas, New Jersey, and Florida follow close behind.[20] Nationwide, 21 percent of the population speaks a language other than English in the home; two-thirds of these speak Spanish.[21] Worldwide, there are 195 recognized independent states, and many more distinct cultures within these countries.[22] What these figures suggest is that audience members will hold different cultural perspectives and employ different styles of communicating that may or may not mesh with your own.

How might you prepare to speak in front of an ethnically and culturally diverse audience, including that of your classroom? In any speaking situation, your foremost concern should be to treat your listeners with dignity and to act with integrity. You do this by infusing your speech with the pillars of character

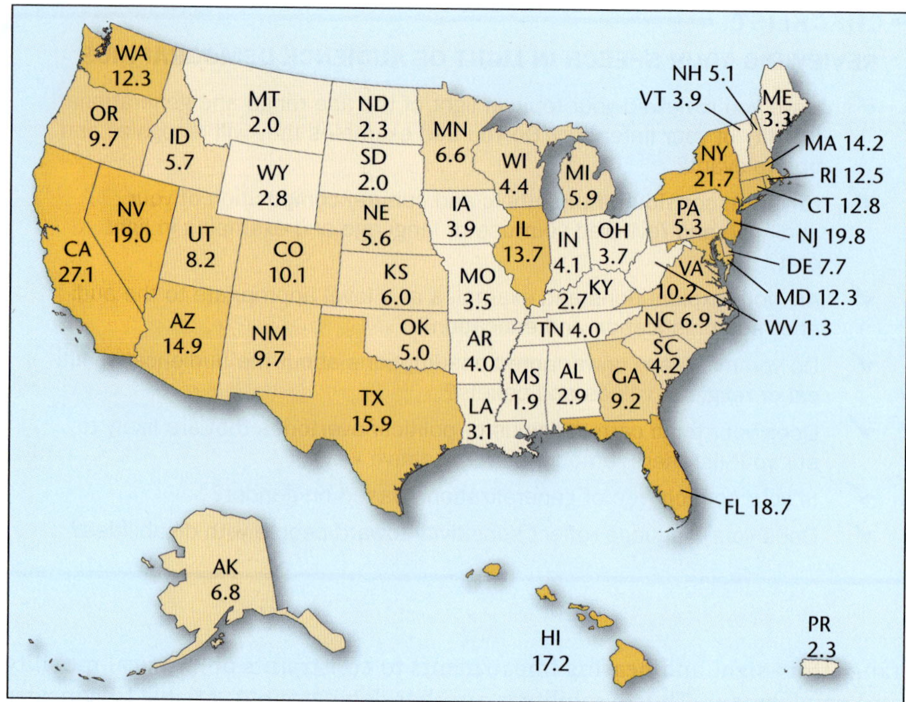

FIGURE 6.1 Foreign-Born Population as a Percentage of State Population
Note: Data are limited to the household population and exclude the population living in institutions, college dormitories, and other group quarters. *Data from:* U.S. Census Bureau, *American Community Survey* (2010), www.census.gov/prod/2012pubs/acs-19.pdf.

described in Chapter 5: trustworthiness, respect, responsibility, and fairness. Since values are central to who we are, identifying those of your listeners with respect to your topic can help you to avoid ethnocentrism and deliver your message in a culturally sensitive manner.

Adapt to Cross-Cultural Values

People in every culture possess **cultural values** related to their personal relationships, religion, occupation, and so forth, and these values can significantly influence how audience members respond to a speaker's message. For example, in Mexico, *familismo*, *respeto*, and *fatalismo*, among others, are important cultural values; surveys of several Asian societies reveal such dominant values as a *spirit of harmony*, *humility toward one's superiors*, *awe of nature*, and a *desire for prosperity*.[23] Becoming familiar with differences, as well as points of sameness, in cultural values can help you to frame messages effectively and with sensitivity.

Hofstede's Value-Dimensions Model: Understanding Differences in National Cultural Values

Dutch cultural anthropologist Geert Hofstede and colleagues' value dimensions model offers revealing data about how values vary across cultures. These researchers have identified six major "value dimensions," or "broad preferences for one state of affairs over another, usually held unconsciously," as being significant across all cultures, but in widely varying degrees; thus far they have studied and ranked 86 countries (scored from 0 to 100) in terms of how they compare on these dimensions (see Figure 6.2, "Value Dimensions by Country").[24] The six value dimensions are individualism versus collectivism, uncertainty avoidance, power distance, masculinity versus femininity, time orientation, and indulgence versus restraint.

Individualism versus Collectivism

The *individualism versus collectivism* dimension refers to how a society's members define themselves in relation to others. In **individualistic cultures**, people tend to emphasize the needs of the individual rather than those of the group, upholding such values as *individual achievement* and *decision making*. In **collectivist cultures**, personal identity, needs, and desires are viewed as secondary to those of the larger group; interdependence among people is much greater. As such, audience members who share collectivist values may be less responsive than members of individualistic cultures to speeches emphasizing personal achievement. The United States is a highly individualist culture, with a score of 91, followed by Australia, Great Britain, and Canada. Ecuador, Venezuela, Peru, Taiwan, and Pakistan rank highest in collectivist characteristics.

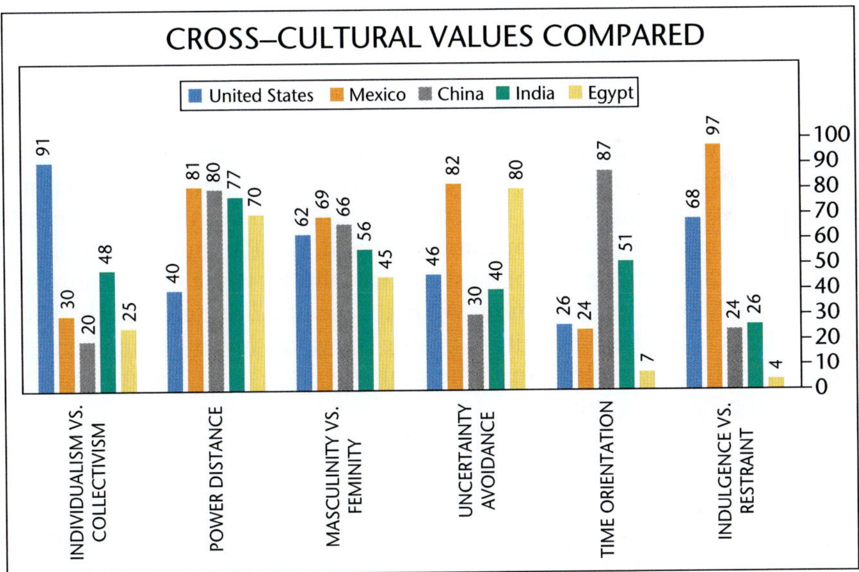

FIGURE 6.2 Values Dimensions by Country
Information drawn from https://geert-hofstede.com/countries.html, "Country Comparison" Tool, accessed May 5, 2017.

Uncertainty Avoidance

Uncertainty avoidance refers to the extent to which people in a given culture feel threatened by ambiguity (e.g., how much they value predictability in their lives). **High-uncertainty avoidance cultures** tend to structure life more rigidly and formally for their members, while **low-uncertainty avoidance cultures** are more accepting of uncertainty in life and therefore allow more variation in individual behavior. Out of a score of 100, the United States scored 46, placing it near the middle of the uncertainty-avoidance value dimension. This dimension suggests that it can be helpful to consider the degree to which audience members might tend to invite or avoid change in the status quo, especially when the speech is persuasive in nature.

Power Distance

Power distance is the extent to which people in a given culture accept inequality and authority as normal. Cultures with *high levels of power distance* tend to be more rigidly organized along hierarchical lines, with greater emphasis placed on honoring authority. Those with *low levels of power distance* place a higher value on social equality. Some very high power distance countries include Malaysia, the Philippines, Indonesia, India, and the Arab nations of Egypt, Iraq, Kuwait, Lebanon, Libya, and Saudi Arabia; the Scandinavian nations, New Zealand, and Israel rank lowest, favoring the most equality among persons of different social levels. With a score of 40, the United States ranks fairly low on the power distance dimension, indicating that social rank is less important than equal rights in the culture. Audience members from high power distance cultures may be more sensitive than members from low power distance cultures to the respect speakers demonstrate in their speech when discussing those in authority.

Masculinity versus Femininity

The *masculinity and femininity* dimension refers to the degree to which a culture values traits that are associated with traditional gender roles. Traditional masculine traits include ambition, assertiveness, and competitiveness. Feminine traits stress nurturance and cooperation. Ireland, the Philippines, Greece, and South Africa rank among the highest in masculinity, while the Scandinavian nations rank highest in femininity. With a score of 62 out of 100, the United States weights toward masculinity. Gauging the value audience members place on traditional gender roles can be helpful when speaking about topics that touch upon gender relations.

Time Orientation

The *time orientation* dimension refers to the degree to which a culture values behavior that is directed to future rewards, with cultures with a long-term orientation valuing such traits as perserverance and thrift, and which encourage a focus on long-term goals; countries with a *short-term orientation* tend to value behavior directed toward the past or present more so than the future. High value is placed on respect for tradition, preservation of face, and fulfillment of social obligations. China, Hong Kong, Taiwan, and South Korea ranked highest in long-term orientation, while Canada, Great Britain, the United States, Germany, and Australia rank highest in short-term orientation.

Indulgence versus Restraint

The *indulgence versus restraint* dimension refers to the degree to which a culture supports activities that lead to the enjoyment of life versus restraining those activities. Nations that score highly on this dimension encourage relatively free gratification of people's own drives; people tend to be happier and enjoy more leisure; nations with low scores tend to have strict social norms that suppress gratification and restrict freedom of speech. Mexico scores very highly on the indulgent side; Egypt is among the most restrained. The United States, with a score of 68, is somewhat high in indulgence.

Bear in mind that the cultural patterns identified by Hofstede reflect those of the *dominant culture*; they do not necessarily reflect the behaviors of all the groups living within a society. Although individualism characterizes the dominant culture of the United States, for example, various co-cultures—such as Hispanic Americans, Native Americans, and (to varying degrees) African Americans—have been described as collectivist in nature. To find out individual country rankings and compare your home culture with another culture, see www.geert-hofstede.com/hofstede_dimensions.php.

Focus on Universal Values

As much as possible, it is important to try to determine the attitudes, beliefs, and values of audience members and plan your speeches accordingly. At the same time, you can focus on certain values that, if not universally shared, are probably universally aspired to in the human heart. These include love, truthfulness, fairness, unity, tolerance, responsibility, and respect for life.[25]

A CULTURAL PERSPECTIVE

Consult Global Opinion Polls

charles taylor/Shutterstock

Cross-cultural surveys can be extremely useful for learning about how values vary across cultures. In addition to Hofstede's research, the *Pew Global Attitudes Project* (www.pewglobal.org/), surveys opinions in 64 countries. *Gallup World Poll* (www.gallup.com; go to "World") surveys people in 150 countries on attitudes ranging from well-being to the environment. The *World Values Survey* (www.worldvaluessurvey.org) offers a fascinating look at the values and beliefs of people in ninety-seven countries. Through these resources you can discover how people of other nations feel about work, family, religion, and even who should do the housework.

Techniques for Learning about Your Audience

Now that you know the kind of information to look for when analyzing an audience, how do you actually uncover it? While you don't have the sophisticated resources of professional pollsters, you can use similar tools to discover information about your audience. These include *interviews*; *online, telephone,* or *in-person surveys*; and *published sources*. Using these methods, often it takes just a few questions to get some idea of the audience members' attitudes and values on a topic and to identify their demographic factors.

Conduct Interviews

Interviews, even brief ones, can reveal a lot about the audience's interests and needs. You can conduct interviews one-on-one or in a group, in person, by telephone, or online. Consider interviewing a sampling of the audience, or even just *one* knowledgeable representative of the group that you will address. As with questionnaires (see "Survey the Audience," which follows), interviews usually consist of a mix of open- and closed-ended questions. (See Chapter 9 for more on conducting interviews.)

Survey the Audience

Surveys can be as informal as a poll of several audience members or as formal as the pre-speech distribution of a written survey, or **questionnaire**—a series of open- and closed-ended questions. **Closed-ended questions** (also called *structured questions*) elicit a small range of specific answers.

> "Do you smoke cigarettes?"
>
> Yes _____ No _____ I quit, but I smoked for _____ years

Answers will be "Yes," "No," or "I smoked for *x* number of years."

Closed-ended questions may be either fixed-alternative or scale questions. **Fixed-alternative questions** contain a limited choice of answers, such as "Yes," "No," or "For *x* years" (as in the preceding example). **Scale questions**—also called *attitude scales*—measure the respondent's level of agreement or disagreement with specific issues.

> "Flag burning should be outlawed."
>
> Strongly agree _____ Agree _____ Undecided _____ Disagree _____ Strongly disagree _____

Scale questions can be used to measure how important listeners judge something to be and how frequently they engage in a particular behavior.

> "How important is religion in your life?"
>
> Very important _____ Important _____ Moderately important _____
>
> Of minor importance _____ Unimportant _____

"How frequently do you attend religious services?"

Very frequently _____ Frequently _____ Occasionally _____ Never _____

Open-ended questions (also called *unstructured questions*) begin with a "how," "what," "when," "where," or "why," and are particularly useful for probing beliefs and opinions. This style of question allows respondents to elaborate as much as they wish.

"How do you feel about using the results of DNA testing to prove innocence or guilt in criminal proceedings?"

Open-ended questions elicit more individual or personal information about audience members' thoughts and feelings. They are also more time-intensive than closed-ended questions, so use them sparingly if at all in written questionnaires.

Often, it takes just a few fixed-alternative and scale questions to draw a fairly clear picture of audience members' backgrounds and attitudes and where they fall in demographic categories. You may wish to use Web-based survey software, such as SurveyMonkey or QuestionPro, to generate surveys electronically using premade templates and distribute them via e-mail.

Sample Audience Analysis Questionnaire

Part I: Demographic Analysis

1. What is your age? _____ years
2. What is your sex? _____ Male _____ Female _____ Other
3. Please indicate your primary heritage:
   _____ Native American _____ African American
   _____ Asian American _____ European
   _____ Latino _____ Middle Eastern _____ Other
4. Please indicate your level of formal education:
   _____ High school _____ Some college
   _____ College degree _____ Other (please specify)
5. What is your approximate annual income range?
   _____ less than $10,000 _____ $10,000–$24,999
   _____ $25,000–$49,999 _____ $50,000–$74,999
   _____ $75,000–$100,000 _____ over $100,000
6. With which political party are your views most closely aligned?
   _____ Democratic _____ Republican _____ Other

7. Please check the box below that most closely matches your religious affiliation:

_____ Buddhist _____ Christian

_____ Hindu _____ Jewish

_____ Muslim _____ Not religious _____ Other (please specify)

8. How would you characterize your religious involvement?

_____ Very religious _____ Somewhat religious _____ Not very religious

9. How would you characterize your political position?

_____ Liberal _____ Conservative _____ Moderate

Part II: Analysis of Attitudes, Values, and Beliefs on a Specific Topic

Indicate your answers to the following questions about stem cell research by checking the appropriate blank.

10. It is unethical and immoral to permit any use of stem cells for medical research.

_____ Strongly agree _____ Agree _____ Undecided

_____ Disagree _____ Strongly disagree

11. Do you think the government should or should not fund stem cell research?

_____ Should _____ Should not _____ Neutral

12. Rather than destroy stem cells left over from *in vitro* fertilization, medical researchers should be allowed to use them to develop treatments for diseases.

_____ Strongly agree _____ Agree _____ Undecided

_____ Disagree _____ Strongly disagree

13. What kind of cells come to mind when you think of stem cell therapy?

____

14. Which of the following has had the biggest influence on your thinking about stem cell research?

_____ Media reports _____ Opinions of friends and family

_____ Your religious beliefs _____ Personal experience

Consult Published Sources

Organizations of all kinds publish information describing their missions, operations, and achievements. Sources include websites and related online articles, brochures, newspaper and magazine articles, and annual reports.

Although *published opinion polls* won't specifically reflect your particular listeners' responses, they can provide valuable insight into how a representative state, national, or international sample feels about the issue in question. (Polls also provide an excellent source of supporting material for your speech.) Consider consulting these and other polling organizations:

- National Opinion Research Center (NORC): **www.norc.uchicago.edu**
- Roper Center for Public Opinion Research: **www.ropercenter.uconn.edu**
- Gallup: **www.gallup.com**
- Pew Research Center U.S. Politics and Policy: **www.people-press.org**

Analyze the Speech Setting and Context

As important as analyzing the audience is assessing (and then preparing for) the setting in which you will give your speech—size of audience; location, time, and length of speech; and rhetorical situation. Planning for these factors will help you further adjust your speech to the actual circumstances in which it will occur.

Size of Audience and Physical Setting

The size of the audience and the physical setting in which a speech occurs can have a significant impact on the outcome of the speech. Some settings are formal, others less so. The atmosphere of a classroom is different from that of a banquet room, an outdoor amphitheater, or a large auditorium. A virtual audience requires unique considerations (see Chapter 28 on online presentations). The larger the group, the less you are likely to interact with the audience—an important factor to consider when planning your delivery (see Chapters 17–19 on methods of delivery). You will also need to plan how to position yourself and adjust your voice, with or without a microphone.

Time and Length of Speech

Both the time at which your speech is scheduled and its length will affect listeners' receptivity to it. People gathered at breakfast, lunch, or dinner meetings, for example, come to the speech occasion with more than one agenda. They may wish to hear you, but they will also want time to eat and converse with other people. Your boss or fellow employees may expect to receive information quickly so that they can proceed to other business.

In any speaking situation, always find out how long you are expected to speak. Bear in mind that few matters of speech etiquette are as annoying to an audience as a speaker's apparent disregard for time. Start on time and end well within the time allotted to you. Table 6.2 includes typical lengths for various presentations.

The Rhetorical Situation

Any speech or presentation you deliver will always occur in a particular circumstance and for a particular reason, defined as the "rhetorical situation"

TABLE 6.2 Typical Length of Presentations

Kind of Presentation	Length
In-depth speech	15–20 minutes
Presentation to boss	1–10 minutes
Toast	1–2 minutes
Award acceptance speech	3–5 minutes

(see Chapter 1). You may be the third of six speakers on a panel, for instance. You might precede or follow a speaker who is more dynamic or well-known than you are. Listeners may be anxious to hear certain information early in the speech, because it addresses matters vital to them. They may be preoccupied with unusual circumstances—a local sports team just won a championship, extreme weather conditions have disrupted everyday life, the president of the company just resigned, and so forth. By being alert to any of these contingencies, you can address them in your speech.

CHECKLIST

ANALYZING THE SPEECH SITUATION

_____ 1. Where will the speech take place?

_____ 2. How long am I expected to speak?

_____ 3. What special events or circumstances of concern to my audience should I acknowledge?

_____ 4. How many people will attend?

_____ 5. Will I need a microphone?

_____ 6. How will any projecting equipment I plan to use in my speech, such as an LCD projector, function in the space?

_____ 7. Where will I stand or sit in relation to the audience?

_____ 8. Will I be able to interact with listeners?

_____ 9. Who else will be speaking?

7 Selecting a Topic and Purpose

LearningCurve can help you review!
Go to LaunchPad: **launchpadworks.com**

The late, great baseball player Yogi Berra, famously prone to mangling popular sayings,[1] once said "You've got to be very careful if you don't know where you're going, because you might not get there." Presumably, Berra meant the actual saying: "You must know where you are going in order to get there."

No words were ever truer for the public speaker. Unless you know what you want to say and why you want to say it—your topic and purpose—you won't get *there*—giving a speech that works. Thus one of the first tasks in preparing any speech is to select a topic and purpose that are *appropriate to the audience, occasion, and overall speech situation* (*rhetorical situation*). You should be able to answer three key questions with total confidence before delivering any speech: "What precisely is my speech about?" "What is my goal in speaking to the audience?" and "What specifically do I want my listeners to know or do?"

Understand Your Constraints

In any given speaking situation, including the public speaking classroom, various constraints exist on what you can do with a topic. For example, there will be times when the topic is assigned and times when it is yours to select. Even when you pick the topic, you are nevertheless usually given some direction as to how your speech should be presented. In the classroom, your instructor might assign a persuasive speech. Persuasive speeches are meant to achieve different aims than informative ones, so you'll need to evaluate your topic's appropriateness for that general speech purpose. There is also the critical task of analyzing the audience's potential interest in the topic, and at what level. Usually, you will be given time constraints, which will limit the amount of material that you can cover. Thus, even in the preliminary stages of choosing a topic, try to consider the specifics of your rhetorical situation. Doing so will help you avoid picking inappropriate or unrealistic topics.

Discovering Good Topics for Your Speech

A good speech topic must pique the audience's curiosity as well as your own. You must feel sufficiently interested and excited about a topic to spend the necessary time to select, narrow, research, and organize the topic into an effective speech. We naturally transmit our interest (or lack of it) in our voice and body language, so allow yourself the space to discover topics to which you are genuinely drawn. Focus on picking topics about which you can speak competently and bring fresh information to your listeners. At the same time, carefully consider each potential topic's appeal to the audience (based on audience analysis, including demographic and psychological information; see Chapter 6). How do you want them to respond to, and benefit by, what you have to say?

Identify Personal Interests

Personal interests run the gamut from favorite activities and hobbies to deeply held goals and values about spiritual, political, and other matters we care about (see Table 7.1). You can translate personal experiences into powerful topics, especially if sharing them in some way benefits the audience. "What it's like" stories, for example, yield captivating topics—what is it like to go hang gliding in the Rocky Mountains or to be part of a medical mission team working in Uganda?

Consider Current Events and Controversial Issues

Few of us have the time to delve into the all of the important events that get reported, yet most of us appreciate learning about them when we can. As an interested and responsible citizen of your community and the world, think about events and issues that most affect you and your audience, and see if you can make a difference. Be aware, however, that audience members rarely respond to perspectives opposed to their core values, so plan speeches on such topics carefully using audience analysis (see Chapter 6 on analyzing the audience).

For trustworthy background information on pressing social, political, environmental, and regional issues, librarians often refer students to two related publications—*CQ Researcher* (published weekly) and *CQ Global Researcher* (published monthly). Available online as part of most libraries' electronic holdings, for each topic they include an overview and assessment of the current situation, pro/con statements from representatives of opposing positions, and bibliographies of key sources. Online, *Opposing Views* features contrasting viewpoints in news articles on politics, societal issues, world affairs, and culture; *I Side With* provides concise overviews on hot-button issues and suggests candidates that support them; and *Rock the Vote* contains polls and articles about political candidates and social issues.

Survey Grassroots Issues: Engage the Community

Audience members, including college students, generally respond with interest to local issues that may affect them directly. Review your community's newspapers, including your school's paper and press releases, and news blogs for

TABLE 7.1 Identifying Topics

Favorite Hobbies	Personal Experiences	Values	Goals
· Sports · Cars · Fashion · Reading · Video games · Music · Travel · Cooking	· Travel destinations · Service in the armed forces · Volunteer work in the United States or abroad · Emigrating to the United States · Surviving a life-threatening disease · Surviving disaster · Growing up in a nontraditional family	· Building a greater sense of community · Spirituality · Philanthropy · Political activism · Living a sustainable life	· Being an entrepreneur · Attending graduate or professional school · Starting a family · Staying fit · Learning more about one's religion
Specific Subject Interests	**Social Problems**	**Health and Nutrition**	**Current Events**
· Local history · Genealogy · U.S. or global politics · Photography and art · Religion · Science	· Driving while black/racial profiling · Gun violence · Bullying in the schools · Unemployment · Racism	· Diets · Insomnia · Exercise regimens · Eating organic or gluten-free · Cell phones and cancer	· Religious Freedom Act and individual state legislation · Anti-discrimination laws · Border security · Federal college tuition programs · Immigration · Political races · Climate and biodiversity · National security
Grassroots Issues	**New or Unusual Angles**	**Issues of Controversy**	
· Student loan relief options · Drought and water conservation · Caring for the homeless	· Unsolved crimes · Unexplained disappearances · Conspiracy theories · Scandals	· Open gun carrying laws · Immigration (illegal, and paths to citizenship; detainment policies; assimilation policies; border security; tuition assistance . . .) · Death penalty · Drug decriminalization · Raising the minimum wage · Animal testing · Mandatory vaccinations	

the local headlines. What social, environmental, health, political, or other hot-button issues currently affect your community? Consider finding a topic about one of these issues.

Steer Clear of Overused and Trivial Topics

To avoid boring your classmates and instructor, stay away from tired issues, such as drunk driving and the health risks of smoking cigarettes, as well as trite topics such as "how to change a tire" (unless you can say something truly new about them). Overused and trite topics appear far too frequently in student classroom speeches. Instead, seek out subject matter that yields new information or different perspectives.

One way to find fresh topics is to check websites that provide information on search trends, hot topics, and ideas that are trending now, such as the following.

- **Google Trends** (www.google.com/trends) allows you to discover the most popular topics on Google's database, along with the latest trending news worldwide or by regions and subregions.
- **Google Zeitgeist** (www.zeitgeistminds.com) events are a series of speeches on social, economic, political, and cultural topics delivered by top global thinkers and leaders.
- **Twitter Trends** (www.twitter.com) Trending topics are listed on the left-hand column of the user's home page.
- **Facebook Trending** (www.facebook.com) Located on Facebook's home page sidebar, trending topics are grouped into five categories, displayed as icons to the right of the "Trending" heading: Top Trends, Politics, Science and Technology, Sports, and Entertainment. The content includes public posts and posts from your network.

Try Brainstorming to Generate Ideas

Brainstorming is a method of spontaneously generating ideas through word association, topic (mind) mapping, or Internet browsing using search engines and directories. Brainstorming works! It is truly a structured and effective way to identify topic ideas in a relatively brief period of time, so give it a try.

Word Association

To brainstorm by **word association**, write down *one* topic that might interest you and your listeners. Then jot down the first thing that comes to mind related to it. Repeat the process until you have a list of fifteen to twenty items. Narrow the list to two or three, and then select a final topic.

- health ⇒ insomnia ⇒ sleep medicine doctors ⇒ cutting-edge treatments for insomnia
- energy ⇒ oil ⇒ solar energy ⇒ solar panels ⇒ Elon Musk's solar company

- exercise ⇒ cold weather ⇒ speed riding ⇒ snowkiting ⇒ junkboarding ⇒ junkboarding pioneer Justin Woods
- video games ⇒ platform games ⇒ shooter games ⇒ artillery games

Topic Mapping

Topic (mind) mapping is a brainstorming technique in which you lay out words in diagram form to show categorical relationships among them (see Figure 7.1). Put a potential topic in the middle of a piece of paper and draw a circle around it. As related ideas come to you, write them down, as shown in Figure 7.1. Keep going until you hit upon an idea that appeals most to you *and* which will appeal to the audience.

Use Internet Tools

As seen in the nearby Source to Speech on "Narrowing Your Topic Using a Library Portal," yet another excellent online means of finding (and narrowing) a topic are the databases available on a library's portal, or its home page (see also p. 135). Consult general databases such as Academic OneFile (for browsing and starting the search process) and *subject-specific databases* such as Ethnic NewsWatch (for in-depth research on a topic). Popular Internet search engines such as Google also offer a wealth of resources to discover and narrow topics. Each search engine offers options for specialized searches within books, news, blogs, finance, images, and other sources. You can further narrow topics by limiting searches to within a range of dates (e.g., 1900–1950), to a geographic region (e.g., Europe), or to a particular language.

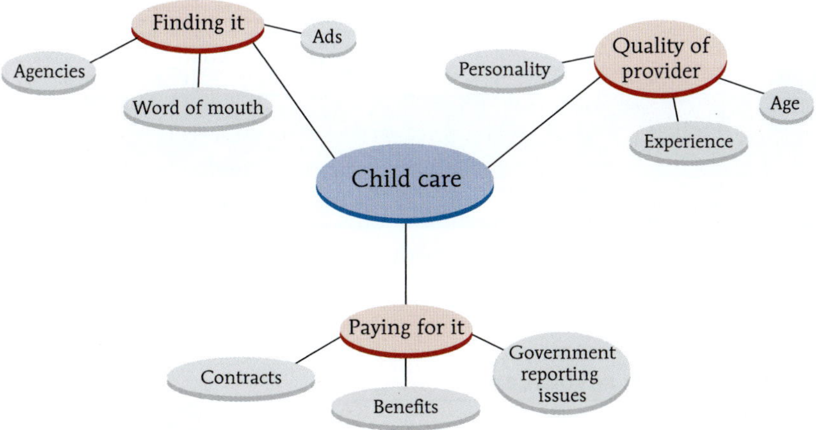

FIGURE 7.1 A Topic Map

Narrowing Your Topic Using a Library Portal

One of several ways to research your topic is to use a library's online portal. Using reputable tools to generate narrower ideas also guarantees that the new ideas are supported by credible sources. For example, to narrow down the topic of *smoking in movies*, you could use your school library's home page to locate relevant books and access online periodical databases that offer full-text articles evaluated for reliability by librarians and other content experts.

Navigating the Library Portal through Basic Searches

To search the portal of the Brooklyn Public Library, you could find sources through links on the home page: "Library Catalog" to find books, and "Articles and Databases" to find full-text articles.

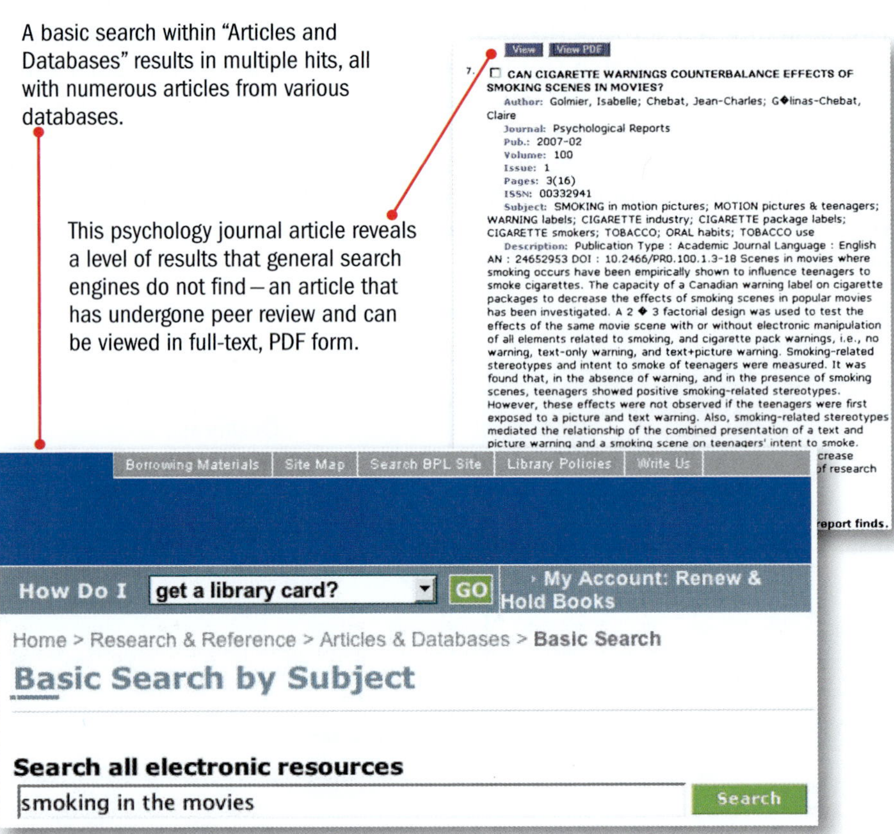

Using Advanced Library Portal Searches

An advanced search allows you to hone in on credible sources that are even more likely to help you. This function will allow you to better distill the specific purpose of your speech and to develop your thesis statement.

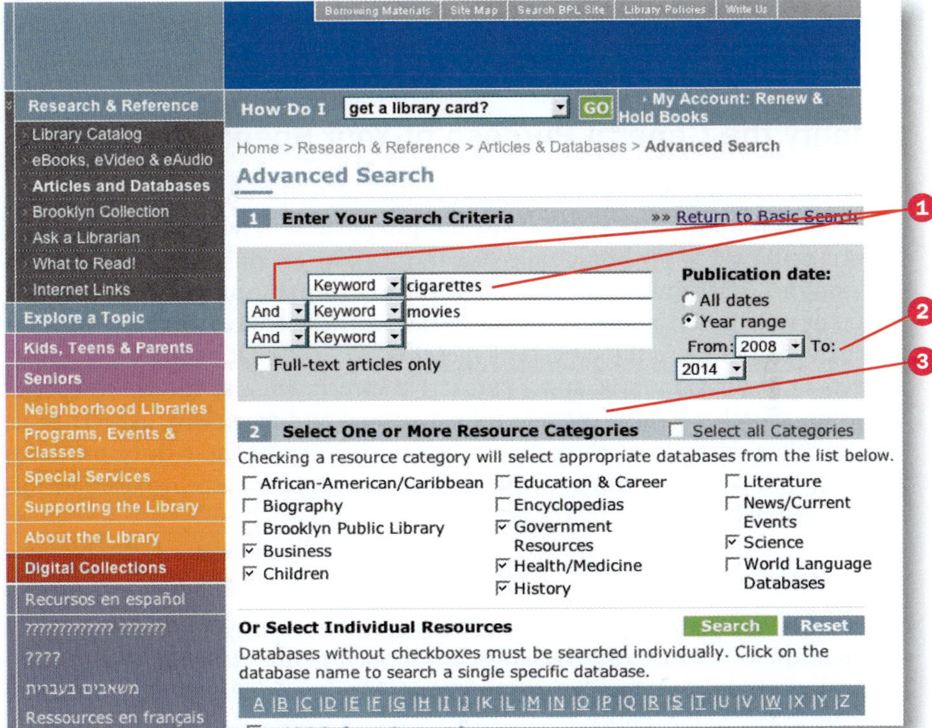

1 Linking search terms *cigarettes* and *movies* by the Boolean operator "AND" results in hits containing both these terms.

2 Limiting the search from 2015 to 2018 ensures that only articles in this period appear.

3 Limiting the resource categories yields results that cover only the areas on which you want to focus your thesis.

CHECKLIST

CRITERIA FOR SELECTING A TOPIC

1. Is the topic appropriate to the audience and occasion?
2. Can I research and report on the topic in the time allotted?
3. Will the topic appeal to my listeners' interests and needs?
4. Is the topic something I can speak about with enthusiasm and insight?
5. Will I be able to offer a fresh perspective on the topic?

Identify the General Purpose of Your Speech

Once you have an idea for a topic, you'll need to refine and adapt it to a general speech purpose. The **general speech purpose** for any speech answers the question: "What is my broad objective in speaking on this topic to this audience on this occasion?" Is my primary focus to *inform* the audience, to *persuade* them, or to help the audience *mark a special occasion?* Note that there is always some overlap in these three types of speeches. An informative speech will have aspects of persuasion in it, and a persuasive speech will also inform. A special occasion speech will also include informational and persuasive aspects to it. Nevertheless, identifying the primary function as one of these three purposes will help you effectively narrow your topic and meet your speech goals. The following will help you identify the general speech purpose.

When the General Speech Purpose Is to Inform

Do you primarily aim to educate or inform listeners about your topic? The general purpose of an **informative speech** is *to increase the audience's understanding and awareness of a topic by defining, describing, explaining, or demonstrating your knowledge of the subject.*

Just about any topic is appropriate for an informative speech (see Tables 7.2 and 7.3), as long as you present it with the goal of giving the audience something new to expand their understanding and awareness.

When the General Speech Purpose Is to Persuade

Is your goal primarily to influence listeners to accept your position on a topic and perhaps to take action (e.g., "only eat wild salmon")? The general purpose of a **persuasive speech** goes beyond informing and educating the audience to instead attempting to *effect some degree of change in the audience's attitudes, beliefs, or even specific behaviors.*

Topics or issues on which there are competing perspectives are particularly suitable for persuasive speeches. Issues such as gun control, immigration policies, Common Core, and affirmative action naturally lend themselves to a persuasive purpose because people hold strongly contrasting opinions about them.

TABLE 7.2 Some General Categories of Informative Topics

Objects	People	Events	Concepts	Processes	Issues
Their origin, construction, function, symbolic or concrete meaning. For example, history of the personal computer; the many facets of a diamond.	Their biographies, noteworthy achievements, anecdotes about them. For example, the poet and activist Maya Angelou; the professional life of Sheryl Sandburg.	Noteworthy or unusual occurrences, both past and present. For example, major storms of the 21st century, so far; high-lights of the most recent Olympics.	Abstract and difficult ideas or theories. For example, the nature of love; the definition of peace; the theory of intelligent design.	A series of steps leading to an end result. For example, how "fracking" works; how to plant an organic garden.	Problems or matters of dispute. For example, U.S. border security; whether reality television is really unscripted.

Most any topic is suitable for a persuasive speech as long as the speaker can fashion it into a message that is intended to effect some degree of change in the audience (see Table 7.4).

When the General Speech Purpose Is to Mark a Special Occasion

In your speech, do you aim primarily to mark a special occasion, such as an awards ceremony, retirement dinner, or funeral? **Special occasion speeches** serve the general purpose to *entertain*, *celebrate*, *commemorate*, *inspire*, or *set a social agenda* and include speeches of introduction, acceptance, and presentation; roasts and toasts; eulogies; and after-dinner speeches, among others. Speeches are often a key, if not featured, part of a special occasion. Special occasion speeches sometimes have secondary specific purposes to inform or to persuade. For example, a speech to mark the occasion of Veterans Day might include a persuasive message to contribute to or volunteer with organizations like the Wounded Warrior Project.

Consider the Speech Occasion to Identify the General Purpose

Note that the speech occasion itself often suggests an appropriate general speech purpose. A town activist, invited to address a civic group about

TABLE 7.3 Sample Informative Speech Topics

- How to Find Summer Internships that Pay
- Taking Distance Courses as a Resident Student
- Using Your Smart Phone as a Learning Aid
- Voting Patterns since 2000
- What's Behind the Immigration Issue

TABLE 7.4 Sample Persuasive Speech Topics

- Prepare for Your Future Career by Pursuing a Summer Internship
- Enroll in Distance Courses to Put Slack in Your Campus Schedule
- Learn by Using Your Smart Phone in Class
- Vote! Your Vote Matters in Local and National Elections
- Take a Stand on Immigration Reform

installing solar panels in town buildings, may choose a *persuasive purpose* to encourage the group to get behind the effort. If invited to describe the initiative to the town finance committee, the activist may choose an *informative purpose*, in which the main goal is to help the committee understand project costs. If asked to speak at an event celebrating the project's completion, the speaker will choose a *special occasion purpose*. Addressing the same topic, the speaker selects a different general speech purpose to suit the audience and occasion.

Refine the Topic and Purpose

Once you have selected a topic and a general speech purpose, you'll need to narrow it to align it with an analysis of the audience, time constraints, and any other relevant factors, such as availability of research. Beyond identifying your general speech purpose of informing, persuading, or marking a special occasion, you will also need to identify precisely what you want to audience to take away from your presentation. This is called the *specific speech purpose*.

Narrow the Topic

Speakers narrow a topic for a variety of reasons, including audience adaptation, speech occasion, and preparation and delivery time constraints. Imagine, for example, how your approach to the topic "Internship Opportunities and Career Development" may change as you consider the following factors.

- The speech is for an informative speaking assignment.
- The time limit is five to seven minutes.
- You have one very busy school week to prepare the speech.

Just as brainstorming and Internet tools can be used to discover a general topic, they can also be instrumental in narrowing one. Using *topic mapping*, you can brainstorm by category (e.g., subtopic). Say your general topic is internships. Some related categories include paid internships, unpaid internships, and cooperative (co-op) education. As you brainstorm, ask yourself, "What questions do I have about the topic? Am I more interested in cooperative (co-op) education or one of the two types of internships? What aspect of internships is my audience most likely to want to hear about?" You can also use trend searching (see p. 106) to narrow your topic.

CHECKLIST

NARROWING YOUR TOPIC

- ✓ What is my audience most likely to know about the subject?
- ✓ What do my listeners most likely want to learn?
- ✓ What aspects of the topic are most relevant to the occasion?
- ✓ Can I develop the topic using just two or three main points?
- ✓ How much can I competently research and report on in the time I am given to speak?

Form a Specific Speech Purpose

After you've narrowed your topic sufficiently, you will have a better idea of what your speech can actually accomplish. At this stage, it is helpful to articulate an even more refined goal for your speech than simply to inform, persuade, or mark a special occasion. The **specific speech purpose** lays out precisely what you want *the audience to take away from your presentation*. As in the fulfillment of any goal, explicitly stating a specific speech purpose makes it more likely that you will achieve it.

Formulating the specific speech purpose is straightforward. Ask yourself, "What is it about my topic that I want the audience to learn/do/reconsider/agree with?" Be specific about your aim, and then state it in action form, as in the following, written for an informative speech.

GENERAL TOPIC:	Binge Drinking
NARROWED TOPIC:	Describe the nature and prevalence of binge drinking on U.S. campuses and offer solutions to avoid it
GENERAL PURPOSE:	To persuade
SPECIFIC PURPOSE:	To persuade my audience that binge drinking is harmful and to convince listeners to consume alcohol safely or not at all.

Although the specific purpose statement may or may not be articulated in the actual speech, it is important to formulate it for yourself in order to keep in mind exactly what you want your speech to accomplish. Recall Yogi Berra's mangled quote about not knowing where you are going and consequently not getting there when you actually deliver the speech.

From Topic and Purpose to Thesis Statement

Once you've formed a specific speech purpose statement, you are ready to formulate a thesis statement. The **thesis statement** (also called the central idea) is the theme of the speech stated as a single declarative sentence. It concisely expresses what the speech will attempt to demonstrate or prove. The main

FROM SOURCE TO SPEECH

Narrowing Your Topic to Fit Your Audience

Why Narrow Your Topic?

Choosing a topic that interests you is only the beginning. A vital step in moving from topic to speech is narrowing your topic and tailoring it to fit your audience and the speech occasion.

A Case Study

Jenny is a member of the campus animal rights club and a student in a public speaking class. She is giving several persuasive speeches this semester: one to her public speaking class, one to the student council, and one in an online video for the website of the animal rights club. For all three presentations, Jenny plans to speak on the broad topic of animal rights and welfare. But she must narrow this topic considerably to fit each audience and the speech occasion, and this means different narrowed topics.

First, Jenny draws a topic map to generate ideas.

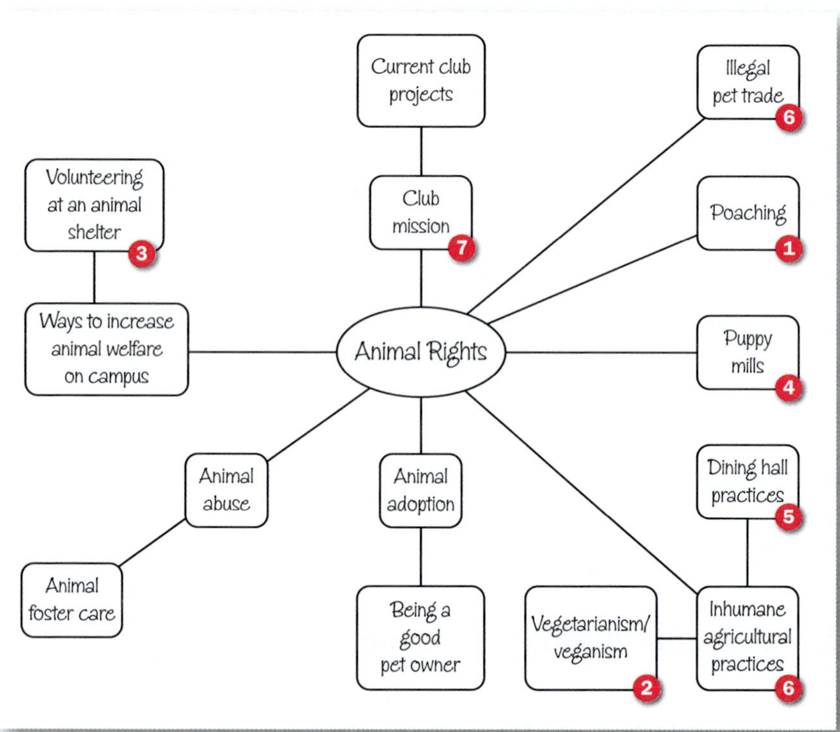

For each presentation, Jenny narrows her topic after considering her audience and the speech occasion.

Public speaking class (25–30 people):

- Mixed ages, races, and ethnicities, and an even mix of males and females
- Busy with classes, jobs, sports, and clubs
- Half live in campus housing, where pets are not allowed

1. Jenny eliminates poaching because it's not an everyday concern for students.
2. She eliminates vegetarianism because she will be unlikely to change listeners' minds in a six-minute speech.
3. Volunteering at an animal shelter may appeal to animal lovers who are not allowed to have pets on campus. Jenny argues that students should donate an hour a week to a nearby shelter, so that busy students can still participate.

Student council (8–10 people):

- Mixed demographic characteristics
- Similar interests: government, maintaining a rich campus life, an investment in ethics and the honor code, and an interest in keeping student affairs within budget

4. Jenny can eliminate the topic of puppy mills — though the student council may agree that they are harmful, it's not likely that they'll be able to do anything about the problem.
5. Jenny zeros in on dining hall practices because they are directly tied to campus life. A resolution to use free-range eggs in the campus dining hall benefits all students and requires the support of the council — an ideal topic for this audience.

Animal rights club website (open to all searchers of the Internet):

- Most diverse audience — unknown mix of demographic characteristics
- Likely interest in animal rights

6. Jenny can easily eliminate many topics, such as inhumane agricultural practices, because they are too complicated for a brief video clip.
7. She opts for the club's mission as a topic. A very brief welcome message that invites Web visitors to attend a longer information session will appeal to both the curious passerby and the dedicated animal rights activist.

(top) Andersen Ross/Getty Images; (mid) Manfred Rutz/Getty Images; (bot) Anne Ackermann/Getty Images

points, the supporting material, and the conclusion all serve to flesh out the thesis.

The thesis statement and the specific purpose are closely linked. Both state the speech topic, but do so in different forms. *The specific purpose describes in action form what outcome you want to achieve with the speech. The thesis statement concisely declares, in a single idea, what the speech is about.* By clearly stating your speech thesis (what it's about), you set in your mind exactly what outcome you want to accomplish (the specific purpose).

The difference between the thesis and specific purpose can be clearly seen in the following examples.

Example 1

SPEECH TOPIC: Blogs

GENERAL SPEECH PURPOSE: To inform

SPECIFIC SPEECH PURPOSE: To inform my audience of three benefits of keeping a blog

THESIS STATEMENT: Maintaining a blog provides the opportunity to practice writing, a means of networking with others who share similar interests, and the chance to develop basic website management skills.

Example 2

SPEECH TOPIC: Service learning courses

GENERAL SPEECH PURPOSE: To persuade

SPECIFIC SPEECH PURPOSE: To persuade my audience that service learning courses are beneficial for gaining employment after schooling

THESIS STATEMENT: Taking service learning courses is a good way to build your resume and increase your chances of gaining employment after graduation

Postpone Development of Main Points

The thesis statement conveys the central idea or core assumption about the topic (see Figure 7.2). It offers your perspective on the topic. For instance, the thesis statement "Three major events caused the United States to go to war in 1941" expresses your view that three factors played a part in the U.S. entry into World War II. The speech is then developed from this thesis, presenting facts and evidence to support it. Thus, you should postpone the development of main points and supporting material until you have correctly formulated the specific purpose and thesis statement (see Chapter 11, "Organizing the Body of the Speech").

Use the Thesis Statement to Guide Your Speech Preparation

As you develop the speech, use the thesis to keep yourself on track. As you research materials, review them in the light of whether they contribute to the thesis or stray from your thesis statement. When you actually draft your speech, work your thesis statement into it and restate it where appropriate. Doing so will encourage your audience to understand and accept your message.

Make the Thesis Statement Relevant and Motivating

As you revise drafts of your speech, try to express the thesis statement so that it will motivate the audience to listen. In many cases, creating a relevant thesis can be accomplished quite easily by adding a few key words or phrases. You can preface an informative thesis statement with a phrase such as "Few of us know" or "Contrary to popular belief" or "Have you ever." A persuasive thesis statement can also be adapted to establish relevance for the audience. Phrases such as "As informed members of the community" or "As concerned adults" can attract listeners' attention and interest and help them see the topic's relevance and create a sense of identification among audience members.

ETHICALLY SPEAKING

Ethical Considerations in Selecting a Topic and Purpose

Radu Bercan/Shutterstock

Respect for your audience members and adaptation to their needs and interests should always guide your topic choices. What makes a speech ethical or unethical depends on how it empowers the audience to think or act. In other words, ethical considerations begin with your speech purpose. Speakers who select persuasive purposes should be particularly careful; under pressure to sway an audience, some speakers may be tempted to tamper with the truth. As you review your speech goal, consider the following.

- Have you deliberately distorted information to achieve a desired result?
- Is it your intent to deceive?
- Do you try to coerce the audience into thinking or acting in a certain way?
- Have you knowingly tried to appeal to harmful biases?

Although few hard-and-fast rules exist when it comes to ethical guidelines for selecting topics, some areas are clearly off-limits—at least in U.S. culture:

- The topic shows an audience how to perform actions prohibited by law.
- The topic provides audience members with information that may result in their physical or psychological harm.
- The topic humiliates or degrades the fundamental values of an audience's culture, religion, or political system.

CHECKLIST

FORMULATING THE THESIS STATEMENT

- ✔ Does my thesis statement sum up in a single sentence what my speech is about?
- ✔ Is it restricted to a single idea?
- ✔ Is it in the form of a complete declarative sentence?
- ✔ Is it stated in a way that is relevant to the audience?

The exact phrasing or rewording of your thesis statement depends on the audience to whom you are speaking. Once you gain some information about your audience members, you won't have trouble making the topic relevant for them.

SUPPORTING THE SPEECH

British actress, model, and activist Emma Watson launches the HeforShe IMPACT 10 × 10 × 10 University Parity Report on gender equality at The United Nations in New York City. Watson promoted education for girls before being appointed UN Women Goodwill Ambassador in 2014.

J. Countess/Getty Images

SUPPORTING THE SPEECH

SPEAKER'S PREVIEW

LearningCurve can help you review.
Go to LaunchPad: **launchpadworks.com**

SUPPORTING THE SPEECH

CHAPTER 8 Developing Supporting Material

Offer a Variety of Supporting Materials

- Illustrate each main point with several different types of supporting material. (p. 125)
- Provide more than your own personal opinions or experiences. (p. 125)

Keep the Audience in Mind When Selecting Sources

- Choose evidence and sources based on audience factors. (p. 126)
- Remember that not every source is appropriate for every audience. (p. 126)

Choose Accurate, Relevant, Motivating, and Audience-Centered Supporting Material

- Seek out compelling *examples* to illustrate or describe your ideas. (p. 126)
- Share *stories*, either real or hypothetical, to drive your point home. (p. 127)
- Use firsthand findings in the form of *testimony*. (p. 129)
- Hunt for relevant *facts* or documented occurrences. (p. 130)
- Consider whether you need *statistics*, or quantified evidence. (p. 130)
- Draw your statistics from reliable sources and present them in context. (p. 131)
- Beware of cherry-picking and other unethical ways of presenting data. (p. 133)

LaunchPad VIDEO ACTIVITY

Go to LaunchPad to watch a video about using supporting material in your speech.

LaunchPad includes:

LearningCurve adaptive quizzing

a curated collection of video clips and full-length speeches.

Additional resources and reference materials such as presentation software tutorials and documentation help.

CHAPTER 9 Finding Credible Print and Online Materials

Assess Your Research Needs

- Assess your thesis before you begin and consider what types of support you need. (p. 135)
- Use sources appropriate to the rhetorical situation. (p. 135)

Start Your Search at Your Library's Home Page

- Library portals provide an entry point for sources that have been vetted for quality. (p. 135)
- Library portals pay for access to proprietary databases containing cutting-edge and credible research. (p. 136)

Learn to Recognize Propaganda, Misinformation, and Disinformation

Consider Using Both Primary and Secondary Sources

- Primary sources provide firsthand testimony or direct evidence of events. (p. 137)
- Consider personal knowledge and experience. (p. 138)
- Consult government publications. (p. 138)
- Search online digital collections. (p. 138)
- Conduct interviews. (p. 139)
- Distribute surveys. (p. 140)

Explore Various Secondary Sources

- Investigate books newspapers, periodicals, and government publications. (p. 141)
- Make use of reference works (e.g., encyclopedias, almanacs, biographical resources, books of quotations, poetry collections, and atlases). (p. 142)

Conduct Smart Searches

- Consult subject guides on your topic to discover resources. (p. 142)
- Use the help section of search tools to determine when to use keywords versus subject headings (as well as other fields). (p. 143)

CHAPTER 10 Citing Sources in Your Speech

Cite Your Sources to Enhance Your Own Authority and Demonstrate Solid Support for Your Reasoning

- Credit information drawn from other people's ideas. (p. 149)
- Information that is common knowledge need not be credited. (p. 149)

Offer Key Source Information

- Cite author or origin of source. (p. 150)
- Cite type of source (e.g., article, book, personal interview). (p. 150)
- Cite title or description of source. (p. 150)
- Cite date of creation or publication. (p. 150)

Demonstrate the Source's Trustworthiness

- If the source is affiliated with a respected institution, identify it. (p. 152)
- If citing a study linked to a reputable institution, identify it. (p. 152)
- If a source has relevant credentials, note them. (p. 152)
- If the source has relevant real-life experience, mention it. (p. 152)

Avoid a Mechanical Delivery of Sources

- Vary the wording and the order. (p. 151)
- Discuss the issue and then reveal the source. (p. 151)

Credit Sources in Presentation Aids

- Put facts and statistics in context. (p. 158)

Identify Whether You Are Summarizing, Paraphrasing, or Quoting a Source

KEY TERMS

Chapter 8

supporting material
evidence
example
brief example
extended example
hypothetical example
story
narrative
anecdote
testimony
expert testimony
lay testimony
facts
statistics
frequency
average
mean
median
mode
cherry-picking

Chapter 9

invention
library portal
deep Web
information
propaganda
misinformation
disinformation
primary sources
secondary sources
blog
encyclopedia
subject guide
keywords
subject heading

Chapter 10

oral citation
source credibility
source qualifier

Go to LaunchPad: **launchpadworks.com** to watch the video clips for this chapter.

8 Developing Supporting Material

LearningCurve can help you review!
Go to LaunchPad: **launchpadworks.com**

Often, the key to a good speech is not just the topic itself, but how it is developed and supported. You can easily see this in speeches on the same theme prepared by different speakers. One speaker's presentation on wind power, for example, consists of little beyond dry facts, while another speaker offers a stream of colorful examples and fascinating stories. Speeches that keep the audience's attention contain relevant, motivating, and audience-centered **supporting material** in the form of examples, stories, testimony, facts, and statistics (see Table 8.1). (In a persuasive speech, these same supporting materials are referred to as **evidence**; see Chapter 25.) These research materials are the essential building blocks for any speech.

The supporting material you select, such as you might discover in a book, news story, or journal article, engages the audience in your topic, illustrates and elaborates upon your ideas, and provides evidence for your arguments. As you comb through the research and decide what to use in your speech, consider how well it fulfills these key functions.

Use a Variety of Supporting Materials

Virtually any speech you deliver will require a variety of supporting material other than your own personal opinion or experience. This holds true whether or not you possess expert knowledge on a topic. People want to know the truth about a given matter, and, unless they view you as a true authority on the subject, they will not merely accept your word for it. In general, listeners respond most favorably to a variety of supporting materials derived from multiple sources to illustrate each main point.[1] Alternating among different types of supporting material—moving from a story to a statistic, for example—will make the presentation more interesting and credible while simultaneously appealing to your audience members' different learning styles (see p. 126).

Consider the Target Audience

Take into account your target audience as you decide upon the research you will offer them (see Chapter 6 on analyzing your audience). Depending on how the audience feels about your topic, it may be wise to weight

TABLE 8.1 Types and Functions of Supporting Material

Type of Supporting Material	Definition	Purpose
Example	A typical instance of something—a fact, incident, or quotation that illustrates a state of things.	Aids understanding by making ideas, items, or events more concrete; creates interest.
Narrative	A story, either real or imaginary, and short or drawn-out in length. Can constitute a small part of the presentation or serve as a basis for the speech itself.	Generates interest and identification.
Testimony	Firsthand findings, eyewitness accounts, and opinions by people, both lay (nonexpert) and expert.	Provides evidence and aids credibility.
Facts	Actual events, dates, times, and places that can be independently verified.	Provides evidence and demonstrates points.
Statistics	Data that demonstrate relationships.	Summarizes information, demonstrates proof, makes points memorable.

your evidence in favor of facts and expert testimony, or, conversely, personal stories and examples (see Table 26.2 on p. 358 on appealing to different types of audiences). Think as well about your choice of sources. *Even if reputable, not every source is appropriate for every audience.* A politically conservative audience may reject testimony you quote from a liberal publication, and a devoutly religious audience may resist examples drawn from certain secular sources. Focusing on the audience, as well as your goals, as you develop supporting materials will help avoid potential mismatches between the audience and support for your speech.

Offer Examples

Examples are indispensable tools public speakers use to clarify their ideas. An **example**, according to the *Oxford English Dictionary*, is a typical instance of something—a fact, incident, or quotation that illustrates a state of things. Without examples to illustrate the points a speaker wants to convey, our listeners would get lost in a sea of abstract statements. Examples are especially important when describing new concepts to audience members, but even the familiar can be made clearer and more compelling with examples.

Examples can be *brief* or *extended* and may be either *factual* or *hypothetical*.

Brief Examples

Brief examples offer a single illustration of a point. In a speech about the need to safeguard free speech, author Ian McEwan uses the following brief example to illustrate restrictions on freedom of expression in China.

> In China, state monitoring of free expression is on an industrial scale. To censor daily the Internet alone, the Chinese government employs as many as fifty thousand bureaucrats—a level of thought repression unprecedented in human history.[2]

Extended Examples

Sometimes it takes more than a brief example to effectively illustrate a point. **Extended examples** offer multifaceted illustrations of the idea, item, or event being described, thereby allowing the speaker to create a more detailed picture for the audience. Here, Jonathan Drori uses an extended example to illustrate how pollen (the fertilizing element of plants) can provide strong circumstantial evidence linking criminals to their crimes.

> [Pollen forensics] is being used now to track where counterfeit drugs have been made, where banknotes have come from, to look at . . . antiques to see that they really did come from the place the seller said they did. And murder suspects have been tracked using their clothing. . . . Some of the people were brought to trial [in Bosnia] because of the evidence of pollen, which showed that bodies had been buried, exhumed, and then reburied somewhere else.[3]

Hypothetical Examples

In some speeches you may need to make a point about something that could happen in the future if certain things occurred. For example, if you argue against reproductive cloning of human embryos to make new humans, you automatically raise the question of what will happen if this comes to pass. Since it hasn't happened yet, you'll need a **hypothetical example** of what you believe the outcome will be. Republican Representative Vernon Ehlers of Michigan offered the following hypothetical example when he spoke at a congressional hearing in support of a bill to ban human cloning.

> What if in the cloning process you produce someone with two heads and three arms? Are you simply going to euthanize and dispose of that person? The answer is no. We're talking about human life.[4]

Offer Stories

One of the most powerful means of conveying a message and connecting with an audience is through a **story** (also called **narrative**)—the telling of a chain of events. Stories help us make sense of our experiences; they tell tales, both real and imaginary, about practically anything under the sun. They can relate personal experiences, folk wisdom, parables, myths, and so forth.

Scholars of narratives have commented that all human history consists of stories. "Most of our experience, our knowledge, and our thinking is organized as stories," notes language scholar Mark Turner. "One story helps us make sense of another."[5] A growing body of neuroscientific evidence also suggests that it is through stories that we actually organize our thinking.[6] As communication theorist Nick Morgan notes, stories have a profound effect on our brain: "If you tell your audience a story, you jump right into the deeper parts of the brain, where emotion and memory work together, the hippocampus and amygdala."[7]

Stories can be relatively short and simple descriptions of brief incidents worked into the body of the speech, or longer accounts that constitute most of the presentation and even serve as the organizing framework for it (see Chapter 12 on the narrative pattern of organization, p. 187). In either case, a successful story will strike a chord with the audience and create an emotional connection between the speaker and audience members. Some stories are powerful enough to spur audiences to act on the speaker's persuasive goal.[8]

However briefly sketched, all stories possess the essential storytelling elements of *character* (or "protagonist"), *challenge* or *conflict*, and *resolution*, or means of dealing with the challenge. Using these elements, many stories, and especially those that describe overcoming obstacles, work well when they follow a three-part trajectory. First, introduce the protagonist (perhaps yourself) in his or her story setting, or context. Next, recount the challenge or conflict the character faces. A compelling description of the challenge or conflict is crucial in storytelling since everyone can relate to struggle and even failure and how to overcome it. Finally, finish with the resolution—how the challenge was either dealt with or overcome.

In a speech on helping more young Americans earn college degrees, Melinda French Gates used this format in the following very brief story to illustrate that although some community college students encounter many barriers to completing their degrees, they persevere.

> Last year, we met a young man named Cornell at Central Piedmont Community College in Charlotte, North Carolina. We asked him to describe his typical day. He clocks into work at 11 P.M. When he gets off at 7 the next morning, he sleeps for an hour. In his car. Then he goes to class until 2 o'clock. "After that," Cornell said, "I just crash."[9]

In just six sentences, Gates includes the elements of character (the student Cornell), challenge (taking classes while working difficult hours), and resolution (gets enough sleep to continue).

Many speakers, whether they're business leaders rallying employees or preachers at the pulpit, liberally sprinkle their speeches with **anecdotes**—brief stories of interesting and often humorous incidents based on real life (often the speaker's own), with a recognizable moral—the lesson the speaker wishes to convey.[10] With its offering of wisdom gained through life's experiences, the moral is the most important part of an anecdote. For example, in a speech to students

CHECKLIST

EVALUATING MY STORY

_____ 1. Is the story credible, or believable?

_____ 2. Is it compelling enough?

_____ 3. Does the example or story truly illustrate or prove the point I need to make?

_____ 4. Is it suitable for my audience's background and experiences?

at Maharishi University, comedian Jim Carrey shared an anecdote about how his father's fear of being impractical led him to become an accountant instead of the comedian he wanted to be. This spurred Carrey to take another path.

> So many of us choose our path out of fear disguised as practicality. . . . I learned many great lessons from my father, not the least of which was that you can fail at what you don't want, so you might as well take a chance on doing what you love.[11]

Draw on Testimony

Another potentially powerful source of support for your speech is **testimony**—firsthand findings, eyewitness accounts, and people's opinions. When you use testimony, you quote or paraphrase people who have an intimate knowledge of your topic (see p. 73, Chapter 5, for guidelines on quoting and paraphrasing). **Expert testimony** includes findings, eyewitness accounts, or opinions by professionals trained to evaluate a given topic. For example, a medical doctor may provide cutting-edge information on the threat of cholesterol. **Lay testimony**, or testimony by nonexperts such as eyewitnesses, can reveal compelling firsthand information that may be unavailable to others, such as that given by volunteers of the International Committee of the Red Cross working in war-torn Syria.

ESL SPEAKER'S NOTES

Broaden Your Listeners' Perspectives

NASA Goddard Space Flight Center

As a non-native speaker of English, consider sharing a personal experience with the audience. Stories from other countries that describe other ways of life often fascinate listeners. Unique cultural traditions, eyewitness accounts of newsworthy events, or tales passed down orally from one generation to the next are just some of the possibilities. Depending on the goal of your speech, you can use your experiences as supporting material for a related topic or as the topic itself.

Credibility plays a key role in the effectiveness of testimony, since a source is only as credible as an audience believes it to be. Briefly establish the person's qualifications and inform listeners of when and where the testimony was offered. It isn't always necessary to cite the exact date (though do keep a written record of it); in the oral presentation, terms such as "recently" and "last year" are fine.

> In testimony before the U.S. House Subcommittee on Human Rights and Wellness last week, Derek Ellerman, co-executive director of the Polaris Project, said, "Many people have little understanding of the enormity and the brutality of the sex trafficking industry in the United States. When they think of sex slavery, they think of Thailand or Nepal — not a suburban house in the DC area, with $400,000 homes and manicured lawns."[12]

CHECKLIST

EVALUATING THE CREDIBILITY OF TESTIMONY

- ✔ Are the experts I've cited proven in their fields?
- ✔ Is the lay testimony reliable?
- ✔ Do the sources have any obvious biases?
- ✔ Is their testimony timely? Is it relevant?
- ✔ Do their views effectively support my thesis?
- ✔ Are there reasons that the audience may not react favorably to the testimony?

Testimony that does not meet these standards is likely to do more harm to your speech than good.

Provide Facts and Statistics

Most people (especially in Western societies) require some type of evidence, usually in the form of facts and statistics, before they will accept someone else's claims or position.[13] **Facts** represent documented occurrences, including actual events, dates, times, people, and places. Facts are truly facts only when they have been independently verified by people other than the source. For example, we accept as true that Abraham Lincoln was the sixteenth president of the United States because this fact has been independently verified by eyewitnesses, journalists, historians, and so forth. Listeners are not likely to accept your statements as factual unless you back them up with credible evidence.

Use Statistics Selectively—and Memorably

Statistics are quantified evidence that summarizes, compares, and predicts things, from batting averages to birthrates. Statistics can clarify complex information and help make abstract concepts or ideas concrete for listeners. Although audience members may want you to offer some statistics in support of your assertions, they don't want an endless parade of them. Rather than overwhelm the audience with numbers, put a few statistics in context to make your message more compelling. For example, instead of citing the actual number of persons belonging to Facebook worldwide (over 1.5 billion and counting), perhaps use a simple ratio and, to drive home the company's enormous reach, provide a down-to-earth example of what the figure represents: "Today, at least 38 percent of people in the world have a Facebook account, roughly the population of China."[14]

Use Statistics Accurately

Statistics add precision to speech claims, *if* you know what the numbers actually mean and use the terms that describe them accurately. Following are some basic statistical terms commonly used in speeches that include statistics.

Use Frequencies to Indicate Counts

A **frequency** is simply a count of the number of times something occurs:

> "On the midterm exam there were 8 As, 15 Bs, 7 Cs, 2 Ds, and 1 F."

Frequencies can indicate size, describe trends, or help listeners understand comparisons between two or more categories. For example:

- Inside the cabin, the Airbus A380 has room for at least 525 passengers—and as many as 853.[15] (*shows size*)
- Since 2007, heroin-involved overdose deaths rose from 2,402 in 2007 to 10,574 in 2014.[16] (*describes a trend*)
- The total population of the state of Colorado comprised 2,744,657 males and 2,711,917 females.[17] (*compares two categories*)

Use Percentages to Express Proportion

As informative as frequencies can be, the similarity or difference in magnitude between things may be more meaningfully indicated in a *percentage*—the quantified portion of a whole. Informing the audience that heroin overdose deaths rose by 340 percent between 2007 and 2014 more quickly shows them the magnitude of the problem than offering counts would. Percentages also help audience members easily grasp comparisons between things, such as the unemployment rate in several states.

> In August 2016, Alaska had the highest rate of unemployment, at 6.8 percent. At 2.9 percent, South Dakota had the lowest rate.[18]

Audience members cannot take the time to pause and reflect on the figures as they would with written text, so consider how you can help listeners interpret the numbers, as in this example:

> As you can see, Alaska's unemployment rate is nearly two and one-half times greater than that of South Dakota.

Use Types of Averages Accurately

An **average** describes information according to its typical characteristics. Usually we think of the average as the sum of the scores divided by the number of scores. This is the **mean**, the arithmetic average. But there are two other kinds of averages—the **median** and the **mode**. As a matter of accuracy, in your speeches you should distinguish among these three kinds of averages.

Consider a teacher whose nine students scored 5, 19, 22, 23, 24, 26, 28, 28, and 30, with 30 points being the highest possible grade. The following illustrates how she would calculate the three types of averages.

- The *mean* score is 22.8, the *arithmetic average*, the sum of the scores divided by nine.
- The *median* score is 24, the *center-most score in a distribution*, or the point above and below which 50 percent of the nine scores fall.
- The *mode* score is 28, the *most frequently occurring score* in the distribution.

The following speaker, claiming that a policy institute misrepresented the "average" tax rate for U.S. families, illustrates how the inaccurate use of the different types of averages can deceive audience members.

> The Tax Foundation determines an *average* [*mean*] tax rate . . . simply by dividing all taxes paid by the total of everyone's income. For example, if four middle-income families pay $3,000, $4,000, $5,000, and $6,000, respectively, in taxes, and one very wealthy family pays $82,000 in taxes, the *average* [*mean*] tax paid by these five families is $20,000 ($100,000 in total taxes divided by five families). But four of the five families [actually] have a tax bill equaling $6,000 or less. . . . [Many] analysts would [more accurately] define a *median* income family—a family for whom half of all families have higher income and half have lower income—to be the "typical family."[19]

Present Statistics Ethically

Offering listeners inaccurate statistics is unethical, and it happens all too often. Following are steps you can take to reduce the likelihood of using false or misleading statistics.

- *Use Only Reliable Statistics.* Include statistics from the most authoritative source you can locate, and evaluate the methods used to generate the data. The more information that is available about how the statistics came about, including how and why they were collected and what researchers hoped to learn from them, the more reliable the source is likely to be.
- *Present Statistics in Context.* Statistics are meaningful only within a proper context. To help audience members accurately interpret statistical information, inform listeners of when the data were collected, the method used to collect the data, and the scope of the research.

These figures represent data collected by the U.S. Department of Education during 2016 from questionnaires distributed to all public and private schools in the United States with students in at least one of grades 9 through 12 in the fifty states and the District of Columbia.

- *Avoid Confusing Statistics with "Absolute Truth."* Even the most recent data will change the next time the data are collected. And statistics are not necessarily any more accurate than the human who collected them. Offer the data as they appropriately represent your point, but refrain from declaring that the data are definitive.
- *Orally Refer to Your Sources.* Clearly identify the source of your information and provide enough context to accurately interpret it. For guidelines on orally citing your sources see Chapter 10, "Citing Sources in Your Speech."
- *Use Visual Aids.* When your speech relies heavily on statistical information, use appropriate tables, graphs, and charts to help audience members process the information (see Chapters 20–22 on presentation aids).

ETHICALLY SPEAKING

Avoid Cherry-Picking

Radu Bercan/ Shutterstock

To **cherry-pick** is to selectively present only those statistics that buttress your point of view while ignoring competing data.[1] Cherry-picking is a popular tool of politicians and policymakers, who are often accused of selectively referring to only those statistics that boost their arguments while ignoring competing information. Cherry-picking is often in evidence when people argue about contentious issues such as hydraulic fracking for oil and natural gas deep underground, with each side cherry-picking bits and pieces of scientific evidence out of context in order to support their own views.

When you find yourself searching for statistics to confirm an opinion or a belief you already hold, you are probably engaging in cherry-picking. Offering the mean when in fact one of the other averages is the better indicator of what your data represent is an instance of cherry-picking. Researching statistical support material is not a trip through a buffet line to select what looks good and discard what doesn't. To be fair to audience members, avoid misrepresenting the truth by offering inaccurate and one-sided data. You must locate as much information as possible that is pertinent to your particular point, and then present it in context or not at all.

1. Roger Pielke Jr., "The Cherry Pick," *Ogmius: Newsletter for the Center for Science and Technology Research* 8 (2004), sciencepolicy.colorado.edu/ogmius/archives/issue_8/intro.html.

SELF-ASSESSMENT CHECKLIST

USING STATISTICS IN YOUR SPEECH: AN ETHICAL INVENTORY

- ✓ Do I include statistics from the most authoritative sources I can locate?
- ✓ Do I briefly tell listeners about the method(s) used to collect the statistics (e.g., a survey), the scope of the research (e.g., sample size), and where the data are drawn from?
- ✓ Do I alert listeners to when the statistics were collected?
- ✓ Do I offer the data as they appropriately represent my point or claim but refrain from declaring that these data are absolute?
- ✓ Do I refrain from using or ignoring statistics selectively to make my point (cherry-picking)?

9 Finding Credible Print and Online Materials

LearningCurve can help you review!
Go to LaunchPad: **launchpadworks.com**

The search for supporting material—for the examples, facts and statistics, opinions, stories, and testimony described in Chapter 8—can be one of the most enjoyable parts of putting together a speech. It is at this stage that you can delve into your subject, sift through sources, and select relevant and audience-centered material that supports your speech points. Classical rhetoricians termed this process of discovery *invention* (see p. 11 in Chapter 1). Rather than simply gathering information, **invention** involves creating valid arguments from evidence and choosing from among the many different types of evidence those sources that are most likely to lead listeners to accept the speaker's point of view.

Assess Your Research Needs

Before beginning your research, review your thesis statement and specific speech purpose (see Chapter 7, "Selecting a Topic and Purpose"). Consider what you need to support them. A little while spent on visualizing a research strategy will result in significant savings of time and energy that might otherwise be wasted in an untargeted search. What do you need to elaborate upon, explain, demonstrate, or prove, and what mix of evidence—personal knowledge, examples, stories, statistics, and testimony—will help you accomplish this? If you find your topic isn't sufficiently narrowed, refine it further before proceeding. Different topics, audiences, purposes, and occasions will suggest different balances of sources, so reflect on what might work best for your particular rhetorical situation.

Use a Library Portal to Access Credible Sources

Easy access to the Internet may lead you to rely heavily or even exclusively on sources you find through general search engines such as Google. In doing so, however, you risk overlooking key sources not found through these sites and finding biased or untrustworthy information. To circumvent this, consider beginning, or certainly continuing, your search at your school library's home page. You might use the Web to brainstorm and narrow topics, locate current news on a topic, review reputable blogs, and so forth. Then switch to your school's **library portal**, or its collection of databases, to find peer-reviewed research articles, books, primary source databases, and other vetted materials.

Access to these scholarly and other sources is a key benefit of searching for materials within library databases versus relying only on Google or another for-profit general search engine. You won't find the latest scholarship on general search engines, or, if you do, you will be unable to access it. Libraries, on the other hand, evaluate and purchase access to proprietary databases and other resources that form part of the **deep Web**—the large and invisible portion of the Web that general search engines cannot access because the information is not indexed by them, or is licensed or fee-based. When you select speech material from a library's resources, you can access its full contents and be assured that an information specialist has vetted that source for reliability and credibility. No such standards exist for popular Web search engines. Table 9.1 lists resources typically found on library portals.

Recognize Propaganda, Misinformation, and Disinformation

Discerning the accuracy of open content—or of any content, whether appearing online, in print, or in another medium—is not always easy. Anyone can post material on the Web and, with a little bit of design savvy, make a website look reputable. And anyone can self-publish a book or produce and distribute a video.

One way to judge a source's trustworthiness is to ask yourself: Is it reliable *information*, or is it *propaganda*, *misinformation*, or *disinformation?*[1] (See Figure 9.1.)

- **Information** is *data* that are presented in an understandable context. Data are raw and unprocessed facts; information makes sense of data. For example, a patient's vital signs (temperature, blood pressure, pulse, etc.) are data. Interpreting the vital signs in the context of health status is information. Information is neutral unto itself but is subject to manipulation, for purposes both good and bad. It then has the potential to become propaganda, misinformation, or disinformation.
- **Propaganda** is information represented in such a way as to provoke a desired response. Many people believe that propaganda is based on false information, but this is not necessarily so. Instead, propaganda may well be based in fact, but its purpose is to instill a particular attitude or

TABLE 9.1 Typical Resources Found on Library Portals

- Full text databases (newspapers, periodicals, journals)
- General reference works (dictionaries, encyclopedias, atlases, almanacs, fact books, biographical reference works, quotation resources, poetry collections)
- Books, e-books, and monographs
- Archives and special collections (collected papers, objects and images, and scholarly works unique to the institution)
- Digital collections (oral histories, letters, old newspapers, image collections, audio and video recordings)

emotion in order to gain public support for a cause or issue. Usually presented as advertising or publicity, propaganda encourages you to think or act according to the ideological, political, or commercial perspective of the message source.

- **Misinformation** always refers to something that is not true. While propaganda may include factual information, misinformation does not. For example, in the summer of 2014, rumors circulated that the Ebola virus had mutated and become airborne when in fact it had not. This common form of misinformation, found so often on the Internet, is called an *urban legend*—a fabricated story passed along by unsuspecting people.
- **Disinformation** is the deliberate falsification of information. Doctored photographs and falsified profit-and-loss statements are examples of disinformation in action. Unfortunately, disinformation thrives on the Internet.

Ethical speeches are based on sound information—on facts put into context—rather than on misinformation, propaganda, or disinformation.

Investigate a Mix of Primary and Secondary Sources

Nearly all types of speeches can benefit from a mix of the two broad categories of supporting material: primary and secondary sources. **Primary sources** provide firsthand testimony or direct evidence concerning events, objects, or people. **Secondary sources** provide analysis or commentary about things not directly observed or created. These include the vast worlds of news, commentary, analysis, and scholarship found in books, articles, and a myriad of sources other than the original. A speech that contains both primary and secondary sources can be more compelling and believable than one that relies on one source type alone. The firsthand nature of a credible primary source can build trust and engage audience members emotionally. Secondary sources can help listeners put the topic in perspective. A speech on an oil spill, for example, can command more attention if it includes testimony by oil riggers and other eyewitnesses (primary sources) along with analyses of the spill from magazines and newspapers (secondary sources).

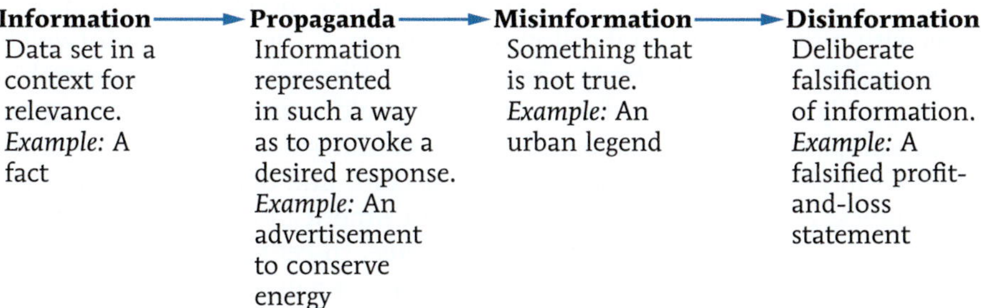

Information
Data set in a context for relevance. Example: A fact
Propaganda
Information represented in such a way as to provoke a desired response. Example: An advertisement to conserve energy
Misinformation
Something that is not true. Example: An urban legend
Disinformation
Deliberate falsification of information. Example: A falsified profit-and-loss statement

FIGURE 9.1 Information, Propaganda, Misinformation, and Disinformation

Explore Primary Sources

A primary source for a speech may be your own personal experience; a firsthand account found in letters, diaries, old newspapers, photographs, or other sources; government documents and data; blogs; or interviews or surveys that you conduct yourself.

Consider Personal Knowledge and Experience

Used effectively, your own knowledge and experience about your topic can serve important functions in a speech, drawing in listeners and creating a sense of connection with them. Sharing experiences and observations about work you've done, people you've known, or places you've visited can add a dimension of authenticity and credibility that a secondhand source might not.

Depending on your topic and the amount of your direct involvement with it, personal knowledge and experience can play a smaller or larger role in a speech. However much information you choose to share, consider whether your experiences will truly clarify and increase the audience's understanding of the topic, omitting anything that does not accomplish this. Keep in mind too that audiences look for a balance of evidence, including other people's expert knowledge and analysis (see Chapter 8 on types of supporting material).

Access Government Information

Many speeches can benefit from citing a statistic from a census or other data set, quoting testimony from a hearing or speech, or otherwise incorporating information discovered in government documents. Nearly all the information contained in these wide-ranging documents, relating to virtually all aspects of social endeavor, comes from highly credible primary sources, so it's well worth the effort to consult them. Start at www.usa.gov, the official portal to all government information and services. To locate reliable statistics related to your topic, go to FedStats (fedstats.sites.usa.gov) and American FactFinder (factfinder.census.gov). To access resources in Spanish, use www.gobiernousa.gov; translations in other languages are also available.

Explore Digital Collections

Another potentially useful source of credible primary speech materials may be found within the online digital collections of libraries. These collections (which are generally organized by topic, material type, time period, and geographic area) typically include oral histories, letters, and old newspapers; photographs, prints, and paintings; and audio and video recordings (see Table 9.1). Sources drawn from these collections can add great color and depth to speeches on many topics. A presentation on early African American actors, for example, might include a passage from a diary of a nineteenth-century actor and a photograph of him or her on stage. One way to discover a digital collection related to your topic is to enter your topic terms into a general search engine (e.g., *African American actors* AND *digital collections*).

Access Blogs

A **blog** is a site containing journal-type entries maintained by individuals or groups. Newest entries appear first. Blogs can offer compelling sources of information of unfolding events and new trends and ideas, *if* the source is reputable. Currently there are few comprehensive or reliable blog search engines; to search for one, try Googling key terms related to *[your topic]* AND *blog.* Many reputable publications, such as *Scientific American*, *The Atlantic*, and *Huffington Post* maintain blog sites for their contributors. If a publication appears likely to contain information about your topic, search for *[publication name]* AND *blogs.*

Conduct Interviews

Oftentimes you can glean considerably more insight into a topic, and get more compelling material to bring to your audience, by speaking personally with someone who has expertise on the subject. Consider how an interview of someone who has completed a 26-mile marathon, for example, could bring the topic of long-distance running alive in ways that a magazine article might not. Getting the information you need from a subject requires research and advance planning, from deciding how you will record the interview to preparing the questions you will ask.

- Begin by learning about the person you will be interviewing so that you can prepare appropriate and informed questions for him or her.
- *Prepare questions for the interview* in advance of the interview date.
- *Word questions carefully.*
    - Avoid *vague questions,* those that don't give the person you are interviewing enough to go on. Vague questions waste the interviewee's time and reflect a lack of preparation.

CHECKLIST

FINDING SPEECHES ONLINE

Online, you can find numerous videos and audio files of speeches. These can be useful as models of speeches *and* as primary source material.

- ✔ TED Talks (www.Ted.com) contains over 2,200 presentations, described by TED as "short, powerful talks of 18 minutes or less."
- ✔ American Rhetoric (www.americanrhetoric.com) contains 5,000+ speeches.
- ✔ Gifts of Speech (gos.sbc.edu) features speeches by women since 1848.
- ✔ The Wake Forest University's Political Speeches gateway (users.wfu.edu/louden/Political%20Communication/Class%20Information/SPEECHES.html) offers links to collections of political speeches.
- ✔ The United States Senate (www.senate.gov) includes speeches by U.S. senators.
- ✔ Vital Speeches of the Day (www.vsotd.com) features current speeches delivered in the United States and is published monthly.

- Avoid *leading questions*, those that encourage, if not force, a certain response and reflect the interviewer's bias (e.g., "Like most of us, are you going to support candidate X?"). Likewise, avoid *loaded questions*, those that are phrased to reinforce the interviewer's agenda or that have a hostile intent (e.g., "Isn't it true that you've never supported school programs?").
  - Focus on asking *neutral questions*, those that don't lead the interviewee to a desired response. Usually, this will consist of a mix of open, closed, primary, and secondary questions. See pages 98–99 for more details on open- and closed-ended questions.
- *Establish a spirit of collaboration at the start.*
  - Acknowledge the interviewee and express respect for his or her expertise.
  - Briefly summarize your topic and informational needs.
  - State a (reasonable) goal—what you would like to accomplish in the interview—and reach agreement on it.
  - Establish a time limit for the interview and stick to it.
- *Use active listening strategies* (see Chapter 4, "Listeners and Speakers").
  - Don't break in when the subject is speaking or interject with leading comments.
  - Paraphrase the interviewee's answers when you are unclear about meaning and repeat back to him or her.
  - Ask for clarification and elaboration when necessary.
- *End the interview by rechecking and confirming.*
  - Confirm that you have covered all the topics (e.g., "Does this cover everything?").
  - Briefly offer a positive summary of important things you learned in the interview.
  - Offer to send the interviewee the results of the interview.

Distribute Surveys

A survey can be useful as both a tool to investigate audience attitudes (see Chapter 6, p. 97) and a source of primary material for your speech. Surveys are an especially effective source for speech topics focused on the attitudes and behavior of people in your immediate environment, such as fellow students' opinions on issues on or off campus or community members' attitudes toward local initiatives (for guidelines on creating surveys, see Chapter 6.)

Remember that any informal survey you conduct is unlikely to be statistically sound enough to be taken as actual proof of your claims. Present your findings to the audience in a manner that acknowledges this, and shore up any informal survey research you conduct with other forms of support. (See Chapter 8 for a discussion of using statistics in speeches.)

CHECKLIST

PREPARING FOR THE INTERVIEW

_____ 1. Have I researched my interviewee's background and accomplishments?

_____ 2. Do I have a written set of questions?

_____ 3. Can the questions be answered within a reasonable time frame?

_____ 4. Are my questions relevant to the purpose of my speech?

_____ 5. Are my questions posed in a well-thought-out sequence?

_____ 6. Are my questions free of bias and hostile intent?

_____ 7. Are controversial questions reserved until the end of the interview?

_____ 8. Have I obtained advance permission to record the interview?

_____ 9. Do I have a working writing implement and ample notepaper or functioning laptop or tablet?

_____ 10. Have I made certain that any recording equipment I plan to use is in working order?

Explore Secondary Sources

Along with primary sources, your speeches will also, if not at times exclusively, rely on secondary sources as found in books, newspapers, periodicals, government publications, print or online reference works (such as encyclopedias, books of quotations, and poetry collections), and social media sites. Social media sites, such as Twitter and Facebook, allow users to submit news stories, articles, and videos to share with other users of the site. As with blogs, only reference those that are affiliated with reputable (local, regional, or national) news agencies and media outlets.

CHECKLIST

USE WATCHDOG SITES TO CHECK THE FACTS

Our most trustworthy elected officials occasionally make false assertions, and even the most reliable news sources publish errors of fact or omission. So whom should you believe—Congresswoman X's dire predictions regarding Social Security or Senator Y's rosier assessment? To check the factual accuracy of information offered by key political players and major journalistic outlets, consult these websites (bearing in mind that they, too, are not infallible).

- ✔ www.factcheck.org, sponsored by the Annenberg Public Policy Center
- ✔ www.politifact.com, sponsored by the *Tampa Bay Times*
- ✔ Fact Checker, a blog sponsored by the *Washington Post*

Encyclopedias

Encyclopedias summarize knowledge that is found in original form elsewhere. Their usefulness lies in providing an overview of subjects and highlighting important terms, people, and concepts to build a search upon. *General encyclopedias* attempt to cover all important subject areas of knowledge. The most comprehensive of the general encyclopedias is the *Encyclopaedia Britannica*. For a more in-depth exploration of one subject area, such as religion, science, art, sports, or engineering, consult a *specialized encyclopedia* devoted to it. To discover encyclopedias in your subject area, go to your library home page and key in *encyclopedias* AND *[your subject]*.

Wikipedia—Dos and Don'ts

When it comes to online research, it is impossible to ignore the presence of Wikipedia, the world's largest experimental free encyclopedia, written collaboratively and often anonymously by anyone who wishes to contribute to it. Though Wikipedia's instant accessibility and vast range make it tantalizingly easy to consult, bear in mind that information may or may not be accurate at any given moment, as people edit material at will. As with any encyclopedia, Wikipedia provides an initial—and sometimes exhaustive—overview of a topic, but to ensure accuracy, use it only as a starting-off point for further research.[2] The references cited in a Wikipedia article can serve as potential research leads—*if* you follow the links provided and carefully evaluate the information for trustworthiness. Be sure to compare the information in the article to credible sources *not* supplied in the entry itself, and do not offer Wikipedia—or any encyclopedia entry—as a source to audience members.

See Table 9.2 for descriptions of selected secondary sources and databases where they can be located; your school library will have its own mix of databases.

Conduct Smart Searches

Armed with an understanding of the nature of primary and secondary sources, consider how you can search most effectively for the research you need. One way to go about this is to use a library portal to

- Access the *subject guides* it offers on your topic to obtain an overview of the types of resources available to your institution and elsewhere,
- Identify when to use *keywords* or *subject headings* to retrieve the best results, and
- Consult the *help guides* for individual databases.

Consult Subject Guides on Your Topic

A **subject guide** (also called a "research guide") is a collection of links to subject-specific article databases, reference works, websites, and other resources

TABLE 9.2 Selected Secondary Sources and Databases for Public Speakers

Books Books explore topics in depth, providing details and perspectives often unavailable elsewhere.	• See *Books in Print* (www.booksinprint.com) to search titles of all books currently in print in the United States. • See *Google Books* (books.google.com) to search the full texts of books by title, author, or keyword. • See *Worldcat.org* to search the library collections in the United States and worldwide; it also includes primary source collections and archives. • Consult Amazon.com or another online bookseller and key in your topic.
Newspapers Newspapers contain a mix of eyewitness accounts, in-depth analyses of local and world events, and human-interest feature stories.	• See *ProQuest Newspapers* to search U.S. newspapers by state. • See *World Newspapers* (www.worldnewspapers.com) or EBSCO's *Newswires* to search world newspapers. • See *Newspaper Archive* (www.newspaperarchive.com) to research historical newspapers from 1753 to the present.
Periodicals **Periodicals** are regularly published magazines or journals and include *peer-reviewed* and *popular journals*, *general-interest magazines* such as *Time* and *Newsweek*, and countless specialized business and technical publications.	• Many general-interest magazines are available in *InfoTrac Online* and *General OneFile*. • To locate both general periodicals and scholarly journals, see *Academic Search Premier* and *Academic Search Elite*. • *LexisNexis Academic* provides access to a myriad of news, business, legal, and medical publications and related information sources. (See also Table 9.3 for selected databases devoted to individual disciplines.)
Books of Quotations and Poetry Collections Public speakers often use quotations and offer lines of poetry.	• *Bartlett's Familiar Quotations* contains passages, phrases, and proverbs traced to their sources. • *Bartlett's Familiar Black Quotations*, by Retha Powers and Henry Louis Gates, contains quotations, lyrics, poems, and proverbs. • *The Yale Book of Quotations* includes 12,000 quotations collected on a wide array of subjects. • *The Columbia Granger's World of Poetry* indexes poems by author, title, and first line and is available in print and online. • The Library of Congress *Poetry Resources Web Guide* offers links to poetry resources. • *Poets.org* is the website of the Academy of American Poets.

for a particular subject available to the library's user. Compiled by in-house librarians, subject guides provide depth and breadth about a topic most users would otherwise not know about, providing at least a partial research road map (see Figure 9.2 for a sample subject guide and Table 9.3 for selected subject-specific databases).

You can research a topic by *keyword* or by *subject heading* (as well as by other fields, such as *author, title,* and *date*); see the help section of the search tools you select for the fields to use. The most effective means of retrieving

FROM SOURCE TO SPEECH

Evaluating Web Sources

Discerning the accuracy of online content is not always easy. Search engines such as Google cannot discern the quality of information; only a human editor can do this. Each time you examine a document, especially one that has not been evaluated by credible editors, ask yourself, "Who put this information here, and why did they do so? What are the source's qualifications? Where is similar information found? When was the information posted, and is it timely?"

Check the Most Authoritative Websites First

Seek out the most authoritative websites on your topic. If your speech explores the NBA draft, investigate the NBA's official website first. For information on legislation, government statistics, health, the environment, and other relevant topics, check government-sponsored sites at the official U.S. government portal, www.usa.gov. Government-sponsored sites are free of commercial influence and contain highly credible primary materials.

Evaluate Authorship and Sponsorship

1. *Examine the domain in the Web address*—the suffix at the end of the address tells you the nature of the site: educational (.edu), government (.gov), military (.mil), nonprofit organization (.org), business/commercial (.com), and network (.net). A tilde (~) in the address usually indicates that it is a personal page rather than part of an institutional website. Make sure to assess the credibility of each site and determine whether it is operated by an individual, a company, a government agency, or a nonprofit group.
2. *Look for an "About" link that describes the organization or a link to a page that gives more information.* These sections can tell a great deal about the nature of the site's content. Be wary of sites that do not include such a link.
3. *Identify the creator of the information.* If an individual operates the site—and such sites are now prolific in the form of blogs and professional profile pages—does the document provide relevant biographical information, such as links to a résumé or a listing of the author's credentials? Look for contact information. A source that doesn't want to be found, at least by e-mail, is not a good source to cite.

Check for Currency

4. *Check for a date that indicates when the page was placed on the Web and when it was last updated.* Is the date current? Websites that do not have this information may contain outdated or inaccurate material.

Check That the Site Credits Trustworthy Sources

5 *Check that the website documents its sources.* Reputable websites document the sources they use. Follow any links to these sources, and apply the same criteria to them that you did to the original source document. Verify the information you find with at least two other independent, reputable sources.

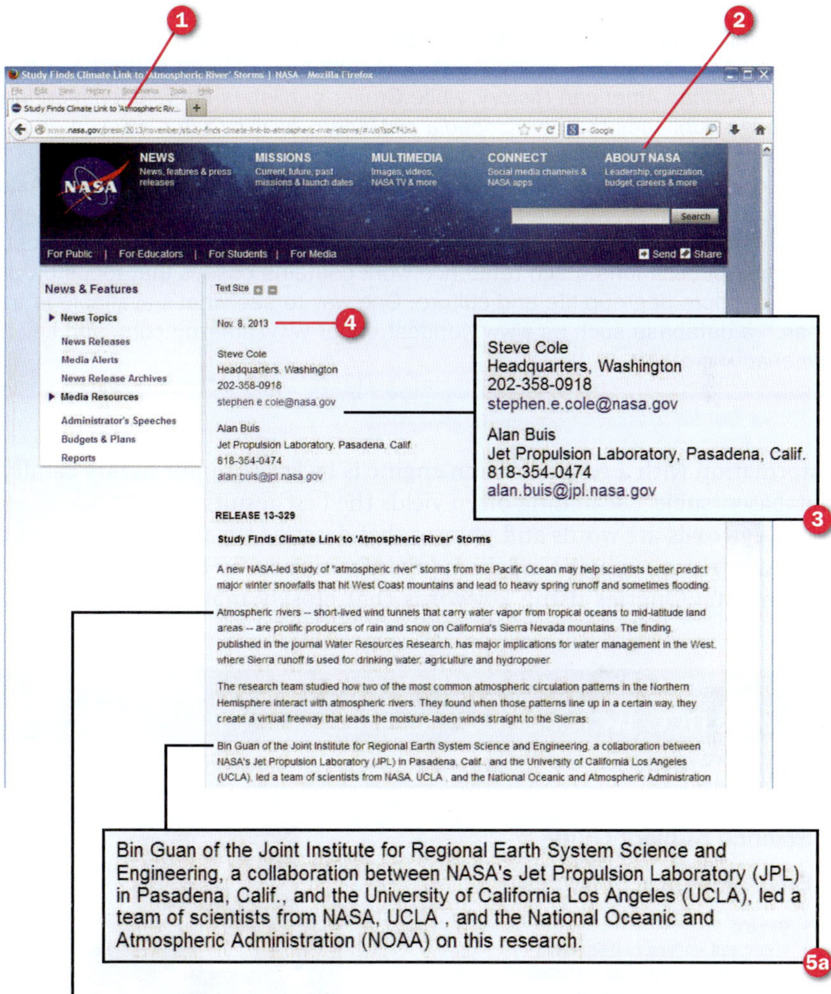

"Atmospheric rivers are the bridge between climate and West Coast snow," said Guan. "If scientists can predict these atmospheric patterns with reasonable lead times, we'll have a better understanding of water availability and flooding in the region." The benefit of improving flood prediction alone would be significant. A single California atmospheric-river storm in 1999 caused 15 deaths and $570 million in damage.

5b

A CULTURAL PERSPECTIVE

Discovering Diversity in Reference Works

charles taylor/Shutterstock

In addition to the rich cultural resources to be found in digital collections (see "Explore Digital Collections," p. 138), a wealth of reference works exists for speakers who seek information on the accomplishments of the many ethnic, cultural, and religious communities that make up the United States. Hundreds of specialized encyclopedias focus on specific ethnic groups and religions. Oxford University Press publishes two volumes of the *Encyclopedia of African-American History*, while Grolier publishes *Encyclopedia Latina*. Routledge publishes the *Encyclopedia of Modern Jewish Culture*. Key in *encyclopedia* AND *[ethnic group]* and see what you find.

Among specialized almanacs, multiple publishers produce versions of Asian American almanacs, Muslim almanacs, Native North American almanacs, African American almanacs, and Hispanic American almanacs, along with a host of similar publications. Each reference work contains essays that focus on all major aspects of group life and culture. One way to see what's available is to search a database such as www.worldcat.org or www.amazon.com, and key in *almanac* AND *ethnic*.

information with a general search engine is by keyword; for library catalogs and databases, subject searching often yields the best results.

Keywords are words and phrases that describe the main concepts of topics. Search engines such as Google index information by keywords tagged within documents. Queries using keywords that closely match those tagged in the

FIGURE 9.2 Library of Congress Subject Guide for Environmental Sciences

TABLE 9.3 Selected Subject-Specific Databases

Subject Area	Databases
Business	*ABI/INFORM* covers journals and news in business, management, economics, and related fields; see also *LexisNexis Academic*, *Business Source Complete*, and *Bloomberg News*.
Education	Proquest Education Journals searches 760 leading education journals; most are available as full texts.
Environment	GreenFILE contains information related to human impact on the environment, including scholarly, government, and general interest titles on topics such as global warming, green building, pollution, sustainable agriculture, and renewable energy.
Arts and Sciences	*JSTOR* is a searchable database of full-text articles from selected scholarly journals focused on a range of arts, social science, humanities, and life science topics; it excludes the last two to five years.
Science	*ScienceDirect* is a leading full-text database offering journal articles; also see *Web of Science*. *ProQuest Science Journals* searches full texts and images within leading journals in science and technology.
Medicine and Allied Health	*PubMed* (MedLine) is the U.S. National Library of Medicine's database of citations for biomedical literature from MEDLINE, life science journals, and online books. *CINAHL* searches nursing and allied health literature. Ebsco's *Alt HealthWatch* focuses on contemporary, holistic, and integrated approaches to health care and wellness.
Public Affairs	*PAIS International* (Public Affairs Information Service) holds political science and public policy articles, books, and government documents. *iPoll Databank* (Roper Center for Public Opinion Research) searches polling data from 1935 to the present; see also Pew Research and Gallup.org.
Contemporary Social Issues	*CQ Researcher* (published weekly) and *CQ Global Researcher* (published monthly) include information on pressing social, political, environmental, and regional issues. They include, for each topic, an overview and assessment of the current situation, pro/con statements from representatives of opposing positions, and bibliographies of key sources.
Ethnic and Minority-Specific Viewpoints and Research	*Ethnic NewsWatch* covers newspapers, magazines, and academic journals of the ethnic, minority, and native press.
Statistics	*FedStats* is a government portal that links to statistics generated by at least one hundred government agencies.

document will therefore return the most relevant results. Keyword searches, while most efficient when using general search engines, may yield unsatisfactory results in a library catalog or database. Here the tool of choice is the **subject heading**—a term selected by information specialists (such as librarians) to describe and group related materials in a library catalog, database, or subject guide (e.g., *cookery* for cooking-related articles). Identifying the correct heading is the key to an effective subject search. If you use the wrong term in a catalog or database (such as keying in *Lou Gehrig's disease* rather than the medical term *amyotrophic lateral sclerosis*), no results may appear, when in fact a wealth of sources exists, organized under another subject heading.

Librarians agree that searching by subject headings is the most precise way to locate information in library databases. But how do you identify the right subject headings? One tactic is to check whether the database includes a *thesaurus of subject headings*. Another option is to do a keyword search of important terms related to your topic in a general search engine. Then try these in your subject search of your library's databases.

10 Citing Sources in Your Speech

LearningCurve can help you review!
Go to LaunchPad: **launchpadworks.com**

If you've ever challenged a speeding ticket in traffic court, you may not be surprised to learn that people rarely win their appeals without offering strong evidence to support their case.[1] Much the same can be said of convincing audience members to accept your speech points. Research confirms that when you back up your claims with evidence, audience members are more likely to process and accept them than if you make unsupported assertions.[2] Alerting the audience to the sources you use, as well as offering ones that they will find authoritative, is thus a critical aspect of delivering a speech or presentation. When you credit speech sources, you:

- Increase the odds that audience members will believe in your message.
- Demonstrate the quality and range of your research to listeners.
- Demonstrate that reliable sources support your position.
- Avoid plagiarism and gain credibility as an ethical speaker who acknowledges the work of others.
- Enhance your own authority.
- Enable listeners to locate your sources and pursue their own research on the topic.

As described in Chapter 5, ethically you are bound to attribute any information drawn from other people's ideas, opinions, and theories—as well as any facts and statistics gathered by others—to their original sources. Remember, you need not credit sources for ideas that are *common knowledge*—established information likely to be known by many people and described in multiple places.

Alert Listeners to Key Source Information

An **oral citation** credits the source of speech material that is derived from other people's ideas. During your speech, always cite your sources as you present the information derived from them, rather than waiting until the end of the speech to disclose them to the audience. For each source, plan on briefly alerting the audience to the following:

1. The *author* or *origin of the source* ("documentary filmmaker Morgan Spurlock . . ." or "On the *National Science Foundation website* . . .")
2. The *type of source* (journal article, book, personal interview, website, blog, online video, etc.)
3. The *title* or a *description of the source* ("In the book *Endangered Minds* . . ." or "In *an article on sharks* . . .")
4. The *date of the source* ("The article, published in the January *10th, 2017,* issue . . ." or "According to a report on financing student loans, posted online on *September 28, 2017,* on the *Daily Beast* . . .")

Of course, spoken citations need not include a complete reference (exact titles, full names of all authors, volume and page numbers); doing so will interrupt the flow of your presentation and distract listeners' attention. However, do keep a running list of source details for a bibliography to appear at the end of your speech draft or outline. (For guidelines on creating a written bibliography for your speeches, see Appendices B, C, and G–I.) In place of bibliographic details, focus on presenting your sources in a way that will encourage audience members to process and believe in the source material.

Establish the Source's Trustworthiness

Too often, inexperienced speakers credit their sources in bare-bones fashion, offering a rote recitation of citation elements. For example, they might cite the publication name and date but leave out key details about the source's background that could convince the audience to accept the source as reliable and that his or her conclusions are true. Discerning listeners will only accept the information you offer if they believe that the sources for it are reliable and accurate, or *credible*. **Source credibility** refers to our level of trust in a source's credentials and track record for providing accurate information. If you support a scientific claim by crediting it to an unknown student's personal blog, for example, listeners won't find it nearly as reliable as if you credited it to a scientist affiliated with a reputable institution.

Be aware that while a source that is credible is usually accurate, this is not always so.[3] Sometimes we have information that contradicts what we are told by a credible source. For example, a soldier might read a news article in the *Washington Post* newspaper about a conflict in which he or she participated. The soldier knows the story contains inaccuracies because the soldier was there. In general, however, the soldier finds the *Washington Post* a credible source. Therefore, *since even the most credible source can sometimes be wrong, it is always better to offer a variety of sources, rather than a single source, to support a major point*. This is especially the case when your claims are controversial.

Qualify the Source

A simple and straightforward way to demonstrate a source's trustworthiness is to include a brief description of the source's qualifications to address the

CHECKLIST

OFFERING KEY SOURCE INFORMATION

_____ 1. Have I identified the author or origin of the source?

_____ 2. Have I indicated the type of source?

_____ 3. Have I offered the title or description of the source?

_____ 4. Have I noted the date of the source?

_____ 5. Have I qualified the source to establish its credibility and accuracy?

topic (a **source qualifier**) along with your oral citation. A brief mention of the source's relevant affiliations and credentials (e.g., "researcher at Duke Cancer Institute," "columnist for *The Economist*") will allow the audience to put the source in perspective and establish his or her *ethos*. And when offering your own insights or experience, don't forget to mention your own qualifications. (Whoever the source, audience members will want to know why they should accept them.) The "Types of Sources and Sample Oral Citations" on p. 154 in this chapter and the From Source to Speech guide "Demonstrating Your Sources' Reliability and Credibility" on p. 152 illustrate how you can orally cite your sources in a way that listeners will accept them.

Avoid a Mechanical Delivery

Acknowledging sources need not interrupt the flow of your speech. On the contrary, audience members will welcome information that adds backing to your assertions. The key is to avoid a formulaic, or mechanical, delivery. Audience members expect a natural style of delivery of your speech, and this includes delivery of speech sources.

Vary the Wording

One way to avoid a mechanical delivery of sources is to vary your wording. If you introduce one source with the phrase "According to . . . ," switch to another construction ("As reported by . . .") for the next one. Alternating introductory phrases, such as "In the words of . . . ," "*Baltimore Sun* reporter Jonathan X writes that . . . ," and so forth, contributes to a natural delivery and provides the necessary variety listeners need.

Vary the Order

Another means of artfully weaving source citations into a speech is to discuss the findings first, before revealing the source. For example, you might state the claim, "Caffeine can cause actual intoxication" and provide evidence to back it up before revealing the source(s) of it—"A chief source for this argument is a report in the July 5th, 2017, issue of the *New England Journal of Medicine* . . ."

Demonstrating Your Sources' Credibility and Accuracy

How Can I Lead the Audience to Accept My Sources as Credible and Accurate?

- If the source is affiliated with a respected institution, identify that affiliation.
- If citing a study linked to a reputable institution, identify the institution.
- If a source has relevant credentials, note the credentials.
- If the source has relevant real-life experience, mention that experience.

In the following excerpt from a speech about becoming a socially conscious consumer, the speaker omits information about key sources that would help convince the audience that his evidence and sources are trustworthy.

> The force behind this new kind of partnership is called "cause marketing." According to the *Financial Times*, cause marketing is when a company and a consumer group — or a charity — tackle a social or environmental problem and create business value for the company at the same time. A survey on consumer responses to cause marketing was conducted by Nielsen. The poll found that two-thirds of consumers around the world would say they prefer to buy products and services from companies that have programs that give back to society. And over 46 percent of consumers were willing to pay more for goods and services from companies that are giving back.

Below we see a much more convincing use of the same sources.

> The force behind this new kind of partnership is called "cause marketing." According to the *Financial Times* Lexicon, an online dictionary found at the publication's website, in *cause marketing* a company and a consumer group — or a charity — tackle a social or environmental problem and create business value for the company at the same time. In March of 2012, the global marketing firm Nielson, which studies consumer behavior in more than one hundred countries, conducted a worldwide study on cause marketing. It found that two-thirds of consumers around the world say they prefer to buy products and services from companies that have programs that give back to society. And over 46 percent said that they were, and I'm quoting here from the survey question, "willing to pay more for goods and services from companies that are giving back."

1

2

3

4

1 The speaker states the date of the study.

2 Rather than merely mentioning the source's name (Nielsen), the speaker identifies the source as a reputable global marketing firm. Listeners are more likely to trust the source if it is connected to a trusted entity.

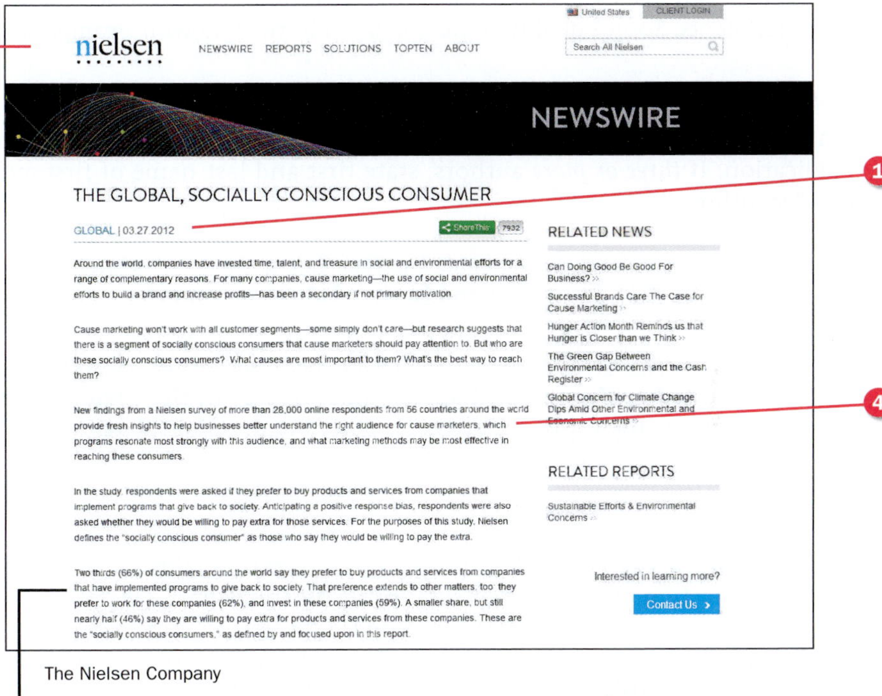

United States | CLIENT LOGIN

nielsen

NEWSWIRE REPORTS SOLUTIONS TOPTEN ABOUT

Search All Nielsen

NEWSWIRE

THE GLOBAL, SOCIALLY CONSCIOUS CONSUMER

GLOBAL | 03.27.2012

ShareThis 7932

Around the world, companies have invested time, talent, and treasure in social and environmental efforts for a range of complementary reasons. For many companies, cause marketing—the use of social and environmental efforts to build a brand and increase profits—has been a secondary if not primary motivation.

Cause marketing won't work with all customer segments—some simply don't care—but research suggests that there is a segment of socially conscious consumers that cause marketers should pay attention to. But who are these socially conscious consumers? What causes are most important to them? What's the best way to reach them?

New findings from a Nielsen survey of more than 28,000 online respondents from 56 countries around the world provide fresh insights to help businesses better understand the right audience for cause marketers, which programs resonate most strongly with this audience, and what marketing methods may be most effective in reaching these consumers.

In the study, respondents were asked if they prefer to buy products and services from companies that implement programs that give back to society. Anticipating a positive response bias, respondents were also asked whether they would be willing to pay extra for those services. For the purposes of this study, Nielsen defines the "socially conscious consumer" as those who say they would be willing to pay the extra.

Two thirds (66%) of consumers around the world say they prefer to buy products and services from companies that have implemented programs to give back to society. That preference extends to other matters, too: they prefer to work for these companies (62%), and invest in these companies (59%). A smaller share, but still nearly half (46%) say they are willing to pay extra for products and services from these companies. These are the "socially conscious consumers," as defined by and focused upon in this report.

RELATED NEWS

Can Doing Good Be Good For Business? >>

Successful Brands Care The Case for Cause Marketing >>

Hunger Action Month Reminds us that Hunger is Closer than we Think >>

The Green Gap Between Environmental Concerns and the Cash Register >>

Global Concern for Climate Change Dips Amid Other Environmental and Economic Concerns >>

RELATED REPORTS

Sustainable Efforts & Environmental Concerns >>

Interested in learning more?

Contact Us >

The Nielsen Company

Two thirds (66%) of consumers around the world say they prefer to buy products and services from companies that have implemented programs to give back to society. That preference extends to other matters, too: They prefer to work for these companies (62%), and invest in these companies (59%). A smaller share, but still nearly half (46%) say they are willing to pay extra for products and services from these companies. These are the "socially conscious consumers," as defined by and focused upon in this report.

3 The speaker informs the audience that he is quoting the source.

4 The speaker describes enough detail about the scope of the study ("world-wide"; "28,000 survey participants from 56 countries") to convince the audience of its credibility and reliability.

Types of Sources and Sample Oral Citations

Following are common types of sources cited in a speech, the specific citation elements to mention, and examples of how you might refer to these elements in a presentation. Note that each example includes a source qualifier describing the source's qualifications to address the topic—for instance, "director of undergraduate studies for four years" or "research scientist at Smith-Kline." Qualifying a source can make the difference between winning and losing acceptance for your arguments. Source qualifiers are boldfaced in the following examples.

Book

If a book has *two* or *fewer* authors, state first and last names, title, and date of publication. If *three or more* authors, state first and last name of first author and "coauthors."

> *Example:* In the book *Dreamland: The True Tale of America's Opiate Epidemic*, published in 2016, **journalist and former *L.A. Times* reporter** Sam Quinones describes how . . .

> *Example:* In *The Civic Potential of Video Games*, published in 2009, Joseph Kahne, **noted professor of education and director of the Civic Education Research Group at Mills College**, and his two coauthors, **both educators**, wrote that . . .

Reference Work

For a reference work (e.g., atlas, directory, encyclopedia, almanac), note title, date of publication, and author or sponsoring organization.

> *Example:* According to the *2017 Literary Marketplace*, **the foremost guide to the U.S. book publishing industry**, Karen Hallard and her coeditors report that . . .

Print Article

When citing from a print article, use the same guidelines as you do for a book.

> *Example:* In an article titled "The False Promise of DNA Testing," published in the June 2016 edition of *Atlantic Monthly* magazine, **journalist and *New York Times* contributing writer** Matthew Shaer argues that forensic testing is becoming ever less reliable.

Online-Only Magazine, Newspaper, Journal

Follow the same guidelines as for a book, and identify the publication as an "online magazine," "online newspaper," or "online journal."

> *Example:* In an *article* titled "The Ethical Quandary of Self-Driving Cars," published in the online magazine *Slate* on June 6, 2016, Jesse Kirkpatric, **a professor of philosophy and public policy at George Mason University** . . .

Organization Website

Name the website, section of website cited (if applicable), and last update.

> *Example:* On its website, last updated July 8, 2017, the Society of Interventional Radiology, **a nationwide organization of physicians and scientists**, explains that radio waves are harmless to healthy cells . . .

If website content is undated or not regularly updated, review the site for credibility before use, using the criteria listed on p. 156.

Blog

Name the blogger, affiliated website (if applicable), and date of posting.

> *Example:* In an April 26, 2017, posting on *Talking Points Memo*, a **news blog that specializes in original reporting on government and politics**, editor Josh Marshall notes that . . .

Television or Radio Program

If you are citing a television or radio program, name the program, segment, reporter, and date aired.

> *Example:* Judy Woodruff, **PBS *NewsHour* cohost**, described in a segment on immigration reform, aired on November 2, 2017 . . .

Online Video

For online videos, name the online video source, program, segment, and date aired (if applicable).

> *Example:* In a session on mindfulness delivered at the University of Miami on October 9, 2015, and broadcast on YouTube, Jon Kabat-Zinn, **scientist, author, and founding director of the Stress Reduction Clinic** . . .

Testimony

Name the person and date and context in which information was offered.

> *Example:* On June 7, 2016, in congressional testimony before the U.S. Senate Foreign Relations Committee, Victoria Nuland, **assistant secretary at the Bureau of European and Eurasian Affairs**, revealed that Russian violations of borders . . .

Interview and Other Personal Communication

Name the person and date of interview.

> *Example:* In an interview I conducted last week, Tim Zeutenhorst, **chairman of the Orange City Area Health System Board, at Orange City Hospital in Iowa,** said . . .

> *Example:* In a June 23 e-mail/twitter post/letter/memorandum from Ron Jones, **a researcher at the Cleveland Clinic . . .**

Recording and Citing Web Sources

When using a Web document as a source, locate and record the following citation elements.

1. Author of the Work
2. Title of the Work
3. Title of the Website
4. Date of Publication/Last Update
5. Site Address (URL)

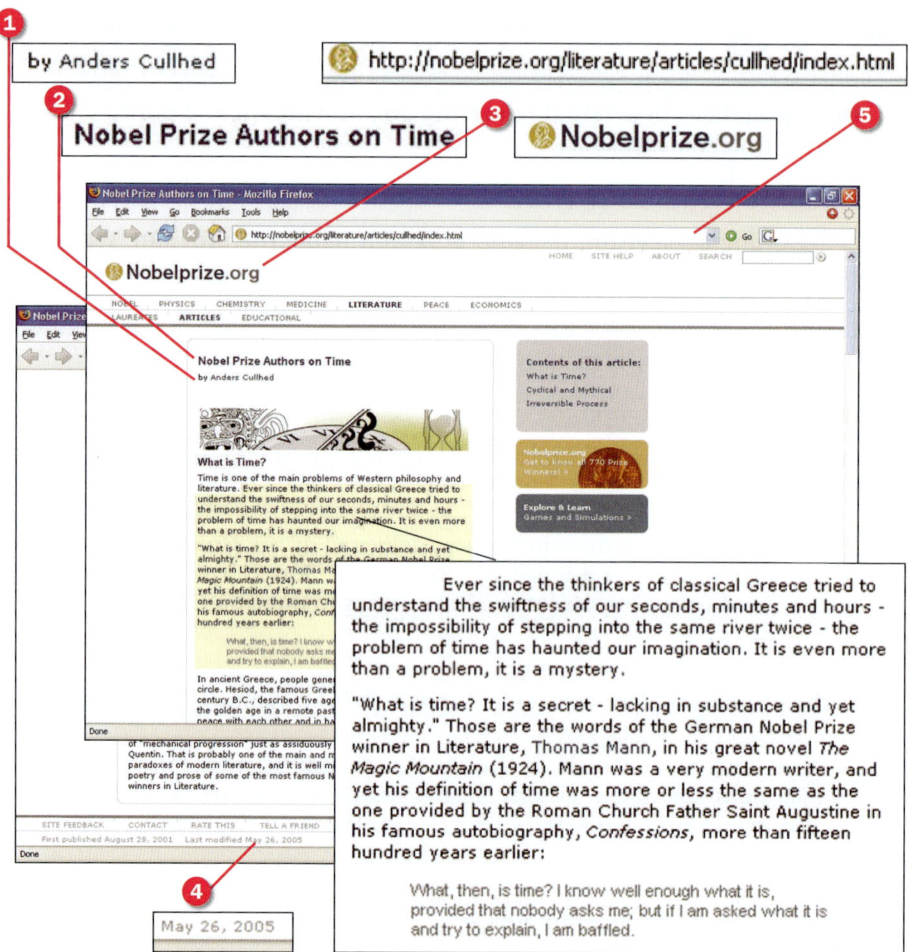

Record Note

When taking notes, create a separate heading for each idea and record the citation elements from your source. Indicate whether the material is a direct quotation, a paraphrase, or a summary of the information.

Following are sample notes for a quotation and a paraphrase.

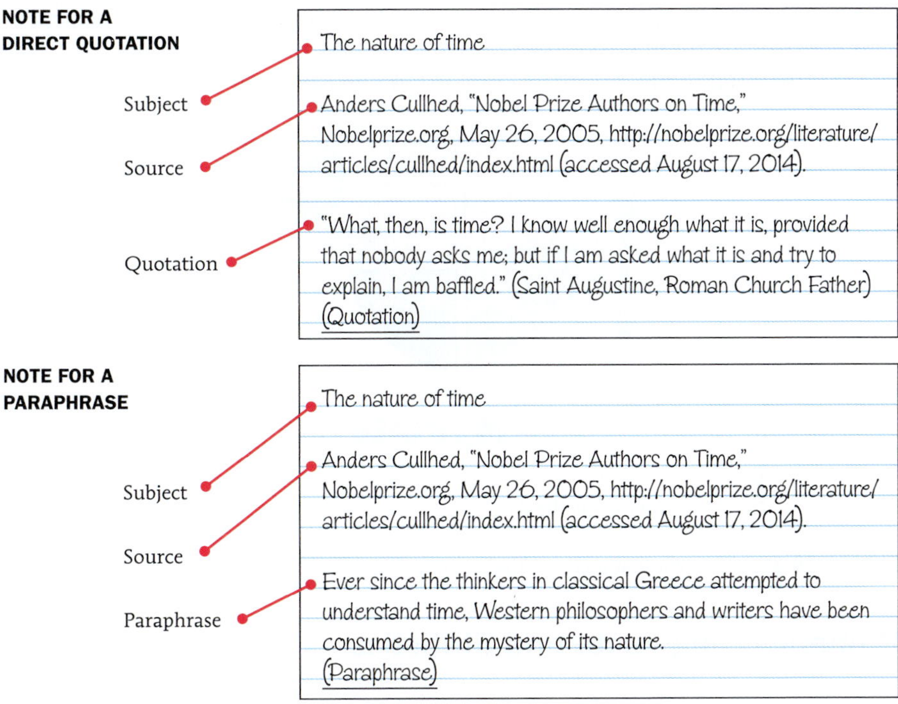

NOTE FOR A DIRECT QUOTATION
Subject
Source
Quotation
The nature of time
Anders Cullhed, "Nobel Prize Authors on Time," Nobelprize.org, May 26, 2005, http://nobelprize.org/literature/articles/cullhed/index.html (accessed August 17, 2014).
"What, then, is time? I know well enough what it is, provided that nobody asks me; but if I am asked what it is and try to explain, I am baffled." (Saint Augustine, Roman Church Father)
(Quotation)
NOTE FOR A PARAPHRASE
Subject
Source
Paraphrase
The nature of time
Anders Cullhed, "Nobel Prize Authors on Time," Nobelprize.org, May 26, 2005, http://nobelprize.org/literature/articles/cullhed/index.html (accessed August 17, 2014).
Ever since the thinkers in classical Greece attempted to understand time, Western philosophers and writers have been consumed by the mystery of its nature.
(Paraphrase)

Orally Cite Sources in Your Speech

In your speech, alert the audience to the source of any ideas that are not your own. You can find information on oral citations earlier in this chapter (p. 149). For guidelines on various citation styles, including *Chicago*, APA, MLA, CBE/CSE, and IEEE, see Appendices B and C, as well as online Appendices G–I.

SPEECH EXCERPT INDICATING A DIRECT QUOTATION

Many famous thinkers have grappled with the concept of time. For example, Saint Augustine wrote in his biography, *Confessions*, "What, then, is time? I know well enough what it is, provided that nobody asks me; but if I am asked what it is and try to explain, I am baffled."

SPEECH EXCERPT INDICATING A PARAPHRASE

In an article on the nature of time posted on the website Nobelprize.org, professor of comparative literature Anders Cullhed notes that beginning with thinkers in ancient Greece, Western philosophers and writers have tried to understand the nature of time.

Credit Sources in Presentation Aids

Just as you acknowledge the ideas of others in the verbal portion of your speech, be sure to credit such material used in any accompanying presentation aids. When reproducing copyrighted material, such as a table or photograph, label it with a copyright symbol (©) and the source information. Even if it is not copyrighted, supporting material listed on a visual aid requires citation. You may cite this material orally, print the citation unobtrusively on the aid, or both.

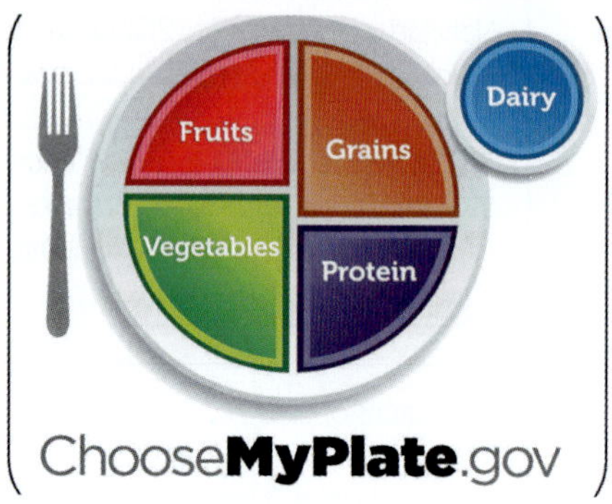

Courtesy of the USDA

FIGURE 10.1 PowerPoint that includes the source ("Courtesy of the USDA")

Properly Citing Facts and Statistics

Facts that are widely disseminated and commonly known—information referred to as **common knowledge**—require no attribution (see Chapter 5). Otherwise, credit the source of the fact in your speech.

> According to the Galileo Project website (*source*), a project supported by Rice University, Galileo was appointed professor of mathematics at the University of Padua in 1592 (*fact*).

Statistics add credibility to speech claims and can make your arguments more persuasive, *if* you tell listeners what the numbers actually mean, use terms that describe them accurately, and reveal the methods and scope of the research.

> According to a nationally representative sample of males ages 15 and older, selected by a random digit sample of telephone numbers (*methods and scope of research*) conducted by the Pew Research Center, a major nonpartisan "fact tank" that provides information on the issues shaping America and the world (*source qualifier*), a record 8 percent of households with children are now headed by single fathers, up from just over 1 percent in 1960 (*what the numbers actually mean*).[4]

Properly Citing Summarized, Paraphrased, and Quoted Information

As discussed in Chapter 5, information that is not your own may be cited in the form of a *summary* (a brief overview of someone else's ideas, opinions, or theories), *paraphrase* (a restatement of someone else's ideas, opinions, or theories in the speaker's own words), or *direct quotation* (statements made verbatim by someone else).

For examples of how to cite different types of supporting materials, including facts and statistics, see Table 10.1.

TABLE 10.1 Types of Supporting Materials and Sample Oral Citations

Type of Supporting Material	Sample Oral Citation
Examples (real or hypothetical)	"One example of a website that evaluates charities is GiveWell. Founded by hedge fund employees, GiveWell conducts research into how much good various charities achieve and then publishes their research . . ."
Stories (extended or anecdotal)	"In J. R. R. Tolkien's classic trilogy, *The Lord of the Rings*, a young Hobbit boy named Frodo . . ."
Testimony (expert or lay)	"Dr. Mary Klein, a stem-cell researcher from the Brown University School of Medicine, echoed this sentiment when she spoke last Monday at the Public Health Committee meeting . . ."
Facts	"According to the *Farmer's Almanac*, published every year since 1818, originally the phrase 'blue moon' referred to the second of two full moons appearing in a single month."
Statistics	"Data from the U.S. Census Bureau, which produces national population estimates annually using the latest available data on births, deaths, and international migration, indicate that in 2016, there was one birth every eight seconds and one death every ten seconds in the United States."

ORGANIZING AND OUTLINING

Malala Yousafzai, age 18 in the photo, speaks during the first focus event on education at the 'Supporting Syria Conference' in London, England, calling on world leaders to pledge funds to help educate Syrian refugee children. Since Yousafzai was a child, she has voiced her support for girls' education in Pakistan, even after she was shot by the Taliban. At age 17 in 2014, she became the youngest person to receive the Nobel Peace Prize. **WPA Pool/Getty Images**

ORGANIZING AND OUTLINING

SPEAKER'S PREVIEW

LearningCurve can help you review.
Go to LaunchPad: **launchpadworks.com**

ORGANIZING AND OUTLINING

CHAPTER 11 Organizing the Body of the Speech

Understand the Value of Organization in a Speech

- Audience understanding is directly linked to speech organization. (p. 167)
- Speech outlines are essential tools in organizing speeches, allowing you to order your ideas into logical divisions. (p. 167)

Recognize the Parts of a Speech

- A speech structure consists of an introduction, body, and conclusion. (p. 168)

Create Main Points That Express Your Major Claims

- Use the thesis and specific purpose statements as guides. (p. 169)
- Check that each main point flows directly from these statements. (p. 169)
- In most cases, restrict the number of main points to between two and five. (p. 169)
- Focus each main point on a single idea. (p. 170)
- Present each main point as a declarative sentence. (p. 170)
- State main points in parallel form. (p. 170)

Use Supporting Points to Substantiate or Prove Your Main Points

- Create supporting points with your research. (p. 171)
- Ensure that supporting points follow logically from main points. (p. 172)
- Check that supporting points are in fact subordinate in weight to main points. (p. 173)

LaunchPad VIDEO ACTIVITY

Go to LaunchPad to watch a video about outlining your speech.

LaunchPad includes:

- LearningCurve adaptive quizzing
- a curated collection of video clips and full-length speeches.

Additional resources and reference materials such as presentation software tutorials and documentation help.

Pay Attention to Coordination and Subordination

- Make ideas of equal weight *coordinate* to one another. (p. 172)
- Make an idea that has less weight than another idea *subordinate* to it. (p. 172)

Create Speech Points That Are Unified, Coherent, and Balanced

- Focus each point, whether main or subordinate, on a single idea. (p. 174)
- Review the logical connections between points. (p. 174)
- Dedicate roughly the same amount of time to each main point. (p. 174)
- Ensure that the introduction and the conclusion are approximately of the same length and that the body is the longest part of the speech. (p. 174)
- Support each main point with at least two supporting points. (p. 174)

Use Transitions to Signal Movement from One Point to Another

- Use transitions to move between main points and between subpoints as needed. (p. 175)
- Use transitions to move from introduction, body, and conclusion. (p. 175)
- Select among full sentences, phrases, and single words. (p. 175)

Use Internal Previews and Summaries as Transitions

- Use internal previews to help listeners anticipate what is ahead. (p. 177)
- Use internal summaries to help listeners review what has been said. (p. 177)

CHAPTER 12 Types of Organizational Arrangements

Use a Pattern to Help Listeners Process and Retain Information

- Select a pattern that emphasizes the points you want to make so that listeners can easily follow. (p. 180)
- Select a pattern that helps you achieve your speech goals. (p. 180)

Choose from a Variety of Organizational Patterns

- To describe a series of developments in time or a set of actions occurring sequentially, consider a *chronological pattern*. (p. 180)
- To emphasize physical arrangement, consider a *spatial pattern*. (p. 183)
- To demonstrate a topic in terms of its underlying causes (or its effects), consider a *causal (cause–effect) pattern*. (p. 184)

- To demonstrate a problem and then provide justification for a solution, consider a *problem–solution pattern*. (p. 185)
- To stress natural divisions or categories in a topic, consider a *topical pattern*. (p. 186)
- To convey speech ideas through a story, consider a *narrative pattern*. (p. 187)

Be Aware That Subpoints Need Not Follow the Pattern Selected for Main Points

CHAPTER 13 Outlining the Speech

Plan on Developing Two Outlines before Delivering Your Speech

- Begin by creating a working outline in sentence format. (p. 190)
- Transfer your ideas to a speaking outline in phrase or key-word format. (p. 190)

Become Familiar with Sentence, Phrase, and Key-Word Outlines

- Sentence outlines express speech points in full sentences. (p. 191)
- Phrase outlines use shortened versions of the sentence form. (p. 191)
- Key-word outlines use just a few words associated with the specific point. (p. 192)

Know the Benefits and Drawbacks of the Three Outline Formats

- The less you rely on your outline notes, the more eye contact you can have with the audience. (p. 192)
- Key-word outlines promote eye contact and natural delivery, *if* you are well rehearsed. (p. 192)
- Sentence outlines offer the most protection against memory lapses but sacrifice eye contact. (p. 192)

Plan Your Speech with a Working Outline

- Treat the working outline as a document to be revised and rearranged. (p. 193)
- Include everything you want to say in your working outline. (p. 193)

Create a Speaking Outline to Deliver the Speech

- Condense the working outline into a phrase or key-word outline. (p. 200)
- Clearly indicate delivery cues. (p. 200)

KEY TERMS

Chapter 11

- canon of arrangement
- outline
- introduction
- body
- conclusion
- main points
- primacy effect
- recency effect
- supporting points
- indentation
- roman numeral outline
- coordination and subordination
- coordinate points
- subordinate points
- transitions (connectives)
- rhetorical question
- preview statement
- internal preview
- internal summary

Chapter 12

- chronological pattern of arrangement
- spatial pattern of arrangement
- causal (cause-effect) pattern of arrangement
- problem-solution pattern of arrangement
- topical pattern of arrangement (or categorical pattern)
- narrative pattern of arrangement

Chapter 13

- outline
- coordination
- subordination
- working outline
- speaking outline
- sentence outline
- phrase outline
- key-word outline
- bibliography
- delivery cues

Go to LaunchPad: **launchpadworks.com** to watch the video clips for this chapter.

11 Organizing the Body of the Speech

LearningCurve can help you review!
Go to LaunchPad: **launchpadworks.com**

Audience members quickly note the difference between a well-organized speech and one that has been put together haphazardly, with decidedly negative results when the speech is disorganized. The reason for this is simple: Our understanding of information is directly linked to how well it is organized.[1] Apparently, a little bit of disorganization won't ruin a speech for us if the topic and speaker are otherwise engaging, but we quickly lose interest, and even become irritated, when the speech is very disorganized.[2] On the other hand, we find speakers whose speeches are well organized more understandable, more believable, and more trustworthy than those who present poorly organized ones.[3] Given all this, you won't want to skip the crucial steps of arranging and outlining speech points.

As in written composition, organizing a speech—a stage in speech development classical speakers called the **canon of arrangement**—is the process of devising a logical and convincing structure for your message. Organizing occurs in stages, in which you decide upon the main points of the speech, select one of several formal patterns or designs for the speech's structure, and, using that design, complete the outline with subpoints. In an **outline**, you determine how to order your ideas and evidence into larger and smaller logical categories, or divisions and subdivisions. Your main points are the larger divisions, and your subpoints are the subdivisions or subcategories of these main points. Rather than making the job of drafting a speech harder, an outline lets you check for logical inconsistencies in the placement of speech points and pinpoint weaknesses in the amount and kind of support for them.

Organizing your speech into an outline provides a vivid snapshot of its strengths and weaknesses and clearly points to how you can fix the flaws. Although a few famous speakers have managed to deliver successful speeches without first arranging and outlining them, for the vast majority of us, the success or failure of a speech will depend on doing so.

Beyond the Speech: Organizing as a Life Skill

As well as being of immense practical value in fashioning better speeches, skill in arranging and outlining information can have far-reaching positive effects on many aspects of your academic and professional life. As noted in

TABLE 11.1 Sample Outline Format

Extended Outline Format

I. Main point
  A. Subordinate to main point I
  B. Coordinate with subpoint A
    1. Subordinate to subpoint B
    2. Coordinate with sub-subpoint 1
      a. Subordinate to sub-subpoint 2
      b. Coordinate with sub-sub-subpoint a
        (1) Subordinate to sub-sub-subpoint b
        (2) Coordinate with sub-sub-sub-subpoint (1)
II. Main point: Coordinate with main point I

Chapter 1, written and verbal skills in communication rank first in employers' "wish list" for employees. Employers seek workers who can communicate ideas logically and convincingly. Nearly all professional-level jobs, for example, require you to prepare well-organized written or oral reports and visual presentations, for both internal and external audiences. Similarly, written assignments in the classroom depend upon how convincingly and logically you present your viewpoint. Learning how to arrange ideas compellingly and gaining proficiency with outlining—a skill that depends on the logical coordination and subordination of ideas (see p. 172)—will serve you well as a public speaker and in these other arenas (see Table 11.1).

Chapters 12 and 26 describe organizational patterns you can use to order speech points to greatest effect, and Chapter 13 illustrates the three types of outline formats speakers use to prepare and deliver speeches. In this chapter we examine the elements of the speech body—main points, supporting points, and transitions—and their function and placement within an outline.

Basic Structure of a Speech

A speech structure is simple, composed of just three general parts: an introduction, a body, and a conclusion. The **introduction** establishes the purpose of the speech and shows its relevance to the audience. It lets listeners know where the speaker is taking them. The **body** of the speech presents main points that are intended to fulfill the speech purpose. Main points are developed with various kinds of supporting material to fulfill this purpose. The **conclusion** brings closure to the speech by restating the purpose, summarizing main points, and reiterating the speech thesis and its relevance to the audience. In essence, the introduction tells listeners where they are going, the body takes them there, and the conclusion lets them know the journey has ended (see Chapters 14 and 15 on Introductions and Conclusions).

Use Main Points to Make Your Major Claims

Main points express the key ideas or arguments of the speech. Their function is to elaborate on the main ideas (in an informative speech) or claims (in a persuasive speech) being made in support of the speech thesis. To create main points, begin by identifying the central ideas and themes of the speech, as reflected in your thesis statement. What are the most important ideas you want to convey in support of it? What key ideas emerge from your research? What ideas can you demonstrate with supporting material? Each of these ideas or claims should be expressed as a main point.

Use the Purpose and Thesis Statements as Guides

You can use the specific purpose and thesis statement as reference points to help generate main points. As discussed in Chapter 7, the *specific purpose statement* expresses what you want the audience to learn or do as a result of your speech. Formulating it in your mind allows you to articulate precisely what you want the speech to accomplish (without necessarily stating it directly in the speech itself). The *thesis statement* (the essence of which *is* stated in some form in the speech, in your introduction) expresses the central idea of the speech, concisely laying out what it is about. Main points should flow directly from your speech purpose and thesis, as in the following example.

SPECIFIC PURPOSE: (what you want the audience to learn or do as a result of your speech; not necessarily stated in speech itself): To show my audience, through a series of easy steps, how to perform meditation.

THESIS: (the central idea of the speech; thesis is expressed in speech): When performed correctly, meditation is an effective and easy way to reduce stress.

Main Points

I. The first step of meditation is "positioning."

II. The second step of meditation is "breathing."

III. The third step of meditation is "relaxation."

Restrict the Number of Main Points

Research indicates that many audiences can comfortably take in only between two and seven main points. For most speeches, and especially those delivered in the classroom, between two and five main points should be sufficient.[4] As a rule, the fewer main points in a speech, the greater are the odds that you will keep your listeners' attention. Importantly, listeners have the best recall of points made at the beginning of a speech, a phenomenon termed the **primacy effect**, and at the end of a speech (the **recency effect**) than of those made in between (unless the ideas made in between are far more striking than the others).[5] Thus, if it is especially important that listeners remember certain ideas, introduce those ideas near the beginning of the speech and reiterate them at the conclusion.

If you find you have too many main points, consider whether your topic is sufficiently narrow (see Chapter 7 on selecting a topic). If the problem does not lie in an overly broad topic, review your main and supporting points for proper subordination (see p. 172 for a discussion on these topics).

Restrict Each Main Point to a Single Idea

A main point should not introduce more than one idea. If it does, split it into two (or more) main points.

Incorrect

I. West Texas has its own Grand Canyon, and South Texas has its own desert.

Correct

I. West Texas boasts its own Grand Canyon.

II. South Texas boasts its own desert.

Main points should be mutually exclusive of one another. If they are not, consider whether a main point more properly serves as a subpoint.

Express each main point as a *declarative sentence*—one that asserts or claims something. This emphasizes the point and alerts audience members to the main thrusts of your speech. For example, if one of your main points is that females who played sports in college outperform other college graduates in important measures of well-being, clearly state, in declarative form, "According to a 2016 nationwide study conducted by the Gallup organization, former female student-athletes lead other college graduates in key measures of well-being."[6] In addition, as shown in the following example, state your main points in *parallel form*—that is, in similar grammatical form and style. (See p. 239 for a discussion of parallelism.) Phrasing points in parallel form helps listeners understand and retain the points (by providing consistency) and lends power and elegance to your words.

THESIS STATEMENT: Female student athletes who played NCAA Division I, II, or III sports in college outperform other college graduates on important career and life outcomes.

Incorrect

I. Female former student athletes are more likely to be employed full time (62 percent), compared with female graduates who were not student athletes (56 percent).

II. They are also more likely to thrive physically than their non-athlete peers.

III. Social well-being is another aspect in which female student atheletes who have graduated college score better than non-athlete peers.

Correct

I. Female former student athletes are more likely to be employed full time (62 percent), compared with female graduates who were not student athletes (56 percent).

II. Female former student athletes are more likely to thrive in their physical well-being, with 47 percent having good health and enough energy to get things done on a daily basis as compared with 33 percent of female non-athletes.

III. Female former student athletes are more likely to thrive in their social well-being, with 53 percent reporting strong, supportive relationships compared with 48 percent of their female non-athlete counterparts.

SELF-ASSESSMENT CHECKLIST

DO THE SPEECH POINTS ILLUSTRATE OR PROVE THE THESIS?

_____ 1. Are the most important ideas in your speech expressed in the main points?

_____ 2. Are any key ideas implied by your thesis not addressed by main points?

_____ 3. Does each supporting point offer sufficient evidence for the corresponding main point?

_____ 4. Do your supporting points reflect a variety of appropriate supporting material, such as examples, narratives, testimony, and facts and statistics?

Use Supporting Points to Substantiate Your Claims

Supporting points organize the evidence you have gathered to explain (in an informative speech) or justify (in a persuasive speech) the main points. It is here that you substantiate or prove the main points with the examples, narratives, testimony, and facts and statistics discovered in your research (see Chapter 8 on supporting materials).

In an outline, supporting points appear in a subordinate position to main points. This is indicated by **indentation**. Just as you arrange main points, order supporting points according to their importance or relevance to the main point.

The most common format is the **roman numeral outline**. Main points are enumerated with uppercase roman numerals (I, II, III, . . .), supporting points are enumerated with capital letters (A, B, C, . . .), third-level points are enumerated with Arabic numerals (1, 2, 3, . . .), and fourth-level points are enumerated with lowercase letters (a, b, c, . . .), as seen in the following.

I. Main point
   A. Supporting point
      1. Subsupporting point
         a. Sub-subsupporting point
         b. Sub-subsupporting point
      2. Subsupporting point
         a. Sub-subsupporting point
         b. Sub-subsupporting point
   B. Supporting point
II. Main point

Note that different levels of points are also distinguished by different levels of indentation. These differences clearly indicate the direction of your speech. They also enhance your recollection of points and make it easy for you to follow the outline as you speak.

Pay Close Attention to Coordination and Subordination

Outlines reflect the principles of **coordination and subordination**—the logical placement of ideas relative to their importance to one another. Ideas that are *coordinate* are given equal weight; **coordinate points** are indicated by their parallel alignment. An idea that is *subordinate* to another is given relatively less weight; **subordinate points** are indicated by their indentation below the more important points.

Here is an example (in phrase outline form, see p. 239) from a speech on using effective subject lines in business-related e-mails: Coordinate points are aligned with one another, while subordinate points are indented below the points that they substantiate. Thus Main Point II is coordinate with Main Point I, Subpoint A is subordinate to Main Point I, Subpoint B is coordinate with Subpoint A, and so forth.

I. Subject line most important, yet neglected, part of e-mail.
   A. Determines if recipient reads message
      1. Needs to specify point of message
      2. Needs to distinguish from spam
   B. Determines if recipient ignores message
      1. May ignore e-mail with missing subject line
      2. May ignore e-mail with unclear subject line

II. Use proven techniques for creating effective subject lines.
- A. Make them informative
    - 1. Give specific details
    - 2. Match central idea of e-mail
    - 3. Be current
- B. Check for sense
    - 1. Convey correct meaning
    - 2. Reflect content of message
- C. Avoid continuing subject line in text
    - 1. May annoy the reader
    - 2. May be unclear
        - a. Could be confused with spam
        - b. Could be misinterpreted

Recheck Division of Main and Subpoints

As you review your outline, evaluate whether any of your main points more properly belong as subpoints to other main points. In a speech draft about interviewing and etiquette training, University of Oklahoma student Amber Pointer found this to be the case when she saw that she had created six main points.

I. Interviewing is competitive and requires preparation.

II. As in sports, interviewing requires training to compete well against others.

III. When you sell yourself in an interview, you want to make your best impression.

IV. When you take a course on interviewing, you become more competitive.

V. Dressing appropriately is critical to making a good impression.

VI. Proper table manners are key to making a positive impression during a luncheon interview.

Upon examination, Amber realized that main points II and IV are actually subpoints of point I.

I. Interviewing is competitive and requires preparation.

~~II.~~ A. As in sports, interviewing requires training to compete well against others.

~~IV.~~ B. When you take a course on interviewing, you become more competitive.

Similarly, points V and VI are subpoints of point III (which now becomes main point II).

II. When you sell yourself in an interview, you want to make your best impression.

~~V.~~ A. Dressing appropriately is critical to making a good impression.

~~VI.~~ B. Proper table manners are key to making a positive impression during a luncheon interview.

As she examined her outline, Amber realized that she had introduced ideas later in her speech that properly supported the first main point and presented other material that was actually subordinate to her second main point. Rather than six main points, Amber's speech in fact consists of just two.

Strive for a Unified, Coherent, and Balanced Outline

A well-organized speech is characterized by unity, coherence, and balance. Try to adhere to these principles as you arrange your speech points.

A speech exhibits *unity* when it contains only those points that are implied by the purpose and thesis statements. The thesis is supported by the main points, main points are strengthened by supporting points, and supporting points consist of carefully chosen evidence and examples. Finally, each point should focus on a single idea.

A speech exhibits *coherence* when it is organized clearly and logically, using the principles of coordination and subordination to align speech points in order of importance (see Table 11.2). In addition, the speech body should expand upon the introduction, and the conclusion should summarize the body. Within the body of the speech itself, main points should support the thesis statement, and supporting points should expand upon the main points. Transitions serve as mental bridges that help establish coherence.

The principle of *balance* suggests that appropriate emphasis or weight be given to each part of the speech relative to the other parts and to the thesis. Inexperienced public speakers may give overly lengthy coverage to one point and insufficient attention to others; or they might provide scanty evidence in the body of the speech after presenting an impressive introduction. The body of a speech should always be the longest part, and the introduction and the conclusion should be of roughly the same length. Stating the main points in parallel form is one aspect of balance. Assigning each main point at least two supporting points is another. If you have only one subpoint, consider how

TABLE 11.2 Principles of Coordination and Subordination

- Assign equal weight to ideas that are coordinate.
- Assign relatively less weight to ideas that are subordinate.
- Indicate coordinate points by their parallel alignment.
- Indicate subordinate points by their indentation below the more important points.
- Assign every point at least two points or none at all (consider how to address one "dangling" point in the point above it).

CHECKLIST

DO YOUR SPEECH POINTS REFLECT THE PRINCIPLES OF COORDINATION AND SUBORDINATION?

- ✓ Do you assign equal weight to ideas that are coordinate?
- ✓ Do you assign relatively less weight to ideas that are subordinate?
- ✓ Do you indicate coordinate points by their parallel alignment?
- ✓ Do you indicate subordinate points by their indentation below the more important points?
- ✓ Do you support each point by at least two points or none at all? (Consider how to address one "dangling" point by including it in the point above it.)

you might incorporate it into the superior point. Think of a main point as a tabletop and supporting points as table legs; without at least two legs, the table cannot stand.

Use Transitions to Give Direction to the Speech

Transitions are words, phrases, or sentences that tie the speech ideas together and enable the listener to follow the speaker as he or she moves from one point to the next. Transitions (also called **connectives**) are a truly critical component of speeches because listeners cannot go back and reread what they might have missed. As you develop your speech, focus on creating transitions to shift listeners from one point to the next, to signal that a new point will be made, and to move the audience from the introduction to the body of the speech, and from the body to the conclusion. Transitions can take the form of full sentences, phrases, or single words (see Table 11.3).

Use Transitions between Speech Points

Use transitions to move between speech points—from one main point to the next, and from one subpoint to another.

When moving from one *main point* to another, full-sentence transitions are especially effective. For example, to move from main point I in a speech about sales contests (*"Top management should sponsor sales contests to halt the decline in sales over the past two years"*) to main point II (*"Sales contests will lead to better sales presentations"*), the speaker might use the following transition:

> Next, let's look at exactly what sales contests can do for us.

Another full-sentence transition is the **rhetorical question**. Rather than inviting actual responses, rhetorical questions make the audience think (see also Chapter 14 on developing an introduction).

Could there really be a way to use radiation without side effects, and to treat more types of cancer with it?

How do the costs of contests stack up against the expense of training new people?

Don't be afraid to get creative with your use of transitions. In a speech on mountain biking, student Zachary Dominique used metaphoric language in this transition to lend color to the speech:

Now, let's do a hopturn—a turn in reverse—and learn about the sport's colorful history.

Transitions between *supporting points* can be handled using single words, phrases, or full sentences, as in the following.

Next, . . .
First, . . . (second, third, and so forth)
Similarly, . . .
We now turn . . .
If you think that's shocking, consider this . . .

Transitions can also serve the dual function of signaling shifts between speech points and indicating relationships between ideas, as seen in Table 11.3.

Very frequently speakers will use internal previews and internal summaries, both described next, as transitions.

TABLE 11.3 Transitional Words and Phrases

Function	Example
To show comparisons	Similarly; In the same way; Likewise; In comparison; Just as
To contrast ideas	On the other hand; And yet; At the same time; In spite of; However; In contrast
To illustrate cause and effect	As a result; Hence; Because; Thus; Consequently
To illustrate sequence of time or events	First, second, third, . . . ; Following this; Before; After; Later; Earlier; At present; In the past
To indicate explanation	For example; To illustrate; In other words; To simplify; To clarify
To indicate additional examples	Not only; In addition to; Let's look at
To emphasize significance	Most importantly; Above all; Remember; Keep in mind
To summarize	As we have seen; In summary; Finally; In conclusion; Let me conclude by saying

Use Previews and Summaries as Transitions

Previews briefly introduce audience members to the ideas that the speaker will address. In a speech introduction, the **preview statement** briefly mentions the main points and thesis of the speech (see pp. 222). Within the body itself, speakers use an **internal preview** to draw the audience in with a glimpse of what he or she will discuss next.

> Victoria Woodhull was a pioneer in many respects. Not only was she the first woman to run her own brokerage firm, but she was also the first to run for the presidency of the United States, though few people know this. Let's see how she accomplished these feats. . . .

Similar to the internal preview, the **internal summary** draws together ideas to reinforce them before the speaker proceeds to another speech point. Often, a speaker will transition from one major idea or main point to the next by using an internal summary and internal preview together.

> We've seen that mountain bikes differ from road bikes in the design of the tires, the seat, the gears, the suspension systems, and the handlebars. (*internal summary*) Now let's take a look at the different types of mountain bikes themselves. As you will see, mountain bikes vary according to the type of riding they're designed to handle—downhill, trails, and cross-country. Let's begin with cross-country. (*internal preview*)

See Chapter 13, "Outlining the Speech," for guidance on including transitions in the outline of your speech.

SELF-ASSESSMENT CHECKLIST

USING TRANSITIONS

_____ 1. Do you include enough transitions to adequately guide your listeners through your speech?

_____ 2. Do you use transitions to signal comparisons, cause and effect, sequences in time, contrasting ideas, summaries, and so forth?

_____ 3. Do you use transitions when moving from one main point to the next?

_____ 4. Do you use internal previews and summaries where appropriate?

_____ 5. Do you use transitions between the introduction and the body and between the body and the conclusion of the speech?

Using Transitions to Guide Your Listeners

Transitions direct your listeners from one point to another in your speech, leading them forward along a logical path while reinforcing key ideas along the way. At a bare minimum, plan on using transitions to move between:

- The introduction and the body of the speech
- The main points
- The subpoints, whenever appropriate
- The body of the speech and the conclusion

Introduction

I. Today I'll explore the steps you can take to create a greener campus.

(**Transition:** Let's begin by considering what "going green" actually means.)

Body

I. "Going green" means taking action to promote and maintain a healthy environment.

(**Transition:** So how do you go green?)

A. Get informed — understand what is physically happening to your planet.

(**Transition:** Understanding the issues is only part of going green, however. Perhaps most important, . . .)

B. Recognize that change starts here, on campus, with you.

While transitions help guide your listeners from point to point, they can also do a lot more, including:

1. Introduce main points
2. Illustrate cause and effect
3. Signal explanations and examples
4. Emphasize, repeat, compare, or contrast ideas
5. Summarize and preview information
6. Suggest conclusions from evidence

Following is an excerpt from a working outline on a speech about campuses going green. Note how the student edits himself to ensure that he (1) uses transitions to help listeners follow along and retain his speech points and (2) uses transitions strategically to achieve his goal of persuading the audience.

Student inserts a transition (**rhetorical question**) to introduce a new point.

Student uses this transitional phrase to signal a **cause-effect relationship**.

Student uses a transition to **move to the next point.**

This transitional phrase **introduces additional examples**.

Student inserts an **internal summary** to help listeners retain information and transition to the next main point.

Student inserts an **internal preview** to move to the next main point.

Student inserts a transition to signal a **shift to the conclusion**.

(Transition: Why are environmentalists targeting college campuses?)

I. College campuses generate the waste equivalent of many large towns

(Transition: As a result . . .)

A. Colleges face disposal issues, especially of electronics . . .

B. Administrators face decisions about mounting energy costs . . .

(**Transition:** Following are some ideas to create a greener campus. First . . .)

II. Promote a campus-wide recycling program

(**Transition:** For example . . .)

A. Decrease the availability of bottled water and disposable . . .

B. Insist on recycling bins at all residence halls . . .

C. Encourage computer centers to recycle . . .

(Transition: Recycling is a critical part of going green. Decreasing the consumption of plastic and paper, installing recycling bins, and responsibly disposing of print cartridges will make a huge difference. Another aspect of going green is using sustainable energy . . .)

III. Lobby administrators to investigate solar, wind, and geothermal

A. Make an argument for "eco-dorms" . . .

B. Explore alternative heating . . .

(Transition: So far, we've talked about practical actions we can take to encourage a greener lifestyle on campus, but what about beyond the campus?)

IV. Get involved at the town government level

A. Town-grown committees . . .

B. Speak up and voice your concerns . . .

(Transition: As you can see, we have work to do . . .)

Conclusion

I. If we want our children and our children's children to live to see a healthy earth, we must take action now.

12 Types of Organizational Arrangements

✓ **LearningCurve** can help you review!
Go to LaunchPad: **launchpadworks.com**

Of all of the aspects of speechmaking, the idea of organizational arrangements may seem the most confusing. But the process of organizing speech points into a pattern is easier and more natural than it might seem. Why be concerned about using an organizational arrangement for your speeches? Very simply, an arrangement suited to your particular topic and purpose offers a highly effective way to link points together to maximum effect. As important, a clear structure allows the audience to follow your ideas and mentally link points together as you wish. A good time to select an arrangement is after you've gathered the supporting materials and prepared main points.

Speeches make use of at least a dozen different organizational arrangements. In this chapter we look at six commonly used patterns, five of which are used for all forms of speeches: chronological, spatial, causal (cause-effect), topical, and narrative; and one, the problem–solution pattern, which is typically used for persuasive speeches. In Chapter 26, you will find three additional patterns designed specifically for persuasive speeches: *Monroe's motivated sequence*, *refutation*, and *comparative advantage*.

As you review these organizational designs, bear in mind that there are multiple ways to organize any given topic, as seen in Table 12.1. Each method communicates something different, even if the broad topic is the same. Regardless of the specific pattern, studies confirm that the way you organize your ideas affects your audience's understanding of them, so you'll want to make use of a pattern.[1] Your goal should be to choose one that your audience can easily follow and that will best achieve your speech purpose.

Arranging Speech Points Chronologically

Some speech topics lend themselves well to the arrangement of main points according to their occurrence in time relative to each other. The **chronological pattern of arrangement** (also called the *temporal pattern*) follows the natural sequential order of the main points. To switch points around would make the arrangement appear unnatural and might confuse the audience. Topics that describe a series of events in time (such as events leading to the adoption of a peace treaty) or develop in line with a set pattern of actions or tasks (such as plans for building a model car or procedures for

TABLE 12.1 One Topic (Immigrants to the United States) Organized Six Ways

Organizational Pattern: Chronological. Also called the temporal pattern, main points describe a series of developments in time or a set of actions that occur sequentially.

Thesis Statement: "Historically, immigration in has gone through a series of peaks and troughs, with the first large wave occurring in 1820 and the most recent wave beginning in 1965."

Sample Main Points

I. First large wave occurred between 1790 and 1820, when English, Scottish, Irish, and Germans immigrated to the North and mid-West and Spanish immigrants headed South.

II. Second wave of immigrants, largely German, British, and Irish, arrived between 1820 and 1860.

III. Asian immigrants arrived in Western states between 1880 and 1914 and constituted the third wave.

IV. The fourth wave, beginning in 1965 and continuing up to today, is bringing Asians, Mexicans and South and Central Americans, and Europeans.

Organizational Pattern: Spatial. Main points follow the physical or geographical arrangement of a place, a scene, or an object.

Thesis Statement: "Of nine Border Patrol sectors ranging across 2,000 miles – from western-most San Diego to eastern-most Brownsville – sectors in Texas have become the deadliest for undocumented migrants entering these areas from Mexico."[1]

Sample Main Points:

I. For many years, the highest migrant apprehension rates occurred, from west to east, for San Diego, Tucson, and El Paso sectors, but these sectors have seen steep declines in recent years.

II. Along the middle of the border, two Texas sectors – Del Rio and Laredo – have shown modest increases in migrant apprehensions since 2010.

III. In the same recent period, the Rio Grande Valley Sector, at the east end of the border, has seen a marked increase in migrant apprehensions, leading all other sectors.

Organizational Pattern: Cause-effect. Main points explain or argue a topic in terms of its underlying causes and effects, or effects and causes.

Thesis Statement: "U.S. children whose parents are unauthorized immigrants **[the cause]** are exposed to numerous risks, including lower preschool enrollment, poverty, and reduced socioeconomic progress **[the effects]**."

Sample Main Points:

I. Children ages 3–4 with unauthorized immigrant parents are less likely to be enrolled in preschool.[2]

II. Three-quarters of children with unauthorized parents had incomes below the threshold for free and reduced price school lunches.[3]

III. Children with unauthorized immigrant parents exited poverty at lower rates than the U.S. population generally.[4]

(continued on next page)

TABLE 12.1 *continued*

Organizational Pattern: Topical (categorical). Main points are subtopics or categories of the speech topic.

Thesis Statement: "Public debates about immigration often focus on the role of immigrants in the labor force, admissions policies, and enforcement policies."

Sample Main Points:

I. Immigrants accounted for nearly 17 percent (26.7 million) of the 159.5 million workers in the civilian labor force in 2014.[5]

II. Immigration admissions policies are largely governed by the Immigration and Naturalization Act (INA), which is based on reunification of families, admitting immigrants with skills the U.S. needs, and protecting refugees.[6]

III. The Criminal Alien Program (CAP), administered by U.S. Immigration and Customs Enforcement (ICE), is now the primary channel through which immigration enforcement occurs.[7]

Organizational Pattern: Problem–solution. Main points demonstrate the nature and significance of a problem and justify a proposed solution.

Thesis Statement: "Persons who enter the country legally but overstay their visas account for about 40 percent of undocumented immigrants in the United States.[8] **[the problem]** To help address the issue, we need a biometric (fingerprint) exit system that will identify visa overstayers." **[the solution]**

Sample Main Points:

I. Up to five million persons who entered the U.S. legally remain here with expired visas.[9]

II. The Department of Homeland Security takes fingerprints and photos of entering visitors with visas but has no similar system to track their exits.

III. DHS plans to launch a biometric exit system at high-volume airports in 2018.[10]

Organizational Pattern: Narrative. Main points convey speech ideas through a story, using character, plot, setting, conflict, and resolution.

Thesis Statement: "I came to the United States illegally, at age 3, as the child of undocumented immigrants. I am about to graduate high school and want to go to college, but because I am undocumented I cannot apply for aid. I'm scared I will be deported. Sometimes I feel hopeless about gaining a path to citizenship."

Sample Main Points:

I. I was brought to the United States at 3 years, by parents who were undocumented.

II. I attended U.S. schools through high school.

III. I remain undocumented and cannot apply for college aid.

admitting patients to a hospital) naturally call out to be organized according to a chronological pattern of arrangement. A speech describing the development of the World Wide Web, for example, immediately suggests a chronological, or time-ordered, sequence of main points.

THESIS STATEMENT: The Internet evolved from a small network designed for military and academic scientists into a vast array of networks used by billions of people around the globe.

I. The Internet was first conceived in 1962 as the ARPANET to promote the sharing of research among scientists in the United States.

II. In the 1980s a team created TCP/IP, a language that could link networks, and the Internet as we know it was born.

III. At the end of the cold war, the ARPANET was decommissioned, and the World Wide Web constituted the bulk of Internet traffic.[2]

In addition to topics that involve time lines, the chronological arrangement is appropriate for any topic that involves a series of sequential steps. A speaker might describe the steps in a research project on fruit flies, for example, or explain the steps in a recipe.

Arranging Speech Points Using a Spatial Pattern

When describing the physical arrangement of a place, a scene, or an object, logic suggests that the main points be arranged in order of their physical proximity or direction relative to each other. This calls for the **spatial pattern of arrangement**. For example, you can select a spatial arrangement when your speech provides the audience with a "tour" of a particular place.

THESIS STATEMENT: El Morro National Monument in New Mexico is captivating for its variety of natural and historical landmarks.

I. Visitors first encounter an abundant variety of plant life native to the high-country desert.

II. Soon visitors come upon an age-old watering hole that has receded beneath the 200-foot cliffs.

III. Beyond are the famous cliff carvings made by hundreds of travelers over several centuries of exploration in the Southwest.

IV. At the farthest reaches of the magnificent park are the ancient ruins of a pueblo dwelling secured high atop "the Rock."

In a speech describing a geothermal heating and cooling company's market growth across regions of the country, a speaker might use the spatial arrangement as follows.

THESIS STATEMENT: Sales of geothermal systems have grown in every region of the country.

I. Sales are strongest in the Eastern Zone.

II. Sales are growing at a rate of 10 percent quarterly in the Central Zone.

III. Sales are up slightly in the Mountain Zone.

IV. Sales in the Western Zone are lagging behind the other regions.

Arranging Speech Points Using a Causal (Cause-Effect) Pattern

Some speech topics represent cause-effect relationships. Examples include (1) events leading to higher interest rates, (2) reasons students drop out of college, and (3) causes of domestic abuse. In speeches on topics such as these, the speaker relates something known to be a "cause" to its "effects." The main points in a **causal (cause-effect) pattern of arrangement** usually take the following form.

I. Cause

II. Effect

Sometimes a topic can be discussed in terms of multiple causes for a single effect, or a single cause for multiple effects.

Multiple Causes for a Single Effect (Reasons Students Drop Out of College)

I. Cause 1 (lack of funds)

II. Cause 2 (unsatisfactory social life)

III. Cause 3 (unsatisfactory academic performance)

IV. Effect (drop out of college)

Single Cause for Multiple Effects (Reasons Students Drop Out of College)

I. Cause (lack of funds)

II. Effect 1 (lowered earnings)

III. Effect 2 (decreased job satisfaction)

IV. Effect 3 (increased stress level)

Some topics are best understood by presenting listeners with the effect(s) before the cause(s). In a speech on health care costs, a student speaker arranges his main points as follows:

THESIS STATEMENT: In response to rising health care costs, large employers are shifting part of the expense to workers.

MAIN POINTS: I. (Effect) Workers are now seeing higher co-pays and deductibles.

II. (Effect) Raising the amount employees must contribute has restricted employer costs to just 5 percent this year.

III. (Cause) The Affordable Care Act mandates that large employers offer more of their workers health care plans.

IV. (Cause) Rising health care costs have led to more expensive plans at all levels of coverage.

Arranging Speech Points Using a Problem–Solution Pattern

The **problem–solution pattern of arrangement** organizes main points both to demonstrate the nature and significance of a problem and to provide justification for a proposed solution. Typically used in persuasive speeches, the problem–solution pattern can be arranged as simply as two main points.

I. Problem (define what it is)

II. Solution (offer a way to overcome the problem)

But many problem–solution speeches require more than two points to adequately explain the problem and to substantiate the recommended solution.

I. The nature of the problem (identify its causes, incidence, etc.)

II. Effects of the problem (explain why it's a problem, for whom, etc.)

III. Unsatisfactory solutions (discuss those that have not worked)

IV. Proposed solution (explain why it's expected to work)

Following is a partial outline of a persuasive speech about cyber-bullying arranged in a problem–solution format.

THESIS STATEMENT: To combat cyber-bullying, we need to educate the public about it, report it when it happens, and punish the offenders.

MAIN POINT: I. Nature of cyber-bullying

- A. Types of activities involved
  1. Name-calling, insults
  2. Circulation of embarrassing pictures
  3. Sharing of private information
  4. Threats
- B. Incidence of bullying
- C. Profile of offenders

MAIN POINT: II. Effects of cyber-bullying on victims

A. Acting out in school

B. Feeling unsafe in school

C. Skipping school

D. Experiencing depression

MAIN POINT: III. Unsuccessful attempts at solving cyber-bullying

A. Let offenders and victims work it out on their own

B. Ignore problem, assuming it will go away

MAIN POINT: IV. Ways to solve cyber-bullying

A. Educate in schools

B. Report incidences to authorities

C. Suspend or expel offenders

For more on using the problem–solution pattern to organize persuasive speeches, see Chapter 26.

Arranging Speech Points Topically

When each of the main points is a subtopic or category of the speech topic, try the **topical pattern of arrangement** (also called the **categorical pattern**). Consider an informative speech about choosing Chicago as a place to establish a career. You plan to emphasize three reasons for choosing Chicago: the strong economic climate of the city, its cultural variety, and its accessible public transportation. Since these three points are of relatively equal importance, they can be arranged in any order without negatively affecting one another. For example:

THESIS STATEMENT: Chicago is an excellent place to establish a career.

I. Accessible transportation

II. Cultural variety

III. Multiple industries

This is not to say that, when using a topical arrangement, you should arrange the main points without careful consideration. Any number of considerations can factor into your ordering of points, not the least of which should be the audience's most immediate needs and interests. You may decide to arrange the points in ascending or descending order according to their relative importance, complexity, or timeliness. Perhaps you have determined that listeners' main concern is the city's multiple industries, followed by an interest in its cultural variety and accessible transportation. You may then decide to arrange the points in the order of the audience's most immediate needs and interests:

I. Multiple industries

II. Cultural variety

III. Accessible transportation

Topical arrangements give you the greatest freedom to structure main points according to the way you wish to present your topic. You can approach a topic by dividing it into two or more categories, for example, such as benefits and drawbacks. You can lead with the strongest evidence or leave your most compelling points until you near the conclusion. If your topic does not call out for one of the other patterns described in this chapter, be sure to experiment with the topical pattern.

Arranging Speech Points Using a Narrative Pattern

Storytelling is often a natural and effective way to get your message across. In the **narrative pattern of arrangement**, the speech consists of a story or a series of short stories, replete with characters, conflict or complications, and resolution (see pp. 127, Chapter 8 on developing supporting materials).

In practice, a speech built largely upon a story (or series of stories) is likely to incorporate elements of other designs. You might organize the main points of the story in an effect-cause design, in which you first reveal why something happened (such as the collapse of a company) and then describe the events that led up to the event (the causes).

Whatever the structure, simply telling a story is no guarantee of giving a good speech. Any speech should include a clear thesis, a preview, well-organized main points, and effective transitions. For example, in a speech entitled "Tales of the Grandmothers,"[3] Anita Taylor uses the real-life history of her grandmothers to illustrate how women in the United States have always worked, even if they were unpaid. Although the story of her grandmothers dominates the speech, Taylor frequently leaves off and picks up the story's thread in order to orient her listeners and drive home her theme. For example, in addition to explicitly stating her thesis, Taylor pauses to preview main points.

> My grandmothers' stories illustrate the points I want to make. . . .

Taylor also makes frequent use of transitions, including internal previews, summaries, and simple signposts, to help her listeners stay on track.

> But, let's go on with Luna's story.

Taylor also pauses in her story to signal the conclusion.

> So here we are today. . . . And finally . . .

CHECKLIST

EVALUATING ORGANIZATIONAL PATTERNS

_____ 1. Does the arrangement move the speech along in a logical and convincing fashion?

_____ 2. Do my ideas flow naturally from one point to another, leading to a satisfying conclusion?

_____ 3. Does the organizational pattern lend my speech momentum?

_____ 4. Does the organizational plan convey the information listeners expect or need in a way that they will be able to grasp?

Subpoints Need Not Match the Pattern of Main Points

Once you select an organizational arrangement, you can proceed to flesh out the main points with subordinate ideas, or subpoints. The pattern of organization you select for your subpoints can differ from the pattern you select for your

A CULTURAL PERSPECTIVE

Organizational Patterns and Diverse Audiences

charles taylor/Shutterstock

Studies confirm that the way you organize your ideas affects your audience's understanding of them.[1] Another factor that may affect how we organize relationships among ideas is culture.[2] Are certain organizational formats better suited to certain cultures? Consider the chronological arrangement format. It assumes a largely North American and Western European orientation to time, because these cultures generally view time as a linear (or chronological) progression in which one event follows another along a continuum, with events strictly segmented. In contrast, some Asian, African, and Latin American cultures view time more fluidly, with events occurring simultaneously or cyclically.[3] When a speaker uses a chronological arrangement of the typical linear fashion, audience members from cultures with different time orientations may have difficulty making the connections among the main points. For these audiences, an alternative arrangement, such as the narrative, may be a more appropriate form in which to express speech ideas.

1. Raymond G. Smith, "Effects of Speech Organization upon Attitudes of College Students," *Speech Monographs* 18 (1951): 547–49; and Ernest Thompson, "An Experimental Investigation of the Relative Effectiveness of Organizational Structure in Oral Communication," *Southern Speech Journal* 26 (1960): 59–69.
2. Devorah A. Lieberman, *Public Speaking in the Multicultural Environment*, 2nd ed. (Englewood Cliffs, NJ: Prentice Hall, 1997).
3. Edward T. Hall, *The Dance of Life: Other Dimensions of Time* (New York: Doubleday, 1983); and Judee K. Burgoon, David B. Buller, and W. Gill Woodall, *Nonverbal Communication: The Unspoken Dialogue* (New York: Harper & Row, 1989).

main points. *Do keep your main points in one pattern—this will be the predominant pattern for the speech,* but feel free to use other patterns for subpoints when it makes sense to do so. For instance, for a speech about the history of tattooing in the United States, you might choose a *chronological pattern* to organize the main points but use a *cause-effect arrangement* for some of your subpoints about why tattooing is on the rise today. (See the following Checklist for descriptions of patterns.) Organization, whether of main points or subpoints, should be driven by what's most effective for the particular rhetorical situation.

CHECKLIST

CHOOSING AN ORGANIZATIONAL PATTERN

Does your speech . . .

- ✓ Describe a series of developments in time or a set of actions that occur sequentially? Use the *chronological pattern of arrangement.*
- ✓ Describe or explain the physical arrangement of a place, a scene, or an object? Use the *spatial pattern of arrangement.*
- ✓ Explain or demonstrate a topic in terms of its underlying causes and effects? Use the *causal (cause-effect) pattern of arrangement.*
- ✓ Stress natural divisions in a topic, in which points can be moved to emphasize audience needs and interests? Use a *topical pattern of arrangement.*
- ✓ Demonstrate the nature and significance of a problem and justify a proposed solution? Use the *problem-solution pattern of arrangement.*
- ✓ Convey ideas through a story, using character, plot, conflict or complications, and resolution? Use a *narrative pattern of arrangement*, perhaps in combination with another pattern.

13 Outlining the Speech

LearningCurve can help you review!
Go to LaunchPad: **launchpadworks.com**

Outlines are enormously helpful in putting together a speech, providing a framework for your research and a blueprint for your presentation. In an **outline** you separate the main and supporting points—the major speech claims and the evidence to support them—into larger and smaller divisions and subdivisions. Plotting ideas into hierarchical fashion based on their relative importance to one another and using indentation to visually represent this hierarchy will allow you to examine the underlying logic of the speech and the relationship of ideas to one another.[1]

Outlines rely on *coordination* and *subordination*. **Coordination** refers to assigning points of equal significance or weight the same level of numbering (e.g., *I*, *II*, *III*, *A*, *B*, *C*, *1*, *2*, *3*, and so on). **Subordination** is the arrangement of points in order of their significance to one another, descending from general to specific or abstract to concrete. (For a review of the principles and the mechanics of outlining, see Chapter 11.)

Plan on Creating Two Outlines

As you develop a speech, plan on creating two outlines: a working outline (also called a *preparation* or *rough* outline) and a speaking, or delivery, outline. The purpose of the **working outline** is to organize and firm up main points, and, using the research you've gathered, develop supporting points to substantiate them. Completed, the working outline should contain your entire speech, organized and supported to your satisfaction.

The **speaking outline** is the one you will use when you are practicing and actually presenting the speech. Speaking outlines contain your ideas in condensed form and are much briefer than working outlines. Figure 13.1 provides an overview of the steps involved in outlining a speech.

Before taking a closer look at constructing the working outline, consider the three types of formats speakers use to outline speeches.

Use Sentences, Phrases, or Key Words

Speeches can be outlined in sentences, phrases, or key words. Working outlines typically contain full or partial sentences, reflecting much of the text of the speech; speaking outlines use key words or short phrases.

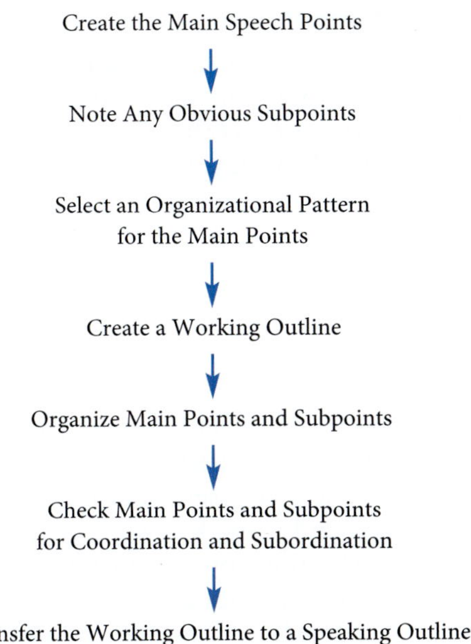

FIGURE 13.1 Steps in Organizing and Outlining the Speech

The Sentence Outline Format

In the **sentence outline** format, each main and supporting point is stated in sentence form as a declarative sentence (e.g., one that makes an assertion about something). These sentences are stated in much the same way the speaker wants to express the idea during delivery. The following is an excerpt in sentence format from a speech by Mark B. McClellan on keeping prescription drugs safe.[2]

I. The prescription drug supply is under attack from a variety of increasingly sophisticated threats.
    A. Technologies for counterfeiting—ranging from pill molding to dyes—have improved across the board.
    B. Inadequately regulated Internet sites have become major portals for unsafe and illegal drugs.

The Phrase Outline Format

A **phrase outline** uses partial construction of the sentence form of each point. Phrase outlines encourage you to become so familiar with the speech that a glance at a few words is enough to remind you of exactly what to say. McClellan's sentence outline would appear as follows in phrase form:

I. Drug supply under attack
    A. Counterfeiting technologies more sophisticated
    B. Unregulated Internet sites

The Key-Word Outline Format

The **key-word outline** uses the smallest possible units of understanding to outline the main and supporting points. Keyword outlines encourage you to become familiar enough with your speech points that a glance at a few words is enough to remind you of exactly what you want to say.

I. Threats
   A. Counterfeiting
   B. Internet

Use a Key-Word Outline for Optimal Eye Contact

The type of outline you select will affect how well you deliver the speech. The less you rely on reading an outline, the more eye contact you can have with audience members. Eye contact is an essential aspect of a successful speech. For this reason, experts recommend using key-word or phrase outlines over sentence outlines for delivery, with the more succinct key-word outline often being the preferred format. Key-word outlines permit not only the greatest degree of eye contact but also greater freedom of movement and better control of your thoughts and actions than either sentence or phrase outlines. With adequate practice, the key words will jog your memory so that the delivery of your ideas becomes more natural.

If there are points in your speech where you want to note exact quotations or precisely state complicated facts or figures, you can write those out in full sentences within the key-word outline. Sentences may help under the following conditions:

1. When the issue is highly controversial or emotion-laden for listeners and precise wording is needed to make the point as clear as possible
2. When the material is highly technical and exact sentence structure is critical to an accurate representation of the material
3. When a good deal of material relies on quotations and facts from another source that must be conveyed precisely as worded

Even with the inclusion of an occasional sentence, if at any time during the speech you experience stage fright or a lapse in memory, a key-word outline may not be of much help. This is why preparation is essential when using one. You must be confident in knowing the topic and the speech arrangement well enough to deliver the speech extemporaneously. An extemporaneous speech is carefully planned and practiced in advance and then delivered from a key-word or phrase outline (see Chapter 17 on methods of delivery). (Note that outlining requirements differ among instructors. Be sure to understand your instructor's specific outlining and formatting requirements before you begin outlining your speech.)

Create a Working Outline First

Unless otherwise instructed, begin drafting your speech with a working outline before transferring your ideas to a speaking outline containing key words or shortened phrases, editing or rearranging as necessary as you work through the mass of information you've collected. Use the working outline to create a well-supported document containing all of your claims and research.

Separate the Introduction and Conclusion from the Body

Regardless of the type of outline you select, prepare the body of the speech *before* the introduction, keeping the introduction (and the conclusion) *separate from* the main points (see sample outlines in this chapter). Since introductions serve as a preview of the main points, you will first need to finalize them in the body. Introductions must also gain the audience's attention, introduce the topic and thesis, and establish the speaker's credibility (see Chapter 14 on developing the introduction). To ensure that you address these elements in your outlines, use such labels as *Attention Getter, Thesis, Credibility Statement,* and *Preview Statement* (see sample speech outlines on p. 201). (Your instructor may assign another format.)

Similarly, in the conclusion you can indicate where you signal the close of the speech, summarize main points, reiterate the thesis and purpose, and leave the audience with something to think about or offer a call to action—or, again, assign it a labeling system as directed by your instructor (see Chapter 15 on developing the conclusion).

Indicate Your Sources

As you work on the outline, clearly indicate both to the audience and to yourself where speech points require source credit and decide on a system to keep track of these sources. Either insert a footnote or otherwise indicate enough information in parentheses to be able to retrieve the full citation later (see sample outlines in this chapter for this latter method). Instructors may ask for a "Works Cited" **bibliography** (a list of sources), in which you list sources alphabetically; the sample outline below includes such a bibliography. For guidelines on what to include in a source note, see the *From Source to Speech* guides in Chapter 9 and online. See Appendices B, C, and G–I for individual citation styles.

Create a Title

As the last step, assign the speech a title, one that informs the audience of its subject in a way that invites them to listen to or read it. Thoughtfully crafted titles communicate the essence of a speech. At times, you might even refer to the title during your speech as a means of previewing or emphasizing your perspective on the topic.

CHECKLIST

STEPS IN CREATING A WORKING OUTLINE

_____ 1. On separate lines, label and write out your topic, general purpose, specific speech purpose, and thesis.

_____ 2. Establish your main points (optimally two to five).

_____ 3. Flesh out supporting points.

_____ 4. Check for correct subordination and coordination; follow the numbering system shown in Table 11.1 (p. 168).

_____ 5. Label each speech part (i.e., "Introduction," "Body," and "Conclusion").

_____ 6. Label and write out transitions.

_____ 7. Note sources for the bibliography.

_____ 8. Assign the speech a title.

Sample Working Outline

The following working outline is from a speech delivered by public speaking student Zachary Dominique. It includes all the elements of the speech, including transitions and reminders ("delivery cues") to show presentation aids ("SHOW SLIDE"). Next to each mention of a source requiring credit is a note in parentheses (e.g., "**For bibliography**: *ABC of Mountain Biking*"). The speech is organized topically or according to natural subdivisions of a topic.

The History and Sport of Mountain Biking

ZACHARY DOMINIQUE
St. Edwards University

TOPIC: Mountain Biking

SPECIFIC PURPOSE: To inform my listeners about the sport of mountain biking

THESIS STATEMENT: Mountain biking is a relatively new, exciting, and diverse sport.

Introduction

(Attention getter:)

I. Imagine that you're on a bike, plunging down a steep, rock-strewn mountain, yet fully in control.

II. Adrenaline courses through your body as you hurtle through the air, touch down on glistening pebbled streams and tangled grasses, and rocket upward again.

III. You should be scared, but you're not; in fact, you're having the time of your life.

IV. Like we say, Nirvana.

V. How many of you like to bike-ride to campus, bike for fitness, or cycle just for fun?

VI. You might own a bike with a lightweight frame and thin wheels, and use it to log some serious mileage—or possibly a comfort bike, with a nice soft seat and solid tires.

(Credibility Statement:)

VII. Good morning, folks. My name is Zachary Dominique, and I'm a mountain biker.

VIII. I've been racing since I was eight years old and won state champion three years ago, so this topic is close to my heart.

(Preview:)

IX. Today, I'm going to take you on a tour of the exciting sport of mountain biking: I'll be your engine-your driver-in mountain bike-speak.

X. Our ride begins with a brief overview of mountain biking; then we'll do a hopturn—a turn in reverse—to learn about the sport's colorful history.

XI. Pedalling ahead in this beautiful autumn air, we'll chat about the various differences in design and function between mountain bikes and road bikes.

XII. We'll conclude our tour at a local bike shop, where you can compare downhill, trail, and cross-country mountain bikes.

XIII. These are the three main types of mountain bikes, designed for the three major types of mountain biking.

XIV. I hope by then that you'll catch a little bit of mountain biking fever and see why I find it such an exciting, intense, and physically challenging sport.

TRANSITION: Mountain biking is a sport that can be extreme, recreational, or somewhere in between. But no matter what kind of rider you are, it's always a great way to get out in the natural world and get the adrenaline going. To start, let me briefly define mountain biking.

Body

I. The website ABC of Mountain Biking offers a good basic definition: "Mountain biking is a form of cycling on off-road or unpaved surfaces such as mountain trails and dirt roads; the biker uses a bicycle with a sturdy frame and fat tires." (**For bibliography**: *ABC of Mountain Biking*)

A. The idea behind mountain biking is to go where other bikes won't take you.
   1. Mountain bikers ride on backcountry roads and on single-track trails winding through fields or forests.
   2. They climb up steep, rock-strewn hills and race down over them.
   3. The focus is on self-reliance, because these bikers often venture miles from help.

B. According to the National Bicycle Dealers Association website, in 2016 mountain bikes accounted for 25 percent of all bikes sold in the United States.
   1. If you factor in sales of the comfort bike, which is actually a mountain bike modified for purely recreational riders, sales jump to nearly 38 percent of all bikes sold.
   2. Some 50 million Americans love riding their mountain bikes, according to data collected by the New England Mountain Bike Association. (**For bibliography**: *National Bicycle Dealers Assn*)

TRANSITION: So you see that mountain biking is popular with a lot of people. But the sport itself is fairly new.

II. The history of mountain biking is less than 50 years old, and its founders are still around.
   A. The man in this picture is Gary Fisher, one of the founders of mountain biking. (SHOW GF SLIDE 1)
   B. According to *The Original Mountain Bike Book*, written in 1998 by pioneering mountain bikers Rob van der Plas and Charles Kelly, they, along with Fisher, Joe Breeze, and other members of the founding posse from the Marin County, California, area, were instrumental in founding the modern sport of mountain biking in the early 1970s. (**For bibliography**: *Original MB Book*)
   C. Mountain bikes—called MTBs or ATBs (for all-terrain bikes)—didn't exist then as we now know them, so as you can see, in this picture of Gary Fisher, he's riding a modified one-speed Schwinn cruiser. (SHOW SCHWINN SLIDE 2)
      1. Cruisers, or "ballooners," aren't made to go off road at all.
      2. Nothing equips them to navigate trails, and their brakes aren't remotely equipped to handle stops on steep descents.
      3. But this is the type of bike Fisher and others started out with.
   D. By the mid-1970s, growing numbers of bikers in California got into using modified cruisers to race downhill on rocky trails.
      1. They'd meet at the bottom of Mount Tamalpais, in Corte Madera, California. (SHOW MT TAM SLIDE 3)

2. They'd walk their bikes a mile or two up its steep slopes, and hurl on down.

E. As even more people got involved, Charles Kelly and others organized the famed Repack Downhill Race on Mt. Tam.

1. Held from 1976 to 1979, the Repack race became a magnet for enthusiasts and put the sport on the map, according to *The Original Mountain Bike Book.*

TRANSITION: The reason why the race was called "Repack" is a story in itself.

2. The trail in the Repack race plummeted 1,300 feet in less than 2 miles, according to Joe Breeze in an article posted on the Mountain Biking Hall of Fame website. (**For bibliography**: MTB Hall of Fame)

a. Such a steep drop meant constant braking, which in turn required riders to replace, or "repack," their bikes' grease after nearly each run.

b. As Breeze recounts in his own words: "The bikes' antiquated hub coaster brake would get so hot that the grease would vaporize, and after a run or two, the hub had to be repacked with new grease." (SHOW BIKE SLIDE 4)

TRANSITION: As you might imagine, these early enthusiasts eventually tired of the routine.

F. The bikers had tinkered with their bikes from the start, adding gearing, drum brakes, and suspension systems.

G. In 1979, Joe Breeze designed a new frame—called the "Breezer"—which became the first actual mountain bike.

H. By 1982, as van der Plas and Kelly write in *The Original Mountain Bike Book*, standardized production of mountain bikes finally took off.

TRANSITION: Now that you've learned a bit of the history of mountain biking, let's look at what today's mountain bike can do. To make things clearer, I'll compare them to road bikes. Road bikes are the class of bikes that cyclists who compete in the Tour de France use.

III. Mountain bikes and road bikes are built for different purposes. (SHOW MB & RB SLIDE 5)

A. Mountain bikes are built to tackle rough ground, while road bikes are designed to ride fast on paved, smooth surfaces.

1. To accomplish their task, mountain bikes feature wide tires with tough tread.

2. In contrast, road bike tires are ultrathin and their frames extremely lightweight.

a. If you take a road bike off road, chances are you'll destroy it.

b. Without the knobby tread and thickness found on mountain bike tires, road bike tires can't grip onto the rocks and other obstacles that cover off-road courses.

B. The handlebars on the bikes also differ.

1. Mountain bikes feature flat handlebars; these keep us in an upright stance, so that we don't flip over when we hit something.

2. The drop handlebars on road bikes require the cyclist to lean far forward; this position suits road cycling, which prizes speed.

C. The gears and suspension systems also differentiate mountain bikes from road bikes.

1. Mountain bikes use lower gears than road bikes and are more widely spaced, giving them more control to ride difficult terrain.

2. As for suspension, road bikes generally don't have any kind of suspension system that can absorb power.

a. That is, they don't have shock absorbers because they're not supposed to hit anything.

b. Imagine riding over rocks and roots without shocks; it wouldn't be pretty.

3. Many mountain bikes have at least a great front shock-absorbing suspension system.

a. Some have rear-suspension systems.

b. Some bikes have dual systems.

TRANSITION: I hope by now you have a sense of the mountain bike design. But there are finer distinctions to draw.

IV. There are actually three different types of mountain bikes, designed to accommodate the three major kinds of mountain biking—downhill, trails, and cross-country.

TRANSITION: Let's start with downhill. (SHOW DH SLIDE 6)

A. Downhill bikes have the fewest gears of the three types of mountain bikes and weigh the most.

1. That's because downhill biking is a daredevil sport—these bikers are crazy!

2. They slide down hills at insane speeds, and they go off jumps.

3. They have lots of what they call *gravity checks*, or falls.

B. As described on the website Trails.com, downhill racers catch a shuttle going up the mountain, then speed downhill while chewing up obstacles.

C. Think of downhill racing as skiing with a bike.

TRANSITION: Now let's swing by trails biking. (SHOW TB SLIDE 7)

D. Trails bikes look quite different than either downhill or cross-country bikes.
   1. They have very small wheels, measuring either 20, 24, or 26 inches, and smaller frames.
   2. These differences in design help trail bikers do what they do best: jump over obstacles—cars, rocks, and large logs.

E. The trail biker's goal is to not put a foot down on the ground.

F. Trail bike racing is one of the few types of biking that's done by time, not all at a mass start.

TRANSITION: The third major type of mountain biking, cross-country, or XC cycling, is my sport. (SHOW XC SLIDE 8)

G. Cross-country biking is also the most common type of mountain biking—and the one sponsored by the Olympics.
   1. That's right. In 1996, mountain biking became an Olympic sport.
   2. This was just two decades after its inception.

H. With cross-country, you get the best of all worlds, at least in my humble opinion.
   1. The courses are creative, incorporating hills and valleys and rough to not-so-rough terrain.
   2. If done competitively, cross-country biking is like competing in a marathon.
   3. Done recreationally, it offers you the chance to see the great outdoors while getting, or staying, in great shape.

I. Cross-country bikes come in two forms.
   1. XC bikes are very lightweight, with either full or partial suspension.
   2. The Trails/Marathon XC hybrid bikes are a bit heavier, with full suspension; XC bikes are designed for seriously long rides.

TRANSITION: Well, it has been quite a tour, folks. ***(Signals close of speech)***

Conclusion

I. Our course began with an overview of mountain biking and a hopturn into a brief history of the sport.

II. We also learned about the differences between mountain bikes and road bikes, and the three major categories of mountain bikes. ***(Summarizes main points)***

III. To me, mountain biking, and especially cross-country, is the perfect sport—fulfilling physical, spiritual, and social needs.

IV. It's a great sport to take up recreationally. ***(Leaves audience with something to think about)***

V. And if you decide to mountain bike competitively, just remember: ride fast, drive hard, and leave your blood on every trail. ***(Memorable close)***

Prepare a Speaking Outline for Delivery

Using the same numbering system as the working outline, condense long phrases or sentences from your working outline into key words or phrases, using just enough words to jog your memory. Note that even though the delivery outline should contain key words or phrases almost exclusively, when exact wording is critical to an accurate representation of your speech material (as in conveying quotations verbatim or when the issue is highly controversial or emotional and precise wording is needed to make the point as clear as possible), you may want to write it out in full sentences.

Indicate Delivery Cues

Include in the speaking outline any **delivery cues** that will be part of the speech (see Table 13.1). To ensure visibility, capitalize the cues, place them in parentheses, and/or highlight them.

Place the outline on large (at least 4 × 6-inch) notecards or 8.5 × 11-inch sheets of paper, or in a speaker's notes software program or app such as Evernote. Print large enough, or use large-enough fonts, so that you can see the words at a glance.

Practice the Speech

The key to the successful delivery of any speech is practice. The more you rehearse your speech, the more comfortable you will become when you speak. For more information on practicing the speech, see Chapter 19.

Sample Speaking Outline

The History and Sport of Mountain Biking

ZACHARY DOMINIQUE
St. Edwards University

Introduction

(Attention getter:)

I. Imagine on bike, plunging rock-strewn, yet control.

II. Adrenaline, hurtle, touch downstream, rocket.

III. Be scared, but not—time of life.

TABLE 13.1 Common Delivery Cues in a Speaking Outline

Delivery Cue	Example
Transitions	(TRANSITION)
Timing	(PAUSE) (SLOW DOWN)
Speaking Rate/Volume	(SLOWLY) (LOUDER)
Presentation Aids	(SHOW MODEL) (SLIDE 3)
Source	(ATLANTA CONSTITUTION, August 2, 2014)
Statistic	(2014, boys to girls = 94,232; U.S. Department of Health and Human Services)
Quotation	Eubie Blake, 100: "If I'd known I was gonna live this long, I'd have taken better care of myself."
Difficult-to-Pronounce-or -Remember Names or Words	Eowyn (A-OH-win)

CHECKLIST

TIPS ON USING NOTECARDS OR SHEETS OF PAPER

_____ 1. Leave some blank space at the margins to find your place as you glance at the cards.

_____ 2. Number the notecards or sheets so that you can follow them with ease.

_____ 3. Instead of turning the cards or sheets, slide them under one another.

_____ 4. Do not staple notes or sheets together.

_____ 5. If you use a lectern, place the notes or sheets near eye level.

_____ 6. Do not use the cards or sheets in hand gestures, as they become distracting pointers or flags.

IV. Nirvana.

V. How many bike, fitness, fun?

VI. Might own lightweight, thin wheels, serious mileage—or comfort, soft seat, solid tires.

(Credibility Statement:)

VII. Morning, Zachary, MTBer

VIII. Eight; champion, heart.

(Preview:)

IX. Today, tour, exciting sport of . . . engine, driver, MTB-speak.

X. Ride begins brief overview; do hopturn—colorful history.

XI. Pedalling ahead autumn, chat differences between mountain, road.

XII. Conclude shop, compare MTBs.

XIII. Three types bikes, designed for three . . .

XIV. Hope catch fever, exciting, intense, and physically.

TRANSITION: MTB sport extreme . . . in-between. But no matter, always great way natural world, adrenaline. Start, define.

Body

I. *ABC/MB def:* "MTB is a form of cycling on off-road or unpaved surfaces such as mountain trails and dirt roads; the biker uses a bicycle with a sturdy frame and fat tires."

  A. The idea—go where others.

    1. MTBs ride backcountry, single-track winding fields, forests.
    2. Climb steep, rock-strewn, race down.
    3. Self-reliance, miles from help.

  B. National Bicycle Dealers Assoc., 2016 MTBs 25 percent sold.

    1. Factor comfort, actually MTB modified recreational, sales 38%.
    2. 50 million love riding, data gathered NE MTB Assn.

TRANSITION: So MTB popular people. But fairly new.

II. History MTB less 50, founders.

  A. Gary Fisher, founders MTB. (SHOW GF SLIDE 1).

  B. *Original Mountain Bike Book*, written 1998 by van der Plas, Kelly; they, along with Fisher, Breeze, other members posse Marin, instrumental founding modern sport early 1970s.

  C. MTBs or ATBs (terrain)—didn't exist, so picture Fisher, modified Schwinn cruiser. (SHOW SCHWINN SLIDE 2)

    1. Cruisers, "ballooners," off-road.
    2. Nothing equips navigate, brakes equipped stops descents.
    3. But bike Fisher, others started.

  D. Mid-1970s, growing numbers using modified race downhill.

    1. Meet bottom Tamalpais, CA. (SHOW MT TAM SLIDE 3)
    2. Walk bikes mile up steep, hurl.

  E. Even involved, Kelly, others organized Repack.

    1. 1976–1979, magnet enthusiasts, on map, *Original MTB*.

TRANSITION: Reason called "Repack" story itself.

2. Trail plummeted 1,300 feet 2 miles, according Breeze article posted MTB Fame website.
    a. Such drop constant braking, required riders replace, "repack," grease each run.
    b. Breeze recounts: "The bikes' antiquated hub coaster brake would get so hot that the grease would vaporize, and after a run or two, the hub had to be repacked with new grease." (SHOW BIKE SLIDE 4)

TRANSITION: Might imagine, early enthusiasts tired.

F. Bikers tinkered, gearing, drum, suspension.

G. 1979, Breeze new frame—"Breezer"—first actual MTB.

H. 1982, as van der Plas, Kelly write in *Original MTB*, standardized took off.

TRANSITION: Now learned history, let's look today's can do. Clearer, compare road. Class cyclists Tour de France use.

III. MTB, road built different purposes. (SHOW MB & RB SLIDE 5)

A. MTB tackle rough, road designed fast, paved, smooth.
1. Accomplish task, wide tire, tough tread.
2. In contrast, road ultrathin, frames lightweight.
    a. Take off road, destroy.
    b. Without knobby tread, thickness MTB tires, road can't grip rocks, obstacles.

B. Handlebars differ.
1. MTB flat; upright stance, don't flip.
2. Drop handlebars require lean forward; suits road cycling, prizes speed.

C. Gears, suspension also differentiate.
1. MTB lower gears, widely spaced—more control difficult terrain.
2. As for suspension, road don't, absorb power.
    a. That is, don't have shock, not supposed to.
    b. Imagine without shocks; wouldn't pretty.
3. Many MTBs at least a great front.
    a. Some rear.
    b. Some dual.

TRANSITION: Hope sense MTB design. But finer distinctions to draw.

IV. Actually three types MTB, accommodate three kinds.

TRANSITION: Let's start with downhill. (SHOW DH SLIDE 6)

A. Downhill fewest gears, weigh most.
   1. Because downhill daredevil—crazy!
   2. Slide insane, off jumps.
   3. Lots *gravity checks*.
B. Trails.com, downhill racers catch shuttle going up, speed downhill chewing up.
C. Think racing skiing bike.

TRANSITION: Now let's swing by trails biking. (SHOW TB SLIDE 7)

D. Trails bikes look different than either.
   1. Small wheels, 20, 24, or 260, smaller frames.
   2. Differences design help trail do best—jump obstacles—cars, rocks, large logs.
E. Trail goal not foot on ground.
F. Trail racing few types done by time, not mass.

TRANSITION: Third major type MTB, cross-country, or XC. (SHOW XC SLIDE 8)

G. Cross-country most common—Olympics.
   1. That's right. In 1996 . . .
   2. Just two decades inception.
H. With XC, best all worlds, humble.
   1. Courses creative, incorporating hills, valleys, rough, not-so-.
   2. Competitively, XC like marathon.
   3. Recreationally, chance see outdoors, shape.
I. XC two forms.
   1. Lightweight, full or partial.
   2. Trails/Marathon XC hybrids heavier, full suspension; designed seriously long.

TRANSITION: Quite tour. (***Signals close of speech***)

Conclusion

I. Course began overview, hopturn history sport.

II. Also learned differences mountain, road, three major categories of MTB, three types MTB accommodate fans. ***(Summarizes main points)***

III. To me, MTB, especially XC, perfect—fulfilling physical, spiritual, social needs.

IV. Great take up recreationally. ***(Leaves audience with something to think about)***

IV. Decide bike competitively, remember: ride fast, drive hard, leave blood. ***(Memorable close)***

Full-Text Speech

Following is the full text of the speech outlined in this chapter. Zachary's assignment was to deliver a ten-minute informative speech citing at least four authoritative sources, incorporating at least two presentation aids, and including a list of references in either APA or MLA style.[3]

CHECKLIST

STEPS IN CREATING A SPEAKING OUTLINE

_____ 1. Create the outline on sheets of paper or large notecards.

_____ 2. Write large and legibly using at least a 14-point font or easy-to-read ink and large letters.

_____ 3. For each main and subpoint, choose a key word or phrase that will jog your memory accurately.

_____ 4. Include delivery cues.

_____ 5. Write out full quotations or other critical information.

_____ 6. Using the speaking outline, practice the speech at least five times.

SAMPLE INFORMATIVE SPEECH

The History and Sport of Mountain Biking

ZACHARY DOMINIQUE
St. Edwards University

Imagine that you're on a bike, plunging down a steep, rock-strewn mountain, yet fully in control. Adrenaline courses through your body as you hurtle through the air, touch down on glistening pebbled streams and tangled grasses, and rocket upward again. You should be scared, but you're not. In fact, you're having the time of your life. Like we say, Nirvana. •

• By asking the audience to visualize racing down a mountain, Zachary effectively captures the audience's attention.

How many of you like to bike? Perhaps you ride to campus, bike for fitness, or cycle just for fun. You might own a bike with a lightweight frame and thin wheels, and use it to log some serious mileage. Or possibly you ride a comfort bike, with a nice soft seat and solid tires.

Good morning, folks. My name is Zachary Dominique, and I'm a mountain biker. I've been racing since I was eight years old and won state champion three years ago, so this topic is close to my heart. •

• Pointing to his lengthy experience with the sport lends Zachary credibility to address the topic.

Today, I'm going to take you on a tour of this exciting sport. I'll be your "engine"—your driver—in mountain bike-speak. Our ride begins with a brief overview of mountain biking; then we'll do a hopturn—a turn in reverse—to learn about the sport's colorful history. • Pedalling ahead in this beautiful autumn air, we'll chat about the differences between mountain bikes and road bikes. We'll conclude our tour at a local bike shop, where you can compare downhill, trail, and cross-country mountain bikes. These are the three main types of mountain bikes, designed for the three major types of mountain biking. I hope by then that you'll catch a little bit of mountain biking fever and see why I find it such an exciting, intense, and physically challenging sport.

• Zachary previews the speech using metaphoric language in which the speech becomes a tour with courses.

To start, let me briefly define mountain biking. •

• Zachary transitions into the speech body.

Mountain biking is a sport that can be extreme, recreational, or somewhere in-between. The website *ABC of Mountain Biking* offers a good basic definition: "Mountain biking is a form of cycling on off-road or unpaved surfaces such as mountain trails and dirt roads; the biker uses a bicycle with a sturdy frame and fat tires." •

• Zachary is careful to define his topic for the audience.

The idea behind mountain biking is to go where other bikes won't take you. Mountain bikers ride on backcountry roads and on single-track trails winding through fields or forests. They climb up steep, rock-strewn hills and race down over them. The focus is on self-reliance, because these bikers often venture miles from help.

According to the National Bicycle Dealers Association website, in 2016 mountain bikes accounted for 25 percent of all bikes sold in the United States. If you factor in sales of the comfort bike, which is actually a mountain bike modified for purely recreational riders, sales jump to nearly 38 percent of all bikes sold. Some 50 million Americans love riding their mountain bikes, according to data published by the New England Mountain Bike Association, or NEMBA. • According to NEMBA, that's one and one-third times the population of Canada. And that's one and one-half times the number of golfers in the U.S.

• Zachary uses reputable sources and informs the audience of where the information can be located.

So you see that mountain biking is popular with a lot of people. But the sport itself is fairly new. •

• Zachary uses a transition to signal a change in focus.

The history of mountain biking is less than 50 years old. The man in this picture is Gary Fisher, one of the founders of mountain biking. • According to *The Original Mountain Bike Book*, written in 1998 by pioneering mountain bikers Rob van der Plas and Charles Kelly, they, along with Fisher, Joe Breeze, and other members of the founding posse from the Marin County, California, area, were instrumental in founding the modern sport of mountain biking in the early 1970s.

• To add interest and involvement, Zachary supplements his description with photographs.

Mountain bikes—called MTBs or ATBs (for all terrain bikes)—didn't exist then as we now know them, so as you can see, in this picture • of Gary Fisher, he's riding a modified one-speed Schwinn cruiser. Cruisers, or "ballooners," aren't made to go off road at all. Nothing equips them to navigate trails, and their brakes aren't remotely equipped to handle stops on steep descents. But this is the type of bike Fisher and others started out with.

• Zachary again supplements his verbal description with a visual aid.

By the mid-1970s, growing numbers of bikers in California got into using modified cruisers to race downhill on rocky trails. They'd meet at the bottom of Mount Tamalpais, in Corte Madera, California, walk their bikes a mile or two up its steep slopes, and hurl on down. As even more people got involved, Charles Kelly and others organized the famed Repack Downhill Race on Mt. Tam. Held from 1976 to 1979, the Repack race became a magnet for enthusiasts and put the sport on the map, according to *The Original Mountain Bike Book*.

The reason why the race was called "Repack" is a story in itself.

The trail in the Repack race plummeted 1300 feet in less than 2 miles, according to Joe Breeze in an article posted on the Mountain Biking Hall of Fame website. Such a steep drop meant constant braking, which in turn required riders to replace, or "repack," their bikes' grease after nearly each run. As Breeze recounts in his own words: "The bikes' antiquated hub coaster brake would get so hot that the grease would vaporize, and after a run or two, the hub had to be repacked with new grease."

As you might imagine, these early enthusiasts eventually tired of the routine: The bikers had tinkered with their bikes from the start, adding gearing, drum brakes, and a suspension system. In 1979, Joe Breeze designed a new frame—called the "Breezer"—which became the first actual mountain bike. By 1982, as van der Plas and Kelly write in *The Original Mountain Bike Book*, • standardized production of mountain bikes finally took off.

• Rather than relying solely on Internet sources, a practice that lessens speaker credibility, Zachary cites a key book on the topic, written by two founders of the sport.

Now that you've learned a bit of the history of mountain biking, let's look at what today's mountain bike can do. To make things clearer, I'll compare them to road bikes. Road bikes are the class of bikes that cyclists who compete in the Tour de France use. •

• To help foster understanding, Zachary compares and contrasts the mountain bike with the more familiar road bike.

Mountain bikes and road bikes are built for different purposes. Mountain bikes are built to tackle rough ground, while road bikes are designed to ride fast on paved, smooth surfaces. To accomplish their task, mountain bikes feature wide tires with tough tread. In contrast, road bike tires are ultrathin and their frames extremely lightweight. If you take a road bike off road, chances are you'll destroy it. Without the knobby tread and thickness found on mountain bike tires, road bike tires can't grip onto the rocks or other obstacles that cover off-road courses.

The handlebars on the bikes also differ. Mountain bikes feature flat handlebars; these keep us in an upright stance, so that we don't flip over when we hit something. The drop handlebars on road bikes require the cyclist to lean far forward; this position suits road cycling, which prizes speed.

The gears and suspension systems also differentiate mountain bikes from road bikes.

Mountain bikes use lower gears than road bikes and the gears are more widely spaced. This gives them more control to ride difficult terrain.

As for suspension, road bikes generally don't have any kind of suspension system that can absorb power. That is, they don't have shock absorbers because they're not supposed to hit anything. Imagine riding over rocks and roots without shocks. It wouldn't be pretty. Many mountain bikes have at least a great front shock-absorbing suspension system; some have rear-suspension systems, and some bikes have dual systems. •

• Zachary internally summarizes the speech points he's covered thus far and previews what he'll discuss next. Note his use of biking jargon to draw the audience in.

I hope by now you have a sense of the mountain bike design. But there are finer distinctions to draw. These are actually three different types of mountain bikes, designed to accommodate the three major kinds of mountain biking—downhill, trails, and cross-country.

Let's start with downhill. Downhill bikes have the fewest gears of the three types of mountain bikes and weigh the most. That's because downhill biking is a dare-devil sport—these bikers are crazy! They slide down hills at insane speeds, and they go off jumps. Lots of what they call *gravity checks*, or falls. As described on the website Trails.com, downhill racers catch a shuttle going up the mountain, then speed downhill while chewing up obstacles. Think of downhill racing as skiing with a bike.

Now let's swing by trails biking. •

• In this transition, Zachary extends the metaphor of his speech as a tour.

Trails bikes look quite different than either downhill or cross-country bikes. They have very small wheels, measuring either 20, 24, or 26 inches, and smaller frames. These differences in design help trail bikers do what they do best—jump over obstacles—cars, rocks, and large logs. The trail biker's goal is not to put a foot down on the ground. In trails biking, the course is set right there in front of you. Trail bike racing is one of the few types of biking that's done by time, not all at a mass start.

The third major type of mountain biking, cross-country, or XC cycling, is my sport.

Cross-country biking is also the most common type of mountain biking—and the one sponsored by the Olympics. That's right. In 1996, mountain biking became an Olympic sport—just two decades after its inception.

With cross-country, you get the best of all worlds, at least in my humble opinion. The courses are creative, incorporating hills and valleys and rough to not-so-rough terrain. If done competitively, cross-country biking is like competing in a marathon. Done recreationally, it offers you the chance to see the great outdoors while getting, or staying, in great shape.

Cross-country bikes come in two forms: XC bikes are very lightweight, with either full or partial suspension. The Trails/Marathon XC hybrid bikes are a bit heavier, with full suspension; XC bikes are designed for seriously long rides.

Well, it has been quite a tour, folks. • Our course began with an overview of mountain biking and a hop-turn into a brief history of the sport. We also learned about the differences between mountain bikes and road bikes, the three major categories of mountain biking, and the three types of mountain bikes made to accommodate fans of each type.

• Zachary signals the close of the speech by reiterating his opening analogy in which he compares the speech to a tour.

To me, mountain biking, and especially cross-country, is the perfect sport—fulfilling physical, spiritual, and social needs. It's a great sport to take up recreationally. And if you decide to mountain bike competitively, just remember: ride fast, drive hard, and leave your blood on every trail. •

• Zachary's use of vivid language makes the conclusion memorable and leaves the audience with something to think about.

Works Cited

"Cycling, Mountain Biking," Olympics.org website, accessed August 22, 2016, www.olympic.org/Assets/OSC%20Section/pdf/QR_sports_summer/Sports_Olympiques_VTT_eng.pdf.

"The Economics and Benefits of Mountain Biking," New England Mountain Bike Association, accessed August 22, 2016, www.nemba.org.

"History of Mountain Biking," Marin Museum of Biking website, accessed August 22, 2016, http://mmbhof.org/mtn-bike -hall-of-fame/history.

"Industry Overview, 2013," National Bicycle Dealers Association, accessed August 22, 2016, http://nbda.com/articles/industry-overview-2012-pg34.htm.

National Bicycle Dealers Association. "Industry Overview, 2012." Accessed October 13, 2013. nbda.com/articles/industry-overview-2012-pg34.htm

"Types of Mountain Bikes," Trails.com. accessed August 22, 2016, www.trails.com/types-of-mountain-bikes.html.

Van der Plas, Rob, and Charles Kelly. *The Original Mountain Bike Book*. Minneapolis: Motorbooks, 1998.

"What Is Mountain Biking?" ABC of Mountain Biking website. Accessed November 23, 2010. www.abc-of-mountainbiking.com/mountain-biking-basics/whatis-mountain-biking.asp.

To see Zachary Dominique deliver his speech, go to LaunchPad: **launchpadworks.com**

INTRODUCTIONS, CONCLUSIONS, AND LANGUAGE

Actress and activist America Ferrera speaks at an immigration reform rally. In 2013, she addressed graduates at the University of Delaware commencement and spoke about the importance of education. Her speaking style exemplifies an effective use of oral style marked by vivid language and compelling personal stories. Kris Connor/Getty Images

INTRODUCTIONS, CONCLUSIONS, AND LANGUAGE

SPEAKER'S PREVIEW

LearningCurve can help you review.
Go to LaunchPad: **launchpadworks.com**

INTRODUCTIONS, CONCLUSIONS, AND LANGUAGE

CHAPTER 14 Developing the Introduction

Prepare the Introduction

- Prepare the introduction after the body of the speech (p. 218)
- Keep the introduction brief—10 to 15 percent of the overall speech. (p. 218)

Use the Introduction to Gain Audience Attention

- Use a quotation. (p. 218)
- Tell a story. (p. 218)
- Establish common ground. (p. 218)
- Refer to the occasion. (p. 219)
- Pose questions. (p. 219)
- Offer unusual information. (p. 220)
- Use humor—perhaps (p. 220)

Preview the Topic and Purpose

- Declare what your speech is about and what you hope to accomplish. (p. 221)

Establish Your Credibility

- Briefly state your qualifications for speaking on the topic. (p. 222)
- Emphasize some experience, knowledge, or perspective you have that is different from or more extensive than that of your audience. (p. 222)

LaunchPad VIDEO ACTIVITY

Go to LaunchPad to watch a video about using examples in your speech.

LaunchPad includes:

LearningCurve adaptive quizzing

a curated collection of video clips and full-length speeches.

Additional resources and reference materials such as presentation software tutorials and documentation help.

Preview the Main Points

- Help listeners mentally organize the speech by introducing the main points and stating the order in which you will address them (the *preview statement*). (p. 222)

Motivate the Audience to Accept Your Goals

- Emphasize the topic's relevance and importance to audience members. (p. 223)
- Alert them to what they stand to gain by listening. (p. 223)
- Demonstrate that the speech purpose is consistent with their values and motives. (p. 223)

CHAPTER 15 Developing the Conclusion

Use the Conclusion to Serve Several Functions

- Signal the close of the speech. (p. 225)
- Summarize key points. (p. 225)
- Reiterate the thesis and specific purpose. (p. 226)
- In a persuasive speech, challenge the audience to respond to your appeals. (p. 226)

Make the Conclusion Meaningful and Memorable

- Use a quotation, tell a story, pose a rhetorical question (p. 227)
- Link back to material in the introduction (*bookending*). (p. 228)

CHAPTER 16 Using Language to Style the Speech

Prepare Your Speeches Using an Oral Style

- Use language that is simpler, more repetitious, more rhythmic, and more interactive than written language. (p. 229)
- Structure the speech clearly, using transitions to indicate beginning, middle, and end. (p. 230)
- Use an organizational pattern. (p. 230)

Strive for Simplicity

- Try to say what you mean in short, clear sentences. (p. 230)
- Avoid words unlikely to be understood by your audience. (p. 230)
- Steer clear of unnecessary jargon. (p. 230)

Aim for Conciseness

- Use fewer words to express your thoughts. (p. 230)
- Experiment with phrases and sentence fragments. (p. 231)

Use Repetition Frequently

- Repeat key words and phrases to emphasize important ideas and to help listeners follow your logic. (p. 231)

Use Personal Pronouns

- Foster a sense of inclusion by using the personal pronouns *I*, *you*, and *we*. (p. 231)

Use Concrete Language and Vivid Imagery

- Use imagery (concrete and colorful language) that plays off the senses. (p. 232)

  Use descriptive adjectives ("the dark *hour") and strong verbs ("gaze" rather than "look").*

- Use figures of speech, including *similes*, *metaphors*, allusion, and irony, to help listeners get the message. (p. 233)

Choose Words That Build Credibility

- Use language that is appropriate to the audience, occasion, and subject. (p. 235)
- Use words accurately. (p. 235)
- Choose words that are both denotatively (literally) and connotatively (subjectively) accurate and appropriate for the audience. (p. 235)
- Use the active voice. (p. 235)
- Use culturally sensitive and gender-neutral language. (p. 236)

Choose Language That Creates a Lasting Impression

- Repeat key words, phrases, or sentences at various intervals. (p. 237)

  Experiment with anaphora and epiphora.

- For a poetic quality, experiment with alliteration. (p. 238)
- Use parallelism (arranging words or sounds in similar form) to emphasize important ideas. (p. 239)

KEY TERMS

Chapter 14

- rhetorical question
- preview statement

Chapter 15

- call to action

Chapter 16

- style
- oral style
- jargon
- concrete language
- abstract language
- imagery
- figures of speech
- simile
- metaphor
- cliche
- mixed metaphor
- analogy
- faulty analogy
- personification
- understatement
- irony
- allusion
- hyperbole
- onomatopoeia
- code-switching
- malapropism
- denotative meaning
- connotative meaning
- voice
- colloquial expressions
- gender-neutral language
- rhetorical devices
- anaphora
- epiphora
- alliteration
- hackneyed
- parallelism
- antithesis

14 Developing the Introduction

LearningCurve can help you review!
Go to LaunchPad: **launchpadworks.com**

The introduction and conclusion, although not more important than the body of the speech, are essential to the speech's overall success. Introductions set the tone and prepare the audience to hear the speech. A good introduction previews what's to come in a way that engages audiences in the topic and establishes a tone of goodwill. An effective conclusion ensures that the audience remembers the key points of the speech and reacts in a way that the speaker intends.

This chapter describes the essential components of the speech introduction. Chapter 15 addresses the conclusion.

Functions of the Introduction

The choices you make about the introduction can affect the outcome of the entire speech. In the first several minutes (one speaker pegs it at ninety seconds), audience members will decide whether they are interested in the topic of your speech, whether they will believe what you say, and whether they will give you their full attention.

A good introduction serves to:

- Arouse your audience's attention and willingness to listen
- Introduce the topic and purpose
- Establish your credibility to speak on the topic
- Preview the main points
- Motivate the audience to accept your speech goals

The introduction comes first in a speech, but plan on preparing it after you've completed the body of the speech. This way, you will know exactly what material you need to preview. Keep the introduction brief—as a rule, it should occupy no more than 10 to 15 percent of the entire speech.

Gain Audience Attention

The first challenge faced by any speaker is to win the audience's attention. The audience must believe at the onset that the speech will interest them and offer them something of benefit. Some time-honored techniques used

CHECKLIST

GUIDELINES FOR PREPARING THE INTRODUCTION

- ✓ Prepare the introduction after you've completed the body of the speech so you will know exactly what you need to preview.
- ✓ Keep the introduction brief—as a rule, no more than 10 to 15 percent of the entire speech.
- ✓ Plan the introduction word for word.
- ✓ Practice delivering your introduction until you feel confident you've got it right.

to do this include sharing a compelling quotation or story, establishing common ground, posing a provocative question, providing unusual information, and using humor.

Use a Quotation

In a 2016 commencement address, Twitter executive Wayne Change advised University of Massachusetts graduates: "Make your own rules, hack the system, and change the world."[1] A quotation that elegantly and succinctly expresses a theme of the speech will draw the audience's attention. Quotations can be culled from books of quotations, literature, poetry, film, news stories, other people's speeches, or directly from people you know.

Tell a Story

Noted speechwriter and language expert William Safire once remarked that stories are "surefire attention getters."[2] Speakers like to use stories, or *narratives*, to illustrate points, and audiences like to hear them, because they make ideas concrete and colorful. Stories personalize issues by encouraging audience identification and making ideas relevant. And they should be, importantly, entertaining.

Brief stories of meaningful and entertaining incidents based on real life, often the speaker's own (called *anecdotes*; see Chapter 8 on developing supporting materials), can serve as powerful tools to command the audience's attention. Dutch researchers discovered this when audience members they studied rated speeches introduced with anecdotes as being more interesting and understandable than those that were not. The anecdotes also boosted speaker credibility and helped the audience retain more of the speech.[3] Scientific studies aside, the key to successfully introducing a speech with any anecdote is choosing one that strikes a chord with the audience and that, like a good joke, can stand on its own without explanation.

Establish Common Ground

Just as friendships are formed by showing interest in others, audiences are won over when speakers express interest in them and show that they share in the audiences' concerns and goals. This creates goodwill and a feeling of common ground (or *identification*; see also Chapter 6 on analyzing the audience). Use your knowledge of the audience to touch briefly on areas of shared experience. You might mention a shared alma mater or hometown, or acknowledge a recent event that touched the audience and yourself, such as a sports team victory or a bout of severe weather.

Refer to the Occasion

Introductions that include references to the speech occasion and to any relevant facts about the audience make listeners feel recognized as individuals, so this is another way of establishing common ground. People appreciate a direct reference to the event, and they are interested in the meaning the speaker assigns to it. In her introduction to a ceremony honoring the fiftieth anniversary of Martin Luther King Jr.'s "I Have a Dream" speech, Oprah Winfrey began this way:

> On this date, in this place, at this time, 50 years ago today, Dr. Martin Luther King shared his dream for America with America. . . . Dr. King was the passionate voice that awakened the conscience of a nation and inspired people all over the world. The power of his words resonated because they were spoken out of an unwavering belief in freedom and justice, equality and opportunity for all. "Let Freedom Ring" was Dr. King's closing call for a better and more just America.[4]

Pose a Provocative Question

"How long do you think your water supply will last?" Posing a question of vital interest to the audience can be an effective way to draw their attention to what you are about to say. These sorts of questions are usually rhetorical. Rather than inviting actual responses, **rhetorical questions** make the audience think.

Whenever you use a rhetorical question in an introduction, always let the audience know that your speech will attempt to answer it.

> Are you concerned about whether you'll be able to find a job when you graduate? Are you worried that unemployment will remain high? If so, we are in this together. Today I'm going to talk about some steps you can take in college that will help you enter the job market sooner once you graduate.

Posing questions that seek an actual response, either in a show of hands or by verbal reply, also sparks interest. Here is an example of how a speech about trends in technology usage might be introduced by using real, or "polling," questions.

> How many of you have gone 24 hours without using any mobile devices? *(Speaker waits for a show of hands.)* How many of you think you'd enjoy doing so? *(Speaker waits for show of hands.)* Do you think you'd be comfortable not using a smart phone, Droid, iPad, laptop, or whatever other devices you own, for a week? *(Speaker waits for a show of hands.)* How many of you are more likely to return home to retrieve your smart phone than your wallet? *(Speaker waits for a show of hands.)* As you can see by looking around this room, not many of us can visualize being comfortable without our electronic devices. Today I'm going to describe trends in technology usage and our dependence on these modern devices. . . .

Polling audience members is an effective way to gain their attention if your questions are thought-provoking and novel, but it has drawbacks. Bear in mind when using this attention-gaining technique that it is possible that no one will respond, or that the responses will be unexpected. Analyzing your audience will be helpful in designing effective rhetorical questions (see Chapter 6).

Offer Unusual Information

"Sean Connery wore a wig in every single one of his James Bond performances." Surprising audience members with startling or unusual information is one of the surest ways to get their attention. Such statements stimulate your listeners' curiosity and make them want to hear more about your topic. Some the most effective such statements are based in statistics, a powerful means of illustrating consequences and relationships that can quickly bring points into focus, as in this opener by Chef James Oliver: "Sadly, in the next eighteen minutes when I do our chat, four Americans that are alive will be dead from the food they eat."[5]

Use Humor—Perhaps

Handled well, humor can build rapport and set a positive tone for a speech. Humor can also enliven a speech about a topic that is dry, difficult, or complex. Using humor can be a challenge, however, and it can backfire easily. Include humor in your speech with caution. Simply telling a series of unrelated jokes without making a relevant point will likely detract from your purpose. And few things turn an audience off more quickly than tasteless or inappropriate humor. Every speaker should strictly avoid humor or sarcasm that belittles others—whether on the basis of race, sex, ability, or otherwise. A good rule of thumb is that speech humor should always match the rhetorical situation.

SELF-ASSESSMENT CHECKLIST

USING HUMOR APPROPRIATELY

_____ 1. Is your humor appropriate to the audience and occasion?

_____ 2. Does your humor help you make a point about your topic or the occasion?

_____ 3. Have you avoided any potentially offensive issues such as race or religion?

_____ 4. Is your humor likely to insult or demean anyone?

_____ 5 Have you given your humor a trial run?

_____ 6. Is your use of humor likely to translate well to the cultural composition of the audience?

A CULTURAL PERSPECTIVE

Humor and Culture: When the Jokes Fall Flat

While humor can be a highly effective tool for introducing speeches, it can also be the cause of communication breakdowns. As one scholar notes:

charles taylor/Shutterstock

> Although humor is present in all human groups, its content varies significantly across cultures. Many jokes don't translate well—or at all—because of differences in social structure and cultural norms. There is no universally appreciated joke; what is funny in one culture may not be amusing in another.[1]

Humor assumes shared understanding. When that understanding is absent, the jokes fall flat. Humor breakdowns can occur any time audience members do not share the same cultural assumptions as the speaker. These assumptions may be based on gender, social class, educational background, ethnicity, or nationality.[2]

How can you avoid using humor that your audience won't understand? The obvious answer is to carefully consider your audience and, if possible, learn about audience members' cultures. Be as confident as possible that your material will make sense and be humorous to your listeners. Be particularly alert to nonverbal feedback. If you receive puzzled stares, consider clarifying your meaning. You might even acknowledge the cultural assumptions that your humor tacitly expresses.

1. Lawrence T. White and Steven B. Jackson, "Culture Conscious," *Psychology Today*, May 2012, www.psychologytoday.com/blog/culture-conscious/201205/whats-funny.
2. William Lee, "Communication about Humor as Procedural Competence in Intercultural Encounters," in *Intercultural Communication: A Reader*, eds. Larry A. Samovar and Richard E. Porter, 7th ed. (Belmont, CA: Wadsworth, 1994), 373.

Preview the Purpose and Topic

Once you've gained the audience's attention, use the introduction to alert listeners to the speech topic and purpose. You may already have alluded to your topic in the attention-getting phase of the introduction. If not, declare what your speech is about and what you hope to accomplish. Note an exception to this rule: When your purpose is to persuade, and the audience is not yet aware of this purpose, "forewarning" may predispose listeners in the opposite direction and thwart your persuasive goal. However, when the audience knows of your persuasive intent, previewing the topic and purpose can enhance understanding.[6]

Topic and purpose are clearly explained in this introduction to a speech by Marvin Runyon, former postmaster general of the United States.

> This afternoon, I want to examine the truth of that statement—"Nothing moves people like the mail, and no one moves the mail like the U.S. Postal Service." I want to look at where we are today as a communications industry, and where we intend to be in the days and years ahead.[7]

Establish Your Credibility as a Speaker

During the introduction, audience members make a decision about whether they are interested not just in your topic but also in you. They want to know why they should believe in you. They want to feel that they can trust what you have to say—that they can believe in your *ethos*, or good character. Thus, another function of the introduction is to establish your credibility to speak.

Recall from Chapter 5 (see p. 63) that you signal positive ethos by demonstrating a solid grasp of your topic, an honest presentation of the material, and respect and concern for the audience's best interests. To build credibility, offer a simple statement of your qualifications for speaking on the topic. Briefly emphasize some experience, knowledge, or perspective you have that is different from or more extensive than that of your audience. If your goal, for example, were to persuade your audience to be more conscientious about protecting city parks, you might state, "I have felt passionate about conservation issues ever since I started volunteering with the city's local chapter of the Nature Conservancy four summers ago."

Although it is always important to establish your credibility in the introduction, it is particularly so when the audience does not know you well.[8] In these situations, be sure to stress the reasons why audience members should trust you and believe what you have to say. To learn more about building your credibility throughout a speech, see pp. 234–36.

Preview the Main Points

Once you've revealed the topic and purpose and established your credibility, briefly preview each of the main points of the speech. Previewing main points helps audience members mentally organize the speech as they follow along. An introductory **preview statement** is straightforward. You simply tell the audience what the main points will be and in what order you will address them.

Robert L. Darbelnet effectively introduces his topic, purpose, and main points.

> Good morning. When I received this invitation, I didn't hesitate to accept. I realized that in this room I would find a powerful coalition: the American Automobile Association and the National Asphalt Pavement Association. Where our two groups come together, no pun intended, is where the rubber meets the road.
>
> Unfortunately, the road needs repair.
>
> My remarks today are intended to give you a sense of AAA's ongoing efforts to improve America's roads. Our hope is that you will join your voices to ours as we call on the federal government to do three things:

> Number one: Perhaps the most important, provide adequate funding for highway maintenance and improvements.
>
> Number two: Play a strong, responsible, yet flexible role in transportation programs.
>
> And number three: Invest in highway safety.
>
> Let's see what our strengths are, what the issues are, and what we can do about them.[9]

When previewing your main points, simply mention those points, saving your in-depth discussion of each one for the body of your speech.

Motivate the Audience to Accept Your Goals

A final and critical function of the introduction is to motivate the audience to care about your topic and make it relevant to them. You may choose to convey what the audience stands to gain by the information you will share or convince audience members that your speech purpose is consistent with their motives and values. A student speech about the value of interview training shows how this can be accomplished.

> Why do you need interview training? It boils down to competition. As in sports, when you're not training, someone else is out there training to beat you. All things being equal, the person who has the best interviewing skills has got the edge.

SELF-ASSESSMENT CHECKLIST

HOW EFFECTIVE IS YOUR INTRODUCTION?

Does your introduction . . .

_____ 1. Capture the audience's attention?

_____ 2. Stimulate their interest in what's to come?

_____ 3. Establish a positive bond with listeners?

_____ 4. Alert listeners to the speech purpose and topic?

_____ 5. Establish your credibility?

_____ 6. Preview the main points of the speech?

_____ 7. Motivate listeners to accept your speech goals?

15 Developing the Conclusion

LearningCurve can help you review!
Go to LaunchPad: **launchpadworks.com**

Just as a well-crafted introduction gets your speech effectively out of the starting gate, a well-constructed conclusion ensures that you go out with a bang and not a whimper. Conclusions give you the opportunity to drive home your purpose, and they offer you a final chance to make the kind of impression that will accomplish the goals of your speech. Conclusions also provide the audience with a sense of logical and emotional closure and provide a final opportunity to create a relationship with them.

Functions of Conclusions

Like introductions, conclusions consist of several elements that work together to make the end of a speech as memorable as the beginning. Conclusions serve to:

- Signal to the audience that the speech is coming to an end and provide closure
- Summarize the key points
- Reiterate the thesis or central idea of the speech
- Remind the audience of how your ideas will benefit them
- Challenge the audience to remember and, especially in persuasive speeches, possibly act upon your ideas
- End the speech memorably

As with the introduction, prepare the conclusion after you've completed the body of the speech. Keep it brief—as a rule, no more than 10 to 15 percent, or about one-sixth, of the overall speech. And, just as you should outline the introduction in full-sentence and then key-word form (see Chapter 14 on developing an introduction), do so for the conclusion. Carefully consider your use of language in the conclusion. More than other parts of the speech, the conclusion can contain words that inspire and motivate (see Chapter 16 on use of language).

CHECKLIST

GUIDELINES FOR PREPARING THE CONCLUSION

- ✔ During the research phase, be on the lookout for material that you can use in the conclusion.
- ✔ Do not leave the conclusion to chance. Include it within your speaking outline.
- ✔ Keep the conclusion brief—as a rule, no more than 10 to 15 percent, or about one-sixth, of the overall speech.
- ✔ Carefully consider your use of language. More than in other parts of the speech, the conclusion can contain words that inspire and motivate (see Chapter 16 on use of language).
- ✔ Practice delivering your conclusion until you feel confident you've got it right.
- ✔ Once you've signaled the end of your speech, conclude in short order (though not abruptly).

Signal the Close of a Speech and Provide Closure

People who listen to speeches are taking a journey of sorts, and they want and need the speaker to acknowledge the journey's end. They look for logical and emotional closure.

One way to signal that a speech is about to end is to use a transitional word or phrase: *finally, looking back, in conclusion,* or *let me close by saying* (see Chapter 11 on transitions). You can also signal closure by adjusting your manner of delivery; for example, you can vary your tone, pitch, rhythm, rate of speech, and even a well-timed pause to indicate that the speech is winding down (see Chapters 17 and 18 on speech delivery). Note that few things annoy listeners more than hearing a speaker say "in conclusion" and then having to sit through another twenty minutes of the speech. Once you've signaled the end of your speech, conclude in short order (though not abruptly).

Summarize the Key Points

One bit of age-old advice for giving a speech is "Tell them what you are going to tell them (in the introduction), tell them (in the body), and tell them what you told them (in the conclusion)." The idea is that emphasizing the main points three times will help the audience to remember them. A restatement of points in the conclusion brings the speech full circle and gives the audience a sense of completion. However, the summary review should be more than a rote recounting. Consider how Holger Kluge, in a speech titled "Reflections on Diversity," summarizes his main points.

> I have covered a lot of ground here today. But as I draw to a close, I'd like to stress three things.
>
> First, diversity is more than equity. . . .
>
> Second, weaving diversity into the very fabric of your organization takes time. . . .

Third, diversity will deliver bottom line results to your businesses and those results will be substantial. . . .[1]

Reiterate the Topic and Speech Purpose

The conclusion should reiterate the topic and speech purpose to imprint it on the audience's memory. In the conclusion to a persuasive speech about the U.S. immigration debate, Elpidio Villarreal reminds his listeners of his central idea.

> Two paths are open to us. One path would keep us true to our fundamental values as a nation and a people. The other would lead us down a dark trail; one marked by 700-mile-long fences, emergency detention centers and vigilante border patrols. Because I really am an American, heart and soul, and because that means never being without hope, I still believe we will ultimately choose the right path. We have to.[2]

Reminding listeners of your speech purpose links their frame of reference to yours, thus allowing your audience to determine how well they've comprehended—and agree or disagree with—your central idea.

Challenge the Audience to Respond

A strong conclusion challenges audience members to put to use what the speaker has shared with them. In an *informative speech*, the speaker challenges audience members to use what they've learned in a way that benefits them. In a *persuasive speech*, the challenge usually comes in the form of a **call to action**. Here the speaker challenges listeners to act in response to the speech, see the problem in a new way, or change both their beliefs and actions about the problem.

A concluding challenge is important because it shows audience members that the problem or issue being addressed is real and personally relevant to them.

Emma Watson, United Nations Women Goodwill Ambassador, makes a strong call to action at the conclusion of her speech at a special event for the HeForShe campaign.

> We are struggling for a uniting word but the good news is we have a uniting movement. It is called HeForShe. I am inviting you to step forward, to be seen to speak up, to be the "he" for "she." And to ask yourself if not me, who? If not now, when?[3]

Make the Conclusion Memorable

Beyond summarizing and providing closure, a key function of the conclusion is to make the speech memorable—to increase the odds that the speaker's message will linger after the speech is over. A speech that makes a lasting impression is one that listeners are most likely to remember and act on. To accomplish this, make use of the same devices for capturing attention described for use in introductions—quotations, stories, startling statements, humor, and references to the audience and occasion. See the following for examples.

Use Quotations

Using a quotation that captures the essence of the speech can be a very effective way to close it. Note how Sue Suter quotes a character in *Star Trek* to conclude her speech on discrimination and the disabled.

> That brings us to the final lesson from *Star Trek*. I'd like to leave you with two quotations from Captain Picard that define what it means to be human. In *The Next Generation*, Picard confronts discrimination by agreeing that, yes, we may be different in appearance. Then he adds, "But we are both living beings. We are born, we grow, we live, and we die. In all the ways that matter, we are alike."[4]

Tell a Story

A short concluding story, or *anecdote*, can bring the entire speech into focus very effectively. It helps the audience to visualize the speech.

> I would conclude with a story that applies to all of us in this industry. In ancient times there was a philosopher who had many disciples. . . .

Another technique is to pick up on a story or an idea that you mentioned in the introduction, bringing the speech full circle. James C. May does this by reminding his audience of the story of Apollo 13 that started his speech.

> If I may draw one final lesson from the crippled spacecraft that made it back to earth on an empty fuel tank, it is that one should never underestimate the human capacity for doing "impossible" things. All through history, enterprising people have surprised themselves—and others around them—by finding ingenious solutions to the most complex problems. We can do that here.[5]

Pose a Rhetorical Question

Another effective way to make a speech memorable is to leave the audience with a *rhetorical question.* Just as such questions focus attention in the introduction, they can drive home the speech theme in the conclusion. Former President Barack Obama concluded his remarks on a speech about immigration with poignant rhetorical questions. These served both to leave a lasting, emotional impression and to reiterate key speech points.

> Are we a nation that educates the world's best and brightest in our universities, only to send them home to create businesses in countries that compete against us? Or are we a nation that encourages them to stay and create jobs here, create businesses here, create industries right here in America?[6]

Bring Your Speech Full Circle

Picking up on a story or idea you mentioned in the introduction—a technique known as "bookending"—can be a memorable way to close a speech and bring the entire presentation full circle. You can provide the resolution of the story ("what happened next?") or reiterate the link between the moral (lesson) of the story and the speech theme. You might also repeat lines from a poem you cited or repeat a quotation you mentioned.

SELF-ASSESSMENT CHECKLIST

HOW EFFECTIVE IS YOUR CONCLUSION?

Does your conclusion . . .

_____ 1. Alert the audience, with the use of a transition, that the speech is ending?

_____ 2. Actually come to an end soon after you say you will finish?

_____ 3. Last no more than about one-sixth of the time spent on the body of the speech?

_____ 4. Reiterate the main points?

_____ 5. Remind listeners of the speech topic and purpose?

_____ 6. Include a challenge or call to action to motivate the audience to respond to your ideas or appeals?

_____ 7. Provide a sense of closure and make a lasting impression?

16 Using Language to Style the Speech

LearningCurve can help you review!
Go to LaunchPad: **launchpadworks.com**

Words are the public speaker's tools of the trade, and the words you choose to style your speech will play a crucial role in creating a dynamic connection with your audience. **Style** is the specific word choices and rhetorical devices (techniques of language) speakers use to express their ideas and achieve their speech purpose.

Used in all its richness, language allows us to visualize an image and even get a sense of sound or smell. Poets and novelists use descriptive language to breathe life into something or someone and to make their words leap off the page into the reader's mind. In public speaking, you, too, can use the evocative power of language to captivate your audience. Carefully choosing the right words and images is crucial to helping listeners understand, believe in, and retain your message.

Use an Oral Style

In an interview in *The Atlantic*, Jayne Benjulian, former chief speechwriter at Apple, was asked what went into making a good speech.

> What is key to writing any speech of quality is a central idea. One idea, not ten. So every great speech has a major concept or message. Second thing, *every speech has language meant to be spoken. They are monologues. They have shape and movement. Speeches are an oral medium.*[1]

Benjulian wrote speeches for some of the most brilliant executives in the tech industry. A master of the spoken word, she was keenly aware that speeches must be prepared for the ear—to be *heard* rather than read. Speeches require an **oral style**—the use of language that is simpler, more repetitious, more rhythmic, and more interactive than written language.[2] An oral style is particularly important because unlike readers, listeners have only one chance to get the message.

The next time you listen to a speech or classroom presentation, consider how the speaker's language differs from that of this textbook. Here are some things you are likely to note:

- More so than written texts, effective speeches use familiar words, easy-to-follow sentences, and even sentence fragments.

- Speeches make much more frequent use of repetition and transitions than do most forms of written communication.
- Speeches make more use of personal pronouns, such as *I*, *we*, *you*, and *our*, than written language.
- Speeches require an even clearer structure than written language, with obvious signals indicating beginning, middle, and end.

Keeping these differences between oral and written language in mind, consider how you can use the following guidelines to write your speeches to be heard rather than read.

Strive for Simplicity

To make certain that your audience understands you, focus on expressing things simply, without pretentious language or unnecessary jargon. When selecting between two synonyms, choose the simpler term. For example, avoid showy or empty terms such as *extrapolate* for "guess" and *utilize* for "use." And unless the audience consists solely of the professionals who use it, translate **jargon**—the specialized, "insider" language of a given profession—into commonly understood terms.

As the celebrated presidential speechwriter Peggy Noonan notes in her book *Simply Speaking*:

> Good hard simple words with good hard clear meanings are good things to use when you speak. They are like pickets in a fence, slim and unimpressive on their own but sturdy and effective when strung together.[3]

The late William Safire, another master of the oral style, put it this way:

> Great speeches steer clear of forty-dollar words. Big words, or terms chosen for their strangeness—I almost said "unfamiliarity"—are a sign of pretension. What do you do when you have a delicious word, one with a little poetry in it, that is just the right word for the meaning—but you know it will sail over the head of your audience? You can use it, just as FDR used "infamy," and thereby stretch the vocabulary of your listeners. But it is best if you subtly define it in passing, as if you were adding emphasis.[4]

In a speech to the 2016 Democratic Convention, former first lady Michelle Obama used the simplest, jargon-free language to describe her party's response to its opponents: "Our motto is, when they go low, we go high." But for the word "motto," each word contains just one syllable, and the motto itself is a mere seven words. Yet the crowd roared with understanding and approval of the values they expressed.[5]

Be Concise

Concise wording is yet another feature of effective oral style. Edit any unnecessary words and phrases, bearing in mind that, in general, easy-to-pronounce words and shorter sentences are more readily understood. Use *contractions*—"I'll" instead of "I will"—and other shortened forms of the verb *to be* in conjunction with pronouns *(I, he, she, you, we)*. Contractions reflect how the English language is actually spoken.

Experiment with Phrases and Sentence Fragments

Although they are often avoided in written language, phrases and sentence fragments in place of full sentences may help to communicate an oral message. This speaker, a physician, demonstrates how they can add punch to a speech:

> I'm just a simple bone-and-joint guy. I can set your broken bones. Take away your bunions. Even give you a new hip. But I don't mess around with the stuff between the ears. . . . That's another specialty.[6]

Make Frequent Use of Repetition

Repetition is key to oral style, serving to compensate for natural lapses in listening and to reinforce information. Indeed, even very brief speeches make use of this extremely important linguistic device. Repetition adds emphasis to important ideas, helps listeners follow your logic, and infuses language with rhythm and drama. For examples of how to introduce repetition into your speeches, see p. 237 in this chapter ("Use Repetition for Rhythm and Reinforcement").

Use Personal Pronouns

Oral style is more interactive and inclusive of the audience than is written language. After all, the audience and speaker are physically together in the same space. Audience members want to know what the speaker thinks and feels, and to be assured that he or she recognizes them and relates them to the message. The direct form of address, using the personal pronouns such as *we, us, I,* and *you*, helps to create this feeling of recognition and inclusion. Note how Sheryl Sandberg, chief operating officer of Facebook, uses personal pronouns to begin a speech on why there are too few women leaders:

> So for any of *us* in this room today, *let's* start out by admitting *we're* lucky. *We* don't live in the world *our* mothers lived in, *our* grandmothers lived in, where

CHECKLIST

PERSONALIZING YOUR SPEECH WITH PERSONAL PRONOUNS

- ✔ "*I* am indebted to the ideas of . . ."
- ✔ "Those of *us* who have lived during a world war . . ."
- ✔ "*We* cannot opt out of this problem . . ."
- ✔ "To *me*, the truly great lessons . . ."
- ✔ "Some of *you* will recall . . ."

career choices for women were so limited. And if *you're* in this room today, most of *us* grew up in a world where *we* had basic civil rights, and amazingly, *we* still live in a world where some women don't have them. But all that aside, *we* still have a problem . . . Women are not making it to the top of any profession anywhere in the world.[7]

Use Concrete Language and Vivid Imagery

Concrete words and vivid imagery make a speech come alive for listeners, engaging their senses and encouraging involvement. **Concrete language** is specific, tangible, and definite. Words such as "mountain," "spoon," "dark," and "heavy" describe things we can physically sense (see, hear, taste, smell, and touch). In contrast, **abstract language** is general or nonspecific, leaving meaning open to interpretation. Abstract words such as "peace," "freedom," and "love" are purely conceptual; they have no physical reference. Politicians use abstract language to appeal to mass audiences or to be noncommittal ("We strive for peace.") In most speaking situations, however, listeners will appreciate concrete nouns and verbs.

Note how concrete words add precision and color:

ABSTRACT:	The old road was bad.
CONCRETE:	The road was pitted with muddy craters and nearly swallowed up by huge outcroppings of dark gray granite.

Offer Vivid Imagery

Imagery is concrete language that brings into play the senses of smell, taste, sight, hearing, and touch to paint mental pictures. Studies show that vivid imagery is more easily recalled than colorless language,[8] and speeches using ample imagery also elicit more positive responses than those that do not.[9]

Adding imagery into your speech need not be difficult if you focus on using concrete and colorful adjectives and strong verbs. Try substituting passive forms of the verb "to be" (e.g., *is, are, was, were, will be* . . .) with more active verb

CHECKLIST

IS YOUR SPEECH LANGUAGE CONCRETE?

As you construct your speech, consider which words and phrases may be abstract. Consult a dictionary or thesaurus to find more concrete words that would strengthen your message. For example, consider the following levels of concreteness:

Abstract	Less Abstract	Concrete
summer →	hot weather →	sweltering heat
congestion →	traffic jam →	gridlock

TABLE 16.1 Choosing Strong Verbs

Mundane Verb	Colorful Alternative
look	behold, gaze, glimpse, peek, stare
walk	stride, amble, stroll, skulk
throw	hurl, fling, pitch
sit	sink, plop, settle
eat	devour, inhale, gorge

forms. For example, rather than state "the houses were empty," use "the houses *stood* empty." You can use descriptive adjectives to modify nouns as well as verbs, as in "*dilapidated* house." President Franklin D. Roosevelt famously did this when he portrayed the Japanese bombing of Pearl Harbor as "the dark hour,"[10] conveying with one simple adjective the gravity of the attack.

Trading weak and mundane verbs with those that are strong and colorful is another means of producing imagery. Rather than "walk," you can say "saunter"; in place of "look," use "gaze." Table 16.1 lists examples of mundane verb forms and more colorful alternatives.

Use Figures of Speech

Figures of speech, including similes, metaphors, and analogies, make striking comparisons that help listeners visualize, identify with, and understand the speaker's ideas. A **simile** explicitly compares one thing to another, using *like* or *as*: "He works *like* a dog" and "The old woman's hands were *as* soft as a baby's." A **metaphor** also compares two things but does so by describing one thing as actually *being* the other. Metaphors do not use *like* or *as*: "Time is a thief" and "All the world's a stage."

Used properly, similes and metaphors express ideas compactly and cleverly. By comparing the unfamiliar to the known, they allow us to more quickly process information. However, try to avoid **clichés**, or predictable and stale comparisons (as in the above examples). Beware, too, of **mixed metaphors**, or those that juxtapose or compare unlike images or expressions: for example, "Burning the midnight oil at both ends" incorrectly joins the expressions "burning the midnight oil" and "burning a candle at both ends."

An **analogy** is simply an extended simile or metaphor that compares an unfamiliar concept or process to a more familiar one to help listeners understand the unfamiliar one. For example, African American minister Phil Wilson used metaphoric language in a sermon to a Los Angeles congregation about the dangers of AIDS.

> Our house is on fire! The fire truck arrives, but we won't come out, because we're afraid the folks from next door will see that we're in that burning house. AIDS is a fire raging in our community and it's out of control![11]

TABLE 16.2 Figures of Speech

Figure of Speech	Description	Example
Personification	Endowing abstract ideas or inanimate objects with human qualities.	"Computers have become important members of our family."
Understatement	Drawing attention to an idea by minimizing, or lowering, its importance.	"Flunking out of college might be a problem."
Irony	Using humor, satire, or sarcasm to suggest a meaning other than the one that is actually being expressed.	"Our football players are great. They may not be big, but they sure are slow."
Allusion	Making vague or indirect reference to people, historical events, or concepts to give deeper meaning to the message.	"His meteoric rise to the top is an example for all of us."
Hyperbole	Using obvious exaggeration to drive home a point.	"Have you seen those students carrying backpacks the size of minivans filled with five-course dinners, cell phones, and an occasional textbook or two?"
Onomatopoeia	The imitation of natural sounds in word form; it adds vividness to the speech.	"The rain dripped a steady *plop plop plop* on the metal roof; the bees *buzzed* through the wood."

Information from Andrea A. Lunsford, *The St. Martin's Handbook,* 8th ed. (Boston: Bedford/St. Martin's, 2015).

As useful as analogies are, they can be misleading if used carelessly—as they often are. A weak or **faulty analogy** is an inaccurate or misleading comparison suggesting that because two things are similar in some ways, they are necessarily similar in others. Some analogies are clearly faulty, as in suggesting that Israel is a "Nazi" state like Germany during World War II because of its clash over territory with the Palestinians. Many other analogies are less obviously so, requiring both speaker and listener to critically examine the limits of comparison and decide for themselves whether or not they agree with a particular analogy. (See Chapter 25 for a discussion of other logical fallacies.)

Table 16.2 lists other figures of speech that contribute to vivid imagery, including **personification**, **understatement**, **irony**, **allusion**, **hyperbole**, and **onomatopoeia**.

Choose Words That Build Credibility

Your use of language in your speech will have an immediate effect on how audience members perceive you. To make that effect positive—to be seen as a competent and credible speaker—you'll want to use language that is appropriate, accurate, assertive, and respectful.

Use Words Appropriately

The language you use in a speech should be appropriate to the audience, the occasion, and the subject matter. As a rule, audience members will expect you to uphold the conventional rules of grammar and usage associated with General American (GA) English, but in oral style. The more formal the occasion, the closer you will want to remain within these conventional bounds. Listeners view speakers who use GA English as more competent—though not necessarily more trustworthy or likable—than those who speak in a distinctive dialect (regional variation of speech).[12]

At times, however, it may be appropriate to mix casual language, dialects, a second language, or even slang in your speech. For example, done carefully, the selective use of these elements, called **code-switching**, can encourage identification and imbue your speech with friendliness, humor, earthiness, honesty, and nostalgia.[13] The key is to ensure that your meaning is clear and your use is appropriate for the audience. Consider the following excerpt.

> On the gulf where I was raised, *el valle del Rio Grande* in South Texas—that triangular piece of land wedged between the river *y el golfo* which serves as the Texas-U.S./Mexican border—is a Mexican *pueblito* called Hargill.[14]

An important aspect of using language appropriately is avoidance of the "shock jock" syndrome—an informal term for a radio host who uses suggestive language, bathroom humor, and obscene references. These (ab)uses of language are never appropriate in a public speech event. Even those audience members who otherwise might not object to off-color material will react to it unfavorably.

Use Words Accurately

Audiences lose confidence in speakers who misuse words. Check that your words mean what you intend, and beware of the **malapropism**—the inadvertent use of a word or a phrase in place of one that sounds like it.[15] ("It's a strange *receptacle*" for "It's a strange *spectacle*.")

More broadly, choose words that are both denotatively and connotatively appropriate for the audience. The **denotative meaning** of a word is its literal, or dictionary, definition. Although some concrete words have mainly denotative meanings—*surgery* and *saline*, for example—through long use most words have acquired special associations that go beyond their dictionary definitions. The **connotative meaning** of a word is the special (often emotional) association that different people bring to bear on it. For example, you may agree that you are "angry" but not "irate," and "thrifty" but not "cheap." Consider how the connotative meanings of your word choices might affect the audience's response to your message, including those of non-native speakers of English.

Use the Active Voice

Voice is the feature of verbs that indicates the subject's relationship to the action. Speaking in the active rather than passive voice will make your

TABLE 16.3 Gender-Neutral Terms

Instead of	Use
mankind, early man, man	humankind, early peoples, humans
he, his	he or she, his or her, one, you, our, they
policeman, mailman, anchorman, chairman, middleman	police officer, mail carrier, news anchor, chair, intermediary

statements—and the audience's perception of you as the speaker—clear and assertive instead of indirect and weak. A verb is in the *active voice* when the subject performs the action, and in the *passive voice* when the subject is acted upon or is the receiver of the action.

PASSIVE: A test was announced by Ms. Carlos for Tuesday.

A president was elected by the voters every four years.

ACTIVE: Ms. Carlos announced a test for Tuesday.

The voters elect a president every four years.

Use Culturally Sensitive and Gender-Neutral Language

Be alert to using language that reflects respect for audience members' cultural beliefs, norms, and traditions. Review and eliminate any language that reflects unfounded assumptions, negative descriptions, or stereotypes of a given group's age, class, gender, or ability and geographic, ethnic, racial, or religious characteristics. Consider, too, whether certain seemingly well-known names and terms may be foreign to some listeners, and include brief explanations for them. Sayings specific to a certain region or group of people—termed **colloquial expressions** or idioms—such as "back the wrong horse" and "ballpark figure"—can add color and richness to a speech, but only if listeners understand them.

Word your speech with **gender-neutral language**: Avoid using third-person generic masculine pronouns (*his, he*) in favor of inclusive pronouns such as *his or her, he or she, we, ours, you, your,* or other gender-neutral terms (see Table 16.3).

Choose Language That Creates a Lasting Impression

Oral speech that is artfully arranged and infused with rhythm draws listeners in and leaves a lasting impression on audience members. Throughout the ages, speakers have created the cadenced arrangement of language through **rhetorical devices** such as repetition, alliteration, and parallelism. After reviewing some of these techniques, you will find it surprisingly easy to incorporate them into your speeches.

A CULTURAL PERSPECTIVE

Adapting Your Language to Diverse Audiences

charles taylor/Shutterstock

Using language that is appropriate to each of your listeners is one of the most important challenges facing you as a public speaker. It isn't an easy task, given the nation's many *co-cultures*, or groups of people who share values, norms, and interests beyond their national citizenship. Consider, for example, that many students at your school may be Latino (or may identify as Hispanic), African, Arab, Jewish, or Asian American. Others may have families that come from Europe, Canada, and elsewhere.

How do members of the co-cultures in your audience want you to refer to them? Are there important regional differences in languages you should address? Instead of being a monolithic group, for example, the 16.6 million Asian Americans and Pacific Islanders in the United States, or about 5.4 percent of the total U.S. population of over 325 million Americans in 2016,[1] include those of Chinese, Samoan, Pakistani, Bangladeshi, Native Hawaiian, Vietnamese, Korean, Thai, and Japanese descent, and this is merely a partial listing of countries of origin! Rather than treating any individual merely as a member of a broad category, address audience members as individuals and recognize them for their unique characteristics and life circumstances.

Similarly, many people believe that all Arab Americans, who number about 3.7 million,[2] are practicing Muslims. In fact, the largest portion are Catholics (35 percent); only 26 percent are Muslim, though numbers are rising rapidly.[3] Rather than sharing a religion, Arab Americans belong to many religions, including Islam, Christianity, Druze, Judaism, and others.[4] Using biased language based on these and other misconceptions can only alienate your listeners.

All people look to speakers to use language that is respectful and inclusive of them. As you prepare your speeches, consider whether you include terms that might leave your listeners feeling less than respected. For the long term, make learning about other cultures an ongoing endeavor. In this way, you will truly be able to address the sensitivities of diverse audiences.

1. "Asian Americans and Pacific Islanders," U.S. Social Security website, accessed September 12, 2016, www.ssa.gov/aapi/.
2. Arab American Institute, "Demographics," accessed September 12, 2016, www.aaiusa.org/demographics.
3. Lanouar Ben Hafsa, "Ethnic Identity vs. Religious Affiliation: Understanding the Divide between Arab American Christians and Muslims," *World Journal of Social Science Research*, vol. 3, no. 3, 2016, accessed August 29, 2016, www.scholink.org/ojs/index.php/wjssr.
4. Ibid.

Use Repetition for Rhythm and Reinforcement

Repetition is one of the most effective strategies for creating a lasting impression in a speech. Repeating key words, phrases, or even sentences at various intervals throughout a speech creates a distinctive rhythm and thereby implants important ideas in listeners' minds. Repetition works particularly well when delivered with the appropriate voice inflections and pauses.

In a form of repetition called **anaphora**, the speaker repeats a word or phrase at the beginning of successive phrases, clauses, or sentences. For example, in his speech delivered in 1963 in Washington, D.C., Martin Luther King Jr. repeated the phrase "I have a dream" eleven times in eight successive sentences, each with an upward inflection followed by a pause. Former President Barack Obama made frequent use of anaphora in his speeches, as in this excerpt from his second inaugural address (italics added).

> *We, the people,* still believe that our obligations as Americans are not just to ourselves, but to all posterity.
>
> *We, the people,* still believe that enduring security and lasting peace do not require perpetual war.
>
> *We, the people,* declare today that the most evident of truths—that all of us are created equal—is the star that guides us still.[16]

Speakers have used anaphora since early times. For example, Jesus preached:

> *Blessed are* the poor in spirit. . . . *Blessed are* the meek. . . . *Blessed are* the peacemakers. . . .[17]

In addition to reinforcing key ideas and imbuing a speech with unmistakable rhythm, repetition can help you create a thematic focus. Speakers often do this by using both anaphora and *epiphora* in the same speech. In **epiphora** (also called *epistrophe*) the repetition of a word or phrase appears at the end of successive statements. In a speech to his New Hampshire supporters, former President Obama used both anaphora and epiphora to establish a theme of empowerment (italics added).

> *It was* a creed written into the founding documents that declared the destiny of a nation: *Yes we can.*
>
> *It was* whispered by slaves and abolitionists as they blazed a trail toward freedom through the darkest of nights: *Yes we can.*
>
> *It was* sung by immigrants as they struck out from distant shores and pioneers who pushed westward against an unforgiving wilderness: *Yes we can.*[18]

Use Alliteration for a Poetic Quality

Alliteration is the repetition of the same sounds, usually initial consonants, in two or more neighboring words or syllables. Classic examples of alliteration in speeches include phrases such as long-time social activist Jesse Jackson's "Down with dope, up with hope" and former U.S. Vice President Spiro Agnew's disdainful reference to the U.S. press as "nattering nabobs of negativism."

Alliteration lends speech a poetic, musical rhythm. When used well, it drives home themes and leaves listeners with a lasting impression. When alliteration is poorly crafted or **hackneyed**, it can distract from a message.

Experiment with Parallelism

Parallelism is the arrangement of words, phrases, or sentences in a similar form. Parallel structure can help the speaker emphasize important ideas and can be as simple as orally numbering points ("first, second, and third"). Like repetition, parallelism creates a sense of steady or building rhythm. Speakers often make use of three parallel elements, called a *triad.*

> . . . of the people, by the people, and for the people. —Abraham Lincoln

Parallelism in speeches often makes use of **antithesis**—setting off two ideas in balanced (parallel) opposition to each other to create a powerful effect.

> One small step for a man, one giant leap for mankind. —Neil Armstrong on the moon, 1969
>
> To err is human, to forgive divine. —Alexander Pope, 1711
>
> For many are called, but few are chosen. —Matthew 22:14

CHECKLIST

USING EFFECTIVE ORAL STYLE

- ✔ Use familiar words, easy-to-follow sentences, and straightforward syntax.
- ✔ Root out culturally insensitive and biased language.
- ✔ Avoid unnecessary jargon.
- ✔ Use fewer rather than more words to express your thoughts, and choose the simpler of two synonyms.
- ✔ Make striking comparisons with *similes*, *metaphors*, and *analogies*.
- ✔ Use the active voice.
- ✔ Repeat key words, phrases, or sentences at the beginning of successive sentences (*anaphora*) and at their close (*epiphora*).
- ✔ Experiment with *alliteration*—words that repeat the same sounds, usually initial consonants, in two or more neighboring words or syllables.
- ✔ Experiment with *parallelism*—arranging words, phrases, or sentences in similar form.

VOCAL AND NONVERBAL DELIVERY

Award-winning actor and writer Lin-Manuel Miranda, known for his Broadway musicals *Hamilton* and *In the Heights*, takes part in Insight Dialogues presented by The Rockefeller Foundation, on June 23, 2016 in New York City, touching upon the impact of the arts in education, how diversity in the arts impact the Hollywood film industry, and the possibilities of solving the debt crisis in Puerto Rico. **Jennifer Graylock/Getty Images**

VOCAL AND NONVERBAL DELIVERY

SPEAKER'S PREVIEW

LearningCurve can help you review.
Go to LaunchPad: **launchpadworks.com**

VOCAL AND NONVERBAL DELIVERY

CHAPTER 17 Methods of Delivery

Strive for Naturalness in Your Delivery

- Think of your speech as a particularly important conversation. (p. 248)
- Rather than behaving theatrically, strive for naturalness. (p. 249)

Show Enthusiasm

- Speak about what excites you. (p. 249)
- Show enthusiasm for your topic and for the occasion. (p. 249)

Project a Sense of Confidence and Composure

- Inspire audience members' confidence in you by appearing confident. (p. 249)
- Focus on the ideas you want to convey rather than on yourself. (p. 249)

Engage Your Audience by Being Direct

- Establish eye contact with your listeners. (p. 249)
- Use a friendly tone of voice. (p. 249)
- Smile whenever it is appropriate. (p. 249)
- Consider positioning yourself close to the audience. (p. 249)

If You Must Read from a Prepared Text, Do So Naturally

- Vary the rhythm of your words. (p. 251)
- Become familiar with the speech so you can establish some eye contact with the audience. (p. 251)
- Consider using compelling presentation aids. (p. 251)

LaunchPad VIDEO ACTIVITY

Go to LaunchPad to watch a video that offers tips on delivering your speech.

LaunchPad includes:

LearningCurve adaptive quizzing

a curated collection of video clips and full-length speeches.

Additional resources and reference materials such as presentation software tutorials and documentation help.

In General, Don't Try to Memorize Entire Speeches

- Brief remarks, like toasts, can be well served by memorization. (p. 251)
- Consider memorizing parts of your speech, such as quotations. (p. 251)
- When delivering material from memory, know it well enough to do so with enthusiasm and directness. (p. 251)

When Speaking Impromptu, Maximize Any Preparation Time

- Anticipate situations that may require impromptu speaking. (p. 252)
- Consider what would best serve the audience. (p. 252)
- As you wait your turn to speak, listen to and note what others are saying. (p. 252)
- Jot down a few key ideas in key-word form. (p. 252)
- Stay on topic. (p. 252)

In Most Situations, Select the Extemporaneous Method of Delivery

- Prepare and practice your speech in advance of delivery. (p. 253)
- Speak from an outline of key words and phrases. (p. 253)
- Use eye contact, body orientation, and movement to maximize delivery. (p. 253)

CHAPTER 18 The Voice in Delivery

Adjust Your Speaking Volume

- The bigger the room and the larger the audience, the louder you need to speak. (p. 255)
- Be alert to signals from the audience indicating problems in volume. (p. 255)
- Breathe deeply from your diaphragm. (p. 255)

Beware of Speaking in a Monotone

- Vary your intonation to reflect meaning. (p. 256)
- Use pitch to animate your voice. (p. 256)

Adjust Your Speaking Rate for Comprehension and Expressiveness

- To ensure that your speaking rate is comfortable for your listeners (neither too fast nor too slow), be alert to their reactions. (p. 257)
- Vary your speaking rate depending on topic type. (p. 257)

Use Strategic Pauses and Avoid Meaningless Vocal Fillers

- Use pauses to emphasize points, to draw attention to key thoughts, or to allow listeners a moment to contemplate what you've said. (p. 257)
- Eliminate distracting vocal fillers, such as "uh," "hmm," "you know," "I mean," and "it's like." (p. 257)

Use Vocal Variety

- Use the various vocal elements—volume, pitch, rate, and pauses—to create an effective delivery. (p. 258)
- Use a mix of these elements throughout your speech. (p. 258)

Be Conscious of How You Pronounce and Articulate Words

- Learn to pronounce words correctly. (p. 258)
- If you use a dialect, make sure that your audience understands it. (p. 258)
- Don't mumble or slur your words. (p. 258)

CHAPTER 19 The Body in Delivery

Remember the Importance of Your Nonverbal Behavior

- In addition to the speaker's vocal delivery (how you say something), audiences are highly attuned to the speaker's physical actions, or *body language* (facial expressions, gestures, body movement, and physical appearance). (p. 261)
- Audience members interpret speakers' attitudes toward the audience, speech, and occasion largely through their nonverbal behavior. (p. 261)

Use Nonverbal Cues to Enhance Your Credibility

- Nonverbal behaviors such as eye contact, open body posture, and vocal variety can enhance the audience's perception of your credibility. (p. 261)

Animate Your Facial Expressions in Appropriate Ways

- Establish rapport with your audience with a smile. (p. 262)

Maintain Eye Contact with Your Audience

- Establish eye contact to indicate that you recognize and respect listeners. (p. 262)
- Scan the room with your eyes, pausing to gaze at selected listeners. (p. 263)

Use Gestures That Feel Natural

- Use gestures to clarify your message. (p. 263)
- Use gestures that feel comfortable to you. (p. 263)
- Avoid exaggerated gestures, but make them broad enough to be visible. (p. 263)

Use Body Movement to Establish an Appropriate Degree of Formality or Informality

- Use your physical position vis-à-vis the audience to adjust your relationship with them. (p. 264)

  Movement toward listeners stimulates a sense of informality

  Remaining behind the podium fosters a greater degree of formality
- Be aware of your posture, standing erect, but not ramrod straight. (p. 264)

Pay Attention to Your Clothes and Grooming

- Dress appropriately for the occasion. (p. 264)
- Choices of clothing and grooming will probably be the first thing your listeners notice about you. (p. 264)
- Keep your hands free of distracting objects, such as pens and notecards. (p. 265)

Practice the Delivery

- Practice is essential to effective nonverbal delivery. (p. 266)
- After you've practiced several times, videorecord your delivery, incorporating changes and recording it again. (p. 266)
- Practice in surroundings made to simulate the actual speech setting. (p. 266)
- Time your speech and practice to adjust your amount of material and rate of speaking. (p. 267)

KEY TERMS

Chapter 17

- effective delivery
- elocutionary movement
- speaking from manuscript
- TelePrompTer
- speaking from memory
- oratory
- speaking impromptu
- speaking extemporaneously

Chapter 18

- volume
- pitch
- intonation
- lavalier microphone
- handheld or fixed microphone
- speaking rate
- vocal fillers
- pauses
- vocal variety
- pronunciation
- articulation
- mumbling
- lazy speech
- dialects

Chapter 19

- paralanguage
- body language
- nonverbal communication
- scanning
- talking head

17 Methods of Delivery

LearningCurve can help you review!
Go to LaunchPad: **launchpadworks.com**

> *I wish you to see that public speaking is a perfectly normal act, which calls for no strange, artificial methods, but only for an extension and development of that most familiar act, conversation.*
>
> —James Albert Winans, *Public Speaking*[1]

The process of putting together a speech may be challenging, but what often creates the bigger challenge for most of us is contemplating or actually getting up in front of an audience and speaking. Many communication scholars have noted that *anticipating* giving a speech creates as much anxiety as giving one. Added to this uneasiness is the unfounded idea that speech delivery should be formulaic, mechanical, and exaggerated—that it is, in a way, unnatural or artificial. But as the early public speaking scholar James Albert Winans noted, a speech is really just an enlarged conversation, "quite the natural thing."

Natural, however, does not mean unplanned and unrehearsed. Each component of your speech "conversation," from the quality of your voice to your facial expressions, gestures, and manner of dress, affects how your listeners respond to you. As audience members listen to your words, they are simultaneously reacting to you on a nonverbal level—how you look, how you sound, and how you respond to them. If your verbal and nonverbal cues violate audience members' expectations, they will lose confidence in your credibility as a speaker.[2] Developing effective delivery skills is therefore a critical aspect of the speechmaking process.

Keys to Effective Delivery

Effective delivery is the controlled use of voice and body to express the qualities of naturalness, enthusiasm, confidence, and directness. As Winans has noted, effective delivery is characterized by "a style at once simple and effective."[3] Thus an effective delivery style rests on the same natural foundation as everyday conversation, except that it is more rehearsed and purposeful.

Strive for Naturalness

Contemporary audiences expect naturalness from a speaker. Had you been a student in the early 1900s, during the heyday of the **elocutionary movement**, the opposite would have been true. The elocutionists regarded speechmaking as a type of performance, much like acting.[4] Students were given a rigid set of rules on how to use their eyes, faces, gestures, and voices to drive home certain points in the speech and to manipulate audience members' moods. Instructors emphasized delivery to such an extent that it often assumed more importance than the content of the speech.

Today, the content or message itself, rather than the delivery, is seen as being most important. Audience members expect speakers to be without artifice, to be genuine. Conveying these qualities, however, requires practice. Perhaps ironically, it is only by thoroughly rehearsing the message that you gain the confidence to deliver it in a natural manner.

Show Enthusiasm

Enthusiasm is contagious and is seldom criticized. When you talk about something that excites you, you talk more rapidly, use more gestures, look at your listeners more frequently, use more pronounced facial expressions, and probably stand closer to your listeners. Your enthusiasm spills over to your listeners, drawing them into your message. As their own enthusiasm grows, they listen more attentively because they want to know more about the thing that excites you. In turn, you sense their interest and responsiveness and realize that you are truly connecting with them. The value of enthusiastic delivery is thus accomplished: It focuses your audience's attention on the message.

Project a Sense of Confidence

Speeches delivered with confidence and composure inspire the audience's confidence in you and in your message. Your focus is on the ideas that you want to convey, not on memorized words and sentences and not on yourself. Instead of thinking about how you look and sound, think about the idea you're trying to convey and how well your listeners are grasping it. Confident delivery directs the audience's attention to the message and away from the speaker's behavior.

Be Direct

To truly communicate with an audience, you must build rapport with your listeners. You need to show that you care about them and their reasons for listening to you. This is generally done in two ways: by making your message relevant to the interests and attitudes of audience members, and by demonstrating your interest and concern for them in your delivery. The best way to do the latter is by being direct: Maintain eye contact; use a friendly tone of voice; animate your facial expressions, especially positive ones such as smiling and nodding; and position yourself so that you are physically close to the audience. Of course, you don't want to go overboard by becoming annoying or overly familiar with the audience. But neither do you want to appear distant, aloof, or uncaring. Both extremes draw audience attention away from the message. Chapters 18 and 19 focus on techniques for using your voice and body, respectively, to achieve a natural, enthusiastic, confident, and direct delivery. In the following section, we consider the major methods of delivery.

Select a Method of Delivery

For virtually any type of speech or presentation, you can choose from four basic methods of delivery: speaking from manuscript, speaking from memory, speaking impromptu, and speaking extemporaneously. Each method is distinguished by the expressive voice and body behaviors it uses or restricts, and by the qualities of delivery it promotes or impedes (see Table 17.1).

Speaking from Manuscript

When **speaking from manuscript**, you read a speech verbatim—that is, from prepared written text (either on paper or on a **TelePrompTer**) that contains the entire speech, word for word. As a rule, speaking from manuscript restricts eye contact and body movement and may also limit expressiveness in vocal variety and quality. Watching a speaker read a speech can be monotonous and boring for the audience. Quite obviously, the natural, relaxed, enthusiastic, and direct qualities of delivery are all limited by this method. Commenting on the dangers of reading from a TelePrompTer, for instance, the late columnist and former speechwriter William Safire noted that it can make the speaker appear "shifty and untrustworthy."[5] Working effectively with a TelePrompTer requires practice—just like any method of delivery.

At certain times, however, it is advisable or necessary to read a speech, such as when you must convey a very precise message. As with politicians and business leaders, you may know that you will be quoted and must avoid misinterpretation. Or perhaps it is your responsibility to explain an emergency, so you will need to convey exact descriptions and directions (see Chapter 30 on crisis communication). In some speech circumstances, such as when an award is being presented, tradition may dictate that your remarks be read from a manuscript.

TABLE 17.1 Methods of Delivery and Their Probable Uses

When	Method of Delivery
You want to avoid being misquoted or misconstrued, or you need to communicate exact descriptions and directions . . .	Consider *speaking from manuscript* (reading part or all of your speech from fully prepared text).
You must deliver a short special-occasion speech, such as a toast or introduction, or you plan on using direct quotations . . .	Consider *speaking from memory* (memorizing part or all of your speech).
You are called upon to speak without prior planning or preparation . . .	Consider *speaking impromptu* (organizing your thoughts with little or no lead time).
You have time to prepare and practice developing a speech or presentation that achieves a natural conversational style . . .	Consider *speaking extemporaneously* (developing your speech in a working outline and then practicing and delivering it with a phrase or key-word outline).

If you must read from a prepared text, do what you can to deliver the speech naturally.

- Vary the rhythm of your words (see Chapter 18 on voice).
- Become familiar enough with the speech so that you can establish some eye contact.
- Use a large font and double- or triple-space the manuscript so that you can read without straining.
- Consider using some compelling presentation aids (see Chapter 20).
- Paginate your sheets in case the speech is dropped or shuffled.

Speaking from Memory

The formal name for **speaking from memory** is **oratory**. In oratorical style, you put the entire speech, word for word, into writing and then commit it to memory. In the United States, speaking from memory rarely occurs anymore, though this form of delivery is common in other parts of the world.[6]

Memorization is not a natural way to present a message. True eye contact with the audience is unlikely, and memorization invites potential disaster

ESL SPEAKER'S NOTES

Avoiding the Pitfalls of Manuscript Delivery

NASA Goddard Space Flight Center

Speaking from a manuscript may be difficult and perhaps even ill-advised for some ESL speakers. Reading a speech aloud, word for word, is likely to exaggerate existing problems with pronunciation and *word stress*, or the emphasis given to words in a sentence. These emphasized words or syllables are pronounced more loudly and with a higher pitch. Robbin Crabtree and Robert Weissberg note:

> One of the most characteristic features of spoken English is the tendency of native speakers to take one word in every sentence and give it a stronger push than the others. This feature is called *primary stress*. If you try out a couple of sample sentences, you'll note that the primary stress normally falls at the end, or very close to the end, of the sentence: "That was one of the best speeches I've ever heard." "Let me know if you have trouble; and I'll be glad to help."[1]

If you have difficulty with word and sentence stress and you find that you need to deliver a speech from manuscript, spend extra practice time reading your speech with the aim of ensuring that your word and sentence stress align with the meaning you intend.

1. Dan O'Hair, Rob Stewart, Hannah Rubenstein, Robbin Crabtree and Robert Weissberg, *ESL Students in the Public Speaking Classroom: A Guide for Teachers* (Boston: Bedford/St. Martin's, 2012).

during a speech because there is always the possibility of a mental lapse or block. Some kinds of brief speeches, however, such as toasts and introductions, can be well served by memorization. Sometimes it's helpful to memorize a part of the speech, especially when you use direct quotations as a form of support. If you do find an occasion to use memorization, learn that portion of your speech so completely that in actual delivery you can convey enthusiasm and directness.

Speaking Impromptu

Speaking impromptu, a type of delivery that is unpracticed, spontaneous, or improvised, involves speaking on relatively short notice with little time to prepare. Many occasions require that you make some remarks on the spur of the moment. An instructor may ask you to summarize key points from an assignment, for example, or a fellow employee who was scheduled to speak on a new project may be sick and your boss may invite you to take his or her place.

Try to anticipate situations that may require you to speak impromptu, and prepare some remarks beforehand. Otherwise, maximize the time you do have to prepare on the spot.

- *Think first about your listeners.* Consider their interests and needs, and try to shape your remarks accordingly. For example, who are the people present, and what are their views on the topic?
- *Listen to what others around you are saying.* Take notes in a key-word or phrase format and arrange them into ideas or main points from which you can speak.
- If your speech follows someone else's, acknowledge that person's statements. Then make your own points.
- Stay on the topic. Don't wander off track.
- Use transitions such as "first," "second," and "third," both to organize your points and to help listeners follow them.

As much as possible, try to organize your points into a discernible pattern. If addressing a problem, for example, such as a project failure or glitch, consider the problem-solution pattern—state problem(s), then offer solution(s); or the cause-effect pattern of organizational arrangement—state cause(s) first, then address effect(s); see Chapter 12 for various ways of using these patterns. If called upon to defend one proposal as superior to another, consider using the comparative advantage pattern to illustrate various advantages of your favored proposal over the other options (see Chapter 26 on organizing a persuasive speech).

Taking steps like these will enhance your effectiveness because you will maintain the qualities of natural, enthusiastic, and direct delivery. And having even a hastily prepared plan, even hand-written notes, can give you greater confidence than having no plan at all.

ETHICALLY SPEAKING

A Tool for Good and Evil

Radu Bercan/ Shutterstock

The philosopher Plato believed that the art of public speaking—or rhetoric, as the ancients referred to it—was too often corrupt.[1] Plato's cynicism toward public speaking was the result of unethical practices that he witnessed among his peers and other leaders in ancient Greece. From his perspective, rhetoric (at least as practiced) too often distorted the truth. Today, few people condemn public speaking per se as a dishonest form of communication. But many are aware of the power of delivery to corrupt. If history is any guide, these fears are well founded: One has only to think of such dictators as Mao Tse-tung, Joseph Stalin, Adolf Hitler, and Saddam Hussein, all of whom deliberately used delivery as a means of manipulation. Hitler's forceful delivery—a scorching stare, gestures, and a staccato voice—so mesmerized his listeners that millions accepted the horrific idea that an entire people should be annihilated. Historians note how Hitler spent countless hours practicing his vocal delivery and body language to achieve maximum hypnotic effect. As he did this, he would have himself photographed so that he could hone individual gestures to perfection.[2]

Like any tool, delivery can be used for both ethical and unethical purposes. Countless speakers, from Abraham Lincoln to Martin Luther King Jr. to today's company leaders, have used their flair for delivery to uplift and inspire people. Yet there will always be those who try to camouflage weak or false arguments with an overpowering delivery. You can ensure that your own delivery is ethical by reminding yourself of the ground rules for ethical speaking described in Chapter 5: trustworthiness, respect, responsibility, and fairness. Always reveal your true purpose to the audience, review your evidence and reasoning for soundness, and grant your audience the power of rational choice.

1. Thomas M. Conley, *Rhetoric in the European Tradition* (New York: Longman, 1990).
2. Ian Kershaw, "The Hitler Myth," *History Today* 35, no. 11 (1985): 23.

Speaking Extemporaneously

Speaking extemporaneously falls somewhere between impromptu and written or memorized deliveries. In an extemporaneous speech, you prepare well and practice in advance, giving full attention to all facets of the speech—content, arrangement, and delivery alike. Instead of memorizing or writing the speech word for word, you speak from an outline of key words and phrases (see Chapter 13), having concentrated throughout your preparation and practice on the ideas you want to communicate.

More speeches are delivered by extemporaneous delivery than by any other method. Many, if not most, PowerPoint and Prezi presentations are extemporaneous. Because this technique is most conducive to achieving a natural, conversational quality of delivery, many speakers consider it to be the preferred method of the four types of delivery. Knowing your idea well enough to present it without memorization or manuscript gives you greater flexibility in adapting to the specific speaking situation. You can modify wording, rearrange your points, change examples, or omit information in keeping with the audience and the setting. You can have more eye contact, more direct body orientation, greater freedom of movement, and generally better control of your thoughts and actions than any of the other delivery methods allow.

Speaking extemporaneously does present several possible drawbacks. Because you aren't speaking from specifically written or memorized text, you may become repetitive and wordy. Fresh examples or points may come to mind that you want to share, so the speech may take longer than anticipated. Occasionally, even a glance at your speaking notes may fail to jog your memory on a point you wanted to cover, and you may momentarily find yourself searching for what to say next. The remedy for these potential pitfalls is frequent practice using a speaking outline (see p. 200).

CHECKLIST

READY FOR THE CALL: PREPARING FOR THE EXTEMPORANEOUS SPEECH

Follow these general steps to prepare effective extemporaneous speeches.

_____ 1. Focus your topic as assigned or as appropriate to the audience and occasion.

_____ 2. Prepare a thesis statement that will serve as the central point or idea of your speech.

_____ 3. Research your topic in a variety of sources to gather support for your thesis and add credibility to your points.

_____ 4. Outline main and subordinate points.

_____ 5. Practice the speech at least six times.

(See Chapter 2 for more on speech preparation.)

18 The Voice in Delivery

LearningCurve can help you review!
Go to LaunchPad: **launchpadworks.com**

Used properly in the delivery of a speech, your voice is a powerful instrument of expression that conveys who you are and delivers your message in a way that engages listeners. Your voice also indicates your confidence and affects whether the audience perceives you to be in control of the situation.[1] If you have inadequate mastery of your voice, you may lose your audience's attention and fail to deliver a successful speech. Fortunately, as you practice your speech, you can learn to control each of the elements of vocal delivery. These include volume, pitch, rate, pauses, vocal variety, and pronunciation and articulation.

Adjust Your Speaking Volume

Volume, the relative loudness of a speaker's voice while giving a speech, is usually the most obvious and frequently cited vocal element in speechmaking, and with good reason. We need to hear the speaker at a comfortable level. *The proper volume for delivering a speech is somewhat louder than that of normal conversation.* Just how much louder depends on three factors: (1) the size of the room and of the audience, (2) whether or not you use a microphone, and (3) the level of background noise.

Given the large number of things to focus on while delivering a speech, volume may be overlooked. But speaking at the appropriate volume is critical to how credible your listeners will perceive you to be. Audience members view speakers whose volume is too low less positively than those who project their voices at a pleasing volume. Be alert to signals that your volume is slipping or is too loud and make the necessary adjustments. If your tendency is to speak softly—and many speakers do this, usually from a lack of confidence—initially you will need to project more than seems necessary. To project your voice so that it is loud enough to be heard by everyone in the audience, breathe deeply from your diaphragm rather than more shallowly from your vocal cords. The strength of our voices depends on the amount of air the diaphragm—a large, dome-shaped muscle encasing the inner rib cage—pushes from the lungs to the vocal cords. With full but relaxed breaths, the depth of your voice will improve and help your voice sound more confident.[2]

Vary Your Intonation

Imagine the variation in sound between the leftmost and the rightmost keys of a piano. This variation represents the instrument's **pitch**, or range of sounds from high to low (or vice versa). Pitch is determined by the number of vibrations per unit of time; technically, the more vibrations per unit (also called *frequency*), the higher the pitch, and vice versa.[3] The classic warm-up singing exercise "Do re mi fa so la ti do" is an exercise in pitch.

Anatomy determines a person's natural pitch—a bigger or smaller voice box produces a lower- or higher-pitched voice. But within these natural constraints, you can control pitch through **intonation**—the rising and falling of vocal pitch across phrases and sentences.[4] Intonation is important in speechmaking—indeed, in talk of any kind—because it powerfully affects the meaning associated with spoken words. For example, say "Stop." Now, say "*Stop!*" Varying **intonation** conveys two very distinct meanings. Intonation is what distinguishes a question from a statement:

It's time to study already.
It's time to study al*ready*?

Intonation is very useful in highlighting certain aspects or points of your speech. It helps to capture and maintain the audience's attention and aids them in remembering the key point of the speech. Intonation conveys your mood,

CHECKLIST

TIPS ON USING A MICROPHONE

_____ 1. Perform a sound check with the microphone at least several hours before delivering your speech.

_____ 2. When you first speak into the microphone, ask listeners if they can hear you clearly. Never do a sound check by blowing into a microphone.

_____ 3. Speak directly into the microphone; with many mics, if you turn your head or body, you won't be heard.

_____ 4. When wearing a hands-free **lavalier microphone**—also called *lapel* or *personal mic*—clipped to clothing, speak as if you were addressing a small group. The amplifier will do the rest.

_____ 5. When using a **handheld or fixed microphone**, beware of *popping*, which occurs when you use sharp consonants, such as *p*, *t*, and *d*, and the air hits the mike. To prevent popping, move the microphone slightly below your mouth and about six inches away.

_____ 6. If you have never used a microphone, begin your practice well before the event. It takes time to become comfortable speaking with a microphone.

level of enthusiasm, concern for the audience, and overall commitment to the occasion. Without the variation in pitch that intonation produces, speaking becomes monotonous. A monotone voice is the death knell to any speech.

The best way to avoid speaking in monotone is to record yourself as you practice your speech and then listen to the recording. If you have a recording device on your smart phone, you can use it to test your voice. You will readily identify instances that require better intonation.

Adjust Your Speaking Rate

Speaking rate is the pace at which you convey speech. The normal rate of speech for native English-speaking adults is roughly between 120 and 150 words per minute, but there is no standard, ideal, or most effective rate. If the rate is too slow, it may lull the audience to sleep. If your speech is too fast, listeners may see you as unsure about your control of the speech.[5]

Being alert to the audience's reactions is the best way to know whether your rate of speech is too fast or too slow. Of course, there may be instances in a speech where you may want to vary your speech rate strategically—for example, to convey especially important information or drive home a point. In addition, some serious topics benefit from a slower speech rate; a lively pace generally corresponds with a lighter tone. In general, however, an audience will get fidgety, bored, listless, perhaps even sleepy if you speak too slowly. If you speak too rapidly, listeners will appear irritated and confused, as though they can't catch what you're saying. Both slow and fast speaking rates can signal nervousness to your audience. We know from research that a slower speaking style is perceived as less credible than moderate or fast speaking rates.

To control your speaking rate, choose 150 words from your speech and time yourself for one minute as you read them aloud. If you fall very short of finishing, increase your pace. If you finish well before the minute is up, slow down. Practice until you achieve a comfortable speaking rate.

Use Strategic Pauses

Many novice speakers are uncomfortable with pauses. It's as if some social stigma is attached to any silence in a speech. We often react the same way in conversation, covering pauses with unnecessary and undesirable **vocal fillers**, such as "uh," "hmm," "you know," "I mean," and "it's like." Like intonation, however, pauses can be important strategic elements of a speech. **Pauses** enhance meaning by providing a type of punctuation, emphasizing a point, drawing attention to a thought, or just allowing listeners a moment to contemplate what is being said. They make a speech far more effective than it might otherwise be. Both the speaker and the audience need pauses.

In his well-known "I Have a Dream" speech, the great civil rights leader Martin Luther King Jr. exhibits masterful use of strategic pauses. In what is now the most memorable segment of the speech, King pauses, just momentarily, to secure the audience's attention to the next words that are about to be spoken:

> I have a dream [*pause*] that one day on the red hills of Georgia. . . .
> I have a dream [*pause*] that one day even the great state of Mississippi. . . .[6]

Imagine how diminished the impact of this speech would have been if King had uttered "uh" or "you know" at each of these pauses! These unnecessarily filled pauses can make you appear unprepared and cause audience members to be distracted. Rather than vocal fillers, use silent pauses for strategic effect.

Strive for Vocal Variety

Rather than operating separately, all the vocal elements described so far—volume, pitch, rate, and pauses—work together to create an effective delivery. Indeed, the real key to effective vocal delivery is to vary all these elements with a tone of enthusiasm, thereby producing **vocal variety**. For example, as King spoke the words "I have a dream," the pauses were immediately preceded by a combination of reduced speech rate and increased volume and pitch—a crescendo, you might say. The impact of this variety leaves an indelible impression on anyone who has heard his speech. Vocal variety comes naturally when you are excited about what you are saying and feel it is important to share it with the audience.

Carefully Pronounce and Articulate Words

Few things distract an audience more than improper pronunciation or unclear articulation of words. **Pronunciation** is the correct formation of word sounds. **Articulation** is the clarity or forcefulness with which the sounds are made, regardless of whether they are pronounced correctly. Consider these words that are routinely mispronounced:

- effect (*ee-fect*) is stated as *uh-fect.*
- anyway (*any-way*) is said as *any-ways.*
- mobile (*mo-bile*) is said as *mo-bull* or *mo-bill.*
- leaves (*leevz*) is stated as *leephs.*

Incorrect pronunciations are a matter of habit. Normally you may not know that you are mispronouncing a word because most people you talk with probably say the word much the same way you do. This habit may be associated with a regional accent or dialect. In that case, speaking to an audience of local origin may pose few problems if you pronounce words in regionally customary ways. But if you are speaking to members of an audience for

ESL SPEAKER'S NOTES

Vocal Variety and the Non-Native Speaker

NASA Goddard Space Flight Center

Learning to deliver a speech with the vocal variety that English-speaking people in the United States expect can be particularly challenging for non-native speakers. In addition to having concerns about pronunciation and articulation, the non-native speaker may also be accustomed to patterns of vocal variety—volume, pitch, rate, and pauses—that are different from those discussed in this chapter.

The pronunciation of English depends on learning how to combine a series of about forty basic sounds (fifteen vowels and twenty-five consonants) that together serve to distinguish English words from one another. Correct pronunciation also requires that the speaker learn proper word stress, rhythm, and intonation or pitch.[1] As you practice your speeches, pay particular attention to these facets of delivery. Seek feedback from others to ensure that your goal of shared meaning will be met whenever you deliver speeches.

1. MaryAnn Cunningham Florez, "Improving Adult ESL Learners' Pronunciation Skills," National Clearinghouse for ESL Literacy Education, 1998, accessed October 27, 2013, resources.marshalladulteducation.org/pdf/briefs/ImprovingPronun.Florez.pdf.

whom your accent and pronunciation patterns are not the norm, it is especially important to practice using correct pronunciation. In fact, the better your pronunciation all around, the more enhanced will be the audience's perceptions of your competence, and the greater will be the potential impact of your speech. (See Table 18.1 and Appendix A for lists of commonly mispronounced words.)

SELF-ASSESSMENT CHECKLIST

PRACTICE CHECK FOR VOCAL EFFECTIVENESS

_____ 1. As you practice, is your vocal delivery effective?

_____ 2. Is your voice too loud? Too soft?

_____ 3. Do you avoid speaking in a monotone? Do you vary the stress or emphasis you place on words to clearly express your meaning?

_____ 4. Is your rate of speech comfortable for listeners?

_____ 5. Do you avoid unnecessary vocal fillers, such as "uh," "hmm," "you know," and "I mean"?

_____ 6. Do you use silent pauses for strategic effect?

_____ 7. Does your voice reflect a variety of emotional expressions? Do you convey enthusiasm?

A CULTURAL PERSPECTIVE

Using Dialect (Language Variation) with Care

Charles Taylor
Shutterstock

Every culture has subcultural variations on the preferred pronunciation and articulation of its languages. These variations represent **dialects** of the language. In the United States, for example, there is so-called Standard English, Tex-Mex (a combination of Spanish and English spoken with a distinct Texas drawl or accent), and such regional variations as those found in the South, New England, and along the border with Canada. In parts of Texas, for example, a common usage is to say "fixin' to" instead of "about to," as in "We're fixin' to go to a movie."

Your own dialect may be a factor in the effectiveness of your delivery when speaking to an audience of people whose dialect is different. Your dialect might call attention to itself and be a distraction to the audience. One strategy you can use is to determine which words in your usual vocabulary are spoken dialectically and practice articulating them in General American (GA) English pronunciation.

Articulation problems are also a matter of habit. A common pattern of poor articulation is **mumbling**—slurring words together at a very low level of volume and pitch so that they are barely audible. Sometimes the problem is **lazy speech**. Common examples are saying "wanna" instead of "want to" and "theez 'er" instead of "these are."

Like any habit, poor articulation can be overcome by unlearning the problem behavior:

- If you mumble, practice speaking more loudly and with emphatic pronunciation.
- If you tend toward lazy speech, put more effort into your articulation.
- Consciously try to say each word clearly and correctly.
- Practice clear and precise enunciation of proper word sounds. Say *articulation* several times until it rolls off your tongue naturally.
- Do the same for these words: *want to, going to, riding, walking, Atlanta, chocolate, sophomore, California, affect.*
- Another exercise is the pen drill. Practice your entire speech with a pen horizontally between your teeth. This forces you to overemphasize certain syllables, which allows you to have crystal clear articulation once you take the pen out and speak normally.

19 The Body in Delivery

LearningCurve can help you review!
Go to LaunchPad: **launchpadworks.com**

Beyond the actual words that you say, audiences receive important information from any speech you deliver through two nonverbal channels of communication: the aural and the visual. The *aural channel* consists of the vocalizations that form and accompany your spoken words. These vocalizations, or **paralanguage**, include the qualities of volume, pitch, rate, variety, and pronunciation and articulation described in Chapter 18. Paralanguage refers to *how* something is said, not to *what* is said. Audience members simultaneously use their eyes (the *visual channel*) to evaluate messages sent by your physical appearance and **body language** – facial expressions, eye behavior, gestures, and general body movement.

An abundance of research confirms the importance of paying attention to aural and visual cues both during delivery of a speech and when listening to one. One study suggests that when speakers talk about their feelings and attitudes, the audience derives a mere *7 percent* of the speaker's meaning from the words they utter. The balance comes from the speaker's **nonverbal communication**: 38 percent from the speaker's voice, and 55 percent from the speaker's body language and appearance.[1] Learning to become more confident in using body language is certainly possible. Studies demonstrate that a speaker's attention to body language, including using techniques that focus on posture, gestures, and facial expressions, can improve a speaker's self-efficacy (a feeling that you can succeed in speaking).[2]

Enhance Your Credibility through Nonverbal Cues

Nonverbal communication behaviors play a key part in the audience's perception of your competence, trustworthiness, and character.[3] Research shows, for example, that audiences are more readily persuaded by speakers who emphasize vocal variety, eye contact, nodding at listeners, and standing with an open body position than by those who minimize these nonverbal cues.[4] Instructors, for instance, are judged as more credible when they demonstrate nonverbal behaviors such as direct eye contact, open gestures, and smiling. Audience members also respond more positively to speakers whom they perceive to be well dressed and attractive. They are apt to take them more seriously and are more objective in their responses than they are to speakers whom they do not find attractive.

Pay Attention to Body Language

As you practice delivering your speeches, pay attention to the following elements of body language: facial and eye expressions, gestures, whole body movements, and dress.

Animate Your Facial Expressions

From our facial expressions, audiences can gauge whether we are excited about, disenchanted by, or indifferent to our speech — and the audience to whom we are presenting it. Audiences have a tendency to appreciate a friendly speaker.

Universally, few behaviors are more effective for building rapport with an audience than *smiling.*[5] A smile is a sign of mutual welcome at the start of a speech, of mutual comfort and interest during the speech, and of mutual goodwill at the close of a speech. In addition, smiling when you feel nervous or otherwise uncomfortable can help you relax and gain heightened composure. Of course, facial expressions need to correspond to the tenor of the speech. Doing what is natural and normal for the occasion should be the rule. You can portray your friendliness through your eyes and your mouth.[6] Practice smiling while you are speaking in a mirror. You can learn quickly how easy it is to be an outgoing speaker.

Maintain Eye Contact

If smiling is an effective way to build rapport, maintaining eye contact is mandatory in establishing a positive relationship with your listeners. Having eye contact with the audience is one of the most, if not *the* most, important physical actions in public speaking. Eye contact does the following:

- Maintains the quality of directness in speech delivery
- Lets people know they are recognized
- Indicates acknowledgment and respect
- Signals to audience members that you see them as unique human beings

SELF-ASSESSMENT CHECKLIST

TIPS FOR USING EFFECTIVE FACIAL EXPRESSIONS

____ ✔ Use animated expressions that feel natural and express your meaning.

____ ✔ Never use expressions that are out of character for you or inappropriate to the speech occasion.

____ ✔ In practice sessions, loosen your facial features with exercises such as widening the eyes and moving the mouth.

____ ✔ Establish rapport with the audience by smiling naturally when appropriate.

With an audience of a hundred to more than a thousand members, it's impossible to look at every listener. But in most speaking situations you are likely to experience, you should be able to make the audience feel recognized by using a technique called **scanning**. When you scan an audience, you move your gaze from one listener to another and from one section to another, pausing to gaze at one person long enough to complete one thought before removing your gaze and shifting it to another listener. One speaking professional suggests following the "rule of three": Pick three audience members to focus on—one in the middle, one on the right, and one on the left of the room; these audience members will be your anchors as you scan the room.[7] Some experienced speakers have recommended that your eyes could focus on the back row, giving the audience the impression you are taking them all in.

Use Gestures That Feel Natural

Words alone seldom suffice to convey what we want to express. Physical gestures fill in the gaps, as in illustrating the size or shape of an object (e.g., by showing the size of it by extending two hands, palms facing each other) or expressing the depth of an emotion (e.g., by pounding a fist on a podium).[8] Gestures should arise from genuine emotions and should conform to your personality (see the checklist below for tips on gesturing effectively). Take slight deep breaths and gesture naturally—don't become glued to the podium.[9]

Create a Feeling of Immediacy

In most Western cultures, listeners learn more from and respond most positively to speakers who create a perception of physical and psychological closeness, called **nonverbal immediacy**, between themselves and audience members.[10] Among the nonverbal behaviors you can use to improve your connection with the audience are nodding to show understanding and leaning forward.[11]

Audience members soon tire of listening to a **talking head** (think long-winded sports analyst) who remains steadily positioned in one place behind a

CHECKLIST

TIPS FOR EFFECTIVE GESTURING

- ____ ✔ Use natural, spontaneous gestures.
- ____ ✔ Avoid exaggerated gestures, but use gestures that are broad enough to be seen by each audience member.
- ____ ✔ Eliminate distracting gestures, such as fidgeting with pens or pencils or brushing back hair from your eyes.
- ____ ✔ Analyze your gestures for effectiveness in practice sessions.
- ____ ✔ Practice movements that feel natural to you, especially punctuating movements that drive home your points.

CHECKLIST

BROAD DRESS CODE GUIDELINES

_____ 1. For a "power" look, wear a dark-colored suit.

_____ 2. Medium-blue or navy paired with white can enhance your credibility.

_____ 3. Yellow and orange color tones convey friendliness.

_____ 4. The color red focuses attention on you.

_____ 5. Flashy jewelry distracts listeners.

microphone or podium. As space and time allow, use your physical position vis-à-vis audience members to adjust your relationship with them, establishing a level of familiarity and closeness that is appropriate to the topic, purpose, and occasion. Movement toward listeners stimulates a sense of informality and closeness; remaining behind the podium fosters a more formal relationship of speaker to audience.

One way of demonstrating immediacy is to push your hands and arms out wide for maximum effect when demonstrating your points. Walking around is also an effective way to demonstrate that you are interested in the audience.[12]

Maintain Good Posture

A speaker's posture sends a definite message to the audience. Listeners perceive speakers who slouch as being sloppy, unfocused, and even weak. Strive to stand erect, but not ramrod straight. The goal is to appear authoritative, not rigid. Again, looking in a mirror when you practice will help determine an effective posture for you.

Dress Appropriately

Superficial as it may sound, the first thing an audience is likely to notice about you as you approach the speaker's position is your clothing. The critical criteria in determining appropriate dress for a speech are audience expectations and the nature of the speech occasion. If you are speaking as a representative of your business, for example, you will want to complement your company's image.[13] Consider the late Apple co-founder Steve Jobs, who invariably wore jeans and a black shirt when he rolled out a new product. Jobs's attire conveyed a signature style that was casual and "cool," personifying the Apple products he represented.[14]

Although some speaking occasions permit casual dress, take care not to confuse casual with sloppy or unkempt. Even casual attire should be professional in the sense that it conveys a responsible, credible, and confident image. Your attire reveals an attitude about what you are doing and the amount of effort you seem willing to put into it. The more professional you look, the more professional you will feel, and the more positive the attitude you will convey to audience members. This advice is no less important for your classroom speeches than it is for speeches given elsewhere. You should dress for your speeches in class just as you would if you were delivering them to a business or professional group that you wanted to impress. At the very least, it's good practice, and it's likely to benefit your speech by showing your respect for both the occasion and the audience.

An extension of dress is having various objects on or around your person while giving a speech—pencil and pen, a briefcase, a glass of water, or papers with notes on them. Always ask yourself if these objects are really necessary. A sure way to distract an audience from what you're saying is to drag a briefcase or backpack to the speaker's stand and open it while speaking, or to fumble with a pen or other object.

A CULTURAL PERSPECTIVE

Nonverbal Communication Patterns in Different Cultures

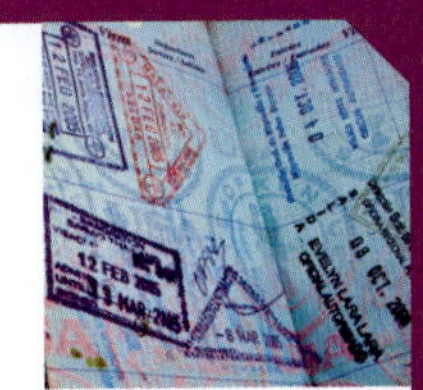
Charles Taylor Shutterstock

As a speaker, it's important to remember that, like verbal communication, nonverbal communication is also profoundly influenced by culture. Gestures, for example, have entirely different meanings in different cultures, and many an unsuspecting speaker has inadvertently made a rude gesture in his or her host's culture. In the late 1950s, for instance, Vice President Richard Nixon made a goodwill tour of Latin America, where there were feelings of hostility toward the United States. On one of his stops, Nixon stepped off his plane and, smiling, gestured with the A-OK sign to the waiting crowd. The crowd booed. In that culture, Nixon's gesture meant "screw you." Days of delicate diplomacy were undone by two seconds of nonverbal behavior.[1] This same gesture, incidentally, means "zero" in French and "money" in Japan. Roger Axtell catalogs a variety of gestures in his book *Gestures: The Do's and Taboos of Body Language around the World*. This eye-opening account demonstrates how something in one culture can mean literally the opposite in another (e.g., nodding means "yes" in the United States but can mean "no" in the former Yugoslavia and Iran).

The display of emotions is also guided by the social rules of the culture. The Japanese are conditioned to mask emotion, whereas Americans express emotion more freely. Speakers in different cultures thus use different facial expressions to convey emotions. Eye behavior also takes quite different forms; people in the United States and Canada use eye contact as a form of acknowledgment or politeness in greeting, but in other cultures—such as in Southeast Asia, Nigeria, and Puerto Rico, among other places—this is often considered disrespectful. Finally, appearance preferences also change from one culture to another.

No speaker should feel obliged to adopt nonverbal behaviors that are not his or her own. At the same time, a successful speech depends on shared meaning. As such, a thorough audience analysis is needed to anticipate potential misunderstandings that might occur nonverbally.

1. Roger Axtell, *Gestures: The Do's and Taboos of Body Language around the World* (New York: Wiley, 1991).

Source: Adapted from Dan O'Hair, Gustav Friedrich, and Lynda Dixon, *Strategic Communication in Business and the Professions* (Boston: Allyn Bacon, 2011), Chapter 3.

Practice the Delivery

One of the most cited recommendations from public speaking experts—whether they appear in books, blogs, or websites—is the importance of practice. Practice is essential to effective delivery. The more you practice, the greater your comfort level will be when you actually deliver the speech. More than anything, it is uncertainty that breeds anxiety. By practicing your speech using a fully developed speaking outline (see Chapter 13), you will know what to expect when you actually stand in front of the audience.

Focus on the Message

The primary purpose of any speech is to get a message across, not to display extraordinary delivery skills. Keep this goal foremost in your mind. Psychologically, too, focusing on your message is likely to make your delivery more natural and more confident.

Record the Speech

Once you've practiced your speech several times, talk it out into an audio recorder. At a later stage in the practice process, you can place the recorder across the room from you and practice projecting your voice to the back row of the audience. To accurately gauge how you sound, use a good-quality recording device.

Videorecording two practice sessions can provide valuable feedback. As you watch your initial recording, make notes of the things you'd like to change. Before rerecording, practice several more times until you are comfortable with the changes you've incorporated. Note that no one is ever entirely thrilled with his or her image on video, so try to avoid unnecessary self-criticism. Even your voice is going to sound different on a recording than what you are used to hearing. Videorecord your speech a second time, paying close attention to the areas of speech delivery that you want to improve.

Be Prepared to Revise Your Speaking Notes

As you practice, revise your speech as needed. If your introduction or conclusion isn't as effective as you would like, rework it. Make other adjustments as necessary to improve your speech and make the notes easier to follow.

Practice under Realistic Conditions

Try to simulate the actual speech setting as you practice. Keep the seating arrangement in mind as you speak, picturing the audience as you go along. Turn various objects in the room into imaginary audience members, and project your voice in their direction. Practice scanning for eye contact. Practice with a podium of some kind (unless you know that you won't be using one). Stack some boxes to form a makeshift podium if you have to. Practice working with your speaking notes until you are confident that you can refer to them without overly relying on them. Practice placing your notes on a podium and moving around the podium for effective delivery.

At some point, practice your speech in front of at least one other person. Ask your volunteer(s) to identify the purpose and key points of your speech. Question them about what they did or did not understand. Seek detailed feedback about the quality of your delivery.

Time Your Speech

As you practice, time each part of the speech (introduction, body, and conclusion) so that if you exceed your time limit you can adjust these sections accordingly. Recall that, as a general rule, the introduction or the conclusion should make up no more than 10 or 15 percent of your entire speech (see Chapters 14 and 15). If the speech is too long, look for extraneous material that can be cut. Consider your rate of speech. If it is too slow, practice speaking more concisely. If the speech is too short, review your evidence and make certain that you adequately support your main points. If your rate of speech is too fast, practice slowing your tempo.

Plan Ahead and Practice Often

If possible, begin practicing your speech at least several days before you are scheduled to deliver it. Many expert speakers recommend practicing your speech about five times in its final form. Since few speeches are longer than twenty minutes, and most are shorter, this represents a maximum of two hours of practice time—two hours well spent.

- Practice with your speaking notes, revising those parts of the speech that aren't satisfactory, and altering the notes as you go.
- Focus on your speech ideas rather than on yourself.
- Time each part of your speech—introduction, body, and conclusion.
- Practice with any presentation aids you plan to use.
- Practice with a pencil in your teeth. When you speak without it, you will find you have a much more articulate style.
- Practice your speech several times, and then record it.
- If possible, videotape yourself twice—once after several practice sessions, and again after you've worked to incorporated any changes into your speech.
- Visualize the setting in which you will speak, and practice the speech under realistic conditions, paying particular attention to projecting your voice to fill the room.
- Practice in front of at least one volunteer, and seek constructive criticism.
- Schedule your practice sessions early in the process so that you have time to prepare.

PRESENTATION AIDS

In the photo, founder and CEO of Facebook Mark Zuckerberg uses presentation aids to support his speech announcing a new product at the company headquarters on April 4, 2013. Combining his description of the features of the new product with the visuals helps his audience understand his message. Justin Sullivan/Getty Images News/Getty Images

PRESENTATION AIDS

SPEAKER'S PREVIEW

LearningCurve can help you review.
Go to LaunchPad: **launchpadworks.com**

PRESENTATION AIDS

CHAPTER 20 Speaking with Presentation Aids

Use Presentation Aids to Increase Understanding and Retention

- Understanding is enhanced when information is received orally *and visually*. (p. 275)
- Aids should not merely repeat spoken points. (p. 275)

Consider Using Props and Models

- Inanimate or live *props* can solidify your descriptions. (p. 275)
- In many areas of study, *models* are a central component of presentations. (p. 275)

Consider Illustrating Key Points with Pictures

- Look for visually arresting *photographs*. (p. 276)
- Create a *diagram* to demonstrate how something is constructed or used. (p. 276)
- Use a *map* to pinpoint an area or illustrate proportions. (p. 276)

Use Graphs and Charts to Show Trends and Demonstrate Relationships

- Select a *line graph* to represent trends and other information that changes over time. (p. 277)
- Choose a *bar graph* to compare quantities or magnitudes. (p. 277)
- Use a *pie graph* to show proportions. (p. 277)
- Use a *pictogram* to characterize comparisons in picture form. (p. 277)

LaunchPad VIDEO ACTIVITY

Go to LaunchPad to watch a video about using presentation aids effectively in your speech.

LaunchPad includes:

LearningCurve adaptive quizzing

a curated collection of video clips and full-length speeches.

Additional resources and reference materials such as presentation software tutorials and documentation help.

- Uses a *chart* to visually organize complex information into compact form. (p. 278)
- Use a *flowchart* to diagram a procedure or process. (p. 278)
- Use a *table* to allow viewers to make comparisons about information quickly. (p. 278)

Use Audio and Video to Add Interest

- Consider incorporating clips into PowerPoint presentations. (p. 279)
- Be familiar with software programs that produce multimedia. (p. 279)
- Become familiar with digital storytelling. (p. 280)

Become Familiar with Options for Displaying Aids

CHAPTER 21 Designing Presentation Aids

Present One Major Idea per Aid

- Limit the amount of information in any single visual. (p. 282)
- Use no more than six words in a line and six lines on one slide. (p. 282)
- Word text in active verb form and use parallel sentence structure. (p. 282)

Apply the Same Design Decisions to Each Aid

- Apply consistent colors, fonts, capitalization, and styling. (p. 283)

Use Type Large Enough to Be Read Comfortably

- Experiment with 36-point type for major headings, 24-point type for subheadings, and 18-point type for the body of the text. (p. 285)
- For slides, use a sans serif typeface for titles and major headings. (p. 283)
- Experiment with a serif typeface for the body of the text. (p. 283)

Use Color Carefully

- Be aware of the effect of color combinations on readability. (p. 285)
- Understand that colors can evoke distinct associations in people and summon various moods. (p. 286)
- For typeface and graphics, use colors that contrast with the background color. (p. 285)
- Restrict the number of colors to three or four. (p. 285)
- Consider subjective interpretations of color. (p. 286)

CHAPTER 22 Using Presentation Software

Remember That You're Giving a Speech, Not a Slide Show

- Focus on your message and audience first rather than the pizzazz of a slide show. (p. 287)
- Help your audience by using presentation aids to help them process information. (p. 287)

Follow a Plan to Avoid Technical Problems

- Use your speaking outline to plan the content, number, and arrangement of aids. (p. 287)
- Carefully consider which points are more suited for visual display than others. (p. 287)
- Check compatibility for operating systems, versions of presentation programs, and other software in advance of your speech. (p. 289)
- Ensure compatibility for input and output devices such as flash drives, projectors, and speakers. (p. 289)
- Save your files to a source recognized by the presentation computer, and make a backup of your presentation. (p. 289)

Refer to LaunchPad for Presentation Software Guidance

- See tips on using Microsoft PowerPoint
- See tips on using Apple Keynote
- See tips on using Prezi

Find Media for Presentations

- Locate downloadable files for digital images, clip art, video, and sound files. (p. 292)

Avoid Copyright Infringement

- Carefully abide by copyright restrictions. (p. 293)
- Even if fair use applies, cite the source of material in your presentation. (p. 293)

KEY TERMS

Chapter 20

- presentation aids
- multimedia effect
- prop
- model
- graph
- pictogram
- chart
- flowchart
- table
- multimedia
- digital storytelling
- flip chart
- handout

Chapter 21

- six-by-six rule
- typeface
- serif typefaces
- sans serif typefaces
- script
- novelty font

Go to LaunchPad: **launchpadworks.com** to watch the video clips for this chapter.

20 Speaking with Presentation Aids

LearningCurve can help you review!
Go to LaunchPad: **launchpadworks.com**

Used judiciously, **presentation aids** can help listeners understand and retain information that is otherwise difficult or time-consuming to convey in words. Indeed, research confirms that most people process information best when it is presented both verbally and visually—a principle dubbed the "**multimedia effect**."[1] However, no matter how powerful a photograph, chart, or other aid may be, if it is unrelated to a speech point, is poorly designed, or simply duplicates what the speaker says, the audience will become distracted and actually retain less information than they would without it.[2]

Select an Appropriate Aid

Presentation aids can be objects, models, pictures, graphs, charts, tables, audio, videos, or multimedia. Choose the aid, or combination of aids, that will help your audience grasp information most effectively.

Props and Models

A **prop** can be any object, inanimate or even live, that helps demonstrate the speaker's points. A **model** is a three-dimensional, scale-size representation of an object. Presentations in engineering, architecture, and many other disciplines often use these aids. The rapidly growing availability of 3D printing is making it possible for speakers and presenters to forge almost any object imaginable. When using a prop or model:

- Practice delivering your speech using it.
- Make sure it is big enough for everyone to see (and read, if applicable).
- In most cases, keep it hidden until you are ready to use it.

FIGURE 20.1 This photo of a wind farm is an example of a picture used in a speaker's presentation.

PASCAL GUYOT/Getty Images

Pictures

Pictures (two-dimensional representations) include photographs, line drawings, diagrams, maps, and posters. A *diagram* or *schematic drawing* depicts how something works or is constructed or operated. *Maps* help audience members visualize geographic areas and understand relationships among them; they also illustrate the proportion of one thing to something else in different areas.

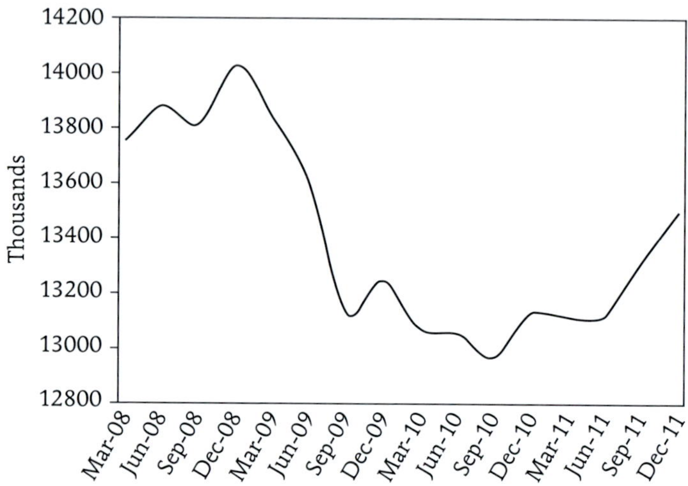

FIGURE 20.2 Line Graph Depicting South Africa Total Employment, 2008–2011

Source: Accessed November 17, 2013, www.sec.gov.

Graphs, Charts, and Tables

A **graph** represents relationships among two or more things.

- A *line graph* uses points connected by lines to demonstrate how something changes or fluctuates over time.
- A *bar and column graph* uses bars of varying lengths to compare quantities or magnitudes.
- *Pie graphs* depict the division of a whole into slices, with each slice constituting a percentage of the whole.
- **Pictograms** use picture symbols (icons) to illustrate relationships and trends; for example, a a generic-looking human figure repeated in a row below a shorter version of the same row can demonstrate increasing college enrollment over time.

Vertical Bar Graph

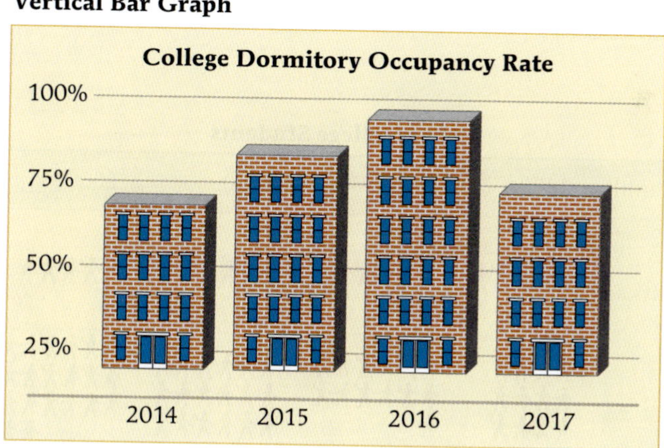

Horizontal Bar Graph

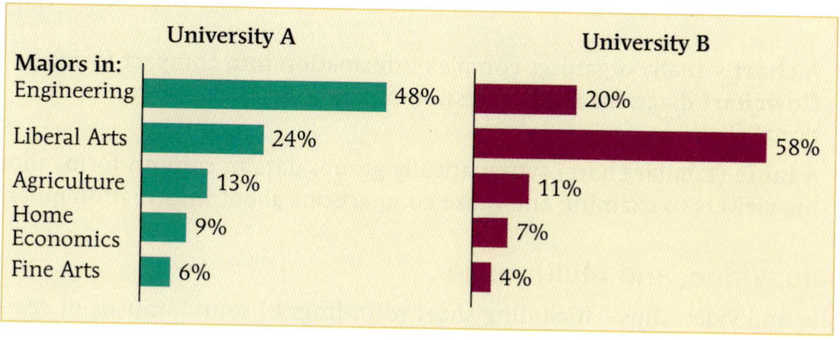

FIGURE 20.3 Bar Graphs of Quantities and Magnitudes

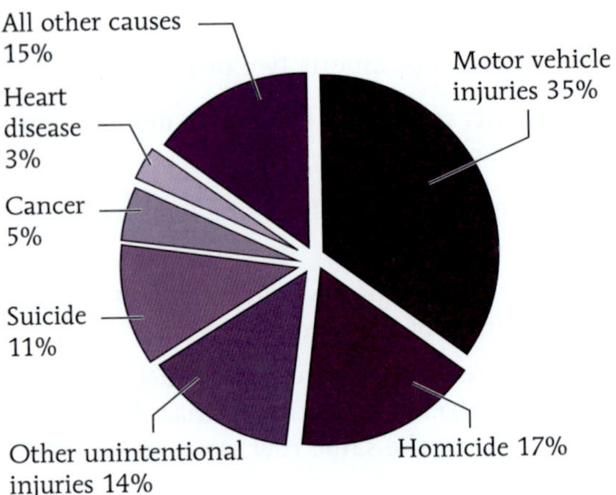

FIGURE 20.4 Pie Graph Showing Various Causes of Teen Deaths

Source: Centers for Disease Control and Prevention, accessed November 17, 2013, www.cdc.gov/motorvehiclesafety/teenbrief/.

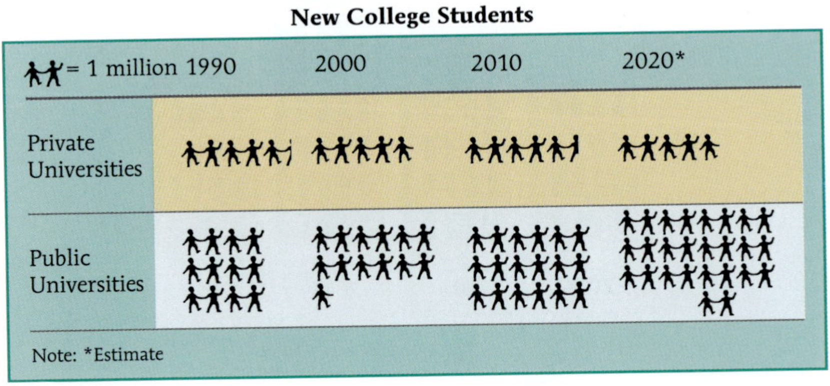

New College Students

= 1 million	1990	2000	2010	2020*
Private Universities				
Public Universities				

Note: *Estimate

FIGURE 20.5 Pictogram Showing Increase in College Students

- A **chart** visually organizes complex information into compact form. A **flowchart** diagrams the progression of a process as a sequence or directional flow.
- A **table** (tabular chart) systematically groups data in column form, allowing viewers to examine and make comparisons about information quickly.

Audio, Video, and Multimedia

Audio and video clips—including short recordings of sound, music, or speech, and clips from movies, television, and other recordings—can motivate attention

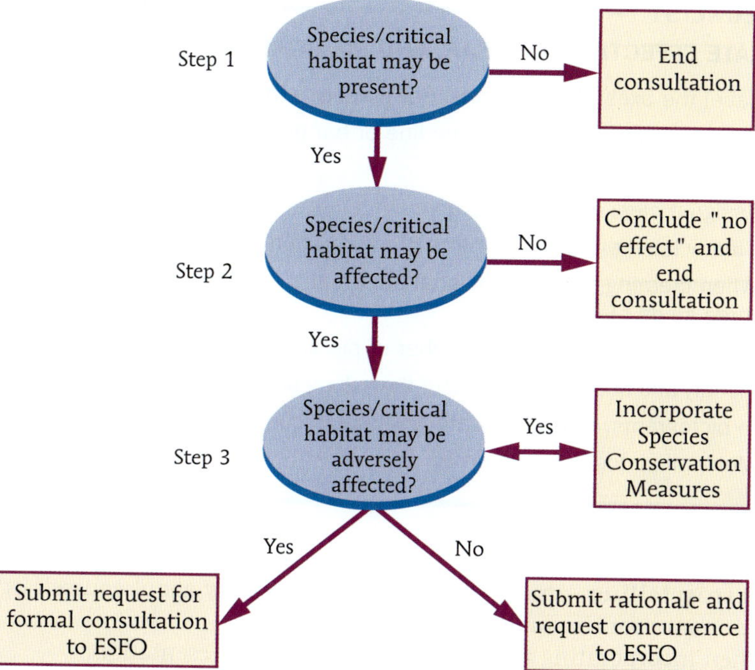

FIGURE 20.6 Flowcharts show a sequence of action.
U.S. Fish and Wildlife Service

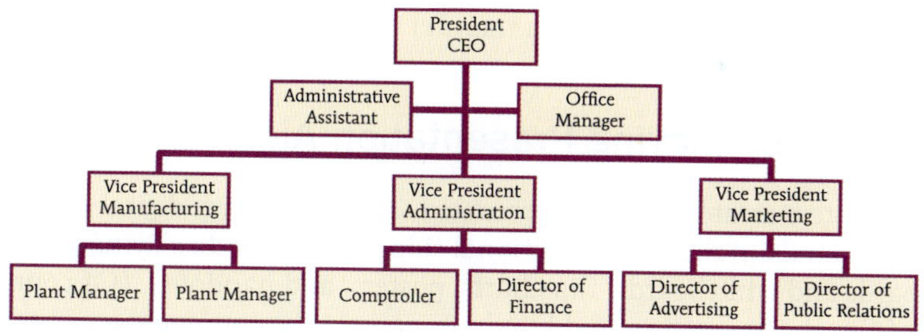

FIGURE 20.7 Organizational Chart Showing Personnel Hierarchy

and help to move among and clarify points.[3] **Multimedia**, which combines stills, sound, video, text, and data into a single production, requires familiarity with presentation software programs such as Windows Movie Maker and Apple iMovie. (See Chapter 22 for guidelines on linking audio and video clips to slides.) This rich variety of information cues can potentially boost audience attention, comprehension, and retention.[4] One application of multimedia is

CHECKLIST

CREATE EFFECTIVE LINE, BAR, AND PIE GRAPHS

- ✔ Label the axes of line graphs, bar graphs, and pictograms.
- ✔ Start the numerical axis of the line or bar graph at zero.
- ✔ Compare only like variables.
- ✔ Assign a clear title to the graph.
- ✔ Clearly label all relevant points of information in the graph.
- ✔ When creating multidimensional bar graphs, do not compare more than three kinds of information.
- ✔ In pie graphs, restrict the number of pie slices to a maximum of seven.
- ✔ Identify and accurately represent the values or percentages of each pie slice.
- ✔ In pictograms, clearly indicate what each icon symbolizes.
- ✔ Make all pictograms the same size.

digital storytelling—using multimedia to tell a story about yourself or others with resonance for the audience.

When incorporating audio and video into your presentation:

- Cue the audio or video clip to the appropriate segment before the presentation.
- Alert audience members to what they will be hearing or viewing before you play it back.
- Reiterate the relevance of the audio or video clip to your key points once it is over.
- Use the audio or video clip in a manner consistent with copyright.

Options for Displaying Presentation Aids

Many presenters create computer-generated aids shown with digital projectors or on LCD displays. On the more traditional side, options for displaying aids include chalkboards and whiteboards, flip charts, posters, and handouts. (Of course, elements of flip charts, posters, and handouts can also be computer generated.)

Computer-Generated Aids and Displays

With software such as Microsoft PowerPoint and Apple Keynote, and their online counterparts such as Prezi, speakers can create slides to project using LCD (liquid crystal display) panels and projectors or DLP presentation software. (See Chapter 22 for guidelines on presentation software.)

Chalkboards and Whiteboards

On the lowest-tech end of the spectrum lies the writing board, on which you can write with chalk (on a chalkboard) or with nonpermanent markers (on a *whiteboard*). Reserve writing boards for impromptu explanations, such as presenting simple processes that are done in steps, or for engaging the audience in short brainstorming sessions. If you have the time to prepare more advanced presentation aids, however, avoid writing boards. They force the speaker to turn his or her back to the audience, make listeners wait while you write, and require legible handwriting that will be clear to all viewers.

Flip Charts

A **flip chart** is simply a large (27–34 inch) pad of paper on which a speaker can write or draw. This aid is often prepared in advance; then, as you progress through the speech, you flip through the pad to the next exhibit. You can also write and draw on the pad as you speak. Sometimes a simple drawing or word written for emphasis can be as or more powerful than a highly polished slide.

Handouts

A **handout** conveys information that either is impractical to give to the audience in another format or is intended to be kept by audience members after the presentation. To avoid distracting listeners, unless you specifically want them to read the information as you speak, wait until you have concluded your presentation before you distribute the handout. If you do want the audience to view a handout during the speech, pass it out only when you are ready to talk about it.

Posters

Speakers use *posters* — large paperboards incorporating text, figures, and images, alone or in combination — to illustrate some aspect of their topic; often the poster rests on an easel. See Chapter 30 for guidelines on using posters in presentations called poster sessions.

CHECKLIST

INCORPORATING PRESENTATION AIDS INTO YOUR SPEECH

- ✔ Practice with the aids until you are confident that you can handle them without causing undue distractions.
- ✔ Talk to your audience rather than to the screen or object—avoid turning your back to the audience.
- ✔ Maintain eye contact with the audience.
- ✔ Place the aid to one side rather than behind you, so that the entire audience can see it.
- ✔ Display the aid only when you are ready to discuss it.
- ✔ If you use a pointer, once you've indicated your point, put it down.
- ✔ In case problems arise, be prepared to give your presentation without the aids.

21 Designing Presentation Aids

LearningCurve can help you review!
Go to LaunchPad: **launchpadworks.com**

The quality of a speaker's presentation aids is a critical factor in the audience's perception of his or her credibility. Well-designed presentation aids signal that the speaker is prepared and professional; poorly designed aids create a negative impression that is difficult to overcome. As you prepare aids, focus on keeping the elements easy to see, and ensure that they are designed in a consistent manner. Audience members can follow only one piece of information at a time, and visuals that are crowded or difficult to decipher will divert attention from your message.[1] This chapter contains guidelines for designing effective presentation aids such as PowerPoint slides, flip charts, and simple posters.

Keep the Design Simple

On average, audience members have only 30 seconds or less[2] to view an aid, so keep the text to a minimum and present only one major idea per slide or page.

- *Follow the* ***six-by-six rule***. Use no more than six words in a line and six lines on one slide. This will keep the audience's attention on you (see Figure 21.1).
- *Word text in active verb form*. Use the active voice and parallel grammatical structure, for example, "Gather Necessary Documents; Apply Early" (see Chapter 16 on language).
- *Avoid clutter*. Allow plenty of white space, or "visual breathing room" for viewers.[3]
- *Create concise titles*. Use titles that succinctly summarize content and reinforce your message.

Beware of "Chartjunk"

Certain kinds of information — especially statistical data and sequences of action — are best understood when presented visually. However, avoid what information design expert Edward Tufte coined as "chartjunk"[4] — visuals jammed with too many graphs, charts, and meaningless design elements that obscure rather than illuminate information. The fewer slides the better, and only use those design elements that truly enhance meaning.

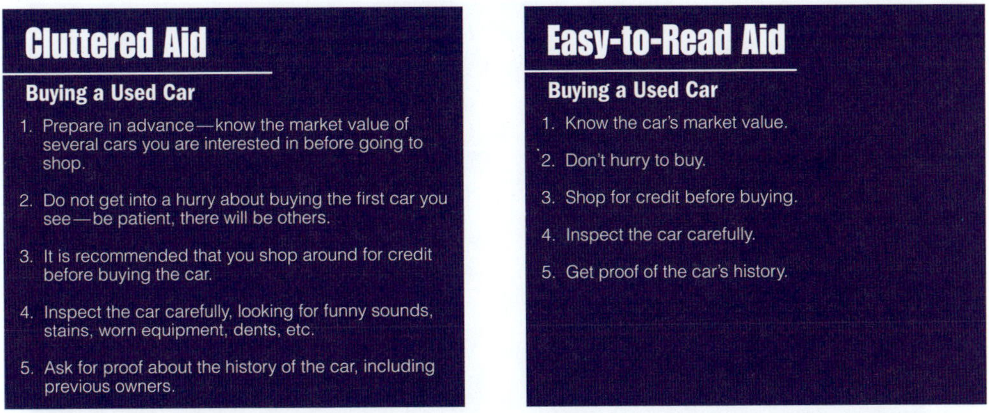

Cluttered Aid

Buying a Used Car

1. Prepare in advance—know the market value of several cars you are interested in before going to shop.
2. Do not get into a hurry about buying the first car you see—be patient, there will be others.
3. It is recommended that you shop around for credit before buying the car.
4. Inspect the car carefully, looking for funny sounds, stains, worn equipment, dents, etc.
5. Ask for proof about the history of the car, including previous owners.

Easy-to-Read Aid

Buying a Used Car

1. Know the car's market value.
2. Don't hurry to buy.
3. Shop for credit before buying.
4. Inspect the car carefully.
5. Get proof of the car's history.

FIGURE 21.1 Cluttered versus Easy-to-Read Presentation Aid

Use Design Elements Consistently

Apply the same design decisions you make for a particular presentation aid in a speech to all of the slides or pages in that aid; this will ensure that viewers aren't distracted by a jumble of unrelated visual elements. Carry your choice of design elements throughout the aid—color, fonts, upper- and lowercase letters, styling (boldface, underlining, italics), general page layout, and repeating elements such as titles and logos.

Select Appropriate Typeface Styles and Fonts

A **typeface** is a specific style of lettering, such as Arial or Times Roman. Typefaces come in a variety of fonts, sizes (called the point size), and upper and lower cases. Designers divide the thousands of available typefaces into two major categories: serif and sans serif. **Serif typefaces** include small flourishes, or strokes, at the tops and bottoms of each letter. Text in serif font conveys confidence, knowledge, and reliability. **Sans serif typefaces** are more blocklike and linear; they are designed without the tiny strokes of a serif font. Sans serif looks clean and modern. For reading a block of text, serif typefaces (like this) are easier on the eye. Small amounts of text, however, such as headings, are best viewed in sans serif type (like this). Thus, consider a sans serif typeface for the heading and a serif typeface for the body of the text. If you include only a few lines of text, use sans serif type throughout.

Two other categories of font are *script* and *novelty*. **Script** is cursive, like handwriting, and conveys friendliness, approachability, or creativity. **Novelty fonts** are unique, flashy, and even cartoonish. They grab attention and convey fun or excitement. Novelty fonts may have a place in some presentation aids

Typefaces

Serif

- Times New Roman
- Courier New
- Garamond
- Book Antiqua

Sans Serif

- Arial Narrow
- Haettenschweiler
- Veranda
- Century Gothic

FIGURE 21.2 Serif and Sans Serif Typefaces

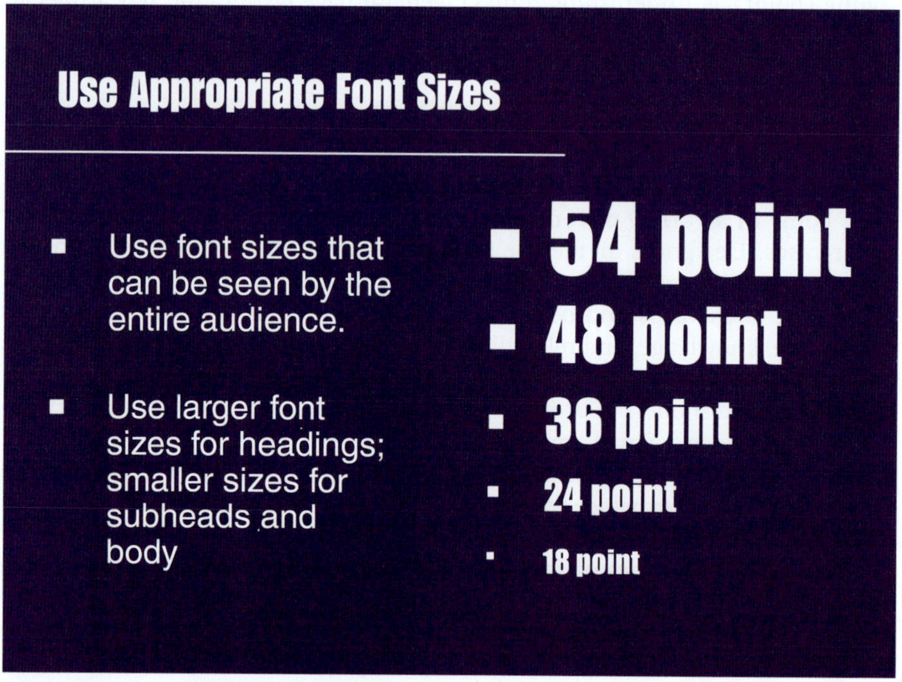

Use Appropriate Font Sizes

- Use font sizes that can be seen by the entire audience.
- Use larger font sizes for headings; smaller sizes for subheads and body

- 54 point
- 48 point
- 36 point
- 24 point
- 18 point

FIGURE 21.3 Use Appropriate Font Sizes

but should be used the least. Script should also be used infrequently as it can be difficult to read and process quickly at a distance.

Consider these guidelines when selecting and composing lettering:

- Check the lettering for legibility, taking into consideration the audience's distance from the visual. On slides, experiment with 36-point type for major headings, 24-point type for subheadings, and *at least* 18-point type for body text.
- Lettering should stand apart from the background. Use either dark text on light background or light text on dark background.
- Use a common typeface that is simple and easy to read and is not distracting.
- Use standard upper- and lowercase type rather than all capitals.
- Use no more than two different typefaces in a single visual aid.
- Use **boldface**, underlining, and *italics* sparingly.

Use Color Carefully

Skillful use of color can draw attention to key points, influence the mood of a presentation, and make things easier to see. Conversely, poor color combinations will set the wrong mood, render an image unattractive, or make it unreadable. Note the effect of the following color combinations.

Effects of Color Combinations

Color	Effect in Combination
Yellow	Warm on white, harsh on black, fiery on red, soothing on light blue
Blue	Warm on white, hard to see on black
Red	Bright on white, warm or difficult to see on black

Color affects both the legibility of text and the mood conveyed. To use color effectively in your presentation aids:

- Keep the *background color* consistent across all slides or pages of your aid.
- Carefully use *bold, bright colors* to emphasize important points.
- For typeface and graphics, use colors that contrast rather than clash with or blend into the background color; check for visibility when projecting. Audiences will remember information just as easily if white text appears on a dark background or dark text appears on a light background, as long as the design is appealing.[5]
- Limit colors to no more than three, with maximum of four in complex and detailed aids.

Consider Subjective Interpretations of Color

Colors can evoke distinct associations for people, so take care not to summon an unintended meaning or mood. For example, control engineers see red and think danger, whereas a financial manager will think unprofitability.

Consider, too, that the meanings associated with certain colors may differ across cultures. Western societies don black for funerals, while the Chinese wear white. If you are presenting in an international cross-cultural context, check the meanings of colors for the relevant nationalities.

CHECKLIST

APPLY THE PRINCIPLES OF SIMPLICITY AND CONTINUITY

- ✓ Concentrate on presenting one major idea per visual aid.
- ✓ Apply design decisions consistently to each aid.
- ✓ Use type that is large enough for audience members to read comfortably.
- ✓ Use color judiciously to highlight key ideas and enhance readability.
- ✓ Check that colors contrast rather than clash.

22 Using Presentation Software

LearningCurve can help you review!
Go to LaunchPad: **launchpadworks.com**

A variety of powerful software programs are available for public speakers to create and display high-quality visual aids. These programs include Microsoft PowerPoint and its Apple counterpart, Keynote, as well as other programs such as Prezi, Prezentit, and SlideRocket.

Give a Speech, Not a Slide Show

Frequently we hear someone say, "I'm giving a PowerPoint (or a Prezi or Keynote) presentation today," instead of "I'm giving a speech today." Some speakers hide behind presentation media, focusing attention on their aids rather than on the audience. They might mistakenly believe that the display itself is the presentation, or that it will somehow save an otherwise poorly planned speech.[1] It can be easy to become so involved in generating glitzy aids that you forget your primary mission: to communicate through the spoken word and your physical presence. Presentation aids can and do help listeners process information and enhance a speech, but only as long as you work to engage the audience and achieve your speech goal.[2] Speaker and message, rather than any presentation media, must take center stage.

Develop a Plan

Visual aids are meant to support certain points in your speech, and the best place to find these points and plan your slides is in your speaking outline (see Chapter 13, p. 190). Think through which points in your speech might be better explained with some kind of visual: Decide what the content of your slides should be, how many slides you'll need, and how they should be arranged. Review and edit the slides as necessary using *Slide Sorter view* (in PowerPoint), *Light Table* or *Outline view* (in Keynote), or *Path tool* (in Prezi). Also, determine the best platform for displaying your slides. A room full of people (say, twenty-five or more) will call for using a projector displaying slides on a large wall screen. A group of ten to twenty-five people could be served by displaying your slides on a large television screen. For fewer than ten people, a laptop computer or tablet set on a table might be large enough to display your slides.

LaunchPad For detailed guidance on creating presentations in PowerPoint, Keynote, and Prezi, go to **launchpadworks.com**

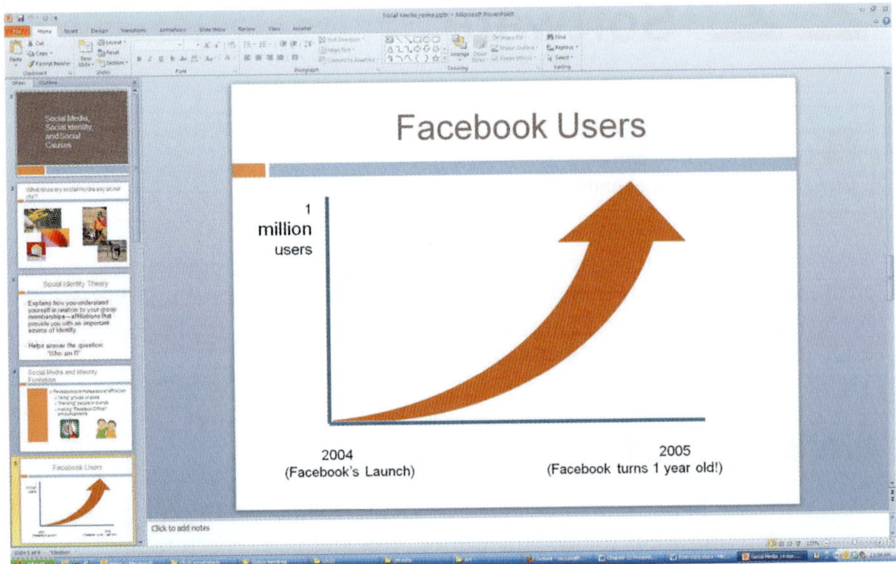

FIGURE 22.1 Normal View in PowerPoint

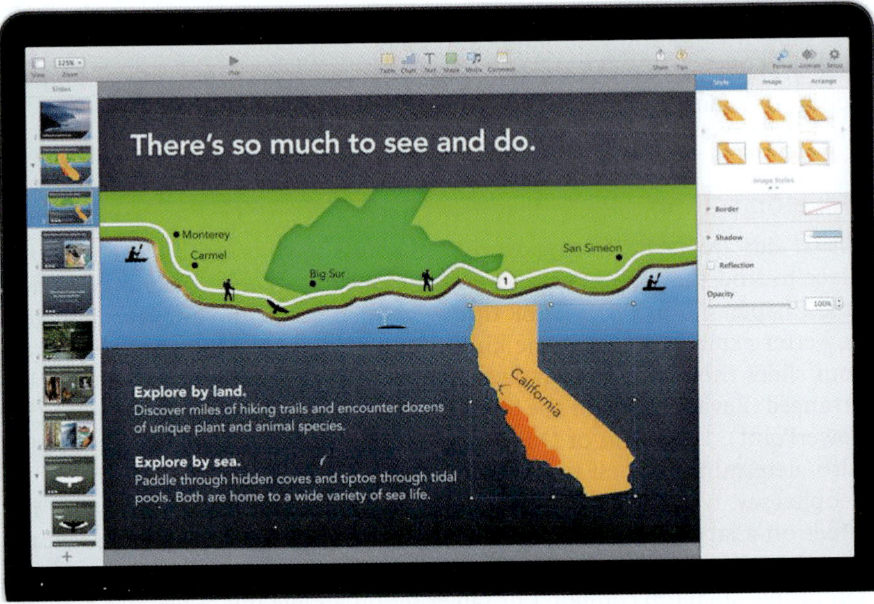

FIGURE 22.2 Keynote is a presentation tool by Apple that allows users to choose different design themes and offers collaboration tools.

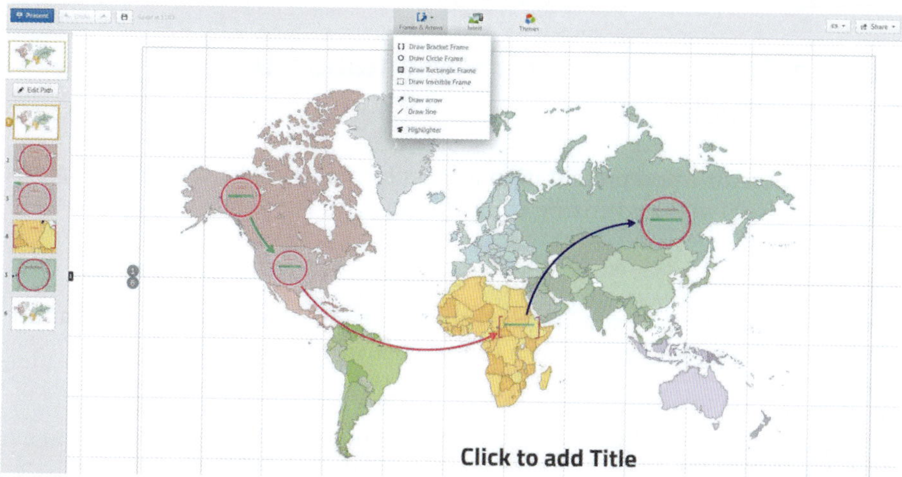

FIGURE 22.3 Prezi allows Users to Flip and Zoom within their Presentations, allowing for a more Conversational Presentation.

Avoid Technical Glitches

Technical errors are always a hazard with presentation software and any hardware required to run it. Common risks include a projector malfunction, incompatibility of a presentation file with an operating system, an Internet connection failing while using files from the Internet, or a computer drive freezing when attempting to play a media file. Follow these steps to avoid such problems.

1. Verify that you've saved the presentation files to a reliable source—flash drive, CD, DVD, website, or e-mail—that will be accessible or recognized by the presentation computer.
2. Save all the files associated with your presentation (i.e., images, sound, videos) into the same folder in the source location.
3. Familiarize yourself with the presentation computer before you give the speech to facilitate smooth operation during the presentation.
4. Check that the operating system on the computer you will use during your speech (e.g., Windows 10, Mac OS X) is compatible with the visual and audio aids.
5. Confirm that the version of the presentation software used to create the aids corresponds to the software on the computer you will use in the presentation; this will prevent distortions in your graphics, sound, and video.
6. Prepare a digital backup and a set of printed handouts of your visual aids in case of technical challenges.

Getting Ready to Deliver a Presentation Using Software Tools

To assure as error-free a presentation as possible, practice delivering your speech with your visual aids and ensure compatibility with the venue's equipment.

Check the Venue

Before your speech, take stock of the equipment and room layout. See the annotated photo for tips on achieving a smooth delivery with digital aids.

(clockwise from bottom) Jeff Presnail/Getty Images; Cinoby/Getty Images; Casper Benson/Getty Images; Purestock/Getty Images

1 **Locate power sources.** Ensure that cords can reach the presentation equipment, and consider taping them to the floor to keep them out of the way.

2 **Computer needs and compatibility.** Make sure that all files, from the slide show to audio and video clips, load successfully to the presentation computer and can be seen and heard in the room. If possible, practice at least once on this computer.

3 **Internet access.** Have wireless log-in information available and/or a cable that reaches an Ethernet jack.

4 **Backup plan.** Create a contingency plan in case of computer or projector failure; for example, print copies of your slides that can be handed out or be prepared to put information on a whiteboard.

5 **Audio.** Determine how you will broadcast any audio aids, and check speaker volume before the speech.

Position Yourself Carefully

Choose a place to stand that gives the audience clear sightlines to you and your slide show. Stand such that you can face forward even when changing slides or gesturing toward your aids. Plan to use a pointer, laser pointer, or mouse cursor to indicate particular details on a slide. This positioning helps you connect with your audience, supports you projecting your voice clearly, and prevents you from reading off your slides.

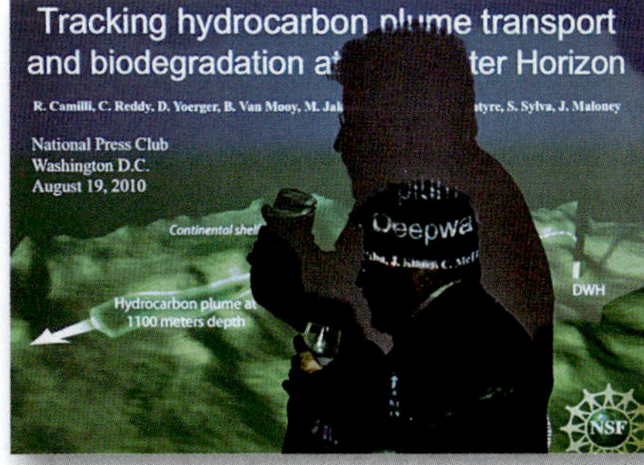

Mark Wilson/Getty; Getty Images

Needs improvement: This speaker's sideways stance discourages eye contact and indicates that he may be reading off his slides.

Good placement: This speaker can access the computer or gesture toward the slides without blocking the audience's sightlines.

Finding Media for Presentations

You can import photos, illustrations, clip art, video, or sound directly into your presentations by downloading your own files or those from the Internet. For downloadable digital images, try the following websites.

- Getty Images (www.gettyimages.com): Contains more than eighty million photographs, illustrations, and paintings, which you can download for your personal use (for a fee).
- Google (www.google.com), Yahoo! (www.yahoo.com), and Bing (www.bing.com) offer extensive image searches.

The following sites contain free photographs and other still images.

- Flickr (www.flickr.com/creativecommons): Access to thousands of photographs shared by amateur and hobbyist photographers.
- Exalead (www.exalead.com/search/image): An innovative image search engine with over two billion images.
- American Memory (http://memory.loc.gov/ammem/index.html): Free access to still and moving images depicting the history of the American experience.

The following sites offer downloadable music files and audio clips.

- MP3.com (www.mp3.com)
- SoundClick (www.soundclick.com)
- Internet Archive (www.archive.org/details/audio)
- The Daily .WAV (www.dailywav.com)
- SoundCloud (www.soundcloud.com)

The following sites contain useful video clips.

- NBC Learn (http://www.nbclearn.com/portal/site/learn)
- CNN Video (www.cnn.com/video) and ABC News Video (abcnews.go.com/video): Especially useful for speech topics on current events or timely social issues.
- YouTube (www.youtube.com)
- New York Times (www.nytimes.com/video)
- Google Videos (video.google.com)
- Bing Videos (www.bing.com/videos/browse)
- Metacafe (www.metacafe.com)

Avoid Copyright Infringement

Be certain to abide by copyright restrictions when using visual and audio material from the Internet or other sources. Some material is available under fair-use provisions (see p. 74). Even if fair use applies, cite the source of the material in your presentation. Consult your school's information technology (IT) office for statements of policy pertaining to copyrighted and fair-use materials, especially from undocumented sources such as peer-to-peer (P2P) sharing.

- Cite the source of all copyrighted material in your presentation. For example, include a bibliographic footnote on the slide containing the material.
- Be wary of sites purporting to offer "royalty free" media objects; there might be other costs associated with the materials.
- When time, resources, and ability allow, create and use your own pictures, video, or audio for your presentation slides.

CHECKLIST

TIPS FOR SUCCESSFULLY USING PRESENTATION SOFTWARE IN YOUR SPEECH

- ✓ Don't let the technology get in the way of relating to your audience.
- ✓ Talk to your audience rather than to the screen.
- ✓ Maintain eye contact as much as possible.
- ✓ Have a backup plan in case of technical errors.
- ✓ If you use a pointer (laser or otherwise), turn it off and put it down as soon as you have made your point.
- ✓ Incorporate the aids into your practice sessions until you are confident that they strengthen, rather than detract from, your core message.

FORMS OF SPEECHES

In his eulogy for former South African president Nelson Mandela's memorial service on December 10, 2013 in Johannesburg, South Africa, former U.S. President Barack Obama urged listeners to honor Mandela's life by following in his footsteps and continuing the fight against inequality and discrimination. In the photo, you can see Obama engage his audience using frequent eye contact and a strong posture. Erhan Sevenler/Anadolu Agency/Getty Images

FORMS OF SPEECHES

SPEAKER'S PREVIEW

LearningCurve can help you review.
Go to LaunchPad: **launchpadworks.com**

FORMS OF SPEECHES

CHAPTER 23 The Informative Speech

Focus on Sharing Knowledge and Demonstrating Relevance

- Strive to enlighten (informative intent) rather than to advocate (persuasive intent). (p. 308)
- Use audience analysis to determine information needs. (p. 309)
- Show the audience why the topic is relevant to them. (p. 309)
- Present new and interesting information. (p. 309)
- Look for ways to increase understanding. (p. 309)

Identify the Subject Matter of Your Informative Speech

- Is it a speech about people—e.g., individuals or groups who have made a difference? (p. 310)
- Is it a speech about an event—e.g., a noteworthy occurrence? (p. 310)
- Is it a speech about a concept—e.g., an idea, theory, or belief? (p. 311)
- Is it a speech about an issue—e.g., a social problem or matter in dispute? (p. 311)
- Is it a speech about a process—e.g., an explanation of how something works, as in a series of steps leading to a product or end result? (p. 311)

Decide How to Convey the Information

- Use *definition* to clarify. (p. 312)
- Provide *descriptions* to paint a picture. (p. 313)
- Provide a *demonstration*. (p. 313)
- Offer an in-depth *explanation*. (p. 313)

LaunchPad VIDEO ACTIVITY

Go to LaunchPad to watch a video about delivering a persuasive speech.

LaunchPad includes:

LearningCurve adaptive quizzing

a curated collection of video clips and full-length speeches.

Additional resources and reference materials such as presentation software tutorials and documentation help.

Clarify Complex Information

- Use analogies that link concepts to something familiar. (p. 314)
- Demonstrate underlying causes. (p. 316)
- Use visual aids, including models and drawings. (p. 315)

Appeal to Different Learning Styles

- Consider listeners' learning styles as part of your audience analysis. (p. 316)
- Offer information in a variety of modes—visually, with sound, with text, and with demonstrations. (p. 316)

Arrange Speech Points in an Organizational Pattern

- Consult Chapters 12 and 26 for possible organizational patterns to use. (p. 316)

CHAPTER 24 Principles of Persuasive Speaking

Select a Persuasive Purpose If Your Goal Is to:

- Influence an audience's attitudes, beliefs, or understanding of an issue. (p. 329)
- Produce a change in an audience's behavior. (p. 329)
- Reinforce existing attitudes, beliefs, or behavior. (p. 329)

Increase the Odds of Achieving Your Persuasive Speech Goal by:

- Seeking minor rather than major changes. (p. 331)
- Establishing credibility with your audience. (p. 331)
- Making your message relevant to the audience. (p. 331)
- Demonstrating positive consequences for listeners. (p. 331)
- Consider including storytelling. (p. 331)

Recognize Classical Persuasive Appeals Using Logos, Pathos, and Ethos

- Appeals to *logos* target the audience's systematic reasoning about an issue. (p. 332)

  Speakers evoke logos with arguments based on factual evidence and logical reasons.
- Appeals to *pathos* target the audience's emotions about an issue. (p. 332)

  Speakers evoke emotion using vivid imagery, compelling stories, and repetition and parallelism.

- Appeals to *ethos* target the audience's feelings about the speaker's competence, moral character, and goodwill (e.g., character). (p. 335)

  Speakers can evoke ethos by knowing the topic well, projecting honesty, and conveying genuine interest in the audience.

Appeal to What Motivates Audience Members

- Contemporary approaches to persuasion highlight audience motives to believe and behave as they do. (p. 336)
- Persuading audience members requires understanding these motivations and showing them how your proposals can fulfill them. (p. 336)

Appeal to Audience Members' Needs

- Identify and appeal to audience members' needs and wants. (p. 336)
- Consider Abraham Maslow's Hierarchy of Needs. (p. 336)

Encourage Mental Engagement

- To encourage audience members to think critically about the message, stress its relevance to them (see *elaboration likelihood model of persuasion*). (p. 336)

  Link arguments to practical concerns.

  Present the message at appropriate level.

  Demonstrate common bonds.

To Change Behavior, Stress Positive Outcomes

- Identify the outcomes audience members expect (through audience analysis) and show them how your proposals will help listeners achieve them (see *expectancy value theory*). (p. 338)

Use Your Own Credibility as a Tool of Persuasion

- Our perceptions of a speaker's expertise and trustworthiness are key contributors to persuasiveness. (p. 339)
- For speeches that involve a lot of facts and analysis, stress your expertise. (p. 340)
- For speeches that concern matters of a more personal nature, emphasize your commonality with the audience. (p. 340)

Build Your Credibility throughout the Speech

- Be aware of the factors that affect initial, derived, and terminal credibility as you move through a speech. (p. 340)

SPEAKER'S PREVIEW

CHAPTER 25 Developing Arguments for the Persuasive Speech

Understand the Features of an Argument

- An *argument* is a stated position, with support for or against an idea or issue. (p. 342)
- The core elements of an argument are claim, evidence, and warrants. (p. 342)

  A claim *makes an assertion about something.*

  Evidence *is supporting material that offers proof of the claim.*

  A warrant is a line of reasoning demonstrating the link between claim and evidence.

Select among Three Types of Claims Made in Arguments

- *Claims of fact* address whether something is or is not true, or whether something will or will not happen. (p. 345)
- *Claims of value* address issues that rely on individual judgment of right and wrong for their resolution. (p. 345)
- *Claims of policy* propose specific actions or solutions to an issue. (p. 345)

Choose the Types of Evidence That Best Support Your Claim

- Secondary sources are a common form of evidence. (p. 348)

  Secondary sources containing new and credible information can be particularly persuasive to audiences.

  Offering evidence related to audience needs and values is often most persuasive.

- The speaker's own knowledge is also a form of evidence. (p. 348)

  In general, offer your own expertise in conjunction with other forms of evidence.

Select among Different Types of Warrants to Gain Acceptance for Your Claims

- Appeal to the audience's needs and emotions with a *motivational warrant.* (p. 349)
- Use an *authoritative warrant* to appeal to the audience members' beliefs about the credibility of a source as the basis of their accepting some evidence. (p. 350)
- Use a *substantive warrant* to appeal to the audience members' beliefs about the reliability of factual evidence as the basis of their accepting some evidence. (p. 350)

  Use causal reasoning *)"warrants by cause") when offering a cause-effect relationship as proof of the claim.*

Use reasoning by analogy ("warrants by analogy") when the topic allows you to compare two similar cases and infer that what is true in one case is true in the other.

Anticipate and Plan on Addressing Counterarguments to Your Position

- One-sided messages ignore opposing claims; two-sided messages mention them. (p. 352)

  Generally it is best to acknowledge and adequately refute opposing claims.
- In most instances, plan on refuting major counterclaims to your position. (p. 352)

Different Types of Audiences Require Different Counterargument Strategies

- When speaking with a hostile audience or one that strongly disagrees, raise counterarguments and try to win support. (p. 352)
- When speaking to a critical or conflicted audience, raise counterarguments and refute them. (p. 352)
- When speaking to a sympathetic audience, you don't need to raise counterarguments. (p. 352)
- When speaking to an uninformed, less educated, or apathetic audience, briefly raise only key counterarguments. (p. 352)

Beware of Logical Fallacies That Will Weaken Your Arguments

- Avoid *begging the question*, or using circular reasoning to state an argument in such a way that it cannot help but be true. (p. 353)
- Avoid *ad hominem arguments* that attack an opponent instead of attacking the opponent's arguments. (p. 353)
- Do not rely on popular opinion as evidence that your claim is true (*bandwagoning*). (p. 353)
- Avoid framing your argument as an either-or proposition (*either-or fallacy*). (p. 354)
- Avoid relying on irrelevant information to argue your point (*red herring fallacy*). (p. 354)
- Avoid using an isolated instance to make an unwarranted general conclusion (*hasty generalization*). (p. 354)

  Avoid claiming that a relationship exists between two states or events merely due to the order in which the events occurred (post hoc ergo propter hoc).

  Avoid claiming that two phenomena are alike when the things compared are not similar enough to warrant the comparison (faulty analogy).
- Avoid offering conclusions that do not connect to your reasoning (*non sequitur*). (p. 354)

- Avoid claiming that something is true by stating that one example or case will inevitably lead to a series of events or actions (*slippery slope*). (p. 354)
- Avoid asking audiences to accept a claim based merely on common practice, or "the way things have always been" (*appeal to tradition*). (p. 354)

CHAPTER 26 Organizing the Persuasive Speech

Select an Organizational Pattern Based on Your Claims, Audience Attitudes, and Desired Response

- Choose a pattern that will work with the nature of your claims—of fact, value, or policy. (p. 355)
- Choose a pattern that will help you appeal to the attitudes of the audience toward the topic. (p. 355)
- Choose a pattern that will help you elicit the reaction you seek from your audience (your *specific speech purpose*). (p. 355)

Use the Problem Solution Pattern for Speeches That Demonstrate the Nature of a Problem and Provide Justification for a Solution

- Define the problem and offer a solution (*problem-solution*). (p. 358)
- Define the problem, cite reasons for the problem, and offer a solution (*problem-cause-solution*). (p. 358)
- *Define the problem, cite reasons, offer solution, offer evidence for solution's feasibility* (*problem-cause-solution-feasibility*). (p.358)

If the Audience Is Already Aware of an Issue and Agrees That It Should Be Addressed, Consider the Comparative Advantage Pattern

- Organize points to favorably compare your position to alternatives. (p. 359)
- Acknowledge familiar alternatives to the problem supported by opposing interests, and then stress your own position. (p. 360)
- Conclude by offering brief but compelling evidence demonstrating the unique advantages of your option over competing ones. (p. 360)

If Listeners Disagree with Your Position or Are Conflicted, Consider the Refutation Pattern

- State the opposing claim. (p. 361)
- Explain the ramifications of the opposing claim. (p. 361)
- Present your argument and the evidence. (p. 361)
- Show the superiority of your claim through contrast. (p. 361)

Consider the Motivated Sequence Pattern When Urging Action

- Step 1: *Attention*—address listeners' core concerns. (p. 362)
- Step 2: *Need*—show listeners they have a need or problem that must be satisfied or solved. (p. 362)
- Step 3: *Satisfaction*—introduce the solution to the problem. (p. 362)
- Step 4: *Visualization*—provide a vision of outcomes associated with the solution. (p. 362)
- Step 5: *Action*—make a direct request of listeners. (p. 362)

CHAPTER 27 Special Occasion Speeches

Identify the Primary Function of Your Special Occasion Speech

- Is it to *entertain* the audience? (p. 372)
- Is it to *celebrate* or recognize a person, a place, or an event? (p. 372)
- Is it to *commemorate* a person or an event? (p. 373)
- Is it to *inspire* your listeners? (p. 373)
- Is it to set a social agenda? (p. 373)

Recognize the Different Types of Special Occasion Speeches

- Special occasion speeches include *speeches of introduction*, *speeches of acceptance*, *award presentations*, *roasts and toasts*, *eulogies and other speeches of tribute*, *after-dinner speeches*, and *speeches of inspiration*. (p. 373)

Focus Your *Speech of Introduction* on Motivating the Audience to Listen to the Speaker

- Establish the speaker's credibility by describing relevant facts about his or her background and qualifications for speaking. (p. 374)
- Briefly describe the speaker's topic and establish its relevance to the audience. (p. 374)
- Keep your remarks brief. (p. 374)
- As the person being introduced, briefly acknowledge and thank the person who introduced you. (p. 375)

Focus Your *Speech of Acceptance* on Expressing Gratitude for the Honor Bestowed on You

- If you know that you are to receive an award or suspect that you may be honored, prepare the speech in advance. (p. 375)
- Express yourself genuinely and with humility. (p. 376)

- Let the audience know what the award means to you. (p. 376)
- Thank each of the individuals or organizations involved in giving you the award. (p. 376)
- Acknowledge others who helped you attain the achievement. (p. 376)

Focus Your *Speech of Presentation* on Explaining the Award and the Reason It Is Being Bestowed on the Recipient

- Explain what the award represents. (p. 376)
- Explain why the recipient is receiving the award. (p. 377)

Focus Remarks Made at *Roasts* and *Toasts* on the Person Being Honored

- For a roast, prepare a humorous tribute to the person. (p. 377)
- For a toast, pay brief tribute to the person or event. (p. 377)
- Prepare your remarks in advance. (p. 377)
- Rehearse any jokes in advance. (p. 377)
- Keep within your time limits. (p. 378)

When Delivering a *Eulogy*, Pay Tribute to the Life of the Deceased

- Stay in control of your emotions. (p. 378)
- Refer to each family member of the deceased by name. (p. 378)
- Focus on the person's life rather than on the circumstances of death. (p. 378)
- Emphasize the person's positive qualities. (p. 379)

When Delivering an *After-Dinner Speech*, Balance Insight and Entertainment

- Begin by recognizing the occasion and linking it to your theme. (p. 379)
- Balance seriousness with light-heartedness. (p. 380)

Focus Your *Speech of Inspiration* on Uplifting the Audience

- Seek to arouse the audience's better instincts. (p. 380)
- Focus on creating positive speaker ethos (see Chapter 5). (p. 380)
- Appeal to the audience's emotions (pathos) through vivid descriptions and emotionally charged words. Consider the use of repetition, alliteration, and parallelism (see Chapter 16). (p. 380)
- Consider using real-life stories and examples. (p. 380)
- Strive for a dynamic delivery style. (p. 380)
- Clearly establish your speech goal. (p. 380)
- Make your conclusion strong. (p. 381)

KEY TERMS

Chapter 23

- informative speech
- preview statement
- backstory
- reportage
- operational definition
- definition by negation
- definition by example
- definition by synonym
- definition by etymology (word origin)
- analogy

Chapter 24

- persuasion
- persuasive speaking
- persuasive appeals ("proofs")
- logos
- argument
- pathos
- demagogue
- fear appeal
- ethos
- motive
- hierarchy of needs
- elaboration likelihood model of persuasion (ELM)
- central processing
- peripheral processing
- expectancy value theory
- speaker credibility

Chapter 25

- claim (proposition)
- evidence
- warrants
- reasoning
- claim of fact
- speculative claim
- claim of value
- claim of policy
- cultural norms
- cultural premises
- motivational warrants
- authoritative warrants
- substantive warrants
- warrants by cause (causal reasoning)
- warrants by analogy (reasoning by analogy)
- one-sided message
- two-sided message
- logical fallacy
- begging the question
- bandwagoning
- either-or fallacy
- ad hominem argument
- red herring fallacy
- hasty generalization
- post hoc ergo propter hoc (fallacy of cause)
- faulty analogy
- non sequitur
- slippery slope
- appeal to tradition

Chapter 26

- target audience
- hostile audience or one that strongly disagrees
- critical and conflicted audience
- sympathetic audience
- uninformed, less educated, or apathetic audience
- problem–solution pattern of arrangement
- problem–cause–solution pattern of arrangement
- motivated sequence pattern of arrangement
- comparative advantage pattern of arrangement
- refutation pattern of arrangement

Chapter 27

- special occasion speech
- speech of introduction
- speech of acceptance
- speech of presentation
- roast
- toast
- eulogy
- after-dinner speech
- canned speech
- social agenda setting speech
- speech of inspiration

23 The Informative Speech

LearningCurve can help you review!
Go to LaunchPad: **launchpadworks.com**

Ever wondered how driverless cars sense the road or what personal DNA testing can reveal about you? How do 3D printers actually work? People are naturally curious about the world's countless mysteries, and with its primary goal of *sharing knowledge*, the informative speech is an ideal vehicle for satisfying this instinct. Audience members are always seeking out thoughtful explanations and different perspectives on topics, and informative speeches can answer this need. The one billion views (and counting) of presentations on TED talks (www.TED.com) confirm the enduring appeal of a well-crafted informative speech.

Focus on Sharing Knowledge

Informative speeches bring new topics to light, offer fresh insights on familiar subjects, provide novel ways of thinking about a topic, or demonstrate how to do things. A few speeches manage to do all of this in a single speech, but most aim for a more modest goal. Your speech might be an in-depth analysis of a complex subject, a compelling interpretation of an event, or a physical demonstration of how something works. As long as your audience learns something new, the options are nearly limitless.

Enlighten Rather Than Advocate

The goal of **informative speaking** is to increase the audience's awareness of some phenomenon and/or deepen understanding of it by imparting knowledge.[1] This stands in contrast to that of the persuasive speech, which explicitly attempts to influence people's attitudes, values, beliefs, or behavior about an issue. Whereas a persuasive speech would seek to modify attitudes or ask an audience to adopt a specific position, an informative speech stops short of this. Yet scholars of public speaking point out that there is no such thing as a purely informative or persuasive speech; that is, there are always elements of persuasion in an informative speech, and vice versa. Rarely are we entirely dispassionate about a subject, especially one that tends to elicit strong reactions. Nevertheless, if you keep in mind the primary purpose of sharing knowledge and deepening understanding, you will be able to deliver an informative speech whose principal function is to enlighten rather than to advocate.

Use Audience Analysis

Audience members must be able to identify with your informative topic and see how they can use and benefit from the information you give them. You therefore will need to gauge what your listeners already know about your informative topic as well as what they want and need to know about it (see Chapter 6, "Analyzing the Audience"). Then, adapt your speech accordingly. If speaking about collecting vintage guitars to a general audience, for example, you might describe the differences between electric and acoustic guitars, the major brands collectors seek, and the most prized models and the astronomical prices they fetch. Only a specialized audience of collectors will want or need to hear about the types of resin used to make the guitars, peghead construction, or other technical information.

The importance of giving listeners a reason to care about your topic cannot be overstated. Early on in your speech (in your **preview statement**, for example; see Chapter 14, on introductions, p. 217) tell audience members why they should listen to you. Use the introduction to point out the topic's relevance to them and describe any concrete benefits they will gain by listening to you.

Present New and Interesting Information

Audiences want to learn something new from a speaker. To satisfy this drive, offer information that is fresh and compelling. Seek out unusual (but credible) sources, novel (but sound) interpretations, moving stories, compelling examples, and striking facts. As professional speaker Vickie K. Sullivan notes, "If the speech does not convey provocative information, audience members feel their time has been wasted (and rightfully will feel offended). They expect their thinking to be challenged."[2]

As important as it is to offer new information, you do not want to overwhelm listeners with too much of it. Most people will recall less than half of the information you tell them, so focus on what you most want to convey and trim material that is not vital to your central idea.[3]

Look for Ways to Increase Understanding

People are not simply empty vessels into which you can pour facts and figures and expect them to recognize and remember all that information. Before we can retain information, we must be motivated to listen to it and be able to recognize and comprehend it.[4] Incorporating the following basic speechmaking techniques discussed in previous chapters will help you motivate the audience to listen and keep them on track as you move through the speech.

- *Prepare a well-organized introduction that clearly previews the thesis and main points and a conclusion that concisely summarizes them*; this will help listeners anticipate and remember information (see Chapters 14 and 15).
- *Make liberal use of transition words and phrases* ("first," "next," "I'll now turn . . .") to signal points and verbally map the flow of ideas. Use *internal previews* to forecast key points and *internal summaries* to reinforce them (see Chapter 11, p. 117).

- *Use* rhetorical devices such as *repetition* and *parallelism* to reinforce information and drive home key ideas (see Chapter 16).
- *Choose an appropriate organizational pattern* to help listeners mentally organize ideas and see relationships among them (see Chapters 12 and 26).
- *Use presentation aids* selectively to help listeners hear *and* see related (but not duplicated) information, with, for instance, charts and diagrams (see Chapters 20–22).

The Subject Matter of Informative Speeches

When searching for topics for an informative speech, it can be useful to brainstorm using the following broad subject categories: people, events, concepts, issues, processes, or objects or phenomena. These are not hard-and-fast divisions—for example, a speech can be about both the *process* of dance and the *people* who perform it—but they do indicate the range of potential subjects suited to an informative purpose.

Speeches about People

Speeches about people inform audiences about individuals and groups who have made contributions to society (both positive and negative) or those who for one reason or another we simply find compelling. For example, what inspired Reshma Saujani to found Girls Who Code and motivate more women to pursue careers in computing and engineering fields?

Speeches about people may also be autobiographical. Each of us has stories to tell, and if they express common themes—love, loss, growth, the overcoming of obstacles—audience members will be drawn in. The key to delivering an effective speech about yourself or another person is to provide a "lesson" that audience members can take away from the speech. How did the person face and overcome obstacles? What steps did the person take on the road to achievement? What human qualities harmed or helped the person? What turning points were noteworthy?

Speeches about Events

Speeches about events focus on noteworthy occurrences, past and present. What is the time line of the rise of the Islamic State (ISIS), and what is their status today? Speeches about events rely on **reportage**—an account of the who, what, where, when, and why of the facts. The key to a speech about an event is to offer new insights and information about the event, and to shed light on its meaning. For example, what was the **backstory**—the story that leads up to the event that listeners might find interesting—that led to Philando Castile's killing in 2016 after a routine traffic stop for a broken taillight? It turns out aggressive police encounters are much more common in Falcon Heights, the racially segregated suburb of St. Paul, Minnesota, in which the arrest took place, than in many other parts of the country.[5] Giving audience members "behind the scenes" information is a guaranteed way of catching their attention.

Speeches about Concepts

Speeches about concepts focus on abstract or complex ideas, theories, or beliefs and attempt to make them concrete and understandable to an audience. What is chaos theory? What do Hindus believe? We've heard the term *hate speech*, but we're confused because it seems to encompass everything from racist expressions to racist actions. Because they address abstract or complex ideas, speeches about concepts have the potential to confuse audience members. To ensure that this does not occur, follow the guidelines in "Take Steps to Reduce Confusion" later in this chapter (p. 314).

Speeches about Issues

An *issue* is a problem or a matter in dispute, one that people seek to bring to a conclusion. Informative *speeches about issues* provide an overview or a report of problems in order to raise awareness and deepen understanding. The high cost of college and controversial police stops are examples of issues that might be addressed in an informative speech.

Of the various types of informative speeches, speeches about issues have the greatest potential of "crossing the line" into the persuasive realm. Yet as long as your primary purpose is to inform rather than to advocate, you can legitimately address issues in an informative speech. Thus, in a speech on immigration law, you might describe current immigration laws at the state and federal levels and discuss Supreme Court rulings. On the other hand, you would refrain from advocating for or against reforms to existing immigration policy.

Speeches about Processes

Speeches about processes refer to a series of steps that lead to a finished product or end result. In this type of speech, you can talk about how something is done, how it is made, or how it works. How do hybrid cars operate? What steps are involved in planting an organic garden?

When discussing a process, you can either explain how something works or develops (*How does the body process fruit sugars?*) or actually teach audience members to perform a process (*how to create a podcast*; see p. 400 to learn how). When describing how to do something, you might perform the actual task during the speech, demonstrating each step as you describe it, or use presentation aids to illustrate the steps involved. Presentation aids, from slides to models to the actual thing being demonstrated, often accompany speeches about processes (see Chapter 20, "Using Presentation Aids in the Speech").

Speeches about Objects or Phenomena

A final category of subject matter for an informative speech, *speeches about objects or phenomena*, explore anything that isn't human; it can be animate, as in the animal kingdom, or inanimate, as in electronic devices or sports equipment. Topics for such speeches run the gamut from ribbons used to raise awareness about diseases to therapy dogs and the making of a musical score. Phenomena such as new inventions, the history of graphic novels, and the evolution of "Texas English" belong to this broad category.

Subject Categories of Informative Speeches

Subject Category	Sample Topics
Speeches about People Address impact of individuals or groups of people who have made a difference	• Athletes • Authors • Inventors • You, the speaker
Speeches about Current or Historical Events Address noteworthy occurrences, past and present	• The refugee crisis • The rise of the Islamic State • The Battle of Britain
Speeches about Concepts Address abstract or complex ideas, theories, or beliefs	• Cybersecurity • String theory • Nanotechnology
Speeches about Issues Address social problems or matters in dispute, about which you want to raise awareness rather than advocate a position	• Blue on Black violence • Regulating drones • U.S. immigration policy • Gun violence
Speeches about Processes Demonstrate and/or explain how something is done, how it is made, or how it works	• Production of algae-based biofuels • Visualization in sports • Power-Yoga routine
Speeches about Objects or Phenomena Address aspects of nonhuman subjects (their history and function, for example)	• Status of self-driving cars • History of UNESCO Heritage Sites • What is the El Niño phenomenon?

Decide How to Communicate Your Information

Whether in conversation, writing, or speeches, typically we communicate information by defining, describing, demonstrating, and/or explaining it. Some informative speeches rely almost exclusively on a single approach (e.g., they focus primarily on *demonstrating* how something works or *explaining* what something means). Many speeches, however, combine strategies within a presentation. As you prepare your speech, ask yourself, "How much emphasis should I give to defining my topic, demonstrating it, describing it, or explaining its meaning?"

Definition

Many informative speeches require that the speaker define the terms under discussion. When you *define* information, you identify the essential qualities and meaning of something. Consider, for example, these speech topics: What is cholesterol? What is a fractal? What is the Americans with Disabilities Act?

When your topic is new to the audience or is a complex concept ("*What is a fractal?*"), pay particular attention to providing clear definitions. Little is more frustrating to audience members than to sit through a presentation about something that they don't quite grasp, and which the speaker never defines adequately. Definition can also be necessary when clarifying a controversial idea or issue. For example, many of us are aware that affirmative action is a strategy to provide special opportunities for historically excluded or underrepresented groups, but how many people know about the various Supreme Court decisions that have defined it in very different ways?

You can approach definition in your speech in a number of ways, including the following:

- Defining something by what it does (**operational definition**); for example, *A computer is something that processes information.*
- Defining something by what it is not (**definition by negation**); for example, *Courage is not the absence of fear.*
- Defining something by providing several concrete examples (**definition by example**); for example, *Health professionals include doctors, nurses, EMTs, and ambulance drivers.*
- Defining something by comparing it to something synonymous (**definition by synonym**); for example, *A friend is a comrade or a buddy.*
- Defining something by illustrating its root meaning (**definition by etymology** [**word origin**]); for example, *The word* rival *derives from the Latin word* rivalis, *"one living near or using the same stream."*[6]

Description

Certain speech topics, such as an overview of postwar architecture in Rotterdam, call for a good deal of description. When you *describe* information, you provide an array of details that paint a mental picture of your topic. For example, you might offer your audience a "virtual tour" of the top of Mount Everest, or describe the physical ravages wrought by drug abuse. The point of description is to provide a mental picture for the audience. Use *concrete words* and *vivid imagery* to help listeners visualize your depictions (see Chapter 16).

Demonstration

Sometimes the purpose of an informative speech is to explain how something works or to provide an actual demonstration, similar to the many "how-to" videos found on the Web. A speech may not include an actual physical demonstration (e.g., *how to use social bookmarks*) but the speaker will nevertheless rely on a verbal demonstration of the steps involved. Speeches that rely on demonstration often work with the actual object, representations or models of it, or visual aids that diagram it.

Explanation

Finally, many informative speech topics are built on *explanation* — providing reasons or causes, demonstrating relationships, and offering interpretation and analysis. The classroom lecture is a classic example of explanation in an informative context (see Chapter 31). But numerous kinds of speeches rely on explanation, from those that address difficult or confusing theories and processes (*What is the relationship between the glycemic index and glycemic load?*) to those that present ideas that challenge conventional thinking (*Why do researchers say that sometimes emotion makes us more rather than less logical?*). See the checklist on strategies for explaining complex processes on p. 315.

Take Steps to Reduce Confusion

New information can be hard to grasp, especially when it addresses a difficult concept or term (such as *equilibrium* in engineering), a difficult-to-envision process (such as *cash-flow management* in business), or a counterintuitive idea—one that challenges commonsense thinking (such as *drinking a glass of red wine a day can be healthy*).

Useful for most any speech, the following strategies for communicating information are especially helpful when attempting to clarify complex ideas.

Use Analogies to Build on Prior Knowledge

Audience members will understand a new concept more easily if the speaker uses an **analogy** to relate it to something that they already know. Indeed, the process of learning itself is sometimes defined as constructing new knowledge from prior knowledge.[7] By linking the unfamiliar with the familiar through an analogy, you will give your listeners an easier way to venture into new territory. For example, to explain the unpredictable paths that satellites often take when they fall to Earth, you can liken the effect to dropping a penny into water: "Sometimes it goes straight down, and sometimes it turns end over end and changes direction. The same thing happens when an object hits the atmosphere."[8]

You can organize part or even all of a speech around an analogy. Bear in mind, however, that no analogy can exactly represent another concept; at a certain point, the similarities will end.[9] Therefore, you may need to alert listeners to the limits of the comparison. The statement "The heart is like a pump, *except that the heart actually changes size as it pushes blood out*" demonstrates that, though similar, a heart and a pump are not the same.[10]

In the following excerpt from a speech about nanotechnology, Wolfgang Porod explains the size of a nanometer by comparing it to the diameter of the moon. Note how he attempts to reduce confusion by first defining the root *nano* and then comparing it to the size of the moon.

> What is a nano and what is special about a nano? *Nano* is a prefix derived from the Greek word for dwarf and it means one billionth of something. So a nanosecond is a billionth of a second. A nanometer is a billionth of a meter. Now, just saying that doesn't really tell you that much. So what does it mean to have the length scale of a billionth of a meter? Well, imagine the diameter of the moon. It just happens to be, roughly . . . a billion meters. So take that and

shrink it down to the length scale of a meter, which is what it means to go a billion size scales. So a nanometer is a billionth of a meter.[11]

Demonstrate Underlying Causes

Listeners may fail to understand a process because they believe that something "obviously" works a certain way when in fact it does not. To counter faulty assumptions, first acknowledge common misperceptions and then offer an accurate explanation of underlying causes.[12]

Appeal to Different Learning Styles

Audience members are more likely to follow your points if you reinforce them with other media. The reason for this is that people have different learning styles, or preferred ways of processing information. One learning theory model suggests four such preferences: visual, aural, read/write, and kinesthetic.[13] *Visual learners* will most quickly grasp ideas by viewing visual representations of them, either through pictures, diagrams, slides, or videos. Understanding for *aural learners* comes most easily through the spoken word, by hearing and speaking. *Read/write learners* are most comfortable processing information that is text-based. *Kinesthetic learners* learn best by experiencing information directly, through real-life demonstrations, simulations, and hands-on experience. Some of us are *multimodal learners*, in that we combine two or more preferences.

CHECKLIST

STRATEGIES FOR EXPLAINING COMPLEX INFORMATION

To explain a concept or term:

- ✓ Build on prior knowledge.
- ✓ Use analogies that link concepts to something familiar.
- ✓ Define terms in several ways (e.g., by example, by what it is not).
- ✓ Simplify terminology wherever possible.
- ✓ Check for understanding.

To explain a complex process or structure:

- ✓ All of the above, and:
- ✓ Make ample use of visual aids, including models and drawings.
- ✓ Make the topic fun.

To explain a counterintuitive idea:

- ✓ All of the above, and:
- ✓ Address the commonly held assumption first, acknowledge its plausibility, and then demonstrate its limitations using familiar examples.

TABLE 23.1 Communicating Information to Different Types of Learners

Type	Advice for Communicating Information
Visual	Will most easily grasp ideas communicated through pictures, diagrams, charts, graphs, flowcharts, or maps.
Aural	Will most easily grasp ideas communicated through the spoken word, whether in live lectures, tapes, group discussions, or podcasts.
Read/Write	Will most easily grasp ideas communicated through text-based delivery, handouts, or with text-based slides.
Kinesthetic	Will most easily grasp ideas communicated through real-life demonstrations, simulations, movies, and hands-on applications.

Audience analysis can sometimes give you a sense of the types of learners in an audience. For example, mechanics of all types have strong spatial visualization abilities and thus would be classified as visual learners; they may also be kinesthetic learners who want to "test" things for themselves. Often, however, you may not have enough information to determine your listeners' learning style, so *plan on conveying and reinforcing information in a variety of modes.* In your speech, use charts, diagrams, and other visual representations of ideas to appeal to visual learners. Use colorful and concrete language and strong examples and stories that will engage aural listeners. Prepare text-based slides containing main ideas (but beware of crowding; see Chapter 21, "Designing Presentation Aids," p. 282) and, if appropriate, consider distributing handouts at the end of your speech. Use demonstrations to appeal to kinesthetic learners. Table 23.1 offers guidelines for presenting information to different types of learners.

Arrange Speech Points in a Pattern

Informative speeches can be organized using any of the patterns described in Chapters 12 and 26, including the topical, chronological, spatial, cause-effect, comparative advantage, and narrative patterns. (Note that although the problem-solution pattern may be used in informative speeches, it usually is a more logical candidate for persuasive speeches.)

There are any number of ways to organize the various types of informative speeches. A speech about the Impressionist movement in painting, for example, could be organized *chronologically,* in which main points are arranged in sequence from the movement's early period to its later falling out of favor (subpoints, as discussed in Chapter 12, can assume a different pattern than that of main points). It could be organized *causally* (cause-effect), by demonstrating that it came about as a reaction to the art movement that preceded it. It could also be organized *topically* (by categories), by focusing on the major figures associated with the movement, famous paintings linked to it, and notable contemporary artists who painted in the style.

Following are some possible pairings of speech types and organizational patterns.

Objects — spatial, topical
People — topical, narrative, chronological
Events — topical, chronological, causal, narrative
Processes — chronological, spatial, causal
Concepts — topical, causal
Issues — topical, chronological, causal

In a speech describing how to buy a guitar, Richard Garza organizes his main points chronologically.

THESIS STATEMENT: Buying and caring for a guitar involves knowing what to look for when purchasing it and understanding how to maintain it once you own it.

MAIN POINTS:

I. Decide what kind of guitar you need.

II. Inspect the guitar for potential flaws.

III. Maintain the guitar.

In a student speech on using radio-frequency waves to cure cancer, David Kruckenberg organizes his main points topically, dividing his points by categories.

THESIS STATEMENT: An engineer outside of the medical establishment discovers how to refine a medical procedure called radio-frequency ablation, potentially making it a critical tool in the fight against certain kinds of cancer.

MAIN POINTS:

I. Radio-frequency ablation, as currently practiced to treat cancer, poses risks to patients.

II. Kanzius's invention uses nanoparticles to improve upon ablation.

III. Kanzius's discovery is currently being tested in several large medical research centers.

CHECKLIST

GUIDELINES FOR CLEARLY COMMUNICATING YOUR INFORMATIVE MESSAGE

- ✓ In your introduction, tell audience members what you hope they will learn by listening to you.
- ✓ Stress the topic's relevance to your listeners.
- ✓ As needed, use definition, description, explanation, and demonstration to convey your ideas.
- ✓ Use analogies to make your examples familiar to the audience.
- ✓ Choose an organizational pattern for your main points that suits your topic (you can use a different pattern for your subpoints; see Chapter 13, p. 190).
- ✓ Use presentation aids to reinforce your points.

SAMPLE VISUALLY ANNOTATED INFORMATIVE SPEECH

To see DJ McCabe deliver his speech, go to LaunchPad: **launchpad-works.com**

Freeganism: More Than a Free Lunch

DJ McCABE

This informative speech by DJ McCabe describes a movement or cause that might be unfamiliar to his audience. To ensure understanding, he is careful to define any potentially confusing or unknown terms, including, of course, the topic term freeganism. *DJ provides a short but effective preview of his thesis and main points, which serves both to create interest in the topic and to signal how the speech will be organized—in this case topically. With strong supporting material in the form of examples and statistics and a compelling conclusion based on a story of a real-life freegan, DJ is able to convey a great deal of information in an engaging way.*

DJ starts the speech by asking the audience a question.

How many people in this audience consider themselves—or know someone who is—vegetarian? How about vegan? • If you're not familiar with veganism, it's the form of strict vegetarianism in which individuals do not eat food containing any animal products, including dairy, eggs, or honey. Although some vegans choose this dietary lifestyle for health reasons, most do so for

• Beginning the speech with a rhetorical question is an effective attention-getter, especially since most people do know someone who is vegetarian.

ideological reasons, ranging from a commitment to animal rights to concerns about pollution resulting from animal farming.

Gestures help DJ define new terms.

To many of you, this may seem like an extreme lifestyle choice. However, there are people who take things a step beyond veganism. How many of you are familiar with the term *freegan*? According to the website Freegan.info, *freegan* is a combination of *free* and *vegan*. • Freegans look for free products – from food to furniture – to minimize the impact of human consumerism on both the planet and other people. In fact, not all freegans are vegan; it is the "free" part that is key. Freegans oppose our consumer culture, in which we buy things we don't need and throw away things that are still usable.

• DJ takes care to define terms that may not be familiar to the audience, or about which they have an incomplete understanding.

Animated facial expressions help DJ connect with the audience.

During this presentation, I will introduce you to the freegan lifestyle – what the Freegan.info website defines as "living based on limited participation in" capitalism and "minimal consumption of resources." • I will first describe a few of the ways that freegans try to minimize their use of resources, then discuss the reasons why some people choose to live this way, and finally explore some legitimate criticisms of the freegan lifestyle.

• Here is DJ's preview statement, in which he states the thesis and main points. He also signals how he will organize the speech – in this case topically, or by focusing on different categories of his topic.

DJ's warm demeanor sparks interest in the topic.

First, the heart of freeganism is a commitment to using fewer resources, and one way to do that is to throw away less trash. • As reported in a 2007 article in the *New York Times* by Steven Kurutz, the Environmental Protection Agency found that we throw away nearly 250 million tons of trash per year, which translates to over 4 pounds on average, per person, every single day. Two freegan practices – waste minimization and waste reclamation – specifically deal with trash and seek to reduce the amount of garbage Americans produce every year.

• DJ uses the signal word "first" to transition into the body of the speech.

Many of us already support one of the tenets of freeganism – *waste minimization* – through recycling; hopefully everyone in this room today will take the time to throw their empty plastic water bottles and soda cans into a recycling container. • But minimizing waste isn't just about recycling. Freegans also reuse everything they can, like using that old mayonnaise jar to hold pens and pencils instead of buying a specially designed pencil holder; this option reduces the demand for resources to make the specialty item and also eliminates the need for energy consumed during recycling. •

DJ checks his note cards when citing data.

Waste reclamation is just a formal term for what many of us know affectionately as "Dumpster diving." You've engaged in this truly free acquisition of items that other people have thrown away if you furnished your dorm or apartment with a chair or a bookcase that someone left on the curb or in a Dumpster. • But would you consider making your meals out of what other people throw away? Freegans do. • In his article on food waste, Robert Fireovid notes a U.S. Department of Agriculture finding: In 2008, the amount of food wasted by restaurants and stores averaged 275 pounds per American, not including what we throw away at home. • For freegans, this is unnecessary waste, and so they will reclaim any still-edible food along with other household items.

If you think it sounds gross to eat food that has been thrown away by someone else, there are certainly legitimate worries about illness from spoiled food. At the same time, recent research shows that a lot of the food thrown away by grocery stores, for example, is perfectly safe to eat. A 2013 report published by the Natural Resources Defense Council and the Harvard Law School Food Law and Policy Clinic noted that $900 million in food was thrown away by retailers in 2001 because the date listed on the product had expired. • Those date labels often refer to the date until which the product will retain its highest quality, not necessarily the date after which the food is no longer safe to eat. That same report confirms that "the FDA's Center for Food Safety and Applied Nutrition has noted that most foods, when kept in optimal storage conditions, are safe to eat and of acceptable quality for periods of time past the label date."

Yet even if freegans reclaim wasted food safely and are mindful of their health, *why* would people who

• Even though this is an informative speech, it contains elements of persuasion, just as persuasive speeches also inform.

• DJ provides plenty of concrete examples that both enlarge understanding and add color and interest.

• DJ encourages engagement in his topic by showing the topic's relevance to the audience members' own lives.

• DJ continues to directly engage listeners, this time by acknowledging that most in the audience probably wouldn't engage in the more radical practices of freeganism.

• When citing this finding DJ should have mentioned the name of the publication, which is the journal *Agricultural Research*.

• DJ offers trustworthy sources throughout the speech.

DJ uses slides with graphics.

could afford to buy food *choose* to dig it out of the trash? •

• This rhetorical question serves as an effective transition to the next point.

As defined at the beginning of my presentation, freegans try to avoid participating in capitalism, which they believe to be inherently exploitative. As the Freegan.info website puts it, "Instead of avoiding the purchase of products from one bad company only to support another, we avoid buying anything to the greatest degree we are able." Although many health- and environmentally conscious people choose to shop at certain stores so that they can buy organic or fair-trade goods, freegans see even those efforts as problematic choices. Organic and fair-trade products still need to be shipped to stores, consuming fossil fuels and producing exhaust emissions in the process. And given the amount of food wasted unnecessarily in the United States, freegans feel an ethical obligation not to contribute to increased consumer demand when so much of the existing supply is already unused.

Maintaining strong eye contact, DJ explains his points.

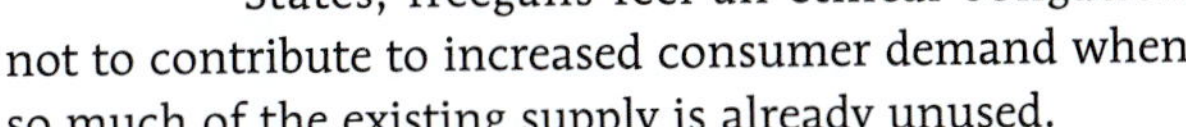

Despite their noble commitment to environmentalism and advocacy of a more humane economic system, freegans are not without critics. In some cities, Dumpster diving is illegal under municipal codes against trespassing and vandalism, although those laws are not often enforced against people "reclaiming" waste from Dumpsters unless the divers create a mess or property owners actively seek to have anti-trespassing laws applied. Harsher objections come from critics who argue that the freegan lifestyle does little to help the truly impoverished and may literally take food out of their mouths. In the words of Jerry Adler in a 2007 *Newsweek* article, "The freegans, most of whom are educated and capable of contributing to the economy, aren't sharing the surplus wealth of the West with those who are destitute by circumstance rather than choice. They are competing with them for it." Given both the small number of Americans who choose to live as freegans and the enormous amount of food wasted in this country, freegans are not very likely to consume all of the still-edible food thrown away by stores and restaurants. But their small numbers also mean they are not likely to have a significant impact on the environmental and economic problems their freegan lifestyle hopes to combat.

During this speech, I have introduced you to the subculture of freegans in the United States. • Through their practices of waste minimization and waste reclamation, freegans hope to avoid the negative impacts of capitalist consumption on both the environment and people. Whether freegans are prophets of a better world or naive idealists living on other people's trash remains an open question, but I hope that the next time you see someone exploring a Dumpster behind a supermarket, you remember that some people do so by choice rather than because it is their only option. And so I want to close by introducing you to one woman who made that choice.

• DJ signals the conclusion of the speech.

As described in the 2007 *New York Times* article by Steven Kurutz, Madeline Nelson lived a life to which many of us aspire, making over $100,000 per year as a communications director for Barnes & Noble bookstores. Frustrated that her job and daily life continued to reinforce the rat race of buying "stuff" only to throw it away before buying more, in 2005 Ms. Nelson sold her posh Manhattan apartment in favor of a small place in Brooklyn and quit her corporate job so she could live as a freegan. When asked if she misses the extravagances that once filled her life, she responds, "Most people work 40-plus hours a week at jobs they don't like to buy things they don't need." We might not wish to become freegans ourselves, but Madeline's life is quite literally food for thought. •

DJ closes the speech with a quotation.

• Concluding the speech with a real-life story of a freegan gives the topic even more relevance and leaves the audience with something to think about.

Works Cited

Adler, J. "The Noble Scavenger on the Living-Room Couch." *Newsweek* 150, no. 14 (2007): 48.

Fireovid, Robert L. "Wasted Food: What We Are Doing to Prevent Costly Losses." *Agricultural Research* 61, no. 3 (2013): 2.

Freegan.info. "What Is a Freegan?" Author, n.d., www.freegan.info.

Kurutz, Steven. "Not Buying It." *New York Times*, June 21, 2007. Retrieved from www.lexis-nexis.com.

Leib, E. B., D. Gunders, J. Ferro, A. Nielsen, G. Nosek, and J. Qu. "The Dating Game: How Confusing Food Date Labels Lead to Food Waste in America." National Resources Defense Council, September 2013, www.nrdc.org/food/files/dating-game-report.pdf.

SAMPLE VISUALLY ANNOTATED INFORMATIVE SPEECH

To see Anna Davis deliver her speech, go to LaunchPad: **launchpadworks.com**

Social Media, Social Identity, and Social Causes

ANNA DAVIS

The following informative speech by student Anna Davis may be characterized as a speech about both a concept *and a* phenomenon *(see p. 311). The concept is social identity theory, which Anna uses to explain the contemporary phenomenon of promoting social causes on the Internet.*

Anna makes ample use of definition and explanation to ensure her audience understands the theory and the terms used in her speech. She also offers analogies to make her explanations easier to understand. Note, too, her frequent use of transitions to help listeners follow along and her careful citation of sources. Anna's speech is organized topically, in which she focuses on different subsets or categories of the topic. Topical arrangements give you the greatest freedom to structure main points according to the way you wish to present your information.

Just before my first year of college, I was excited and nervous about meeting other new students on

Anna begins her speech enthusiastically with a personal story.

campus. As soon as dorm assignments were announced, we all began "friending" each other on Facebook and following each other on Twitter. • This is how I found out that my roommate was an obsessive soccer fan and had seen all of Quentin Tarantino's movies. The school also sponsored online forums, allowing me to learn about different student groups and to find like-minded people across campus. For example, I connected immediately with students who share my interest in animal rescue and adoption. • These online connections and groups helped my college friendships develop quickly and meaningfully, and gave me a sense of belonging on campus before I even arrived.

• This attention-getter works because it references something familiar to nearly everyone in a college-age audience.

• A personal example can help establish the speaker's ethos, or credibility. This particular example also relates to the main theme of the speech, which deals with social identity and the answer to the question "Who am I?"

Today I'd like to share with you how social media is being used, not only to help students connect but also as a powerful tool to advance social causes and motivate us to act on their behalf. We'll start by looking at a compelling theory of why social media is so uniquely suited to forging connections. Next, I'll review some data on social media's meteoric rise. Finally, we'll see how today's activists are harnessing social media to support an array of social causes to make life better for us all. •

• A preview statement, with brief mention of each main point, helps listeners mentally organize and anticipate the entire speech.

Using animated facial expressions, Anna keeps the audience engaged.

Let's begin our conversation about these intriguing developments in communication by considering the underlying reasons why we want to use social media in the first place. What is it that drives us to connect through social media with like-minded people and groups? •

• Anna clearly signals her transition into the body of the speech with the signal phrase "Let's begin" and a rhetorical question.

Social identity theory offers a compelling answer to this question. First, let me define the concept of social identity. *Social identity* refers to how you understand yourself in relation to your group memberships. • Michael Hogg, a professor of social psychology at Claremont University, focuses on social identity research. In his 2006 book on contemporary social psychological theories, Hogg explains that group affiliations provide us with an important source of identity, and we therefore want our groups to be valued positively in relation to other groups. • By "affiliations" I simply mean the groups that we join and perhaps link to online. •

• Anna defines technical terms used within the speech; she can then refer to them later with the assurance that the audience will understand precisely what she means.

• Offering explanations from an expert on the topic helps establish credibility for your speech.

• Anna remembers to define an ambiguous term.

Social psychologist Henry Tajfel—one of the founders of social identity theory—spent years considering how we form our social identities. Tajfel believes that the groups to which we attach ourselves, both online and off, help answer the very important question, "Who am I?" According to Tajfel's 1979 book *The Social Psychology of Intergroup Relations*, we associate with certain groups to help resolve the anxiety brought about by this fundamental question of identity. By selecting certain groups and not others, we define who we are and develop a sense of belonging in the social world. Social media sites such as Facebook provide a platform for this type of social identity formation by offering participants certain tools, such as the ability to "friend" people, groups, and even brands, and to "like" certain posts. The simple act of friending, for example, promotes social affiliation between two individuals, and our Facebook friends are collectively a source of social identity. Because we are proclaiming something important to our groups, announcing that we are in a serious relationship takes on great social significance. • As we all know, it's not official until it's "Facebook official." •

• Applying the key terms of the theory, Anna offers concrete explanations of how we create social identity online. This gives the listener a deeper understanding of the social media phenomena being discussed.

• Taking a common phrase used by your peers, such as "Facebook official," encourages identification with the topic and speaker.

Gesturing at her slides, Anna explains the graph.

As you can see, social identity theory gives us insight into the reasons behind the popularity of social media sites: They let us proclaim to ourselves and the world, "This is who I am." Even so, the near miraculous rate of growth of these sites over the past decade is surprising. •

• Anna offers a helpful internal summary of her points thus far and signals that she will transition to her next point.

Anna uses strong eye contact while making her point.

According to Marcia Clemmit's 2010 *CQ Researcher* article on social networking, Facebook had over one million members in 2005—just one year after its launch. This growth from zero to a million in one year was quite an impressive feat. Today, according to a May 2013 article on the number of active Facebook users published by the Associated Press, Facebook harbors over 1.16 billion members. That's almost four times the population of the United States. • Like Facebook, Twitter's growth has also been astronomical. Shea Bennett, editor of the Mediabistro-sponsored blog *AllTwitter*, reports in an October 2013 article that Twitter had 218 million active users at the end of June 2013. Like

• It's important to present statistics in ways that make sense for listeners—for example, using analogies and comparison. Here, Anna compares the large number of Facebook users to the population of the United States, making the abstract figure "1.16 billion" concrete.

Facebook, its success can be largely attributed to the demand for virtual communities that enable users to connect with one another.

As the data clearly show, people around the world are defining themselves socially and answering the question, "Who am I?" through the use of social media sites. • And social movement organizations have taken note. Organizations of all kinds are using social media to get their messages across to global consumers and spur their members into action.

• The subtle repetition of "Who am I?" reinforces the thesis of the speech.

Anna checks her notecards when relaying facts.

Social movements, defined by Princeton .edu as "a group of people with a common ideology who try together to achieve certain general goals," range across the political and social spectrum. Consider Occupy Wall Street and the Tea Party. • Both of these organizations communicate their messages and build support through social media sites. For example, they use Facebook to announce events and link to petitions. In fact, a nonprofit organization called Social Movement Technologies created a Facebook page to help individual social movement organizations get out their message.

• An informative speech calls for balanced and unbiased examples.

But social media is not just being used as a platform for informing the public of a group's mission and activities, or even merely to get people to sign petitions. Increasingly, activists are deploying social media to motivate like-minded people to get into the fight. To get a sense of what this means, consider the recent efforts of a seventeen-year-old skateboarder from St. Cloud, Minnesota. •

• Here, Anna uses an internal summary to review her points thus far and an internal preview for her next main point.

Using a real-life story, Anna connects to the audience.

For three years, Austin Lee found himself struggling to get support for a skate park in his local community. But when he decided to use Facebook for his cause, things changed nearly overnight. Lee's posting attracted 1,085 members, and even drew a portion of those members to city council meetings on behalf of his cause. David Unze of *USA Today* reported that Lee won the approval — and $500,000 — for his skate park (2010). And it all happened within one day of Lee's original posting on Facebook.

So as you can see, if you can use social media to convince people to identify with what you want to accomplish, success is possible. Lee's accomplishment shows us that not only do we identify and affiliate ourselves with groups, but also we are willing to actively work toward accomplishing their goals.

• Today I hope I've shown that the skyrocketing use of social media sites over the past decade is no accident. The human desire to develop a positive sense of social identity through group affiliation is one reason for this phenomenon. Capitalizing on this universal psychological drive, social movement organizations are harnessing these technologies to accomplish their goals. Social media sites allow us to communicate, express, and identify with one another in ways that encourage affiliation as well as action. Whether it's a major political movement or a teenager's desire for a local skate park, social media technologies are powerful. •

• Anna signals the close of the speech with the phrase, "Today I hope I've shown. . . ."

• Anna concludes by briefly summarizing the main points.

Concluding her speech, Anna ends on a warm note.

So as you tweet about new groups or see the next "Facebook official" status update, think about what groups you like, whom you have friended, and what those affiliations may be able to do for you. See you online! •

• Finishing on a strong note, Anna leaves the audience with something to think about.

Works Cited

Associated Press. "Number of Active Users at Facebook over the Years." *Yahoo! News*, May 1, 2013, http://news.yahoo.com/number-active-users-facebook-over-230449748.html.

Bennett, S. "How Many Active Users Does Twitter Have, and How Fast Is It Growing?" Media Bistro blog, October 4, 2013, accessed October 16, 2013, www.mediabistro.com/alltwitter/tag/twitter-active-users.

Brenner, J., and A. Smith. "72% of Online Adults Are Social Networking Site Users." Pew Internet and American Life Project, August 5, 2013, www.pewinternet.org/~/media//Files/Reports/2013/PIP_Social_networking_sites_update.pdf.

Clemmitt, M. "Social Networking." *CQ Researcher* 20, no. 32 (2010), accessed August 17, 2013, www.cqpress

.com/product/Researcher-Social-Networking-v20-32.html.

Constine, J. "Pinterest Hits 10 Million U.S. Monthly Uniques Faster Than Any Standalone Site Ever." TechCrunch, February 12, 2012, accessed August 17, 2013, http://techcrunch.com/2012/02/07/pinterest-monthly-uniques.

Hogg, M. "Social Identity Theory." In *Contemporary Social Psychological Theories*, edited by P. J. Burke, 111–36. Palo Alto, CA: Stanford University Press, 2006.

Lipsman, A. "Tumblr Defies Its Name as User Growth Accelerates." ComScore, August 30, 2011, accessed August 17, 2013, www.comscore.com/Insights/Blog/Tumblr_Defies_its_Name_as_User_Growth_Accelerates.

Madden, M., et al. "Teens, Social Media, and Privacy." *Pew Internet and American Life Project*, May 21, 2013, www.pewinternet.org/Reports/2013/Teens-Social-Media-And-Privacy.aspx.

Occupy Wall Street. In *Facebook* [Group page], accessed August 17, 2013, www.facebook.com/OccupyWallSt Socialmovement.

"Social Movement." *Wordnetweb.Princeton.edu*. Retrieved from http://wordnetweb.princeton.edu/perl/webwn?s=social%20movement.

Social Movement Technologies. In *Facebook* [Group page], accessed August 17, 2013, www.facebook.com/SocialMovementTechnologies.

Tajfel, H., and J. C. Turner. "An Integrative Theory of Intergroup Conflict." *The Social Psychology of Intergroup Relations* 33 (1979): 47.

The Tea Party. In *Facebook* [Group page], accessed August 17, 2013, www.facebook.com/TheTeaParty.net.

Twitter. "#numbers." Author, March 14, 2011, https://blog.twitter.com/2011/numbers.

Unze, D. "Facebook Helps Spark Movements." *USA Today*, March 26, 2010, http://usatoday30.usatoday.com/news/nation/2010-03-25-facebook_N.htm.

24 Principles of Persuasive Speaking

LearningCurve can help you review!
Go to LaunchPad: **launchpadworks.com**

Virtually every human interaction includes elements of persuasion, from extending invitations to friends, to asking people for help, to simply getting along with others. A persuasive speaker likewise attempts to generate a desired response from audience members. Related to the Greek verb "to induce by words to believe,"[1] **persuasion** is a deliberate process of influence, of convincing others to share your beliefs.

Of all the types of public speaking, persuasive speaking may be the one you do most frequently—and the one that offers the greatest potential for professional and personal rewards. Skilled persuasive speakers often achieve positions of leadership for their motivational abilities and earn the respect of their communities for making a difference. They are able to make their voices count during public conversations about issues that are important to them. Practiced persuasive speakers also tend to be skilled *evaluators* of persuasive communications. In a world in which persuasive, but not necessarily trustworthy, messages bombard us from all sides, being a critical receiver of persuasion has never been more necessary. Platforms such as Twitter, for example, empower political figures as well as average people to instantaneously share their opinions with millions of people through their tweets.

Perhaps most important of all, the ability to speak persuasively ensures a healthy democracy. "In a Republican nation," Thomas Jefferson said in a speech during his term as the third president of the United States, "whose citizens are to be led by reason and persuasion and not by force, the art of reasoning becomes of first importance."

What Is a Persuasive Speech?

A **persuasive speech** is meant to influence audience members' attitudes, beliefs, values, and/or behavior by appealing to some combination of their needs, desires, interests, and even fears. When you speak persuasively, you want to produce some shift in the audience's emotions and reasoning about an issue—to arouse involvement and perhaps motivate action for an issue or a cause, or to strengthen (or weaken) beliefs about a certain controversy. Whatever the topic, the goal is to reinforce, stimulate, or change the audience's attitudes and beliefs about the issue in question to more closely match your own.

Persuasive Speeches Attempt to Influence Audience Choices

Similar to informative speeches, persuasive speeches also serve to increase understanding and awareness. They present an audience with new information, new insights, and new ways of thinking about an issue. In fact, persuasive speeches do all the things informative speeches do. But unlike the informative speech, which seeks foremost to increase understanding, the explicit goal of the persuasive speech is to influence audience choices.[2] These choices may range from slight shifts in opinion to actual changes in behavior. A persuasive speech about prison reform, for example, may aim to encourage awareness of certain issues and influence attitudes about them, or spur audience members to take specific actions.

Persuasive Speeches Limit Alternatives

Any issue that would constitute the topic of a persuasive speech represents at least two viewpoints. For example, there are "pro-choice" advocates and "right-to-life" advocates; there are those who prefer a Samsung Galaxy over an iPhone. With any such issue, it is the objective of the persuasive speaker to limit the audience's alternatives to the side the speaker represents. This is done not by ignoring the unfavorable alternatives altogether but by contrasting them with the favorable alternative and showing it to be of greater value or usefulness to the audience than the other alternatives.

Persuasive Speeches Appeal to Human Psychology

Success in persuasive speaking requires attention to human psychology—to what motivates people. Audience analysis is therefore extremely important in persuasive appeals, both to identify what your target audience cares about and to build common ground (see Chapter 6 on analyzing your audience). But persuasion is a complex process, and getting people to change their minds, even a little, is challenging.[3] Rarely do audiences respond immediately or completely to a persuasive appeal. An audience can be immediately "stirred," as the Roman orator Cicero put it, with relative ease. However, producing a lasting impact is more difficult. Changes tend to be small, even imperceptible, especially at first.

CHECKLIST

CONDITIONS FOR CHOOSING A PERSUASIVE PURPOSE

You should select a persuasive purpose if:

_____ 1. Your goal is to influence an audience's beliefs or attitude about something.

_____ 2. Your goal is to influence an audience's behavior.

_____ 3. Your goal is to reinforce audience members' existing attitudes, beliefs, or behavior so the audience will continue to possess or practice them.

ETHICALLY SPEAKING

Persuasive Speeches Respect Audience Choices

Radu Bercan/ Shutterstock

Even though persuasive speeches present audiences with a choice, the ethical persuasive speaker recognizes that the choice is ultimately the audience members' to make—and he or she respects their right to do so. People take time to consider what they've heard and how it affects them. They make their own choices in light of or despite the best evidence. Your role as a persuasive speaker is not to coerce or force your listeners to accept your viewpoint but to present as convincing a case as possible so that they might do so willingly. For instance, you might want to persuade members of your audience to become vegetarians, but you must also respect their choice not to adopt this path. By illustrating the positive impact on both your health and the environment, you give the listener all they need to choose vegetarianism without coercing them into the decision.

Research confirms that you can increase the odds of influencing the audience in the direction you seek if you:

- Set modest goals. Expect minor rather than major changes in your listeners' attitudes and behavior.[4]
- Establish credibility and build common bonds to encourage the audience's trust in and identification with you (see p. 87).
- Make your message personally relevant to the audience.
- Expect to be more successful when addressing an audience whose position differs only moderately from your own.[5] The more strongly audience members feel about a given issue, the less likely they are to be persuaded of an alternative viewpoint.[6]
- If asking for the audience to support a position or cause, demonstrate plenty of positive consequences of your position.
- Consider using narratives (storytelling) in your persuasive speeches. Audiences react positively to them, both cognitively and behaviorally.[7]

Persuasion is both an ancient art and modern science, with roots in Greek and Roman *rhetoric*, as persuasion was first named, and branches in contemporary social science. Following is a brief overview of how the first scholars of rhetoric in the Western tradition viewed the process of persuasion. Many of their ideas about how to persuade an audience remain as relevant now as then. Following that discussion is an overview of several leading contemporary theories of persuasion. Both classical and contemporary perspectives recognize that successful persuasion requires a balance of reason and emotion, and that audience members must be well disposed toward the speaker.

Classical Persuasive Appeals: Ethos, Pathos, and Logos

In his treatise on rhetoric, written in the fourth century B.C.E., Aristotle explained that persuasion could be brought about by the speaker's use of three types of **persuasive appeals** or **proofs**—termed *logos, pathos*, and *ethos*. The first appeal uses *reason* and *logic*, the second targets listeners' *emotions*, and the third enlists *speaker credibility* to further the persuasive aims (see Table 24.1). According to Aristotle, and generations who follow him to the present day, you can build an effective argument with any one or a combination of these appeals or proofs. An **argument** is a stated position, with support, for or against an idea or issue; arguments serve as the framework for these appeals (see Chapter 25, on developing arguments for the persuasive speech).

Logos: Appeals to Reason

Many persuasive speeches focus on issues that require considerable thought. Aristotle used the term **logos** to refer to persuasive appeals directed at the audience's rational thinking, or systematic reasoning, on a topic. Are entities in the United States too easily susceptible to hacking by foreign governments? Does the U.S. banking industry require more oversight? When you ask audience members to make an important decision or reach a conclusion regarding a complicated issue, they will look to you to provide arguments based on factual evidence and logical reasons—to offer appeals to logos.

Pathos: Appeals to Emotion

A second powerful means of persuasion first described by classical theorists is appealing to listeners' emotions. The term Aristotle used for this is **pathos**. Making appeals to pathos requires "creating a certain disposition in the audience."[8] Feelings such as pride, love, compassion, anger, shame, and fear underlie many of our actions and motivate us to think and feel as we do. Appealing to these emotions helps establish a personal connection with the audience and makes issues more relatable and arguments more compelling.

How might you evoke these emotions in a speech? One way is by telling *compelling stories* (especially ones that touch upon shared values such as patriotism, selflessness, faith, and hope). Using *vivid imagery* (to tap into the senses and emotions of audience members) and *repetition* and *parallelism* (to create

TABLE 24.1 Applying Aristotle's Three Persuasive Appeals

Appeal to Logos	Targets audience members' rationality and logic using factual evidence and logical reasoning.
Appeal to Pathos	Targets audience members' emotions using dramatic storytelling and techniques of language such as vivid imagery, repetition, and parallelism, and figures of speech such as metaphor.
Appeal to Ethos	Targets audience members' feelings about the speaker's character through demonstrations of trustworthiness, competence, and concern for their welfare.

rhythm and drama) and other stylistic devices of language can help you evoke emotional responses (see Chapter 16 on using language).

You can see the evocation of emotion in the following excerpt from the famous "Battle of Britain" speech by Winston Churchill, delivered in June 1940 to the British House of Commons following the mass retreat by British and Allied forces from northern France. Here Churchill sought to motivate the nation for the battles ahead through his use of vivid imagery of where he would take the battle ("on the seas and the oceans;" "in the fields and in the streets"); with emotionally charged words ("odious apparatus of Nazi rule"); and with the cadenced repetition of sentences beginning with the same phrases ("We shall"; see anaphora, p. 238):

> Even though large tracts of Europe and many *old and famous* states have fallen or may fall into the *grip of the Gestapo* and all the *odious apparatus* of Nazi rule, *we shall not flag or fail. We shall go on* to the end, *we shall fight* in France, *we shall fight* on the seas and oceans, *we shall fight* with growing confidence and growing strength in the air, *we shall defend* our island, whatever the cost may be, *we shall fight* on the beaches, *we shall fight* on the landing grounds, *we shall fight* in the fields and in the streets, *we shall fight* in the hills; *we shall never surrender* . . .[9]

Churchill's powerful use of pathos galvanized the nation to fight on after the French had fallen to the Germans. Science bears out the obvious effect of pathos. For example, experiments by the Cambridge Experimentation Review Board demonstrated that pathos plays a vital role in influencing public policy.[10] By using a healthy amount of pathos in a speech, you increase the odds that listeners will to connect emotionally with your message. If this occurs, you are more likely to keep their attention once you delve into the more logos driven parts of your arguments, which tend to be drier and less interesting.

Base Emotional Appeals on Sound Reasoning

Although emotion is a powerful means of moving an audience, relying solely on naked emotion to persuade will fail most of the time. What actually persuades is the interplay between emotion and logic.[11] As Aristotle stressed, *pathos functions as a means to persuasion not by any persuasive power inherent in emotions per se but by the interplay of emotions—or desire—and sound reasoning.* Emotion gets the audience's attention and arouses their feelings—either positive or negative—about the issue in question. Reason provides the justification for these feelings, and emotion and reason together may dispose audience members to believe in or act upon your suggestions. For example, a popular television advertisement depicts a grandfatherly man in a series of activities with family members. An announcer makes the logical appeal that people with high blood pressure should maintain their prescribed regimen of medication; this is followed by the emotional appeal "If not for yourself, do it for them" (see "Motivational Warrants," Chapter 25, p. 349).

Appealing to an audience's emotions on the basis of sound reasoning ensures that your speech is ethical. However, as seen in the accompanying Ethically Speaking box, there are a host of ways in which emotions can be used unethically.

ETHICALLY SPEAKING

Using Emotions Ethically

Radu Bercan/ Shutterstock

The most successful persuaders are those who are able to understand the mind-set of others. With such insight comes the responsibility to use emotional appeals in speeches for ethical purposes. As history attests only too well, not all speakers follow an ethical path in this regard. Demagogues, for example, clutter the historical landscape. A **demagogue** relies heavily on irrelevant emotional appeals to short-circuit the listeners' rational decision-making process.[1] Senator Joseph McCarthy, who conducted "witch hunts" against alleged Communists in the 1950s, was one such speaker. Adolf Hitler, who played on the fears and dreams of German citizens to urge them toward despicable ends, was another master manipulator.

Persuasive speakers can influence their listeners' emotions by arousing fear and anxiety and by using propaganda.

- *Fear and anxiety.* Some speakers deliberately arouse fear and anxiety in an audience so that listeners will follow their recommendations. Sometimes this is done by offering a graphic description of what will happen if the audience doesn't comply (e.g., people will get hurt, children will starve). If used fairly and carefully, the **fear appeal** has a legitimate place in persuasive speaking. For example, it can be used in health campaigns, as in demonstrating the harm caused by smoking or texting while driving. It can also encourage civic involvement to address pressing social problems, as Josh Fox does in his documentaries *Gasland* and *Gasland 2*, which argue against the environmental harm done by fracking and encourage audiences to speak out against it. The effectiveness of fear appeals depends on whether audience members feel they are able to act on the subject in question after they have heard the speaker's message.[2]
- *Propaganda.* Speakers who employ **propaganda** aim to manipulate an audience's emotions for the purpose of promoting a belief system or dogma. Propagandists tell audiences only what they want their listeners to know, deliberately hiding or distorting opposing viewpoints. Kim Jong-un, chairman of the Workers' Party of Korea (commonly referred to as North Korea), is known for relying on propaganda to keep his people consumed by fear of the outside world. Another example is filmmaker Michael Moore, who has been called a "docugandist" for his selective portrayal of events in his documentary films.[3] Propagandists engage in name-calling and stereotyping to arouse their listeners' emotions.

The propagandist does not respect the audience's right to choose; nor does the speaker who irresponsibly uses fear appeals. Ethically, speakers who use appeals to emotion should avoid these practices.

1. Charles U. Larson, *Persuasion: Reception and Responsibility*, 13th ed. (Belmont, CA: Wadsworth, 2013).
2. Erin K. Maloney, Maria K. Lapinski, and Kim Witte, "Fear Appeals and Persuasion: A Review and Update of the Extended Parallel Process Model," *Social & Personality Psychology Compass* 5, no. 4 (2011): 206–219.
3. Brian Anse Patrick, *The Ten Commandments of Propaganda* (Arktos Media, 2013).

CHECKLIST

DISPLAYING ETHOS IN THE PERSUASIVE SPEECH

- ✓ Demonstrate your competence as a speaker by knowing your subject well and by emphasizing your expertise.
- ✓ Be straightforward and honest in presenting the facts of your argument.
- ✓ Reveal early your personal moral standards vis-à-vis your topic.
- ✓ Demonstrate a genuine interest in and concern for your listeners' welfare.

Ethos: Appeals Based on the Speaker's Character

Imagine how you would respond if the president of your country presented him- or herself as seeming not to care about the country's citizens, as untrustworthy, and even as unkempt. No matter how well reasoned a message is or which strong emotions its words target, if audience members have little or no regard for the speaker, they will not respond positively to his or her persuasive appeals. Aristotle recognized that the nature of the speaker's character and personality also plays an important role in how well the audience listens to and accepts the message. He referred to this effect of the speaker as **ethos**, or moral character.

What does a persuasive appeal based on ethos include? The first element is *competence*, or the speaker's mastery of the subject matter. Skillfully preparing the speech at all stages, from research to delivery, as well as emphasizing your own expertise, evokes this quality.

The second element of an ethos-based appeal is *moral character*, as reflected in a straightforward and honest presentation of the message. The speaker's own ethical standards are central to this element. Current research suggests, for example, that a brief disclosure of personal moral standards relevant to the speech or the occasion made in the introduction of a speech will boost audience regard for the speaker.[12]

The final element of ethos is *goodwill* toward the audience. A strong ethos-based appeal demonstrates an interest in and a concern for the welfare of your audience. Speakers who understand the concerns of their listeners and who address their needs and expectations relative to the speech exhibit this aspect of the ethos-based appeal.

Contemporary Persuasive Appeals: Needs and Motivations

Current research confirms the persuasive power of ethos, pathos, and logos in persuasive appeals.[13] For example, advertisers consciously create ads aimed at evoking an emotional response (pathos) in consumers that convince us that their company or product is reliable or credible (ethos) and that offer factual reasons (logos) for why we should buy something.[14] At the same time, today's social scientists have developed additional strategies for appealing to audience members and for reinforcing or changing attitudes. These strategies suggest that for persuasion to succeed, the message must effectively (1) target audience members' *motivations* for feeling and acting as they do, (2) appeal to audience members' *needs*, and (3) appeal to how they are likely to *mentally process* the *persuasive message*.

Appeal to What Motivates Audience Members

Winning over audience members to your point of view requires appealing to their **motives**, or predispositions to behave in certain ways.[15] Motives arise from needs and desires that we seek to satisfy (see below). If as a speaker you can demonstrate how an attitude or a behavior might keep listeners from feeling satisfied and competent, or that by taking an action you propose they will be rewarded in some way, you are likely to encourage receptivity to change. For example, to motivate people to lose weight and keep it off, you must make them believe that they will be healthier and seem more attractive if they do so. Persuaders who achieve this are skilled at motivating their listeners to help themselves.[16]

Appeal to Audience Members' Needs

The multibillion-dollar advertising industry focuses on one goal: appealing to consumers' needs. Likewise, one effective way to persuade an audience is to point to some need they want fulfilled and then show them a way to fulfill it. According to psychologist Abraham Maslow's classic **hierarchy of needs**, each of us has a set of basic needs ranging from the essential, life-sustaining ones to the less critical, self-improvement ones (see Figure 24.1). Our needs at the lower, essential levels (physiological and safety needs) must be fulfilled before the higher levels (social, self-esteem, and self-actualization needs) become important and motivating. Using Maslow's hierarchy to persuade your listeners to wear seat belts, for example, you would appeal to their need for safety.

Critics of this approach suggest that we may be driven as much by *wants* as by needs,[17] but recent studies confirm that persuasive attempts demonstrating benefits to audience members' social needs, including an enhanced sense of belonging, self-esteem, control, and meaningful existence, are more likely to succeed than those that ignore these needs.[18] Table 24.2 describes Maslow's five basic needs, along with suggested actions a speaker can take to appeal to them.

Encourage Mental Engagement

Audience members will mentally process your persuasive message by one of two routes, depending on the degree of their involvement in the message.[19] According to the **elaboration likelihood model of persuasion (ELM)**, when listeners are motivated and able to think critically about a message, they engage in **central processing**. That is, listeners who seriously consider what your message means to them are the ones most likely to act on it. When audience members

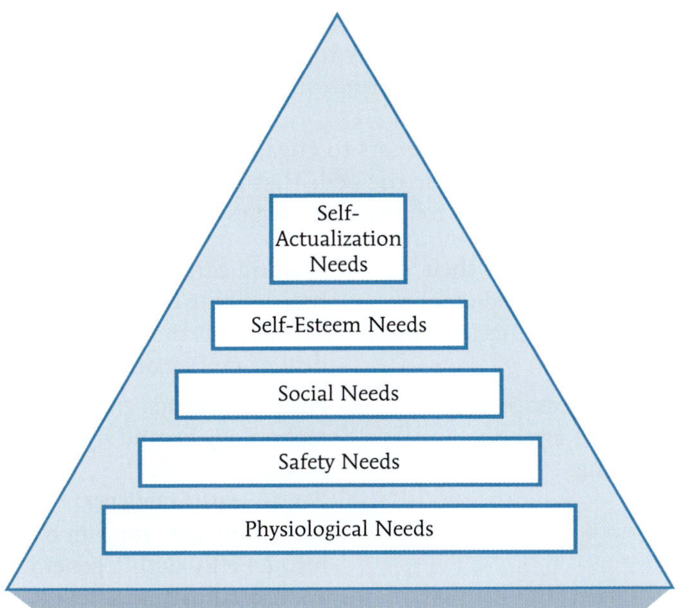

FIGURE 24.1 Maslow's Hierarchy of Needs

lack the motivation or ability to judge the argument based on its merits, they engage in **peripheral processing** of information—they pay little attention and respond to the message as being irrelevant, too complex to follow, or just plain unimportant. Even though such listeners may buy into your message, they do so not on the strength of the arguments but on the basis of such superficial

TABLE 24.2 Using Needs to Motivate Listeners

Need	Speech Action
Physiological needs (to have access to basic sustenance, including food, water, and air)	• Plan for and accommodate the audience's physiological needs—are they likely to be hot, cold, hungry, or thirsty?
Safety needs (to feel protected and secure)	• Appeal to safety benefits—voting for a clean air bill will remove a threat or protect audience members from harm.
Social needs (to find acceptance; to have lasting, meaningful relationships)	• Appeal to social benefits—adopting a healthier diet will lead to being more physically fit and attractive to peers.
Self-esteem needs (to feel good about ourselves; to feel self-worth)	• Appeal to emotional benefits—volunteering as a high school mentor will make listeners feel better about themselves.
Self-actualization needs (to achieve goals; to reach our highest potential)	• Appeal to your listeners' need to fulfill their potential—stress how adopting daily meditation will help them reduce stress and increase self-awareness.

factors as reputation, entertainment value, or personal style.[20] Listeners who use peripheral processing are unlikely to experience any meaningful changes in attitudes or behavior. Central processing produces the more long-lasting changes in audience perspective.

You can encourage your listeners to engage in central rather than peripheral processing and thus increase the odds that your persuasive appeal will produce lasting changes with the following strategies:

• Link your argument to their practical concerns and emphasize direct consequences to them.	"Hybrid cars may not be the best-looking or fastest cars on the market, but they will save you a great deal of money on fuel."
• Present your message at an appropriate level of understanding.	For a *general audience*: "The technology behind hybrid cars is relatively simple." For an *expert audience*: "To save even more gas, you can turn an EV into a PHEV with a generator and additional batteries."
• Demonstrate common bonds (i.e., foster identification) and stress your credibility to offer the claims.	"It took me a while to convince myself to buy a hybrid, but once I did, I found I saved nearly $3,000 this year."

When Targeting Behavior, Identify Audience Expectations and Stress Positive Outcomes

The audience is not merely a collection of empty vessels waiting to be filled with whatever wisdom and knowledge you have to offer. Members of an audience are rational, thinking, choice-making individuals. Their day-to-day behavior is directed mainly by their own volition, or will. According to **expectancy value theory**, developed by Icek Ajzen and Martin Fishbein,[21] each of us consciously evaluates the potential costs and benefits (or "value") associated with taking a particular action. As we weigh these costs and benefits, we consider our attitudes about the behavior in question (e.g., "Is this a good or a bad behavior?") as well as what other people who are important to us might think about the behavior (e.g., "My friend would approve of my taking this action"). On the basis of these self-assessments, we develop expectations about what will happen if we do or do not take a certain action (e.g., "My friend will think more highly of me if I do this"). These expected outcomes become our rationale for acting in a certain way. *Thus when you want to persuade listeners to change their behavior, you should try to identify these expectations and use them to appeal to your audience.*[22] For instance, when trying to motivate people to participate in physical activity, the most effective messages that actually move people to action are those that accurately address the outcomes people want from exercise, such as losing weight, lowering blood pressure and blood sugar, and so forth.[23]

The principles of expectancy value theory can help you plan a persuasive speech in which the specific purpose is to target behavior. A thorough audience analysis (in the form of a questionnaire) is critical to this approach, however (see the section on surveys in Chapter 6). Putting the theory into practice as you conduct your audience analysis, you will need to include questions that uncover (1) your listeners' attitudes about the behavior you are proposing that they change, as well as (2) their feelings about the consequences associated with that behavior. Knowing these attitudes, you have a good foundation for presenting your listeners with evidence that will support their attitudes and strengthen your argument. Third (3), try to determine what audience members believe other significant people in their lives think about the behavior in question, as well as the audience members' willingness to comply with those beliefs. You now have a basis for appealing to your audience's concerns. Figure 24.2 illustrates the steps to take when seeking to persuade an audience to adopt a course of action, based on the principles of expectancy values theory.

Demonstrate Speaker Credibility

You've learned about the qualities of speaker knowledge, moral character, and goodwill toward the audience that ancient scholars such as Aristotle described in terms of *ethos*. Research by contemporary social scientists confirms the vital importance of these qualities on gaining the audience's trust. A contemporary term for ethos is **speaker credibility**. Research shows that the audience's perceptions of a speaker's *expertise* and *trustworthiness* are critical contributors to persuasiveness.

1. Investigate listeners' attitudes toward the specific behavior you are targeting in your speech (e.g., taking vitamin supplements, purchasing a hybrid car, adopting a vegetarian diet, etc.).

↓

2. Identify listeners' beliefs about the consequences of their behavior (e.g., "I believe I will damage the environment if I don't buy a hybrid car" or "I believe hybrids aren't fun and are boring to look at").

↓

3. Investigate what the audience members believe *significant others in their lives* think about the behavior in question (e.g., my girlfriend is very environmentally conscious).

↓

4. Demonstrate the positive outcomes of adopting a course of action *favored by audience members' significant others* (e.g., "Choosing a hybrid car will lead to greater love and admiration from my girlfriend/boyfriend").

FIGURE 24.2 Using Expectancy Value Theory to Change Behavior

Trustworthiness

If there is one speaker attribute that is more important than others, it is probably *trustworthiness*. It's a matter of the "goodwill" that Aristotle taught—audiences want more than information and arguments; they want what's relevant to them from someone who cares. Indeed, audience members who perceive the speaker to be high in credibility will regard the communication as more truthful than a message delivered by someone who is seen to have low credibility.[24]

Expertise

Speaker *expertise* contributes to the persuasive outcomes of a speech under two conditions. First, when audience members are relatively unmotivated or unable to fully grasp a message, their responses to the speech will probably be in the speaker's favor if the speaker is perceived as an expert on the subject. Second, when audience members themselves are well informed about the message and perceive the speaker as someone who has expertise, he or she will be more apt to persuade them. Note that "expert" doesn't mean you're a world authority on the topic or issue of your speech. What it does mean is that you have enough knowledge and experience on the subject to be able to help the audience to better understand and accept it.

Speaker Similarity

An additional element in the speaker–audience relationship that influences the outcome of a persuasive message is *speaker similarity*—listeners' perceptions of how similar the speaker is to themselves, especially in terms of attitudes and moral character. Generally, audience members are more likely to respond favorably to the persuasive appeals of a speaker whom they perceive to be a lot like them. However, in certain situations we actually attach more credibility to people who are dissimilar to us. For example, we are more likely to be persuaded by a dissimilar speaker, especially one viewed as an "expert," when the topic or issue emphasizes facts and analysis. This is why lawyers seek the expert testimony of psychiatrists and specialists to provide insight into the personality of a suspect, the features of a crime scene, and the like. On the other hand, an audience is more likely to be persuaded by a similar speaker when the subject is personal or relational. For example, we prefer to watch *The Dr. Phil Show* instead of a news show when the subject is fathers and daughters, or bosses and secretaries. But if the issue involves new details in a political scandal or a foreign agreement, we would probably turn to news commentators as our preferred source. These facts point to an important lesson for the persuasive speaker: *For speeches that involve a lot of facts and analysis, play on whatever amount of expertise you can summon. For speeches that concern matters of a more personal nature, however, it's best to emphasize your commonality with the audience.*

Building Credibility in a Speech

For audience members, speaker credibility builds in phases as the speaker moves through the speech. It begins with the impressions audience members form even before you speak.

Initial credibility is based on factors such as information provided about the speaker ahead of the event and/or their reputation. Also influencing the speaker's initial credibility is his or her physical appearance and nonverbal behavior; listeners respond most positively to speakers who establish eye contact and dress appropriately for the occasion.

Beyond first impressions, audience members will assign speakers more or less credibility based on their actual message, including the quality of evidence and the skill with which the speech is delivered. This is called *derived credibility,* since it derives from the speaker's actual performance. Here is where expertise, or competence, plays a major role—where everything discussed in this textbook comes into play.

Audience members continue to make judgments about credibility up until and even after the conclusion of the speech. *Terminal credibility* encompasses the totality of the audience's impressions. It includes their impression of the strength of the speaker's conclusion as well as the overall speech performance. Ending abruptly, without a good summation, and hurrying away from the venue will negatively impact terminal credibility.[25]

SELF-ASSESSMENT CHECKLIST

TIPS FOR INCREASING SPEAKER CREDIBILITY

_____ 1. For speeches that involve a lot of facts and analysis, emphasize your expertise on the topic.

_____ 2. Enlighten your audience with new and relevant information.

_____ 3. Demonstrate your trustworthiness by presenting your topic honestly and in a way that shows concern for your listeners.

_____ 4. For speeches of a more personal nature, emphasize your commonality with the audience.

25 Developing Arguments for the Persuasive Speech

LearningCurve can help you review!
Go to LaunchPad: **launchpadworks.com**

The persuasive power of any speech depends on the strength of the arguments within it. This chapter describes how to use argument as a framework for making appeals in persuasive speeches (see Chapter 24, "The Persuasive Speech"). Most persuasive speeches consist of several arguments.

What Is an Argument?

An *argument* is a stated position with support for or against an idea or issue. In an argument, you ask listeners to accept a conclusion about some state of affairs, support it with evidence, and provide reasons demonstrating that the evidence supports the claim. The core elements of an argument consist of a claim, evidence, and warrants:[1]

1. The *claim* states the speaker's conclusion about some state of affairs.
2. The *evidence* substantiates the claim.
3. The *warrant* provides reasons or justifications for why the claim follows from the evidence; it may be stated or implied (see Figure 25.1).

A good argument offers accurate claims and supporting evidence and provides convincing reasons why the audience should accept them.

Stating a Claim

To state a **claim** (also called a **proposition**) is to declare a state of affairs. Claims convey the speaker's position on a matter; they answer the question "What is the speaker trying to prove?" If you want to convince audience members to purchase goods from producers who are fair-trade certified, you might make this claim: "By purchasing goods from fair-trade producers, you can help ensure that farmers and workers are justly compensated." This claim asserts that buying fair-trade products will help farmers and workers. But unless your listeners already agree with the claim, it's unlikely that they'll accept it at face value. To make the claim convincingly, the speaker must provide proof, or evidence, in support of the claim.

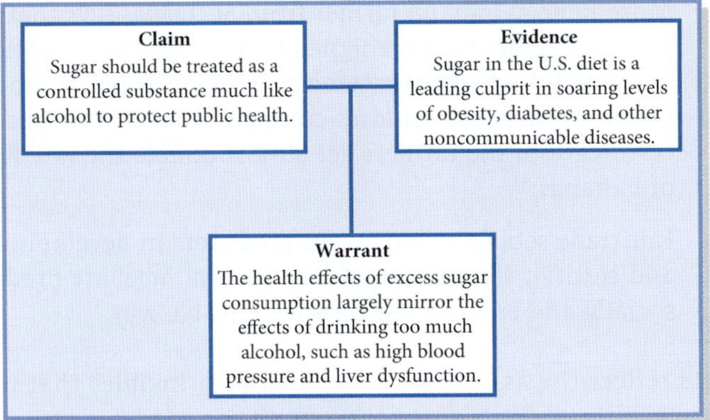

FIGURE 25.1 Core Components of Argument

Providing Evidence

Every key claim you make in a speech must be supported with **evidence**, or supporting material that provides grounds for belief in the speaker's claim. Evidence answers the question, "What is your proof for the claim?" In the speech about fair-trade certified products, you might provide *statistics* showing the number of farmers and workers that the certification program actually benefits. You might then couple these data with *testimony* from some farmers and workers (see Chapter 8, on developing supporting material).

The goal in using evidence is to make a claim more acceptable, or believable, to the audience. If the evidence itself is believable, then the claim is more likely to be found acceptable by the audience.

Providing Reasons

A **warrant**, the third component of an argument, helps to justify in the audience's mind why the evidence proves the claim; it is a line of reasoning that provides a *rationale* for accepting that the evidence is valid for the claim, or *warranted*. Audiences must believe warrants or else they will not accept the argument. Note that the explanation of warrant closely follows the definition of **reasoning** itself: "the process of drawing inferences or conclusions from evidence."[2] For listeners to accept the argument, the connection between the claim and the evidence must be made clear and justified in their minds; one or more warrants serve this purpose. For example, a warrant behind the claim that "purchasing fair-trade certified products helps the farmers and workers who produce them" might be that "people want what's fair for others and to spend their money on goods produced in a socially and environmentally responsible manner."

CLAIM: Purchasing products certified as fair trade assures just compensation to the farmers and workers who produce them.

EVIDENCE: Mose Rene, a banana farmer from St. Lucia, says that his local group of eighty farmers signed up for fair trade certification at the point when they were thinking of stopping producing bananas; they just couldn't compete. Now, under fair trade certification, the farmers get almost double the rate for a box of bananas.[3]

WARRANT: Fair trade sets fairer prices for producers in developing countries and certifies that goods sold under that label are produced in a socially and environmentally responsible way.

Warrants reflect the assumptions, beliefs, or principles that underlie the claim. Critically, *if the audience does not accept these underlying assumptions, they will not accept your argument.* For example, some evidence suggests that while the owners of farms in developing countries benefit from fair trade, their hired workers do not necessarily share in these benefits.[4] Audience members who are aware of this evidence may not fully accept the speaker's warrant. Similarly, if a claim addresses an emotionally charged topic such as "prayer should be permitted in public schools," audience members' beliefs about the separation of church and state may be such that no amount of reasoning would change their minds. Thus, it is crucial when preparing claims for an audience to (1) identify the assumptions behind your warrant, and (2) consider whether the audience is likely to accept it.[5] The more controversial your claims, the more important this step becomes. For less controversial topics, the warrants may be shared by most people and thus not be necessary to state.[6] For example, when urging people to

ETHICALLY SPEAKING

Engaging in Arguments in the Public Arena

Radu Bercan/Shutterstock

Because the potential to do harm is greater when more people are involved in a communication event, public discourse carries a greater scope of responsibility and accountability than does private discourse. Consider the following guidelines when engaged in arguments in the public arena:

- Arguing does not mean "fighting," name-calling, or attacking personalities (see "Avoid Fallacies in Reasoning," pp. 353–54).
- Arguing involves sound reasoning about claims that are ethically supportable.
- Arguing strives for accuracy in the claims made and the evidence offered.
- Arguing responds to alternative or opposing views with sound counterclaims.
- Arguing begins and ends with civil discourse.

take care of their teeth, the warrant may be as widely understood as "you want to protect your health." The warrant is implied but not necessarily stated.

Diagramming your argument allows you to visualize how evidence and warrants can be presented in support of your claim. Figure 25.1 illustrates the three core components of an argument. As you consider formulating an argument, try to diagram it in a similar fashion.

1. Write down the claim.
2. List each possible piece of evidence you have in support of the claim.
3. Write down the corresponding warrants, or justifications, that link the evidence to the claim.

Types of Claims Used in Persuasive Speeches

An argument may address three different kinds of claims: of fact, of value, and of policy. A persuasive speech may contain only one type of claim or, often, consist of several arguments addressing different kinds of claims.

Claims of Fact

Claims of fact focus on whether something is or is not true or whether something will or will not happen. They usually address issues for which two or more competing answers exist, or those for which an answer does not yet exist (called a **speculative claim**). An example of the first is "Global warming is causing hotter and dryer weather patterns." An example of the second, a speculative claim, is "Drones will deliver groceries to most homes in the United States by 2025."

Claims of Value

Claims of value address issues of judgment. Rather than attempting to prove the truth of something, as in claims of fact, speakers arguing claims of value try to show that something is right or wrong, good or bad, worthy or unworthy. Examples include "Is assisted suicide ethical?" and "Is any painting worth 100 million dollars?"

Like claims of fact, claims of value require evidence. However, the evidence in support of a value claim tends to be more subjective than factual. In defending assisted suicide, for example, a speaker might be able to show that in certain situations compassion requires us to help terminally ill people take their own lives. Likewise, public opinion polls can be used to sway attitudes about a value ("after all, X percent of Americans support the death penalty").

Claims of Policy

Claims of policy recommend that a specific course of action be taken or approved. Legislators regularly construct arguments based on claims of policy: "Should we pass law X restricting the use of assault weapons/genetically modified foods/firecrackers?" Anyone can argue for a claim of policy as long as he or she advocates for or against a given plan. Such claims might include "Voluntary prayer should be permitted in public schools" and "Stop-and-frisk programs (the 'Terry Stop') should be banned." Notice that in each claim the word *should* appears. A claim of policy speaks to an "ought" condition, arguing that better outcomes would be realized if the proposed condition was met.

By nature, claims of policy involve claims of fact and often claims of value as well. Consider the following example.

POLICY CLAIM: The city should provide walking paths in all municipal parks.

FACT: Almost every park in the city is busy several times each day with recreational walkers. This activity is noticeably greater on weekends.

VALUE: Walking on properly maintained paths is healthier both for walkers and for the park landscape.

The fact and value claims become, essentially, pieces of evidence in support of the policy claim. The fact statement provides objective evidence, and the value statement offers a more subjective justification of the policy. See Table 25.1 for a summary and example of each type, and see Chapter 26 for guidelines on matching organizational patterns to the different types of claims.

Types of Evidence

As in claims, you can choose among different types of evidence to support claims of fact, value, and policy, including the supporting materials described in Chapter 8 ("secondary sources") and your own knowledge and experience, or "speaker expertise."

TABLE 25.1 Sample Claims for Arguments of Fact, Value, and Policy

Type of Argument	Claim of Fact	Claim of Value	Claim of Policy
	(Focuses on whether something is or is not true or whether something will or will not happen)	*(Addresses issues of judgment)*	*(Recommends that a specific course of action be taken, or approved of, by an audience)*
Sample Claim	• Demand for online college courses will outpace bricks-and-mortar classes in the next decade.	• Solitary confinement in prisons for lengthy periods is unethical. • Assisted suicide is immoral.	• Until final legislation on immigration is passed, all deportations of illegal immigrants should cease. • Taxes on inheritance should be abolished.

A CULTURAL PERSPECTIVE

Addressing Culture in the Persuasive Speech

charles taylor/ Shutterstock

Audience members' cultural orientations will significantly affect their responses to persuasion due to culture-specific core values, norms, and premises.[1]

CORE VALUES Audience members of the same culture share core values, such as *self-reliance* and *individual achievement* (in individualist cultures such as the United States) and *interdependence* and *group harmony* (in collectivist cultures such as those of China and India; see also Chapter 6 on cultural differences). Usually, appeals that clash with core values are unsuccessful, although globalization may be leading to some cross-pollination of values.[2]

CULTURAL NORMS Cultural norms are a group's rules for behavior. Attempts to persuade listeners to think or do things contrary to important norms will usually fail.[3] Failure to positively acknowledge the central role of family—*familismo*—in Mexican culture, for example, when making appeals to modify various health practices will likely fail.

CULTURAL PREMISES Listeners sharing a common culture usually hold culturally specific values about identity and relationships, called **cultural premises**. Prevalent among the Danes and Israelis, for example, is the premise of egalitarianism, the belief that everyone should be equal. A different premise exists in Korea, Japan, and other Asian societies, where status most often is aligned strictly with one's place in the social hierarchy. Bear in mind that it is difficult to challenge deeply held cultural premises.[4]

EMOTIONS Culture also influences our responses to emotional appeals. Appeals that touch on *ego-focused* emotions such as pride, anger, happiness, and frustration, for example, tend to find more acceptance among members of individualist cultures;[5] those that use *other-focused* emotions such as empathy, indebtedness, and shame are more apt to encourage identification in collectivist cultures.[6] Usually, it is best to appeal to emotions that lie within the audience's "comfort zone."[7]

Persuasion depends on appeals to values; culture shapes these values. Eliciting a range of emotions may therefore help you appeal to diverse audience members.

1. Jennifer Aaker and Durairaj Maheswaran, "The Impact of Cultural Orientation on Persuasion," *Journal of Consumer Research* 24 (1997): 315–28.
2. Jennifer L. Aaker, "Accessibility or Diagnosticity? Disentangling the Influence of Culture on Persuasion Processes and Attitudes," *Journal of Consumer Research* 26 (2000): 340–57.
3. Kristine L. Fitch, "Cultural Persuadables," *Communication Theory* 13 (2003): 100–23.
4. Ibid.
5. Jennifer L. Aaker and Patti Williams, "Empathy versus Pride: The Influence of Emotional Appeals across Cultures," *Journal of Consumer Research* 25 (1998): 241–61.
6. Ibid.
7. Ibid.

Secondary Sources ("External Evidence")

The most common form of evidence is secondary sources—the examples, narratives, testimony, facts, and statistics described in Chapter 8. Sometimes called *external evidence* because the knowledge comes from outside the speaker's own experience, secondary sources are most powerful when they impart new information that the audience has not previously used in forming an opinion.[7] Thus, for a persuasive speech it can be particularly effective to offer supporting material that your audience is not likely to know but will find both persuasive and credible.

Speaker Expertise as Evidence

When the audience will find your opinions credible and convincing, consider using your own *speaker expertise* as evidence. Few persuasive speeches can be convincingly built on speaker experience and knowledge alone. Offered in conjunction with other forms of evidence, however, your expertise can help audience members identify with you and add some credibility to your claims. Using speaker expertise as evidence for a claim on the need to purchase health insurance might work like this:

CLAIM:	Young adults need the protection of a health insurance plan.
SPEAKER EXPERTISE AS EVIDENCE:	I thought that being young and healthy, I didn't need insurance . . . until I suffered a complex fracture requiring surgery and costing many thousands of dollars . . .
WARRANT:	The young and healthy are also vulnerable and need to protect themselves against unforeseen events.

Note that even seemingly overwhelming evidence may not be enough to convince audience members of certain claims *unless they can see how it relates to their own needs and values*. This is especially the case with claims of *policy* and of *value*. For example, if making a claim of policy that your college administration should change its free speech policies, you might cite evidence that relates directly to the students: "In our college, the administration's Student Code of Conduct infringes on your First Amendment rights of freedom of expression by . . ."

Types of Warrants

As with claims and evidence, you can also use different types of warrants to justify the links you make between your claim and evidence.

- Motivational warrants offer reasons targeted at the audience's needs and emotions. In Aristotle's terms, the motivational warrant makes use of *pathos*, or *emotional appeals*.

CHECKLIST

TESTING THE STRENGTH OF YOUR EVIDENCE

As you identify and apply evidence to a claim, keep in mind the three tests of evidence:

_____ 1. Is the evidence directly relevant to the claim?

_____ 2. Is it timely (recent and up to date)?

_____ 3. Will listeners find it credible, or from a source they can trust?

- Authoritative warrants appeal to the credibility the audience assigns to the *source of the evidence*; this appeal is based on *ethos*.
- Substantive warrants, based on *logos*, appeal to the audience's beliefs in the reliability of any factual evidence you offer. (See Chapter 24 for a review of ethos, logos, and pathos.)

Motivational Warrants: Appeal to Audience Needs and Values

No doubt you have seen television and magazine advertisements asking viewers to give just pennies a day to sponsor a starving child in a distant land. The claim may say, "You can easily afford to join this organization dedicated to ending the hunger of thousands of children." The evidence may be stated as "For the price of one soft drink you can feed a child for a week." The warrant is something like, "You don't want any child to starve or go without proper medical care." **Motivational warrants** use the needs, desires, emotions, and values of audience members as the basis for accepting some evidence as support for a claim, and thus accepting the claim itself. More often than not, motivational warrants are *implied* rather than stated outright. In terms of the ad to support a starving child, we don't have to be told that we don't want children to starve; if the value or desire is meaningful to us, we realize it instinctively.

The following is a motivational warrant for a claim of policy advocating a higher minimum wage.

CLAIM:	We should support Legislation Bill No. 12 raising the minimum wage.
EVIDENCE:	In our school, most of us — 73 percent — work at least fifteen hours a week and earn the minimum wage . . .
MOTIVATIONAL WARRANT:	Every person who works hard and does the job he or she is hired to do deserves the dignity of a living wage . . .

Although appealing to the needs, desires, and values of audience members requires audience analysis (see Chapter 6), some values — such as *fairness, human dignity, financial security, health*, and *happiness* — are universally shared and generally can serve safely across various audiences as the basis for motivational warrants.

Authoritative Warrants: Appeal to the Audience's Trust in the Source

Just as one form of evidence relies on the speaker's own expertise, **authoritative warrants** rely on an audience's beliefs about the credibility of a source of evidence. For example, in terms of sponsoring a hungry child, the speaker might make the claim that "We should contribute financially to agency x that feeds hungry children." The speaker's evidence includes brief stories of children who have been helped by the agency. As a warrant, the speaker notes that a former U.S. senator works with the agency and its recipients; perhaps she is even the person delivering the message.

The success or failure of authoritative warrants rests on how highly the audience regards the authority figure. If listeners hold the person in high esteem, they are more likely to find the evidence and the claim acceptable. Thus, authoritative warrants make the credibility of sources of evidence all the more important.

In support of the claim that "in war zones, rape should be prosecuted as a war crime," you could offer an authoritative warrant as follows: "According to Angelina Jolie, Hollywood actress and Special Envoy to the United Nations Refugee Agency, there are hundreds of thousands of survivors of sexual violence, but only a handful of prosecutions because the world has not made the issue a priority";[8] this gives both the evidence (rapes in war zones) and the warrant (the specific famous person is Angelina Jolie)[9] in the same sentence.

If you happen to be highly knowledgeable on a subject, an authoritative warrant can be made by reference to yourself. In this case, the warrant provides the speaker's knowledge and opinions as evidence. Your experience offers evidence for the claim, and you, having had the experience, give warrant to the evidence.

Substantive Warrants: Appeal to Factual Evidence

Rather than appealing to audience needs and values (as with a motivational warrant) or source credibility (as with an authoritative warrant), **substantive warrants** target the audience's faith in your factual evidence as justification for the argument. For example, if you claim that "climate change is linked to stronger hurricanes," and offer as evidence that "we have seen a consistent pattern of stronger hurricanes and warmer oceans," a substantive warrant might be "hurricanes and tropical storms get their energy from warm water." The warrant is based on factual evidence.

There are several types of substantive warrants, or rationales for accepting a claim on the basis of factual evidence. Two that occur commonly in speeches are *causation* and *analogy*. A **warrant by cause** uses causal reasoning to offer a cause-and-effect relationship as proof of the claim. In **causal reasoning**, the speaker argues that one factual event, circumstance, or idea (the cause) is the reason (effect) for another. The example above about climate change offers an instance of causal reasoning, or warrant by cause. The warrant proves the relationship of cause (climate change) to effect (stronger hurricanes) on the scientific (i.e., factual) basis of the process of hurricane formation.

Critics of the federal deficit often reason by cause when they suggest too much government spending leads to debt. Their opponents also reason by cause when they claim that the actual cause of the debt is insufficient taxes on the rich. Rather than suggesting a cause-to-effect relationship, however, either the critic or the opponent might suggest an effect-to-cause relationship, as in: "Overspending on social programs [EFFECT] leads to the deficit [CAUSE]." Similarly, a speaker might argue the following:

CLAIM:	Candidate X lost his bid for the Senate largely because of his age.
EVIDENCE:	Many available media reports refer to the age issue with which Candidate X had to contend.
WARRANT BY CAUSE:	Our society attributes less competence to people who are older versus those who are younger.

Older age is assumed to be a cause of Candidate X's loss in the senatorial campaign. The warrant justifies the relationship of cause (age) to effect (loss of race) on the basis of society's negative stereotypes of older people.

As pointed out in the accompanying checklist, when using warrants based on causal reasoning, it is essential to make relevant and accurate assertions about cause and effect.

A second type of substantive warrant, the **warrants by analogy**, uses **reasoning by analogy** to compare two similar cases and imply that what is true in one case is true in the other. The assumption is that the characteristics of Case A and Case B are similar, if not the same, and that what is true for B must also be true for A.

Offering arguments based on reason by analogy occurs frequently in persuasive speeches, especially those addressing claims of policy. Consider the example at the top of the next page.

CHECKLIST

MAKING EFFECTIVE USE OF WARRANTS BASED ON CAUSAL REASONING

- ✓ Avoid making hasty assertions of cause or effect on the basis of stereotypes.
- ✓ Avoid making hasty assertions of cause or effect based on hearsay or tradition.
- ✓ Be certain that you don't offer a single cause or effect as the only possibility when others are known to exist.
- ✓ When multiple causes or effects can be given, be sure to note their importance relative to one another.

CLAIM: Lifting economic sanctions on Iran in exchange for a suspension in its pursuit of nuclear weapons risks creating another North Korea.

EVIDENCE: Under previous U.S. administrations, North Korea used the loosening of sanctions as an opportunity to redouble its program, just as the Iranians are doing now under the current administration . . .

WARRANT BY ANALOGY: Iran, like Korea, is an anti-American regime and sponsor of terror that cannot be trusted to do as they say.

Counterarguments: Addressing the Other Side

All attempts at persuasion are subject to counterpersuasion. Listeners may be persuaded to accept your claims, but once they are exposed to counterclaims they may change their minds. As a persuasive speaker, you can choose to offer only one side of the argument or acknowledge opposing views. A **one-sided message** does not mention opposing claims; a **two-sided message** mentions opposing points of view and sometimes refutes them. Research suggests that two-sided messages generally are more persuasive than one-sided messages, as long as the speaker adequately refutes opposing claims.[10]

If listeners are aware of opposing claims and you ignore them, you risk a loss of credibility. This is especially the case when the audience disagrees with your position. Yet you need not painstakingly acknowledge and refute all opposing claims. Instead, *raise and refute the most important counterclaims and evidence that the audience would know about*. Ethically, you can ignore counterclaims that don't significantly weaken your argument.

Persuasion scholar Herbert Simon describes four types of potential audiences, including the hostile audience or one that strongly disagrees; the critical and conflicted audience; the sympathetic audience; and the uninformed, less educated, or apathetic audience. Table 25.2 suggests various counterargument strategies for appealing to them.

TABLE 25.2 Counterargument Strategies for Appealing to Different Audience Types*

Audience Type	Counterargument Strategy
Hostile audience or those that strongly disagree	• Raise counterarguments, focusing on those the audience is most likely to disagree with and try to win support.
Critical and/or conflicted audience	• Address major counterarguments and refute them; introduce new evidence as above.
Sympathetic audience	• Unnecessary to raise counterarguments if no time; otherwise, briefly address only most important ones.
Uninformed, less-educated, or apathetic audience	• If you have time, briefly raise only key counterarguments the audience may hear in future and offer counterarguments.

*Audience types based on Herbert Simons, *Persuasion in Society*, 2nd ed. (New York: Routledge, 2011).

CHECKLIST

STRATEGIES FOR ADDRESSING COUNTERARGUMENTS

- ✓ Gently challenge preconceptions associated with the counterarguments, but do not insult the audience.
- ✓ Acknowledge counterclaims the audience is most likely to disagree with and demonstrate why those claims are weaker than your argument.
- ✓ If you can introduce new evidence to demonstrate that the counterclaim is outdated or inaccurate, do so.
- ✓ Consider where in the speech to introduce the counterclaims: when addressing a hostile audience about a controversial topic, addressing the counterclaim early in the speech and revisiting it just before the conclusion works well; otherwise, you can address counterclaims just before the conclusion.

Avoid Fallacies in Reasoning

A **logical fallacy** is either a false or erroneous statement or an invalid or deceptive line of reasoning. In either case, you need to be aware of fallacies in order to avoid making them in your own speeches and to be able to identify them in the speeches of others. Unfortunately, logical fallacies appear frequently in arguments of all types and can easily evade our detection, leaving us with misrepresentations and distortions of the truth. Many fallacies of reasoning exist; the following lists several that occur frequently in communication.

LOGICAL FALLACY	EXAMPLE
Begging the question An argument that is stated in such a way that it cannot help but be true, even though no evidence has been presented. Characteristic of begging-the-question fallacy is circular thinking and a lack of evidence for the assumptions offered.	"Intelligent Design is the correct explanation for biological change over time because we can see godly evidence in our complex natural world." "War Kills."
Ad hominem argument An argument that targets a person instead of the issue at hand in an attempt to incite an audience's dislike for that person.	"I'm a better candidate than X because, unlike X, I work for a living." "How can you accept my opponent's position on education when he has been divorced?"
Bandwagoning An argument that uses (unsubstantiated) general opinion as its (false) basis for asserting the truth of something. The critical listener of the bandwagoning fallacy will ask, "Whose opinion is it?"	"Nikes are superior to other brands of shoes because everyone wears Nikes."

LOGICAL FALLACY	EXAMPLE
Either-or fallacy (false dichotomy) An argument stated in terms of only two alternatives, even though there may be many additional alternatives.	"Either you're with us or against us."
Red herring fallacy An argument that introduces an irrelevant or unrelated topic into the discussion to divert attention from the issue at hand. The red herring fallacy replaces an objective discussion of facts with an essentially unrelated topic.	"The previous speaker suggests that Medicare is in shambles. I disagree and recommend that we study why the young don't respect their elders."
Hasty generalization An argument that uses an isolated instance to make an unwarranted general conclusion.	"My neighbor who works for Xmart is untrustworthy; therefore, Xmart is not a trustworthy company."
Post hoc ergo propter hoc (post hoc) *("after this, therefore because of this")* An argument suggesting that a causal relationship exists between two states or events due to the order in which the events occurred, rather than taking other factors into consideration: e.g., since Event A followed Event B, Event B must have caused Event A. Also called ***fallacy of false cause***.	"The child was vaccinated in June and became ill the following week, clearly as a result of the vaccine."
Faulty analogy An argument claiming that two phenomena are alike when in fact the things compared are not similar enough to warrant the comparison. Instead, the comparison is weak, misleading, and/or illogical. (Note that an *analogy* compares two like phenomena. Analogies work when the similarities between two things outweigh their differences.)	"Banning guns for law-abiding citizens because criminals use them to kill people is like banning cars because some people use them to drive drunk and kill people."[11]
Non sequitur *("does not follow")* An argument in which the conclusion does not follow from the evidence.	"Because they live in the richest country in the world, they must be extremely wealthy."
Slippery slope An argument based on a faulty assumption that a single case will lead inevitably to another event or series of events or actions.	"Legalizing marijuana for medical use will lead to widespread recreational use of heroin."
Appeal to tradition An argument that bases its acceptance on historical tradition, on the fact that if something has traditionally been done, it must be "right."	"A marriage should be between a man and a woman because that is how it has always been."

26 Organizing the Persuasive Speech

LearningCurve can help you review!
Go to LaunchPad: **launchpadworks.com**

Once you've developed your arguments, with major claims as main points, the next step is to structure your speech using an organizational pattern. Chapter 12 describes six patterns: topical/categorical, narrative, chronological, spatial, causal, and problem-solution. Of these, the *problem-solution* pattern is typically reserved for organizing persuasive rather than informative speeches; the *cause-effect* pattern also appears frequently in persuasive speeches but works well in many informative speeches too. In this chapter we demonstrate how to apply these two patterns to persuasive topics and illustrate three additional organizational patterns designed specifically for persuasive speeches: *Monroe's Motivated Sequence, comparative advantage,* and *refutation.* Table 26.1 summarizes the patterns discussed in this chapter and in Chapter 12.

Keep in mind that there is no one "right" way to organize a persuasive speech—or any kind of speech—but only choices that will be more or less effective for your particular message, audience, and goal. Experimenting with the various patterns can help you to decide; often an effective choice will become apparent fairly quickly.

Factors to Consider When Choosing an Organizational Pattern

Beyond experimentation, what criteria should you consider when choosing an organizational pattern? Depending on (1) the nature of your claims (whether of fact, value, or policy), (2) audience members' attitudes toward the topic, and (3) the response you want to elicit from them, certain patterns can be more effective than others (see Figure 26.1).

What Do Your Claims and Evidence Suggest?

You've seen that persuasive speeches contain arguments, which in turn consist of claims, evidence, and warrants. Examining the nature of your claims can help to identify a pattern for your persuasive speech.

Some claims clearly suggest a specific design. A claim of policy arguing that "junk" foods in school cafeterias should be limited, for example,

TABLE 26.1 Sample Organizational Formats

Organizational Format	Description
Problem-Cause-Solution *(Used in persuasive speeches)*	Speech points arranged in order to demonstrate problem, reasons for problem, and solution to problem
Monroe's Motivated Sequence *(Used in persuasive speeches)*	Speech points arranged to motivate listeners to act on something or to shift their attitudes in direction of speaker's
Comparative Advantage *(Used in persuasive speeches)*	Speech points arranged to demonstrate that your viewpoint or proposal contrasts favorably with (is superior or preferable to) one or more alternative positions
Refutation *(Used in persuasive speeches)*	Speech points arranged to disprove opposing claims
Causal (cause-effect) *(Often used in persuasive speeches; see Chapter 12)*	Speech points arranged to demonstrate that a particular set of circumstances (causes) leads to a specific result (effects) or, conversely, that various results (effects) follow from a particular set of circumstances (causes)
Topical/Categorical *(May be used in any type of speech; see Chapter 12)*	Speech points arranged according to different subtopics within a larger topic
Chronological *(May be used in any type of speech; see Chapter 12)*	Speech points arranged according to their occurrence in time relative to each other
Spatial *(May be used in any type of speech; see Chapter 12)*	Speech points arranged in order of their physical proximity or direction relative to each other
Narrative *(May be used in any type of speech; see Chapter 12)*	Speech points tell a story; they can use any design as long as together the points convey the story

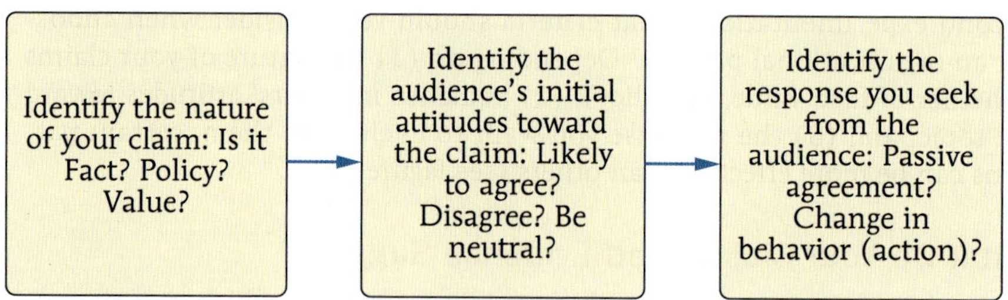

Identify the nature of your claim: Is it Fact? Policy? Value?
Identify the audience's initial attitudes toward the claim: Likely to agree? Disagree? Be neutral?
Identify the response you seek from the audience: Passive agreement? Change in behavior (action)?

FIGURE 26.1 Selecting an Organizational Pattern for Your Persuasive Speech

implies that unrestricted sales of these foods represents a *problem* and that limiting them represents a *solution*. Thus, one obvious way to arrange main points is with the *problem-solution pattern* (see Chapter 12 and p. 358 below). Many claims of policy—claims that recommend a specific course of action—fit naturally into the problem-solution pattern. However, another pattern may be equally or more effective for this argument. Perhaps your research convincingly points to several advantages associated with limiting junk food and several disadvantages associated with not doing so. In this event, the *comparative advantage pattern of arrangement* (see p. 359 in this chapter) might serve you well.

Similarly, consider a claim of value (i.e., a claim that addresses issues of judgment): "Religious freedom dictates that people should be legally free to practice polygamy, or to marry multiple partners." One potentially effective way of ordering this (and many other) claims of value is with the *topical* (also called *categorical*) *pattern of arrangement*. Here, you arrange main points to reflect a series of reasons in support of the claim. (A topical pattern arranges information according to different subtopics or categories of relatively equal importance within a larger topic; see p. 186 in Chapter 12.)

Finally, consider the *claim of fact* (i.e., a claim addressing whether something is or is not true or will or will not happen) that "deficits are projected to rise again as the last of the baby boomers begin drawing from Medicare, Medicaid, and Social Security." The claim implies a cause-effect relationship in which a large aging population drawing on services (CAUSE) leads to rising deficits (EFFECT). Alternatively, you could argue this claim in a *problem-solution* or *problem-cause-solution pattern* (see Chapter 12), so that the first point establishes the problem (rising deficits) and subsequent points explain reasons for the problem (aging population/need for more services) and provide a solution (raise taxes/lower benefits).

What Response Do You Seek?

All persuasive speeches seek to influence attitudes, but some speeches focus on passive agreement while others encourage action, such as donating to a cause or signing a petition. Thus, yet another consideration in choosing how you will order speech points is your *specific speech purpose*—how you want your audience to react to your message. If you want them to actually do something—buy a product, donate to a cause—you may wish to choose *Monroe's Motivated Sequence*—a particularly effective pattern for getting people to act on the speaker's suggestions (see p. 362 below).

What Is the Attitude of the Audience?

A final consideration of potential importance when selecting an organizational arrangement is where your **target audience** stands in relation to your topic (see Chapter 6 on analyzing your audience). How receptive to or critical of your claims are they likely to be? As demonstrated in Table 26.2, depending on the audience's attitudes toward the topic, certain organizational patterns and various persuasive strategies can be more effective than others.[1]

TABLE 26.2 Persuasive Strategies and Organizational Patterns for Different Types of Audiences

Audience Disposition	Possible Strategies and Organizational Patterns
Hostile audience or one that strongly disagrees	• Stress areas of agreement; focus on diffusing anger or suspicion by demonstrating respect • Address opposing views • Don't expect major changes in attitudes • Wait until the end before asking audience to act, if at all • Reason *inductively*—start with evidence, leaving conclusion until last ("tuition should be raised") • Consider the *refutation* pattern, in which you present both sides of the argument and demonstrate the strength of your position in contrast to the other side (see p. 360 in this chapter)
Critical and conflicted audience	• Present strong arguments and audience evidence • Address opposing views, perhaps by using the *refutation* pattern (see p. 360)
Sympathetic audience	• Use motivational stories and emotional appeals to reinforce positive attitudes • Stress your commonality with listeners • Clearly tell audience what you want them to think or do • Refutation isn't necessary; most patterns appropriate, including the *narrative* (storytelling) pattern (see Chapter 12, p. 187)
Uninformed, less-educated, or apathetic audience	• Focus on capturing their attention • Stress personal credibility and "likability" • Stress the topic's relevance to listeners • Consider *Monroe's Motivated Sequence*

Problem-Solution Pattern of Arrangement

As seen above, one commonly used design for persuasive speeches, especially (but not restricted to) those based on *claims of policy*, is the **problem-solution pattern of arrangement**. Here you organize speech points to demonstrate the nature and significance of a problem and then to provide justification for a proposed solution:

I. Problem (define what it is)

II. Solution (offer a way to overcome the problem)

But many problem-solution speeches require more than two points to adequately explain the problem and to substantiate the recommended solution. Thus a **problem-cause-solution pattern of arrangement** may be in order:

I. The nature of the problem (define what it is)

II. Reasons for the problem (explain why it's a problem, for whom, etc.)

III. Proposed solution (explain why it's expected to work)

When arguing a claim of policy, it may be important to demonstrate the proposal's feasibility. To do this, use a four-point *problem-cause-solution-feasibility* pattern: (1) a need or a problem, (2) reasons for the problem, (3) a solution to the need or problem, and (4) evidence of the solution's feasibility.

First comes a *need* or a *problem*. The policy must speak to a real issue that the audience would like to have resolved. If your claim is that "to prevent the collapse of the Social Security system, we should change eligibility requirements," the *need* is for a lessening of financial challenges to funding Social Security. Second, the justification for a policy must provide *reasons for the problem*. One reason that the Social Security program faces financial shortfalls is that too many people are taking money out of the system and too few are putting money into it. (You can list multiple reasons.) Next, you must provide a *solution to the problem*, a specific way to address the need. The policy claim that Social Security should be changed must then offer an alternative policy, such as "the Social Security program needs to raise the normal retirement age from 67 to 70." Fourth, the justification for the policy claim should offer *evidence of the solution's feasibility*. In this case, the speaker could provide evidence showing that based on a retirement age of 70, budget analysts project X amount of savings over a thirty-year period.

THESIS STATED AS NEED OR PROBLEM: Serious financial challenges to our nation's Social Security program require that we take steps to ensure it will be able to meets its obligations to citizens.

MAIN POINTS:

I. To keep Social Security funded, we need to raise both the full benefits age and the early eligibility age. *(Need/problem)*

II. People are living longer in retirement, which means they are collecting Social Security over a longer period. *(Reasons for the problem; can offer single or multiple reasons)*

III. Congress needs to raise the early eligibility age from 62 to 67 and the normal retirement age from 67 to 70. *(Solution to the problem)*

IV. Social Security programs in countries X and Y have done this successfully. *(Evidence of the solution's feasibility)*

Comparative Advantage Pattern of Arrangement

Another way to organize speech points is to show how your viewpoint or proposal is superior to one or more alternative viewpoints or proposals. This **comparative advantage pattern of arrangement** is most effective when your audience is already aware of the issue or problem and agrees that a need for a solution (or an alternative view) exists. Because listeners are alert to the issue,

CHECKLIST

ORGANIZING A CLAIM OF POLICY USING THE PROBLEM-CAUSE-SOLUTION PATTERN

- ✔ Describe the need or problem.
- ✔ Discuss reasons for the problem.
- ✔ Offer a solution to the need or problem.
- ✔ Offer evidence of the solution's feasibility.

you don't have to spend time establishing its existence. Instead, you can proceed directly to favorably comparing your position with the alternatives.

Using the comparative advantage pattern, the main points in a speech addressing the best way to control the deer population might look like the following:

THESIS:	Rather than hunting, fencing, or contraception alone, the best way to reduce the deer population is by a dual strategy of hunting and contraception.
MAIN POINT I:	A combination strategy is superior to hunting alone because many areas are too densely populated by humans to permit hunting; in such cases contraceptive darts and vaccines can address the problem. *(Advantage over alternative No. 1)*
MAIN POINT II:	A combination strategy is superior to relying solely on fencing because fencing is far too expensive for widespread use. *(Advantage over alternative No. 2)*
MAIN POINT III:	A dual strategy is superior to relying on contraception alone because only a limited number of deer are candidates for contraceptive darts and vaccines. *(Advantage over alternative No. 3)*

Refutation Pattern of Arrangement

Similar to debate, the **refutation pattern of arrangement** addresses each main point and then refutes (disproves) an opposing claim to your position. The aim here is to bolster your own position by disproving the opposing claim. This pattern can effectively address competing arguments (see Chapter 25, p. 352). Refutation is a favorite tool of political candidates, who use it to strengthen their position on an issue and debunk the position taken by the opposing candidate.

Refutation may influence audience members who either disagree with you or are conflicted about where they stand. Note that it is important to refute *strong* rather than *weak* objections to the claim, since refuting weak objections won't sway the audience.[2] Consider this pattern when you are confident that the opposing argument is vulnerable to attack.

Main points arranged in a refutation pattern follow a format similar to the following:

MAIN POINT I: State the opposing position.

MAIN POINT II: Describe the implications or ramifications of the opposing claim.

MAIN POINT III: Offer arguments and evidence for your position.

MAIN POINT IV: Contrast your position with the opposing claim to drive home the superiority of your position.

Consider the speaker who argues for increased energy conservation versus a policy of drilling for oil in protected land in Alaska.

THESIS: Rather than drilling for oil in Alaska's Arctic National Wildlife Refuge (ANWR), we should focus on energy conservation measures as a way of protecting the environment.

MAIN POINT I: Proponents claim that drilling in the Arctic refuge is necessary to decrease dependence on foreign oil sources and hold down fuel costs while adding jobs, and that modern drilling techniques along with certain environmental restrictions will result in little negative impact on the environment. *(Describes opposing claims)*

MAIN POINT II: By calling for drilling, these proponents sidestep our need for stricter energy conservation policies, overlook the need to protect one of the last great pristine lands, and ignore the fact that the oil would make a negligible dent in oil imports—from 68 percent to 65 percent by 2025. *(Describes implications and ramifications of opposing claims)*

MAIN POINT III: The massive construction needed to access the tundra will disturb the habitat of caribou, polar bear, and thousands of species of birds and shift the focus from energy conservation to increased energy consumption, when the focus should be the reverse. *(Offers arguments and evidence for the speaker's position, as developed in subpoints)*

MAIN POINT IV: The proponents' plan would encourage consumption and endanger the environment; my plan would encourage energy conservation and protect one of the world's few remaining wildernesses. *(Contrasts the speaker's position with the opposition's to drive home the former's superiority)*

Monroe's Motivated Sequence

The **motivated sequence pattern of arrangement**, developed in the mid-1930s by Alan Monroe,[3] is a five-step process that begins with arousing listeners' attention and ends with calling for action. This time-tested variant of the problem-solution pattern of arrangement is particularly effective when you want the audience to do something—buy a product, donate to a cause, and so forth. Yet it is equally useful when you want listeners to reconsider their present way of thinking about something or continue to believe as they do but with greater commitment.

Step 1: Attention

The *attention step* addresses listeners' core concerns, making the speech highly relevant to them.

Step 2: Need

The *need step* isolates the issue to be addressed. If you can show the members of an audience that they have an important need that must be satisfied or a problem that must be solved, they will have a reason to listen to your propositions.

Step 3: Satisfaction

The *satisfaction step* identifies the solution. This step begins the crux of the speech, offering audience members a proposal to reinforce or change their attitudes, beliefs, and values regarding the need at hand.

Step 4: Visualization

The *visualization step* provides the audience with a vision of anticipated outcomes associated with the solution. The purpose of the step is to carry audience members beyond accepting the feasibility of your proposal to seeing how it will actually benefit them.

Step 5: Action

Finally, in the *action step* the speaker asks audience members to act according to their acceptance of the message. This may involve reconsidering their present way of thinking about something, continuing to believe as they do but with greater commitment, or implementing a new set of behaviors. Here, the speaker makes an explicit call to action.

Jacob Hahn selected the Monroe Motivated Sequence pattern to organize the speech that follows about being a socially conscious consumer. Jacob's specific purpose was to convince his audience to change their purchasing habits. See the page at the end of the book that lists the speeches in the text and the organizational patterns they make use of, including the problem-solution, comparative advantage, refutation, topical, and chronological.

CHECKLIST

STEPS IN THE MOTIVATED SEQUENCE

- ✓ Step 1: *Attention*—address listeners' core concerns, making the speech highly relevant to them.
- ✓ Step 2: *Need*—show listeners that they have an important need that must be satisfied or a problem that must be solved.
- ✓ Step 3: *Satisfaction*—introduce your proposed solution.
- ✓ Step 4: *Visualization*—provide listeners with a vision of anticipated outcomes associated with the solution.
- ✓ Step 5: *Action*—make a direct request of listeners that involves changing or strengthening their present way of thinking or acting.

SAMPLE VISUALLY ANNOTATED PERSUASIVE SPEECH

To see Jacob Hahn deliver his speech, go to LaunchPad: **launchpadworks.com**

Becoming a Socially Conscious Consumer

JACOB HAHN

In this carefully planned persuasive speech, Jacob Hahn offers strong evidence and reasons for his claims in support of socially responsible consumerism. Jacob organizes the speech using Monroe's five-step motivated sequence. He begins with the attention step, making the speech relevant to listeners, and ends with the action step, demonstrating clearly what audience members can do. Note Jacob's persuasive use of language throughout, especially in the strong imagery that helps listeners visualize the tragedy that occurred in a factory in Bangladesh ("bodies, bricks, and garments left in the rubble") and use of personal pronouns to involve audience members personally ("The thousands of miles that separate ***us*** *from tragedies like this can make them seem unrelated to* ***our*** *everyday lives. But what if . . . by purchasing the products these companies make, individuals such as* ***you*** *and* ***me*** *are also somewhat responsible for what happened?).*

It started with a few cracks in the wall. But then, on April 24, 2013, it became the worst disaster in the history of the garment industry. According to BBC News,

Jacob uses his own clothing as a visual to show the audience how his topic relates to everyday life.

on that day the Rana Plaza garment factory in Dhaka, Bangladesh, completely collapsed, leading to the deaths of over 1,100 people. •

• Jacob starts the persuasive speech with a dramatic story line ("a few cracks . . .") that serves as an effective attention getter.

Along with the bodies, bricks, and garments left in the rubble, questions remained about who was to blame for the tragedy. Sure, there were the obvious culprits—the plaza owner, the construction company. But, there were other suspects too. What about the companies whose goods were manufactured there? • As Emran Hossain and Dave Jamieson pointed out in their May 2, 2013, *Huffington Post* article, garment industry insiders partially blame Western retailers for the tragedy. They claim that it is retailer demand for low-priced labor that creates these poorly constructed and unsafe work factories, which then leads to disasters like the factory collapse.

• Continuing with the "story" keeps the audience involved and wanting to know more.

Gesturing to the audience in an inviting way indicates that Jacob wants the audience to feel involved.

The thousands of miles that separate us from tragedies like this can make them seem unrelated to our everyday lives. But what if they are not? What if, by purchasing the products these companies make, individuals such as you and me are also somewhat responsible for what happened? •

• Step 1, the *attention* step of Monroe's sequence, demonstrates the topic's relevance to audience members.

Jacob deliberately makes eye contact with audience members in every area of the room.

As we'll see today, there is evidence to support the idea that consumers and companies share a responsibility to ensure safer conditions for factory workers. • This is why I encourage all of you to become socially conscious consumers and help convince companies to adopt ethical manufacturing standards. Being a socially conscious consumer means being aware of the issues communities face worldwide and actively trying to correct them.

• Jacob states his thesis.

Why would companies do business with factories that allow dangerous working conditions? It's actually quite simple: Corporations want bigger profit margins. The cheaper the production costs, the more money they make when the product sells. And since consumers show more interest in buying lower-priced products than in thinking about how such items are produced, the pressure is on to provide inexpensive goods.

The only way to do this and still make money is to make the goods at the lowest cost possible.

But there is a way to break this cycle of cheap labor and deadly working conditions. You, me, all of us as consumers, must be willing to step up and take an active role in the system. •

• Step 2, the *need* step, shows listeners why they should listen to the speaker's propositions – in this case, to help factory workers obtain safer working conditions.

We can do this in two ways: First, we can pressure companies to improve working conditions for factory laborers, and second, we can pay fairer prices. Some consumer groups are now signaling their willingness to do this, and corporations are responding. •

• Step 3, the *satisfaction* step, identifies how to meet the need.

The force behind this new kind of partnership is called "cause-related marketing." According to the *Financial Times*, *cause-related marketing* is when a company and a charity (or a consumer group) tackle a social or an environmental problem and create business value for the company at the same time. •

• Jacob clearly defines a potentially confusing term, offering an explanation from a credible source.

In March 2012, the global marketing firm Nielsen conducted a worldwide study on consumer responses to cause marketing. The poll found that two-thirds of consumers around the world say they prefer to buy products and services from companies that give back to society. Nearly 50 percent of consumers said that they were, and I'm quoting here, "willing to pay more for goods and services from companies that are giving back." •

• Jacob provides convincing evidence from a credible source.

Coordinating body movement with his speech drives home his main points.

The fact that large numbers of consumers are concerned enough about fairness to pay more for products is key to solving the problems that surround the ethical manufacture of clothing. Corporations can appeal to this group of socially conscious consumers, as they are called, by addressing concerns about ethical manufacturing. What do corporations gain by meeting these concerns? It allows them to charge more for their products while also raising their profit margins and improving their brand image. This means that as socially conscious consumers, we can set the standards that corporations must meet if they wish to maximize their profit from our purchasing power.

You may find yourself asking, Can this actually work? The answer is a simple yes. • In both the food and apparel industries, calls for changes in working conditions led to the now widely known nonprofit

• Here is step 4: *visualization*. Jacob offers a vision of outcomes associated with the proposed solution.

organization Fair Trade USA. According to its website, Fair Trade USA is an organization that seeks "to inspire the rise of the [socially] Conscious Consumer and eliminate exploitation" worldwide. If products are stamped with the Fair Trade logo, it means the farmers and workers who created those products were fairly treated and justly compensated through an internationally established price.

Fair Trade USA made its mark in the food industry through its relationship to coffee production in third-world nations. Its success helped major companies such as Starbucks and Whole Foods recognize the strength of cause marketing: If you appeal to the high ethical standards of socially conscious consumers, they will pay more for your product. •

• Is this a claim of fact, value, or policy?

Appealing to high ethical standards is often directly related to tragedies like the one that occurred in Bangladesh. After the factory collapsed, the major apparel sellers faced intense criticism over their lax labor practices. In response, these companies are now much more interested in establishing their products as Fair Trade to meet socially conscious consumer standards. For example, as Jason Burke, Saad Hammadi, and Simon Neville report in the May 13, 2013, edition of the *Guardian,* major fashion chains like H&M, Zara, C&A, Tesco, and Primark have pledged to help raise the standards for working conditions. According to the article, they will be helping to "finance fire safety and building improvements in the factories they use in Bangladesh." •

• Note that Jacob provides evidence in support of his claim.

Emotional facial expressions add to the seriousness of Jacob's topic.

So, what exactly can you do to help bring about ethical labor practices within the clothing industry? The two steps I encourage you to take are these: Become informed, and ask questions about what you're buying—whether it's shoes, a t-shirt, or any other type of apparel. •

• Here begins step 5 of Monroe's Motivated Sequence: the *action* step—a direct request of listeners to act on the speaker's suggestions and concrete directions for doing so.

To be informed, go to websites such as fairtradeusa.org, thirdworldtraveler.com, and tenthousandvillages.com, which list and sell products from clothing manufacturers who have worked to meet the Fair Trade conditions. This list grows monthly, and by supporting these companies through your purchases, you can become a socially conscious consumer.

Additionally, ask questions of other retailers. Whether you shop online or at local retail stores, ask direct questions before purchasing clothes — for example: Where are your products made? Do you have proof of fair-trade practices? Where can I find this information before I make my purchase? Such questions define the socially conscious consumer, and they ensure that you will not be directly contributing to unsafe and unfair labor practices.

Although several factors contributed to the tragedy in Bangladesh, there is one clear way to help prevent future disasters: become a socially conscious consumer. By being informed and asking questions, you, too, can make a difference in the lives of workers around the world. •

• Jacob concludes by reinforcing his call to action and leaves the audience with a new perspective to consider.

SAMPLE PHRASE OUTLINE

Becoming a Socially Conscious Consumer

JACOB HAHN

Following is a phrase outline Jacob created for delivering his speech. As explained in Chapter 13, a ***phrase outline*** *uses partial construction of the sentence form of each point; it encourages you to become so familiar with the speech that a glance at a few words is enough to remind you of exactly what to say. (At the same time, a phrase outline offers a bit more content than a* ***key word outline****, which uses the smallest possible units of understanding to outline the main and supporting points.) Knowing a speech well enough to comfortably use a phrase or keyword outline will permit you to maintain eye contact with the audience and use a natural style of delivery. Practice, of course, is key. (Note that transitions and quotations are written out in full, as some speakers find that this helpful. For his outline, Jacob used "SCC" to indicate "socially conscious consumer" and "FT" to indicate "Fair Trade.")*

PHRASE DELIVERY OUTLINE

INTRODUCTION

I. Started few cracks wall.
   a. BUT April 24, 2013, worst disaster history garment.
   b. (BBC News), on that day Rana Plaza factory, Dhaka, Bangladesh collapsed, deaths 1,100.

II. Bodies, bricks, garments, rubble, questions who blame?
   a. Sure, obvious culprits—plaza owner, construction company.
   b. But other suspects—companies who manufactured there?
   c. Emran Hossain, Dave Jamieson, May 2, 2013, *Huffington*: insiders blame Western retailers: demand low-priced labor creates poorly constructed factories, leads disasters.

III. Thousands miles separate us, seem unrelated, but what if not. . . . what if by purchasing, you, me also responsible?

IV. Evidence supports idea consumers, companies share responsibility safer conditions
   a. . . . Why I encourage you become SCC, help convince companies ethical manufacturing standards.
   b. Being an SCC—being aware issues communities face worldwide, correct them.

BODY

I. Why companies do business with factories, allow dangerous conditions?
   a. Actually simple, bigger margins.
      1. Cheaper production costs, more money when product sells.

2. Consumers more interest lower-priced than how produced, pressure on provide inexpensive.
3. Only way do this, still make money, make goods lowest cost.

(TRANSITION: *But there is a way to break the cycle of cheap labor and deadly working conditions.*)

II. You, me, step up, take active role in system (two ways).
  a. Pressure companies improving conditions.
  b. Pay fairer prices.
  c. Some groups willing to do, and corporations responding.

III. Force behind new partnership SCC and business: "cause-related marketing."
  a. *Financial Times defined*—when company/charity/consumer group tackle social/environmental problem to create business value same time.
  b. March 2012, Nielsen worldwide study results.
    1. 2/3rds consumers prefer buy product from companies give back society.
    2. 50% [QUOTE] "Willing to pay more for goods and services from companies that are giving back."

IV. Consumers concerned enough about fairness to pay more key to solving problems surround ethical manufacture.
  a. Corporations can appeal to group SCC by addressing concerns.
  b. What do corporations gain?
    1. Charge more while raising profit, improving brand image.
    2. Means as SCC, *we* set standards corporations meet if wish to maximize profit from our purchasing power.

(TRANSITION: *You may find yourself asking, Can this actually work? The answer is a simple yes.*)

V. In both food, apparel industries' calls for changes led to FT USA.

   a. FT website: [QUOTE] "Seeks to inspire the rise of the SCC and eliminate exploitation" worldwide.

   b. If products stamped w/FT logo, means farmers, workers treated fairly, justly compensated through internationally established price.

   c. FT USA made mark in food industry through relationship coffee third-world nations.

   d. Success FT helped companies (Starbucks . . .) recognize strength of CM: appeal to high ethical standards—socially conscious will pay more.

VI. Attention to ethical standards often precipitated by tragedy

   a. After . . . collapsed, sellers faced intense criticism lax practices.

   b. Apparel sellers now much interested establishing products as FT, meet SCC standards.

      1. Jason Burke, Saad Hammadi, Simon Neville, May 13, 2013 *Guardian,* chains H&M, Zara, C&A, Tesco, Primark pledged raise standards for working conditions.

      2. Will be helping [QUOTE] "finance fire safety and building improvements in the factories they use in Bangladesh."

VII. What can you . . . help . . . ethical practices clothing industry . . . two steps . . . *become informed, ask questions* about buying—whether shoes . . . other apparel.

   a. To be informed—websites fairtradeusa.org, thirdworldtraveler.com, tenthousandvillages.com—list, sell products from manufacturers worked to meet FT conditions.

b. Ask questions retailers.

1. Whether shop online/local, before purchasing clothes—where made, proof FT practices, where find information before purchase?
2. Questions define SCC, ensure not contributing to unsafe, unfair labor practices.

CONCLUSION

VIII. Although several factors Bangladesh, one clear way prevent future: become SCC. Being informed, asking questions, you, too, make difference workers around world.

27 Special Occasion Speeches

LearningCurve can help you review!
Go to LaunchPad: **launchpadworks.com**

Special occasions stand out from the ordinary rhythm of life, marking passages, celebrating life's highlights, and commemorating events. Such occasions often include the observance of important ceremonies and rituals as well as speeches. When it is delivered well, a special occasion speech forges a bond among audience members and helps them put the significance of the occasion in perspective.

Functions of Special Occasion Speeches

There are many kinds of occasions that call for speeches, some serious and some lighthearted. As is suggested by its name, a **special occasion speech** is one that is prepared for a specific occasion and for a purpose dictated by that occasion. In the special occasion speech, the rhetorical situation truly gives rise to the speech content. Awards ceremonies call for remarks that acknowledge accomplishments, for example, and acceptance speeches call for a display of gratitude.

Special occasion speeches can be informative or persuasive or a mix of both. However, neither of these functions is the main goal; the underlying function of a special occasion speech is to entertain, celebrate, commemorate, inspire, or set a social agenda.

Entertainment

Many kinds of special occasions call for a speech that entertains. Venues such as banquets, awards dinners, and roasts, for example, frequently feature speakers whose main purpose is to entertain those in attendance. In such cases, listeners expect a lighthearted, amusing speech; they may also expect the speaker to offer a certain degree of insight into the topic at hand.

Celebration

Often a special occasion speech will celebrate a person, a place, or an event. Weddings, anniversaries, retirement parties, and awards banquets all call for speeches that recognize the person(s) or event being celebrated. The audience expects the speaker to praise the subject of the celebration and to cast him or her in a positive light. The listeners also expect a certain degree of ceremony in accordance with the norms of the occasion.

Commemoration

Certain special occasion speeches, called *commemorative speeches*, focus on remembrance and tribute. Commemorative speeches mark important anniversaries, such as the anniversary of the attack on Pearl Harbor or of the first moon landing. Speakers deliver commemorative speeches about events or people of note at memorials dedicated to them or at gatherings otherwise held in their honor.

Inspiration

Inaugural addresses, keynote speeches at conventions, and commencement speeches all have inspiration as their main function. With their examples of accomplishments, achievement, and heroism, many commemorative speeches also inspire audiences as well as pay homage to the person or event being commemorated.

Agenda Setting

Yet another function of the special occasion speech is **social agenda setting** – articulating or reinforcing the goals and values of the group sponsoring the event. Occasions that call for agenda-setting speeches include gatherings of issues- or cause-oriented organizations, fundraisers, campaign banquets, conferences, and conventions. Speakers asked to deliver keynote addresses at conferences or conventions are charged with establishing the theme of the meeting and with offering a plan of action related to that theme. Similarly, politically oriented organizations also routinely hold meetings at which invited speakers perform the function of agenda setting.

Types of Special Occasion Speeches

Special occasion speeches include (but are not limited to) speeches of introduction, speeches of acceptance, award presentations, roasts and toasts, eulogies and other speeches of tribute, after-dinner speeches, and speeches of inspiration.

Speeches of Introduction

A **speech of introduction** is a short speech with two goals: to prepare or "warm up" the audience for the speaker, and to motivate audience members to listen to what the main speaker has to say. Many occasions call for speeches of introduction. You might be asked to introduce a guest speaker at a monthly meeting of a social organization to which you belong, to introduce an award presenter at your company's annual banquet, or to introduce an outside expert at a quarterly sales meeting. A good speech of introduction balances four elements: the speaker's background, the subject or topic of the speaker's message, the occasion, and the audience.

Describe the Speaker's Background

A key part of the introducer's task is to tell the audience something about the speaker's background and qualifications for speaking. The object is to heighten audience interest and build the speaker's credibility. If you don't know the background of the person you will introduce, inquire ahead about his or her important achievements, offices held, and other activities relevant to the occasion that will show audience members what kind of speaker they are about to hear and why they should listen.

Briefly Preview the Speaker's Topic

Part of the introducer's job is to give audience members a sense of why the speaker's subject is of interest to them. Is the subject timely? What significance does it have for the audience? What special connections exist between the subject or the speaker and the occasion? Is he or she an expert on the topic? Why was the speaker invited? Keep in mind, however, that it is not the introducer's job to evaluate the speech or otherwise offer critical commentary on it. The rule is: *Get in and out quickly with a few well-chosen remarks.* Introducers who linger on their own thoughts run the risk of stealing the speaker's thunder.

Ask the Audience to Welcome the Speaker

A final part of the introducer's task is to cue the audience to welcome the speaker. This can be done very simply by saying something like "Please welcome Anthony Svetlana." Hearing this, the audience will provide applause, thereby paving the way for the speaker to take his or her place at the podium.

In the following excerpt from a speech by Frank D. Stella, of F. D. Stella Products Company, Stella introduces Richard A. Grasso, former chairman and chief executive officer of the New York Stock Exchange, to the Economic Club of Detroit. Notice how Stella makes use of the date of the occasion—April 15, or Tax Day—to engage the audience. Stella also provides a quick overview of who the speaker is and a reference to why he was a good choice for this occasion.

> Happy April 15! This may be only a quirk of history, but do you realize that not only is today Tax Day, it is also the anniversary of the sinking of the *Titanic!* Talk about double jeopardy!
>
> It's interesting, therefore, that we have scheduled today's speaker for April 15: If your company or individual stock did well and was listed on the New York Stock Exchange, you can, in part, thank Dick Grasso for keeping the Exchange so strong and competitive; but if your taxes went up because your stocks did so well, you can thank Dick for capital gains, the market upsurge, and profitability.
>
> It is a distinct honor for me to introduce Richard A. Grasso, chairman and chief executive officer of the New York Stock Exchange. He has enjoyed a remarkable twenty-eight-year-career at the Exchange. [Mr. Stella goes on to provide a more detailed background on Mr. Grasso.][1]

CHECKLIST

GUIDELINES FOR INTRODUCING OTHER SPEAKERS

- ✓ Identify the speaker correctly. Assign him or her the proper title, such as "vice president for public relations" or "professor emeritus."
- ✓ Practice difficult-to-pronounce names several times before actually introducing the speaker.
- ✓ Contact the speaker ahead of time to verify the accuracy of any facts about him or her that you plan to cite.
- ✓ Consider devices that will capture the audience's attention, such as quotes, short anecdotes, and startling statements (see Chapter 14 on developing introductions).

Respond to Introductions

Whenever you are introduced by another speaker, acknowledge and thank him or her for the introduction. For example:

- I appreciate those kind words.
- Thank you for making me feel welcome today.
- This is a wonderful event, and I appreciate being a part of it.

Most of us are not used to being publicly honored, and accepting praise and accolades from a speaker who introduces us can be awkward. One of the ways to show your humility toward a gracious introduction is through humor:

- That introduction was so gracious; you were more than halfway through it before I realized you were talking about me.[2]
- Thank you, Mr. Secretary, for that incredible introduction. If I had known you were going to eulogize me, I would have done the only decent thing and died.[3]
- I'm really not as good as she said, but neither am I as bad as my mother-in-law thinks. So I guess it averages out.[4]

Speeches of Acceptance

A **speech of acceptance** is made in response to receiving an award of some sort. Its purpose is to express gratitude for the honor bestowed on the speaker. The speech should reflect that gratitude.

Prepare in Advance

If you know or even suspect that you will be given an award, be sure to prepare an acceptance speech. If the award is not a surprise, you may be asked to prepare extended remarks. Otherwise, if it appears at all likely that you will be honored, prepare and practice your speech just as you would any other. Doing so will ensure that you avoid using standard—and cringe-worthy—responses such as "I really just don't know what to say."

React Genuinely and with Humility

Genuineness and humility are possibly the most important parts of expressing gratitude. Offering a sincere response shows your audience how much the award means to you. Explain why the award is important to you, perhaps tell your listeners how it will affect your future, and speak about how it gives meaning to whatever you did in the past that led to its receipt. Express your gratitude with humility, acknowledging your good fortune in having received it.

Thank Those Giving the Award

Even though the attention is focused on you, don't forget to express your gratitude to the people who are giving you the award. If the award is given by an organization, specifically thank that organization by name. If it is given by a combination of organizations, remember to mention all of them. If there is a sponsor of the award, such as a donor that makes the award possible, remember to acknowledge the donor as well.

If the reason for your award represents a team effort, be sure to thank all members. If there are people who gave you the inspiration that helped you achieve the award, thank them. You might even ask them to stand up to be recognized if they are in attendance.

Speeches of Presentation

The job of presenting an award can be an honor in itself. Whether you are presenting a bowling trophy or a Grammy music award, your goal in the **speech of presentation** is twofold: to communicate the meaning of the award and to explain why the recipient is receiving it.

Convey the Meaning of the Award

It is the presenter's task to explain the meaning of the award to the audience. What is the award for? What kind of achievement does it celebrate? Who or

CHECKLIST

GUIDELINES FOR DELIVERING SPEECHES OF ACCEPTANCE

- ✓ Prepare an acceptance speech in advance of the event.
- ✓ Explain why the award is important to you.
- ✓ Express your gratitude to the people who are giving you the award.
- ✓ Thank those who helped you attain the achievement.
- ✓ Do not belabor your acknowledgments.
- ✓ Accept the award gracefully by showing that you value it.
- ✓ End your speech with an explicit expression of gratitude.

what does the award represent? What is the significance of its special name or title? You might offer a brief history of the award, such as when it was founded and the names of some of its previous recipients. Because you are a presenter, it is also your job to identify the sponsors or organizations that made the award possible and to describe the link between the sponsor's goals and values and the award.

The following example is a common way of communicating to the audience the significance of an award:

> It is an honor and a privilege to be the one making this presentation today. This plaque is only a token of our appreciation for Seamus's achievements, but we hope that this symbol will serve as a daily reminder of our admiration for his great work. Let me read the inscription. "Seamus O'Leary, in appreciation for the outstanding work. . . ."

Talk about the Recipient of the Award

The second part of the presenter's task is to explain why the recipient is receiving the award. Tell the audience why the recipient has been singled out for special recognition. Describe this person's achievements and special attributes that qualify him or her as deserving of the award. If relevant, explain how the recipient was selected. What kind of selection process was used? The following example illustrates how this can be done:

> And, I might add, these were just some of the accomplishments of Carol Brown. When the selection committee reviewed all the nominees (some eighty-four of them), it became clear that Carol would be our choice. The committee met four times to narrow the list of nominees, and at each meeting it was clear who our winner would be. The other nominees were outstanding in their own right, but Carol stood apart. . . .

Roasts and Toasts

A **roast** is a humorous tribute to a person, one in which a series of speakers jokingly poke fun at him or her. Examples of famous annual roasts are the Comedy Central Roast and the White House Correspondents' Dinner. A **toast** is a brief tribute to a person or an event being celebrated. Both roasts and toasts call for short speeches whose goal is to celebrate an individual and his or her achievements. Should you be asked to speak at such events, it will be helpful to follow these guidelines.

Prepare

Impromptu though they might appear, the best roasts and toasts reflect time spent drafting, and importantly, rehearsing the remarks. Many speakers rehearse in front of trusted friends. This is especially helpful if you are considering telling a joke that you are unsure about. Practicing with friends also allows them to time your speech. People often speak for much longer than they realize.

Highlight Remarkable Traits of the Person Being Honored

Because these speeches are usually short, restrict your remarks to one or two of the person's most unusual or recognizable attributes. Convey the qualities that have made him or her worthy of celebrating.

Be Positive and Be Brief

Even if the speech pokes fun at someone, as in a roast, keep the tone good natured and brief. Remember, the overall purpose of your speech is to pay tribute to the honoree. It's great to have fun, but avoid saying anything that might embarrass the person being honored. For example, at the 2016 annual White House Correspondents' Dinner roast, *Saturday Night Live* cast member Cecily Strong struck the right balance of humor and social satire when she joked to then-President Barack Obama: "Your hair is so white now, it can talk back to the police."[5]

Eulogies and Other Tributes

The word **eulogy** derives from the Greek word meaning "to praise." Those delivering eulogies, usually close friends or family members of the deceased, are charged with celebrating and commemorating the life of someone while consoling those who have been left behind. Given these goals, the eulogy can be one of the most difficult and challenging special occasion speeches to deliver. At the same time, probably more people with little or no experience in public speaking deliver a eulogy at one time or another than any other type of special occasion speech.

Should you be called upon to give a eulogy, the following guidelines will help to ensure an effective speech.

Balance Delivery and Emotions

Many speakers fight the tendency to become overly emotional while giving a eulogy. Despite the sense of grief the speaker may be feeling, his or her job is to help others feel better. The audience looks to the speaker for guidance in dealing with the loss, and for a sense of closure, so stay in control. If you do feel that you are about to break down, pause, take a breath, and focus on your next thought.

Refer to the Family of the Deceased

Families suffer the greatest loss, and a memorial service is primarily for their benefit. Show respect for the family, mentioning each family member by name. Make it clear that the deceased was an important part of a family by humanizing that family.

Commemorate Life—Not Death

A eulogy should pay tribute to the deceased as an individual and remind the audience that he or she is still alive, in a sense, in our memories. Rather than focus on the circumstances of death, focus on the life of the person. Talk about the person's contributions and achievements, and demonstrate the person's

CHECKLIST

TIPS FOR DELIVERING EFFECTIVE EULOGIES

- ✓ Stay in control of your emotions.
- ✓ Refer to the family of the deceased, mentioning each family member by name.
- ✓ Rather than focusing on the circumstances of the death, talk about the contributions the deceased person made during his or her lifetime.
- ✓ Consider telling a story or an anecdote that illustrates the type of person you are eulogizing. Humor that is respectful may be appropriate.
- ✓ Emphasize the person's positive qualities, but do not be insincere.

character. Consider telling an anecdote that illustrates the type of person you are eulogizing. Even humorous stories and anecdotes may be appropriate if they effectively humanize the deceased.

Be Positive but Realistic

Emphasize the deceased's positive qualities. This seems obvious, but care must be taken in selecting stories and anecdotes, as well as in planning descriptions of the person, to ensure that none of the speech is interpreted as casting the deceased in a negative light. At the same time, avoid excessive praise that will ring false to those who loved the deceased.

After-Dinner Speeches

In the course of his career, Mark Twain, the nineteenth-century humorist and writer, was said to have given more than 150 after-dinner speeches. Extremely popular at the time, lavish dinner affairs were attended by a host of male notables who spent several hours eating and drinking, after which they spent several more hours listening to humorous toasts and speeches.[6] Twain's speeches were so well received that many of them were reprinted in the next day's newspaper.

Today, the **after-dinner speech** is just as likely to occur before, during, or after a breakfast or lunch seminar or other type of business, professional, or civic meeting or family event as it is to follow a formal dinner. In general, an after-dinner speech is expected to be lighthearted and entertaining (see the following exceptions). At the same time, listeners expect the speaker to provide insight into the topic at hand and/or to hear an outline of priorities and goals for the group. Thus, social agenda setting is a simultaneous goal of many after-dinner speeches.

Recognize the Occasion

Be sure to connect the speech with the occasion. Delivering a speech that is unrelated to the event that has given rise to it may leave the impression that it is a **canned speech**—that is, one that the speaker uses again and again in different settings.

Balance Seriousness with Lightheartedness

Even when charged with addressing a serious topic, the after-dinner speaker should make an effort to keep his or her remarks low-key enough to accompany the digestion of a meal. Low-key does not mean stand-up comedy, however, which should be avoided. The most convincing speakers are the ones who are most naturally believable. Trying to become funnier—or more serious—than you normally are will probably set you up to fail because it will make your job harder. The speech becomes an acting challenge. If you are naturally very funny, use that skill. If you have a dry sense of humor, plan jokes that reflect that kind of humor. Do not be fooled into thinking that expressing humor means that you have to become Amy Schumer or Kevin Hart.

Speeches of Inspiration

While many special occasion speeches may well be inspiring, a **speech of inspiration** deliberately seeks to uplift members of the audience and to help them see things in a positive light. Sermons, commencement addresses, pep talks, and nomination speeches are all inspirational in nature. In the business world, occasions for inspirational speeches are so numerous that some people earn their living as inspirational speakers.

Effective speeches of inspiration touch on deep feelings in the audience. Through emotional force, they urge us toward purer motives and harder effort and remind us of a common good.

As in a persuasive speech, to create an effective inspirational speech you'll need to appeal to the audience's emotions (pathos) and display positive ethos. Three means of evoking emotion, or pathos, are touching upon shared values (Chapter 24) using *vivid imagery* (Chapter 16), and *telling stories* (Chapter 8). Repetition, alliteration, and parallelism can also help transport the audience from the mundane to a loftier level (see Chapter 16 on using language). To find inspiration for your speech, see TED Talks (www.ted.com/talks), which has become a favorite venue for such speeches.

Use Real-Life Stories

Few things move us as much as the example of the ordinary person who achieves the extraordinary, whose struggles result in triumph over adversity and the realization of a dream. Real-life stories and examples of achievement and overcoming obstacles can be very moving. Recognizing this, several recent U.S. presidents have taken to weaving stories about "ordinary American heroes" into their State of the Union addresses.

Be Dynamic

If it fits your personality, use a dynamic speaking style to inspire through delivery. Combining an energetic style with a powerful message can be one of the most successful strategies for inspirational speaking.

Make Your Goal Clear

Inspirational speeches run the risk of being vague, leaving the audience unsure about what the message was. Whatever you are trying to motivate your listeners

CHECKLIST

DELIVERING A SUCCESSFUL SPEECH OF INSPIRATION

- ✔ Focus the speech on uplifting the audience.
- ✔ Seek to arouse the audience's better instincts.
- ✔ Use emotional appeals.
- ✔ Concentrate on creating positive speaker ethos (see Chapter 5, on ethics, and Chapter 24, on ethos and speaker credibility).
- ✔ Appeal to the audience's emotions through vivid descriptions and emotionally charged words.
- ✔ Consider the use of repetition, alliteration, and parallelism (see Chapter 16, on using language).
- ✔ Consider using real-life stories and examples.
- ✔ Strive for a dynamic style of delivery.
- ✔ Clearly establish your speech goal.
- ✔ Consider using an acronym to organize your inspirational message.
- ✔ Make your conclusion strong.

to do, let them know. If you are speaking about a general goal, such as remaining positive in life, let your listeners know that. If you are trying to motivate your listeners to perform a specific action, such as donating money to a particular charity, clearly state so.

Close with a Dramatic Ending

Using a dramatic ending is one of the best means of inspiring your audience to feel or act in the ways suggested by the theme of your speech. Recall from Chapter 15 the various methods of concluding a speech, including a quotation, story, or call to action.

ETHICALLY SPEAKING

Tailor Your Message to the Audience and Occasion

Radu Bercan/ Shutterstock

More so than for other kinds of speeches, audiences have high expectations that the speaker of a special occasion speech will fulfill a specific need. People listening to a eulogy, for example, will be very sensitive to what they perceive to be inappropriate use of humor or a lack of respect shown to the deceased. Those attending a dedication ceremony for a war memorial will expect the speaker to offer words of inspiration. When a speaker violates audience expectations in situations like these, audience reaction is usually pronounced. When giving a special occasion speech, it is therefore critical to plan your speech with audience expectations firmly in mind.

SAMPLE VISUALLY ANNOTATED SPECIAL OCCASION SPEECH

President Obama Speaks at a Memorial Service for Nelson Mandela

December 10, 2013

JOHANNESBURG, SOUTH AFRICA

Following is a eulogy for former South African president Nelson Mandela by President Barack Obama. Delivered to some seventy thousand persons in attendance at the First National Bank stadium, including one hundred heads of state, and broadcast to millions more worldwide, Obama's speech gave praise to one of his—and the world's—greatest heroes of the twentieth century. A eulogist is charged with celebrating and commemorating the life of the deceased, and in this stirring address Obama does this with great skill.

Note that as with most eulogies, Obama's speech is largely organized using the topical pattern, with Obama describing various characteristics of the deceased (recall that the topical pattern organizes main points according to various divisions, categories, or subtopics as the speaker sees fit; see p. 186). Another pattern commonly used in eulogies is the chronological pattern, especially for some subpoints. Obama does that here.

Thank you. Thank you so much. Thank you. To Graça Machel and the Mandela family; • to President Zuma and members of the government; to heads of states and government, past and present; distinguished guests—it is a singular honor to be with you today, to celebrate a life like no other. To the people of South Africa, people of every race and walk of life—the world thanks you for sharing Nelson Mandela with us. His struggle was your struggle. His triumph was your triumph. Your dignity and your hope found expression in his life. And your freedom, your democracy is his cherished legacy. •

• A eulogist should always first recognize the family of the deceased.

• Throughout this eulogy, note how often Obama uses a personal pronoun—"you," "us," "we"—to create a sense of inclusion and identification.

It is hard to eulogize any man—to capture in words not just the facts and the dates that make a life, but the essential truth of a person—their private joys and sorrows; the quiet moments and unique qualities that illuminate someone's soul. How much harder to do so for a giant of history, who moved a nation toward justice, and in the process moved billions around the world.

Born during World War I, far from the corridors of power, a boy raised herding cattle and tutored by the elders of his Thembu tribe, Madiba would emerge as the last great liberator of the twentieth century. • Like Gandhi, he would lead a resistance movement—a movement that at its start had little prospect for success. Like Dr. King, he would give potent voice to the claims of the oppressed and the moral necessity of racial justice. He would endure a brutal imprisonment that began in the time of Kennedy and Khrushchev, and reached the final days of the Cold War. Emerging from prison, without the force of arms, he would—like Abraham Lincoln—hold his country together when it threatened to break apart. And like America's Founding Fathers, he would erect a constitutional order to preserve freedom for future generations—a commitment to democracy and rule of law ratified not only by his election, but by his willingness to step down from power after only one term. •

Given the sweep of his life, the scope of his accomplishments, the adoration that he so rightly earned, it's tempting I think to remember Nelson Mandela as an icon, smiling and serene, detached from the tawdry affairs of lesser men. But Madiba himself strongly resisted such a lifeless portrait. Instead, Madiba insisted on sharing with us his doubts and his fears; his miscalculations along with his victories. "I am not a saint," he said, "unless you think of a saint as a sinner who keeps on trying."

It was precisely because he could admit to imperfection—because he could be so full of good humor, even mischief, despite the heavy burdens he carried—that we loved him so. He was not a bust made of marble; he was a man of flesh and blood—a son and a husband, a father and a friend. • And that's why we learned so much from him, and that's why we can learn from him still. For nothing he achieved was inevitable. In the arc of his life, we see a man who earned his place in history through struggle and shrewdness, and persistence and faith. He tells us what is possible not just in the pages of history books, but in our own lives as well.

Mandela showed us the power of action; of taking risks on behalf of our ideals. Perhaps Madiba was right that he inherited, "a proud rebelliousness, a stubborn sense of fairness" from his father. • And we know

• A eulogist should talk about and celebrate the positive contributions of the deceased—an easy task in the case of Mandela.

• Note that in three successive sentences, Obama begins with the word "Like." This rhetorical device, termed anaphora, lends the speech a rhythmic quality.

• Obama emphasizes Mandela's humanity with this strong image. Note the many concrete nouns and verbs Obama uses throughout. The colorful and vibrant language makes the words come alive for listeners.

• Obama uses Mandela's traditional clan name, creating an even deeper sense of connection between himself and Mandela—and between the audience and Mandela.

he shared with millions of black and colored South Africans the anger born of, "a thousand slights, a thousand indignities, a thousand unremembered moments . . . a desire to fight the system that imprisoned my people," he said. •

• With a person as renowned as Mandela, it's fitting to quote him.

But like other early giants of the ANC—the Sisulus and Tambos—Madiba disciplined his anger and channeled his desire to fight into organization, and platforms, and strategies for action, so men and women could stand up for their God-given dignity. Moreover, he accepted the consequences of his actions, knowing that standing up to powerful interests and injustice carries a price. "I have fought against white domination and I have fought against black domination. I've cherished the ideal of a democratic and free society in which all persons live together in harmony and [with] equal opportunities. It is an ideal which I hope to live for and to achieve. But if needs be, it is an ideal for which I am prepared to die."

Mandela taught us the power of action, but he also taught us the power of ideas; the importance of reason and arguments; the need to study not only those who you agree with, but also those who you don't agree with. • He understood that ideas cannot be contained by prison walls, or extinguished by a sniper's bullet. He turned his trial into an indictment of apartheid because of his eloquence and his passion, but also because of his training as an advocate. He used decades in prison to sharpen his arguments, but also to spread his thirst for knowledge to others in the movement. And he learned the language and the customs of his oppressor so that one day he might better convey to them how their own freedom depends upon his.

• Note again Obama's use of personal pronouns—in this case the inclusive "us."

Mandela demonstrated that action and ideas are not enough. No matter how right, they must be chiseled into law and institutions. • He was practical, testing his beliefs against the hard surface of circumstance and history. On core principles he was unyielding, which is why he could rebuff offers of unconditional release, reminding the Apartheid regime that "prisoners cannot enter into contracts."

• The concrete verb "chiseled" produces a vivid image.

But as he showed in painstaking negotiations to transfer power and draft new laws, he was not afraid to compromise for the sake of a larger goal. And because he was not only a leader of a movement but a skillful politician, the Constitution that emerged was worthy of this multiracial democracy, true to his vision of laws that protect minority as well as majority rights, and the precious freedoms of every South African.

And finally, Mandela understood the ties that bind the human spirit. There is a word in South Africa—Ubuntu—a word that captures Mandela's greatest gift: his recognition that we are all bound together in ways that are invisible to the eye; that there is a oneness to humanity; that we achieve ourselves by sharing ourselves with others, and caring for those around us.

We can never know how much of this sense was innate in him, or how much was shaped in a dark and solitary cell. But we remember the gestures, large and small—introducing his jailers as honored guests at his inauguration; taking a pitch in a Springbok uniform; turning his family's heartbreak into a call to confront HIV/AIDS—that revealed the depth of his empathy and his understanding. He not only embodied Ubuntu, he taught millions to find that truth within themselves.

It took a man like Madiba to free not just the prisoner, but the jailer as well, to show that you must trust others so that they may trust you; to teach that reconciliation is not a matter of ignoring a cruel past, but a means of confronting it with inclusion and generosity and truth. He changed laws, but he also changed hearts.

For the people of South Africa, for those he inspired around the globe, Madiba's passing is rightly a time of mourning, and a time to celebrate a heroic life. But I believe it should also prompt in each of us a time for self-reflection. With honesty, regardless of our station or our circumstance, we must ask: How well have I applied his lessons in my own life? It's a question I ask myself, as a man and as a president.

We know that, like South Africa, the United States had to overcome centuries of racial subjugation. As was true here, it took sacrifice—the sacrifice of countless people, known and unknown, to see the dawn of a new day. Michelle and I are beneficiaries of that struggle. But in America, and in South Africa, and in countries all around the globe, we cannot allow our progress to cloud the fact that our work is not yet done.

The struggles that follow the victory of formal equality or universal franchise may not be as filled with drama and moral clarity as those that came before, but they are no less important. For around the world today, we still see children suffering from hunger and disease. We still see run-down schools. We still see young people without prospects for the future. Around the world today, men and women are still imprisoned for their political beliefs, and are still persecuted for what they look like, and how they worship, and who they love. That is happening today.

And so we, too, must act on behalf of justice. We, too, must act on behalf of peace. There are too many people who happily embrace Madiba's legacy of racial reconciliation, but passionately resist even modest reforms that would challenge chronic poverty and growing inequality. There are too many leaders who claim solidarity with Madiba's struggle for freedom, but do not tolerate dissent from their own people. And there are too many of us on the sidelines, comfortable in complacency or cynicism when our voices must be heard.

The questions we face today — how to promote equality and justice; how to uphold freedom and human rights; how to end conflict and sectarian war — these things do not have easy answers. But there were no easy answers in front of that child born in World War I. Nelson Mandela reminds us that it always seems impossible until it is done. South Africa shows that is true. South Africa shows we can change, that we can choose a world defined not by our differences, but by our common hopes. We can choose a world defined not by conflict, but by peace and justice and opportunity.

We will never see the likes of Nelson Mandela again. But let me say to the young people of Africa and the young people around the world — you, too, can make his life's work your own. Over thirty years ago, while still a student, I learned of Nelson Mandela and the struggles taking place in this beautiful land, and it stirred something in me. It woke me up to my responsibilities to others and to myself, and it set me on an improbable journey that finds me here today. And while I will always fall short of Madiba's example, he makes me want to be a better man. He speaks to what's best inside us.

After this great liberator is laid to rest, and when we have returned to our cities and villages and rejoined our daily routines, let us search for his strength. • Let us search for his largeness of spirit somewhere inside of ourselves. And when the night grows dark, when injustice weighs heavy on our hearts, when our best-laid plans seem beyond our reach, let us think of Madiba and the words that brought him comfort within the four walls of his cell: "It matters not how straight the gate, how charged with punishments the scroll, I am the master of my fate: I am the captain of my soul."

What a magnificent soul it was. We will miss him deeply. May God bless the memory of Nelson Mandela. May God bless the people of South Africa.

• As he concludes, Obama issues a final inspirational call to action.

SPEAKING BEYOND THE SPEECH CLASSROOM

Sheryl Sandberg, Facebook executive and author of Lean In, speaks about women and leadership to an audience in Beijing, China. She talks about equality in business and at home, at an event co-sponsored by the Cheung Kong Graduate School of Business (CKGSB) and China CITIC Press on September 13, 2013. VCG/Getty Images

SPEAKING BEYOND THE SPEECH CLASSROOM

SPEAKER'S REFERENCE

LearningCurve can help you review.
Go to LaunchPad: **launchpadworks.com**

SPEAKING BEYOND THE SPEECH CLASSROOM

CHAPTER 28 Preparing Online Presentations

Apply Your Knowledge of Face-to-Face Speaking

- *Online presentations* require the same elements of planning and delivery as in-person speeches. (p. 397)

Understand the Unique Demands of Online Delivery

- Review the equipment you will use, and become comfortable with using it. (p. 397)
- Focus on *vocal variety* to hold audience interest and a conversational style to convey naturalness. (p. 398)
- Provide superior presentation aids to give the audience a compelling visual experience. (p. 398)

Plan for the Delivery Mode

- Use *real-time, synchronous presentations* for immediate interactivity with your online audience. (p. 399)
- *Recorded, or asynchronous, presentations* provide the advantage of long-term availability to your audience—who can access them on their time. (p. 399)

Select the Appropriate Online Presentation Format

- *Video* is one of the most common ways people get their message out. (p. 399)

LaunchPad VIDEO ACTIVITY

Go to LaunchPad to watch a video about group communication.

LaunchPad includes:

LearningCurve adaptive quizzing

a curated collection of video clips and full-length speeches.

Additional resources and reference materials such as presentation software tutorials and documentation help.

- *Podcasts* and *vodcasts* are digital audio recordings (with or without video) stored in a Web-accessible form. (p. 400)
- *Webinars* connect presenters and audiences from their desktops regardless of where they are. (p. 400)

CHAPTER 29 Communicating in Groups

Focus on the Goals of the Group

- Many speaking experiences occur in group settings, so learning how to work cooperatively within them will benefit you. (p. 403)
- Keep sight of the group goals and avoid behaviors that detract from them. (p. 403)
- Creating and following an *agenda* will help keep the group on task. (p. 403)

Plan on Assuming Dual Roles

- Adopt constructive *task roles* to accomplish concrete needs of the group. (p. 403)
- Adopt constructive *social roles* to facilitate group interaction. (p. 403)
- Avoid *antigroup roles* that hinder group efforts. (p. 403)

Center Disagreements on Issues Rather Than Personalities

- Productive conflict is issues-based rather than personal-based. (p. 404)

Don't Accept Ideas Uncritically Merely to Get Along

- Resist *groupthink*. (p. 404)
- Engage in *devil's advocacy* and *dialectical inquiry*. (p. 405)

As a Leader, Adopt an Effective Leadership Style

- Choose among directive, supportive, achievement-oriented, and participative styles. (p. 405)
- Hold members accountable for achieving results. (p. 405)
- Encourage active participation. (p. 406)
- Set a positive tone. (p. 406)
- Use reflective thinking. (p. 406)

Plan Carefully When Delivering Group Presentations

- Analyze your audience and set goals for the presentation. (p. 407)
- Establish information needs. (p. 408)
- Assign roles and tasks. (p. 408)
- Decide on the transitions to be used between speakers. (p. 408)

- Control the team's nonverbal behavior during the presentation. (p. 408)
- Consider team member strengths to construct a better presentation. (p. 408)
- Coordinate presentation aids. (p. 408)
- Rehearse the presentation as a group and with any presentation aids. (p. 408)

CHAPTER 30 Business and Professional Presentations

Understand the Differences between a Presentation and a Speech

- Presentations are less formal than public speeches. (p. 410)
- Presentations tend to be more interactive than speeches. (p. 410)
- Presentations generally do not presume special speaker expertise. (p. 410)

Become Familiar with Reports and Proposals

- A *report* is a systematic and objective description of facts and observations related to business or professional interests. (p. 411)
- A *proposal* recommends a product, procedure, or policy to a client or company. (p. 411)

Prepare a Sales Proposal ("Sales Pitch") to Persuade Potential Buyers to Purchase a Service or Product

- Organize the presentation as a persuasive speech, selecting among the problem-solution, comparative advantage pattern, or Monroe's Motivated Sequence (also called the *basic sales technique*), which follows. (p. 413)

    Draw the potential buyer's attention to the product. (p. 414)

    Isolate and clarify the buyer's need for the product. (p. 414)

    Describe how the product will satisfy the buyer's need. (p. 414)

    Invite the buyer to purchase the product. (p. 414)

Prepare a Staff Report When Informing Personnel of Developments Affecting Them or When Reporting on the Completion of a Task

- A *staff report* will state the problem, describe how it was addressed, analyze major issues, and offer recommendations. (p. 414)

Prepare a Progress Report to Offer Updates on Developments in an Ongoing Project

- A *progress report* is similar to a staff report, but its audience can include people from outside the organization. (p. 415)

CHAPTER 31 Presentations in Other College Courses

Expect to Prepare Oral Presentations in a Variety of Formats

- You will be asked to prepare *journal article reviews*. (p. 418)
- You may give a *service learning presentation*. (p. 419)
- You may prepare *poster presentations*. (p. 419)
- You may engage in *debates*. (p. 420)
- You may prepare a *case study*. (p. 421)

Prepare to Present to a Variety of Audiences

- *Expert or insider audience*. (p. 422)
- *Colleagues within the field*. (p. 422)
- *Lay audience*. (p. 422)
- *Mixed audience*. (p. 422)

Ground Scientific and Mathematical Presentations in the Scientific Method

- Be prepared to use observations, proofs, and experiments as support for the presentation. (p. 424)
- Be selective in your choice of details. (p. 424)
- Use analogies to build on prior knowledge. (p. 424)
- Use presentation aids. (p. 424)

In Science and Mathematics Presentations, Expect to Present the Results of Experiments or Solutions to Problems

- The *research presentation* (or *scientific talk*) describes original research you have done, either alone or as part of a team. (p. 424)
- The *methods/procedure presentation* describes and sometimes demonstrates an experimental or mathematical process, including the conditions under which the report can be applied. (p. 425)
- The *field study presentation* describes research conducted in naturalistic surroundings. (p. 426)

In Technical Presentations in Engineering, Computer Science, and Architecture, Expect to Describe Projects

- An *engineering design review* explains the problem-solving steps in devising a product or system. (p. 427)
- An *architecture design review* enables the audience to visualize the design. (p. 428)
- The *request for funding presentation* provides evidence that a project is worth funding. (p. 428)

In Social Science Presentations, Expect to Explain the Research Question

- Refer to current research. (p. 429)
- Use theory to build explanations. (p. 429)

In Social Science Presentations, Expect to Review and Evaluate Research and Propose Policies

- The *review of the literature presentation* examines the body of research related to a given topic or issue and offers conclusions about the topic based on this research. (p. 429)
- The *program evaluation presentation* examines the effectiveness of programs developed to address various issues. (p. 430)
- The *policy proposal report* offers recommendations to solve a problem or address an issue. (p. 430)

In Arts and Humanities Presentations, Expect to Interpret and Analyze Topics

- Expect to identify a work's key themes and the author's method of communicating them. (p. 431)
- Be prepared to provide original interpretations of works. (p. 431)
- Be prepared to compare and contrast events, stories, people, or artifacts in order to highlight the similarities or differences. (p. 432)

In Education Presentations, Expect to Deliver Lectures, Lead Group Activities, and Direct Classroom Discussions

- Focus on clear organization and fostering understanding. (p. 432)
- Use a learning framework. (p. 433)
- Use student-friendly examples as evidence and support. (p. 433)

In Nursing and Allied Health Courses, Expect to Address a Range of Audiences on Health Care Practices and Techniques

- You may be assigned an *evidence-based practice (EBP) presentation*, in which you review the scientific literature on a clinical problem and suggest best practices. (p. 434)
- You may be assigned a *clinical case study*, in which you offer an analysis of a case. (p. 435)
- You may prepare a *quality improvement proposal*, in which you recommend adoption of new practices or policies. (p. 435)
- You may prepare one of several *treatment plan reports*, in which you report on a patient's condition and outline plans of treatment. (p. 435)

- The *case conference* describes the patient's status, outlines steps for treatment, reviews goals and financial needs, and assesses resources. (p. 435)
- The *shift report* provides the oncoming caregiver a concise report of the patient's status and needs. (p. 436)

KEY TERMS

Chapter 28

online presentation
vocal variety
real-time presentation
synchronous communication
recorded presentation
asynchronous communication
video capture software
screencast
podcast
vodcast
webinar

Chapter 29

small group
virtual group
agenda
task roles
social roles
antigroup roles
productive conflict
groupthink
devil's advocacy
dialectical inquiry
group presentation

Chapter 30

presentational speaking
report
proposal
call to action
sales proposal (sales pitch)
motivated sequence
staff report
progress report

Chapter 31

journal article review
service learning presentation
poster presentation
debate
case study
expert or insider audience
colleagues within the field audience
lay audience
mixed audience
research presentation (scientific talk)
methods/procedure presentation
field study presentation
engineering design review
prototype
architecture design review
request for funding presentation
review of the literature presentation
program evaluation presentation
policy proposal report
lecture
group activity presentation
classroom discussion
evidence-based practice (EBP) presentation
clinical case study
quality improvement proposal
case conference
shift report

Go to LaunchPad: **launchpadworks.com** to watch the video clips for this chapter.

28 Preparing Online Presentations

 **LearningCurve** can help you review!
Go to LaunchPad: **launchpadworks.com**

The demand for people skilled in connecting with audiences in mediated environments continues to grow as online and mobile communication technologies become a routine part of everyday life. Experience in this speaking environment could set you apart when seeking a new job or advancement.

Apply Your Knowledge of Face-to-Face Speaking

Online presentations require the same basic elements of planning and delivery as in-person presentations. As in traditional public speaking, an online speaker will select among the three general speech purposes of informing, persuading, or marking a special occasion (see p. 110). Online speaking also calls for careful audience analysis, credible supporting materials, a clear organizational structure, and a natural delivery style. And because speaker and audience are separated physically during online presentations, it becomes all the more critical to focus on engaging the audience.

Plan for the Unique Demands of Online Delivery

While much is similar, important differences exist between online and in-person speaking, in both the means of delivery and nature of the audience. As you plan online presentations, follow the fundamental techniques of public speaking you already know while making the necessary adjustments to transmit your message effectively online.

 **LaunchPad** Go to LaunchPad to watch a video of the online speech "Preventing Cyberbullying" at **launchpadworks.com**

Know the Equipment

Online presentations require some familiarity with digital communication tools. Well before your actual presentation, familiarize yourself with the equipment you'll be using and rehearse with it several times.

Tools used to produce and display online presentations include:

- High-speed Internet connection
- Website or app for distribution to audience (e.g., GoToMeeting, Adobe Connect, Skype, Facebook Live)
- Hardware for recording audio and video (Webcam/video camera/microphone)
- Software for recording and editing audio and video (e.g., Adobe Audition)
- Video capture software (e.g., ScreenFlow, Camtasia)
- Web-based presentation software (e.g., Prezi, SlideRocket)
- Podcasting software (e.g., GarageBand, Audacity)
- Popular commercial websites (e.g., YouTube, Vimeo)
- Online conferencing tools (e.g., Huddle, GoToMeeting, Yugma, Skype)

Focus on Vocal Variety

In an online presentation, the audience cannot interact with your physical presence, making your voice an even more critical conduit of communication. In place of body movement, **vocal variety**—alterations in volume, pitch, speaking rate, pauses, and pronunciation and articulation—must hold audience interest. Especially important to eliminate are vocal fillers such as "umm" and "aah." Instead, strategically use pauses to help audience members process information.

Focus on Projecting Enthusiasm and Naturalness

Staring into a computer screen rather than listeners' eyes makes it difficult to infuse your voice with the enthusiasm and naturalness that eye contact encourages. But a lively conversational style is key for most online presentations. Consider delivering your first presentations with someone else in the room, talking to that person rather than to the screen. Alternatively, experiment with addressing your remarks to a picture, photograph, or even your own reflection in a mirror.[1]

Provide Superior Visual Aids

The audience might not see you in person, but with presentation aids you can still provide them with a compelling visual experience. Consider how you can illustrate your talking points in eye-catching text form or with photos, animations, and video clips (see Chapters 20–22). Software and Web platforms can help you easily create slides, screencasts, and video for online presentations (see later in this chapter).

Plan the Delivery Mode

Online presentations can be streamed in real time or recorded for distribution later, whenever an audience wants to access them. Understanding the advantages and limitations of both delivery modes can help you plan more effectively.

Real-Time Presentations

Real-time presentations connect the presenter and audience in live, **synchronous communication**. Interactivity is a chief advantage of this type of presentation: Speaker and audience can communicate with one another in real time either orally or via chat, text, or e-mail. As in traditional speaking situations, audience feedback allows you to adapt topic coverage according to audience input and questions, or adjust technical issues as they occur.

A chief limitation of real-time presentations is scheduling them around people's available times and different time zones. The more geographically dispersed the audience, the greater the logistical challenge. As such, many speakers reserve real-time online presentations for occasions when they are in time zones close to the audience, or they will give the presentation more than once for different time zones.

Recorded Presentations

In a **recorded presentation**, transmission and reception occur at different times, in **asynchronous communication**. The audience can access the presentation at their convenience, such as listening to a podcast at night. Lack of direct interaction with the audience poses challenges, however. Without immediate feedback from the audience to enliven the presentation, you must work harder to produce something polished and engaging, especially by providing compelling content, delivery style, and presentation aids. Consider including contact information (e.g., e-mail address, Twitter address, or URL) as part of your presentation so that audience members can send you feedback shortly after the presentation. That way, you will receive their feedback as soon as possible after they have viewed or listened to the presentation.

Choose an Online Presentation Format

Online presentation formats include videos, podcasts, vodcasts, and Webinars, any of which may be streamed in real time or recorded for later delivery.

Video

Many people use video to present online: from individuals using a smart phone camera or Webcam, to professional companies sending out messages using high-definition digital video cameras. With **video capture software**, such as Camtasia or Adobe Audition, you can seamlessly incorporate video clips into an online presentation. The "Record Slideshow" feature in the Tools menu of PowerPoint can serve a similar purpose.

You can also use video capture software or dedicated screencasting software to create screencasts. A **screencast** captures whatever is displayed on your computer screen, from text to slides to streaming video. Screencasts can be streamed in real time, recorded for playback, or exported to a hosting website. The screencast format is especially useful for training purposes. For example,

CHECKLIST

CREATING A PODCAST

The basic equipment and software needed to create a podcast are included on most current personal computers, tablets, and smart phones. The only other pieces you may need are an external microphone and audio recording software such as Audacity. Then try these steps:

- ✓ Plan what you want to say.
- ✓ Seat yourself in an upright, direct position facing your computer, with the microphone no more than 8 inches from your mouth.
- ✓ Make sure that your external microphone is plugged into your computer, or that your built-in microphone is operational.
- ✓ Open your audio recording software. Be familiar with how to start, pause, and stop a recording.
- ✓ Activate the recording software and begin speaking into the microphone. You're now making your presentation.
- ✓ At the conclusion of your presentation, stop the recording.
- ✓ Save the new recording as an audio file, such as .mp3.
- ✓ Close your audio recording software and disengage the microphone.
- ✓ Go to the new audio file saved to your computer, and open and play it. Now you are listening to your recorded presentation.
- ✓ Transfer the saved file to a website, blog, or podcast hosting site.

a presentation relying on screencasts can be used to demonstrate how to set up an e-mail account with your own personal or business domain name (e.g., yourname@yourbusiness.com).

Podcasts and Vodcasts

A **podcast** is a digital audio recording of a speech or presentation captured and stored in a form that is accessible via the Web or an app. A **vodcast** (also called *vidcast* and *video podcasting*) is a podcast containing video clips. A variety of computer, tablet, and smart phone apps (e.g., Audacity, Stitcher, iTunes, Google Play Music, Soundcloud) are available by which listeners can subscribe to podcasts and vodcasts.

Recording, storing, and delivering a speech via podcast requires a microphone attached to a computer; simple, free digital audio recording software (e.g., Audacity); and a website to host the podcast and provide your audience with access to it. Using PowerPoint, you can use the "Record Audio" feature to produce a podcast-like presentation file; the file can be used and distributed as you would any PowerPoint file, even via e-mail.

Webinars

Webinars are real-time seminars, meetings, training sessions, or other presentations that connect presenters and audiences from their computers or mobile devices.[2] Webinars typically include live video conversation, video capture and screencasting, and other functions such as chat, instant messaging, and polling.

As in any speech or presentation, planning a Webinar starts with considering the audience's needs and wants. Many Webinars are *team presentations*, so use the guidelines on p. 409 during the planning stages.[3]

CHECKLIST

ONLINE PRESENTATION PLANNING

Keeping in mind both the fundamental guidelines for preparing and presenting an in-person speech as well as those unique considerations of online presentations, here are some additional tips to follow.[4]

- ✓ *Be well organized*. Offer a clear statement of purpose and preview of main points. Proceed with a solid structure that the audience can easily follow. Conclude by restating your purpose, reviewing the main points, and encouraging the audience to watch or listen for more.
- ✓ *Design powerful presentation aids*. For video and Webcasts, plan for meaningful graphics and images that properly convey your ideas.
- ✓ *Keep your audience engaged*. In real-time presentations, encourage audience interaction by incorporating chat, instant messaging, or polling features. In recorded presentations, offer an e-mail address, Twitter address, or URL where audience members can submit comments and questions. Use these tools to gather feedback from your audience, much the way you would use eye contact in a face-to-face speech or presentation.
- ✓ *Prepare a contingency plan in case of technology glitches*. For example, have a backup computer running simultaneously with the one used to deliver the presentation. Provide a list of FAQs or a Web page with instructions for audience members to manage technology problems.
- ✓ *Maintain ethical standards*. Use the same degree of decorum as you would in an in-person speech, bearing in mind that online presentations have the potential to go viral.
- ✓ *Get in plenty of practice time*. Rehearse, record, and listen to yourself as many times as needed.

1. Start with a title that indicates what the Webinar will do for the audience (e.g., "How Company Travel Policies Will Affect You").
2. Time each aspect of the Webinar and distribute the following information to each presenter:

   Introduction of speaker(s) and purpose

   Length and order of each speaker's remarks

   Length of question-and-answer session, if separate
3. Rehearse the Webinar (remotely if necessary).
4. Check meeting room for noise and visual distractions; check equipment.
5. Create a backup plan in case of technical problems.

Put a Face to the Speaker(s)

To encourage a feeling of connection between yourself and the audience during a webinar, consider displaying a headshot of yourself, along with your name and title. A second slide might announce start and finish times; a third, a list of speech objectives.[5] During the presentation, you can alternate displays of text and graphic slides with views of your photograph (and/or other presenters) or, in some cases, side-by-side with the aids.

29 Communicating in Groups

LearningCurve can help you review!
Go to LaunchPad: **launchpadworks.com**

Most of us will spend a substantial portion of our educational and professional lives communicating in **small groups** or teams (usually between three and twenty people), and many of the experiences we have as speakers — in the classroom, workforce, or in **virtual groups**, online — occur in a group setting. Groups often report on the results they've achieved, and some groups form solely for the purposes of coordinating oral presentations. Thus, understanding how to work cooperatively within a group setting, as described in this chapter, can be an important life skill.

Focus on Goals

How well or poorly you meet the objectives of the group — whether to coordinate a team presentation or meet some other purpose — is largely a function of how you keep sight of the group's goals and avoid behaviors that detract from these goals. The more you use the group's goals as a steadying guide, the less likely you are to be diverted from your real responsibilities as a participant. Setting an **agenda** can help participants stay on track by identifying the items to be accomplished during a meeting; often it will specify time limits for each item of business. Figure 29.1 offers an example of an agenda.

Plan on Assuming Dual Roles

In a work group, you will generally assume a task role and a social role, and sometimes both.[1] **Task roles** are the hands-on roles that directly relate to the group's accomplishment of its objectives. Examples include "recording secretary" (takes notes) and "moderator" (facilitates discussion). Members also adopt various **social roles** reflecting individual members' personality traits. Social roles function to help facilitate effective group interaction, such as *harmonizer* (smooths over tension by settling differences) and *gatekeeper* (keeps the discussion moving forward and gets everyone's input).

Sometimes, group members focus on individual needs irrelevant to the tasks on hand. **Antigroup roles** — such as *floor hogger* (not allowing others to speak), *blocker* (being overly negative about group ideas; raising issues that have

Meeting Agenda

Product team meeting, June 8, 2017
Macmillan Learning
Roslin Room, 46th floor
9:30 a.m.-11:30 a.m.

Participants: Jesse Hassenger, Kate George, Will Stonefield, Angela Beckett, Jennifer Yee, Adam McDonnell

1. Welcome and introduction of participants
2. Review of team goals
3. Sales updates based on sales manager's report
4. Update on project management. Each participant gives a summary of what's done and what needs to be done
5. Update on resource needs
6. Training plans: new software programs
   Schedules and dates
   Possible venues
7. Plans for next quarter
   Conferences
   Customer focus groups
8. Questions and answers
9. Closing and thank you

FIGURE 29.1 Sample Meeting Agenda

been settled), and *recognition seeker* (acts to call attention to oneself rather than to group tasks)—do not further the group's goals and should be avoided.

Center Disagreement around Issues, not Personalities

Whenever people come together to consider an important issue, conflict is inevitable. But conflict doesn't have to be destructive. In fact, the best decisions are usually those that emerge from productive conflict.[2] In **productive conflict**, group members clarify questions, challenge ideas, present counterexamples, consider worst-case scenarios, and reformulate proposals.[3] After a process like this, the group can be confident that its decision has been put to a good test. Productive conflict centers disagreements around issues rather than personalities. Rather than wasting time with one another over personal motives or perceived shortcomings, productive conflict encourages members to rigorously test and debate ideas and potential solutions. It requires each member to ask tough questions, press for clarification, and present alternative views.[4]

Resist Groupthink

For a group to be truly effective, its members need to form a cohesive unit with a common goal. At the same time, they must avoid **groupthink**—the tendency to minimize conflict by refusing to examine ideas critically or test solutions.[5] Groups prone to groupthink typically exhibit these behaviors:

- Participants reach a consensus and avoid conflict in order not to hurt others' feelings, but without genuinely agreeing.
- Members who do not agree with the majority of the group feel pressured to conform.
- Disagreement, tough questions, and counterproposals are discouraged.
- More effort is spent justifying the decision than testing it.

Research suggests that groups can reach the best decisions by adopting two methods of argument: **devil's advocacy** (arguing for the sake of raising issues or concerns about the idea under discussion) or **dialectical inquiry** (devil's advocacy that goes a step further by proposing a countersolution to the idea).[6] Both approaches help expose underlying assumptions that may be preventing participants from making the best decision. As you lead a group, consider how you can encourage both methods of argument.

Adopt an Effective Leadership Style

When called upon to lead a group, bear in mind the four broad styles of leadership, and mix and match the leadership style that best suits your group's needs.[7]

- *Directive:* Leader controls group communication by conveying specific instructions to members.
- *Supportive:* Leader attends to group members' emotional needs, stressing positive relationships.
- *Achievement-oriented:* Leader sets challenging goals and high standards.
- *Participative:* Leader views members as equals, welcoming their opinions, summarizing points, and identifying problems that must be solved rather than dictating solutions.

Whatever style or styles of leadership you adopt, remember that the most effective leaders (1) remain focused on their group's goals, (2) hold themselves and the group accountable for achieving results, (3) treat all group members in an ethical manner, and (4) inspire members to contribute their best.[8]

Set Goals

Most negative experiences in groups result from a lack of a clear goal. Each member of a group should be able to clearly identify the purpose(s) of the group and the goals it is charged with reaching. As a leader, aim to be a catalyst in setting and reaching these goals in collaboration with other group members. The accompanying checklist contains guidelines for setting group goals.

CHECKLIST

GUIDELINES FOR SETTING GROUP GOALS

- ✔ Identify the problem.
- ✔ Map out a strategy.
- ✔ Set a performance goal.
- ✔ Identify the resources necessary for achieving the goal.
- ✔ Recognize contingencies that may arise.
- ✔ Obtain feedback.

Encourage Active Participation

Groups tend to adopt solutions that receive the largest number of favorable comments, whether these comments emanate from one individual or many. If only one or two members participate, it is their input that sets the agenda, whether or not their solution is optimal.[9]

When you lead a group, take these steps to encourage active participation:

- *Directly ask members to contribute.* Sometimes one person, or a few people, dominates the discussion. Encourage the others to contribute by redirecting the discussion in their direction ("Patrice, we haven't heard from you yet," or "Juan, what do you think about this?").
- *Set a positive tone.* Some people are reluctant to express their views because they fear ridicule or attack. Minimize such fears by setting a positive tone, stressing fairness, and encouraging politeness and active listening.
- *Make use of devil's advocacy and dialectical inquiry.* Raise pertinent issues or concerns, and entertain solutions other than the one under consideration.

Use Reflective Thinking

To reach a decision or solution that all participants understand and are committed to, guide participants through the six-step process of reflective thinking shown in Figure 29.2, which is based on the work of the educator John Dewey.[10] Dewey suggested that this sequence of steps encourages group members to "think reflectively" about their task. In this way, all the relevant facts and opinions can be discussed and evaluated, thereby ensuring a better decision.

Delivering Group Presentations

Group presentations are oral presentations prepared and delivered by a group of three or more individuals (see Chapter 30 for discussion of the differences between a presentation and a speech). While in an individual presentation one person assumes all responsibility for presenting a topic, in a *team presentation*

Step 1 Identify the Problem

- What is being decided upon?

Group leader summarizes problem, ensures that all group members understand problem, and gains agreement from all members.

Step 2 Conduct Research and Analysis

- What information is needed to solve the problem?

Conduct research to gather relevant information.
Ensure that all members have relevant information.

Step 3 Establish Guidelines and Criteria

- Establish criteria by which proposed solutions will be judged.

Reach criteria through consensus and record criteria.

Step 4 Generate Solutions

- Conduct brainstorming session.

Don't debate ideas; simply gather and record all ideas.

Step 5 Select the Best Solution

- Weigh the relative merits of each idea against criteria. Select one alternative that can best fulfill criteria.

If more than one solution survives, select solution that best meets criteria.
Consider merging two solutions if both meet criteria.
If no solution survives, return to problem identification step.

Step 6 Evaluate Solution

- Does the solution have any weaknesses or disadvantages?
- Does the solution resemble the criteria that were developed?
- What other criteria would have been helpful in arriving at a better solution?

FIGURE 29.2 Making Decisions in Groups: John Dewey's Six-Step Process of Reflective Thinking

some or all of the group members share responsibility. Regularly assigned in the classroom and frequently delivered in the workplace, successful group presentations require close cooperation and planning.

Analyze the Audience and Set Goals

Even if the topic is assigned and the audience consists solely of the instructor and classmates (perhaps in an online setting; see Chapter 28), consider the audience's interests and needs with respect to the topic and how you can meet them. For example, if your group is delivering a business proposal presentation, is it for an internal or external audience—fellow employees or customers/outside contractors? Just as you would prepare an individual speech, brainstorm and set down in writing the central idea and goals for the presentation.

Establish Information Needs

Gain agreement among members on the scope and type of research needed. What types of sources best suit the topic, purpose, and audience—for example, surveys your team does itself, scholarly articles, government data, or other sources?

Assign Roles and Tasks

First, designate a *group leader* to help guide coordination among members, beginning with the selection of roles and tasks. Assign team members responsibility for various aspects of the research, and decide what parts of the presentation team members will present—introduction, body, or conclusion. Set firm time limits for each portion of the presentation.

Establish Transitions between Speakers

Work out transitions between speakers ahead of time—for example, whether a designated group member will introduce every speaker or whether each speaker will introduce the next speaker upon the close of his or her presentation. The quality of the presentation will depend in great part on smooth transitions between speakers!

Consider the Presenters' Strengths

Audiences become distracted by marked disparities in style, such as hearing a captivating speaker followed by an extremely dull one. If you are concerned about an uneven delivery, consider choosing the person with the strongest presentation style and credibility level for the opening. Put the more cautious presenters in the middle of the presentation. Select another strong speaker to conclude the presentation.[11]

Be Mindful of Your Nonverbal Behavior

During a team presentation, the audience's eyes will fall on everyone involved, not just the person speaking. Thus any signs of disinterest or boredom by a team member will be easily noticed. Give your full attention to the other speakers and project an attitude of interest toward audience members.

Coordinate the Presentation Aids

To ensure design consistency, consider assigning one person the job of coordinating templates for slides, videos, and/or audio (see Chapter 21). The team can also assign a single individual the task of presenting the aids as the other members speak. If this is done, be sure to position the person presenting the aids unobtrusively so as not to distract the audience from the speaker.

Rehearse the Presentation Several Times

Together with the whole group, members should practice their portions of the presentation, *with* any presentation aids they will use, in the order they will be given in the final form. Rehearse with group members several times, until the presentation proceeds smoothly (see p. 23 on practicing the delivery). Assign at least one member to set up and check any equipment needed to display the aids.

CHECKLIST

TEAM PRESENTATION TIPS

- ✓ Establish in writing the specific purpose and goals of the presentation.
- ✓ Decide on the scope and types of research needed.
- ✓ Specify each team member's responsibilities regarding content and presentation aids.
- ✓ Determine how introductions will be made—all at once at the beginning or by having each speaker introduce the next one.
- ✓ Practice introductions and transitions to create a seamless presentation.
- ✓ Establish an agreed-upon set of hand signals to indicate when a speaker is speaking too loud or soft, too slow or fast.
- ✓ Assign someone to manage the question-and-answer session.
- ✓ Rehearse the presentation with all group members and *with* presentation aids several times from start to finish.

30 Business and Professional Presentations

LearningCurve can help you review!
Go to LaunchPad: **launchpadworks.com**

In many business and professional positions, delivering presentations is part of the job. Whether the task is informing managers of a project's progress or pitching a service to customers, the skilled speaker will get noticed and, often, promoted. In the classroom, your instructor will assign presentations that mirror those delivered in the workplace, giving you the opportunity to practice what you may be required to do on the job.

Presentational versus Public Speaking

Rather than being types of formal public speeches described in previous chapters, business and professional presentations are forms of **presentational speaking** — oral presentations delivered by individuals or teams addressing people in the classroom, workplace, or other group settings. Presentational speaking has much in common with formal public speaking, yet important differences exist:[1]

- *Degree of formality.* Presentational speaking is *less formal* than public speaking; on a continuum, it would lie midway between public speaking at one end and conversational speaking at the other.
- *Audience factors.* Public-speaking audiences tend to be self-selected or voluntary participants, and they regard the speech as a onetime event. Attendees of oral presentations are more likely to be part of a "captive" audience, as occurs in the workplace or classroom, and may be required to attend frequent presentations. Due to the ongoing relationship among the participants, attendees also share more information with one another than those who attend a public speech and thus can be considered to have a common knowledge base.
- *Speaker expertise.* Listeners generally assume that a public speaker has more expertise or firsthand knowledge than they do on a topic. Presentational speakers, by contrast, are more properly thought of as "first among equals."

Apart from these differences, the speaking guidelines described throughout this book apply equally to both oral presentations and public speeches.

Become Familiar with Reports and Proposals

The majority of business and professional presentations (both oral and written) take the form of *reports* or *proposals*. Corporations and nonprofit, educational, and government organizations alike depend on reports and proposals, both formal and informal, to supply information and shape decisions.

A **report** is a systematic and objective description of facts and observations related to business or professional interests; it may or may not contain recommendations. Reports without recommendations are strictly informative; those that offer analysis and recommendations combine both informative and persuasive intent.

Reports address literally thousands of different topics, audiences, and objectives; some require extensive research and offer lengthy analyses while others may simply summarize weekly changes in personnel or projects. Formats for reports vary accordingly, but many reports include the following:

1. Preview/summary of reasons for the report, including its scope, methods, limitations, and main conclusions and recommendations
2. Discussion of findings/presentation of evidence
3. Key conclusions drawn from evidence
4. Recommendations based on the evidence

A **proposal** recommends a product, procedure, or policy to a client or company. Organizations must constantly make decisions such as whether to switch to a new health plan or implement a new employee grievance procedure, and proposals offer a plan on how to proceed. Usually, proposals advocate for a specific solution, with the presenter arguing in favor of one course of action over another. Careful adaptation to the audience is therefore critical to an effective presentation (see Chapter 6 on analyzing the audience).

Proposals may be assigned by a superior, solicited by a potential client (by a written *request for proposal* or *"RFP"*), or offered unsolicited to either superiors or clients. Frequently, proposals incorporate or respond to information communicated in reports. The audience for a proposal can be a single individual or a group; in either event the audience will have primary or sole decision-making responsibility for evaluating the proposal.

Proposals can be quite lengthy and formally organized or relatively brief and loosely structured. As in reports, individual organizations have their own templates for organizing proposals, but many proposals follow these general steps:

1. Introduce the issue.
2. State the problem.
3. Describe the method by which the problem was investigated.
4. Describe the facts learned.
5. Offer explanations and an interpretation of the findings.
6. Offer recommendations, including time lines and budgets.
7. Leave them with a **call to action**, reiterating your recommendation persuasively.

TABLE 30.1 Sample Types of Reports and Proposals in Business and the Professions

Reports	Proposals
• Progress report	• Sales proposal
• Audit report	• Business plan proposal
• Market research report	• Request for funding
• Quality testing report	• Research proposal
• Staff report	• Quality improvement proposal
• Committee report	• Policy proposal

Table 30.1 list some of the many different types of reports and proposals delivered in the business and professional environment. Following are descriptions of the *sales proposal*, *staff report*, and *progress report*.

The Sales Proposal

A **sales proposal** or **sales pitch** is a presentation that attempts to lead a potential buyer to purchase a service or a product. Successful sales pitches, which are persuasive by nature, clearly show how the product or service meets the needs of the potential buyer and demonstrate how it surpasses other options available.

Audience for the Sales Proposals

The target audience for a sales proposal depends on who has the authority to make the purchase under consideration. Some sales proposals are invited by the potential buyer; others are "cold sales" in which the presenter/seller approaches a first-time potential buyer with a product or a service. In some cases, the audience might be an intermediary—a firm's office manager, for example, who then makes a recommendation to the company's director.

Recent research reported by the *Harvard Business Review* suggests that persons delivering sales pitches encounter two general groups of buyers—talkers and mobilizers.[2] Talkers don't get the presenter very far because while they have much to say about issues, they are unable to build a consensus among those who make the sales decision. Mobilizers keep their focus on the needs of the business and approach the sales pitch with skepticism; they will only advocate for the sale if they believe it will truly help the business. As a result, mobilizers generate trust among their colleagues so that when they make recommendations, people listen.

Successful sales pitches clearly show how the product or service meets the needs of the potential buyer and demonstrate how it surpasses other options available. In fact, studies have shown that exceptional salespeople uncover and expose unrecognized needs in the organization and clearly help the customer pinpoint solutions.[3] It is these "insightful" salespeople who guide their audience to a more productive place and provide support along the way.

ESL SPEAKER'S NOTES

Steps to Counteract Problems in Being Understood

NASA Goddard Space Flight Center

With the exception of young children, virtually everyone who learns to speak another language will speak that language with an accent. This issue is especially important in business and professional settings, where being understood can have a direct impact on your career. What steps can you take when your accent will make your oral presentation difficult for the audience to understand?

In the long term, interacting with native speakers in everyday life will help enormously. Engaging in dialogue with cross-cultural partners is an excellent way to adjust to native communication styles.[1] With immersion, non-native speakers can begin to stop translating word for word and start thinking in English. Using a tape recorder and practicing your speech in front of others is also very important.

But what if, although your experience with English is limited, you must nonetheless give an oral presentation? Robert Anholt, a scientist and author, suggests the following:

1. Practice the presentation often, preferably with a friend who is a native English speaker.
2. Learn the presentation almost by heart.
3. Create strong presentation aids that will convey most of the story by themselves, even if your speech is hard to understand.[2]

By practicing often and ensuring that your presentation aids convey the bulk of your meaning, you can be confident that you will get your message across. And with time and effort, be assured that even the most difficult accent can be tamed to the point where speech is clearly understood.

1. Z. Yuxia, "Using Authentic Cross-Cultural Dialogues to Encourage International Students' Participation in Tutorial Activities," *Business Communication Quarterly* 70 (2007): 43–47.
2. Robert Anholt, *Dazzle 'Em with Style: The Art of Oral Scientific Presentation,* 2nd ed. (New York: Academic Press, 2005).

Organizing the Sales Proposal

Plan on organizing a sales proposal as you would a persuasive speech, selecting among the motivated sequence, problem-solution/problem-cause-solution, or comparative advantage patterns (see Chapter 26). The *comparative advantage pattern* works well when the buyer must choose between competing products and seeks reassurance that the product being presented is indeed superior. The *problem-solution* or *problem-cause-solution* pattern is especially effective when selling to a buyer who clearly needs a product to solve a problem.

CHECKLIST

APPLYING MONROE'S MOTIVATED SEQUENCE IN A SALES PROPOSAL

- ✔ Identify the potential buyer's needs and wants and appeal to them.
- ✔ Using the product's features, match its benefits to the customer's needs and wants.
- ✔ Stress what the product can do for the customer.
- ✔ Engage the customer's senses, using sight, sound, smell, and touch.
- ✔ Ask for the sale. Do not leave the sales encounter without making the ask.[1]
- ✔ Get the buyer to do something (look something up, promise to call someone, or schedule a meeting). Buyers who invest their time are more likely to invest in what you are selling.[2]

1. Stephen Shiffman, "Ten Tips Guaranteed to Improve Sales," *American Salesman* 55 (2010): 28–30.
2. Ibid.

Sometimes called the *basic sales technique*, the **motivated sequence**, with its focus on audience needs, offers an excellent means of appealing to buyer psychology. To use it to organize a sales proposal, do the following:

1. Draw the potential buyer's attention to the product.
2. Isolate and clarify the buyer's need for the product.
3. Describe how the product will satisfy the buyer's need.
4. Invite the buyer to purchase the product.

When making a sales pitch following the motivated sequence, the extent to which you focus on each step depends on the nature of the selling situation. In cold-call sales situations, consider spending more time discovering the potential buyer's needs.[4] For invited sales proposals, including RFPs (request for proposals), spend more time detailing characteristics of the product and showing how it will satisfy the buyer's needs.

Staff Reports

A **staff report** informs managers and other employees of new developments that affect them and their work, or reports on the completion of a project or task. A company's personnel division might implement a new plan for subscribers to the company's health insurance program. To explain the changes, the personnel director will present the plan at a meeting of the sales division, review the reasons for the plan, explain how it works, and describe its ramifications. Another function of a staff report is to provide information on the completion of a project or task. A district manager of a restaurant chain might assign three local restaurant managers the task of devising a plan for expanding the seating capacity at each location. The managers will present their designs at the next district meeting.

Audience for a Staff Report

The audience for a staff report is usually a group, but it can be an individual. The recipients of a staff report then use the information to implement new policy, to coordinate other plans, or to make other reports to other groups.

Organizing the Staff Report

Organize a formal staff report as follows.

1. State the problem or question under consideration (sometimes called a "charge" to a committee or a subcommittee).
2. Provide a description of procedures and facts used to address the issue.
3. Discuss and analyze the facts that are most pertinent to the issue.
4. Provide a concluding statement.
5. Offer recommendations.

The Progress Report

A progress report is similar to a staff report, with the exception that the audience can include people *outside* the organization as well as within it. A **progress report** updates clients or principals on developments in an ongoing project. On long-term projects, progress reports may be delivered at designated intervals or at the time of specific task completions. For example, subcontractors on a housing-construction project meet weekly with the project developers. On short-term projects, reports can occur daily. For example, medical personnel in the intensive-care unit of a hospital meet each morning to review the treatment protocol and progress of each patient. Progress reports have become increasingly important to managers as a means to determine the value of employees and uncover hidden costs of doing business.[5]

Audience for Progress Reports

The audience for a progress report might be supervisors, clients, or customers; developers and investors; company officers; media representatives; or same-level co-workers assigned to the same project. For example, a work team consisting of workers from various departments (engineering, marketing, and cost analysis) may be assigned to the development of a new product. Progress reports are commonplace in staff and committee meetings in which subcommittees report on their designated tasks.

Organizing the Progress Report

Different audiences may want different kinds of reports, so establish expectations with your intended audience, then modify the following accordingly:

1. Briefly review progress made up to the time of the previous report.
2. Describe new developments since the previous report.
3. Describe the personnel involved and their activities.
4. Detail time spent on tasks.
5. Explain supplies used and costs incurred.
6. Explain any problems and their resolution.
7. Provide an estimate of tasks to be completed for the next reporting period.

ETHICALLY SPEAKING

Code of Ethics for Professional Communicators from the International Association of Business Communicators

Radu Bercan/Shutterstock

Because hundreds of thousands of business communicators worldwide engage in activities that affect the lives of millions of people and because this power carries with it significant social responsibilities, the International Association of Business Communicators developed the Code of Ethics for Professional Communicators. The IABC requires its members to follow this code of ethics. The code serves as a guide to making ethical communication decisions as a professional.

IABC's Code of Ethics

1. **I am honest**—my actions bring respect for and trust in the communication profession.
2. **I communicate accurate information** and promptly correct any errors.
3. **I obey laws and public policies**; if I violate any law or public policy, I act promptly to correct the situation.
4. **I protect confidential information** while acting within the law.
5. **I support the ideals of free speech**, freedom of assembly, and access to an open marketplace of ideas.
6. **I am sensitive to others'** cultural values and beliefs.
7. **I give credit to others for their work** and cite my sources.
8. **I do not use confidential information** for personal benefit.
9. **I do not represent conflicting or competing interests** without full disclosure and the written consent of those involved.

10. **I do not accept undisclosed gifts or payments** for professional services from anyone other than a client or employer.
11. **I do not guarantee results** that are beyond my power to deliver.

Source: International Association of Business Communicators (IABC), accessed August 8, 2017, https://www.iabc.com/about-us/governance/code-of-ethics/

About the International Association of Business Communicators

The IABC is a global membership association that was founded in 1970 and that supports business communicators through sharing ideas, best practices, and career development resources. Members of the International Association of Business Communicators include Fortune 500 companies across the world. Representing a diverse group of industries, the IABC strives to foster connections among its members. Chapters of the IABC are located in North America, Africa, Europe, and Asia. The IABC also hosts an annual World Conference that focuses on business communication.

This code of ethics was developed by the Ethics Committee for the International Association of Business Communicators. The IABC nominates its Ethics Committee in an open process, and the members are selected by the IABC Executive Committee. The Ethics Committee can offer guidance to business communicators who seek advice on individual situations.

31 Presentations in Other College Courses

LearningCurve can help you review!
Go to LaunchPad: **launchpadworks.com**

No matter which major you select, oral presentations will be part of your academic career. As an engineering major, for example, you might prepare a *design review* of your major project. A student of history might deliver a presentation linking a historical event with a contemporary issue. Nursing majors might be asked to prepare a *treatment plan* delivered to a mock medical team. Rather than being a formal public speech, classroom presentations are forms of *presentational speaking*; see Chapter 30, p. 410, for a review of the differences between public and presentational speaking.

This chapter contains guidelines for preparing specialized oral presentations assigned in science, mathematics, and technical courses, as well as courses on the social sciences, arts and humanities, education, and nursing and allied health. First, however, are helpful strategies for preparing five types of presentations you are likely to be assigned across the curriculum, from psychology to chemistry to language classes. These include the *journal article review*, *service learning presentation*, *poster presentation*, *debate*, and *case study*.

Journal Article Review

A frequent speaking assignment in many courses is the **journal article review**. A biology instructor might ask you to provide an overview of a peer-reviewed study on cell regulation, for example, or a psychology teacher might require that you talk about a study on fetal alcohol syndrome. Typically, when delivering a talk on a journal article, your instructor will expect you to do the following, in this order:

1. Identify the author's thesis or hypothesis.
2. Explain the methods by which the author arrived at his or her conclusions.
3. Explain the results of the study.
4. Identify the author's methods and, if applicable, theoretical perspective.
5. Evaluate the study's quality, originality, and validity.
6. Describe the author's sources and evaluate their credibility.
7. Show how the findings advance knowledge in the field.

The Service Learning Presentation

Many courses offer the opportunity to engage in service learning projects, in which students learn about and help address a need or problem in a community agency or nonprofit organization, such as may exist in a mental health facility, an economic development agency, or an antipoverty organization. Presentations may be delivered individually, as part of a group presentation, or as a poster presentation (see p. 281). Typically, the **service learning presentation** describes your participation in the project and includes the following information:

1. Description of the service task
   a. What organization, group, or agency did your project serve?
   b. What is the problem or issue, and how did you address it?
2. Description of what the service task taught you about those you served
   a. How were they affected by the problem or issue?
   b. How did your solution help them? What differences did you observe?
3. Explanation of how the service task and outcome related to your service learning course
   a. What course concepts, principles, or theories relate to your service project, and how?
   b. What observations give you evidence that the principles apply to your project?
4. Application of what was learned to future understanding and practice
   a. How was your understanding of the course subject improved or expanded?
   b. How was your interest in or motivation for working in this capacity affected by the project?
   c. What do you most want to tell others about the experience and how it could affect them?

The Poster Presentation

Another common speaking assignment across many college disciplines is the **poster presentation**, which displays information about a study, an issue, or a concept on a large (usually roughly 4 × 3-foot or 4 × 6-foot) poster. Poster presentations typically follow the structure of a scientific journal article, including an *abstract*, *introduction*, *description of methods*, a *results* section, *conclusion*, and *references*. Presenters display their key findings on posters, arranged so session participants can examine them freely; on hand are copies of the written report, with full details of the study. The presenter is prepared to answer questions as they arise.

A good poster presenter considers his or her audience, understanding that with so much competing information, the poster must be concise, visually appealing, and focused on the most important points of the study.

When preparing the poster, follow these guidelines:

- Select a succinct and informative title; make it 84-point type or larger.
- Include blocks of text in columns beginning from the upper left to lower right side of the poster.
- Include an *abstract* (a brief summary of the study) describing the essence of the report and how it relates to other research in the field. Offer compelling and "must know" points to hook viewers and summarize information for those who will only read the abstract.
- Ensure a logical and easy-to-follow flow from one part of the poster to another.
- Edit text to a minimum, using clear graphics wherever possible.
- Select a muted color for the poster itself—such as gray, beige, light blue, or white, and use a contrasting, clear font color (usually black).
- Make your font size large enough to be read comfortably from at least three feet away.
- Design figures and diagrams to be viewed from a distance, and label each one. Audiences are drawn to visuals, so be prepared for questions about them.
- Label and include a concise summary of each figure in a legend below each one.
- Be prepared to provide brief descriptions of your poster and to answer questions; keep your explanations short.[1]

Address your audience while presenting and explain your research without reading verbatim from the poster; if needed, prepare a speaking outline (see Chapter 13). Rehearse your poster presentation as you would any other speech.

The Debate

Debate is a popular oral presentation format in many college courses, calling upon skills in persuasion (especially the reasoned use of evidence; see Chapter 25 on argument), delivery, and the ability to think quickly and critically. This presentation format allows students to analyze arguments in depth and to argue different points of view, including positions with which they disagree. Debates are characterized by refutation, in which each side attacks the arguments of the other. As in any public speaking event, careful research and adequate practice in delivering arguments are critical to success.

Debate Formats, Sides, and Resolutions

In the classroom, opposing sides in debates often take one of two formats. In the *individual debate* format, one person takes a side against another person. In the *team debate* format, each side consists of two or more debaters. The *affirmative ("pro") side* supports the topic with a *resolution*—a declarative statement asking for change or consideration of a controversial issue: "Resolved, that the

United States should provide amnesty to undocumented immigrants." The *negative ("con") side* opposes the affirmative side's arguments. Each side alternates turns at presenting their arguments and rebutting the opposition, with either the instructor or classmates judging the winner.

Depending on the topic and debate format, a debate resolution will address one of three types of claims, or propositions: of *fact*, of *value*, and of *policy* (see Chapter 25). For example, in the individual *Lincoln-Douglas (L-D)* format, two individuals argue the resolution as a *proposition of value* ("Resolved, that the U.S. government is morally obligated to provide amnesty to undocumented immigrants"). In the *team policy debate* format, opposing teams argue resolutions as *propositions of policy*, as in the resolution about amnesty or tax reform.

Advance Strong Arguments

Whether you take the affirmative or negative side, you must advance strong arguments in support of your position. Strong claims, evidence, and reasoning are key to arguing for or against a debate proposition. Equally important is refuting weaknesses in these elements put forth by your opponent. For example, you might refute an opponent's evidence for being outdated: "The survey results used by my opponent are ten years old, and a new study indicates that opinion has changed by X percent." Another strong refutation strategy is criticizing the source of an opponent's evidence ("*People Magazine* can hardly be considered an authoritative source for missions to Mars"). You should also be prepared to rebuild arguments that your opponent has refuted or attacked. You can do this by adding new evidence or attacking the opponent's reasoning or evidence.

"Flow" the Debate

In formal debates (in which judges take notes and keep track of arguments), debaters must attack and defend each argument. "Dropping" or ignoring an argument can seriously compromise the credibility of the debater and her or his side. Thus, note taking is critical to success in debates to ensure that you respond to each of your opponent's arguments.

One useful note-taking technique is the "flowing the debate" method. On a sheet of paper or spreadsheet, write down each of your opponent's arguments and evidence that you want to refute, noting evidence and sources that you want to challenge as unreliable and/or outdated. Write checkmarks next to points you have addressed. Flowchart formats vary according to debate type; your instructor may be able to assist you in constructing an appropriate one.

The Case Study

An exciting and effective learning tool, a **case study** documents a real (or realistic) situation, relating to business, law, medicine, science, or other discipline, which poses difficult dilemmas or problems requiring solutions. Students read a detailed account and then apply what they have studied to analyze and resolve the problems. Instructors typically ask students to report orally on the case study, either alone or in teams. Students are expected to consider the case carefully and then report on the following items:

1. Description/overview of the major issues involved in the case
2. Statement of the major problems and issues involved
3. Identification of any relevant alternatives to the case
4. Presentation of the best solutions to the case, with a brief explanation of the logic behind them
5. Recommendations for implementing the solutions, along with acknowledgment of any impediments

Prepare for Different Types of Audiences

In the workplace, presentations may be delivered to fellow workers, colleagues, managers, clients, or others. As preparation for presenting to these different types of audiences, instructors in disciplines ranging from business to the sciences may ask that you tailor your talk to a mock (practice) on-the-job audience, with your classmates serving as stand-ins. Audiences include the **expert or insider audience**, **colleagues within the field audience**, the **lay audience**, and the **mixed audience** (see Table 31.1 for descriptions). The nearby checklist "Tips on Presenting to a Mixed Audience" offers guidelines on addressing one of the most common types of audiences.

TABLE 31.1 Types of On-the-Job Audiences

Type of Audience	Characteristics
Expert or insider audience	People who have intimate knowledge of the topic, issue, product, or idea being discussed (e.g., an investment analyst presents a financial plan to a group of portfolio managers).
Colleagues within the field audience	People who share the speaker's knowledge of the general field under question (e.g., psychology or computer science) but who may not be familiar with the specific topic under discussion (e.g., short-term memory or voice-recognition systems).
Lay audience	People who have no specialized knowledge of the field related to the speaker's topic (e.g., a city engineer describes failure of water treatment system to the finance department).
Mixed audience	An audience composed of a combination of people—some with expert knowledge of the field and topic and others with no specialized knowledge. This is perhaps the most difficult audience to satisfy (e.g., an attending surgeon describes experimental cancer treatment to a hospital board comprised of medical professionals, financial supporters, and administrative personnel).

CHECKLIST

TIPS ON PRESENTING TO A MIXED AUDIENCE

- ✓ Research the audience and gear your talk to the appropriate level of knowledge and interests.
- ✓ Avoid technical or specialized terms and explain any that you must use.
- ✓ Carefully construct the introduction and clearly identify the central idea and main points of the talk. If possible, present a compelling "story" that listeners can follow.
- ✓ Alert the audience to the order of your coverage: "I will first focus on the big picture and on marketing/sales issues. I will then present design specifications and data analysis."
- ✓ Devote half to two-thirds of your time to an introduction and overview of your subject and save any highly technical material for the remaining time.
- ✓ Include everyone. Try to address different levels of knowledge and different perspectives in turn.
- ✓ Be clear about the level at which you are speaking: "I am going to present the primary results of this project with minimal detailed information, but I'm happy to review the statistics or experimental results in more detail following the presentation."
- ✓ Be alert to audience reactions. If you notice that your listeners are experiencing discomfort, consider stopping and asking for feedback about what they want. You might then change course and opt for a more in-depth, high-level approach, depending on what they say.

Presentations in Science and Mathematics Courses

The purpose of most science and math presentations is to inform listeners of the results of original or replicated research or problem solving. Instructors want to know the processes by which you arrived at your experimental results. For example, your biology instructor may assign an oral report on the extent to which you were able to replicate an experiment on cell mitosis. A math instructor may ask you to apply a concept to an experiment or issue facing the field. A key challenge in these presentations is communicating complex information to audiences with varying levels of knowledge (e.g., a "mixed audience"; see Table 31.1).

Known for their focus on exacting processes, science-related disciplines include the physical sciences (e.g., chemistry and physics), the natural sciences (e.g., biology and medicine), and the earth sciences (e.g., geology, meteorology, and oceanography). Fields related to mathematics include accounting, statistics, and applied math.

Preparing Effective Presentations in Science and Mathematics

Science and mathematics presentations must first of all be grounded in the scientific method. Presentations must clearly illustrate the nature of the research question – describe the methods used in gathering and analyzing data, and explain the results. However, presentations need not be dry and merely factual. Experimentation is a process of discovery, and the fits and starts that often accompany its completion can make for compelling stories during your talk.

Pay particular attention to the introduction of your talk. If you lose the audience at the beginning of a scientific presentation, chances are slim that you'll regain their attention. Listeners want to know what the point of the talk is about (e.g., what key question did you investigate), so make certain that you communicate it in the first few minutes of your scientific talk. Follow this by telling the audience why you believe the research is important and why solving the problem is relevant.

Typically, instructors will expect you to do the following in a science or mathematics presentation:

- Use observation, proofs, and experiments as support for your points.
- Be selective in your focus on details, highlighting critical information but not overwhelming listeners with information they can refer to in the written paper.
- Use analogies to build on prior knowledge and demonstrate underlying causes (see Chapter 23, pp. 315, for guidelines on explaining difficult concepts).
- Use well-executed presentation aids, from slides to equations drawn on a whiteboard, to illustrate important concepts (see Chapters 20–22 on presentation aids).

Three frequently assigned presentations in science and mathematics courses include the *research*, *methods/procedure*, and *field study* presentations.

Research Presentation

In the **research presentation** (also called the **scientific talk** or *oral scientific presentation*) you describe research you conducted, either alone or as part of a team. You may deliver this information as a stand-alone oral presentation or as a poster session (see p. 419).

A research presentation usually follows the standard model used in scientific investigation (see Figure 31.1) and includes the following elements:

1. An *introduction* describing the research question and the scope and objective of the study.
2. A *description of methods* used to investigate the research question, including where it took place and the conditions under which it was carried out.

3. The *results of the study* summarizing key findings and highlighting insights regarding the questions/hypotheses investigated; this is the "body" of the presentation.
4. A *conclusion* (or *"discussion"*) in which the speaker interprets the data or results and discusses their significance. As in any speech, the conclusion should link back to the introduction, reiterating the research question and highlighting key findings.

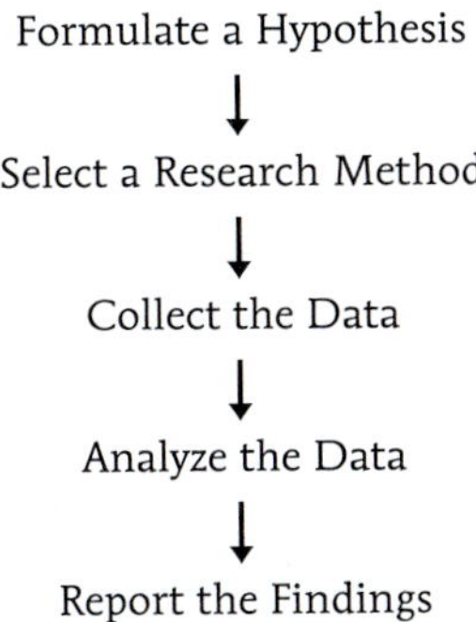

FIGURE 31.1 Steps in a Scientific Investigation

Methods/Procedure Presentation

The **methods/procedure presentation** describes how an experimental or mathematical process works and under what conditions it can be used. This is generally a ten- to fifteen-minute individual presentation. In a mathematics class, for example, your assignment might be to describe an approach to solving a problem, including examples of how this approach has been used, either inappropriately or appropriately. This type of methods/procedure presentation generally does the following:

1. Identifies the conditions under which this particular process should be used
2. Offers a detailed description of the process (at times including a demonstration)
3. Discusses the benefits and shortcomings of the process

CHECKLIST

FOCUSING YOUR SCIENTIFIC TALK

- ✓ State the research question accurately and in a way that will motivate listeners to pay attention.
- ✓ Clearly state the hypothesis to the research question.
- ✓ Describe the study's research design and rationales.
- ✓ Describe the methods used to obtain the results and why you used them.
- ✓ Explain and evaluate the results of the study using the data.
- ✓ Address the significance of the study.

CHECKLIST

STEPS IN PREPARING A FOCUSED SCIENTIFIC PRESENTATION

- ✓ Create an informative title that describes the research.
- ✓ Place your presentation in the context of a major scientific principle.
- ✓ Focus on a single issue that becomes "the story" and adjust it to the interests of your audience.
- ✓ Identify the underlying questions you will address, divide it into subquestions, and answer each question.
- ✓ Follow a logical line of thought.
- ✓ Explain scientific concepts unambiguously, with a minimum of professional jargon.
- ✓ Use analogies to increase understanding.
- ✓ End with a concise, clearly formulated conclusion in the context of your chosen scientific principle.

Information from Robert Anholt, *Dazzle 'Em with Style: The Art of Oral Scientific Presentation*, 2nd ed. (New York: Academic Press, 2005).

Field Study Presentation

A **field study presentation** describes research conducted in natural settings, using methods such as direct observation, surveys, and interviews. For example, a biology major might research links between soil erosion and hiking activity in a public park, or an environmental studies major might describe animal behavior in an oil spill. Field study presentations may be assigned as individual, team, or poster-session presentations. Whatever the topic under investigation and the methods of data collection, field study presentations address the following:

1. Overview and scope of the field research (e.g., if explaining animal behavior in an oil spill, describe the prevalence of oil spills and the effects on environment and wildlife)
2. Description of the site (e.g., describe the habitat before and after the spill, noting ecological interactions)
3. Methods used in the research (e.g., participant observation, type of sample collection, measurement techniques; also: How were the behaviors observed? Who provided the observations? When and for how long?)[2]
4. Interpretation/analysis of the data
5. Future directions for the research

Presentations in Technical Courses

Oral presentations in technical courses often focus on the design of a product or system, whether it is a set of plans for a building, a prototype robot, or an innovative computer-circuit design. Technical presentations include reports and proposals that provide instructions, advocate a product or service, update progress, make recommendations, or request funding. (See Chapter 30 on reports and proposals and the progress report; see below for requests for funding.) Assignments in engineering, architecture, and other technical courses also typically include the *design review*, described below.

Technical disciplines include, but are not limited to the STEM fields (science, technology, engineering, and mathematics) as well as the design-oriented disciplines of graphic design, architecture, and industrial design.

Preparing Effective Technical Presentations

The technical presenter faces the challenge of scaling complex information and processes to audience members with differing levels of technical expertise. Carefully conceived presentation aids—including diagrams, prototypes, drawings, computer simulations, design specifications, and spreadsheets—are key to the technical presentation, yet the aids must not overwhelm it. Presentations are often delivered in teams, so close coordination among members is essential (see Chapter 29 on presenting in groups).

Typically, people who attend technical presentations possess a range of technical knowledge, and effective technical speakers gear the presentation to the appropriate level for the audience, using accessible language, avoiding jargon (see Chapter 16 on language), and offering analogies to clarify hard-to-understand concepts and processes (see Chapter 23 on informative speaking).

Both informative and persuasive strategies come into play in technical presentations, and the best technical presenters know how to appeal to their audiences' needs and motivations to gain agreement for a proposal or design[3] (see Chapter 30).

Effective technical presentations *sell ideas*. The technical presenter must persuade clients, managers, or classmates that a design, an idea, or a product is a good one. As one instructor notes, "You can never assume that your product or design will just sell—*you* have to do that."[4]

Effective technical presentations are also detailed and specific and use numbers as evidence. Instead of offering general, sweeping statements, they provide hard data and clearly stated experimental results.

Professionals working in technical fields point to three major obstacles to designing and delivering a successful technical presentation: (1) too much information crammed into aids and failure to construct and practice with them early in the process, (2) insufficient preparation and practice with fellow team members, and (3) failure to select an appropriate organization and structure for the presentation. Keeping these pitfalls in mind during preparation will set you on a winning path.

Engineering Design Review

The **engineering design review** explains the problem-solving steps in devising a product or system in response to an identified need. Virtually all capstone engineering courses require that students prepare design reviews, which are generally informative in nature—although their purpose may include convincing the audience that the design decisions are sound. (In varying formats, design reviews are also assigned in basic science and mathematics courses.) Design reviews may incorporate a **prototype** (model) demonstration and are usually delivered as team presentations. Design reviews typically include the following:

1. Identification of problem to be solved/need to be met and overview of objectives
2. Description of the design concept and specifications
3. Discussion of why the proposed design will solve the problem
4. Discussion of any experimental testing that has been completed on the design
5. Discussion of future plans and unresolved problems
6. Discussion of schedule, budget, and marketing issues

Architecture Design Review

The **architecture design review** combines two functions: it enables the audience to visualize the design, and it sells it. Using a narrative structure, in which you tell the "story" of the design, combined with a *spatial organizational pattern*, in which you arrange main points in order of physical proximity within the design (see p. 183), can help you do this. At a minimum, architecture design reviews typically cover the following:

1. Background on the site
2. Discussion of the design concept
3. Description and interpretation of the design

Request for Funding

In the **request for funding presentation**, a team member or the entire team provides evidence that a project, proposal, or design idea is worth funding. Requests for funding usually cover the following ground:

1. Overview of customer specifications and needs
2. Analysis of the market and its needs
3. Overview of the design idea or project and how it meets those needs
4. Projected costs for the project
5. Specific reasons why the project or idea should be funded

Presentations in Social Science Courses

Students taking social science courses learn to evaluate and conduct *qualitative research,* in which the emphasis is on observing, describing, and interpreting behavior, as well as *quantitative research,* in which the emphasis is on statistical measurement. Often the focus of inquiry in the social sciences is explaining or predicting human behavior or social forces, answering questions such as what, how, and why.

Oral presentation assignments in social science courses frequently include the *review of the literature presentation*, *theoretical research presentation*, *program evaluation presentation*, and *policy proposal*. Other commonly assigned presentations are described elsewhere in this guide: see the *poster presentation* (p. 419), *research presentation ("scientific talk")* (p. 424), *methods/procedure presentation* (p. 425), *field study presentation* (p. 426), *evidence-based practice presentation* (p. 434), and *case study presentation* (p. 435).

Social science courses include such academic disciplines as psychology, sociology, political science, economics, anthropology, geography, and communication studies.

Preparing Effective Presentations in the Social Sciences

Good social science presentations clearly explain the research question, refer to current research, support arguments with evidence, use theory to build explanations, and use timely data.

- *Illustrate the research question.* Pay special attention to illustrating the nature of the research question and the methods used to investigate it.
- *Refer to current research.* Credible social science presentations refer to recent findings in the field. Instructors are more likely to accept experimental evidence if it is replicable over time and is supported by current research.
- *Use theory to build explanations.* Theory is central to social science research, informing the types of questions asked, the research methods used, and the means by which evidence is interpreted. Thus, your discussion of the research should reflect the theoretical framework within which the research was conducted.[5]
- *Support arguments with evidence.* Each of your assertions or claims must be accompanied by evidence for or against it, which can be used by others to evaluate the claims.

Since most of your social science presentations will be relatively brief, make sure to sufficiently narrow your topic or research question and scale your findings to fit the time allotted (see Chapter 7). For example, rather than selecting an overly broad topic such as "substance abuse," consider "frequency of alcohol-related deaths among U.S. college students in year X."

Review of the Literature Presentation

Frequently, instructors ask students to summarize and evaluate the existing research related to a given topic. A communications student, for example, might review the literature on gender bias in the hiring of journalists. After considering key studies related to the topic, the student would describe the conclusions uncovered by the research and suggest directions for future work. A **review of the literature presentation** typically includes the following:

1. Statement of the topic under review
2. Description of the available research, including specific points of agreement and disagreement among sources
3. Evaluation of the strengths and weaknesses of the research, including the methodology used and whether findings can be generalized to other studies
4. Conclusions that can be drawn from the research
5. Suggested directions for future study

When including a literature review in conjunction *with your own research study*, follow these broad guidelines.

1. Introduce your topic.
2. Review the literature pertinent to your topic.
3. State your research question or hypothesis and describe how it relates to the literature.
4. Discuss your research methods.
5. Discuss your results, including shortcomings and implications for future research.

Program Evaluation Presentation

In addition to explaining social phenomena, social scientists often measure the effectiveness of programs developed to address these issues. Instructors may ask you to evaluate a program or policy, perhaps one you observed in a service learning assignment (see p. 419). Typically, the **program evaluation presentation** includes the following:

1. Explanation of the program's mission
2. Description of the program's accomplishments
3. Discussion of how the accomplishments were measured (e.g., the evaluation methods and questions), including any problems in collecting and/or assessing the evaluation research
4. Conclusions regarding how well or poorly the program met its stated objectives

Policy Proposal Presentation

In addition to evaluating programs and policies, you may be asked to recommend a course of action on a current issue or problem. A **policy proposal report** typically includes the following:

1. Definition and background review of the current policy and its shortcomings
2. Discussion of alternatives to policy, including pros and cons of each

3. Recommendations of a specific policy with clear argument for why this option is better than each of the alternatives
4. Application of forecasting methods to show likely results of the recommended policy
5. Plan for implementation of the recommendations
6. Discussion of future needs or parameters to monitor and evaluate the policy option

Presentations in Arts and Humanities Courses

Speaking assignments in arts and humanities courses often require that you interpret the meaning of a particular idea, event, person, story, or artifact. Instructors expect that these interpretations will be grounded in the conventions of the field and build on the research within it. An instructor of literature may ask you to explain the theme of a novel or a poem, for example, or an art history professor may ask that you identify the various artistic and historical influences on a sculpture or painting. Some presentations may be performative in nature, with students expressing artistic content. Assignments include summaries of works; presentations of interpretation and analysis; presentations that compare and contrast an idea, an event, or a work; and individual and team debates (see pp. 420–21).

Arts and humanties typically includes English, literature, history, religion, philosophy, foreign languages, art history, theater, and music.

Preparing Effective Arts and Humanities Presentations

Good presentations in the arts and humanities help audiences understand and put into context the meaning of original works or scholarship. Working from within the conventions of the discipline, the presenter identifies the work's key themes and the means by which the author or creator communicates them. Instructors will expect you to investigate the following:

- What is the thesis or central message in the text or work?
- What questions/issues/themes does the author address?
- How does the author or creator organize or structure the work?
- Who is the audience for the work?
- What influences or sources inform the work?

Presentations of Interpretation and Analysis

Often in the arts and humanities, instructors assign presentations requiring students to interpret the relevance of a historical or contemporary person or event; a genre or school of philosophical thought; or a piece of literature, music, or art. Instructors look to students to think of topics in new ways by providing original interpretations. A presentation on the historical significance of Reconstruction after the Civil War of 1861–1865, for example, will be more effective if you offer a new way of viewing the topic rather than reiterating what other people have said or what is already generally accepted knowledge. A debate on two philosophical ideas will be most effective when you assert issues and arguments that are different from those that the audience has thought of before. The more original the interpretation (while remaining logical and supported by evidence), the more compelling the presentation will be for the audience.

Presentations That Compare and Contrast

A common assignment in the arts and humanities is to *compare and contrast* events, stories, people, or artifacts in order to highlight similarities or differences. For example, you might compare two works of literature from different time periods, or two historical figures or works of art. These presentations may be informative or persuasive; if the latter, the student will argue in favor of one idea, figure, or time period over another. Presentations that compare and contrast include the following elements:

1. *Thesis statement* outlining the connection between the events, stories, people, or artifacts
2. *Discussion of main points*, including several examples that highlight the similarities and differences
3. *Concluding evaluative statement* about the comparison (e.g., if the presentation is persuasive, why one piece of literature was more effective than another; if informative, a restatement of similarities and differences)

Presentations in Education Courses

In education courses, the most common speaking assignments focus on teaching and related instructional tasks, such as giving a lecture or demonstrating an activity. In a mathematics education course, you may prepare a mini-lecture on a particular geometric theorem. In a learning-styles course, you may tailor an activity to a variety of different learners.

Education courses include subfields such as curriculum and instruction, physical education, secondary and elementary education, and education administration.

Preparing Effective Education Presentations

Good presentations in education are marked by clear organization, integration of the material into the broader course content, two-way communication, and student-friendly supporting material. Above all, effective educational presentations succeed in fostering understanding. Follow these strategies as you prepare your presentation.

- *Use a learning framework.* Select one or more cognitive learning frameworks, such as the Bloom or Marazano taxonomy, and frame the information accordingly.
- *Organize material logically.* Presentations in education must be tightly organized so that the audience can easily access information. The simpler the organizational structure, the better (see Chapters 12 and 26). Use organizing devices such as preview statements, internal summaries, and transitions to help listeners follow ideas in a lecture, for example.
- *Integrate discussion to overall course content.* Describe how the lecture for the day relates to the previous day's lecture, and articulate learning objectives for the presentation. In a discussion or group activity, make clear connections between students' comments and other topics that have been raised or will be raised later in the course.
- *Tailor examples and evidence to the audience.* Use familiar examples and evidence that the audience can grasp easily. Don't support an idea with a statistical proof, for example, unless students are trained in statistics. Using familiar examples will enhance learning (see section on analogies in Chapter 23); try to choose examples that are close to the students' experiences.

Delivering a Lecture

A **lecture** is an informational speech for an audience of student learners. Standard lectures range from thirty minutes to one hour in length; a *mini-lecture presentation* generally lasts about ten to fifteen minutes.

Good lecturers actively engage students in the learning process, pausing to pose questions about the topic, allowing time for discussion, and incorporating short activities into the mix.[6] Rather than delivering a monologue, they encourage student participation. Typically, lectures include the following:

1. A clear introduction of the topic (see Chapter 15)
2. Statement of the central idea of the lecture
3. Statement of the connection to previous topics covered
4. Discussion of the main points
5. Summary of the lecture and preview of the next assigned topic
6. Question-and-answer period

Facilitating a Group Activity

In the **group activity presentation**, you describe an activity to be completed following a lecture. Typically this short presentation includes the following:

1. A brief review of the main idea of the lecture
2. An explanation of the goal of the activity
3. Directions on carrying out the activity

4. A preview of what students will gain from the activity and what the discussion following it will cover

Facilitating a Classroom Discussion

In a **classroom discussion**, you will lead a discussion following a lecture, offering brief remarks, and then guiding the discussion as it proceeds.

1. Begin by outlining critical points to be covered
2. Prepare several general guiding questions to launch the discussion
3. Prepare relevant questions and examples to use during the discussion

Presentations in Nursing and Allied Health Courses

Speaking assignments in nursing and allied health courses range from the *service learning presentation*, *poster presentation*, and *journal article review* (see pp. 418–19 for detailed guidelines) to the *evidence-based practice presentation*, *clinical case study*, *quality improvement proposal*, *case conference*, and *shift report* (see the following sections).[7] Students are assigned a mix of individual and group presentations.

Fields within nursing and allied health include physical therapy, occupational therapy, radiology, pharmacy, and other areas of health care.

Preparing Effective Presentations in Nursing and Allied Health

Good presentations in health-related courses accurately communicate scientific knowledge while reviewing the patient's clinical status and potential treatment options. The presenter will support any assertions and recommendations with relevant scientific literature supporting evidence-based clinical practice. Instructors will expect you to do the following:

1. Use evidence-based guidelines.
2. Demonstrate a solid grasp of the relevant scientific data.
3. Organize the presentation in order of severity of patient problems.
4. Present the patient as well as the illness. That is, remember that the patient is a human being with thoughts and feelings, not merely a collection of symptoms.
5. Include only essential facts, but be prepared to answer any questions about all aspects of the patient and their care.

Evidence-Based Practice Presentation

The **evidence-based practice (EBP) presentation** reviews the scientific literature on a clinical problem, critically evaluates the findings, and suggests best practices for standards of care. To fulfill these criteria, EBP presentations do the following:

1. Define the research problem (e.g., the clinical issue).
2. Critically review the scientific literature on a practice related to the clinical issue, describing method/design, sample size, and reliability.
3. Discuss the strength of the evidence and indicate whether or not the practice should be adopted into clinical practice.[8]

Clinical Case Study Presentation

A **clinical case study** is a detailed analysis of a person or group with a particular disease or condition. Clinical case studies inform medical teams or other audiences about the following:

1. Overview of patient information (presentation and background)
2. Description of pretreatment workup, including results
3. Review of treatment options/plan of care
4. Outcome of treatment plan
5. Surveillance plan (follow-up patient care based on evidence-based practice)

Quality Improvement Proposal

In the **quality improvement proposal**, the speaker recommends the adoption of a new (or modified) health practice or policy, such as introducing an improved treatment regimen at a burn center. This report (sometimes assigned as part of a capstone course) addresses the following:

1. Review of existing practice
2. Description of proposed quality improvement
3. Review of the scientific literature on the proposed practice
4. Plan of action for implementation

Treatment Plan Reports

The ability to communicate information about patients or clients is important for all health care providers. Either individually or as part of a health care team, people in the helping professions routinely report patients' conditions and outline plans of treatment to other health care providers. One form of treatment plan report, called the **case conference**, includes the following:

1. Description of patient status
2. Explanation of the disease process
3. Steps in the treatment regimen
4. Goals for patient and family
5. Plans for patient's care at home
6. Review of financial needs
7. Assessment of resources available

The **shift report** is a concise overview of the patient's status and needs, delivered to the oncoming caregiver. It includes the following information:

1. Patient name, location, and reason for care
2. Current physical status
3. Day on clinical pathway for particular diagnosis
4. Pertinent psychosocial data, including plans for discharge and involvement of caregivers
5. Care needs (physical, hygiene, activity, medication, nutritional needs)

SAMPLE SPEECHES

Merging two timely topics of smartphone applications and refugees, Mia delivers an informative speech on how emigrants use smartphones. She presents what challenges refugees faced, what resources they used to overcome them, and then how a smartphone could be used to solve these challenges.

SAMPLE SPEECHES

Sample Speeches

SAMPLE VISUALLY ANNOTATED INFORMATIVE SPEECH

To see Mia Roberts deliver her speech, go to **launchpadworks.com**

HOW EMIGRANTS USE SMART PHONES

MIA ROBERTS

Mia gains audience attention with a rhetorical question.

Following is a speech by student Mia Roberts about the essential role that smart phones play in refugees' attempts to escape war-torn lands. This speech uses a topical pattern of arrangement.

Imagine that you are a refugee from a war-torn country, trying to migrate across Europe with what you can carry in your backpack. What would be the most important possession to bring with you? Most of you have one with you right now. And although your water bottle and the California roll you brought for lunch would help, I'm not referring to these necessities. The answer, for many emigrants, is a smart phone.

Mia's facial expressions enhance the delivery of her speech.

Today, we'll take a look at how smart phones are central to the success of emigrants' journeys. • Many members of this class have their own stories of how their families came to the United States. And most of you are very familiar with a multitude of apps on your own smart phones. So let's put these two ideas together and see why smart phones are so useful for migrants. • I have always been interested in my own family's story of emigration through Europe and on to North America and have been fascinated while researching the twenty-first-century version of this narrative. We'll get that narrative going by first taking a look at the widespread use of smart phones by emigrants, next, considering how smart phones are vital to emigrants' journeys, and finally, seeing how smart phones

• Mia introduces the thesis.

• Mia creates audience identification with her topic.

are especially essential in dangerous situations. • So let's begin by observing that smart phones are used extensively during emigration. •

• Mia offers a preview of the main points of the speech.

• She uses a transition to signal the start of the speech body.

Mia's gestures help her convey her points.

Smart phones are one of the most important possessions of many college students, and our class surveys indicated that many of you spend hours each day on yours. Smart phones are even more vital for emigrants. Hannah Kozlowska, staff reporter for *Quartz*, • indicated on September 14, 2015, that "more than a billion people around the world rely on smart phones and their ubiquitous messaging and social media apps, but none more so than the hundreds of thousands of people who are fleeing war, hunger, and famine in the Middle East and Africa." •

• For added credibility, Mia might have qualified *Quartz* as "an online business news site."

• Since this is a quotation, Mia should have made this clear. Better yet would be to paraphrase in her own words.

In an October 9, 2015, *MTV News* article, Melita Šunjić, a United Nations Relief and Works Agency senior public information officer, stated that at refugee camps, emigrants not only ask about where to eat and sleep but also where they might get Wi-Fi and be able to charge their phones.

For example, a music teacher named Osama Aljasem, who migrated from Syria to Belgrade, Serbia, told the *New York Times* on August 25, 2015, that "Every time I go to a new country, I buy a SIM card and activate the Internet and download the map to locate myself." Mr. Aljasem acknowledges that "I get stressed out when the battery even starts to get low."

The need for Internet access can spur creative solutions. When refugees experienced connectivity problems after crossing the border into Croatia, Louise Dewast, a digital news associate for *ABC News*, described a unique fix on September 22, 2015. Otvorena mreža (Project Open Network), a tech startup, sent volunteers carrying backpacks with mobile Wi-Fi devices, creating human hotspots.

Now that you have seen that many emigrants rely on smart phones, let's take a look at how and why these phones are so helpful. •

• This helpful transition summarizes what's been said and previews what's to come.

Imagine that you have just arrived in a country for the first time and you need to cross it on your journey. You don't speak the language, could be all alone, have

Mia uses gestures to emphasize important points in her speech.

no local currency, and don't know where you can stay or how to travel safely. What apps on your phones might you use? Don't say "order a pizza," because the closest Domino's is over one hundred miles away and they won't deliver. And what new apps would you download before you left? Your phone could be your lifeline.

Communicating with family members is one important use of smart phones. In *Time* magazine, October 19, 2015, news photographer • Patrick Witty tells the story of Rami Shahhoud, who uses his phone to connect with his wife and family back in Damascus. Rami explains that "if it were five years ago, they'd maybe be thinking what's happening to me and I'd be wondering what's happening to them. . . . But now, thank God for this technology." Emigrants who have become separated from family members can use the Red Cross website *Trace the Face: People Looking for Missing Migrants* in Europe to post their own picture or search for pictures of loved ones that have been posted.

• Mia qualifies her source nicely here.

Another helpful app is a foreign currency conversion calculator. Picture yourself newly arrived in Macedonia with $1,000—your life savings. If a trader offers you 30,000 denars for these dollars, the right decision could determine whether you can afford to make it through Macedonia and on to your ultimate destination. That sounds like a lot of denars. Should you make this deal?

Mia maintains eye contact while using her visual aids.

The answer is no!

If you accepted the 30,000 denars for your $1,000, you would get only about half of what your money was worth. No emigrant could finance travel for long at this rate. Fortunately, as Rob Price, a technology reporter, writes in *Business Insider*, September 9, 2015, "Foreign currency conversion calculators are [a] popular choice, helping people to avoid getting ripped off as they cross borders and currency areas." •

• Mia uses too many quotations. She should paraphrase or summarize information more.

After obtaining the right currency, another question is where to eat and stay. Emigrants share this information with one another online. For instance, on September 15, 2015, *CNN* reported the experience of Kenan al Beni and six friends who relied on the Facebook pages of other migrants. These pages included advice about which tent to purchase and directions to a reasonably priced Athens hotel. They relied on social media sites for everything they need, according to Kenan.

Nonprofit organizations' sites also can be accessed. The International Rescue Committee's website, *Refugee Info*, can be accessed to find information about lodging, services, and food in a number of different European cities. In *Wired*, December 5, 2015, Rey Rodrigues, the organization's technology coordinator, reported that to ensure information wasn't outdated, the organization was trying to reach as many people in as many spots as possible. Rodrigues said that his team then goes in to map those services and validates it across peer groups in each city.

The next morning, it may be time to move on toward the ultimate destination, and again smart phones play a useful role. Investigative journalist Matthew Brunwasser wrote in the *New York Times*, August 25, 2015, that emigrants share photographic evidence on their smart phones of their journeys with Facebook groups such as *How to Emigrate to Europe*, which has over 39,000 members.

In *The Telegraph*, September 20, 2015, reporters Josie Ensor and Magdy Samaan describe a 120,000-member Facebook group, Karajat Al Mushuntiteen (Travelers' Platform) as "an eBay or one-stop shop for migrants" from Africa and the Middle East. On this site, members provide maps that they describe as containing the best routes and stopping points. When one route is closed off, this is noted, and new options are suggested.

We have seen • how emigrants use smart phones to take care of daily needs. Next, let's look at uses of these phones in riskier situations.

• Again, Mia uses transitions effectively.

One problem is coping with traffickers. In his *Business Insider* article, Rob Price noted that thanks to apps such as Google Maps, refugees can find their own way without having to endure the terrible conditions and exorbitant prices associated with people traffickers. In the previously cited *New York Times* article, Mohammed Haj Ali of the Adventist Development and Relief Agency concurs that traffickers are losing out as refugees brave it themselves while relying on Facebook for help.

Smart phones also provide vital information for emigrants who do decide to rely on traffickers for all or part of their journey. Many members of our class have relied on reviews on sites such as Uber and Yelp to make decisions as consumers. And according to social media manager Alessandra Ram in *Wired*, December 5, 2015, social media allows migrants to review trafficking services and to compare prices. Matthew Brunwasser, the *New York Times* reporter I mentioned previously, provides an example of one trafficker who offered a half-price discount for young children and received thirty-nine Facebook "likes." In a September 11, 2015, *CNBC* article, Kate Coyer, director of the Civil Society and Technology Project at Central European University, indicates that although online tools may not bring an end to trafficking, they can reduce the costs and dangers of trafficking.

A second danger is crossing the high seas, often in substandard and overcrowded watercraft. In the *World Post*, October 14, 2015, International Rescue Committee press manager Paul Donohoe reports that smart phones have become a "fundamental" tool, allowing refugees to survive the deadly water crossing from Turkey to Greece, a passage that has claimed almost three thousand lives in 2015 alone, according to the U.N. Human Rights Council.

The visual aid conveys the dangerous conditions that Mia describes.

In *The Independent*, September 3, 2015, reporter Lizzie Dearden related the story of a twenty-year-old emigrant that she calls Firas (Dearden kept the man's real name private). Here he describes the experience of being on a boat that was heading to Greece when the engine died after one half hour at sea:

> Quickly the boat became full of water and started to sink. . . . So I sent a Whatsapp message giving my GPS and asking them [the Greek coast guard] to help us. . . . Me and my three friends from Syria jumped

into the sea. We didn't have any life jackets, just two children's rubber rings for the four of us. . . . The water was very cold, and the waves were very strong. . . . But I never lost my faith or my hope. . . . I was picked up by the coast guard after seven hours of swimming. . . . I've managed to call my mother and tell her I made it.

Mia connects with her audience through animated gestures and expressions.

So you can see that a smart phone can literally make the difference between life and death.

Today, I hope you have learned more about how refugees are benefiting from the use of smart phones. We've seen that smart phones are a prized possession for many migrants, how they help emigrants with the logistics of their journey through Europe, and how they are a valued asset in times of danger. •

• Mia effectively summarizes her main points and signals the close of the speech.

Mia concludes her speech with a compelling story.

We'll end with the experience of Mohamed, a twenty-seven-year-old former deejay, as related on October 3, 2015, by reporter Mallika Rao in the *World Post*. He was adrift with fifty migrants in the Mediterranean Sea after their overcrowded boat lost its engine. Mohamed had the foresight to wrap his iPhone in sheets of plastic, and despite the waves, he was able to get a signal. He used Maps.me to track the group's latitude and longitude and texted the coordinates to his cousin Danya in Hawaii. Danya's family was able to contact the coast guard on the Greek island of Chios. They texted Mohamed. After the Greek coast guard transported Mohamed and his group to Chios, he soon found a hairdryer to dry the ports on his phone and sent Danya a Facebook message explaining how they had survived.

Works Cited

Brunwaser, M. "A Twenty-first-Century Migrant's Essentials: Food, Shelter, Smartphone." *New York Times*, August 26, 2015, A1.

Dearden, L. "Syrian Refugee Tells How He Survived Boat Sinking in Waters Where Aylan Kurdi Drowned." *Independent*, September 3, 2015, http://www.independent.co.uk/news/world/europe

/syrian-refugee-tells-how-he-survived-boat-sinking-in-waters-where-aylan-kurdi-drowned-10484607.html.

Dewast, L. "Volunteers Bring Wi-Fi to Refugees in Europe on Backpacks." *ABC News*, September 22, 2015, http://abcnews.go.com/International/volunteers-bring-wi-fi-refugees-europe-backpacks/story?id=33953223.

Ensor, J., and M. Samaan. "The Facebook Group Helping Migrants Reach Europe." *The Telegraph*, September 20, 2015, http://www.telegraph.co.uk/news/worldnews/europe/croatia/11877508/The-Facebook-group-helping-migrants-reach-Europe.html.

Graham, L. "How Smartphones Are Helping Refugees in Europe." *CNBC*, September 11, 2015, http://www.cnbc.com/2015/09/11/how-smartphones-are-helping-refugees-in-europe.html.

International Committee of the Red Cross. *Trace the Face: People Looking for Missing Migrants in Europe*, August 27, 2015, https://www.icrc.org/en/document/trace-face-people-looking-missing-migrants-europe.

International Rescue Committee. *Refugee Info*, 2015, https://refugeeinfo.eu/.

Kaufman, G. "Young Refugees Are Using Their Smartphones for Way More Than Snapchatting and Selfies." *MTV News*, October 9, 2015, http://www.mtv.com/news/2285755/refugees-europe-facebook-smartphones-wifi/.

Kozlowska, H. "The Most Crucial Item That Migrants and Refugees Carry Is a Smartphone." *Quartz*, September 14, 2015, http://qz.com/500062/the-most-crucial-item-that-migrants-and-refugees-carry-is-a-smartphone/.

Price, R. "Google Maps Is Putting Europe's Human-Traffickers Out of Business." *Business Insider*, September 9, 2015, http://www.businessinsider.com/refugee-crisis-how-syrian-migrants-use-smartphones-avoid-traffickers-2015-9?r=UK&IR=T.

Ram, A. "Smartphones Bring Solace and Aid to Desperate Refugees." *Wired*, December 5, 2015, http://www.wired.com/2015/12/smartphone-syrian-refugee-crisis/.

Rao, M. "Lost at Sea and Texting for Help." *The World Post*, October 3, 2015, http://www

.huffingtonpost.com/entry/syrian-refugees-technology_560c13e2e4b07681270024d9.

Watson, I., C. Nagel, and Z. Bilginsoy. "'Facebook Refugees Chart Escape from Syria on Cell Phones." *CNN*, September 15, 2015, http://www.cnn.com/2015/09/10/europe/migrant-facebook-refugees/.

Witty, P. "Searching for Signal: The Smartphone Is the Refugee's Best Friend." *Time*, October 19, 2015, 56.

SAMPLE VISUALLY ANNOTATED PERSUASIVE SPEECH

To see Elijah Lui deliver his speech online, go to **launchpadworks.com**

Preventing Cyberbullying

ELIJAH LUI

Elijah Lui gives an online speech that helps the audience recognize how problematic cyberbullying is and lets them know how they can address and prevent it. Organizationally, the speech is arranged along the lines of the problem-solution pattern. Note that Elijah uses a variety of sources, from books to scholarly articles to publications posted on reputable websites, to support his arguments. •

• For guidelines on preparing an online presentation, see Chapter 28, "Preparing Online Presentations".

On the evening of September 22, 2010, Rutgers University freshman Tyler Clementi updated his Facebook status: "Jumping off the gw [George Washington] Bridge sorry." According to Lisa Foderaro's report in the *New York Times*, a few hours later Clementi did just that. But what would cause Clementi, recognized as a bright student and talented musician with a promising future, to take his own life? The answer, unhappily, involves a bully with a Web cam.

According to a May 21, 2012, report on CNN, Clementi's roommate was sentenced to 30 days in jail, 3 years of probation, 300 hours of community service, and $11,000 in restitution for using a Web cam to view and transmit images of Clementi in an intimate encounter with another young man.

Tyler Clementi's story is tragic, but it's not an isolated event. On September 9, 2013, 12-year-old Rebecca

Elijah cleans up to provide an appropriate background for his online speech.

Sedwick jumped to her death allegedly after being tormented by two girls on Facebook. And a few months earlier, Rehtaeh Parsons, a 17-year-old Canadian high school student, hanged herself after cell phone pictures of her being sexually assaulted were distributed by the alleged attackers. •

What is going on here? In a word—it's *cyberbullying*.

My name is Elijah and I'm here today to confront the growing problem of electronic harassment experienced by Tyler Clementi and so many others. I'll start with a look at the various forms cyberbullying takes and describe the scope of the problem. • But I'm not here just to talk about one more social ill. I want to show you how you and your loved ones can stay safe—both by scrupulously guarding your personal information and by actively thwarting cyberbullies.

And should you or someone you know become a victim, I want you to be able to respond constructively.

As you can imagine from the heartbreaking story that I've shared about Tyler Clementi, cyberbullying poses serious mental health risks to the nation's children, teens, and young adults. The Cyberbullying Research Center, a leading resource on the topic, • defines *cyberbullying* as "willful and repeated harm inflicted through the use of computers, cell phones, and other electronic devices." • Cyberbullying can take many forms, including the following: posting or sending harassing messages via websites, blogs, or text messages; posting embarrassing or private photos of someone without their permission; recording or videotaping someone and sharing it without permission; and creating fake websites or social networking profiles in someone else's name to humiliate them. Often these acts are done anonymously.

Recent research paints a chilling picture of the frequency and harms of electronic harassment. • According to Hani Morgan, an education professor at the University of Southern Mississippi, the statistics vary widely, but 42 percent of teens in a 2011 study reported being the victims of cyberbullying. Although most of the research to date has focused on cyberbullying among middle and high school students, a 2012 study published in the *Journal of*

• Elijah begins his speech with several dramatic examples that capture the audience's attention; these serve as appeals to pathos.

• Here, Elijah sets up the organizational pattern of the speech, indicating that he will describe a problem and offer solutions; he also previews the main points.

• Elijah qualifies his source and demonstrates its credibility.

• He begins the body of the speech by ensuring that the audience knows what cyberbullying means.

• Words such as "chilling" strike an emotional chord (pathos) and serve to persuade.

School Violence confirmed that the problem of electronic harassment continues into college. Psychologists Allison Schenk and William Fremouw found that nearly 9 percent of university students reported having experienced cyberbullying; that means that at least two or three people listening to this speech know what I'm describing because they've felt it. •

• Translating the statistic into something concrete related to audience members makes the evidence more persuasive.

Sitting a safe distance from the camera allows Elijah's body movements and gestures to be seen.

We have seen with Tyler, Rebecca, Rehtaeh, and too many others that cyberbullying has tragically cut short promising lives. But other consequences less dramatic than suicide take a serious toll on victims. The same study by Schenk and Fremouw reported more symptoms of depression and anxiety, as well as difficulty concentrating, among bullied college students.

As Professor Morgan explains, the anonymity of unsigned messages and fake user names marks cyberbullying as a dangerous evolution of a long-standing face-to-face bullying problem, but you can take steps to protect yourself. • For one, you can be vigilant about safeguarding your personal information. Our school's information technology office lists the following advice on its website. First, never, ever, leave your laptops unattended. Second, keep your account passwords and Social Security numbers completely private. Third, use the most secure privacy settings on your social networking sites. Finally, think carefully about the types of pictures of yourself and your friends that you post online, and restrict views of them to "friends" only. Each of these steps can minimize opportunities for bullies to harm or embarrass you in some way. •

• Elijah now moves from describing the problem to offering solutions.

• Elijah helps listeners follow along by using the signal words *first*, *second*, *third*, and *finally*.

Elijah maintains strong eye contact to evoke confidence and assurance in his speech.

In addition to zealously guarding your personal information, you can help combat cyberbullying by being a voice against it whenever you see it happening. Several organizations have websites that provide information you can use to be part of the solution. The Facebook Group "Don't Stand By, Stand Up!" is a student-led organization formed soon after Tyler Clementi's suicide. The group urges Internet users to take a stand against cyberbullying by recognizing that bullies—in all forms—rarely succeed in their harassment without the support and attention of bystanders. The National Crime Prevention Council website gives specific tips on how to thwart a bully's attempts. The first is to refuse to pass bullying messages along to others—whether via text or photo messaging, social networking, or e-mail—and to let the original sender know that you find the message offensive or stupid.

Despite your best efforts to keep your personal information private and speak out against cyberbullying, you may still become a victim. •

• Elijah transitions to his next point.

Online safety expert Parry Aftab's website, stopcyberbullying.org, advises victims to use the "Stop, Block, and Tell" method to respond to bullying behaviors directed against them. While often taught to younger children, this response makes sense in any case of cyberbullying. After receiving a bullying message you should first "Stop." In other words, do nothing. Take five minutes to cool down, take a walk, breathe deeply, or do whatever helps to calm down the understandable anger you are feeling. Then, "Block": Prevent the cyberbully from having any future communication with you. This may mean anything from removing him or her from your social networking sites' "friends" list to having your cell phone service provider block the bully from being able to call or text you. The third step is to "Tell" someone about the abuse without embarrassment or shame. For example, you might call campus security or confide in a counselor at the Health and Counseling Center—particularly if the abuse has been going on for a long time and you feel that your self-esteem or relationships have been affected. Similarly, parents of younger children should encourage their children to report any bullying to a trusted adult.

Today we've ventured into the very real—and very dangerous—world of cyberbullying. We've seen cyberbullying's negative impact on people of all ages. We've also seen how you can counter this potentially deadly problem by being vigilant about protecting your personal information and speaking out against cyberbullying. And if you or someone you know experiences cyberbullying, you can react constructively with the "Stop, Block, and Tell" method. •

• Elijah signals the conclusion of the speech with a summary of the main points.

Elijah's facial expressions exemplify the seriousness of the subject of his speech.

Cyberbullying isn't just someone else's problem. It's very likely something you need to guard against, now or in the future, as a student today or as a parent tomorrow. I urge each of you to make a personal commitment to do your part to combat the problem. • Refuse to stay silent in the face of cyberbullying. Resolve that you will neither send nor pass along cyberbullying messages of any kind, no matter how harmless doing so might seem. This act alone can make a world of difference in the life of the intended victim. And wouldn't you want someone to take this simple step for you?

• Elijah issues a call to action.

We must never forget Tyler Clementi, and the other young lives cut short by unnecessary bullying. Who knows? Your best friend, your younger brother, or your future son could just have easily been on that bridge that fateful September evening. •

• By stressing the personal relevance of the topic to the audience, Elijah leaves them with something to think about

Works Cited

Foderaro, Lisa W. "Private Moment Made Public, Then a Fatal Jump." *New York Times*, September 29, 2010. http://query.nytimes.com/gst/fullpage.html?res=9B07E6D91638F933A0575AC0A9669D8B63

Hayes, Ashley. "Prosecutors to Appeal 30-Day Sentence in Rutgers Gay Bullying Case." *CNN*, May 21, 2012. www.cnn.com/2012/05/21/justice/new-jersey-rutgers-sentencing/index.html

Hinduja, Sameer, and Justin W. Patchin. "Cyberbullying: Identification, Prevention, and Response." Fact Sheet. Cyberbullying Research Center website. 2010. www.cyberbullying.us/Cyberbullying_Identification_Prevention_Response_Fact_Sheet.pdf

Martinez, Michael. "Charges in Rebecca Sedwick's Suicide Suggest 'Tipping Point' in Bullying Cases." *CNN*, October 28, 2013. www.cnn.com/2013/10/25/us/rebecca-sedwick-bullying-suicide-case/index.html

Morgan, Hani. "Malicious Use of Technology: What Schools, Parents, and Teachers Can Do to Prevent Cyberbullying." *Childhood Education* 89, no. 3 (May/June 2013): 146–51.

Newton, Paula. "Canadian Teen Commits Suicide after Alleged Rape, Bullying." *CNN*, April 10, 2013. www.cnn.com/2013/04/10/justice/canada-teen-suicide/index.html

Schenk, Allison M., and William J. Fremouw. "Prevalence, Psychological Impact, and Coping of Cyberbully Victims among College Students." *Journal of School Violence* 11, no. 1 (January 2012): 21–37.

"Stop, Block, and Tell!" Stopcyberbullying.org website. Accessed November 1, 2013. http://www.stopcyberbullying.org/take_action/stop_block_and_tell.html

"Stop Cyberbullying before It Starts." National Crime Prevention Council website. Accessed February 9, 2011. www.ncpc.org/resources/files/pdf/bullying/cyberbullying.pdf

SAMPLE SPECIAL OCCASION SPEECH

Welcome Remarks to Employees

REX TILLERSON, SECRETARY OF STATE

Following is a speech delivered on February 2, 2017, by the newly appointed U.S. Secretary of State Rex Tillerson, on the occasion of his first day in office (see https://www.state.gov/secretary/remarks/2017/02/267401.htm). *The purpose of Tillerson's talk was to introduce himself to State Department staff, who had gathered to greet him in the atrium of State Department headquarters in Washington, D.C. As you read his remarks, note the many ways that Tillerson establishes rapport with his immediate audience, along with the approximately seventy-five thousand State Department employees worldwide who were likely viewing the event as it was broadcast. Note too Tillerson's effective use of oral style, in which he makes ample use of personal pronouns such as* I, you, *and* we; *down-to-earth language; and the occasional sentence fragment.*

Well, good morning, all. We apologize for being late. It seemed that this year's prayer breakfast, people felt the need to pray a little longer. • (Laughter.) But I certainly welcomed them all, so—thank you for such a warm reception. And it's a pleasure to be here, obviously. I've been anxious to be here, and I'm so pleased to have my wife, Renda, of more than 30 years. And she has been just steadfast through this process, encouraging me on and reminding me what this is really all about. And so thank you. (Applause.)

• Political tensions were at an all-time high when Tillerson took office, and his joke cleverly acknowledges these tensions.

I also want to thank Acting Secretary Tom Shannon, who has just been superb through this entire process. And Tom, thank you so much. (Applause.) It was truly and indeed an honor that Tom joined us in the Oval Office last night for my swearing-in, and I appreciated that he was there. •

• Acknowledging others is critical in special occasion speeches such as this.

Obviously, I also want to recognize and thank all of you here at headquarters of our State Department, the staff and partners around the world, who have faithfully performed your duties regardless of who was in charge. It was so important. I know many of you have assisted ambassadors and other officials during the Senate confirmation process, and indeed some of you have been through it yourself. Having just come through it for the first time, I can assure you the Senate still takes it as serious as ever, they're as energetic as ever, they're as thorough as ever—but we're here. (Laughter and applause.)

So in the days and weeks ahead we're going to have plenty of opportunity to discuss in more detail the goals, the priorities, and the strategic direction for our organization. But for now I really want to take a few minutes to communicate my high regard for the men and women of the State Department and share with you some principles for all of us to live by as we pursue our shared mission. •

• Tillerson expresses respect for the staff and their mission.

The individuals who comprise this department are among the finest public servants in the world. Many of you serve our nation abroad and have served our nation abroad. State Department staffers in the field are not just conduits for policies and plans; you are our emissaries of our nation and the ideals we stand for. When people see you, they see America. •

• Tillerson emphasizes the important role undertaken by employees.

When I wake up each morning, the very first thing I ask myself is: Are all of our people safe? The safety of every single member of our State Department family, regardless of where he or she is posted, is not just a priority for me. It's a core value, and it will become a core value of this department. • (Applause.) This means the State Department family here in the U.S. and all those agencies serving under chief of missions abroad, including Civil Service; Foreign Service officers and specialists; locally engaged staff of host country and third-country nationals; interns, fellows, support contractors, and implementing partners; and not least of all, the family members who support us at home and in our service to our country overseas. •

• Tillerson articulates a core value of his leadership.

• Tillerson acknowledges and offers recognition to the many employees he will now lead.

The Foreign Service is not the only component of the State Department. The Civil Service workforce at the State Department plays an indispensable role in all we achieve, and we cannot attain success without the mission-critical services that you provide.

Though we often live in a world of headlines, working outside of the public eye does not make you any less essential to our operations. Your dedication, your intelligence, and your sound judgment are the brick and mortar elements of all we do. We all depend on your good work, and I know it will continue.

One of the great—(applause)—one of the great challenges and thrills for the State Department staff is deciding how to confront changing conditions in every corner of the world. And I encourage all of you to use your natural and well-developed skills to adapt to changes here at home as well.

I know this was a hotly contested election, and we do not all feel the same way about the outcome. Each of us is entitled to the expression of our political beliefs, but we cannot let our personal convictions overwhelm our ability to work as one team. Let us be understanding with each other about the times we live in as we focus our energies on our departmental goals. •

• Tillerson offers a forthright acknowledgement of divided politics but sets a tone of teamwork.

As Secretary, I will deploy the talent and resources of the State Department in the most efficient ways possible. That may entail making some changes to how things are traditionally done in this department.

Change for the sake of change can be counterproductive, and that will never be my approach.

But we cannot sustain ineffective traditions over optimal outcomes. I will gather information on what processes should be reformed, and do my part to make sure we are functioning in the most productive and efficient way possible.

Regardless of the circumstances shaping our country or our department, we must all remain focused on the mission at hand before us. I remind you that our undertakings are larger than ourselves or our personal careers.

Our duty is to faithfully represent our nation in the arena of foreign affairs. If we stay focused on the work before us, I promise I will work to ensure you achieve your own personal success and your professional satisfaction in what you are doing.

For every individual who works at the State Department, I ask that we adopt a few core principles.

First, I believe that any organization runs best when all of its members embrace accountability. From the mailroom to the boardroom, every member of a team has a job to do. I know nobody will always be perfect, and that certainly includes me. But I ask that everyone strive for excellence and assume responsibility for their actions and their decisions.

The New England Patriots have signs posted all over their team facilities that simply say, "Do your job." It is a brief message, but one with profound importance. If we all do our jobs and embrace a willingness to be held accountable for our performance, we work better as a unit and move closer to attaining our goals. It's worked pretty well for the Patriots over the years, as I must admit. (Laughter.)

Secondly, I want us to be honest with one another. We're on the same team. We share the same mission. Honesty will undergird our foreign policy, and we'll start by making it the basis of how we interact with each other.

Lastly, we're going to treat each other with respect. No one will tolerate disrespect of anyone. Before we are employees of the State Department, we are human beings first. Let us extend respect to each other, especially when we may disagree.

What I ask of you and what I demand of myself—I will embrace accountability, honesty, and respect no less than anyone.

Before President Trump called me, I thought I would be entering retirement this spring after four decades of business experience. (Laughter.) Renda and I were ready to head off to the ranch and enjoy our grandchildren. But when I came back from my first meeting with President Trump and he asked me to do this, Renda said, "You didn't know it, but you've been in a 41-year training program for this job." (Laughter and applause.) So despite our own dreams, she said, "You're supposed to do this."

Well, my first day is here. I'm on the job. Hi, I'm the new guy. • (Applause.). . .

• This is a wonderful way to establish rapport with his audience!

As such, I will depend on the expertise of this institution. There are over 75,000 members of the State Department workforce, both Foreign and Civil Service employees, with an average of over 11 years of service in the department. I have 25 minutes. (Laughter.) You have accumulated knowledge and experience that cannot be replicated anywhere else. Your wisdom, your work ethic and patriotism, is as important as ever. And as your Secretary, I will be proud to draw upon all these qualities in my decision-making.

I ask that you join me in upholding high standards of ethics and professionalism, committing to personal accountability and honesty, and respecting your colleagues. There will undoubtably be times of victory, but there will also be many times of difficulty. Let's go forward as a team through all of it. Let's make the American people proud of what we do in this building and beyond.

Inscribed on the walls in this lobby are the names of fallen Foreign Service personnel, who, in the words of Abraham Lincoln, gave their last full measure of devotion. They died in service of causes far greater than themselves. As we move forward in a new era, it is important to honor the sacrifices of those who have come before us, and reflect on the legacy that we inherit.

In closing, I am honored to be serving alongside each of you as I serve our nation as the Secretary of State. So now I am going to take a moment and pay my respects to those individuals that are memorialized on this wall, and then I look forward to making the rounds and greeting you personally. It may take me a few days. (Laughter.) But in all sincerity, I do hope to have the opportunity to shake the hand of every one of you that's here. Thank you so much. (Applause.)

REFERENCE AND RESEARCH APPENDICES

Online Appendices
Go to LaunchPad: launchpadworks.com

REFERENCE AND RESEARCH APPENDICES

Go to LaunchPad for digital resources: **launchpadworks.com**

Online Appendices

Commonly Mispronounced Words

The following lists of errors in pronunciation are from Paul L. Soper, *Basic Public Speaking, Third Edition* (New York: Oxford University Press, 1968), with gratitude. The correct pronunciation or proper spelling is given in parentheses.

Misplacing the Accent

admir'able (ad'mirable)
applic'able (ap'plicable)
ce'ment (cement')
compar'able (com'parable)
exemplar'y (exemp'lary)
exig'ency (ex'igency)
finan'cier (financier')
formid'able (for'midable)
hor'izon (hori'zon)
i'dea (ide'a)
impi'ous (im'pious)
impot'ent (im'potent)
incompar'able (incom'parable)
incongru'ous (incon'gruous)
infam'ous (in'famous)
in'terest'ed (in'terested)
irrepar'able (irrep'arable)
municip'al (munic'ipal)
prefer'able (pref'erable)
proj'ectile (projec'tile)
reg'ime (regime')
respite' (res'pite)
superflu'ous (super'fluous)
u'nited (unit'ed)
vehe'ment (ve'hement)
vehi'cle (ve'hicle)

Addition of Sounds

athaletics (athletics)
attack-ted (attacked)
barbarious (barbarous)
colyum (column)
corpse (corps)
drawr (draw)
drownded (drowned)
elum (elm)
enterance (entrance)
ekscape (escape)
filum (film)
grievious (grievous)
height-th (height)
hinderance (hindrance)
idear (idea)
lightening (lightning)
mischievious (mischievous)
of-ten (of[t]en)
rememberance (remembrance)
sing-ger (singer)
stastistics (statistics)
sub-tle (su[b]tle)

sufferage (suffrage)
umberella (umbrella)
warsh (wash)

Omission of Sounds

assessory (accessory)
accerate (accurate)
actully (actually)
blong (belong)
canidate (candidate)
defnite (definite)
jography (geography)
guarntee (guarantee)
ineffecshal (ineffectual)
nuclus (nucleus)
particlar (particular)
pome (poem)
plice (police)
quite (quiet)
reconize (recognize)
resume (résumé)
sedimentry (sedimentary)
simlar (similar)
sussinct (succinct)
superntenent (superintendent)
temperture (temperature)
uzhal (usual)
vilent (violent)

Sound Substitutions

agin (again)
blaytant (blatant)
boquet (bouquet)
brochr (brochure)
capsl (capsule)
calvary (cavalry)
tshasm (chasm)
click (clique)
conscious (conscience)
crooks (crux)
cullinary (culinary)
dictionury (dictionary)
diptheria (diphtheria)
dipthong (diphthong)
dis-hevel (dishevel)
fewtyle (futile)
genuwine (genuine)
gesture (*g* is soft)
gigantic (first *g* is soft)
hiccough (hiccup)
homidge (homage)
ullusion (illusion)
interduce (introduce)
irrevelent (irrelevant)
jist (just)
larnyx (larynx)
lenth (length)
longgevity (longevity)
loose (lose)
memor (memoir)
miradge (mirage)
preform (perform)
prespiration (perspiration)
preelude (prelude)
prestidge (prestige)
rench (rinse)
saloon (salon)
statue (stature)
strenth (strength)
substantuate (substantiate)
tedjius (tedious)
theayter (theater)

Chicago Documentation

B

Two widely used systems of documentation are outlined in *The Chicago Manual of Style*, Sixteenth Edition (2010). The first, typically used by public speakers, provides for bibliographic citations in endnotes or footnotes. This method, which is also frequently used by journalists and scholars in the humanities, is illustrated in this appendix. The second system, often used by writers in the physical and natural sciences, employs an author-date system: Sources are cited in the text with full bibliographic information given in a concluding list of references.

For information about the author-date system—and more information generally about Chicago-style documentation—consult the *Chicago Manual*, Sixteenth Edition, Chapters 14 and 15.

1. Book by a Single Author Give the author's full name followed by a comma. Then italicize the book's title. In parentheses, give the city of publication followed by a colon, the publisher's name followed by a comma, and the publication date. Place a comma after the parentheses, and then give the page numbers from which your paraphrase or quotation is taken.

1. Eric Alterman, *What Liberal Media? The Truth about Bias and the News* (New York: Basic Books, 2003), 180–85.

2. Book by Multiple Authors Give all the authors' full names, the book's title in italics, the publication information in parentheses, and the pages from which your paraphrase or quotation is taken.

2. Bill Kovach and Tom Rosenstiel, *The Elements of Journalism: What Newspeople Should Know and the Public Should Expect* (New York: Three Rivers Press, 2001), 57–58.

2. Bill Kovach and Tom Rosenstiel, *The Elements of Journalism: What Newspeople Should Know and the Public Should Expect*, rev. ed. (New York: Three Rivers Press, 2007), 61–62.

2. Leonard Downie Jr. and Robert G. Kaiser, *The News about the News: American Journalism in Peril* (New York: Knopf, 2002), 72–75.

3. Edited Work without an Author Give the editor's full name followed by a comma, "ed." for *editor*, and another comma. Then give the title in italics, publication information in parentheses, and the pages you're citing.

3. Joseph B. Atkins, ed., *The Mission: Journalism, Ethics, and the World* (Ames: Iowa State University Press, 2002), 150–57.

4. Encyclopedia or Dictionary Give the title of the work in italics followed by a comma, the edition (if any), the letters "s.v." (from the Latin *sub verbo*, "under the word"), and then the term you looked up, in quotation marks, and a period. If the citation is from an online reference work, add the publication date or date of last revision; if neither is available, add your date of access. Conclude with the URL (Internet address).

4. *Routledge Encyclopedia of Philosophy*, s.v. "Ethics of journalism."

4. *Encyclopaedia Britannica Online*, s.v. "Yellow Journalism," accessed October 17, 2010, www.britannica.com/EBchecked/topic/652632/yellow-journalism.

5. Article in a Magazine Include the author's full name, the title of the article in quotation marks, the title of the magazine in italics, and the publication date. If you use a quotation, give the page number of the quotation. Otherwise, there is no need to cite the page numbers of the article.

5. John Leo, "With Bias toward All," *U.S. News & World Report*, March 18, 2002, 8.

6. Article in a Journal Give the author's full name, the title of the article in quotation marks, the title of the journal in italics, the volume number, the issue number (if available), the year of publication in parentheses followed by a colon, and the pages used. If the journal article was found online, list the URL of the article or use the DOI (digital object identifier) instead of the URL if one is available. It is not necessary to include page numbers for articles accessed online.

6. Tom Goldstein, "Wanted: More Outspoken Views; Coverage of the Press Is Up, but Criticism Is Down," *Columbia Journalism Review* 40, no. 4 (2001): 144–45.

6. Bree Nordenson, "Vanity Fire," *Columbia Journalism Review* 45, no. 5 (2007), www.cjr.org/profile/vanity_fire.php.

7. Article in a Newspaper Include the author's full name, the title of the article in quotation marks, the title of the newspaper in italics, the date of publication, the edition (such as "national edition") if relevant, and the section of the paper in which the article appeared. Omit page numbers, even for a citation to a quotation. If the article was found online, give the URL to the article itself (or to the newspaper's home page, if the article is archived).

7. Felicity Barringer, "Sports Reporting: Rules on Rumors," *New York Times*, February 18, 2002, sec. C.

7. Peter M. Shane, "Repair the Electoral College: Four Steps Would Help Balance Majority Rule with Minority Rights," *Washington Post*, October 31, 2004, final edition, www.washingtonpost.com.

8. Website Give the name of the author (if available), the title or description of the site, the name of any sponsoring organization, the date of publication or modification, and an address (URL) that links directly to the site or site section. If there is no author, give the owner of the site as the author. Italicize the title of the website only if it is an online book, periodical, or blog. Use quotation marks for titles of articles, pages, or sections of a website. Include the access date only if there is no publication date or date of modification.

8. FAIR (Fairness & Accuracy in Reporting), "Challenging Hate Radio: A Guide for Activists," accessed September 21, 2010, www.fair.org/index.php?page=112.

9. E-mail Message Treat e-mail messages like personal communications. Give the sender's full name, the phrase "e-mail message to author," and the date of the message.

9. Grace Talusan, e-mail message to author, March 20, 2010.

10. Discussion Lists, Newsgroups, or Online Postings Give the author's full name, followed by the name of the discussion list, the date of the posting, and the URL of the posting.

10. Ola Seifert to Society of Professional Journalists discussion list, August 23, 2011, http://f05n16.cac.psu.edu.

11. Blog Posts Include the author's full name, the title of the blog entry (in quotation marks), followed by the name of the blog (in italics). Include "(blog)" after the name if it is not part of the name. If the blog is part of a larger publication, include the name of the publication as well. End with the date of the blog post and the URL.

11. Brian Stetler, "Study: Some Viewers Were Misinformed by TV News," *Media Decoder* (blog), *New York Times*, December 17, 2010, http://mediadecoder.blogs.nytimes.com.

12. Article in an Electronic Database Give the author's full name, the title of the article (in quotation marks), the title of the periodical (in italics), publication information for the periodical, and the pages you are citing. Then cite the DOI (if available) or the name of the database and the document number.

12. Mark J. Miller, "Tough Calls: Deciding When a Suicide Is Newsworthy and What Details to Include Are among Journalism's More Sensitive Decisions," *American Journalism Review* 24, no. 10 (2002): 43, Expanded Academic ASAP (A95153129).

13. Government Document Use the governmental body or office as the author. Give the governmental body's name ("U.S. Congress," "U.S. House," "Senate Committee on Foreign Relations"), the title of the article (in quotation marks) or publication (italicized), the usual publication information, and the page numbers you are citing.

13. U.S. Congress, *Electronic Freedom of Information Amendments of 1996* (Washington, D.C.: GPO, 1996), 22.

14. Personal Communication Give the author's name, the type of communication (e.g., "letter to author," "e-mail message to author," "conversation with author," "telephone conversation with author"), and the date.

14. Soo Jin Oh, letter to author, August 13, 2010.

15. Interview Give the name of the interviewee, the interviewer, the name of the program or forum, the publication or network, and the date. Interviews that have not been published or broadcast should be cited with a description of the type of interview (e.g., "audio recording") and the place the interview was conducted.

15. Walter Cronkite, interview by Daniel Schorr, *Frontline*, PBS, April 2, 1996.

16. Video Recording Give the title of the video, film, or other work; the director; the date of the original release; the place and name of the distribution company; the date of the recording; and the medium (VHS, DVD).

16. *All the President's Men*, directed by Alan J. Pakula (1976; Burbank, CA: Warner Home Video, 1997), DVD.

17. Sound Recording List the composer or writer, the title of the work, the performer or conductor, the recording company or publisher, the recording number or date of release, and the medium.

17. Noam Chomsky, *The Emerging Framework of World Power*, read by the author (AK Press, 2003), compact disc.

APA Documentation

C

Most disciplines in the social sciences—psychology, anthropology, sociology, political science, education, and economics—use the author-date system of documentation established by the American Psychological Association (APA). This citation style highlights dates of publication because the currency of published material is of primary importance in these fields. For more information about APA format, see the *Publication Manual of the American Psychological Association*, Sixth Edition (2010).

This new edition now advises users to omit retrieval dates for content that is unlikely to change, such as published journal articles, and to omit the database from which material is retrieved as long as an identifier such as a URL (Internet address) or DOI (digital object identifier) is included.

The numbered entries that follow introduce and explain some conventions of this citation style using examples relating to the topic of stress management. Note that in the titles of books and articles only the first word of the title and subtitle and proper nouns are capitalized.

1. Book by a Single Author Begin with the author's last name and initials followed by the date of publication in parentheses. Next, italicize the book's title and end with the place of publication and the publisher.

Nakazawa, D. J. (2008). *The autoimmune epidemic.* New York, NY: Simon & Schuster.

2. Book by Multiple Authors or Editors Begin with the authors' last names and initials followed by the date of publication in parentheses. Next, italicize the book's title and end with the place of publication and the publisher. Invert all authors' names and use an ampersand before the last name.

Williams, S., & Cooper, L. (2002). *Managing workplace stress: A best practice blueprint.* New York, NY: Wiley.

3. Article in a Reference Work List the author of the article, the publication date, and the article title. This information is followed by the word *In* and the italicized title of the reference work. Include the volume number and inclusive page numbers of the article in parentheses, followed by the place of publication and the publisher. If an online edition of the reference work is cited, give the retrieval date and the URL. Omit end punctuation after the URL.

Beins, B. C. (2010). Barnum effect. In I. B. Weiner & W. E. Craighead (Eds.), *The Corsini encyclopedia of psychology* (4th ed., Vol. 4, pp. 203–204). Hoboken, NJ: Wiley.

Biofeedback. (1998). In *Encyclopaedia Britannica online*. Retrieved from www.britannica.com/EBchecked/topic/65856/biofeedback

4. Government Document Use the office or governmental department as the author followed by the publication date. Italicize the title of the document and end with the place of publication and the publisher (usually "Washington, DC," and "Government Printing Office").

The Interagency Security Committee. (2013). *Violence in the federal workplace: A Guide for prevention and response*. Washington, DC: Government Printing Office.

5. Journal Article Begin with the author's last name and initials followed by the date of publication in parentheses. Next, list the title of the article, and italicize the title of the journal in which it is printed. Then give the volume number, italicized, and the issue number in parentheses if the journal is paginated by issue. End with the inclusive page numbers of the article.

Dollard, M. F., & Metzer, J. C. (1999). Psychological research, practice, and production: The occupational stress problem. *International Journal of Stress Management, 6*(4), 241–253.

6. Journal Article Online If a DOI number is given, add "doi:" and the number after the publication information. If there is no DOI, add "Retrieved from" and the URL for the journal home page. It is no longer necessary to include the database from which an article is retrieved or the date of retrieval for a published article. Omit the end period after a DOI or URL.

Christian, M. S., Bradley, J. C., Wallace, J. C., & Burke, M. J. (2009, September). Workplace safety: A meta-analysis of the roles of person and situation factors. *Journal of Applied Psychology, 94,* 1103–1127. doi:10.1037/a0016172

7. Magazine Article Begin with the author's last name and initials followed by the date of publication, including the month or the month and day, in parentheses. Next, list the title of the article and the title of the magazine, italicized. Give the volume number, italicized, followed by the inclusive page numbers of the article.

Cobb, K. (2002, July 20). Sleepy heads: Low fuel may drive brain's need to sleep. *Science News, 162,* 38.

8. Newspaper Article Begin with the author's last name and initials followed by the date of publication, including the month and day, in parentheses.

Next, list the title of the article and, in italics, the newspaper in which it is printed. End with the section and page or pages on which the article appears. Note that the abbreviation *p.* or *pp.* is used for newspaper page numbers. If the article was found online, omit page numbers, give the URL for the home page, and do not add end punctuation.

Zimmerman, E. (2010, December 19). Learning to tame your office anxiety. *The New York Times*, p. BU8.

Zimmerman, E. (2010, December 19). Learning to tame your office anxiety. *The New York Times*. Retrieved from www.nytimes.com

9. Unsigned Newspaper Article If a newspaper article does not list an author, give the title, the publication date in parentheses, the name of the newspaper in italics, and the page on which the article appears.

Stress less: It's time to wrap it up. (2002, December 18). *Houston Chronicle*, p. A1.

10. Document from a website List the author; the date of publication (use "n.d." if there is no date); the title of the document, italicized; the words "Retrieved from"; and the URL for the document. If there is no author, begin the entry with the document title followed by the date. Do not include a retrieval date unless the content is likely to change. Do not add punctuation at the end of the URL.

Centers for Disease Control and Prevention. (1999). *Stress . . . at work* (NIOSH Publication No. 99-101). Retrieved from www.cdc.gov/niosh/docs/99-101

11. Entire website To cite an entire website, including personal websites, it is usually sufficient to simply note the site in your speech. For example,

Dr. Wesley Sime's stress management page is an excellent resource (http://www.unl.edu/stress/mgmt).

It is not necessary to include a citation in the reference list.

12. Electronic Mailing List, Newsgroup, Online Forum, or Discussion Group Message Cite the author's name, the posting date in parentheses, the subject line, and a description of the message in brackets, followed by "Retrieved from" and the URL for the list or an archived copy of the message. Include the name of the list if this is not part of the URL.

Lippin, R. (2008, November 2). Re: The relation between work-related psychosocial factors and the development of depression [Electronic mailing list message]. Retrieved from Occupational & Environmental Medicine Mailing List, http://lists.unc.edu/read/archive?id=4872034

Dimitrakov, J. (2001, February 21). Re: Immune effects of psychological stress [Online discussion group message]. Retrieved from http://groups.google.com/group/sci.med.prostate.prostatitis/ browse_thread/thread/5cd921bc1b52688b/b28274accd8aec0f?lnk=gst& q=immune+effects+of+psychological+stress#b28274accd8aec0f

13. Blog Post or Comment Cite the author's name, the date of the post, the title of the post, and the description "Web log post" in brackets, and then give the URL for the post. For a comment to a blog post, add "Re:" before the title and use "Web log comment" for the description.

Lippin, R. (2007, July 31). US corporate EAP programs: Oversight, Orwellian or Soviet psychiatry redux? [Web log post]. Retrieved from http://medicalcrises.blogspot.com/2007/07/us-corporate-eap-programs-oversight.html

14. E-mail Message To cite personal e-mail correspondence, it's sufficient to simply note the message in your speech. For example,

An e-mail message from the staff of AltaVista clarifies this point (D. Emanuel, personal communication, May 12, 2005).

The APA manual states that e-mail correspondence, like other personal communications, should not be included in the reference list; check with your instructor to see what his or her expectations are for your APA reference list.

15. Abstract from an Information Service or Online Database Begin the entry with the publication information as for a print article. End the entry with "Abstract retrieved" followed by the URL of the database or the name of the database and any identifying number.

Viswesvaran, C., Sanchez, J., & Fisher, J. (1999). The role of social support in the process of work stress: A meta-analysis. *Journal of Vocational Behavior, 54,* 314–334. Abstract retrieved from ERIC database. (EJ581024)

16. Personal Interview To cite a personal, unpublished interview, it's usually sufficient to note the interview in your speech. For example,

During her interview, Senator Cole revealed her enthusiasm for the new state-funded stress management center (M. Cole, personal communication, October 7, 2005).

The APA manual states that personal interviews, like other personal communications, should not be included in a bibliography; check with your instructor to see what his or her expectations are for your APA bibliography.

Glossary

abstract language Language that is general or nonspecific. See also *concrete language*.

active listening A multistep, focused, and purposeful process of gathering and evaluating information.

ad hominem argument A form of fallacious argument that targets a person instead of the issue at hand in an attempt to incite an audience's dislike for that person.

after-dinner speech A speech that is likely to occur before, after, or during a formal dinner, a breakfast or lunch seminar, or other type of business, professional, or civic meeting.

agora In ancient Greece, a public square or marketplace. See also *forum*.

alliteration The repetition of the same sounds, usually initial consonants, in two or more neighboring words or syllables.

allusion A figure of speech in which the speaker makes vague or indirect reference to people, historical events, or concepts to give deeper meaning to the message.

analogy An extended metaphor or simile that compares an unfamiliar concept or process with a more familiar one in order to help the listener understand the one that is unfamiliar.

anaphora A rhetorical device in which the speaker repeats a word or phrase at the beginning of successive phrases, clauses, or sentences.

anecdote A brief story of an interesting, humorous, or real-life incident that links back to the speaker's theme.

antigroup roles Negative interpersonal roles of group members who focus on individual versus group needs. These needs are usually irrelevant to the task at hand and are not oriented toward maintenance of the group as a team.

antithesis A rhetorical device in which two ideas are set off in balanced (parallel) opposition to each other.

anxiety stop-time A technique for dealing with pre-performance anxiety by allowing the anxiety to present itself for a few minutes and then declaring time for confidence to step in to help complete practicing a speech.

appeal to tradition A fallacy of reasoning in which the speaker argues for the truth of a claim based solely on common practices in the past.

architecture design review Oral presentation with the dual goal of helping listeners visualize the design concept while also selling it.

argument A stated position, with support, for or against an idea or issue; contains the core elements of claim, evidence, and warrants.

arrangement (of the speech) The strategic process of deciding how to order speech points into a coherent and convincing pattern for your topic and audience.

articulation The clarity or forcefulness with which sounds are made, regardless of whether they are pronounced correctly.

asynchronous communication Communication in which interaction between speaker and receiver does not occur simultaneously. See also *recorded presentation*.

attitudes Our general evaluations of people, ideas, objects, or events.

audience analysis The process of gathering and analyzing demographic and psychological information about audience members.

audience-centered perspective An approach to speech preparation in which each phase of the speech preparation process—from selection and treatment of the speech topic to making decisions about organization, language, and method of delivery—is geared toward communicating a meaningful message to the audience.

audience segmentation Dividing a general audience into smaller groups, called *target audiences*, with similar characteristics, wants, and needs.

authoritative warrant A warrant that appeals to the credibility (ethos) that the audience assigns to the source of the evidence.

average A summary of a set of data according to its typical or average characteristics; may refer to the *mean*, *median*, or *mode*.

backstory The story that leads up to an event that listeners might find interesting; offering a backstory can enliven an informative speech, especially one about events.

bandwagoning A fallacious argument that presents itself as true because "general opinion" supports it.

begging the question A fallacious argument presented in such a way that it is necessarily true, even though no evidence has been presented.

beliefs The ways in which people perceive reality or determine the very existence or validity of something.

bibliography An alphabetical list of sources.

blog Short for "Weblog"; an online personal journal.

body language Facial expressions, eye behavior, gestures, and general body movement; audiences are sensitive to a speaker's body language.

body (of speech) The part of the speech in which the speaker develops the main points intended to fulfill the speech purpose.

brainstorming A problem-solving technique, useful for developing speech topics, that involves the spontaneous generation of ideas. You can brainstorm by making lists, using word association, and mapping a topic, among other techniques.

brief example A single illustration of a point.

call to action A challenge to audience members to act in response to a speech, see the problem in a new way, change their beliefs about the problem, or change both their actions and their beliefs with respect to the problem; placed at the conclusion of a speech.

canned speech A speech used repeatedly and without sufficient adaptation to the rhetorical speech situation.

canon of arrangement The process of devising a logical and convincing structure for a message.

canons of rhetoric A classical approach to speechmaking in which the speaker divides a speech into five parts: invention, arrangement, style, memory, and delivery.

captive audience An audience required to attend the speech event. See also *voluntary audience*.

case conference An oral report prepared by health care professionals evaluating a patient's condition and outlining a treatment plan.

causal (cause-effect) pattern of arrangement A pattern of organizing speech points in order, first of causes and then of effects or vice versa; it is used when the cause-effect relationship is well established.

central processing A mode of processing a persuasive message that involves thinking critically about the contents of the message and the strength and quality of the speaker's arguments; described in the *elaboration likelihood model (ELM) of persuasion*. People who seriously consider what the speaker's message means to them are most likely to experience a relatively enduring change in thinking. See also *peripheral processing*.

channel The medium through which the speaker sends a message (e.g., sound waves, air waves, and electronic transmission).

chart A method of visually organizing complex information into compact form. Several different types of charts are helpful for speakers: flowcharts, organization charts, and tabular charts or tables.

cherry-picking Selectively presenting only those facts and statistics that buttress your point of view while ignoring competing data.

chronological pattern of arrangement A pattern of organizing speech points in a natural sequential order; it is used when describing a series of events in time or when the topic develops in line with a set pattern of actions or tasks.

civic-minded Caring about your community, as expressed in your speeches and in your deeds.

civic virtues Characteristics thought to exemplify excellence of character.

claim (proposition) The declaration of a state of affairs, in which a speaker attempts to prove something by providing evidence and reasons (warrants).

claim of fact An argument that focuses on whether something is or is not true or whether something will or will not happen.

claim of policy A claim that recommends that a specific course of action be taken, or approved, by an audience.

claim of value A claim that addresses issues of judgment.

classroom discussion presentation A presentation in which the speaker presents a brief overview of the topic under discussion and introduces a series of questions to guide students through the topic.

cliché An overused expression such as "works like a dog."

clinical case study A presentation delivered in nursing and allied health contexts; provides medical personnel with a detailed analysis of a person or group with a particular disease or condition and reviews plans for treatment.

closed-ended question A question designed to elicit a small range of specific answers supplied by the interviewer. See also *open-ended question*.

co-culture A community of people whose perceptions and beliefs differ significantly from those of other groups within the larger culture.

code-switching The selective use of casual language, dialect, a second language, or even slang within a speech.

colleagues within the field audience An audience of persons who share the speaker's knowledge of the general field under question but who may not be familiar with the specific topic under discussion.

collectivist culture A culture that tends to emphasize the needs and desires of the larger group rather than those of the individual. See also *individualist culture*.

colloquial expression An informal expression, often with regional variations of speech.

common knowledge Information that is likely to be known by many people and is therefore in the public domain; the source of such information need not be cited in a speech.

communication ethics Our ethical responsibilities when seeking influence over other people and for which there are positive and negative, or "right" or "wrong," choices of action.

comparative advantage pattern of arrangement A pattern of organizing speech points so that the speaker's viewpoint or proposal is shown to be superior to one or more alternative viewpoints or proposals.

conclusion (of speech) The part of the speech in which the speaker reiterates the speech theme, summarizes main points, and leaves the audience with something to think about or act upon.

concrete language Nouns and verbs that convey specific and tangible (as opposed to abstract) language. See also *abstract language*.

connotative meaning The individual associations that different people bring to bear on a word.

consequentialist ethics An approach to ethical standards that suggests that it is the outcome or consequence of our conduct that ultimately determines its rightness.

conversation stoppers Speech that discredits, demeans, and/or belittles those with whom one disagrees.

coordinate points Ideas that are given the same weight in an outline and are aligned with one another; thus, Main Point II is coordinate with Main Point I.

coordination and subordination The logical placement of ideas relative to their importance to one another. Ideas that are coordinate are given equal weight. An idea that is subordinate to another is given relatively less weight.

copyright A legal protection afforded original creators of literary or artistic works, including works classified as literary, musical, dramatic, choreographic, pictorial, graphic, sculptural, audiovisual, sound recording, or architectural. See also *intellectual property*.

critical or conflicted audience Audience members whose attitudes are critical of or conflicted about the speaker's topic.

critical thinking The ability to evaluate claims on the basis of well-supported reasons.

cultural intelligence The willingness to learn about other cultures and gradually reshape one's thinking and behavior in response to what one has learned.

cultural norms A group's rules for behavior; attempts to persuade people to do things contrary to their cultural norms will usually fail.

cultural premises A group's shared beliefs and values about personal identity and relationships; persuasive attempts that challenge cultural premises will usually fail.

cultural values Values related to audience members' personal relationships, religion, occupation, and so forth that can significantly influence how they respond to a speaker's message.

culture The language, beliefs, values, norms, behaviors, and even material objects that are passed from one generation to the next.

debate An oral presentation in which two individuals or groups consider or argue an issue from opposing viewpoints.

decoding The process of interpreting a message.

Deep Web The large portion of the Web that general search engines cannot access because the information is licensed and/or fee-based; libraries subscribe to many such fee-based databases that can be accessed through their portals.

defensive listening A poor listening behavior in which the listener reacts defensively to a speaker's message.

definition by etymology (word origin) Defining something by providing an account of a word's history.
definition by example Defining something by providing an example of it.
definition by negation Defining something by explaining what it is not.
definition by synonym Defining something by comparing it with another term that has an equivalent meaning. For example: A friend is a comrade or a buddy.
deliberative oratory In ancient Greece, speech addressing legislative or political policy issues.
delivery The vocal and nonverbal behavior that a speaker uses in a public speech; one of the five *canons of rhetoric*.
delivery cues Brief reminder notes or prompts placed in the speaking outline; can refer to transitions, timing, speaking rate and volume, presentation aids, quotations, statistics, and difficult-to-pronounce or remember names or words.
demagogue An unethical speaker who relies heavily on irrelevant emotional appeals to short-circuit listeners' rational decision-making process.
demographics Statistical characteristics of a given population. Characteristics typically considered in the analysis of audience members include age, gender, ethnic or cultural background, socioeconomic status (including income, occupation, and education), and religious and political affiliation.
denotative meaning The literal or dictionary definition of a word.
dialect A distinctive way of speaking associated with a particular region or social group.
dialogic communication The sharing of ideas and open discussion through civil discourse.
digital storytelling Using multimedia to present a multisensory narrative about your topic.
dignity The feeling that one is worthy, honored, or respected as a person.
direct quotation A statement quoted verbatim, or word for word, from a source. Direct quotations should always be acknowledged in a speech. See also *paraphrase*.
disinformation The deliberate falsification of information.
dyadic communication Communication between two people, as in a conversation.
effective delivery The skillful application of natural conversational behavior to a speech in a way that is relaxed, enthusiastic, and direct.
either-or fallacy A fallacious argument that is stated in terms of two alternatives only, even though there may be multiple ways of viewing the issue.
elaboration likelihood model of persuasion (ELM) A model of persuasion that states that people process persuasive messages by one of two routes—either central processing or peripheral processing—depending on their degree of involvement in the message.
elocutionary movement An approach to public speaking in which speechmaking is regarded as a type of performance, much like acting.
encoding The process of organizing a message, choosing words and sentence structure, and verbalizing the message.
encyclopedia A reference work that summarizes knowledge found in original form elsewhere and provides an overview of subjects.
engineering design review An oral presentation providing information on the results of a design project.
epideictic oratory In ancient Greece, speech addressing special occasions, such as celebrations and funerals.

epiphora A rhetorical device in which the speaker repeats a word or phrase at the end of successive statements.

ethical theory A theory that attempts to answer questions by proposing criteria or standards with which to distinguish ethical behavior from nonethical behavior.

ethics The rules or standards of moral conduct, or how people should act toward one another. In terms of public speaking, *ethics* refers to the responsibilities speakers have toward both their audience and themselves. It also encompasses the responsibilities that listeners have toward speakers.

ethnocentrism The belief that the ways of one's own culture are superior to those of other cultures. Ethnocentric speakers act as though everyone shares their point of view and points of reference, whether or not this is in fact the case.

ethos The Greek word for "character." According to the ancient Greek rhetorician Aristotle, audiences listen to and trust speakers if they exhibit competence (as demonstrated by the speaker's grasp of the subject matter) and good moral character.

eulogy A speech whose purpose is to celebrate and commemorate the life of someone while consoling those who are left behind; typically delivered by close friends and family members.

evidence Supporting material that provides grounds for belief; a core component of an argument. See also *claims* and *warrants*.

evidence-based practice (EBP) presentation A presentation that reviews the scientific literature on a clinical problem, critically evaluates the findings, and suggests best practices for standards of care.

example (as form of support) An illustration in a speech whose purpose is to aid understanding by making ideas, items, or events more concrete and by clarifying and amplifying meaning. See also *extended example* and *hypothetical example*.

expectancy values theory A theory of persuasion developed by Icek Aizen and Martin Fishbein positing that audience members act according to the perceived costs and benefits ("value") associated with a particular action; useful when developing a persuasive speech targeting behavior.

expert or insider audience An audience composed of individuals who have an intimate knowledge of the topic, issue, product, or idea being discussed.

expert testimony Any findings, eyewitness accounts, or opinions by professionals who are trained to evaluate or report on a given topic; a form of supporting material.

extended example Multifaceted illustrations of the idea, item, or event being described, thereby getting the point across and reiterating it effectively.

facts Documented occurrences, including actual events, dates, times, places, and people involved.

fair use doctrine Legal guidelines permitting the limited use of copyrighted works without permission for the purposes of scholarship teaching and research, among other uses.

fairness One of four "ground rules" of ethical speaking, fairness is the act of making a genuine effort to see all sides of an issue and to be open-minded.

faulty analogy An inaccurate or misleading comparison suggesting that because two things are similar in some ways, they are necessarily similar in others.

fear appeal A persuasive appeal to audience members that deliberately arouses their fear and anxiety.

feedback Audience response to a message, which can be conveyed both verbally and nonverbally through gestures. Feedback from the audience often indicates whether a speaker's message has been understood.

field study presentation A type of oral presentation typically delivered in the context of science-related disciplines, in which the speaker provides (1) an overview of field research, (2) the methods used in the research, (3) an analysis of the results of the research, and (4) a time line indicating how the research results will be used going forward.

"fighting words" Speech that provokes people to violence; such speech is not protected under the First Amendment.

"fight or flight response" The body's automatic physiological reactions in response to a threatening or fear-inducing event, including public speaking.

figures of speech Expressions, such as metaphors, similes, analogies, and hyperbole, in which words are used in a nonliteral fashion.

First Amendment The amendment to the U.S. Constitution that guarantees freedom of speech ("Congress shall make no law . . . abridging the freedom of speech . . . ").

fixed alternative question A closed-ended question that contains a limited choice of answers, such as "Yes," "No," or "Sometimes."

flip chart A large (27–34 inches) pad of paper on which a speaker can illustrate speech points.

flowchart A diagram that shows step-by-step progression through a procedure, relationship, or process.

forensic oratory In ancient Greece, speech addressing legal matters, such as the settlement of disputes.

forum In ancient Rome, a public space in which people gathered to deliberate about the issues of the day. See also *agora* and *public forum.*

free speech The right to be free from unreasonable constraints on expression.

frequency A count of the number of times something occurs or appears.

gender Social and psychological sense of self as male or female.

gender-neutral language Language that avoids the use of third-person generic masculine pronouns (*his, he*) in favor of inclusive pronouns such as *his or her, he or she, we, ours, you, your,* or other gender-neutral terms.

gender stereotype A stereotype based on oversimplified and often severely distorted ideas about the innate nature of what it means to be male or female.

general speech purpose A statement of the broad speech purpose that answers the question "Why am I speaking on this topic for this particular audience and occasion?" Usually the general speech goal is to inform, to persuade, or to mark a special occasion. See also *specific speech purpose.*

generational identity The collective cultural identity of a generation or a cohort.

graph A graphical representation of numerical data. Graphs neatly illustrate relationships among components or units and demonstrate trends. Four major types of graphs are line graphs, bar graphs, pie graphs, and pictograms.

group (activity) presentation An oral presentation that introduces students to an activity and provides them with clear directions for its completion.

groupthink The tendency of a group to accept information and ideas without subjecting them to critical analysis. Groupthink results from strong feelings of loyalty and unity within a group and can lead to a decline in the quality of the group's decisions.

hackneyed language Language that is poorly crafted and lacking in freshness.

handout Printed information that is either impractical to give to the audience in another manner or is intended to be kept by audience members after a presentation.

hasty generalization A fallacy of reasoning in which the speaker attempts to support a claim by asserting that a particular piece of evidence (an isolated case) is true for all individuals or conditions concerned.

hate speech Any offensive communication—verbal or nonverbal—directed against people's racial, ethnic, religious, gender, disability, or other characteristics. Racist, sexist, or ageist slurs, gay bashing, and cross burnings are all forms of hate speech.

hearing The physiological, largely involuntary process of perceiving sound.

hierarchy of needs A classic model of human action developed by Abraham Maslow built on the principle that people are motivated to act on the basis of needs.

high-uncertainty avoidance culture One of five "value dimensions," or major cultural patterns, that are significant across all cultures to varying degrees; identified by Geert Hofstede.

hostile audience or one that strongly disagrees One of four potential types of audiences the persuasive speaker may encounter.

hyperbole A figure of speech in which the speaker uses obvious exaggeration to drive home a point.

hypothetical example An illustration of something that could happen in the future if certain things occurred. See also *example* and *extended example*.

identification A feeling of commonality with another; when appropriate, effective speakers attempt to foster a sense of identification between themselves and audience members.

illusion of transparency Experience in which a speaker thinks his or her anxiety is more noticeable than it is.

imagery Colorful and concrete words that appeal to the senses. See also *analogy*, *metaphor*, and *simile*.

indentation In an outline, the plotting of speech points to indicate their weight relative to one another; subordinate points are placed underneath and to the right of higher-order points.

individualistic culture A culture that tends to emphasize personal identity and the needs of the individual rather than those of the group, upholding such values as individual achievement and decision making. See also *collectivist culture*.

information Data set in a context for relevance.

informative speaking See *informative speech*.

informative speech Speech providing new information, new insights, or new ways of thinking about a topic. The general purpose of informative speaking is to increase the audience's understanding and awareness of a topic.

integrity The quality of being incorruptible, of being able to avoid compromise for the sake of personal expediency.

intellectual property The ownership of an individual's creative expression. See also *copyright*.

internal preview An extended transition used within the body of a speech that alerts audience members to ensuing speech content.

internal summary An extended transition that draws together important ideas before proceeding to another speech point.

interview A type of communication conducted for the purpose of gathering information. Interviews can be conducted one on one or in a group.

introduction (of speech) The first part of a speech, in which the speaker establishes the speech purpose and its relevance to the audience and previews the topic and the main points.

invective Abusive speech; accusatory and attacking speech.

irony A figure of speech in which the speaker uses humor, satire, or sarcasm to suggest a meaning other than the one that is actually being expressed.

jargon Specialized terminology developed within a given endeavor or field of study.

journal article review An oral presentation in which the speaker reports on an article or a study published in a scholarly journal.

key-word outline The briefest of the three forms of outlines, the key-word outline uses the smallest possible units of understanding associated with a specific point to outline the main and supporting points. See also *phrase outline* and *sentence outline.*

keywords Words and phrases that describe the main concepts of topics. Internet search engines index information by keywords tagged within documents.

lay audience An audience of individuals who have no specialized knowledge of the general field related to a speaker's topic or of the topic itself.

lay testimony Testimony by a nonexpert; a form of supporting material.

lazy speech A poor speech habit in which the speaker fails to properly articulate words.

lecture An informative speech prepared for an audience of student learners.

library portal An entry point into a large collection of research and reference information that has been selected and reviewed by librarians.

listening The conscious act of receiving, constructing meaning from, and responding to spoken and nonverbal messages.

listening distraction Anything that competes for a listener's attention; the source of the distraction may be internal or external.

logical fallacy A statement that is either false or erroneous or is based on an invalid or deceptive line of reasoning. See also *ad hominem argument, appeal to tradition, bandwagoning, begging the question, either-or fallacy, hasty generalization, non sequitur, red herring fallacy,* and *slippery slope.*

logos The Greek rhetorician Aristotle used this term to refer to persuasive appeals to the audience's reason and logic.

low-uncertainty avoidance culture One of five "value dimensions" or major cultural patterns that are significant across all cultures to varying degrees; identified by Geert Hofstede. See also *high-uncertainty avoidance culture.*

main points Statements that express the key ideas and major themes of a speech. Their function is to make claims in support of the thesis. See also *subordinate points.*

malapropism The inadvertent use of a word or phrase in place of one that sounds like it.

mass communication Communication that occurs between a speaker and a large audience of unknown people. The receivers of the message are not present with the speaker, or they are part of such an immense crowd that there can be little or no interaction between speaker and listeners. Television, radio news broadcasts, and mass rallies are examples of mass communication.

mean The sum of the scores divided by the number of scores; the arithmetic (or computed) average.

median A type of average that represents the centermost score in a distribution; the point above and below which 50 percent of the scores fall.

memory One of five parts of the classical canons of rhetoric; refers to the practice of the speech until it can be artfully delivered.

message The content of the communication process—thoughts and ideas put into meaningful expressions. A message can be expressed both verbally (through the sentences and points of a speech) and nonverbally (through eye contact, body language, and gestures).

metaphor A figure of speech used to make an implicit comparison without the use of *like* or *as* (e.g., "Love is a rose"). See also *simile.*

methods/procedure presentation An oral presentation describing and sometimes demonstrating an experimental or mathematical process, including the conditions under which that process can be applied; frequently delivered in scientific and mathematical fields.

misinformation Information that is false.

mixed audience An audience composed of a combination of individuals, some of whom have expert knowledge of the field and topic while others have no specialized knowledge.

mixed metaphor A comparison that inappropriately juxtaposes two unlike images or expressions, often clichéd, such as "He went off the deep end like a bull in a china shop."

mode A type of average that represents the most frequently occurring score(s) in a distribution.

model A three-dimensional, scale-size representation of an object such as a building.

Monroe's Motivated Sequence See *motivated sequence pattern of arrangement.*

motivated sequence pattern of arrangement A five-step process of persuasion developed by Alan Monroe.

motivational warrant A warrant that uses the needs, desires, emotions, and values of audience members as the basis for accepting evidence in support of a claim.

motive A predisposition to behave in certain ways; persuading audience members requires paying attention to what motivates them.

multimedia A single production that combines several types of media (stills, sound, video, text, and data).

multimedia effect A learning principle that suggests that we learn better from words and pictures than from words alone, provided that the aids complement, or add to, the information rather than simply match the spoken point.

mumbling Slurring words together at a very low level of volume and pitch so that they are barely audible.

narrative A story; it can be based on personal experiences or imaginary incidents.

narrative pattern of arrangement A pattern of organizing speech points so that the speech unfolds as a story, with characters, plot, setting, and vivid imagery. In practice, this pattern often is combined with other organizational patterns.

noise Anything that interferes with the communication process between a speaker and an audience so that the message cannot be understood; noise can derive from external sources in the environment or from internal psychological factors.

non sequitur ("does not follow") An argument in which the conclusion does not connect to the reasoning.

nonverbal communication Communication other than the spoken word; includes body language, voice, and appearance.

one-sided message An argument in which the speaker does not acknowledge opposing views. See also *two-sided message.*

online presentation A presentation delivered via the Internet; can include both a *real-time presentation* and a *recorded presentation.*

onomatopoeia A figure of speech in which the speaker imitates natural sounds in word form to add vividness to a speech (e.g., "The rain dripped a steady plop, plop, plop").

open-ended question A survey or interview question designed to allow respondents to elaborate as much as they want. See also *closed-ended question*.

operational definition Defining something by describing what it does (e.g., "A computer is something that processes information").

oral citation An oral acknowledgment by a speaker of the source of speech material that is derived from other people's ideas.

oral style The use of language that is simpler, more repetitious, more rhythmic, and more interactive than written language; effective speeches use oral style.

oratory In classical terms, the art of public speaking.

organizational pattern A form of arrangement used to structure the main points, transitions, and subordinate points of a speech to obtain the speaker's intended purpose. Seven common organizational patterns described in this text are topical, causal (cause-effect), chronological, spatial, problem-solution, narrative, and circular, plus three forms applicable specifically to persuasive speechs: Monroe's Motivated Sequence, refutational, and comparative advantage.

outline A document in which main and supporting points—the major speech claims and the evidence to support them—are separated into larger and smaller divisions and subdivisions. See also *outlining* and *Roman numeral outline*.

outlining The physical process of plotting speech points on the page in hierarchical order of importance.

paralanguage Vocalizations that include the qualities of volume, pitch, rate, variety, and pronunciation and articulation.

parallelism The arrangement of words, phrases, or sentences in similar grammatical and stylistic form. Parallel structure can help speakers emphasize important ideas in a speech.

paraphrase A restatement of someone else's statements or written work that alters the form or phrasing but not the substance of that person's ideas. See also *direct quotation*.

pathos The Greek rhetorician Aristotle used this term for appeals to an audience's emotions. Such appeals can get the audience's attention and stimulate a desire to act but must be used ethically.

pauses Strategic elements of a speech used to enhance meaning by providing a type of punctuation emphasizing a point, drawing attention to a key thought, or allowing listeners a moment to contemplate.

performance anxiety A form of *public speaking anxiety* (*PSA*) that occurs the moment a speaker begins to deliver a speech. See also *preparation anxiety*.

periodical A regularly published magazine, journal, or newspaper.

peripheral processing A mode of processing a persuasive message that does not consider the quality of the speaker's message but is influenced by such noncontent issues as the speaker's appearance or reputation, certain slogans or one-liners, or obvious attempts to manipulate emotions; described in the *elaboration likelihood model (ELM) of persuasion*. Peripheral processing of messages occurs when people lack the motivation or the ability to pay close attention to the issues. See also *central processing*.

personification A figure of speech in which the speaker endows an abstract idea or inanimate object with human qualities (e.g., "Computers have become important members of our family").

persons with disabilities (PWD) Persons whose physical or mental impairments substantially limit their major life activities; sensitivity to PWD is important for the public speaker.

persuasion The process of influencing others' attitudes, beliefs, values, and behavior.

persuasive appeals See *proofs*.

persuasive speech A speech meant to influence audience members' attitudes, beliefs, values, and/or behavior by appealing to some combination of their needs, desires, interests, and even fears.

phrase outline A delivery outline that uses a partial construction of the sentence form of each point instead of using complete sentences that present precise wording for each point. See also *key-word outline* and *sentence outline.*

pictogram A type of graph that illustrates comparisons in picture form. The pictures represent numerical units and are drawn to relate the items being compared.

pitch The range of sounds from high to low (or vice versa). Pitch is determined by the number of vibrations per unit of time; the more vibrations per unit (also called frequency), the higher the pitch.

plagiarism The act of using other people's ideas or words without acknowledging the source.

podcast A digital audio recording of a presentation captured and stored in a form accessible via the Internet.

policy recommendation report An oral presentation that offers recommendations for solving a problem or addressing an issue.

post hoc ego propter hoc ("post hoc") An argument suggesting that a causal relationship exists between two states or events due to the order in which the events occurred, rather than taking other factors into consideration (e.g., since Event A followed Event B, Event B must have caused Event A). Also called "fallacy of false cause."

poster presentation A presentation that displays information about a study, an issue, or a concept on a large (usually roughly 4 × 3 or 4 × 6 foot) poster.

power distance As developed by Geert Hofstede, a measure of the extent to which a culture values social equality versus tradition and authority.

preparation anxiety A form of *public speaking anxiety* (*PSA*) that arises when the speaker begins to prepare for a speech, at which point he or she might feel overwhelmed at the amount of time and planning required. See also *performance anxiety.*

pre-performance anxiety A form of *public speaking anxiety* (*PSA*) that occurs when the speaker begins to rehearse a speech.

pre-preparation anxiety A form of *public speaking anxiety* (*PSA*) that occurs the moment speakers learn they must give a speech.

presentation aids Objects, models, pictures, graphs, charts, video, audio, or multimedia, used alone or in combination to illustrate speech points.

presentational speaking A type of oral presentation in which individuals or groups deliver reports addressing colleagues, clients, or customers within a business or professional environment.

preview statement Statement included in the introduction of a speech in which the speaker alerts the audience to the main speech points.

primacy effect Psychological principle in which listeners have a better recall of the main points made at the beginning of a speech than of those made later (unless the ideas made later are far more striking than the others).

primary source Firsthand accounts or direct evidence of events, objects, or people. See also *secondary source.*

problem-cause-solution pattern of arrangement A pattern of organizing speech points so that they demonstrate (1) the nature of the problem, (2) reasons for the problem, (3) unsatisfactory solutions, and (4) proposed solutions.

problem-solution pattern of arrangement A pattern of organizing speech points so that they demonstrate the nature and significance of a problem first, and then provide justification for a proposed solution.

program evaluation presentation A report on a program's mission with a description of its accomplishments and how they were measured, and conclusions on how well or poorly the program has met its stated objectives

progress report A report that updates clients or principals on developments in an ongoing project.

pronunciation The formation of word sounds.

proof (also called "rhetorical proof") In classical terms, a persuasive appeal based on *ethos*, *pathos*, or *logos* or some combination of these.

prop Any live or inanimate object used by a speaker as a presentation aid.

propaganda Information represented in such a way as to provoke a desired response.

proposal A presentation that recommends a product, procedure, or policy to a client or company.

prototype A model of a design.

psychographics The study and analysis of audience members' attitudes, beliefs, and values as they relate to the topic under investigation.

public discourse Open conversation or discussion in a public forum.

public domain Bodies of work, including publications and processes, available for public use without permission; not protected by copyright or patent.

public forum Any space (physical or virtual) in which people gather to voice their ideas about public issues.

public speaking A type of communication in which the speaker delivers a message with a specific purpose to an audience of people who are physically present during the delivery of the speech. Public speaking always includes a speaker who has a reason for speaking, an audience that gives the speaker its attention, and a message that is meant to accomplish a purpose.

public speaking anxiety (PSA) Fear or anxiety associated with a speaker's actual or anticipated communication to an audience.

quality improvement proposal A type of presentation delivered by persons in the allied health professions in which the speaker recommends the adoption of a health practice or policy.

questionnaire A written survey designed to gather information from a large pool of respondents. See also *open-ended* and *closed-ended questions.*

real-time presentation A presentation broadcast at the time of delivery via the Internet; real-time presentations connect the presenter and audience live and at the same time. See also *synchronous communication.*

reasoning Drawing inferences or conclusions from evidence.

receiver The recipient (an individual or a group) of a source's message.

recency effect Psychological principle in which listeners have a better recall of the most recent points in the speech (unless the ideas made earlier are far more striking than the others).

reckless disregard for the truth Statements made with the awareness that they are false; this form of speech is illegal. See also *slander.*

recorded presentation A presentation in which speaker and audience are separated by time and space and the presentation is stored and played back from a digital medium. See also *asynchronous communication.*

red herring fallacy A fallacy of reasoning in which the speaker relies on irrelevant information to support an argument.

refutation pattern of arrangement A pattern of organizing speech points in which each main point addresses and then refutes (disproves) an opposing claim to the speaker's position.

report A presentation that includes a systematic and objective description of facts and observations related to business or professional interests; it may or may not contain recommendations.

reportage An account of the who, what, where, when, and why of the facts.

request for funding presentation An oral presentation that provides evidence that a project, proposal, or design idea is worth funding; it is frequently delivered in such technical fields as engineering, computer science, and architecture.

research presentation An oral presentation describing original research undertaken by the speaker, either alone or as part of a team; frequently delivered in scientific and social scientific fields. Also called "scientific talk" and "oral scientific presentation."

respect To feel or show deferential regard. For the ethical speaker, respect ranges from addressing audience members as unique human beings to refraining from rudeness and other forms of personal attack.

responsibility A charge, trust, or duty for which one is accountable.

review of the literature presentation An oral presentation in which the speaker reviews the body of research related to a given topic or issue and offers conclusions about the topic based on this research; it is frequently delivered in social scientific fields.

rhetoric The practice of oratory, or public speaking. More broadly, the term has multiple meanings, all of which relate to an aspect of human communication.

rhetorical device A technique of language to achieve a desired effect.

rhetorical question A question that does not invite an actual response but is used to make the audience think.

rhetorical situation The circumstances that call for a public response and for the speech itself; in broad terms, consideration of the audience, occasion, and overall speech situation when planning a speech.

roast A humorous tribute to a person, one in which a series of speakers jokingly poke fun at the individual being honored.

roman numeral outline A form of outline in which main points are enumerated with uppercase roman numerals (I, II, III, . . .), supporting points are enumerated with capital letters (A, B, C, . . .), third-level points are enumerated with Arabic numerals (1, 2, 3, . . .), and fourth-level points are enumerated with lowercase letters (a, b, c, . . .).

rules-based ethics An approach to ethical standards that focuses on our duty to do what is inherently right, as established in widely accepted moral rules or norms.

rules of engagement Standards of conduct for communicating with others in the public arena, including speaking the truth, listening, and responding civilly.

sales presentation (sales pitch) A type of oral presentation that attempts to lead a potential buyer to purchase a service or product described by the presenter.

scale question A closed-ended question that measures the respondent's level of agreement or disagreement with specific issues.

scanning A technique for creating eye contact with audiences; the speaker moves his or her gaze across an audience from one listener to another and from one section to another, pausing to gaze briefly at individual listeners.

screencast (also called *video screen capture*) A video recording ("capture") of whatever is on a computer screen that allows the presenter to show all of the actions that are happening on the screen while he or she narrates.

secondary source Analysis or commentary about things not directly observed or created; news, commentary, analysis, and scholarship found in books, articles, and a myriad of sources other than the original. See also *primary source.*

selective perception A psychological principle that posits that listeners pay attention selectively to certain messages and ignore others.

sentence outline An outline in which each main and supporting point is stated in sentence form; generally used for working outlines. See also *key-word outline* and *phrase outline.*

service learning presentation Presentation in which students report on how they helped to address a need or problem in a community agency or nonprofit organization.

shared meaning The mutual understanding of a message between speaker and audience.

shift report An oral presentation by health care workers that concisely relays patient status and needs to incoming caregivers.

simile A figure of speech used to compare one thing with another by using the word *like* or *as* (e.g., "He works *like* a dog"). See also *metaphor.*

six-by-six rule A rule of design suggesting having no more than six words in a line and six lines or bullet points per slide or other kind of visual aid.

slander Defamatory speech.

slippery slope A logical fallacy in which one instance of an event is offered as leading to a series of events or actions.

small group A group that consists of between three and twenty people as opposed to a large public audience.

small group communication Communication involving a small number of people who can see and speak directly with one another, as in a business meeting.

social roles Roles that reflect individual group members' personality traits and function to help facilitate effective group interaction.

socioeconomic status (SES) A cluster of demographic characteristics of audience members, including income, occupation, and education.

source The source, or sender, is the person who creates a message. The speaker transforms ideas and thoughts into messages and sends them to a receiver, or an audience.

source credibility A contemporary term for *ethos*; refers to our level of trust in a source's credentials and track record for providing accurate information.

source qualifier A brief description of the source's qualifications to address the topic (e.g., "Pulitzer-Prize–winning author," "researcher at the Mayo Clinic").

spatial pattern of arrangement A pattern of organizing main points in order of their physical proximity or direction relative to each other; it is used when the purpose of a speech is to describe or explain the physical arrangement of a place, a scene, or an object.

speaking extemporaneously A type of delivery that falls somewhere between impromptu and written or memorized deliveries. Speakers delivering an extemporaneous speech prepare well and practice in advance, giving full attention to all facets of the speech—content, arrangement, and delivery. Instead of memorizing or writing the speech word for word, they speak from a *key-word outline* or *phrase outline*.

speaking from manuscript A style of delivery in which the speaker reads the speech verbatim—that is, from a prepared written text (either on paper or on a TelePrompTer) containing the entire speech.

speaking from memory A type of delivery in which the speaker puts the entire speech, word for word, into writing and then commits it to memory.

speaking impromptu A type of delivery that is unpracticed, spontaneous, or improvised.

speaking outline A delivery outline to be used when practicing and actually presenting a speech.

speaking rate The pace at which a speech is delivered. The typical public speech occurs at a rate slightly less than 120 words per minute.

special occasion speech A speech whose general purpose is to entertain, celebrate, commemorate, inspire, or set a social agenda.

specific speech purpose A statement of precisely what you want the audience to gain from the speech: "To inform (or persuade) my audience about the factors to consider when purchasing an electric car." See also *general speech purpose*.

speculative claim A type of *claim of fact* that addresses questions for which answers are not yet available.

speech codes University regulations prohibiting expressions on campus that would be constitutionally protected in society at large.

speech context Anything that influences the speaker, the audience, the occasion — and thus, ultimately, the speech (see also *rhetorical situation*).

speech of acceptance A special occasion speech made in response to receiving an award. Its purpose is to express gratitude for the honor bestowed on the speaker.

speech of inspiration A special occasion speech whose purpose is to inspire or motivate the audience to positively consider, reflect on, and sometimes even act on the speaker's words.

speech of introduction A special occasion short speech defined by two goals: to prepare or "warm up" audience members for the main speaker and to motivate them to listen to what that speaker has to say.

speech of presentation A special occasion speech whose purpose is twofold: to communicate the meaning of an award and to explain why the recipient is receiving it.

staff report A presentation that informs managers and other employees of new developments relating to personnel that affect them and their work.

statistic Quantified evidence; data that measures the size or magnitude of something, demonstrates trends, or shows relationships with the purpose of summarizing information, demonstrating proof, and making points memorable.

stereotype A generalization about an apparent characteristic of a group, culture, or ethnicity that falsely claims to define all of its members.

story See *narrative*.

style The specific word choices and rhetorical devices (techniques of language) speakers use to express their ideas and achieve their speech purpose.

subject guide A collection of article databases, reference works, websites, and other resources for a particular subject.

subject heading A term used to describe and group related material in a library catalog, database, or subject guide.

substantive warrant A warrant that relies on factual evidence to link a claim to evidence. See also *warrant by analogy* and *warrant by cause.*

summary (of supporting material) A brief overview of someone else's ideas, opinions, or theories. See also *direct quotation* and *paraphrase.*

supporting material Examples, narratives, testimony, facts, and statistics that support the speech thesis and form the speech.

supporting points Information (examples, narratives, testimony, and facts and statistics) that clarifies, elaborates, and verifies the speaker's assertions.

sympathetic audience An audience that already shares much agreement with the speaker; one of four types of potential audiences that persuasive speakers may encounter.

synchronous communication Communication in which people exchange messages simultaneously, in real time. See also *real-time presentation.*

table A systematic grouping of data or numerical information in column format.

talking head A speaker who remains static, standing stiffly behind a podium, and so resembles a televised shot of a speaker's head and shoulders.

target audience Those individuals within the broader audience who are most likely to be influenced in the direction the speaker seeks.

task roles Types of roles that directly relate to the accomplishment of the objectives and missions of a group. Examples include "recording secretary" and "moderator."

TelePrompTer A device that contains a magnified script of a speech; it is commonly used when a speaker's remarks are televised.

testimony Firsthand findings, eyewitness accounts, and opinions by people, both lay (nonexpert) and expert.

thesis statement The theme, or central idea, of a speech that serves to connect all the parts of the speech in a single line. The main points, supporting material, and the conclusion all bear upon the thesis.

toast A brief tribute to a person or an event being celebrated.

topic mapping Also called "mind mapping." A brainstorming technique in which you lay out words in diagram form to show categorical relationships among them; a technique useful for selecting and narrowing a speech topic.

topical pattern of arrangement (also called *categorical pattern*) A pattern of organizing main points as subtopics or categories of the speech topic; of all organizational patterns, this one offers the most freedom to order speech points as desired.

trait anxiety A person's general baseline level of anxiety. People with high trait anxiety are naturally anxious much of the time, whereas people with low trait anxiety will usually experience nervousness only in novel situations.

transitions (connectives) Words, phrases, or sentences that tie speech ideas together and enable a speaker to move smoothly from one point to the next.

trustworthiness The quality of displaying both honesty and dependability.

two-sided message An argument in which the speaker mentions opposing points of view and sometimes refutes them. See also *one-sided message.*

uncertainty avoidance The extent to which people feel threatened by ambiguity.

understatement A figure of speech in which a speaker draws attention to an idea by minimizing its importance (e.g., "Flunking out of college might be a problem").

uninformed, less educated, or apathetic audience An audience that knows or cares little about a specific topic.

values Our most enduring judgments or standards of what's important to us (e.g., equal opportunity, democracy, change and progress, or perseverance).

video capture software Software that allows you to incorporate video clips into an online presentation.

virtue ethics An approach to ethical standards that emphasizes the role of individual moral character in guiding ethical decisions.

visualization The practice of summoning feelings and actions consistent with successful performance; useful for speakers in overcoming speech anxiety

vocal fillers Unnecessary and undesirable phrases or utterances that are used by a speaker to cover pauses in a speech or conversation, such as "uh," "hmm," "you know," "I mean," and "it's like."

vocal variety The variation of volume, pitch, rate, and pauses to create an effective delivery.

vodcast (also called *vidcast* and *video podcasting*) A podcast containing video clips.

voice The feature of verbs in written and spoken text that indicates the subject's relationship to the action; verbs can be either active or passive.

volume The relative loudness of a speaker's voice while giving a speech.

voluntary audience As opposed to a *captive audience*, an audience whose members have chosen to attend the speech event.

warrant by analogy (also called *reasoning by analogy*) A means of justifying a claim by comparing two similar cases and implying that what is true for one case is true in the other.

warrant by cause (also called *causal reasoning*) A means of justifying a claim on the basis of providing a cause-effect relationship as proof of the claim.

webinar Real-time presentations, including training sessions, seminars, and other presentations that connect presenters and audiences from their desktops, regardless of where they are in the world.

word association A brainstorming technique in which one writes down ideas as they come to mind, beginning with a single word; used to generate and narrow speech topics.

working outline A preparation or rough outline, often using full sentences, in which the speaker firms up and organizes speech points and incorporates supporting material to support them.

Notes

Chapter 1

1. "Why Warren Buffett's Most Valuable Skill Wasn't from a Diploma," Fox on Stocks, December 19, 2012, accessed August 13, 2013, at www.foxonstocks.com/why-warren-buffetts-most-valuable0skill-wasn't-from-a-diploma/.
2. "It Takes More than a Major: Employer Priorities for College Learning and Student Success," Hart Research Associates (on behalf of The Association of American Colleges and Universities), April 10, 2013, accessed June 13, 2016, at www.aacu.org/leap/documents/2013_EmployerSurvey.pdf.
3. Pew Research Center, "U.S. Voters Trail Most Developed Countries," May 6, 2015, www.pewresearch.org/fact-tank/2015/05/06/u-s-voter-turnout-trails-most-developed-countries/.
4. Zoltan L. Hajnal, "Where Does America's Low Voter Turnout Matter the Most? In Local Elections," *Washington Post*, March 24, 2015.
5. For a discussion of conversation stoppers and rules of engagement, see W. Barnett Pearce, "Toward a National Conversation about Public Issues," in *The Changing Conversation in America: Lectures from the Smithsonian*, eds. William F. Eadie and Paul E. Nelson (Thousand Oaks, CA: Sage, 2002), 16.
6. Nick Damiris and Helga Wild, "The Internet. A New Agora?" in *An Ethical Global Information Society: Culture and Democracy Revisited*, eds. J. Baleur and D. Whitehouse (Boston: Kluwer Publishing, 1997).
7. James L. Golden, Goodwin F. Berquist, William E. Coleman, and J. Michael Sproule, *The Rhetoric of Western Thought: From the Mediterranean World to the Global Setting*, 8th ed. (Dubuque, IA: Kendall/Hunt, 2003), 37–43.
8. Robert Perrin, "The Speaking-Writing Connection: Enhancing the Symbiotic Relationship," *Contemporary Education* 65 (1994): 62–64.
9. Kristine Bruss, "Writing for the Ear: Strengthening Oral Style in Manuscript Speeches," *Communication Teacher* 26, no. 2 (April 2012): 76–81.
10. David C. Thomas and Kerr Inkson, *Cultural Intelligence: People Skills for a Global Business* (San Francisco: Berrett-Koehler Publishers, 2004), 14.
11. Lloyd F. Bitzer, "The Rhetorical Situation," *Philosophy and Rhetoric* (Winter 1968): 1–14.

Chapter 3

1. Erica Crome and Andrew J. Baillie, "Mild to Severe Social Fears: Ranking Types of Feared Social Situations Using Item Response Theory," *Journal of Anxiety Disorders* 28 (2014): 471–479.
2. Matthew Jacobs, "Celebrities with Stage Fright Include Adele, Hayden Panettiere, Barbra Streisand, Megan Fox, and Many More," *The Huffington Post*, April 5, 2013, accessed July 20, 2013, www.huffingtonpost.com/2013/04/05/celebrities-with-stage-fright_n_3022146.html.
3. Michael J. Beatty, "Situational and Predispositional Correlates of Public Speaking Anxiety," *Communication Education* 37 (1988): 28–39; Ralph Behnke and Chris R. Sawyer, "Milestones of Anticipatory Public Speaking Anxiety," *Communication Education* 48 (April 1999): 165–72.
4. Graham D. Bodie, "A Racing Heart, Rattling Knees, and Ruminative Thoughts: Defining, Explaining, and Treating Public Speaking Anxiety," *Communication Education* 59 (2010): 70–105.

5. Alexander M. Goberman, Stephanie Hughes, and Todd Haydock, "Acoustic Characteristics of Public Speaking: Anxiety and Practice Effects," *Speech Communication* 53 (2011): 867–76.
6. Paul L. Witt and Ralph R. Behnke, "Anticipatory Speech Anxiety as a Function of Public Speaking Assignment Type," *Communication Education* 55 (2006): 167–77.
7. Graham D. Bodie, "A Racing Heart, Rattling Knees, and Ruminative Thoughts: Defining, Explaining, and Treating Public Speaking Anxiety."
8. Brigitte Hertz, Peter Kerkhof, and Cees van Woerkum, "PowerPoint Slides as Speaking Notes: The Influence of Speaking Anxiety on the Use of Text on Slides," *Business and Professional Communication Quarterly* 79 (2016): 1–12.
9. Christine Kane, "Overcoming Stage Fright—Here's What to Do," *Christinekane* (blog), April 24, 2007, http://christinekane.com/blog/overcoming-stage-fright-heres-what-to-do/.
10. Behnke and Sawyer, "Milestones of Anticipatory Public Speaking Anxiety."
11. David-Paul Pertaub, Mel Slater, and Chris Barker, "An Experiment on Public Speaking Anxiety in Response to Three Different Types of Virtual Audience," *Presence: Teleoperators and Virtual Environments* 11 (2002): 670–78.
12. Lenny Laskowski, "Overcoming Speaking Anxiety in Meetings and Presentations," Speakers Platform website, accessed July 26, 2007, www.speaking.com/articles_html/LennyLaskowski_532.html.
13. John Robert Colombo, "Speech Anxiety: Overcoming the Fear of Public Speaking," SpeechCoachforExecutives.com, accessed July 25, 2007, www.speechcoachforexecutives.com/speech_anxiety.html.
14. Ibid.
15. Shi et al.
16. Michael T. Motley, "Public Speaking Anxiety qua Performance Anxiety: A Revised Model and Alternative Therapy," *Journal of Social Behavior and Personality* 5 (1990): 85–104.
17. Joe Ayres, Chia-Fang "Sandy" Hsu, and Tim Hopf, "Does Exposure to Visualization Alter Speech Preparation Processes?" *Communication Research Reports* 17 (2000): 366–74.
18. Elizabeth Quinn, "Visualization in Sport: Imagery Can Improve Performance," About.com: SportsMedicine, accessed August 29, 2007, http://sportsmedicine.about.com/cs/sport_psych/a/aa091700a.htm; and Joe Ayres and Tim Hopf, "Visualization: Is It More Than Extra Attention?" *Communication Education* 38 (1989): 1–5.
19. Joe Ayers and Tim Hopf, *Coping with Speech Anxiety* (Norwood, NJ: Ablex, 1993).
20. U.S. Department of Health and Human Services, "Etiology of Anxiety Disorders," Chapter 4, "Adults and Mental Health," in *Mental Health: A Report of the Surgeon General,* U.S. Department of Health and Human Services, 1999, accessed May 30, 2010, www.surgeongeneral.gov/library/mentalhealth/chapter4/sec2_1.html.
21. Herbert Benson and Miriam Z. Klipper, *The Relaxation Response* (New York: Harper Collins, 2000).
22. Mayo Clinic Staff, "Relaxation Techniques: Learn Ways to Calm Your Stress," MayoClinic.com, accessed May 30, 2010, www.mayoclinic.com/health/relaxation-technique/SR00007.
23. Christine Kane, "Overcoming Stage Fright—Here's What to Do."
24. Lars-Gunnar Lundh, Britta Berg, Helena Johansson, Linda Kjellén Nilsson, Jenny Sandberg, and Anna Segerstedt, "Social Anxiety Is Associated with a Negatively Distorted Perception of One's Own Voice," *Cognitive Behavior Therapy* 31 (2002): 25–30.

Chapter 4

1. Modified from Andrew D. Wolvin and Carolyn G. Coakley, "A Listening Taxonomy," in *Perspectives on Listening*, eds. Andrew D. Wolvin and Carolyn G. Coakley (Norwood, NJ: Ablex, 1993), 15–22.
2. Laura A. Janusik and Andrew D. Wolvin, "24 Hours in a Day: Listening Update to the Time Studies," *International Journal of Listening* 23 (2009): 104–20; see also Richard

Emanuel, Jim Adams, Kim Baker, E. K. Daufin, Coke Ellington, Elizabeth Fitts et al., "How College Students Spend Their Time Communicating," *International Journal of Listening* 22 (2008): 13–28.

3. Joann Keyton, Jennifer M. Caputo, Emily A. Ford, Rong Fu, Samantha A. Leibowitz, Tingting Liu et al., "Investigating Verbal Workplace Communication Behaviors," *Journal of Business Communication* 50, no. 3 (2013): 152–69.
4. Avraham N. Kluger and Keren Zaidel, "Are Listeners Perceived as Leaders?" *International Journal of Listening* 27, no. 2 (2013): 73–84; S. A. Welch and William T. Mickelson, "A Listening Competence Comparison of Working Professionals," *International Journal of Listening* 27, no. 2 (2013): 85–99.
5. Laura A. Janusik, "Listening Pedagogy: Where Do We Go from Here?" in *Listening and Human Communication in the Twenty-First Century*, ed. Andrew D. Wolvin (Boston: Wiley-Blackwell, 2010), 193–224.
6. Donald L. Rubin, Teresa Hafer, and Kevin Arata, "Reading and Listening to Oral-Based versus Literate-Based Discourse," *Communication Education* 49, no. 2 (2000): 121–33.
7. "Noise-Induced Hearing Loss," Centers for Disease Control and Prevention, August 12, 2016, www.cdc.gov/healthyyouth/noise/.
8. "An ILA Definition of Listening," *The Listening Post* 53, no. 1 (1995): 4–5.
9. Ethel Glenn, "A Content Analysis of Fifty Definitions of Listening," *Journal of the International Listening Association* 3 (1989): 21–31.
10. Albert H. Hastorf and Hadley Cantril, *Journal of Abnormal and Social Psychology* 49, no. 1 (1954): 129–34; Gordon W. Allport, and Lee J. Postman, "The Basic Psychology of Rumor," *Transactions of the New York Academy of Sciences* 8 (1945): 61–81.
11. Thomas E. Anastasi Jr., *Listen! Techniques for Improving Communication Skills* (Boston: CBI Publishing, 1982); thanks to Barry Antokoletz of New York City College of Technology for suggesting the inclusion of these strategies.
12. Ronald D. Gordon, "Communication, Dialogue, and Transformation," *Human Communication* 9, no. 1 (2006): 17–30.
13. James Floyd, "Provocation: Dialogic Listening as Reachable Goal," *International Journal of Listening* 24 (2010): 170–73.

Chapter 5

1. Michael Josephson, in discussion with the author, May 10, 1996, and May 23, 2013.
2. *Oxford English Dictionary Online*, s. v. "responsibility," accessed June 17, 2013, www.oed.com/view/Entry/163862?redirectedFrom=responsibility.
3. Adapted from Richard L. Johannesen, Kathleen S. Valde, and Karen E. Whedbee, *Ethics in Human Communication* (Long Grove, IL: Waveland Press, 2007).
4. Cited in Edward P. J. Corbett, *Classical Rhetoric for the Modern Student* (New York: Oxford University Press, 1999): 71–77.
5. Shalom H. Schwartz, "An Overview of the Schwartz Theory of Basic Values," *Online Readings in Psychology and Culture* 2, no. 1 (2012), http://dx.doi.org/10.9707/2307-0919.1116.
6. "Trends in American Values: 1987–2012," Pew Center for People and the Press, June 4, 2012, www.people-press.org/files/legacy-pdf/06-04-12%20Values%20Release.pdf.
7. Ibid.
8. Stephen J. A. Ward, "Ethics in a Nutshell," School of Journalism and Mass Communication, University of Madison–Wisconsin, accessed August 10, 2013, http://ethics.journalism.wisc.edu/resources/ethics-in-a-nutshell/.
9. Quoted in Josh Chafetz, "The Political Animal and the Ethics of Constitutional Commitment," *Harvard Law Review Forum* 124, no. 1 (2011).
10. Walter Barnett Pearce, "Toward a National Conversation about Public Issues," in *The Changing Conversation in America: Lectures from the Smithsonian*, eds. William F. Eadie and Paul E. Nelson (Thousand Oaks, CA: Sage, 2002), 16.
11. Douglas M. Fraleigh and Joseph S. Tuman, *Freedom of Speech in the Marketplace of Ideas* (New York: Bedford/St. Martin's, 1997).

12. "Frequently Asked Questions about Speech" First Amendment Center, May 9, 2016, www.firstamendmentcenter.org/faq/frequently-asked-questions-speech.
13. Ibid.
14. William Gudykunst, Stella Ting-Toomey, Sandra Suweeks, and Leah Stewart, *Building Bridges: Interpersonal Skills for a Changing World* (Boston: Houghton Mifflin, 1995), 92.
15. Michael Josephson, *Making Ethical Decisions: The Six Pillars of Character* (Josephson Institute of Ethics, 2002).
16. Josephson, *Making Ethical Decisions.*
17. Rebecca Moore Howard, "A Plagiarism Pentimento," *Journal of Teaching Writing* 11 (1993): 233.
18. Vance, Noelle, "Cross-Cultural Perspectives on Source Referencing and Plagiarism," Research Starters Education: Academic Topic Overviews, accessed October 19, 2016, http://subjectguides.wcupa.edu/ld.php?content_id=2185825.
19. U.S. Copyright Office website, accessed May19, 2016, www.copyright.gov.

Chapter 6

1. For a useful overview of the history of attitudes and attitude change, see Pablo Briñol and Richard E. Petty, "The History of Attitudes and Persuasion Research," in *Handbook of the History of Social Psychology*, eds. Arie Kruglanski and Wolfgang Stroebe (New York: Psychology Press, 2011).
2. Richard E. Petty and John T. Cacioppo, *Attitudes and Persuasion: Classic and Contemporary Approaches* (Dubuque, IA: Wm. C. Brown, 1981); M. Fishbein and I. Ajzen, *Belief, Attitude, Intention, and Behavior: An Introduction to Theory and Research* (Reading, MA: Addison-Wesley, 1975); I. Ajzen and M. Fishbein, "The Influence of Attitudes on Behavior," in *The Handbook of Attitudes*, eds. Dolores Albarracín, Blair T. Johnson, and Mark P. Zanna (Mahwah, NJ: Erlbaum, 2005), 173–221.
3. Richard E. Petty, S. Christian Wheeler, and Zakary L. Tormala, "Persuasion and Attitude Change," in *Handbook of Psychology, Personality, and Social Psychology*, Vol. 5, eds. Theodore Millon, Melvin Lerner, and Irving B. Weiner (New York: John Wiley & Sons, 2003).
4. *The Stanford Encyclopedia of Philosophy*, s.v. "Belief," Winter 2011 edition, http://plato.stanford.edu/archives/win2011/entries/belief/.
5. Edward D. Steele and W. Charles Redding, "The American Value System: Premises for Persuasion," *Western Speech* 26 (1962): 83–91; Robin M. Williams Jr., *American Society: A Sociological Interpretation*, 3rd ed. (New York: Alfred A. Knopf, 1970).
6. Hannah Fingerhut, "Support Steady for Same-Sex Marriage and Acceptance of Homosexuality," Pew Research Center FactTank, May 12, 2016, www.pewresearch.org/fact-tank/2016/05/12/support-steady-for-same-sex-marriage-and-acceptance-of-homosexuality/
7. "Human Values and Nature's Future: Americans' Attitudes on Biological Diversity," BlueStem Communications, accessed January 22, 2014, http://bluestemcommunications.org/changing-behaviors-not-minds-a-communications-workshop/
8. Herbert Simon, *Persuasion in Society*, 2nd ed. (New York: Routledge, 2011).
9. Ibid.
10. Kenneth Burke, *A Rhetoric of Motives* (Berkeley, CA: University of California Press, 1969).
11. Hillary Rodham Clinton, "Abortion Is a Tragedy," *Vital Speeches of the Day* 71, no. 9 (2005): 266–70.
12. Kim Parker, "The Big Generation Gap at the Polls Is Echoed in Attitudes on Budget Tradeoffs," Pew Research Social and Demographic Trends, December 20, 2012, www.pewsocialtrends.org/2012/12/20/the-big-generation-gap-at-the-polls-is-echoed-in-attitudes-on-budget-tradeoffs.
13. Jere R. Behrman and Nevzer Stacey, eds., *The Social Benefits of Going to College* (Ann Arbor, MI: University of Michigan Press, 2000).

14. "America's Changing Religious Landscape," Pew Research Center, May 12, 2015, www.pewforum.org/2015/05/12/americas-changing-religious-landscape/.
15. Ibid.
16. Daniel Canary and Kathryn Dindia, eds., *Sex Differences and Similarities in Communication*, 2nd ed. (Mahwah, NJ: Lawrence Erlbaum, 2006).
17. U.S. Census Bureau Newsroom, June 2, 2016, www.census.gov/newsroom/facts-for-features/2016/cb16-ff12.html (accessed Sept. 6, 2016).
18. U.S. Department of Education, National Center for Education Statistics. (2016). *Digest of Education Statistics, 2014* (2016-006), Chapter 3. Retrieved September 6, 2016, from https://nces.ed.gov/fastfacts/display.asp?id=60.
19. U.S. Census Bureau Newsroom, June 2, 2016, www.census.gov/newsroom/facts-forfeatures/2016/cb16-ff12.html (accessed Sept. 6, 2016).
20. "Statistical Portrait of the Foreign-Born Population of the United States," Pew Research Center, April 16, 2016, www.pewhispanic.org/2016/04/19/statistical-portrait-of-the-foreign-born-population-in-the-united-states-key-charts/.
21. Ibid.
22. "Fact Sheet: Bureau of Intelligence and Research," U.S. Department of State, July 22, 2016, www.state.gov/s/inr/rls/4250.htm
23. Inter-University Consortium for Political and Social Research, *World Values Survey, 1981–1984 and 1990–1993* (Irvine, CA: Social Science Data Archives, University Libraries, University of California, 1997). The 1990 World Values Survey covers four Asian countries (China, India, Japan, and South Korea) and eighteen Western countries.
24. Geert Hofstede, Gert Jan Hofsted, and Michael Minkov, *Culture and Organizations: Software of the Mind*, 3rd ed. (New York: McGraw Hill, 2010). (Kindle edition)
25. Rushworth M. Kidder, *Shared Values for a Troubled World: Conversations with Men and Women of Conscience* (San Francisco: Jossey-Bass Publishers, 1994).

Chapter 7

1. Yogi Berra Quotes on BrainyQuote, accessed January 22, 2014, www.brainyquote.com/quotes/quotes/y/yogiberra124868.html.

Chapter 8

1. Yaacov Schul and Ruth Mayo, "Two Sources Are Better Than One: The Effects of Ignoring One Message on Using a Different Message from the Same Source," *Journal of Experimental Social Psychology* 35 (1999): 327–45; Mike Allen, Rebecca Bruflat, Renée Fucilla, Michael Kramer, Steve McKellips, Daniel J. Ryan et al., "Testing the Persuasiveness of Evidence: Combining Narrative and Statistical Forms," *Communication Research Reports* 17 (2000): 331–36. Cited in Rodney Reynolds and J. Lynn Reynolds, "Evidence," in *The Persuasion Handbook: Developments in Theory and Practice*, eds. James P. Dillard and Michael Pfau (Thousand Oaks, CA: Sage, 2002), 427–44, doi:10.4135/9781412976046.n22.
2. Ian McEwan, "Freedom of Expression Sustains All Other Freedoms We Enjoy," Speech delivered at Dickinson College, Carlise, PA, May 17, 2015, *Vital Speeches of the Day*, Vol XXXI, No. 8, August 2015, pp. 245–47.
3. Jonathan Drori, "Every Pollen Grain Has a Story" (TED Talk, April 2010), www.ted.com/talks/jonathan_drori_every_pollen_grain_has_a_story.html.
4. Quoted in Katharine Q. Seelye, "Congressman Offers Bill to Ban Cloning of Humans," *New York Times*, March 6, 1997, sec. A.
5. Mark Turner, *The Literary Mind* (New York: Oxford University Press, 1996).
6. Ibid.
7. Nick Morgan, "Why You Must Tell Stories, Not Dump Information, in Your Presentations," *Forbes*, May 9, 2013, accessed May 18, 2016, www.forbes.com/sites/nickmorgan/2013/05/09/why-you-must-tell-stories-not-dump-information-in-your-presentations/#426926dd78bb.

8. Kurt Braddock and James Price Dillard, "Meta-analytic Evidence for the Persuasive Effect of Narratives on Beliefs, Attitudes, Intentions, and Behaviors," *Communication Monographs*, 2016, doi:10.1080/03637
9. Melinda French Gates, "Raising the Bar on College Completion" (keynote address, American Association of Community Colleges, April 20, 2010), www.gatesfoundation.org/media-center/speeches/2010/04/raising-the-bar-on-college-completion.
10. Steven D. Cohen, "The Art of Public Narrative: Teaching Students How to Construct Memorable Anecdotes," *Communication Teacher* 25, no. 4 (2011): 197–204, doi:10.1080/17404622.2011.601726
11. Jim Carrey, Commencement Address, Maharishi University of Management, May 24, 2014, www.mum.edu/whats-happening/graduation-2014/full-jim-carrey-address-video-and-transcript/.
12. Derek P. Ellerman, "Testimony to Subcommittee on Human Rights and Wellness, Committee on Government Reform," U.S. House of Representatives, July 8, 2004, www.polarisproject.org/what-we-do/policy-advocacy/national-policy/congressional-testimony/congressional-testimony-2004-derek-ellerman.
13. Rodney A. Reynolds and J. Lynn Reynolds, "Evidence," in *The Persuasion Handbook: Developments in Theory and Practice*, eds. James P. Dillard and Michael Pfau (Thousand Oaks, CA: Sage, 2002), 427–44, doi:10.4135/9781412976046.n22.
14. Facebook, "Stats," Company Info, newsroom.fb.com/company-info/, accessed September 27, 2016.
15. "State and County QuickFacts," U.S. Census Bureau, accessed September 27, 2016, quickfacts.census.gov/qfd/states/08000.html.
16. Centers for Disease Control and Prevention, National Center for Health Statistics, "Multiple Cause of Death, 1999–2014," on CDC WONDER Online Database, released 2015. Extracted by ONDCP from wonder.cdc.gov/mcd-icd10.html on December 9, 2015.
17. "State and County QuickFacts."
18. U.S. Department of Labor, Bureau of Labor Statistics, Local Area Unemployment Statistics by State, www.bls.gov/web/laus/laumstrk.htm, September 20, 2016, accessed September 27, 2016.
19. Chuck Marr and Chye-Ching Huang, "Tax Foundation Figures Do Not Represent Typical Households' Tax Burdens," Center on Budget and Policy Priorities, April 2, 2013, www.cbpp.org/cms/index.cfm?fa=view&id=3946.

Chapter 9

1. Elizabeth E. Kirk, "Information and Its Counterfeits," Sheridan Libraries of Johns Hopkins University, 2001.
2. Ibid.

Chapter 10

1. M. L. McLaughlin, Michael J. Cody, and K. French, "Account-Giving and the Attribution of Responsibility: Impressions of Traffic Offenders," in *The Psychology of Tactical Communication*, eds. M. J. Cody and M. L. McLaughlin (Bristol, PA: Multilingual Matters, 1990), 244–67. Cited in Rodney Reynolds and J. Lynn Reynolds, "Evidence," in *The Persuasion Handbook: Developments in Theory and Practice*, eds. James P. Dillard and Michael Pfau (Thousand Oaks, CA: Sage, 2002), 427–44, doi:10.4135/9781412976046.n22.
2. Ibid.
3. Ralph Underwager and Hollida Wakefield, "The Taint Hearing" (presented at the 13th Annual Symposium in Forensic Psychology, Vancouver, BC, April 17, 1997), www.ipt-forensics.com/journal/volume10/j10_7.htm#en0.
4. Gretchen Livingston, "The Rise of Single Fathers," Pew Research Social and Demographic Trends, July 2, 2013, www.pewsocialtrends.org/2013/07/02/the-rise-of-single-fathers/.

Chapter 11

1. Ernest Thompson, "An Experimental Investigation of the Relative Effectiveness of Organization Structure in Oral Communication," *Southern Speech Journal* 26 (1960): 59–69; C. Spicer and R. E. Bassett, "The Effects of Organization on Learning from an Informative Message," *Southern Speech Journal* 41 (1976): 290–99.
2. Raymond G. Smith, "Effects of Speech Organization upon Attitudes of College Students," *Speech Monographs* 18 (1951): 292–301.
3. Harry Sharp Jr. and Thomas McClung, "Effects of Organization on the Speaker's Ethos," *Speech Monographs* 33 (1966): 182ff; Eldon E. Baker, "The Immediate Effects of Perceived Speaker Disorganization on Speaker Credibility and Audience Attitude Change in Persuasive Speaking," *Western Speech* 29 (1965): 148–61.
4. Gordon H. Bower, "Organizational Factors in Memory," *Cognitive Psychology* 1 (1970): 18–46.
5. Murray Glanzer and Anita R. Cunitz, "Two Storage Mechanisms in Free Recall," *Journal of Verbal Learning and Verbal Behavior* 5 (1966): 351–60.
6. Brandon Busteed and Julie Ray, "Former Student-Athletes Are Winners in Well-being," Gallup, February 17, 2016, www.gallup.com/poll/189206/former-student-athletes-winners.aspx#share-article-modal.

Chapter 12

1. Raymond G. Smith, "Effects of Speech Organization upon Attitudes of College Students," *Speech Monographs* 18 (1951): 547–49; and Ernest Thompson, "An Experimental Investigation of the Relative Effectiveness of Organizational Structure in Oral Communication," *Southern Speech Journal* 26 (1960): 59–69.
2. "Life on the Internet Timeline," Public Broadcasting System, accessed April 3, 2000, www.pbs.org/internet/timeline/index.html.
3. Anita Taylor, "Tales of the Grandmothers: Women and Work," *Vital Speeches of the Day* 71, no. 7 (2005): 209–12.

Notes for Table 12.1: One Topic Organized Six Ways:

1. Melissa Del Bosque, "Beyond the Border: Into the Wilderness," *The Guardian*, August 6, 2014, www.theguardian.com/world/ng-interactive/2014/aug/06/-sp-texas-border-deadliest-state-undocumented-migrants.
2. Randy Capps, Michael Fix, and Jie Zong, "A Profile of U.S. Children with Unauthorized Immigrant Parents," Migration Policy Institute Fact Sheet, January, 2016, www.migrationpolicy.org/research/profile-us-children-unauthorized-immigrant-parents.
3. Ibid.
4. Ibid.
5. Jie Zong and Jeanne Batalova, "Frequently Requested Statistics on Immigrants and Immigration in the United States," Migration Policy Institute, April 14, 2016, www.migrationpolicy.org/article/frequently-requested-statistics-immigrants-and-immigration-united-states.
6. "How the United States Immigration System Works: A Fact Sheet," American Immigration Council, March 1, 2014, www.immigrationpolicy.org/just-facts/how-united-states-immigration-system-works-fact-sheet.
7. "Enforcement Overdrive: A Comprehensive Assessment of ICE's Criminal Alien Program," American Immigration Council, November 2, 2015, www.immigrationpolicy.org/special-reports/enforcement-overdrive-comprehensive-assessment-criminal-alien-program.
8. Brian Eakin, "Homeland Security Grilled on Visa Overstays," Courthouse News Service, June 14, 2016, www.courthousenews.com/2016/06/14/homeland-security-grilled-on-visa-overstays.htm.
9. Ibid.

10. Joe Davidson, "Visa Overstays a Security Risk When 99% of Foreigners Leave U.S. on Time?," *Washington Post*, June 15, 2016, www.washingtonpost.com/news/powerpost/wp/2016/06/15/visa-overstays-a-security-risk-when-99-of-foreigners-leave-u-s-on-time/.

Chapter 13

1. For an enlightening review of the history of outlining from Cicero to electronic software, see Jonathan Price, "STOP: Light on the History of Outlining," *Journal of Computer Documentation* 23, no. 3 (1999): 69–78.
2. Mark B. McClellan (speech, fifth annual David A. Winston lecture, Washington, DC, October 20, 2003), www.fda.gov/oc/speeches/2003/winston1020.htmlwww.fda.gov/newsevents/speeches/speecharchives/ucm053609.htm.
3. Gratitude goes to Carolyn Clark, Ph.D., of Salt Lake Community College for sharing this assignment with us.

Chapter 14

1. Laurie Loisel, "Twitter Exec tells UMASS Amherst Grads to 'Hack the System'," Boston Globe, May 6, 2016, www.bostonglobe.com/metro/2016/05/06/twitter-exec-tells-umass-amherst-grads-hack-system/uAYypkmN3v1QlHMSsalyaJ/story.html.
2. William Safire, *Lend Me Your Ears: Great Speeches in History* (New York: Norton, 1992), 676.
3. Bas A. Andeweg, Jaap C. de Jong, and Hans Hoeken, "'May I Have Your Attention?': Exordial Techniques in Informative Oral Presentations," *Technical Communication Quarterly* 7 (2009): 271–84, doi:10.1080/10572259809364631.
4. Oprah Winfrey, (speech, 50th anniversary of March on Washington, DC, August 28, 2013), www.washingtonpost.com/politics/full-transcript-oprah-winfreys-speech-on-50th-anniversary-of-march-on-washington/2013/08/28/3fee1ba4-101d-11e3-8cdd-bcdc09410972_story.html.
5. James Oliver, "Teach Every Child about Food," Filmed February 2010, TED video, 21:53, www.ted.com/talks/jamie_oliver.
6. Charles A. Kiesler and Sara B. Kiesler, "Role of Forewarning in Persuasive Communication," *Journal of Abnormal and Social Psychology* 68 (1964): 547–69. Cited in James C. McCroskey, *An Introduction to Rhetorical Communication*, 8th ed. (Boston, MA: Allyn & Bacon, 2001), 253.
7. Marvin Runyon, "No One Moves the Mail Like the U.S. Postal Service," *Vital Speeches of the Day* 61, no. 2 (1994): 52–55.
8. Andeweg, de Jong, and Hoeken, "'May I Have Your Attention?'"
9. Robert L. Darbelnet, "U.S. Roads and Bridges: Highway Funding at a Crossroads," *Vital Speeches of the Day* 63, no. 12 (1997): 379.

Chapter 15

1. Holger Kluge, "Reflections on Diversity," *Vital Speeches of the Day* 63, no. 6 (1997): 171–72.
2. Elpidio Villarreal, "Choosing the Right Path," *Vital Speeches of the Day* 72, no. 26 (2007): 784–86.
3. Emma Watson, "Gender Equality Is Your Issue Too" (speech, United Nations, New York, NY, September 20, 2014).
4. Sue Suter, "Adapting to Change, While Holding on to Values: *Star Trek*'s Lessons for the Disability Community" (speech, Annual Conference of the Association for the Severely Handicapped, Springfield, IL, September 22, 1999).
5. James C. May (address, European Aviation Club, Brussels, Belgium, October 30, 2008), www.airlines.org/News/Speeches/Pages/speech_10-30-08May.aspx.
6. Barack Obama, "Remarks by the President in Address to the Nation on Immigration," The White House, November 20, 2014, www.whitehouse.gov/the-press-office/2014/11/20/remarks-president-address-nation-immigration.

Chapter 16

1. Bourree Lam, "What It Was Like to Write Speeches for Apple Executives," *The Atlantic*, June 10, 2016.
2. Kristine Bruss, "Writing for the Ear: Strengthening Oral Style in Manuscript Speeches," *Communication Teacher* 26, no. 2 (April 2012): 76–81.
3. Peggy Noonan, *Simply Speaking: How to Communicate Your Ideas with Style, Substance, and Clarity* (New York: Regan Books, 1998), 51.
4. William Safire, *Lend Me Your Ears: Great Speeches in History* (New York: Norton, 1992), 26.
5. Michelle Obama, "Remarks by the First Lady at the Democratic National Convention," delivered at the Wells Fargo Center, Philadelphia, PA. The White House Briefing Room, July 25, 2016.
6. Dan Hooley, "The Lessons of the Ring," *Vital Speeches of the Day* 70, no. 20 (2004): 660–63.
7. Sheryl Sandberg, "Why We Have Too Few Women Leaders" (TED Talk, December 2010), www.ted.com/talks/sheryl_sandberg_why_we_have_too_few_women_leaders.html.
8. Susan T. Fiske and Shelley E. Taylor, "Vivid Information Is More Easily Recalled Than Dull or Pallid Stimuli," *Social Cognition*, 2nd ed. (New York: McGraw Hill). Quoted in Jennifer Jerit and Jason Barabas, "Bankrupt Rhetoric: How Misleading Information Affects Knowledge about Social Security," *Public Opinion Quarterly* 70, no. 3 (2006): 278–304.
9. Loren J. Naidoo and Robert G. Lord, "Speech Imagery and Perceptions of Charisma: The Mediating Role of Positive Affect," *Leadership Quarterly* 19, no. 3 (2008): 283–96.
10. Ibid; phrase taken from President Franklin Delano Roosevelt's 1933 inaugural address.
11. L. Clemetson and J. Gordon-Thomas, "Our House Is on Fire," *Newsweek*, June 11, 2001, 50.
12. Andrew C. Billings, "Beyond the Ebonics Debate: Attitudes about Black and Standard American English," *Journal of Black Studies* 36 (2005): 68–81.
13. Sylvie Dubois, "Sounding Cajun: The Rhetorical Use of Dialect in Speech and Writing," *American Speech* 77, no. 3 (2002): 264–87.
14. Gloria Anzaldúa, "Entering into the Serpent," in *The St. Martin's Handbook*, 3rd ed., eds. Andrea Lunsford and Robert Connors (New York: St. Martin's Press, 1995), 25.
15. P. H. Matthews, *The Concise Oxford Dictionary of Linguistics* (New York: Oxford University Press, 1997).
16. "Inaugural Address by President Barack Obama," The White House, January 21, 2013, accessed November 1, 2013, www.whitehouse.gov/the-press-office/2013/01/21/inaugural-address-president-barack-obama.
17. Cited in William Safire, *Lend Me Your Ears: Great Speeches in History* (New York: Norton, 1992), 22.
18. "Barack Obama's New Hampshire Primary Speech," *New York Times*, January 8, 2008, www.nytimes.com/2008/01/08/us/politics/08text-obama.html?r=0.

Chapter 17

1. James A. Winans, *Public Speaking* (New York: Century, 1925). Professor Winans was among the first Americans to contribute significantly to the study of rhetoric. His explanation of delivery is considered by many to be the best coverage of the topic in the English language. His perspective infuses this chapter.
2. Judee K. Burgoon, Thomas Birk, and Michael Pfau, "Nonverbal Behaviors, Persuasion, and Credibility," *Human Communication Research* 17, no. 1 (1990): 140+, *Academic OneFile*.
3. Winans, *Public Speaking*, 17.
4. Thomas M. Conley, *Rhetoric in the European Tradition* (New York: Longman, 1990).
5. William Safire, PBS *NewsHour*, aired August 15, 1996 (Public Broadcasting System), www.pbs.org/newshour/gergen/july-dec96/safire_8-15.html.
6. Dan O'Hair, Rob Stewart, Hannah Rubenstein, Robbin Crabtree, and Robert Weissberg, *ESL Students in the Public Speaking Classroom: A Guide for Teachers* (Boston: Bedford/St. Martin's, 2012), 24.

Chapter 18

1. Kyle James Tusing and James Price Dillard, "The Sounds of Dominance: Vocal Precursors of Perceived Dominance during Interpersonal Influence," *Human Communication Research* 26 (2000): 148–71.
2. Gwen Moran, "6 Simple Ways to Improve the Way You Speak," Fast Company, accessed August 17, 2016, www.fastcompany.com/3035634/how-to-be-a-success-at-everything/6-simple-ways-to-improve-the-way-you-speak.
3. Caryl Raye Krannich, *101 Secrets of Highly Effective Speakers* (Manassas Park, VA: Impact Publications, 1998), 121–22.
4. Kenneth C. Crannell, *Voice and Articulation*, 4th ed. (Belmont, CA: Wadsworth, 2000), 41.
5. MaryAnn Cunningham Florez, "Improving Adult ESL Learners' Pronunciation Skills," National Clearinghouse for ESL Literacy Education, 1998, accessed October 27, 2013, resources.marshalladulteducation.org/pdf/briefs/ImprovingPronun.Florez.pdf.
6. The digitized audio of King's "I Have a Dream" speech can be accessed at American Rhetoric, www.americanrhetoric.com/speeches/mlkihaveadream.htm.

Chapter 19

1. Robert Rivlin and Karen Gravelle, *Deciphering the Senses: The Expanding World of Human Perception* (New York: Simon & Schuster, 1998), 98; see also Anne Warfield, "Do You Speak Body Language?" *Training & Development* 55, no. 4 (2001): 60.
2. A. Hawani, H. Melki, M. Mrayeh, M. Bouzid, N. Souissi, and M. Mrabet, "Impact of 'Body Language and Public Speaking' Training on Physical Education Trainees' Self-Efficacy Pedagoguique," *Creative Education* 7 (2016): 1861–68. doi:10.4236/ce.2016.714188.
3. C. F. Bond and the Global Deception Research Team, "A World of Lies," *Journal of Cross-Cultural Psychology* 37 (2006): 60–74; and Timothy R. Levine, Kelli Jean K. Asada, and Hee Sun Park, "The Lying Chicken and the Gaze Avoidant Egg: Eye Contact, Deception, and Causal Order," *Southern Communication Journal* 71 (2006): 401–11.
4. Ibid.
5. Eva Krumburger, "Effects of Dynamic Attributes of Smiles in Human and Synthetic Faces: A Simulated Job Interview Setting," *Journal of Nonverbal Behavior* 33 (2009): 1–15.
6. Alex Rister, "First Impressions: Nonverbal Communication Tips," Creating Communication: 21st Century Presentation and Communication Tips, December 22, 2011, accessed September 27, 2016, https://alexrister1.wordpress.com/2011/12/22/first-impressions-nonverbal-communication-tips/.
7. Laurie Schloff and Marcia Yudkin, *Smart Speaking* (New York: Plume, 1991), 108.
8. Alissa Melinger and Willem M. Levelt, "Gesture and the Communicative Intention of the Speaker," *Gesture* 4 (2004): 119–41.
9. Bonnie Ellis, "8/15—Are You Scared Speechless? Learn the Awareness and Control Method," *Integral Leadership Review* 14, no. 3 (2014): 10–14.
10. Albert Mehrabian, *Silent Messages* (Belmont, CA: Wadsworth, 1981); and Mike Allen, Paul L. Witt, and Lawrence R. Wheeless, "The Role of Teacher Immediacy as a Motivational Factor in Student Learning: Using Meta-Analysis to Test a Causal Model," *Communication Education* 55, no. 6 (2006): 21–31.
11. A. Sanow, "Improve Your Body Language," *American Speaker* 3 (2012), accessed August 30, 2016, via ebscohost.com.ezproxy.uky.edu.
12. L. Polevoi, "Four Tips for Advanced Public Speakers," *Managing People at Work* 370, no. 4 (2013).
13. J. P. Davidson, "Shaping an Image That Boosts Your Career," *Marketing Communications* 13 (1988): 55–56.
14. Carmine Gallo, *The Presentation Secrets of Steve Jobs* (New York: McGraw-Hill, 2009), 181.

Chapter 20

1. Richard E. Mayer, *The Multimedia Principle* (New York: Cambridge University Press, 2001).
2. See discussion of the redundancy effect in Richard E. Mayer, ed., *The Cambridge Handbook of Multimedia Learning* (New York: Cambridge University Press, 2005).
3. Gary Jones, "Message First: Using Films to Power the Point," *Business Communication Quarterly* 67, no. 1 (2004): 88–91.
4. Kulwadee M. Axtell, "The Effect of Presentation Software on Classroom Verbal Interaction and on Student Retention of Higher Education Lecture Content," *Journal of Technology in Teaching and Learning* 4, no. 1 (2008): 21–23.

Chapter 21

1. Nancy Duarte, "Avoiding the Road to Powerpoint Hell," *Wall Street Journal*, January 22, 2011; and Rebecca Worley, "Presentations and the PowerPoint Problem," *Business Communication Quarterly* 67, no. 1 (2004): 78–80.
2. Edward Tufte, *The Visual Display of Quantitative Information* (Graphics Press, 2001).
3. A. C. Moller, A. J. Elliot, and M. A. Maier, "Red Is for Failure and Green for Success: Achievement-Related Implicit Associations to Color," poster presented at the Society for Personality and Social Psychology Conference, Tampa, FL, February 2009.
4. Edward Tufte, The Visual Display of Quantitative Information (Graphics Press, 2001).
5. Ronald Larson, "Slide Composition for Electronic Presentations," *Journal of Educational Computing Research*, 31, no. 1 (2004): 61–76.

Chapter 22

1. Rebecca B. Worley and Marilyn A. Dyrud, "Presentations and the PowerPoint Problem," *Business Communication Quarterly* 67, no. 1 (2004): 78–80.
2. Dale Cyphert, "Presentation Technology in the Age of Electronic Eloquence: From Visual Aid to Visual Rhetoric," *Communication Education* 56, no. 2 (2007): 168–92; and Dale Cyphert, "The Problem of PowerPoint: Visual Aid or Visual Rhetoric?" *Business Communication Quarterly* 67, no. 1 (2004): 80–84. Jon Thomas, "PowerPoint Is Not the Problem with Presentations Today," Presentation Advisors, March 21, 2010, http://blog.presentationadvisors.com/presentationadvisors/2010/03/powerpoint-is-not-the-problem-with-presentations.html.

Chapter 23

1. Katherine E. Rowan subdivides informative communication into *informatory discourse*, in which the primary aim is to represent reality by increasing an audience's awareness of some phenomenon; and *explanatory discourse*, with the aim to represent reality by deepening understanding. See Katherine E. Rowan, "Informing and Explaining Skills: Theory and Research on Informative Communication," in *Handbook of Communication and Social Interaction Skills*, edited by John O. Greene and Brant R. Burleson (Mahwah, NJ: Erlbaum, 2003), 403–38.
2. Vickie K. Sullivan, "Public Speaking: The Secret Weapon in Career Development," *USA Today*, May 2005, 24.
3. Nick Morgan, "Two Rules for a Successful Presentation," *Harvard Business Review* Blog ("The Conversation"), May 14, 2010, blogs.hbr.org/2010/05/two-rules-for-a-successful-pre/; and Harry E. Chambers, *Effective Communication Skills for Scientific and Technical Professionals* (Cambridge, MA: Perseus Publishing, 2001).
4. Tina Blythe et al., *The Teaching for Understanding Guide* (Hoboken, NJ: Jossey-Bass, 1997); and Kenneth D. Frandsen and Donald A. Clement, "The Functions of Human Communication in Informing: Communicating and Processing Information," in *Handbook of Rhetorical and Communication Theory*, edited by Carroll C. Arnold and John Waite Bowers (Needham, MA: Allyn & Bacon, 1984), 334.

5. Bryce Covert, "Housing, Race, and Police Stops: The Backstory to Philando Castile's Killing," *ThinkProgress*, July 12, 2016, www.thinkprogress.org.
6. Howard K. Battles and Charles Packard, *Words and Sentences*, bk. 6 (Lexington, MA: Ginn & Company, 1984), 459.
7. Sandra Kujawa and Lynne Huske, *The Strategic Teaching and Reading Project Guidebook*, rev. ed. (Oak Brook, IL: North Central Regional Educational Laboratory, 1995).
8. Shawn M. Glynn et al., "Teaching Science with Analogies: A Resource for Teachers and Textbook Authors," *National Reading Research Center: Instructional Resource, 7* (Fall 1994).
9. Shawn M. Glynn et al., "Teaching Science," 19.
10. "Altoona List of Medical Analogies: How to Use Analogies," Altoona Family Physicians Residency, accessed August 5, 2010, www.altoonafp.org/analogies.htm.
11. Wolfgang Porod, "Nanotechnology," *Vital Speeches of the Day* 71, no. 4 (2004): 125–28.
12. Tina A. Grotzer, "How Conceptual Leaps in Understanding the Nature of Causality Can Limit Learning: An Example from Electrical Circuits," paper presented at the annual conference of the American Educational Research Association, New Orleans, LA, April 2000, http://citeseerx.ist.psu.edu/viewdoc/download?doi=10.1.1.36.774&rep=rep1&type=pdf.
13. Neil D. Fleming and Colleen Mills, "Helping Students Understand How They Learn," *Teaching Professor* 7, no. 4 (1992).

Chapter 24

1. Joseph Thayer, *Thayer's Greek-English Lexicon of the New Testament* (Peabody, MA: Hendrickson Publishers, 1996).
2. Winston L. Brembeck and William S. Howell, *Persuasion: A Means of Social Influence*, 2nd ed. (Englewood Cliffs, NJ: Prentice Hall, 1976).
3. Erin S. Knowles and Jay A. Linn, *Resistance and Persuasion* (Mahwah, NJ: Erlbaum, 2004).
4. Carolyn W. Sherif, Muzafer Sherif, and Roger E. Nebergall, *Attitude and Attitude Change: The Social Judgment-Involvement Approach* (Philadelphia: W. B. Saunders, 1965).
5. W. Hart, Dolores Albarracín, A. H. Eagly, I. Brechan, M. J. Lindberg, and L. Merrill, "Feeling Validated versus Being Correct: A Meta-Analysis of Selective Exposure to Information," *Psychological Bulletin* 135 (2009): 555–88.
6. Russel H. Fazio, "How Do Attitudes Guide Behavior?" in *The Handbook of Motivation and Cognition: Foundations of Social Behavior*, eds. Richard M. Sorrentino and E. Tory Higgins (New York: Guilford, 1986).
7. Kurt Braddock and James Price Dillard, "Meta-Analytic Evidence for the Persuasive Effect of Narratives on Beliefs, Attitudes, Intentions, and Behaviors," *Communication Monographs* 83 (2016): 1–24.
8. Edward P. J. Corbett, *Classical Rhetoric for the Modern Student*, 4th ed. (New York: Oxford University Press, 1999).
9. Winston Churchill, "We Shall Fight on the Beaches," speech delivered to the House of Commons, June 4, 1940. The Churchill Centre and Museum at the Churchill War Rooms, http://www.winstonchurchill.org/learn/speeches/speeches-of-winston-churchill/128-we-shall-fight-on-the-beaches
10. Craig Waddell, "The Role of Pathos in the Decision-making Process: A Study in the Rhetoric of Science Policy," *Quarterly Journal of Speech* 76 (1990): 381–400.
11. John S. Nelson, "Emotions as Reasons in Public Arguments," *Poroi* 4, no. 1 (2005): 1–26, doi: 10.13008/2151-2957.1028.
12. Robert A. Stewart, "Perceptions of a Speaker's Initial Credibility as a Function of Religious Involvement and Religious Disclosiveness," *Communication Research Reports* 11 (1994): 169–76.

13. For an extensive review of the history of the field of communication from the classical period to the present era, see Dominic A. Infante, Andrew S. Rancer, and Deanna F. Womack, *Building Communication Theory*, 4th ed. (Prospect Heights, IL: Waveland Press, 2003).
14. Ojenike Bolatito, "Linkage between Persuasion Principles and Advertising," *New Media and Mass Communication* 8 (2012): 7–11.
15. Susan T. Fiske, "Core Social Motivations: Views from the Couch, Consciousness, Classroom, Computers, and Collectives," in *Handbook of Motivation Science*, eds. James Y. Shah and Wendi L. Garner (New York: Guilford Press, 2008).
16. A. E. Latimer, T. A. Rench, S. E. Rivers, N. A. Katulak, S. A. Materese, L. Cadmus, A. Hicks, J. Keamy-Hodorowski, and P. Salovey, "Promoting Participation in Physical Activity Using Framed Messages: An Application of Prospect Theory," *British Journal of Health Psychology* 13, no. 4 (2008): 659–81.
17. Barlow Soper, Gary E. Milford, and Gary T. Rosenthal, "Belief When Evidence Does Not Support the Theory," *Psychology and Marketing* 12 (1995): 415–22. Cited in Stephen M. Kosslyn and Robin S. Rosenberg, *Psychology: The Brain, the Person, the World* (Boston: Allyn & Bacon, 2004), 330.
18. Susan T. Fiske, *Social Beings: A Core Motives Approach to Social Psychology* (New York: Wiley, 2004).
19. Richard Petty and John T. Cacioppo, "The Elaboration Likelihood Model of Persuasion," in *Advances in Experimental Social Psychology*, ed. L. Berkowitz (San Diego, CA: Academic Press, 1986), vol. 19, 123–205
20. Mary Lynn Miller Henningsen, David Dryden Henningsen, Michael Cruz, and Joshua Morrill, "Social influence in Groups: A Comparative Application of Relational Framing Theory and the Elaboration Likelihood Model of Persuasion," *Communication Monographs*, 70 (2003): 175–97.
21. Martin Fishbein and Icek Ajzen, *Belief, Attitude, Intention and Behavior: An Introduction to Theory and Research* (CA: Addison-Wesley, 1975); Martin Fishbein and Icek Ajzen, *Predicting and Changing Behavior: The Reasoned Action Approach* (New York: Psychology Press, 2010); Icek Ajzen and Martin Fishbein, "The Influence of Attitudes on Behavior," in *The Handbook of Attitudes*, eds. Dolores Albarracín, Blair T. Johnson, and Mark P. Zanna (Mahwah, NJ: Erlbaum, 2005), 173–221.
22. Icek Ajzen and Martin Fishbein, *Understanding Attitudes and Predicting Social Behavior* (Englewood Cliffs, NJ: Prentice Hall, 1980).
23. Latimer et al., "Promoting Participation."
24. For good reviews of the literature on source credibility in general, see Richard M. Perloff, *The Dynamics of Persuasion* (Hillsdale, NJ: Lawrence Erlbaum, 1993), and Dominic A. Infante, Andrew S. Rancer, and Deanna F. Womack, *Building Communication Theory.*
25. James A. McCroskey, *An Introduction to Rhetorical Communication*, 9th ed. (Boston, MA: Allyn and Bacon, 2006) 84-97.

Chapter 25

1. The model of argument presented here follows Stephen Toulmin, *The Uses of Argument* (New York: Cambridge University Press, 1958), as described in James C. McCroskey, *An Introduction to Rhetorical Communication,* 9th ed. (Boston, MA: Allyn and Bacon) 108–130.
2. Austin J. Freeley and David L. Steinberg, *Argumentation and Debate,* 13th ed. (Boston, MA: Cengage, 2013).
3. Sarah Morrison, "Fair Trade: Is It Really Fair?" *The Independent*, May 6, 2012.
4. Ralaca Dragusanu, Daniele Giovannucci, and Nathan Nunn, "The Economics of Fair Trade," *Journal of Economic Perspectives* 28, no. 3, 2014): 217–36.
5. Annette T. Rottenberg and Donna Haisty Winchell, *Elements of Argument,* 10th ed. (New York: Bedford/St. Martin's, 2012), 24–25.

6. Ibid.
7. Rottenberg and Winchell, *Elements of Argument*.
8. Michelle Nichols, "Angelina Jolie Urges U.N. Security Council to Act on War Zone Rape," Reuters, June 24, 2013, www.reuters.com/article/2013/06/24/entertainment-us-sexualviolence-un-jolie-idUSBRE95N0ZP20130624.
9. Maria De Los Salmones, Rafael Dominguez, and Angel Herrero, "Communication Using Celebrities in the Non-Profit Sector: Determinants of Its Effectiveness," *International Journal of Advertising* 32, no. 1 (2013): 101–19, www.douglaserice.com/celebrities-non-profits/#sthash.HlIfWIXv.dpuf.
10. Mike Allen, "Comparing the Persuasive Effectiveness of One- and Two-Sided Messages," in *Persuasion: Advances through Meta-Analysis*, eds. Mike Allen and Raymond W. Preiss (Cresskill, NJ: Hampton Press, 1998), 87–98.
11. Elizabeth Sheld, "A Gun Control Analogy," *Breitbart*, January 11, 2013, www.breitbart.com/blog/2013/01/11/a-gun-control-analogy/.

Chapter 26

1. Herbert W. Simons, *Persuasion in Society*, 2nd ed. (Routledge, 2011).
2. C. Ilie, "Strategies of Refutation by Definition: A Pragma-Rhetorical Approach to Refutations in a Public Speech," in *Pondering on Problems of Argumentation: Twenty Essays on Theoretical Issues*, eds. F. H. van Eemeren and B. Garssen (Springer Science + Business Media, 2009), doi:10.1007/978-1-4020-9165-0_4.
3. Alan H. Monroe, *Principles and Types of Speeches* (Chicago: Scott, Foresman, 1935).

Chapter 27

1. Frank D. Stella, "Introductory Remarks Delivered to the Economic Club of Detroit, Detroit, MI," *Executive Speaker* 17 (April 15, 1996): 3.
2. Gene Parret, *I Love My Boss and 969 Other Business Jokes* (New York: Sterling Publishing, 1993).
3. H. H. Shelton, "Victory, Honor, Sacrifice," *Vital Speeches of the Day* 66, no. 20 (2000): 627.
4. Ibid.
5. "Obama, Cecily Strong Joke Around at White House Correspondents' Dinner," NBC News Online, April 26, 2016.
6. Paul Fatout, ed., *Mark Twain Speaks for Himself* (West Lafayette, IN: Purdue University Press, 1978).

Chapter 28

1. Sheri Jeavons, "Webinars That Wow: How to Deliver a Dynamic Webinar," Webinar hosted by Citrix GoToMeeting, December, 12 2011.
2. Chris Peters and Kami Griffiths, "10 Steps for Planning a Successful Webinar," TechSoup, January 31, 2012, www.techsoup.org/support/articles-and-how-tos/10-steps-for-planning-a-successful-webinar; and American Marketing Association, "Best Practices for Webinar Planning and Execution," www.readytalk.com/sites/default/files/docs/support-training/ReadyTalk_and_AMA_Webinar_Best_Practices.pdf.
3. Ken Molay, "Best Practices for Webinars," Adobe Connect, www.images.adobe.com/www.adobe.com/content/dam/Adobe/en/products/adobeconnect/pdfs/web-conferencing/best-practices-webinars-wp.pdf
4. Patricia Fripp, "15 Tips for Webinars: How to Add Impact When You Present Online," *eLearn Magazine*, July 7, 2009, www.elearnmag.acm.org/featured.cfm?aid=1595445
5. Ibid.

Chapter 29

1. Discussion of group roles based on Dan O'Hair, Mary Wiemann, Dorothy Mullin, and Jason Tevon, *Real Communication*, 3rd ed. (New York: Bedford/St. Martin's, 2015); C. M. Anderson, B. L. Riddle, and M. M. Martin, "Socialization in Groups," in *Handbook of Group Communication Theory and Research*, ed. Lawrence R. Frey, Dennis S. Gouran, and Marshall Scott Poole (Thousand Oaks, CA: Sage, 1999), 139–63; A. J. Salazar, "An Analysis of the Development and Evolution of Roles in the Small Group," *Small Group Research* 27 (1996): 475–503; K. D. Benne and P. Sheats, "Functional Roles of Group Members," *Journal of Social Issues* 4 (1948): 41–49; and A. Sapru and H. Bourlard, "Automatic Recognition of Emergent Social Roles in Small Group Interactions," *IEEE Transactions on Multimedia* 7, no. 5(2015). doi:10.1109/TMM.2015.2408437.
2. Dan O'Hair, Gustav Friedrich, and Lynda Dixon, *Strategic Communication for Business and the Professions*, 8th ed. (Boston: Pearson, 2015); and Carsten K. W. Dreu, "Productive Conflict: The Importance of Conflict Management and Conflict Issue," in Carsten K. W. Dreu, Evert Van de Viert (eds.), *Using Conflict in Organizations* (London: Sage Publications, 1997), 9–22.
3. O'Hair, Friedrich, and Dixon, *Strategic Communication.*
4. O'Hair, Wiemann, Mullin, and Tevon, *Real Communication*; Crina I. Damşa, "The Multi-layered Nature of Small-Group Learning: Productive Interactions in Object-Oriented Collaboration," *International Journal of Computer-Supported Collaborative Learning* 9, no. 3 (2014): 247–81; and Ruth Anna Abigail and Dudley D. Cahn, *Managing Conflict through Communication* (Boston, MA: Pearson, 2013).
5. Irving Lester Janis, *Groupthink: Psychological Studies of Policy Decisions and Fiascoes* (Berkeley: University of California Press, 1982).
6. O'Hair, Friedrich, and Dixon, *Strategic Communication.*
7. S. Ruggieri and C. S. Abbate, "Leadership Style, Self-Sacrifice, and Team Identification," *Social Behavior and Personality* 41 (2013): 1171–78.
8. Ibid.
9. L. Richard Hoffman and Norman R. F. Maier, "Valence in the Adoption of Solutions by Problem-Solving Groups: Concept, Method, and Results," *Journal of Abnormal and Social Psychology* 69 (1964): 264–71.
10. John Dewey, *How We Think* (Boston: D.C. Heath, 1950).
11. Lin Kroeger, *The Complete Idiot's Guide to Successful Business Presentation* (New York: Alpha Books, 1997), 113.

Chapter 30

1. For a review, see Priscilla S. Rogers, "Distinguishing Public and Presentational Speaking," *Management Communication Quarterly* 2 (1988): 102–15; Frank E. X. Dance, "What Do You Mean 'Presentational' Speaking?" *Management Communication Quarterly* 1 (1987): 270–81.
2. Brent Adamson, Matthew Dixon, and Nicholas Toman, "The End of Solution Sales," *Harvard Business Review* (2012): 60–68.
3. Ibid.
4. Stephen Shiffman, "Ten Tips Guaranteed to Improve Sales," *American Salesman* 55 (2010): 28–30.
5. Sharon Cunningham, "Progress Reports," *Best's Review* (2010): 54.

Chapter 31

1. Several points derived from Robert Anholt, *Dazzle 'Em with Style: The Art of Oral Scientific Presentation*, 2nd ed. (New York: Academic Press, 2005).
2. With thanks to Professor Calvin Young, Biology Department, Fullerton College, for his input.
3. Deanna P. Daniels, "Communicating across the Curriculum and in the Disciplines: Speaking in Engineering," *Communication Education* 51 (July 2002): 3.

4. Deanna P. Dannels, "Features of Success in Engineering Design Presentations: A Call for Relational Genre Knowledge," *Journal of Business and Technical Communication* 23, no. 4 (2009): 399–427, doi:10.1177/1050651909338790.
5. Peter Redman and Wendy Maples, *Good Essay Writing: A Social Sciences Guide*, 4th ed. (Thousand Oaks, CA: Sage, 2011).
6. Rick Sullivan and Noel McIntosh, "Delivering Effective Lectures," ReproLinePlus, December 2014, www.reproline.jhu.edu/english/6read/6training/lecture/delivering_lecture.htm.
7. With thanks to Patricia Gowland, RN, MSN, OCN, CCRC, executive director of Cancer Research and Patient Navigation, Vanguard Health, Chicago, and associate director of Clinical Research, University of Illinois at Chicago Cancer Center, for her expert counsel and review of presentation types.
8. J. M. Brown and N. A. Schmidt, "Strategies for Making Oral Presentations about Clinical Issues: Part I. At the Workplace," *Journal of Continuing Education in Nursing* 40, no. 4 (2009): 152–53, accessed January 19, 2012, CINAHL with Full Text, EBSCOhost.

Acknowledgments

Text Credits

Index

F

G

N

O

P

T

Y

Z

ESL SPEAKER'S NOTES

ETHICALLY SPEAKING

A CULTURAL PERSPECTIVE

CITING SOURCES

Photos: (top) NASA Goddard Space Flight Center; (mid) Radu Bercan/Shutterstock; (bot) Charles Taylor/Shutterstock

CHECKLISTS

Visual Guides

TOPIC SELECTION

SUPPORTING THE SPEECH

ORGANIZING THE SPEECH

PRESENTATION AIDS

Sample Speech Videos

LaunchPad macmillan learning Go to LaunchPad: **launchpadworks.com** to find a variety of videos, including model speech clips and "needs improvement" clips, on a variety of speech topics that show you how to improve your technique and deliver a strong, effective speech.

Here's a list of topics and the number of videos available for each one noted:

- Ethics (4)
- Audience Analysis (3)
- Supporting Material (21)
- New Information (4)
- Organization (16)
- Thesis Statement (19)
- Introductions (29)
- Conclusions (20)
- Language (31)
- Methods of Delivery (13)
- Body in Delivery (10)
- Vocal Delivery (11)
- Informative Speaking (47)
- Persuasive Speaking (53)
- Argument (24)
- Presentation Aids (10)

Sample Speeches

LaunchPad macmillan learning Speeches marked with a video icon are also available in LaunchPad. Go to LaunchPad: **launchpadworks.com.** To see a list of video clips, see the previous page.

Teresa Gorrell

SPEECHES OF INTRODUCTION

INFORMATIVE SPEECHES

DJ McCabe

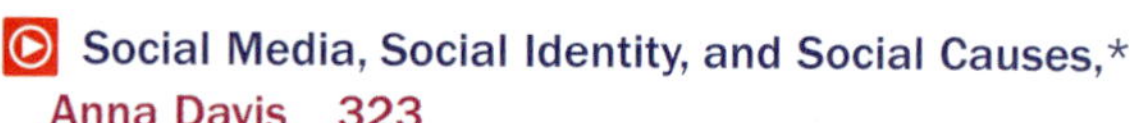

Elijah Lui

PERSUASIVE SPEECHES

SPECIAL OCCASION SPEECHES

Erhan Sevenler/ Anadolu Agency/

*These speeches feature visual annotations and photographs of the speakers delivering their presentations, in addition to textual annotations.